desserts

ILLUSTRATED

AMERICA'S TEST KITCHEN

Library of Congress Cataloging-in-Publication Data has been applied for.

ISBN 978-1-954210-06-6

AMERICA'S —
TEST KITCHEN ®

America's Test Kitchen
21 Drydock Avenue, Boston, MA 02210

Printed in Canada
10 9 8 7 6 5 4 3 2 1

Distributed by Penguin Random House Publisher Services
Tel: 800.733.3000

Pictured on Front Cover **Lemon–Olive Oil Tart (page 428)**

Pictured on Back Cover **Strawberry Ripple Ice Cream (page 540), Blackberry-Mascarpone Layer Cake (page 252), Chocolate Soufflé (page 212), Sour Cherry Cobbler (page 154)**

Editorial Director, Books **Adam Kowit**

Executive Food Editor **Dan Zuccarello**

Deputy Food Editor **Stephanie Pixley**

Executive Managing Editor **Debra Hudak**

Project Editor **Sacha Madadian**

Contributing Editor **Elizabeth Wray Emery**

Senior Editor **Joseph Gitter**

Test Cooks **Sāsha Coleman, Olivia Counter, Jacqueline Gochenouer, Eric Haessler, and Hisham Hassan**

Associate Editor **Sara Zatopek**

Assistant Editor **Emily Rahravan**

Design Director **Lindsey Timko Chandler**

Deputy Art Director **Katie Barranger**

Photography Director **Julie Bozzo Cote**

Senior Photography Producer **Meredith Mulcahy**

Senior Staff Photographers **Steve Klise and Daniel J. van Ackere**

Staff Photographer **Kevin White**

Additional Photography **Carl Tremblay, Joseph Keller, and Nina Gallant**

Food Styling **Joy Howard, Catrine Kelty, Chantal Lambeth, Gina McCreadie, Kendra McNight, Ashley Moore, Christie Morrison, Marie Piraino, Elle Simone Scott, Kendra Smith, and Sally Staub**

Project Manager, Creative Operations **Katie Kimmerer**

Senior Print Production Specialist **Lauren Robbins**

Production and Imaging Coordinator **Amanda Yong**

Production and Imaging Specialists **Tricia Neumyer and Dennis Noble**

Copy Editor **Cheryl Redmond**

Proofreader **Christine Corcoran Cox**

Indexer **Elizabeth Parson**

Chief Creative Officer **Jack Bishop**

Executive Editorial Directors **Julia Collin Davison and Bridget Lancaster**

CONTENTS

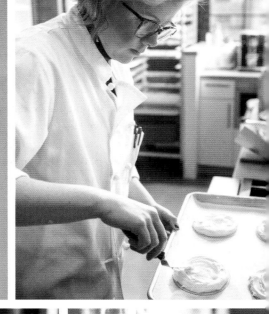

WELCOME TO AMERICA'S TEST KITCHEN

This book has been tested, written, and edited by the folks at America's Test Kitchen, where curious cooks become confident cooks. Located in Boston's Seaport District in the historic Innovation and Design Building, it features 15,000 square feet of kitchen space, including multiple photography and video studios. It is the home of *Cook's Illustrated* magazine and *Cook's Country* magazine and is the workday destination for more than 60 test cooks, editors, and cookware specialists. Our mission is to empower and inspire confidence, community, and creativity in the kitchen.

We start the process of testing a recipe with a complete lack of preconceptions, which means that we accept no claim, no technique, and no recipe at face value. We simply assemble as many variations as possible, test a half dozen of the most promising ones, and taste the results blind. We then construct our own recipe and continue to test it, varying ingredients, techniques, and cooking times until we reach a consensus. As we like to say in the test kitchen, "We make the mistakes so you don't have to." The result, we hope, is the best version of a particular recipe, but we realize that only you can be the final judge of our success (or failure). We use the same rigorous approach when we test equipment and taste ingredients.

None of this would be possible without a belief that good cooking, much like good music, is based on a foundation of objective technique. Some people like spicy foods and others don't, but there is a right way to sauté; there is a best way to cook a pot roast; and there are measurable scientific principles involved in producing perfectly beaten, stable egg whites. Our ultimate goal is to investigate the fundamental principles of cooking to give you the techniques, tools, and ingredients you need to become a better cook. It is as simple as that.

To see what goes on behind the scenes at America's Test Kitchen, check out our social media channels for kitchen snapshots, exclusive content, video tips, and much more. You can watch us work (in our actual test kitchen) by tuning in to *America's Test Kitchen* or *Cook's Country* on public television or on our websites. Listen to *Proof*, *Mystery Recipe*, and *The Walk-In* (AmericasTestKitchen. com/podcasts) to hear engaging, complex stories about people and food. Want to hone your cooking skills or finally learn how to bake—with an America's Test Kitchen test cook? Enroll in one of our online cooking classes. And you can engage the next generation of home cooks with kid-tested recipes from America's Test Kitchen Kids.

Our community of home recipe testers provides valuable feedback on recipes under development by ensuring that they are foolproof. You can help us investigate the how and why behind successful recipes from your home kitchen. (Sign up at AmericasTestKitchen.com/recipe_testing.)

However you choose to visit us, we welcome you into our kitchen, where you can stand by our side as we test our way to the best recipes in America.

facebook.com/AmericasTestKitchen

instagram.com/TestKitchen

youtube.com/AmericasTestKitchen

tiktok.com/@TestKitchen

twitter.com/TestKitchen

pinterest.com/TestKitchen

AmericasTestKitchen.com

CooksIllustrated.com

CooksCountry.com

OnlineCookingSchool.com

AmericasTestKitchen.com/kids

the dessert kitchen

CHANCES ARE YOU WERE ENCOURAGED FROM YOUTH TO FINISH YOUR DINNER BEFORE YOU GOT DESSERT. Something sweet ends a meal on a high note; it's tempting to skip ahead. And while it's true that you can go without dessert, that's part of what makes it so special, comforting, luxurious even.

These descriptors carry importance: if you're taking the extra time and care to make that sweet treat, it's important that it comes out right and satisfies your craving. Ethereal layers of sponge cake sandwiching a rich filling can perk your taste buds and mood, but a heavy, dense slice of cake can be a real disappointment. A scoop of sorbet cleanses the palate after a meal unless it's marred with large icy crystals. Since expectations are high, dessert can intimidate in a way savory dishes do not. It's common to hear people, even those with a sweet tooth, say they "can't" or "don't" bake. Some home cooks won't venture beyond cookies and simply stirred cakes. And there's a thriving market of prepared doughs and boxed mixes to prove it. But we know dessert lovers of any skill level can prepare their favorites at home with some know-how. Get ready to surpass your expectations.

In this book, we've foolproofed nearly any dessert you can think of—from those simple cookies and cakes to patisserie case desserts and even supersmooth frozen scoops. We've taught key techniques—some traditional and some developed in the test kitchen's 30 years of making dessert—in clear terms and with instructional (and beautiful) illustrations. And we've broken down more difficult recipes with step-by-step photography so you can see exactly how a batter should look after folding in an egg foam, how to handle every turn of puff pastry dough to maximize flakiness, or how to know when pastry cream is adequately thickened on the stove.

To facilitate learning, we've structured the book in a unique way. The sections are broken into a tasty taxonomy of dessert categories. Nestled under 10 broad sections like Cookies, Fruit Desserts, and Tarts are 91 types of desserts. Discovering these desserts' similarities takes the intimidation out of trying new recipes, and discovering their differences highlights how key techniques work. You won't just learn about cookies; you'll learn what ingredients and mixing methods turn out a drop cookie that's chewy like Snickerdoodles, cakey like Black and White Cookies, or crispy like Gingersnaps (everyone has a favorite). Read about how to make what comes out of the ice cream machine thick, rich, and almost unctuous like Pistachio Gelato or light, fruity, and hydrating like Raspberry Sorbet. And feel like a pastry chef as you master transferable techniques; once you've tempered eggs, for example, you can make any custard, pudding, or cream pie.

We'd like to convince you that baking is easy once you have the codes, but if you still don't want to turn on the oven, you'll find far more than baked goods in this book. Skillet-roasted fruit lacquered in its own caramelly juices, gelatin-set creamy spoon desserts, and the perfect lemon curd—special items that are afterthoughts or accompaniments in many dessert books are some of the most impressive. These are restaurant classics like buttermilk panna cotta and chocolate semifreddo, and their simple profile really highlights their main ingredients.

This is the last collection you'll need on desserts and with it, something sweet can be an anytime treat. You'll confidently turn elegant desserts out to end a dinner party, or prepare something homey on a weeknight with a seasonal fruit bounty. The only prior skill required for opening this book is loving dessert, and you'll close it with a master class under your belt.

THE PANTRY

Desserts Illustrated is a comprehensive guide to any dessert you'd want to make. You have the ingredients? We have the recipes. These are the pantry items you'll want to keep on hand so you can whip up something sweet whenever you'd like.

Flour

Flour is arguably the most important ingredient for any dessert that goes in the oven; it gives baked goods structure, crumb, and texture, whether tough (bad), tender (good), or something in between (sometimes desired). Most of our recipes call for basic all-purpose flour, although we also use cake flour (you guessed it, for cakes) and occasionally bread flour. The main difference between types of flour is the amount of protein they contain. More protein leads to more gluten development, which translates to more structured baked goods—or, depending on the proportion of other ingredients, tough, dense desserts. It's best to store flour in the pantry, away from light and heat. Here are the flours we use in this book.

ALL-PURPOSE FLOUR All-purpose flour has a moderate protein content (10 to 11.7 percent, depending on the brand) and is by far the most versatile variety for baking. We develop our recipes with easy-to-find Gold Medal Unbleached All-Purpose Flour (10.5 percent protein). Pillsbury All-Purpose Unbleached Flour (also 10.5 percent protein) offers comparable results. If you use an all-purpose flour with a higher protein content (such as King Arthur Unbleached All-Purpose Flour, with 11.7 percent protein) in our recipes that call for all-purpose flour, the baked good may be a bit drier and denser.

CAKE FLOUR Cake flour has a low protein content (6 to 8 percent) and delivers delicate, fine-crumbed cakes. You can approximate cake flour by mixing cornstarch with all-purpose flour. For each cup of cake flour, use ⅞ cup of all-purpose flour mixed with 2 tablespoons cornstarch. Most cake flour is bleached, which affects the starches in the flour and enables it to absorb greater amounts of liquid and fat.

GLUTEN-FREE FLOUR BLENDS We have included some gluten-free recipes throughout this book that rely on a gluten-free all-purpose flour blend. You can certainly purchase this. Each store-bought gluten-free flour blend relies on a different mix of ingredients, yielding baked goods with varying textures, colors, and flavors. Some work well, while others carry off-flavors or result in less-than-satisfactory textures. We've had good luck with and recommend King Arthur Gluten-Free All-Purpose Flour and Betty Crocker All-Purpose Gluten Free Rice Flour Blend, which both turned out tender but structured pie crusts. Bob's Red Mill Gluten Free All-Purpose Baking Flour also works, but it will add a noticeable bean flavor in most instances. If you want to make your own, we've provided our recipe. It is our favorite gluten-free flour blend. We often add a little xanthan gum to recipes; this binder provides additional structure and elasticity by strengthening the protein networks in the flour blend.

THE AMERICA'S TEST KITCHEN ALL-PURPOSE GLUTEN-FREE FLOUR BLEND

Makes 42 ounces (about 9⅓ cups)

Be sure to use potato starch, not potato flour, with this recipe. Tapioca starch is also sold as tapioca flour; they are interchangeable. We strongly recommend that you use Bob's Red Mill white and brown rice flours. We also recommend that you weigh your ingredients; if you measure by volume, spoon each ingredient into the measuring cup (do not pack or tap) and scrape off the excess.

24 ounces (4½ cups plus ⅓ cup) white rice flour
7½ ounces (1⅔ cups) brown rice flour
7 ounces (1⅓ cups) potato starch
3 ounces (¾ cup) tapioca starch
¾ ounce (¼ cup) nonfat dry milk powder

Whisk all ingredients in large bowl until well combined. Transfer to airtight container and refrigerate for up to 3 months.

NUT FLOURS Grinding nuts to a fine flour can add a beautiful aroma and delicate flavor to desserts. We use ground sweet, buttery pecans in the dough for our Chocolate-Nut Thumbprints (page 53). A small amount of ground almonds can fortify the structure of an almost-flourless cake, like our Chocolate-Raspberry Torte (page 321), while a larger amount can provide the bulk for one like Torta Caprese (page 320). You can purchase preground nut flours but they're expensive and prone to rancidity (store them in the freezer), so we like to grind our own; we provide instruction in the recipes for doing so.

CORNMEAL While you might not think of cornmeal as a flour, it functions like one in recipes like Gluten-Free Blueberry Cobbler with Cornmeal Biscuits (page 156). However, because it doesn't contain gluten, it won't provide baked goods with much structure. What it does provide: nutty, sweet flavor and a pleasant texture. Because the texture of cornmeal varies, it's important to use the variety that a recipe calls for. Coarse stone-ground cornmeal, for example, doesn't soften and can make cakes gritty.

Butter

Most of the recipes in this book use butter—rather than oil or shortening—for its satisfyingly rich flavor. But fat isn't just for flavor. Fat can emulsify a dessert sauce, for example. And the amount of fat in a recipe helps to determine the texture of a baked good's crumb; the more fat you add, the more tender your dessert because fat coats the flour proteins, inhibiting their ability to form a strong gluten network.

Butter can be used in its many phases. Chilled butter, cut into a recipe's flour, can give pie doughs and pastries flakes, softened butter creams with sugar in the mixer to aerate batters, and melted butter incorporates easily into cookie doughs.

We usually use regular unsalted butter. Land O'Lakes Unsalted Sweet Butter has received top ratings in our taste tests for its clean dairy flavor. Regular supermarket butter contains about 82 percent fat or less. (The rest is mostly water, with some milk solids too.) Premium butters, many of which are imported from Europe, have a slightly higher fat level—up to 86 percent—and price tag. But in baking tests, we've had trouble telling the difference, except for in laminated pastries, where the higher fat butter has a rich flavor and can improve workability. Similar goes for cultured butter. Culturing, or fermenting, cream before churning it into butter builds tangy, complex flavors—which are lost when baked.

Butter can pick up off-flavors and turn rancid when kept in the refrigerator for longer than a month, as its fatty acids oxidize. For longer storage (up to four months), move it to the freezer. For more information on how butter acts in baked goods, see pages 10 and 227.

You will occasionally see other fats used in this book: olive oil for unique flavor, vegetable oil for moisture and neutral flavor, vegetable shortening for cakey cookies, and coconut oil for vegan baked goods (use refined for a neutral flavor).

Sugar

Sweets obviously require sugar. But in addition to sweetness, sugar can affect the moisture level of a dessert or a baked good's structure or browning; you'll learn about these factors within specific dessert categories. Sweeteners come in many forms, from conventional white sugar to sticky-sweet honey or molasses. These are the sweeteners we use in this book. (If you are baking vegan desserts and are a strict vegan, you'll want organic sugars.)

GRANULATED SUGAR White granulated sugar, made from either sugarcane or sugar beets, is the type of sugar used most often in our recipes. It has a clean flavor and an evenly ground, loose texture that incorporates well with other ingredients and dissolves relatively quickly.

CONFECTIONERS' SUGAR Also called powdered sugar, confectioners' sugar is the most finely ground sugar. It's commonly used for dusting finished desserts, but it's also used for sweetening glazes, icings, and frostings because its fine texture can go undetected in raw applications and because it thickens and stabilizes these mixtures. You can approximate confectioners' sugar with this substitution: For 1 cup of confectioners' sugar, process 1 cup granulated sugar with 1 tablespoon cornstarch in a blender (not a food processor) until fine, 30 to 40 seconds.

BROWN SUGAR Brown sugar is granulated sugar that's combined with molasses, giving it a caramel flavor. An ingredient list will indicate "light" or "dark" brown sugar; if either can be used, we call for "brown sugar." Store brown sugar in an airtight container to prevent it from drying out. (We pop in a Sugar Bears Inc. Brown Sugar Bear [$3.25], a clay bear that keeps the sugar soft.) If the sugar becomes hard, place it in a bowl with a slice of sandwich bread, cover, and microwave for 10 to 20 seconds to revive it.

To approximate 1 cup of light brown sugar, pulse 1 cup of granulated sugar with 1 tablespoon of mild molasses in a food processor until blended. Use 2 tablespoons molasses for dark brown sugar. Brown sugar must be packed into a measuring cup to get an accurate reading. Press it with your fingers or the bottom of a smaller cup.

MOLASSES Molasses is a dark, thick syrup that's the by-product of sugarcane refining. It comes in three types: light or mild, dark or robust, and blackstrap. We prefer either light or dark molasses in baking and generally avoid using bitter blackstrap molasses. Store molasses in the pantry, not in the fridge, where it turns into a thick sludge.

HONEY Made by bees from flower nectar, honey is mechanically filtered and strained to remove wax and debris. Color can indicate depth of flavor: Lighter shades will be more mellow, while darker shades tend to be richer or even slightly bitter. Honey crystallizes in the refrigerator; store it in the pantry. If your honey is crystallized, put the opened jar in a saucepan filled with 1 inch of water, and heat the honey until it reaches 160 degrees.

MAPLE SYRUP This syrup is made by boiling down sap from maple trees. It has a high moisture level, so you should refrigerate it not only to retain flavor but also to prevent microorganisms from growing. It will keep for six months to a year. For long-term storage, freeze maple syrup. If it crystallizes, a zap in the microwave will restore it.

CORN SYRUP Corn syrup is made by adding enzymes to a mixture of cornstarch and water to break the long starch strands into glucose molecules. It's valuable in caramel-making (see page 549, for example) because it discourages crystallization; it also helps baked goods retain moisture. Corn syrup is less sweet than granulated sugar. It is not the same as high-fructose corn syrup (HFCS), a newer product that came on the market in the 1960s, which is widely used in processed foods, but it is not sold directly to consumers.

LYLE'S GOLDEN SYRUP We sometimes use this syrup in frozen desserts. It has a caramel flavor. It is an invert syrup (as is corn syrup), which is made up of smaller glucose and fructose molecules. These smaller molecules are much better at depressing the freezing point, so more of the water in our Frozen Yogurt (page 545) base stays liquid, delivering a treat that not only contains fewer ice crystals but also is more scoopable straight from the freezer.

Eggs

Eggs are a dessert essential. Their yolks and whites have different properties and functions, but together they can bind, thicken, emulsify, and leaven. Theoretically, eggs come in three grades (AA, A, and B), six sizes (from peewee to jumbo), and a rainbow of colors. But the only grade you'll find in a standard supermarket is grade A, the only colors brown and white, and the only sizes jumbo, extra-large, large, and medium. We could not discern any flavor differences among egg sizes or the two colors. For consistency's sake, however, size is important. We use large eggs.

Properly stored eggs will last up to three months, but both the yolks and the whites will become looser and they'll begin to lose their structure-lending properties. To be sure your eggs are fresh, check the sell-by date on the carton. By law, the sell-by date must be no more than 30 days after the packing date. To ensure freshness, store eggs in the back of the refrigerator (the coldest area), not in the door (the warmest area), and keep them in the carton; it holds in moisture and protects the eggs from odors.

The structure, moisture, richness, or lightness eggs can provide are still needed in vegan baking. We turn to aquafaba as a "plant-based egg" in our vegan desserts. Learn more about its properties and how to use it on page 497.

Milk

Liquid thins out batters and contributes to a cakey crumb in baked goods as it generates steam in the oven. It's responsible for gluten development; when liquid interacts with flour, it allows the proteins in wheat to cross-link into strands of gluten. It gives spoon desserts their soft texture and clean dairy flavor, and it lightens ice creams. We most often use whole milk in our recipes to encourage tenderness in baked goods and to impart richness.

CREAM Cream is the fat-rich layer skimmed from the top of unhomogenized milk. Cream is categorized based on its milk-fat content; it needs to be at least 30 percent milk fat to hold enough air to whip properly. Heavy cream is also called heavy whipping cream and this is what we want when we call for cream for a rich and dreamy custard filling or a whipped cream pie topping. Heavy cream contains 36 percent or more milk fat. Avoid whipping cream or light whipping cream (30 to 36 percent milk fat), light cream, or half-and-half (unless specifically called for).

ACIDIC DAIRY Buttermilk can add a tangy flavor to baked goods or panna cotta, but its inclusion is often more about texture: As an acidic ingredient, buttermilk tenderizes. Also, when an acidic ingredient is used, baking soda (or a combination of baking soda and powder) is typically the leavener of choice; the two interact for extra fluffiness.

If a recipe calls for just a cup or so of buttermilk, you may not want to buy an entire quart. We tested a couple of substitutes—shelf-stable powdered buttermilk and soured milk (a tablespoon of vinegar to a cup of milk)—in cakes. Cakes made with powdered buttermilk were more mellow-tasting, whereas cakes made with liquid buttermilk had a detectable, rich tang. However, cake made with powdered buttermilk had the fluffiest, most even texture, making it an able stand-in. The soured-milk cakes were flat-tasting and overly moist, but work in a pinch.

Yogurt and sour cream, both acidic, produce similar results to buttermilk, but sour cream can make for an even more tender baked good, as it's higher in fat than low-fat buttermilk and thus has two tenderizing properties.

DAIRY-FREE There are a lot of dairy-free milk products on the market. We've tested them all and we generally prefer oat milk for baked goods. Its natural sugar content is much higher than that of the other milks, so it helps baked goods brown. This is a particular boon in vegan baking. Without the milk proteins from dairy, vegan baked goods can be quite pale. Ultrarich coconut milk (for more information see page 537) has the rich fat content and body to make creamy vegan desserts like custard-like fillings and ice cream.

Chemical Leaveners
A majority of baked goods include some kind of chemical leavener to help them rise during baking. Baking soda is an alkali and therefore must be used in conjunction with an acidic ingredient—such as buttermilk, sour cream, molasses, or brown sugar—in order to produce carbon dioxide. The leavening action happens right after mixing, so you should bake right away. In addition to leavening, baking soda also promotes browning. Baking powder is a mixture of baking soda, a dry acid, and double-dried cornstarch. The cornstarch absorbs moisture and prevents the premature production of gas. Baking powder works twice—when it first comes in contact with a liquid, and again in response

to heat. Once a container is opened, it will lose its effectiveness after six months. Our favorite baking powder is Argo Double Acting Baking Powder.

Sometimes it's best to use both, especially in cakes. This can give you better control over rise and over the alkalinity of the batter. If a batter with powder is highly acidic, we'll add soda as well for extra support so that the powder isn't neutralized and deactivated. The soda will make the batter more alkaline. Alkaline batters brown more (amino acids thrive in an alkaline environment and react with sugar to create browning) and have a weaker gluten structure so they bake up with a more tender, porous crumb. So while baking powder alone is sufficient for leavening, in the presence of acid, the addition of soda can lighten a cake's crumb when desired and create better browning, which means more flavor.

Vanilla Extract
Vanilla is the most commonly used flavoring in desserts. It's sold in pure and imitation varieties. Which should you buy? If you want to buy just one bottle of extract for all kitchen tasks, our top choice is a real extract—real vanilla has around 250 flavor compounds compared to imitation vanilla's one, giving it a complexity tasters appreciated when we tried it in cooked applications and in cold and creamy desserts. Our favorite pure vanilla is McCormick Pure Vanilla Extract. But if you use vanilla only for baked goods, synthetic is OK (the flavor and aroma compounds in pure vanilla begin to bake off at higher temperatures, so the subtleties are lost). Our top-rated imitation vanilla is CF Sauer Co. Gold Medal Imitation Vanilla Extract.

Vanilla Beans
For creations in which you're really going to taste the vanilla—such as Pastry Cream (page 186) or the elegant topping on our Lavender Tea Cakes with Vanilla Bean Glaze (page 276)—we've found that beans impart deeper flavor than extract. We recommend splurging on McCormick Madagascar Vanilla Beans ($15.99 for two) for their plump, seed-filled pods and complex caramel-like flavor.

Nuts

We love the richness and texture nuts contribute to desserts. We grind them into flour for cookies, cakes, and pie doughs throughout this book (for more information on nut flours, see page 2), and also use them for toppings for fruit desserts and decoration.

All nuts are high in oil and will become rancid rather quickly. We store nuts in the freezer in zipper-lock bags. Frozen nuts will keep for months, and there's no need to defrost before toasting or chopping. Do defrost before grinding.

Nut nomenclature can be confusing. Recipes may call for raw, roasted, blanched, slivered, or sliced nuts. If there is no descriptor in the ingredient list, raw is assumed. Roasted nuts have already been toasted but we rarely use these, as we like to control the degree of toasting ourselves. However, roasted is a good choice for peanuts because we like the flavor of salted peanuts, which are nearly always roasted. We often use blanched nuts for grinding because the sweet nuts are stripped of their skins, which can add too much nuttiness or even bitterness to nut flours. If almonds aren't whole, they're often slivered or sliced. Slivered almonds are blanched and easier than whole nuts to break down, so we use them for grinding. Sliced almonds are just that: almonds that are sliced very thin lengthwise. They most often still have the skin so they're a great choice for decorating.

Peanut Butter

Peanut butter is a popular flavoring, making it into whimsical pies like our Peanut Butter and Concord Grape Pie (page 361) or surprise-filled cookies like Peanut Butter–Stuffed Chocolate Cookies (page 23). It comes salted and unsalted; in creamy, chunky, and even extra-chunky varieties; and conventional and natural. Natural peanut butters can be made simply from ground peanuts without added partially hydrogenated fats or emulsifiers (these butters exhibit natural oil separation and require stirring) or they can be made with only ground peanuts and palm oil (these do not require stirring). We avoid no-stir varieties as they make for oily frostings and fillings. And we like the flavor boost provided by salt. Our favorite creamy peanut butter is Skippy Peanut Butter.

Baking Spices

The addition of spices is a great way to round out the flavor of a cake or to give it a bolder profile. We recommend following a few tips: Label spices with the purchase date; store them in a cool, dry place; and use within 12 months. Buy whole spices when you can and grind them in a coffee grinder devoted solely to this purpose; the flavors of pre-ground spices fade fast. We most commonly use cinnamon, nutmeg, cardamom, and ground ginger in our baking. You'll find other less common baking spices like black pepper, lavender, saffron, turmeric, and cayenne as well.

EVERYTHING CHOCOLATE

There's no doubt about it, chocolate is one of if not *the* ultimate dessert flavoring. The best chocolate flavor starts with buying the best product; learn all about it below.

Unsweetened Chocolate

Unsweetened chocolate is simply chocolate liquor formed into bars. It's used for recipes in which we want a bold chocolate hit and not too much sweetness. But why not skip the step of melting bars and simply use cocoa powder? Cocoa powder has been largely defatted, while unsweetened chocolate still contains the cocoa butter from the cacao bean. We use unsweetened chocolate in confections where the fat contributes to an appropriately dense, fudgy texture, like Cream Cheese Brownies (page 86), and Classic Hot Fudge Sauce (page 548). Our winning unsweetened chocolate is American-classic Baker's Unsweetened Baking Chocolate Bar 100% Cacao.

Cocoa Powder

Cocoa powder is chocolate liquor that has been processed to remove all but 10 to 24 percent of the cocoa butter. Cocoa powder comes in natural and Dutched versions. Dutching, which was invented in the 19th century by a Dutch chemist and chocolatier, raises the powder's pH, which neutralizes its acids and astringent notes and rounds out its flavor. (It also darkens the color.) We often bloom cocoa powder in a hot liquid such as water or coffee. This dissolves the remaining cocoa butter and disperses water-soluble flavor compounds for a deeper, stronger flavor. Our favorites? All-purpose: Hershey's Natural Cocoa Unsweetened. Dutched: Droste Cocoa.

Dark Chocolate: The Semi- and the Bittersweet

There is some confusion surrounding the world of dark chocolate. Is what's labeled "bittersweet chocolate" the same thing as dark chocolate? What about "semisweet"? Legally speaking, both bittersweet and semisweet are considered dark chocolate, which is made when chocolate liquor is blended with additional cocoa butter and mixed with sugar. The FDA doesn't set an identity for dark chocolate except that "bittersweet" and "semisweet" chocolate must contain at least 35 percent cacao—although most contain more than 50 percent (up to 99 percent).

That said, we specify semisweet or bittersweet in our recipes' ingredient lists. Why? Most manufacturers use the term "bittersweet" for chocolates that are higher in cacao (and hence less sweet) than their "semisweet" offering. Thus, "bittersweet" and "semisweet" can be useful terms for comparing products within one brand even if they are imprecise across different brands. There is some flexibility, though. Our overall favorite dark chocolate, Ghirardelli 60% Cacao Bittersweet Chocolate Premium Baking Bar, will work in every recipe calling for semisweet or bittersweet chocolate. Just don't choose 85 percent cacao or higher; you are likely to experience compromised texture and too-bitter flavor.

Milk Chocolate

Milk chocolate is created when milk and sugar are processed with chocolate liquor. Milk chocolate must contain at least 10 percent chocolate liquor and 12 percent milk solids. The result is a smooth but mellow flavor (milk chocolate is usually more than 50 percent sugar). Our favorites are on the higher end of the cacao percentage range, with our winner, Endangered Species Chocolate Smooth + Creamy Milk Chocolate, containing 48 percent. The higher percentage helps creamy desserts set up better because there are more cocoa solids to thicken them.

White Chocolate

White chocolate is made from cocoa butter alone and not cocoa solids, the element responsible for milk and dark chocolate's brown color and nutty roasted flavor. White chocolate must contain at least 20 percent cocoa butter. Many products rely on palm oil in place of some or all of the cocoa butter and so can't be labeled "chocolate." These are labeled "white chips" or "white confection." We're not too picky: White chocolate derives its flavor from milk and sugar, not

from the fat, so we find this distinction makes little difference. The chocolate that worked in all our recipes was Guittard Choc-Au-Lait White Chips. (Yes, a chip: It can be used in any recipe calling for chopped chocolate.)

Chipping Chocolate

Chocolate chips have a similar cacao percentage as but less cocoa butter (i.e., fat) than bar chocolate, which allows them to maintain their shape when baked. (They also tend to have higher levels of emulsifiers, which further helps them hold their shape.) We tried both melted chopped semisweet or bittersweet chocolate (what we call for) and chocolate chips in Pots de Crème (page 190) and Chocolate Sheet Cake (page 262). In the pots de crème, the chips produced a slightly grainy, overly viscous texture. The crumb of the cake masked any textural difference. But we did find chips a better choice in a couple of applications that need extra stability, such as Creamy Vegan Chocolate Frosting (page 246). The emulsifiers make a difference in the two-ingredient vegan frosting; the frosting we made with chopped bar chocolate and coconut milk broke. Our favorite dark chocolate chips are Ghirardelli 60% Premium Baking Chips and our favorite milk chocolate chips are Hershey's Kitchens Milk Chocolate Chips.

It All Starts with a Sheet

Throughout the sections of this book, you'll find our winning choices for the equipment you'll want for the desserts at hand. And while every recipe will require some measuring spoons, bowls, and a kitchen scale if you're exacting (our favorite is the **OXO Good Grips 11 lb Food Scale with Pull Out Display,** $49.99), one foundational piece of equipment that you'll use for nearly every dessert is the baking sheet. It's critical to get a workhorse (preferably three). For evenly baked cookies that fit on the sheet, a sturdy vessel for transferring pie to the oven, and a mold for roulade cakes, buy large (18 by 13 inches is ideal), heavy-duty rimmed baking sheets. We like the thick **Nordic Ware Baker's Half Sheet** ($14.97).

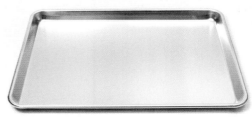

PART 01

cookies

IN THE WORLD OF BAKING, the cookie might just be the most beloved treat—and the most versatile. Whether they're an afternoon snack or the sweet ending to a meal, cookies are welcome anywhere and anytime. They can be as simple to make as mixing the ingredients by hand and dropping the dough onto a sheet, or they can be a more complex process involving layers of pastry and intricate shaping. Cookies are a blank canvas: You can include mix-ins such as oats, chocolate chips, dried fruit, and candies; you can frost or fill them; you can coat them in sugar; and you can even fry them. The possibilities are virtually limitless.

Cookies have a long and varied history. Some can be traced back centuries (the first shortbread dates back to at least 12th-century Scotland), while others are significantly more modern creations (such as Hazelnut Lemon Curd Thumbprints on page 52). Many have stories of how they came to be. Other cookies can be directly traced to newspaper articles, old-fashioned bake-offs, traditional cookbooks, and beloved bakeries. Some invoke spirited arguments as to their origins and others have clear regional ties (Snickerdoodles on page 20 are an undeniably New England creation and Whoopie Pies on page 73 are, well, we'll let you decide). And, of course, everyone is familiar with classic cookie recipes from the back of an ingredient package (Toll House chocolate chip cookies perhaps being the most famous).

This section covers cookies of all kinds. But while different types of cookies may require different techniques and methods to achieve the desired outcome, all cookie recipes have five key steps in common: measuring, mixing, forming, baking, and cooling.

Like most baking, cookie recipes are complex chemical formulas. Texture is the most challenging part of any cookie recipe. Cookie dough is relatively dry—many recipes contain no liquid ingredients, other than perhaps an egg. For that reason, small changes to a single ingredient can have a big effect. Add more sugar, for instance, and the cookies will not only taste sweeter but will also spread more. These changes are especially important in simple cookies, such as many butter cookies, where there aren't big flavors that might otherwise hide textural imperfections. We'll cover what many of these changes look like. There are also different ways to mix cookie dough, and each method serves a specific textural purpose, so it's important to use the right technique for a certain type of cookie.

Placing cookies into categories is a subjective task. Here we have organized our cookie recipes in a way that highlights differences in ingredients, mixing methods, and shaping techniques.

BUTTER: A KEY COOKIE INGREDIENT

Most of the cookie recipes in this book use butter—rather than oil or shortening—for its satisfyingly rich flavor. But fat in cookies isn't just for flavor; the amount of fat in a recipe helps determine the texture of the cookies' crumb as well. When you add fat in large amounts, your cookies will be more tender, and sometimes, more crumbly; the fat coats the flour proteins, inhibiting their ability to form a strong gluten network.

Use Unsalted Butter for Cookies—and Anytime

In the test kitchen, we use only unsalted butter. The amount of salt in salted butter varies from brand to brand, which is problematic in cookie recipes for a couple of reasons: First, it makes it impossible to know how much salt to call for in a recipe. Second, salted butter often contains more water than unsalted does, and the excess water can affect gluten development.

Butter Temperatures for Your Desired Cookie Texture

The temperature of butter affects the texture of finished cookies. We soften butter for creaming so it's malleable enough to be whipped but firm enough to retain air—vital to providing structure and leavening for drop cookies. In reverse creaming, softened butter coats the flour particles for a tender texture. We chill small cubes of butter when we need to cut the butter into the flour to create flaky layers. When we melt butter, whether to create chew or to encourage spread (for a thin and crispy cookie), it should be cooled so you don't warm up the other ingredients.

What About Other Fats?

We prefer the flavor of butter, but other fats serve a specific purpose in some of our recipes. Shortening has a bland flavor, but it's OK to use in strongly flavored cookies. We sometimes use it when we want crispy edges and/or a tall and tender cookie (see Angeletti on page 27). Shortening is 100 percent fat, so it adds no extra moisture to dough. It also has a higher melting point than butter; the structure of cookies made with shortening sets before the shortening fully melts, resulting in a taller cookie.

Sometimes we add vegetable oil (a largely unsaturated fat) in addition to butter (a largely saturated fat) to cookie doughs for a 3:1 ratio of unsaturated to saturated fat that makes cookies chewy (see Chewy Sugar Cookies on page 18). This combination of fats forms a sturdier crystal-line structure than butter does alone, and it requires more force to bite through. But we rarely use oil as the sole fat in a cookie; cookies made with only oil tend to be greasy and stodgy since oil doesn't aerate. Also, cookies made with an abundance of oil can develop an almost fried exterior after baking.

Made with Butter
This cookie is moderately chewy with a rich flavor.

Made with Shortening
This cookie is taller and more cakey.

Made with Oil
This cookie is greasy and has fried edges.

STORING COOKIES

Cookies are perfect for any occasion—holidays, bake sales, school lunches, everyday dessert—so it makes sense that you might need to make them ahead. Here's how we keep cookies at their best.

Refrigerating Doughs

If you're making cookies just for your family, you may want to refrigerate the dough and bake cookies a few at a time. Is this OK? It depends on the type of leavener in the cookies. We made four sugar cookie doughs: one with baking powder, one with baking soda, one with both, and the last (an icebox cookie) with neither. The dough with baking soda held well for two days but baked up a little flatter on the third. Cookies with both baking powder and soda began to lose lift after four days of dough storage (though we wouldn't recommend refrigerating a dough beyond three days so it doesn't pick up off-flavors). The cookie dough with only baking powder maintained good lift for seven days, with the same caveat. The unleavened cookies held just as long.

The dough with baking soda lasted for a shorter amount of time because baking soda is a single-acting leavener: It begins to produce lift-giving air bubbles as soon as it gets wet and comes in contact with an acid. Once started, this action continues until all the leavening power is spent—so there's a time limit. Baking powder is double acting, so it releases gas twice: once when it gets wet, and again when it heats up. So even if the first batch of air bubbles is spent, the second action will allow cookies to rise in the oven.

Freezing Doughs

By keeping unbaked cookie dough in the freezer, you can satisfy your craving for freshly baked cookies—just one or a whole batch—anytime. After making the dough, portion it out as you would for baking right away and place the portions on parchment-lined baking sheets or on large plates. Place in the freezer until the dough is frozen solid, at least 30 minutes. Remove the frozen unbaked cookies from the sheet, arrange them in a zipper-lock bag or in layers in an airtight storage container, and place them back in the freezer for up to two months. You may need to increase the recipe's baking time, but no defrosting is necessary.

Storing Baked Cookies

Many of the cookies in this book can be stored according to the methods below. Exceptions are noted in the recipes.

COOKIE TYPE	HOW TO STORE
Drop Cookies	About 3 days in an airtight container at room temperature.
Rolled and Slice-and-Bake Cookies	About 1 week in an airtight container at room temperature.
Brownies and Blondies	About 5 days in an airtight container at room temperature. Topped brownies may require refrigeration. Uncut brownies last longer than cut brownies.

Reviving Stale Cookies

To restore cookies to just-baked freshness, recrisp them in a 425-degree oven for 4 to 5 minutes. Let the cookies cool on the sheet for a couple of minutes and serve them warm.

PACKING COOKIES FOR SHIPPING

Cookies are baked confections that lend themselves to gifting. Here are our tips for shipping cookies so they arrive in perfect condition.

Select Wisely

Cookies that are baked until dried throughout, such as gingersnaps, remain intact, crunchy, and fresh-tasting. Moist, dense brownies and bar cookies also fare well. But chewy cookies that start out moist end up stale, and delicate lace cookies can be reduced to shards.

Keep Them Separated

Moist cookies will transfer their moisture and make crispy cookies soft, which will in turn make your moist cookies stale. Aromatic cookies will also transfer their flavors to their neighbors, which could potentially taint the flavor of more mild cookies. To prevent this, give each type its own bag.

Stack Bars

Bar cookies such as brownies or blondies can get stuck together while in transit. This can be avoided by placing a small piece of parchment paper in between each brownie in stacks of four or five. Wrap the stacks tightly in plastic wrap to keep them fresh for their journey, and then put them in a zipper-lock bag and close tightly.

Pack with Padding

Surround wrapped cookies with lightweight bulk such as packing peanuts, bubble wrap, or even popcorn. Place the most delicate items in the center of the box and cover everything on each side and on top.

Cookie Equipment Corner

While many cookie recipes require no special equipment at all—a bowl, a spatula, and a baking sheet might be all you need—there are a few items that will make shaping and transferring your cookies a more consistent and enjoyable process.

PORTION SCOOP

A spring-loaded ice cream scoop is helpful for portioning drop cookie dough into even-size mounds. Manufacturers identify scoops in different ways: by volume, by diameter, or, most commonly—and most confusingly—according to a numbered system. In this system, scoops are given numerical "sizes" based on the number of level scoops it would take to empty a quart; for example, it would take twenty level scoops with a #20 scoop (a bit more than 3 tablespoons per scoop). The **OXO Good Grips Large Cookie Scoop** holds about this much—great for our larger drop cookie dough balls (see page 15). And we love the **OXO Good Grips Medium Cookie Scoop** (a #40 scoop) for smaller cookie recipes that call for 1½ tablespoons. The **OXO Good Grips Small Cookie Scoop** (a #70 scoop) has a scant tablespoon volume.

COOKIE SPATULA

Reaching between cookies on a crowded baking sheet and removing brownies from a pan are tricky with a full-size spatula. Enter the **OXO Good Grips Silicone Cookie Spatula** ($7.99), a remarkably small, maneuverable silicone spatula that's safe for nonstick cookware. The flexible edge of its 2⅝ by 3-inch head, attached to an angled handle, glides effortlessly beneath cookies and bars.

COOKIE CUTTERS

We prefer metal cutters to plastic ones because the former are sharper and more likely to make clean cuts. Look at the cutting edges and make sure they are thin and sharp. Ideally, cutters will be at least 1 inch tall (so they can cut through thicker cookie dough). A rounded or rubber top offers nice protection for your hands.

COOKIE PRESSES

Cookie presses are handheld gadgets that portion soft cookie doughs into a variety of shapes, from hearts and flowers to snowmen and turkeys. We found that three qualities mattered most in a cookie press: consistency of shaping, durability, and—most important—the appearance of the cookies. The **MARCATO Biscuit Maker** ($42.00) consistently produces well-defined cookies, and it produces mostly uniform designs even when the dough is warm. This machine's many moving parts do require a small learning curve, but the payoff—beautiful cookies—and the press's excellent durability are worth it.

COOKIE JARS

Cookie jars come in shapes and sizes of all sorts. But while novelty jars may look nice, you want a cookie jar that actually keeps cookies fresh, intact, and easy to grab. Unlike most cookie jars, **OXO Good Grips Pop Storage Container, Big Square 4 Quart** ($16.99) has an airtight seal (activated by a pop-up button on the lid). It also has an opening wide enough to reach into for really big cookies.

Holiday Sugar Cookies

DROP COOKIES

Simple to execute

Can be chewy, crispy, or cakey

Melt or soften butter

Roll dough into balls

Space apart for spreading

DROP COOKIES ARE AMERICAN CLASSICS, and they're one of the first types of cookies most bakers learn how to make: Think chocolate chip, oatmeal raisin, and sugar. This style of cookie gets its name from the process of dropping a medium-soft dough from a spoon onto the baking sheet, although we prefer to measure the dough with a portion scoop and then roll the dough into a ball. (The exception is for soft doughs or cakier cookies that have loose batters, which makes it difficult to roll them between your hands.) A spring-loaded ice cream scoop (see page 12) makes portioning faster, neater, and more consistent than using a tablespoon measure, which results in cookies of uniform shape that bake evenly; this method also allows for freezing some (or all) of the dough balls for later. Having a few scoops in different sizes means you can use them to portion out cookie doughs for a variety of cookie recipes. But if you're going to have just one, we recommend getting one that holds about 3 tablespoons of dough, a serving size we use frequently.

But while most drop cookies are formed in similar fashion, the end results can differ greatly, particularly when it comes to texture: This type of cookie can be thick and chewy, thin and crisp, or even soft and cakelike. Ingredients, mixing method, baking time, and cookie size all play a role in the texture of a cookie. Everyone has a favorite cookie texture. Explore the different types and learn how to manipulate dough to achieve the result you like.

Chewy

When we think about chewy cookies, an oatmeal cookie comes to mind. The ideal version of this cookie features crisp edges and an irresistible center that yields when you take a bite. This supremely satisfying texture is the result of the right ingredients and techniques. All-purpose flour is typically the best choice; it has just enough protein for gluten development, which in turn translates to chewier cookies (too much protein can result in tough, dense cookies). Brown sugar or a liquid sweetener—rather than regular white sugar—and plenty of fat also play key roles in developing a chewy texture. Oftentimes the fat is in liquid form (such as oil or melted butter), so it makes sense to simply stir together the soft dough by hand. But there's another reason to do this: Mixing the ingredients together in a bowl doesn't incorporate air the way a stand mixer does (air contributes to a cakier texture). For superlative chew, take the cookies out of the oven when they still look raw between the cracks and seem underdone; the edges should be set, but the centers should still be soft and puffy.

BROWN SUGAR IS BEST FOR CHEW

In addition to imparting a caramel flavor, brown sugar tends to make cookies more moist and chewy. Why? Molasses is an invert sugar. With invert sugars, sucrose breaks down into individual glucose and fructose molecules when heated with acid—as with molasses—or when treated with enzymes. Invert sugar is especially hygroscopic, pulling water from wherever it can be found—the best source being the air. Cookies made with brown sugar tend to stay chewy because the invert sugar pulls in moisture even after the cookies cool. The cookie on the left was made with dark brown sugar; it baked up chewy and easily bent around a rolling pin. The cookie on the right was made with granulated sugar; it emerged from the oven dry and snapped immediately when bent.

BAKING A BIGGER, BETTER COOKIE

We have pulled out lots of tricks to produce a cookie with great chew. But there's one particularly easy way to get a cookie with a gradation of textures: Simply make the cookie bigger. That's because a larger diameter increases the contrast between the crispy edges and the chewy centers.

Less Dough
One tablespoon of dough per cookie creates a more uniform texture from edge to center.

More Dough
Three tablespoons of dough per cookie increases its crisp-chewy contrast.

STORING CHEWY COOKIES

To keep chewy cookies from turning dry and brittle, store them in a zipper-lock bag at room temperature with a small piece of bread (no more than half of a slice) placed inside. The cookies absorb moisture from the bread and hold on to that moisture so they stay at their peak chewy softness for longer.

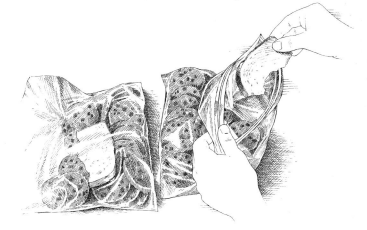

Thin and Crispy

While a thick, substantial cookie with a chewy center is sure to satisfy, sometimes we get a hankering for another style—one with the delicate snap of a gingersnap or the praline crunch of a thin chocolate chip cookie. How do you get that thin, crispy texture? Adding a small amount of a liquid ingredient such as milk to the dough is one way; this creates a looser dough that spreads in the oven, resulting in a thinner cookie. Other ways: We often like to use at least some granulated sugar, as it doesn't hold on to moisture as readily as brown and it also crystallizes as the cookie cools, making it crunchier. We call for a more modest amount of tenderizing butter. Finally, a little extra baking soda helps dry out the cookies by causing a rapid collapse that creates fissures and allows moisture to escape. This is one type of drop cookie you won't want to underbake—baking the cookies until deep golden brown dries them out and crisps them even further.

LEAVENERS—NOT JUST FOR LIFT

Why do so many cookies call for a combination of leaveners? The two work in tandem to create cookies that rise—and spread—to the right degree. Baking powder is responsible for lift since it's engineered to produce most of its gas after the cookies go into the oven, where the dough sets before the bubbles can burst. But too much lift can mean cookies that turn out domed and cakey rather than thin and crispy. Here's where baking soda comes in: As long as there's an acidic ingredient in the dough for it to react with, baking soda can even things out. Baking soda raises the pH of the dough (baking powder does too, but not as high), weakening gluten. Weaker gluten means less structure and cookies that spread nicely. It also allows for the crackly tops to form on cookies like our Chewy Sugar Cookies (page 18); the baking soda reacts immediately in the wet dough to produce large bubbles of carbon dioxide that can't all be contained by the weakened dough. Before the cookies can set in the oven, the bubbles rise to the top and burst, leaving fissures in their wake.

Baking Soda at Work

In our Gingersnaps (page 24), we use a dramatic amount of baking soda—a full 2 teaspoons—and no baking powder to create a cookie with extra snap and large fissures. The weaker gluten structure created in this environment means a more porous structure from which air bubbles and moisture can escape. It also means that the dough will collapse after its initial rise in the oven, leading to cracks that also allow more moisture to evaporate.

No Baking Soda

½ Teaspoon Baking Soda

1 Teaspoon Baking Soda

1½ Teaspoons Baking Soda

2 Teaspoons Baking Soda

Cakey

Sometimes it's a soft, tender cookie that we want—one with an almost cakelike texture. A cakey cookie should have a fluffy-yet-sturdy crumb that is simultaneously moist and light and airy. There are several ways to achieve this unique texture. Introducing some cake flour is one simple way to ensure more tender cookies, but the tradeoff can be structure. The addition of an acidic ingredient such as sour cream or buttermilk works in two ways: It adds moisture, which turns to steam in the oven to produce a cakier crumb, and it also reacts with the leavener for a higher rise. More eggs will also provide more lift, while creaming the butter with sugar helps aerate the dough and open the cookie's crumb. A frosting or glaze is a nice finishing touch and provides a contrast in flavor and texture to the light, fluffy cookie.

MOISTURE MAKERS

Have you ever noticed that cookies made with sour cream or applesauce are often softer and cakier than other drop cookies? You're not imagining it. These ingredients all contain a significant amount of water, and this extra liquid creates a thinner, batter-like dough. As the moisture converts to steam in the oven, it results in a more open crumb and cakey lift.

PERFECT CHOCOLATE CHIP COOKIES

Makes 16 cookies | 2 rimmed baking sheets

WHY THIS RECIPE WORKS There's no question that the chocolate chip cookie is the most iconic American treat. We wanted a reliably moist and chewy cookie with crisp edges and deep butterscotch notes. The key ingredient was browned butter. Melting the butter made its water content readily available to interact with the flour, thus creating more gluten and a chewier texture. Continuing to cook the butter until it browned contributed deep caramel notes, as did dissolving the sugar in the melted butter. Using two egg yolks but only one white added richness without giving the cookies a cakey texture. Studded with gooey chocolate and boasting a complex toffee flavor, these are chocolate chip cookies, perfected. Light brown sugar can be used in place of the dark, but the cookies won't be as full-flavored.

1¾ cups (8¾ ounces) all-purpose flour
½ teaspoon baking soda
14 tablespoons unsalted butter, divided
¾ cup packed (5¼ ounces) dark brown sugar
½ cup (3½ ounces) granulated sugar
2 teaspoons vanilla extract
1 teaspoon table salt
1 large egg plus 1 large yolk
1¼ cups (7½ ounces) semisweet or bittersweet chocolate chips
¾ cup pecans or walnuts, toasted and chopped (optional)

1. Adjust oven rack to middle position and heat oven to 375 degrees. Line 2 rimmed baking sheets with parchment paper. Whisk flour and baking soda together in bowl.

2. Melt 10 tablespoons butter in 10-inch skillet over medium-high heat. Continue to cook, swirling skillet constantly, until butter is dark golden brown and has nutty aroma, 1 to 3 minutes. Transfer browned butter to large bowl and stir in remaining 4 tablespoons butter until melted. Whisk in brown sugar, granulated sugar, vanilla, and salt until incorporated. Whisk in egg and yolk until smooth and no lumps remain, about 30 seconds.

3. Let mixture stand for 3 minutes, then whisk for 30 seconds. Repeat process of resting and whisking 2 more times until mixture is thick, smooth, and shiny. Using rubber spatula, stir in flour mixture until just combined, about 1 minute. Stir in chocolate chips and pecans, if using.

4. Working with 3 tablespoons dough at a time, roll into balls and space them 2 inches apart on prepared sheets. (Dough balls can be frozen for up to 1 month; bake frozen dough balls in 300-degree oven for 30 to 35 minutes.)

Perfect Chocolate Chip Cookies

5. Bake cookies, 1 sheet at a time, until golden brown and edges have begun to set but centers are still soft and puffy, 10 to 14 minutes, rotating sheet halfway through baking. Transfer sheet to wire rack and let cookies cool completely before serving.

VEGAN CHOCOLATE CHIP COOKIES

Makes 16 cookies | 2 rimmed baking sheets

WHY THIS RECIPE WORKS A vegan chocolate chip cookie deserves all the flavor and texture of a traditional one. We started by removing the egg from our classic recipe and found that we simply didn't need a substitute for it. Brown sugar gave the cookies a rich flavor and its moisture provided a softer center. For more chew, we let the dough rest for 1 to 4 hours to give the proteins and starches in the flour a jump-start at breaking down; meanwhile, the sugar dissolved, hydrated, and later retained this moisture better during baking, preventing the cookie from becoming brittle. A little almond butter added toffee-like richness that butter typically provides. If you are a strict vegan, use organic sugar. Not all semisweet chocolate chips are vegan, so check ingredient lists carefully. Use processed almond butter for the best texture; natural almond butter will make the cookies too greasy, and they will spread too much.

2 cups (10 ounces) all-purpose flour
1½ teaspoons baking powder
¼ teaspoon baking soda
½ teaspoon table salt
1⅓ cups packed (9⅓ ounces) light brown sugar
½ cup coconut oil, melted and cooled
6 tablespoons water, room temperature
⅓ cup unsalted creamy almond butter
2 teaspoons vanilla extract
1¼ cups (7½ ounces) semisweet chocolate chips or chunks

1. Whisk flour, baking powder, baking soda, and salt together in bowl. Whisk sugar, melted oil, water, almond butter, and vanilla in large bowl until well combined and smooth. Using rubber spatula, stir flour mixture into oil mixture until just combined; fold in chocolate chips.

2. Cover bowl with plastic wrap and let rest at room temperature for at least 1 hour or up to 4 hours. (Dough can be refrigerated for up to 24 hours; let sit at room temperature for 30 minutes before portioning.)

3. Adjust oven rack to middle position and heat oven to 350 degrees. Line 2 rimmed baking sheets with parchment paper. Divide dough into 16 portions, each about 3 tablespoons, then arrange dough mounds 2 inches apart on prepared sheets.

4. Bake, 1 sheet at a time, until light golden and edges have begun to set but centers are still soft, 12 to 14 minutes, rotating sheet halfway through baking. Transfer sheet to wire rack and let cookies cool completely before serving. (Cookies can be stored at room temperature for up to 3 days.)

CHEWY SUGAR COOKIES
Makes 24 cookies | 2 rimmed baking sheets
WHY THIS RECIPE WORKS The hallmark of a standout sugar cookie is satisfying chew. But sugar cookie recipes can be surprisingly fussy: If the butter temperature isn't just right or the measurements are a bit off, the resulting cookies are brittle. Knowing that the right proportions of saturated and unsaturated fats can enhance chewiness, we replaced some of the butter in the recipe with oil. To mitigate the sweetness, we added an unconventional ingredient: cream cheese. A small amount contributed a slight tang that provided the perfect counterpoint to the sugar without compromising the cookie's texture. As a bonus, its acidic presence enabled us to include baking soda as an additional leavener, which gave the cookies a beautiful crackly surface. For the best results, handle the soft dough as briefly and as gently as possible; overworking the dough will result in flatter cookies.

2¼ cups (11¼ ounces) all-purpose flour
1 teaspoon baking powder
½ teaspoon baking soda
½ teaspoon table salt
1½ cups (10½ ounces) sugar, plus ⅓ cup for rolling
2 ounces cream cheese, cut into 8 pieces
6 tablespoons unsalted butter, melted and still warm
⅓ cup vegetable oil
1 large egg
1 tablespoon whole milk
2 teaspoons vanilla extract

1. Adjust oven rack to middle position and heat oven to 350 degrees. Line 2 rimmed baking sheets with parchment paper. Whisk flour, baking powder, baking soda, and salt together in bowl.

2. Place 1½ cups sugar and cream cheese in large bowl. Whisk in warm melted butter (some lumps of cream cheese will remain). Whisk in oil until incorporated. Whisk in egg, milk, and vanilla until smooth. Using rubber spatula, fold in flour mixture until soft, homogeneous dough forms.

3. Spread remaining ⅓ cup sugar in shallow dish. Working with 2 tablespoons dough at a time, roll into balls, then roll in sugar to coat; space dough balls 2 inches apart on prepared sheets. Using bottom of greased dry measuring cup, press each ball until 3 inches in diameter. Using sugar left in dish, sprinkle 2 teaspoons sugar over each sheet of cookies; discard extra sugar. (Raw cookies can be frozen for up to 1 month; bake frozen cookies in 350-degree oven for 17 to 22 minutes.)

4. Bake cookies, 1 sheet at a time, until edges are set and beginning to brown, 11 to 13 minutes, rotating sheet halfway through baking. Let cookies cool on sheet for 5 minutes, then transfer to wire rack and let cool completely before serving.

Chewy Chai Spice Sugar Cookies
Add ¼ teaspoon ground cinnamon, ¼ teaspoon ground ginger, ¼ teaspoon ground cardamom, ¼ teaspoon ground cloves, and pinch pepper to bowl with sugar and cream cheese in step 2. Reduce vanilla to 1 teaspoon.

Chewy Coconut-Lime Sugar Cookies
Whisk ½ cup finely chopped sweetened shredded coconut into flour mixture in step 1. Add 1 teaspoon finely grated lime zest to bowl with sugar and cream cheese in step 2. Substitute 1 tablespoon lime juice for vanilla.

Chewy Olive Oil, Anise, and Orange Sugar Cookies
Add 1 teaspoon ground anise to flour, rub ¼ teaspoon grated orange zest into sugar in dough, and substitute extra-virgin olive oil for vegetable oil.

TUTORIAL
Chewy Sugar Cookies

The process of making sugar cookies is very exemplary of drop cookies (some of the best and easiest) except that it adds cream cheese to the chewy mix.

1. Place sugar and cream cheese in large bowl. Whisk in warm melted butter (some lumps of cream cheese will remain).

2. Whisk in oil until incorporated. Whisk in egg, milk, and vanilla until smooth.

3. Using rubber spatula, fold in flour mixture until soft, homogeneous dough forms.

4. Working with 2 tablespoons dough at a time, roll into balls, then roll in sugar to coat; space dough balls 2 inches apart on prepared sheets.

5. Using bottom of greased dry measuring cup, press each ball until 3 inches in diameter. Sprinkle with remaining sugar.

6. Bake cookies, 1 sheet at a time, until edges are set and beginning to brown, 11 to 13 minutes, rotating sheet halfway through baking.

GLUTEN-FREE PEANUT BUTTER COOKIES

Makes 24 cookies | 2 rimmed baking sheets

WHY THIS RECIPE WORKS Gluten-free or not, most peanut butter cookies are either dry and sandy or overly cakey, and they all come up short on peanut butter flavor. Our goal was a chewy, really peanut-buttery cookie that was also gluten-free. We found we could pack a full cup of peanut butter into our cookies as long as we kept the butter in check to avoid greasiness. We rested the dough for 30 minutes to hydrate it. Granulated sugar was necessary for crisp edges and structure, while brown sugar contributed chew and a molasses flavor that complemented the peanut butter. The cookies will look underdone after 12 to 14 minutes, but they will set up as they cool. The baking time is very important; 2 minutes can be the difference between a soft, chewy cookie and a dry, crisp cookie. Do not shortchange the dough's 30-minute rest.

- 8 ounces (1¾ cups) all-purpose gluten-free flour blend (see page 2)
- 1 teaspoon baking soda
- ½ teaspoon table salt
- ¼ teaspoon xanthan gum (see page 2)
- 7 ounces packed (1 cup) light brown sugar
- 5¼ ounces (¾ cup) granulated sugar
- 1 cup creamy peanut butter
- 8 tablespoons unsalted butter, melted and still warm
- 2 large eggs
- 1 teaspoon vanilla extract
- ⅓ cup dry-roasted peanuts, chopped fine

1. Whisk flour blend, baking soda, salt, and xanthan gum together in medium bowl; set aside. Combine brown sugar, granulated sugar, and peanut butter in large bowl. Pour warm butter over sugar mixture and whisk to combine. Whisk in eggs and vanilla and continue to whisk until smooth. Stir in flour mixture with rubber spatula and mix until soft, homogeneous dough forms. Cover bowl with plastic wrap and let dough rest for 30 minutes. (Dough will be slightly shiny and soft.)

2. Adjust oven rack to middle position and heat oven to 325 degrees. Line 2 rimmed baking sheets with parchment paper. Working with 2 generous tablespoons dough at a time, roll into balls and space 2 inches apart on prepared sheets. Using bottom of greased dry measuring cup, press each ball to ¾-inch thickness. Sprinkle tops evenly with peanuts.

3. Bake cookies, 1 sheet at a time, until puffed and edges have begun to set but centers are still soft (cookies will look under-done), 12 to 14 minutes, rotating sheet halfway through baking. Let cookies cool on sheet for 5 minutes, then transfer to wire rack. Serve warm or at room temperature.

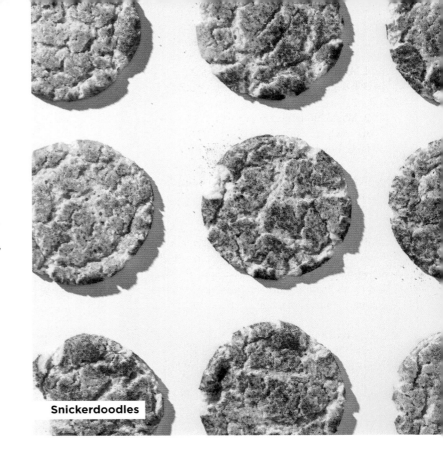

Snickerdoodles

SNICKERDOODLES

Makes 24 cookies | 2 rimless baking sheets

WHY THIS RECIPE WORKS We wanted a streamlined recipe for snickerdoodles that would still give us their trademark subtly tangy flavor and crinkly tops. We replaced the shortening with better-tasting butter, along with a bit of oil for cookies with satisfyingly chewy centers but crispy, crunchy edges. Melting the butter until the water evaporated and the milk solids caramelized gave it a pleasantly nutty flavor. Cream cheese reinforced the tanginess supplied by cream of tartar. Baking soda caused the cookies to rise in the oven and then collapse into that winning crinkled look. Trust the times in the recipe; the cookies may seem underbaked when you pull them from the oven, but they will deflate and set as they cool.

- 2¼ cups (11¼ ounces) all-purpose flour
- 1 teaspoon cream of tartar
- 1 teaspoon baking soda
- ¾ teaspoon table salt
- 1½ cups (10½ ounces) sugar, plus ⅓ cup for rolling
- 3 ounces cream cheese, cut into 3 pieces
- 8 tablespoons unsalted butter
- ¼ cup vegetable oil
- 1 large egg
- 1 teaspoon vanilla extract
- 1 tablespoon ground cinnamon

1. Adjust oven rack to middle position and heat oven to 350 degrees. Line 2 rimless baking sheets with parchment paper.

2. Whisk flour, cream of tartar, baking soda, and salt together in bowl; set aside. Place 1½ cups sugar and cream cheese in large bowl.

3. Melt butter in 8-inch skillet over medium heat. Cook, swirling skillet constantly, until milk solids in butter are color of milk chocolate and have toasty aroma, 3 to 5 minutes.

4. Immediately remove skillet from heat and scrape browned butter into bowl with sugar and cream cheese. Stir and mash with rubber spatula until combined. Whisk in oil. Whisk in egg and vanilla until smooth. Stir in flour mixture with rubber spatula until soft, homogeneous dough forms.

5. Mix cinnamon and remaining ⅓ cup sugar together in shallow dish. Working with 2 tablespoons dough at a time, roll into balls, then roll in cinnamon sugar to coat; evenly space dough balls on prepared sheets, 12 balls per sheet. Using bottom of drinking glass, flatten balls into 2-inch-wide disks, about ½ inch thick.

6. Bake cookies, 1 sheet at a time, until puffed and covered with small cracks (cookies will look raw between cracks and seem underdone; they will deflate and set as they cool), 11 to 13 minutes, rotating sheet halfway through baking.

7. Let cookies cool on sheet for 5 minutes, then transfer to wire rack and let cool completely before serving.

**Chewy Browned
Coconut Butter Cookies**

CHEWY BROWNED COCONUT BUTTER COOKIES

Makes 16 cookies | 2 rimmed baking sheets

WHY THIS RECIPE WOKS After discovering that store-bought coconut butter could be slowly browned to produce a paste with the intense flavors of toasted coconut and toffee, we knew we had to use it in a cookie. Here we achieve the crisp-chewy texture of a good sugar cookie and the toffee-like flavor of a chocolate chip cookie—without using butter. Or eggs. Or even vanilla. In fact, this vegan cookie contains only six ingredients (plus a little water), so the browned coconut butter flavor is front and center. In the absence of eggs or butter, water plays an important role in hydrating this cookie dough. Coconut butter, not to be confused with coconut oil (which is a pure fat), is pureed coconut flesh. We love Maldon Sea Salt for this recipe. The large flakes add crunch and pops of salinity.

1 (15-ounce) jar coconut butter
1½ cups (7½ ounces) all-purpose flour
¾ teaspoon baking powder
½ teaspoon baking soda
½ teaspoon table salt
1⅓ cups packed (9⅓ ounces) brown sugar
6 tablespoons plus 2 teaspoons water
Flake sea salt

1. Place jar of coconut butter in pot of just-simmering water until coconut butter is softened enough to be easily scooped from jar. (Avoid using microwave for this step as coconut butter may heat unevenly and burn in spots.)

2. Transfer coconut butter to large saucepan and cook over medium-low heat, stirring frequently, until medium brown, 6 to 8 minutes. Remove from heat and let cool slightly, about 20 minutes. Measure out ¾ cup (6⅛ ounces) browned coconut butter and set aside. (Remaining browned coconut butter can be refrigerated in airtight container for up to 1 month.)

3. Adjust oven rack to middle position and heat oven to 350 degrees. Line 2 rimmed baking sheets with parchment paper. Whisk flour, baking powder, baking soda, and salt together in medium bowl. Whisk sugar, water, and reserved browned butter in large bowl until well combined and smooth. Using rubber spatula, stir flour mixture into coconut butter mixture until just combined.

4. Divide dough into 16 pieces (about 2 tablespoons [1⅔ ounces] each) and, using your hands, roll into balls. Evenly space dough balls on prepared sheets. Using bottom of drinking glass, flatten dough balls until 2½ inches in diameter. Sprinkle with salt and gently press tops with bottom of drinking glass to help salt adhere.

5. Bake, 1 sheet at a time, until edges are set and just beginning to brown, 15 to 17 minutes, rotating sheet after 7 minutes. Let cookies cool on sheets for 5 minutes, then transfer to wire rack and let cool completely before serving. (Cooled cookies can be stored at room temperature for up to 5 days.)

LOADED COOKIES-AND-CREAM COOKIES

Makes 16 cookies | 2 rimmed baking sheets

WHY THIS RECIPE WORKS We jam-packed these cookies with even more cookies. Chopped Oreos and chunks of white chocolate give these unapologetically loaded treats a cookies-and-cream profile. We started with a simple and easy-to-make cookie dough that would taste great on its own and have satisfying chew. For this base we used a combination of flour, butter, sugar, eggs, vanilla, baking soda, and salt. Melting the butter and adding some brown sugar to the mix gave us the chewy texture we were after. Underbaking the cookies ensured that they remain chewy once cool.

2¼ cups (11¼ ounces) all-purpose flour
  1 teaspoon table salt
¾ teaspoon baking soda
  1 cup packed (7 ounces) light brown sugar
12 tablespoons unsalted butter, melted
½ cup (3½ ounces) granulated sugar
  2 large eggs
1½ teaspoons vanilla extract
15 Oreo cookies, chopped (1½ cups)
  4 ounces white chocolate, chopped

1. Adjust oven rack to middle position and heat oven to 425 degrees. Line 2 rimmed baking sheets with parchment paper. Combine flour, salt, and baking soda in bowl.

2. Using stand mixer fitted with paddle, beat brown sugar, melted butter, and granulated sugar on medium speed until well combined, about 1 minute, scraping down bowl as needed. Add eggs and vanilla and beat until fully incorporated, about 30 seconds.

3. Reduce speed to low. Slowly add flour mixture and mix until mostly incorporated but some streaks of flour remain, about 30 seconds. Add cookies and chocolate and mix until evenly distributed throughout dough, about 30 seconds.

4. Divide dough into sixteen 2½-ounce portions, about ¼ cup each. Divide any remaining dough evenly among dough portions. Roll dough portions between your wet hands to make dough balls.

5. Evenly space dough balls on prepared sheets, 8 balls per sheet. Using your hand, flatten dough balls to ¾-inch thickness.

6. Bake cookies, 1 sheet at a time, until centers of cookies are puffed and still very blond, 8 to 10 minutes. (Cookies will seem underdone but will continue to bake as they cool.) Let cookies cool on sheet for 5 minutes, then transfer to wire rack and let cool for 10 minutes. Serve warm.

CHOCOLATE CHUNK OATMEAL COOKIES WITH PECANS AND DRIED CHERRIES

Makes 16 cookies | 2 rimmed baking sheets

WHY THIS RECIPE WORKS Oatmeal cookies provide an ideal backdrop for almost any addition. But it's easy to lapse into a kitchen-sink mentality, overloading the dough with a jumble of ingredients. We achieved the perfect combination of oats, nuts, chocolate, and fruit in a superlatively chewy package. We used dark brown sugar for deep molasses flavor and the chewiest texture. Making big cookies and baking them just until set yet slightly underdone further ensured good chew. For our carefully curated mix-ins we opted for bittersweet chocolate, toasted pecans, and tart dried cherries for the perfect balance of flavors and textures. You can substitute walnuts or skinned hazelnuts for the pecans and dried cranberries for the cherries. Quick oats can be used in place of the old-fashioned oats, but they will yield a cookie with slightly less chew.

1¼ cups (6¼ ounces) all-purpose flour
¾ teaspoon baking powder
½ teaspoon baking soda
½ teaspoon table salt
1¼ cups (3¾ ounces) old-fashioned rolled oats
  1 cup pecans, toasted and chopped
  1 cup (4 ounces) dried sour cherries, chopped coarse
  4 ounces bittersweet chocolate, chopped into chunks about size of chocolate chips
12 tablespoons unsalted butter, softened
1½ cups packed (10½ ounces) dark brown sugar
  1 large egg
  1 teaspoon vanilla extract

Chocolate Chunk Oatmeal Cookies with Pecans and Dried Cherries

1. Adjust oven racks to upper-middle and lower-middle positions and heat oven to 350 degrees. Line 2 rimmed baking sheets with parchment paper. Whisk flour, baking powder, baking soda, and salt together in bowl. Stir oats, pecans, cherries, and chocolate together in second bowl.

2. Using stand mixer fitted with paddle, beat butter and sugar on medium speed until no sugar lumps remain, about 1 minute, scraping down bowl as needed. Reduce speed to medium-low, add egg and vanilla, and beat until fully incorporated, about 30 seconds, scraping down bowl as needed. Reduce speed to low, add flour mixture, and mix until just combined, about 30 seconds. Gradually add oat mixture until just incorporated. Give dough final stir by hand to ensure that no flour pockets remain and ingredients are evenly distributed.

3. Working with ¼ cup dough at a time, roll into balls and space them 2½ inches apart on prepared sheets. Using bottom of greased dry measuring cup, press each ball to 1-inch thickness.

4. Bake cookies until medium brown and edges have begun to set but centers are still soft (cookies will look raw between cracks and seem underdone), 20 to 22 minutes, switching and rotating sheets halfway through baking. Let cookies cool on sheets for 5 minutes, then transfer to wire rack and let cool completely before serving.

PEANUT BUTTER–STUFFED CHOCOLATE COOKIES

Makes 16 cookies | 2 rimmed baking sheets

WHY THIS RECIPE WORKS For fudgy cookies that pack all the lovable flavors of a peanut butter cup, we started by creating a double-chocolate cookie dough that was easy to work with and stuff with a Reese's-like filling. Adding bittersweet chocolate as well as Dutch-processed cocoa powder to the dough layered in potent chocolate flavor, and the cocoa powder helped keep the cookies rich and fudgy. Increasing the standard ratio of flour to sugar, fat, and egg kept the dough from becoming sticky, making it easy to portion and flatten dough balls to be stuffed with a simple mixture of chilled peanut butter, confectioners' sugar, and salt. Finally, rolling the stuffed dough balls in granulated sugar and more confectioners' sugar made the baked cookies crinkly and stunningly beautiful. Once baked and cooled, these cookies are best stored in the refrigerator.

FILLING
- ½ cup creamy peanut butter
- ½ cup (2 ounces) confectioners' sugar
- ¼ teaspoon table salt

DOUGH
- 1½ cups (7½ ounces) all-purpose flour
- ¼ cup (¾ ounce) Dutch-processed cocoa powder
- 1 teaspoon baking powder
- ¼ teaspoon baking soda
- ¾ teaspoon table salt
- 10 ounces bittersweet chocolate, chopped fine, divided
- 3 tablespoons vegetable oil
- 1 tablespoon unsalted butter
- 1 tablespoon vanilla extract
- 1 cup (7 ounces) granulated sugar, plus ⅓ cup for rolling
- 2 large eggs
- ½ cup confectioners' sugar for rolling

1. FOR THE FILLING: Combine peanut butter, sugar, and salt in bowl. Using fork or your hands, stir and mash mixture until thoroughly combined and no dry pockets of sugar remain. Divide filling into 16 equal portions (about 2 teaspoons each). Roll each portion into ball and place on large plate. Freeze until firm, about 30 minutes.

2. FOR THE DOUGH: Meanwhile, adjust oven racks to upper-middle and lower-middle positions and heat oven to 300 degrees. Line 2 rimmed baking sheets with parchment paper.

3. Whisk flour, cocoa, baking powder, baking soda, and salt together in medium bowl. Microwave 6 ounces chocolate, oil, and butter in second medium bowl at 50 percent power, stirring occasionally, until melted, about 3 minutes. Whisk vanilla into melted chocolate mixture until combined.

4. Whisk 1 cup granulated sugar and eggs in large bowl until thoroughly combined. Add melted chocolate mixture and whisk until uniform. Using rubber spatula, fold in flour mixture until combined. Fold in remaining 4 ounces chocolate.

5. Divide dough into 16 equal portions, about scant 3 tablespoons (1 ⅞ ounces) each; divide any remaining dough evenly among portions. Use your fingers to flatten 1 dough portion into disk with roughly 3-inch diameter. Place 1 ball of filling in center of disk. Wrap edges of dough up and around filling, seal dough, and shape into smooth ball. Repeat with remaining dough portions and filling.

6. Place confectioners' sugar and remaining ⅓ cup granulated sugar in 2 separate shallow dishes. Working in batches, roll dough balls first in granulated sugar, then in confectioners' sugar, to coat. Evenly space dough balls on prepared sheets, 8 dough balls per sheet.

7. Using bottom of drinking glass, flatten dough balls into 2-inch-wide disks. (Dough balls will crack at edges; this is OK. If filling shows through any large cracks, pinch dough together to seal cracks.) Bake until cookies are puffed, edges are just set, and cookies no longer look raw between cracks, about 22 minutes, switching and rotating sheets halfway through baking. Transfer sheets to wire rack and let cookies cool completely before serving.

THIN AND CRISPY CHOCOLATE CHIP COOKIES

Makes 16 cookies | 2 rimmed baking sheets

WHY THIS RECIPE WORKS While our Perfect Chocolate Chip Cookies (page 17) are rich and buttery with an irresistibly chewy center, sometimes we get a hankering for another style: a thin, crisp cookie—one that's perfectly flat, almost praline in appearance, and that packs a big crunch. While brown sugar gives chocolate chip cookies nice flavor, it also contributes moisture; substituting white sugar for some of the brown gave our cookies just the right balance of butterscotch flavor and good crunch. Melted butter helped the dough spread quickly so that the cookies baked without burning. While a traditional chewy cookie contains whole eggs, which encourage the cookies to rise, we used only yolks to thin out the structure of our crispy cookies. Note that this recipe calls for cake flour and mini (not full-size) chocolate chips.

1¼ cups (5 ounces) cake flour
¾   teaspoon table salt
¼   teaspoon baking soda
8   tablespoons unsalted butter, melted and cooled
⅓   cup (2⅓ ounces) granulated sugar
⅓   cup packed (2⅓ ounces) dark brown sugar

2   large egg yolks
1½ tablespoons whole milk
2   teaspoons vanilla extract
¾   cup (4½ ounces) mini semisweet chocolate chips

1. Adjust oven rack to middle position and heat oven to 350 degrees. Line 2 rimmed baking sheets with parchment paper. Whisk flour, salt, and baking soda together in bowl.

2. Using stand mixer fitted with paddle, mix melted butter, granulated sugar, and brown sugar on low speed until fully combined. Increase speed to medium-high and beat until mixture is lightened in color, about 1 minute. Reduce speed to low; add egg yolks, milk, and vanilla; and mix until combined. Slowly add flour mixture and mix until just combined, scraping down bowl as needed. Using rubber spatula, stir in chocolate chips.

3. Using greased 1-tablespoon measure, divide dough into 16 heaping-tablespoon portions on prepared sheets, 8 portions per sheet. Divide any remaining dough evenly among portions. Using your moistened fingers, press dough portions to ½-inch thickness. Bake cookies, 1 sheet at a time, until deep golden brown, 16 to 18 minutes, rotating sheet halfway through baking. Transfer sheet to wire rack and let cookies cool completely before serving.

GINGERSNAPS

Makes 80 cookies | 2 rimmed baking sheets

WHY THIS RECIPE WORKS Most gingersnap recipes don't live up to their name on either account. We wanted homemade gingersnaps to rival the snap and spice of the store-bought kind. Cutting back on the brown sugar reduced moisture as did browning the butter for noticeably drier, crunchier cookies. Using plenty of baking soda resulted in attractive fissures on the tops of our cookies, which also served as channels for moisture to escape. Finally, a lower oven temperature and longer baking time dried them out enough to yield our desired snappy texture. For cookies with real bite, we doubled the amount of dried ginger called for in most recipes and added fresh ginger, black pepper, and a secret weapon: cayenne pepper. For efficiency, form the second batch of cookies while the first batch bakes. The 2 teaspoons of baking soda is essential to getting the right texture.

2½ cups (12½ ounces) all-purpose flour
2   teaspoons baking soda
½   teaspoon table salt
12 tablespoons unsalted butter
2   tablespoons ground ginger
1   teaspoon ground cinnamon
¼   teaspoon ground cloves

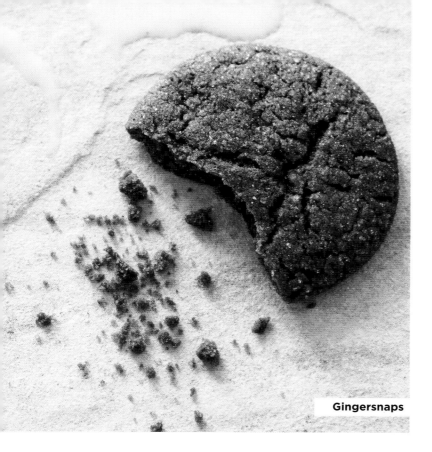

Gingersnaps

4. Place 1 sheet on upper rack and bake for 15 minutes. Transfer partially baked top sheet to lower rack, rotating sheet, and place second sheet of dough balls on upper rack. Continue to bake until cookies on lower sheet just begin to darken around edges, 10 to 12 minutes longer. Remove lower sheet of cookies and transfer upper sheet to lower rack, rotating sheet; continue to bake until cookies begin to darken around edges, 15 to 17 minutes longer.

5. Slide baked cookies, still on parchment, onto wire rack and let cool completely before serving. Repeat with remaining dough balls.

SAND TARTS

Makes 36 cookies | 2 rimmed baking sheets

WHY THIS RECIPE WORKS These buttery, crisp, cinnamon-sugar cookies may have fallen out of favor because the firm dough can be hard to work with. A food processor and reverse creaming eliminated excess air in the dough for cookies that baked flat and crisp. Removing an egg white also helped prevent the cookies from doming. This rich, sticky dough was easily formed into balls, rolled in cinnamon sugar, and flattened. Carefully arranged sliced almonds gave our cookies their signature sand dollar look. Both sliced natural almonds and blanched slices work well here.

   2 cups (10 ounces) all-purpose flour
1½ cups (10½ ounces) sugar, plus ¼ cup for rolling
  ¾ teaspoon table salt
 16 tablespoons unsalted butter, softened
  1 large egg plus 1 large yolk
1½ teaspoons ground cinnamon
  ¼ cup sliced almonds

1. Adjust oven racks to upper-middle and lower-middle positions and heat oven to 350 degrees. Line 2 rimmed baking sheets with parchment paper. Process flour, 1½ cups sugar, and salt in food processor until combined. Add butter, 1 tablespoon at a time, and pulse until just incorporated. Add egg and yolk and pulse until soft dough forms.

2. Wrap dough in plastic wrap and flatten into 1-inch-thick disk. Transfer to freezer until firm, about 15 minutes. Combine cinnamon and remaining ¼ cup sugar in small bowl. Break disk of chilled dough into 2 pieces and return 1 piece to freezer. Working with 1½ tablespoons chilled dough at a time, use your floured hands to roll into balls, then roll in cinnamon-sugar mixture to coat. Space balls 3 inches apart on prepared baking sheets. Press balls into 2½-inch disks with greased measuring cup, sprinkle with cinnamon-sugar, and garnish with almonds.

  ¼ teaspoon pepper
     Pinch cayenne pepper
1¼ cups packed (8¾ ounces) dark brown sugar
  ¼ cup molasses
  2 tablespoons finely grated fresh ginger
  1 large egg plus 1 large yolk
  ½ cup granulated sugar for rolling

1. Whisk flour, baking soda, and salt together in bowl; set aside. Melt butter in 10-inch skillet over medium heat. Reduce heat to medium-low and continue to cook, swirling skillet frequently, until butter is just beginning to brown, 2 to 4 minutes. Transfer browned butter to large bowl and whisk in ground ginger, cinnamon, cloves, pepper, and cayenne. Let cool slightly, about 2 minutes.

2. Whisk brown sugar, molasses, and fresh ginger into butter mixture until combined. Whisk in egg and yolk until combined. Stir in flour mixture until just combined. Cover bowl tightly with plastic wrap and refrigerate until dough is firm, about 1 hour.

3. Adjust oven racks to upper-middle and lower-middle positions and heat oven to 300 degrees. Line 2 rimmed baking sheets with parchment paper. Spread granulated sugar in shallow dish. Divide dough into heaping teaspoon portions; roll dough into 1-inch balls. Working in batches of 10, roll balls in sugar to coat; space dough balls evenly on prepared sheets, 20 dough balls per sheet.

3. Bake cookies until edges are lightly browned, 10 to 12 minutes, switching and rotating sheets halfway through baking. Let cool for 5 minutes on sheets, then transfer to wire rack and let cool completely before serving. Repeat with remaining dough.

BLACK AND WHITE COOKIES

Makes 12 cookies | 2 rimmed baking sheets

WHY THIS RECIPE WORKS These gigantic, tender, cakey cookies, a mainstay of New York City bakeries, sport a two-toned coat of icing—half chocolate and half vanilla. To create this iconic cookie, we started with a basic creamed batter, then swapped in sour cream for the milk to add tenderness and rich flavor. All-purpose flour provided enough structure to hold them together. We quickly determined that the flat undersides of the cookies were far easier to frost. We made a simple glaze with confectioners' sugar, milk, vanilla, and corn syrup that formed a crisp shell as it dried yet stayed creamy underneath. Creating the chocolate glaze was as simple as adding cocoa to the vanilla glaze. You'll get neater cookies if you spread on the vanilla glaze first. This recipe provides a little extra glaze, just in case.

COOKIES

1¾ cups (8¾ ounces) all-purpose flour
½ teaspoon baking powder
¼ teaspoon baking soda
⅛ teaspoon table salt
10 tablespoons unsalted butter, softened
1 cup (7 ounces) granulated sugar
1 large egg
2 teaspoons vanilla extract
⅓ cup sour cream

GLAZE

5 cups (20 ounces) confectioners' sugar, sifted
7 tablespoons whole milk, divided
2 tablespoons corn syrup
1 teaspoon vanilla extract
½ teaspoon table salt
3 tablespoons Dutch-processed cocoa powder, sifted

1. **FOR THE COOKIES:** Adjust oven racks to upper-middle and lower-middle positions and heat oven to 350 degrees. Line 2 rimmed baking sheets with parchment paper. Whisk flour, baking powder, baking soda, and salt together in bowl.

2. Using stand mixer fitted with paddle, beat butter and sugar on medium speed until pale and fluffy, about 3 minutes. Add egg and vanilla and beat until combined. Reduce speed to low and add flour mixture in 3 additions, alternating with sour cream in 2 additions, scraping down bowl as needed. Give dough final stir by hand to ensure that no dry pockets of flour remain.

Using greased ¼-cup dry measuring cup, drop mounds of dough 3 inches apart on prepared sheets. Bake until edges are lightly browned, 15 to 18 minutes, switching and rotating sheets halfway through baking. Let cookies cool on sheets for 5 minutes, then transfer to wire rack and let cool completely.

3. **FOR THE GLAZE:** Whisk sugar, 6 tablespoons milk, corn syrup, vanilla, and salt together in bowl until smooth. Transfer 1 cup glaze to small bowl; reserve. Whisk cocoa and remaining 1 tablespoon milk into remaining glaze until combined.

4. Working with 1 cookie at a time, spread 1 tablespoon vanilla glaze over half of flat side of cookies. Refrigerate until glaze is dry, about 15 minutes. Glaze other half of each cookie with 1 tablespoon chocolate glaze. Let glaze dry for at least 1 hour before serving.

APPLESAUCE COOKIES

Makes 22 cookies | 2 rimmed baking sheets

WHY THIS RECIPE WORKS Applesauce spice cake is a comforting snack; it made sense to transform its flavors into a portable treat—a light, fluffy cookie loaded with apple flavor. We needed to find ways to eliminate water in the dough without decreasing the applesauce. Because applesauce acts as a binder, we found we didn't need a lot of egg; just one yolk gave us structure and richness without added water from the white. Browning the butter further cut down on water and imparted a nutty depth. Finally, a healthy amount of baking soda gave the cookies lift, lightening the crumb; it also contributed to a nicely browned exterior. To give our soft, tender cookies some textural contrast, we mixed in crunchy toasted walnuts and drizzled the finished cookies with a tangy spiced glaze.

1½ cups (7½ ounces) all-purpose flour
½ cup walnuts, toasted and chopped
¾ teaspoon baking soda
½ teaspoon table salt
8 tablespoons unsalted butter
¾ teaspoon plus ⅛ teaspoon ground cinnamon, divided
¾ cup unsweetened applesauce
¾ cup packed (5¼ ounces) light brown sugar
1 large egg yolk
6 tablespoons (1½ ounces) confectioners' sugar
2 tablespoons sour cream

1. Adjust oven racks to upper-middle and lower-middle positions and heat oven to 375 degrees. Line 2 rimmed baking sheets with parchment paper. Whisk flour, walnuts, baking soda, and salt together in bowl.

2. Melt butter in 10-inch skillet over medium-high heat. Continue to cook, swirling skillet constantly, until butter is dark golden and has nutty aroma, 1 to 3 minutes. Add ¾ teaspoon cinnamon and continue to cook, stirring constantly, for 5 seconds. Transfer butter mixture to bowl; let cool for 15 minutes.

3. Whisk applesauce, brown sugar, and egg yolk together in large bowl. Add butter mixture and whisk until combined. Stir in flour mixture until smooth. Drop 2-tablespoon mounds of dough onto prepared sheets, spacing them about 1½ inches apart.

4. Bake cookies until edges are golden brown and centers are firm, 13 to 15 minutes, switching and rotating sheets halfway through baking. Let cookies cool on sheets for 10 minutes, then transfer to wire rack and let cool completely.

5. Whisk confectioners' sugar, sour cream, and remaining ⅛ teaspoon cinnamon in bowl until smooth. Drizzle cookies with glaze and let dry for at least 15 minutes before serving.

Applesauce Cookies

ANGELETTI

Makes 32 cookies | 2 rimmed baking sheets

WHY THIS RECIPE WORKS Angeletti, also known as anisette cookies, are a staple at any big Italian celebration. Cakey, with a little heft, the anise cookies share similarities with a scone or a biscuit. To achieve their unique texture, we used shortening in addition to butter. The shortening gave the cookies a lighter texture and an appealing crisp edge, while butter contributed plenty of flavor. Lemon zest and juice ably complemented the refreshing hit of anise. To ensure that the anise flavor fully permeated our cookies, we used extract in both the dough and the glaze. These cookies are traditionally decorated with cheery multicolored nonpareils after their bright white glaze is applied, but feel free to use any sprinkles you like. Just be sure to glaze and decorate only a few cookies at a time so the sprinkles stick before the glaze dries.

  2 cups (10 ounces) all-purpose flour
  ½ cup (3½ ounces) granulated sugar
  2 teaspoons baking powder
  ½ teaspoon table salt
  4 tablespoons unsalted butter, cut into ½-inch pieces and chilled
  4 tablespoons vegetable shortening, cut into ½-inch pieces and chilled
  2 large eggs
1¼ teaspoons anise extract, divided
  1 teaspoon vanilla extract
  1 teaspoon grated lemon zest plus 2 tablespoons juice
1½ cups (6 ounces) confectioners' sugar
     Multicolored nonpareils (optional)

1. Adjust oven racks to upper-middle and lower-middle positions and heat oven to 375 degrees. Line 2 baking rimmed sheets with parchment paper.

2. Process flour, granulated sugar, baking powder, and salt in food processor until combined, about 5 seconds. Scatter butter and shortening over top and pulse until mixture appears sandy, 10 to 12 pulses. Add eggs, 1 teaspoon anise extract, vanilla, and lemon zest and process until dough forms, 20 to 30 seconds.

3. Working with 1 tablespoon dough at a time, roll into balls and space them 2 inches apart on prepared sheets. Bake until tops have puffed and cracked and bottoms are light golden brown, 14 to 16 minutes, switching and rotating sheets halfway through baking. Let cookies cool on sheets for 5 minutes, then transfer to wire rack and let cool completely.

4. Whisk confectioners' sugar, lemon juice, and remaining ¼ teaspoon anise extract in bowl until smooth. Working with a few cookies at a time, spread each cookie with glaze and decorate with nonpareils, if using. Let glaze dry for at least 30 minutes before serving.

Angeletti

LEMON–SOUR CREAM COOKIES

Makes 42 cookies | 2 rimmed baking sheets

WHY THIS RECIPE WORKS When it's a plush, tender cookie we want, a soft-baked lemon cookie topped with a tangy glaze fits the bill. To achieve a fluffy-yet-sturdy texture and crumb that is simultaneously moist and light and airy, we reached for sour cream, and plenty of it; a full cup contributed moisture and richness. It also tenderized the cookies' crumb, and, in conjunction with the lemon juice in this recipe, reacted with the leavener to create fluffy lift. This generous amount of sour cream also added a pleasant tang, which we reinforced with a couple teaspoons of floral lemon zest. Creaming the butter and sugar and adding two whole eggs to the recipe also helped aerate the dough. A lemon–cream cheese glaze was a nice finishing touch that delivered a second hit of clean citrusy flavor.

- 3 cups (15 ounces) all-purpose flour
- 1 teaspoon baking powder
- ½ teaspoon baking soda
- ½ teaspoon table salt
- 16 tablespoons unsalted butter, softened
- 1½ cups (10½ ounces) granulated sugar
- 2 large eggs
- 1 cup sour cream
- 2 teaspoons grated lemon zest plus ¼ cup juice (2 lemons)
- 1 ounce cream cheese, softened
- 3 cups (12 ounces) confectioners' sugar

1. Whisk flour, baking powder, baking soda, and salt together in large bowl. Using stand mixer fitted with paddle, beat butter and granulated sugar on medium-high speed until pale and fluffy, about 3 minutes. Add eggs, one at a time, and beat until incorporated, about 30 seconds. Reduce speed to low, add sour cream and lemon zest, and beat until just combined. Add flour mixture until incorporated, about 30 seconds. Cover bowl tightly with plastic wrap and refrigerate for 1 hour.

2. Adjust oven racks to upper-middle and lower-middle positions and heat oven to 375 degrees. Line 2 rimmed baking sheets with parchment paper.

3. Drop heaping 1-tablespoon mounds of dough onto prepared sheets, spacing them about 2 inches apart. Bake until just golden around edges, about 15 minutes, switching and rotating sheets halfway through baking. Transfer sheets to wire rack and let cookies cool completely. Repeat with remaining dough.

4. Whisk lemon juice and cream cheese in bowl until combined. Add confectioners' sugar and whisk until smooth. Spread 1 teaspoon glaze onto each cooled cookie before serving.

RICOTTA–CHOCOLATE CHIP COOKIES

Makes 36 cookies | 2 rimmed baking sheets

WHY THIS RECIPE WORKS Ricotta may not immediately come to mind as a cookie ingredient, but its pillowy texture makes for an incredibly delicate, cake-like crumb. Inspired by the combination of chocolate and ricotta in cannoli, we set out to create a unique cookie that was light and tender. We creamed the butter and sugar in a stand mixer until pale and fluffy and then mixed in the flour and ricotta slowly in several additions. One egg plus an extra yolk provided just the right amount of structure and richness. Mini chocolate chips provided the perfect contrast to the sweet, soft ricotta. Do not use standard-size chocolate chips in this recipe; they will overpower the ricotta.

- 2 cups (10 ounces) all-purpose flour
- ½ teaspoon baking soda
- ½ teaspoon table salt
- 8 tablespoons unsalted butter, softened
- 1 cup (7 ounces) sugar
- 1 large egg plus 1 large yolk
- 1 teaspoon vanilla extract
- 8 ounces (1 cup) whole-milk ricotta cheese
- ¾ cup (4½ ounces) mini semisweet chocolate chips

1. Adjust oven racks to upper-middle and lower-middle positions and heat oven to 350 degrees. Line 2 rimmed baking sheets with parchment paper. Whisk flour, baking soda, and salt together in bowl; set aside.

2. Using stand mixer fitted with paddle, beat butter and sugar on medium-high speed until pale and fluffy, about 3 minutes. Add egg and yolk and vanilla and beat until combined, about 15 seconds. Reduce speed to low and add flour mixture in 3 additions, alternating with ricotta in 2 additions, scraping down bowl as needed. Stir in chocolate chips by hand.

3. Working with 1 heaping tablespoon dough at a time, drop dough evenly onto prepared sheets. Bake until cookies are set around edges, 12 to 14 minutes, switching and rotating sheets halfway through baking. Let cookies cool on sheets for 5 minutes, then transfer to wire rack and let cool completely. (Cookies can be stored in airtight container for up to 5 days.)

BUTTER COOKIES

STANDARD BUTTER-COOKIE DOUGH includes just a few main ingredients: all-purpose flour, butter, sugar, and (sometimes) eggs. But don't let the short ingredient list fool you: Not all butter cookies are alike. Butter cookies come in a variety of shapes and present in a gradient of textures from finer to crumblier, all offering sophistication and style with simple pantry ingredients. These variations are largely determined by the ratio of butter to flour, as well as the temperature of the butter and the way it is combined with the other ingredients. Some cookies are relatively thick and sturdy with a pleasantly sandy texture, while others are delicate, flat, and crisp. The flavor of butter takes center stage, but the butter is also what can make the dough challenging to handle, especially when there is a lot of it; chilling the dough is typically an easy solution and prevents it from being overly sticky. Because this type of cookie is meant to be crispy or crumbly, not chewy, limiting gluten development is important; this is typically achieved by reducing moisture and/or replacing some of the flour with another ingredient such as oats, nuts, or cornstarch.

Shortbread

The best shortbread crumbles in the mouth with a pure, buttery richness. Its high butter-to-flour ratio is partially responsible for its distinctive texture and sets it apart from other types of butter cookies, which can be thin and crisp. The type of sugar used can make a difference as well: Granulated sugar contributes a slightly grainier, more rustic texture, whereas finely ground confectioners' sugar yields a finer, more delicate crumb.

THE SHAPES OF SHORTBREAD

Shortbread originated as a way to turn leftover oat bread into something special: The scraps were sprinkled with sugar and left to harden overnight in an oven still hot from the day's baking. Over time, wheat flour replaced oat flour in the recipe for a more refined confection. In traditional Scottish versions of shortbread, the dough is simply shaped into a round, baked, and then scored into wedges. But shortbread can come in all shapes and sizes; it can be cut into rectangles or squares after baking (or before, as with Swedish Walnut Fingers on page 37), rolled and stamped with a cookie cutter, even shaped into a log and sliced. And while butter is always the star of the show, the flavor of shortbread can be enhanced with everything from chocolate to spices to nuts.

MIX SHORTBREAD IN REVERSE

Classic shortbread should have a substantial texture, one that crumbles in your mouth—but not in your hand. For our Shortbread Cookies (page 35) we found that the right mixing method was essential for producing a cookie with the ideal texture. The most traditional approach is akin to making pie crust: Cut the butter and dry ingredients together until they form wet crumbs and then pack the crumbs together into a dough. But we found this technique produced cookies that were crumbly in some spots and brittle in others. Creaming the butter and sugar before adding the flour was also out. This method incorporated too much air into the dough, making for soft, airy, cakelike cookies. Reverse creaming—mixing the flour and sugar before adding the butter—created less aeration, yielded the most reliable results, and was clearly the way to go.

Standard Butter Cookies

Classic butter cookies come in a variety of shapes and sizes, from petite ball-shaped treats to standard cookie-cutter rounds to elegant golden swirls. They have a unique texture that can vary from delicate and crisp to granular and almost crumbly. You'd recognize them if you're familiar with the Royal Dansk blue tin, a fixture for many at the holidays. What unites them is their moderate butter-to-flour ratio, which is lower than that of shortbread styles. Creaming the butter and sugar is the usual mixing method of choice and results in a light, tender cookie.

SEARCHING FOR SAND

Sablés are a type of French butter cookie with an inviting granular texture. (Sablé is French for "sandy," which reflects the cookies' crisp crumble.) For cookies to have a sandy texture, eliminating some moisture is key; with less liquid, only a portion of the sugar dissolves, leaving behind intact granules that deliver a sandy consistency. Reducing the butter is a good start—butter is 20 percent water—but you can't reduce it too much, as you need enough butterfat to coat the flour and provide tenderness. Removing the egg completely, or using just the yolk (which is about 50 percent water compared to the white's 90 percent) is another option. In fact, some recipes (such as our own recipe for Sablés on page 38) go so far as to use a hard-cooked egg yolk—once cooked, its water becomes unavailable to dissolve sugar, which means the sugar's crystalline texture remains.

Butter Cookie Shapes

Butter cookies offer sophistication and style with simple pantry ingredients. With rich flavor and satisfying texture, they require little adornment other than perhaps a sprinkling of crunchy sugar. At their simplest they are shaped like icebox cookies; the dough is rolled into a log, chilled, and then sliced into rounds. But this style of cookies lends itself well to all sorts of fanciful shapes (just think of the cookies from the blue tin). Pretzels and spirals are two of our favorites.

FORMING BLACK AND WHITE SPIRAL COOKIES

FORMING PRETZEL SABLÉS

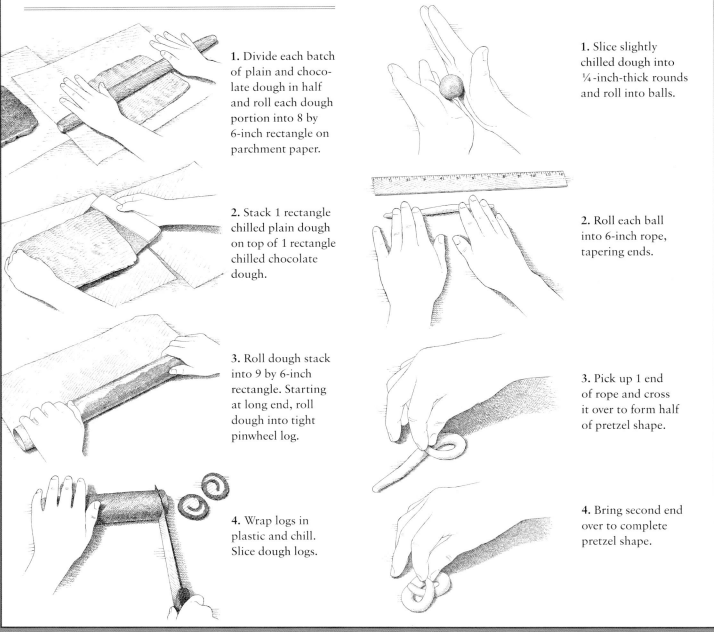

1. Divide each batch of plain and chocolate dough in half and roll each dough portion into 8 by 6-inch rectangle on parchment paper.

2. Stack 1 rectangle chilled plain dough on top of 1 rectangle chilled chocolate dough.

3. Roll dough stack into 9 by 6-inch rectangle. Starting at long end, roll dough into tight pinwheel log.

4. Wrap logs in plastic and chill. Slice dough logs.

1. Slice slightly chilled dough into ¼-inch-thick rounds and roll into balls.

2. Roll each ball into 6-inch rope, tapering ends.

3. Pick up 1 end of rope and cross it over to form half of pretzel shape.

4. Bring second end over to complete pretzel shape.

SNOWBALLS INTERNATIONAL

Snowballs, those familiar petite round cookies dusted with confectioners' sugar, go by many names in many different countries: wedding cookies in Mexico, tea cakes in Russia, kourabiedes in Greece, and polvorones in Spain. Thought to have originated in the Middle East, these cookies eventually made their way to Europe and beyond. Today, variations abound, but most recipes follow a similar path: Chopped or ground nuts and sometimes spices are added to a butter cookie base and the dough is shaped (often into balls or crescents); once baked, the cookies are tossed in confectioners' sugar for a festive finish. Buttery, nutty, slightly crisp, always crumbly, and with a melt-in-your-mouth texture, these treats are irresistible—no matter what you call them.

Sugar Cookies

A favorite for the holidays and other celebrations, this type of cookie features a dough that is rolled and stamped with a cookie cutter or cut into shapes. Of all the butter cookies, this type has the lowest ratio of fat to flour, which facilitates rolling. Chilling the dough is essential, making it much easier to work with (warm butter creates sticky dough that's difficult to manage). The chilling typically happens once the dough is shaped into disks, but sometimes you might chill the dough after rolling it out; for our Holiday Sugar Cookies (page 39) we discovered that we could use chilled butter in the dough and then roll it out right away. These cutout cookies bake up flat and crisp yet sturdy, making them the perfect vehicle for festive additions—though they're just as delicious unadorned. Discover ways to shape, decorate, and enjoy sugar cookies on pages 42–43.

FASHIONING FLAT COOKIES

Cookies with minimal rise and flat tops are ideal for decorating. Here are a few ways we achieve this.

Use Reverse Creaming
This mixing method starts by combining all the dry ingredients before incorporating softened butter and finally any liquids. Since the butter isn't beaten with sugar, less air is incorporated, which translates to less rise and a sturdier cookie.

Skip the Leavener
Baking soda and baking powder create lift—and sometimes a domed top. Eliminating them is one way to ensure minimal rise.

Mix in a Food Processor
Not only does a food processor make mixing dough a breeze, the speed with which the blades combine the ingredients means less air is incorporated.

TUTORIAL
Shortbread Cookies

A springform pan collar helps achieve the traditional shape and slices of this model shortbread.

1. Press dough evenly into springform pan collar, smoothing top of dough with back of spoon.

2. Using 2-inch cutter, cut out center of dough and place extracted 2-inch cookie on sheet next to collar.

3. Replace cutter in center of dough. Open springform collar, but leave it in place. Bake for 5 minutes.

4. Reduce oven temperature to 250 degrees and continue to bake until edges turn pale golden, 10 to 15 minutes. Remove baking sheet and turn off oven. Remove pan collar. Score shortbread into 16 even wedges, cutting down halfway through shortbread.

5. Using wooden skewer, poke 8 to 10 holes in each wedge. Return shortbread to oven, prop door open with handle of wooden spoon, and let shortbread dry in turned-off oven until center is firm but giving to touch, about 1 hour.

6. Remove shortbread from oven and let cool completely on sheet, about 2 hours. Cut shortbread at scored marks and serve.

SHORTBREAD COOKIES

Makes 16 wedges | 9-inch springform pan

WHY THIS RECIPE WORKS We wanted shortbread worthy of its royal reputation: tawny brown cookies with a distinctive texture and pure buttery richness. We tinkered with the time-honored ratio of butter to flour, settling on slightly less butter than flour by weight for rich-tasting—but not greasy—shortbread. Cutting the butter into the flour resulted in cookies that were crumbly in some spots and brittle in others, while creaming the butter and sugar incorporated too much air and resulted in cakey shortbread. Reverse creaming resulted in less aeration and produced substantial shortbread. Replacing some of the flour with ground oats and cornstarch minimized gluten development for tender cookies. We baked the shortbread briefly in a hot oven and then turned the temperature down to finish. Finally, we scored the shortbread and returned it to a turned-off oven, where it dried and finished cooking.

½   cup (1½ ounces) old-fashioned rolled oats
1½ cups (7½ ounces) all-purpose flour
⅔   cup (2⅔ ounces) confectioners' sugar
¼   cup (1 ounce) cornstarch
½   teaspoon table salt
14 tablespoons unsalted butter, cut into
    ⅛-inch-thick slices and chilled

1. Adjust oven rack to middle position and heat oven to 450 degrees. Pulse oats in spice grinder or blender to fine powder, about 10 pulses. Using stand mixer fitted with paddle, mix flour, sugar, cornstarch, salt, and processed oats on low speed until combined. Add butter, 1 piece at a time, and mix until dough just forms and pulls away from sides of bowl, 5 to 10 minutes.

2. Place collar of 9- or 9½-inch springform pan on parchment paper–lined rimmed baking sheet (do not use springform pan bottom). Press dough evenly into collar, smoothing top of dough with back of spoon. Using 2-inch cutter, cut out center of dough, place extracted 2-inch cookie on sheet next to collar, and replace cutter in center of dough. Open springform collar, but leave it in place.

3. Bake for 5 minutes. Reduce oven temperature to 250 degrees and continue to bake until edges turn pale golden, 10 to 15 minutes.

4. Remove baking sheet from oven and turn off oven. Remove springform pan collar. Using knife, score surface of shortbread into 16 even wedges, cutting down halfway through shortbread. Using wooden skewer, poke 8 to 10 holes in each wedge. Return shortbread to oven, prop door open with handle of wooden spoon, and let shortbread dry in turned-off oven until center is firm but giving to touch, about 1 hour.

5. Remove shortbread from oven and let cool completely on sheet, about 2 hours. Cut shortbread at scored marks before serving.

Chocolate-Dipped Pistachio Shortbread

Add ½ cup shelled pistachios, toasted and finely chopped, to flour mixture in step 1. Once shortbread is cool, microwave 8 ounces finely chopped bittersweet chocolate in bowl at 50 percent power for 2 minutes. Stir chocolate and continue to microwave until melted, stirring once every minute. Stir in additional 2 ounces finely chopped bittersweet chocolate until smooth. Carefully dip base of each wedge in chocolate, allowing chocolate to come halfway up cookie. Scrape off excess with your finger and place on parchment paper–lined baking sheet. Refrigerate until chocolate sets, about 15 minutes.

Ginger Shortbread

Add ½ cup chopped crystallized ginger to flour mixture in step 1. Sprinkle shortbread with 1 tablespoon turbinado sugar after poking holes in shortbread in step 4.

Toasted Oat Shortbread

We prefer the texture and flavor of a coarse-grained flake sea salt like Maldon or fleur de sel, but kosher salt can be used.

Toast ½ cup additional oats in 8-inch skillet over medium-high heat until light golden brown, 5 to 8 minutes. Add toasted oats to flour mixture in step 1. Sprinkle ½ teaspoon flake sea salt evenly over surface of dough before baking.

CHOCOLATE SHORTBREAD

Makes 16 wedges | rimmed baking sheet

WHY THIS RECIPE WORKS At its simplest, shortbread contains just four ingredients—flour, sugar, salt, and butter—and features a fine yet substantial texture. We had our sights set on a rich chocolate shortbread, but with so few ingredients we wondered if the addition of chocolate would throw off this careful balance. Indeed it did: When we tried mixing melted bittersweet chocolate into our standard shortbread dough, the dough became very soft and the baked cookie greasy. With so much butter in the recipe the chocolate's high fat content upset our carefully calibrated ratios. Substituting cocoa powder for a portion of the flour worked much better; with its high proportion of cocoa solids, ¼ cup cocoa powder was all we needed for intense flavor. We found that baking the shortbread on a double layer of parchment helped absorb some of the butter during baking and cooling.

2   cups (10 ounces) all-purpose flour
¼   cup (¾ ounce) unsweetened cocoa powder
½   teaspoon table salt
16 tablespoons unsalted butter, softened
½   cup (2 ounces) confectioners' sugar
1   tablespoon granulated sugar (optional)

Chocolate Shortbread

COCONUT SNOWDROPS

Makes 72 sandwich cookies | 2 rimmed baking sheets

WHY THIS RECIPE WORKS These petite, festive treats are like chocolate-covered macaroons turned inside out, with a layer of rich creamy chocolate sandwiched by buttery coconut cookies. In addition to sweetened, shredded coconut and coconut extract, the shortbread dough contains finely chopped almonds and brown sugar for tenderness and flavor. Like other butter-rich doughs, this one is very temperature-sensitive; it can go from chilled and firm to soft and sticky in the blink of an eye. To avoid this problem, we portioned the dough and refrigerated it before cutting it and rolling the pieces into balls. A food processor makes quick work of chopping the nuts.

19 tablespoons unsalted butter, softened, divided
1 cup (7 ounces) granulated sugar
¼ cup packed (1¾ ounces) light brown sugar
1 large egg plus 1 large yolk
1 teaspoon vanilla extract
1 teaspoon coconut extract
2 cups (10 ounces) all-purpose flour
2 cups (6 ounces) sweetened shredded coconut
½ cup whole blanched almonds, chopped fine
¾ cup (4½ ounces) semisweet chocolate chips

1. Using stand mixer fitted with paddle, beat 16 tablespoons butter, granulated sugar, and brown sugar on medium-high speed until fluffy, about 2 minutes. Add egg and yolk, vanilla, and coconut extract and beat until combined. Reduce speed to low; add flour, coconut, and almonds; and mix until just combined. Divide dough in half, form each half into 1-inch-thick square, wrap squares in plastic wrap, and refrigerate for 1 hour.

2. Adjust oven racks to upper-middle and lower-middle positions and heat oven to 350 degrees. Line 2 rimmed baking sheets with parchment paper. Cut 1 square of dough into ½-inch squares. Roll squares into ¾-inch balls; space balls 1 inch apart on prepared sheets. Bake until edges are just golden, 12 to 14 minutes, switching and rotating sheets halfway through baking. Let cookies cool on sheets for 10 minutes, then transfer to wire rack and let cool completely. Repeat with remaining dough square.

3. Microwave chocolate and remaining 3 tablespoons butter in bowl at 50 percent power, stirring frequently, until melted, about 2 minutes. Spread ½ teaspoon chocolate mixture over bottoms of half of cookies, then top with remaining cookies, pressing lightly to adhere, before serving.

1. Whisk flour, cocoa, and salt together in bowl. Using handheld mixer set at medium speed, beat butter and confectioners' sugar in large bowl until light and fluffy, 3 to 6 minutes, scraping down bowl and beaters as needed. Reduce mixer speed to low and slowly add flour mixture until combined, about 30 seconds.

2. Using your hands, press dough into ball in bowl. Transfer dough to lightly floured counter and knead until very smooth, about 3 minutes. Press dough into disk. Roll dough into 9-inch round (about ½ inch thick) on sheet of parchment paper.

3. Transfer dough and parchment to parchment-lined rimmed baking sheet. Using your fingers, flute dough edge, then poke dough all over with fork and score into 16 wedges. Cover with plastic wrap and refrigerate dough for at least 20 minutes or up to 24 hours.

4. Adjust oven rack to middle position and heat oven to 300 degrees. Sprinkle granulated sugar, if using, evenly over dough. Bake shortbread until edges are firm and center springs back slightly when pressed, 40 to 45 minutes, rotating sheet halfway through baking.

5. Transfer sheet to wire rack and, using sharp knife, cut through scored marks to separate wedges. Let shortbread cool on sheet for 10 minutes, then transfer wedges to wire rack and let cool completely before serving, about 1 hour.

SWEDISH WALNUT FINGERS

Makes 40 cookies | 2 rimmed baking sheets

WHY THIS RECIPE WORKS These buttery, nut-topped cookies have a shortbread-like texture but they're lighter, crumbling delicately with each bite. A mixture of lightly beaten egg white and sugar brushed on the exterior gives them a sweet crunch; it also helps the walnuts adhere. These cookies traditionally sport a rustic ridged surface, which further ensures that the walnuts stay in place. To create these grooves, we simply dragged a floured fork across the dough. Chilling the sticky dough before cutting it into rectangles made it easier to work with. To prevent the bottoms from overbrowning, we baked the cookies at a moderate 350 degrees and then let them sit on the baking sheet for only 1 minute—just enough time for them to set up before being transferred to a wire rack to cool.

2¾ cups (13¾ ounces) all-purpose flour
   Pinch table salt
24 tablespoons unsalted butter, softened
¾ cup (5¼ ounces) plus 1 teaspoon sugar, divided
1 large egg, separated
1 teaspoon almond or vanilla extract
½ cup walnuts, chopped fine

1. Line rimmed baking sheet with parchment paper. Whisk flour and salt together in bowl. Using stand mixer fitted with paddle, beat butter and ¾ cup sugar on medium speed until pale and fluffy, 3 to 6 minutes. Add egg yolk and almond extract and beat until combined. Reduce speed to low, slowly add flour mixture, and mix until just combined.

2. Transfer dough to prepared sheet and press into 10 by 8-inch rectangle, about ½ inch thick. Using floured fork, press tines into dough and pull across rectangle to make washboard design. Lightly beat egg white with remaining 1 teaspoon sugar in small bowl, then brush evenly over dough. Sprinkle dough with walnuts, pressing gently to adhere. Cover baking sheet tightly with plastic wrap and refrigerate for 30 minutes.

3. Adjust oven racks to upper-middle and lower-middle positions and heat oven to 350 degrees. Slide dough, still on parchment, onto cutting board. Line baking sheet with fresh parchment; line second baking sheet with parchment.

4. Cut dough into 2 by 1-inch rectangles and space them 1½ inches apart on prepared sheets. Bake until lightly browned and set, 20 to 25 minutes, switching and rotating sheets halfway through baking. Let cookies cool on sheets for 1 minute, then transfer to wire rack and let cool completely before serving.

Mexican Wedding Cookies

MEXICAN WEDDING COOKIES

Makes 48 cookies | 2 rimmed baking sheets

WHY THIS RECIPE WORKS Mexican wedding cookies boast a delicate, melt-in-your-mouth texture plus a rich, deeply nutty flavor. In order to really reinforce the nut flavor, we found it necessary to use equal amounts of nuts (we liked pecans and walnuts) and flour. But with all of those nuts, it was hard to get the dough to hold together. Eggs made the cookies too cakey; instead, we found that grinding a portion of the nuts very finely (almost to a butter) released their natural oil and did the trick. The dough was cohesive, the texture of the cookies was delicate, and each bite still included the pleasing crunch of the coarsely chopped nuts. The thick confectioners' sugar coating is a defining characteristic of these cookies; we found it best to roll them in sugar twice to ensure a thorough coating.

2 cups pecans or walnuts, divided
2 cups (10 ounces) all-purpose flour
¾ teaspoon table salt
16 tablespoons unsalted butter, softened
⅓ cup (2⅓ ounces) superfine sugar
1½ teaspoons vanilla extract
1½ cups (6 ounces) confectioners' sugar

1. Adjust oven racks to upper-middle and lower-middle positions and heat oven to 325 degrees. Line 2 rimmed baking sheets with parchment paper. Process 1 cup pecans in food processor until texture of coarse cornmeal, 10 to 15 seconds; transfer pecans to bowl. Process remaining 1 cup pecans in now-empty food processor until coarsely chopped, about 5 seconds; transfer to bowl with ground pecans. Stir flour and salt into pecans.

2. Using stand mixer fitted with paddle, beat butter and superfine sugar at medium speed until pale and fluffy, about 3 minutes. Beat in vanilla. Reduce speed to low and slowly add nut mixture until combined, about 30 seconds. Scrape down bowl and continue to mix on low speed until dough is cohesive, about 7 seconds. Give dough final stir by hand to ensure that no dry pockets of flour remain.

3. Working with 1 tablespoon dough at a time, roll into balls and space them 1 inch apart on prepared sheets. Bake until tops are pale golden and bottoms are just beginning to brown, about 18 minutes, switching and rotating sheets halfway through baking. Let cookies cool on sheets for 5 minutes, then transfer to wire rack and let cool completely.

4. Spread confectioners' sugar in shallow dish. Working with several cookies at a time, roll in sugar to coat. Before serving, reroll cookies in confectioners' sugar and gently shake off excess.

Sablés

SABLÉS

Makes 40 cookies | 2 rimmed baking sheets

WHY THIS RECIPE WORKS French butter cookies known as sablés offer sophistication and style—if you can capture their elusive sandy texture. The moisture content of a cookie plays a big role in determining sandiness; liquid in the dough dissolves sugar crystals, and it's those sugar crystals that help create the perception of sandiness. To decrease liquid, we started by cutting back on butter but that still didn't give us the texture we sought. Switching from a whole egg to just the rich yolk was a giant step in the right direction, but we wanted to push our efforts further. Based on our research we tried hard-boiling the egg and adding the cooked, mashed yolk. This unusual step eliminated the last bit of moisture and perfected the texture.

  1 large egg
 10 tablespoons unsalted butter, softened
 ⅓ cup plus 1 tablespoon (2¾ ounces) granulated sugar
 ¼ teaspoon table salt
  1 teaspoon vanilla extract
1½ cups (7½ ounces) all-purpose flour
  1 large egg white, lightly beaten with 1 teaspoon water
  4 teaspoons turbinado sugar

1. Place egg in small saucepan, cover with water by 1 inch, and bring to boil over high heat. Remove pan from heat, cover, and let sit for 10 minutes. Meanwhile, fill small bowl with ice water. Using slotted spoon, transfer egg to ice water and let stand for 5 minutes. Crack egg and peel shell. Separate yolk from white; discard white. Press yolk through fine-mesh strainer into small bowl.

2. Using stand mixer fitted with paddle, beat butter, granulated sugar, salt, and cooked egg yolk on medium speed until pale and fluffy, about 4 minutes, scraping down bowl as needed. Reduce speed to low, add vanilla, and mix until incorporated. Stop mixer; add flour and mix on low speed until just combined, about 30 seconds. Using rubber spatula, press dough into cohesive mass.

3. Transfer dough to counter and divide in half. Roll each piece of dough into 6-inch log. Wrap logs tightly in plastic wrap and twist ends tightly to seal and chill until firm, about 2 hours in refrigerator or 45 minutes in freezer.

4. Adjust oven racks to upper-middle and lower-middle positions and heat oven to 350 degrees. Line 2 rimmed baking sheets with parchment paper. Working with 1 dough log at a time, slice chilled dough into ¼-inch-thick rounds and space them 1 inch apart on prepared sheets. Using pastry brush, gently brush cookies with egg white mixture and sprinkle evenly with turbinado sugar.

5. Bake cookies until centers are pale golden brown and edges are slightly darker than centers, about 15 minutes, switching and rotating sheets halfway through baking. Let cookies cool on sheets for 5 minutes, then transfer to wire rack and let cool completely before serving.

Almond Sablés

Substitute 1½ teaspoons almond extract for vanilla. Add ⅓ cup finely ground almonds to dough with flour in step 2. After brushing cookies with egg white mixture, press 3 almond slices in petal shape in center of each cookie instead of sprinkling with turbinado sugar.

Chocolate Sablés

Reduce flour to 1⅓ cups and add ¼ cup Dutch-processed cocoa powder with flour in step 2.

Black and White Spiral Sablés
Makes about 80 cookies

Make 1 batch Sablés cookie dough and 1 batch Chocolate Sablés cookie dough (through step 2). Divide each dough in half and roll each portion into 8 by 6-inch rectangle on parchment paper. Chill doughs briefly until easy to handle. Stack 1 rectangle plain dough on top of 1 rectangle chocolate dough and roll into 9 by 6-inch rectangle. Starting at long end, roll dough into tight pinwheel log. Repeat with remaining doughs. Wrap logs in plastic and chill as directed before slicing and baking.

Vanilla Pretzel Sablés

Increase vanilla extract to 1 tablespoon and reduce refrigerator chilling time in step 3 to 30 minutes (dough will not be completely firm). Slice dough into ¼-inch-thick rounds and roll into balls. Roll each ball into 6-inch rope, tapering ends. Form ropes into pretzel shapes. Brush cookies with egg, sprinkle with turbinado sugar, and bake as directed.

HOLIDAY SUGAR COOKIES

Makes about forty 2½-inch cookies | rimless baking sheet

WHY THIS RECIPE WORKS Our ideal holiday cookies would be firm enough to shape with cutters, bake up crisp and flat with sharp edges, and have buttery flavor. For a crisp texture and no hint of graininess, we made superfine sugar by grinding granulated in the food processor. Whizzing cold butter with the sugar let the dough come together quickly, which meant it was cold enough to be rolled out immediately; most recipes call for refrigerating the dough, which makes it stiff to roll. For an even, golden color and a crunchy texture from edge to edge, we baked the cookies for adequate time at a gentle 300 degrees on a rimless cookie sheet. In step 3, use a combination of rolling and a pushing or smearing motion to form the dough into an oval. Dough scraps can be combined and rerolled once, though the cookies will be slightly less tender.

1 large egg
1 teaspoon vanilla extract
¾ teaspoon table salt
¼ teaspoon almond extract
2½ cups (12½ ounces) all-purpose flour
¼ teaspoon baking powder
¼ teaspoon baking soda
1 cup (7 ounces) granulated sugar
16 tablespoons unsalted butter, cut into ½-inch pieces and chilled
1 recipe Decorating Icing (page 42)

1. Whisk egg, vanilla, salt, and almond extract together in small bowl. Whisk flour, baking powder, and baking soda together in second bowl.

2. Process sugar in food processor until finely ground, about 30 seconds. Add butter and process until uniform mass forms and no large pieces of butter are visible, about 30 seconds, scraping down sides of bowl as needed. Add egg mixture and process until smooth and paste-like, about 10 seconds. Add flour mixture and process until no dry flour remains but mixture remains crumbly, about 30 seconds, scraping down sides of bowl as needed.

3. Turn out dough onto counter and knead gently by hand until smooth, about 10 seconds. Divide dough in half. Place 1 piece of dough in center of large sheet of parchment paper and press into 7 by 9-inch oval. Place second large sheet of parchment over dough and roll dough into 10 by 14-inch oval of even ⅛-inch thickness. Transfer dough with parchment to rimmed baking sheet. Repeat pressing and rolling with second piece of dough, then stack on top of first piece on sheet. Refrigerate until dough is firm, at least 1½ hours (or freeze for 30 minutes). (Rolled dough can be wrapped in plastic wrap and refrigerated for up to 5 days.)

4. Adjust oven rack to lower-middle position and heat oven to 300 degrees. Line rimless cookie sheet with parchment. Working with 1 piece of rolled dough, gently peel off top layer of parchment. Replace parchment, loosely covering dough. (Peeling off parchment and returning it will make cutting and removing cookies easier.) Turn over dough and parchment and gently peel off and discard second piece of parchment. Using cookie cutter, cut dough into shapes. Transfer shapes to prepared cookie sheet, spacing them about ½ inch apart. Bake until cookies are lightly and evenly browned around edges, 14 to 17 minutes, rotating sheet halfway through baking. Let cookies cool on sheet for 5 minutes, then transfer to wire rack and let cool completely. Repeat with remaining dough. (Dough scraps can be patted together, rerolled, and chilled once before cutting and baking.)

5. Spread icing onto cooled cookies. Let icing dry completely, about 1½ hours, before serving.

SPRITZ COOKIES

Makes 72 cookies | 2 rimmed baking sheets

WHY THIS RECIPE WORKS Spritz cookies are beautiful in appearance with their golden swirled shape, but their flavor frequently falls short. We set out to spruce up spritz and make them the light, crisp, buttery treats they were meant to be. For rich flavor, we used a whopping 16 tablespoons of butter. Since these cookies are pressed or piped, the dough needs to be smooth. Adding a little heavy cream made the dough workable. Some recipes for spritz cookies call for whole eggs, while others use just yolks or even no eggs at all. Cookies made without eggs were too tender and crumbly, with an ill-defined shape. A whole egg made for chewy, tough cookies. Using just one yolk made spritz that were tender and crisp yet sturdy. You can use a cookie press or a pastry bag fitted with a star tip to create these cookies.

- 1 large egg yolk
- 1 tablespoon heavy cream
- 1 teaspoon vanilla extract
- 16 tablespoons unsalted butter, softened
- ⅔ cup (4⅔ ounces) sugar
- ¼ teaspoon table salt
- 2 cups (10 ounces) all-purpose flour

1. Adjust oven rack to middle position and heat oven to 375 degrees. Line 2 rimmed baking sheets with parchment paper. Whisk egg yolk, cream, and vanilla in small bowl until combined; set aside.

2. Using stand mixer fitted with paddle, beat butter, sugar, and salt on medium-high speed until pale and fluffy, about 3 minutes, scraping down bowl as needed. Reduce speed to medium, add egg yolk mixture, and beat until incorporated, about 30 seconds. Reduce speed to low and gradually add flour until combined, scraping down bowl as needed. Give dough final stir by hand. (Dough can be wrapped in plastic wrap and refrigerated for up to 4 days. Before using, let sit on counter until softened, about 45 minutes.)

3. If using cookie press to form cookies, follow manufacturer's instructions to fill press. If using pastry bag, fill pastry bag fitted with star tip with half of dough. Push dough down toward tip and twist top of bag tightly. Holding bag at base of twist and holding tip at 90-degree angle ½ inch above baking sheet, pipe cookies, spacing them about 1½ inches apart. Refill cookie press or pastry bag as needed. Bake, 1 sheet at a time, until cookies are light golden brown, 10 to 12 minutes, rotating sheet halfway through baking. Let cookies cool on sheets for 10 to 15 minutes, then transfer to wire rack and let cool completely before serving.

NEW MEXICO BISCOCHITOS

Makes 48 cookies | 2 rimmed baking sheets

WHY THIS RECIPE WORKS Biscochitos are cinnamon-and-anise-flavored shortbread cookies that have rightly earned the title of New Mexico's state cookie. After mixing we shaped the dough into logs to chill so that we could slice and bake the dough for biscochitos with clean, crisp edges. Tossing the baked cookies in cinnamon sugar gave each cookie a sweet-spicy, crunchy exterior. We developed this recipe using John Morrell Snow Cap Lard. We prefer the flavor and melt-in-your-mouth texture lard gives these cookies, but ⅔ cup of softened unsalted butter or vegetable shortening can be substituted.

- 1¾ cups (8¾ ounces) all-purpose flour
- ¼ teaspoon baking powder
- ¼ teaspoon plus pinch table salt, divided
- 1½ teaspoons anise seeds
- ⅔ cup (4⅔ ounces) lard
- ¾ cup (5¼ ounces) sugar, divided
- 1 large egg
- ½ teaspoon vanilla extract
- ¼ teaspoon ground cinnamon

1. Whisk flour, baking powder, and ¼ teaspoon salt together in bowl; set aside. Place anise seeds in zipper-lock bag, seal bag, and crush seeds coarse with rolling pin or meat pounder.

2. Using stand mixer fitted with paddle, beat lard, ½ cup sugar, and crushed anise seeds on medium-high speed until light and fluffy, about 3 minutes. Add egg and vanilla and beat until combined, scraping down bowl as needed. Reduce speed to low, slowly add flour mixture, and mix until just combined.

3. Turn out dough onto counter. Divide dough in half (about 9 ounces per half) and roll each half into 6-inch log. Wrap dough logs tightly in plastic wrap, roll against counter to form tight cylinder, and refrigerate until firm, at least 3 hours or up to 3 days.

4. Adjust oven rack to middle position and heat oven to 350 degrees. Line 2 rimmed baking sheets with parchment paper. Slice dough logs into ¼-inch-thick rounds, rolling logs as you cut to keep circular shape of dough. Evenly space cookies on prepared sheets (about 24 cookies per sheet). Bake cookies, 1 sheet at a time, until edges are lightly browned, 13 to 15 minutes, rotating sheet halfway through baking. Let cookies cool on sheets for at least 5 minutes.

5. Combine cinnamon, remaining pinch salt, and remaining ¼ cup sugar in shallow dish. Gently toss cookies, a few at a time, in cinnamon sugar. Transfer to wire rack and let cookies cool completely, at least 30 minutes, before serving. (Cookies can be stored in airtight container for up to 3 days.)

TUTORIAL
Spritz Cookies

An intricate-looking cookie doesn't have to be intricate to make. Follow how to pipe pretty cookies, even without a cookie press.

1. Fill pastry bag fitted with star tip with half of dough.

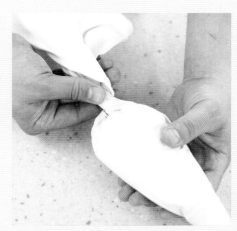

2. Push dough down toward tip and twist top of bag tightly.

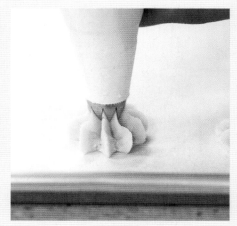

3a. To create stars: Hold pastry bag at 90-degree angle to baking sheet and pipe dough straight down, until it is about 1 inch in diameter.

3b. To create rosettes: Pipe dough while moving bag in circular motion, ending at center; rosettes should be about 1¼ inches in diameter.

3c. To create S shapes: Pipe dough following curves of compact S; they should be about 2 inches long and 1 inch wide.

4. Refill pastry bag as needed. Bake, 1 sheet at a time, until cookies are light golden brown, 10 to 12 minutes, rotating sheet halfway through baking.

Decorating Cookies

Whisk up some glazes and then try these decorating techniques for making Holiday Sugar Cookies (page 39) (and anything with a decorating surface) the brightest on the dessert table.

EASY ALL-PURPOSE GLAZE
Makes about 1 cup
Feel free to use this glaze, dyed or not, on any flat cookie that could use a festive flourish. The cream cheese in the glaze gives it a slightly thicker consistency that's good for spreading, and it cuts the sweetness of the glaze with its tang.

  2 cups (8 ounces) confectioners' sugar
  3 tablespoons milk
  1 ounce cream cheese, softened
     Food coloring (optional)

Whisk all ingredients in bowl until smooth.

Citrus Glaze
Substitute lemon, lime, or orange juice for milk.

Coffee Glaze
Add 1¼ teaspoons instant espresso powder or instant coffee to glaze ingredients.

Nutty Glaze
Add ½ teaspoon almond or coconut extract to glaze ingredients.

DECORATING ICING
Makes 1⅓ cups
A piping of royal icing gives a cookie upscale elegance with its clean lines and stark white color. It's also stunning dotted with silver dragées. After decorating with royal icing, let it dry for 1½ hours before serving.

2⅔ cups (10⅔ ounces) confectioners' sugar
  2 large egg whites
  ½ teaspoon vanilla extract
  ⅛ teaspoon table salt

Using stand mixer fitted with whisk attachment, whip all ingredients on medium-low speed until combined, about 1 minute. Increase speed to medium-high and whip until glossy, soft peaks form, 3 to 4 minutes, scraping down bowl as needed.

BITTERSWEET CHOCOLATE GLAZE
Makes ⅔ cup

Some chocolate glazes only look like chocolate; this one has a pleasantly intense chocolate flavor. Let the glazed cookies dry for at least 20 minutes before serving.

  4 ounces bittersweet chocolate, chopped
  4 tablespoons unsalted butter
  2 tablespoons corn syrup
  1 teaspoon vanilla extract

Melt chocolate and butter in medium heatproof bowl set over saucepan filled with 1 inch barely simmering water, making sure that water does not touch bottom of bowl and stirring occasionally until butter and chocolate are melted. Remove bowl from saucepan; add corn syrup and vanilla and mix until smooth and shiny.

Make Your Own Colored Sugar

Spread ½ cup granulated sugar into a pie plate. Mix 5 drops of food coloring into the sugar. Push the sugar through a fine-mesh strainer and spread back into the plate. Dry sugar thoroughly; this might take several hours. Brush water on the cookies and apply the sugar before baking.

Three Ways to Glaze

Our Easy All-Purpose Glaze spreads smoothly but doesn't hold as firm a line as stiffer Decorating Icing, so it's best used for simple decorating tips like those below. Be sure to start with completely cooled cookies; the glaze will liquefy and fail to set if it's piped onto warm cookies.

Spread Spoon a small amount of glaze in the center of the cookie, then spread it into an even layer. Moving outward from the center ensures even coverage. Use the back of the spoon or a small offset spatula. Let the glaze dry before storing or serving the cookies.

Drag Two Glazes Together Glaze the entire cookie and then pipe small drops of a second glaze in a pattern. Drag a toothpick through the glazes to create a design. As long as both glazes are still wet, you can create a range of designs, from hearts to stars, wiggly lines, and swirls. This idea works best with glazes that are two very different hues.

Fill in Piped Borders For glazed cookies with cleaner edges than those made using the spreading technique, carefully pipe the glaze around the border of the cookie and then add more glaze to the center of the cookie and spread the extra glaze into an even layer. Use the same-colored glaze for both if you want to hide the piped edges, or use different-colored glazes to make the piped border stand out. Note that piping with glaze will be less detailed and neat than piping with decorating icing.

Taking Your Cookies to the Next Level

Our Decorating Icing is less runny and sets up more firmly than a glaze, so it's ideally suited for more intricate, detailed piping work. Here are a few of our favorite ways to step up your cookie decoration game by using icing and other embellishments.

Pipe To apply more intricate designs, such as dots or fine lines, to cookies, pipe the icing directly onto the cookie. Use a pastry bag fitted with a $\frac{1}{16}$-inch or $\frac{1}{8}$-inch round tip or a zipper-lock bag with a small snip in one corner to pipe the icing.

Layer Icing and Play with Patterns Create visual interest and a sense of depth by piping layers of icing over one another. Start by coating the cookie with a thin, smooth layer of icing. Let the first layer dry before piping dots, lines, or other patterns in a second layer on top. Play around with combinations of lines, dots, and swirls to make different patterns, from snowflake fractals to freeform loops to orderly rows.

Add Embellishments While the icing is still soft, place decorations on top and then allow it to dry. Small confections, such as shiny silver or gold balls known as dragées, can be used to dress up cookies. Other small candies—gumdrops, mini chocolate morsels, jelly beans—can be used in a similar fashion. Add these candies immediately after applying the icing. As the icing dries, it will affix the candies in place.

SLICE-AND-BAKE COOKIES

KEY POINTS

Use softened butter

Dough is rolled into log

Chill dough logs before slicing

Try to keep logs round

THESE COOKIES ARE AN OLD-FASHIONED FAVORITE.
Slice-and-bake cookies have a bit more polish than drop cookies but are still quite easy to make. You might also know them as icebox cookies; that's because they're typically rolled into logs and then conveniently stored in the refrigerator, or icebox, until you're ready to cut them into cookies and bake them. While the texture of these cookies can vary—they are typically thin, with a shortbread-like texture, though occasionally they are softer and cakier—they are united in their simplicity. The dough is shaped into a cylindrical or rectangular log, chilled until firm, and then sliced into thin cookies. Unlike other types of cookies, many slice-and-bake cookies don't contain any leaveners—this means they don't spread as much, so you can fit more on one sheet. Softened butter is key to this type of cookie: It's soft enough to be whipped in a mixer or food processor yet just firm enough to retain some air (this helps provide a bit of structure). These cookies are delicious when they're plain and simple, but they can easily be dressed up a bit with a nut garnish or a dip in melted chocolate.

FORMING SLICE-AND-BAKE COOKIES

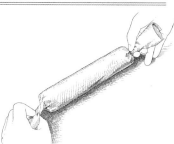

1. Roll After mixing, transfer dough to counter and roll it into log length specified in recipe. (Some recipes may call for dividing dough into pieces first.)

2. Twist and Chill Wrap log of dough tightly in plastic wrap and twist ends to help dough hold its shape. (Try to square off ends as much as possible.) Refrigerate wrapped dough log until firm.

3. Slice the Dough Cut chilled dough into slices as specified in recipe. (Cutting cookies of uniform thickness ensures that they bake evenly.)

4. Arrange and Bake Space cookies evenly on parchment paper–lined baking sheet. (Icebox cookies don't spread very much, so you can fit more on the baking sheet than you would for drop cookies.)

KEEPING DOUGH ROUND

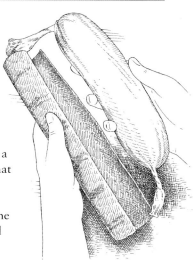

To help dough logs keep their shape in the refrigerator, you can place each wrapped log in a paper towel tube that's been cut open to form a large semicircle. This keeps the dough from flattening out on the refrigerator shelf. And when you cut the log, rotate the dough a quarter turn after each slice so that it won't become misshapen from the weight of the knife. If the dough seems sticky, return it to the refrigerator to chill. This too will prevent misshapen cookies.

STORING ICEBOX COOKIE DOUGH

Most wrapped logs of dough can be refrigerated for up to three days. But you can also freeze the logs for up to one month. Simply wrap them in an additional layer of aluminum foil. Slice and bake frozen cookies as directed, increasing the time if needed. (To slice frozen dough, dip the blade of the knife in flour after every couple of cuts to prevent it from dragging.)

VANILLA ICEBOX COOKIES

Makes 40 cookies | 2 rimmed baking sheets

WHY THIS RECIPE WORKS Essentially shortbread shaped into a log, slice-and-bake (or icebox) cookies have so few ingredients that imperfections are hard to hide. With too much flour, the cookies are crisp but dry and bland; go overboard with the butter, sugar, or egg, and the cookies are rich but soft and misshapen. For crisp texture and rich flavor, we added as much butter as we could without the cookies losing their crisp edge; 12 tablespoons was as high as we could go. Most recipes use a whole egg, but we found that using only the yolk made the cookies firmer. Replacing some of the granulated sugar with brown sugar added complexity. And for the ideal texture, we turned to the food processor, which combined the ingredients in seconds without whipping in much air.

⅓ cup (2⅓ ounces) granulated sugar
2 tablespoons packed light brown sugar
½ teaspoon table salt
12 tablespoons unsalted butter, cut into pieces and softened
1 large egg yolk
2 teaspoons vanilla extract
1½ cups (7½ ounces) all-purpose flour

Vanilla Icebox Cookies

1. Process granulated sugar, brown sugar, and salt in food processor until no lumps of brown sugar remain, about 30 seconds. Add butter, egg yolk, and vanilla and process until smooth and creamy, about 20 seconds. Scrape down bowl, add flour, and pulse until cohesive dough forms, about 20 pulses.

2. Transfer dough to lightly floured counter and roll into 10-inch log. Wrap log tightly in plastic wrap and refrigerate until firm, at least 2 hours or up to 3 days.

3. Adjust oven racks to upper-middle and lower-middle positions and heat oven to 350 degrees. Line 2 rimmed baking sheets with parchment paper.

4. Slice chilled dough into ¼-inch-thick rounds and space them 1 inch apart on prepared baking sheets. Bake until edges are just golden, about 15 minutes, switching and rotating sheets halfway through baking. Let cookies cool on sheets for 10 minutes, then transfer to wire rack and let cool completely before serving. Repeat with remaining dough.

Brown Sugar–Walnut Icebox Cookies
Increase brown sugar to ¼ cup. Add 1 cup walnuts to food processor with sugars and salt in step 1 and process until walnuts are finely ground, about 1 minute.

Coconut-Lime Icebox Cookies
Add 2 cups sweetened shredded coconut and 2 teaspoons grated lime zest to food processor with sugars and salt in step 1.

Orange–Poppy Seed Icebox Cookies
Add ¼ cup poppy seeds and 1 tablespoon grated orange zest to food processor with sugars and salt in step 1.

CHECKERBOARD ICEBOX COOKIES

Makes 36 cookies | 2 rimmed baking sheets

WHY THIS RECIPE WORKS Like swirled soft-serve ice cream, this cookie is a gift to the indecisive. We puzzle together logs of chocolate and vanilla dough to form an attractive checkerboard shape that's as fun to make as it is to eat. To save ourselves the work of making two separate cookie doughs, we mixed up an easy basic vanilla dough, divided it in half, and then incorporated melted semisweet chocolate and cocoa powder into one portion. A combination of granulated and confectioners' sugars allowed the dough to hold its striking geometric pattern during baking, and created a cookie that was tender with just enough snap. These cookies may look intricate, but forming them was a breeze. The cookies don't spread much, so we were able to space them closely together and bake them all at once.

TUTORIAL
Checkerboard Icebox Cookies

Fashioning square slices sporting a striking checkerboard pattern is the key to this cookie—and a lot simpler than you may think.

1. Set aside half of vanilla dough. Add chocolate and cocoa to remaining dough in mixer bowl and mix on low until fully combined.

2. Transfer dough to counter and form each piece into 9 by 2-inch rectangle, about 1 inch thick.

3. Stack rectangles to create 2-inch-square log. Wrap log tightly in plastic wrap and refrigerate.

4. Slice chilled dough in half lengthwise, rotating 1 half to create checkerboard pattern.

5. Press gently to re-adhere halves.

6. Slice dough into ¼-inch-thick squares and space them ¾ inch apart on prepared sheets.

Checkerboard
Icebox Cookies

16 tablespoons unsalted butter, softened
¾ cup (5¼ ounces) granulated sugar
½ cup (2 ounces) confectioners' sugar
½ teaspoon table salt
2 large egg yolks
2 teaspoons vanilla extract
2¼ cups (11¼ ounces) all-purpose flour
1 ounce semisweet chocolate, melted
2 tablespoons Dutch-processed cocoa powder

1. Using stand mixer fitted with paddle, beat butter, granulated sugar, confectioners' sugar, and salt on medium-high speed until pale and fluffy, about 3 minutes. Add egg yolks and vanilla and beat until combined. Reduce speed to low, slowly add flour, and mix until combined. Set aside half of dough; add chocolate and cocoa to remaining dough in mixer bowl and mix on low until fully combined.

2. Transfer dough to counter and form each piece into 9 by 2-inch rectangle, about 1 inch thick. Stack rectangles to create 2-inch-square log. Wrap log tightly in plastic wrap and refrigerate for at least 2 hours or up to 3 days.

3. Adjust oven racks to upper-middle and lower-middle positions and heat oven to 325 degrees. Line 2 rimmed baking sheets with parchment paper.

4. Slice chilled dough in half lengthwise, rotating 1 half to create checkerboard pattern, then press gently to re-adhere halves. Slice dough into ¼-inch-thick squares and space them ¾ inch apart on prepared sheets. Bake until edges are light golden brown, 12 to 15 minutes, switching and rotating sheets halfway through baking. Let cookies cool on sheets for 5 minutes, then transfer to wire rack and let cool completely before serving.

WASHBOARDS

Makes 36 cookies | 2 rimmed baking sheets

WHY THIS RECIPE WORKS We love the old-fashioned washboard shape of these tea cookies, which are crisp, coconutty, and mildly sweet—perfect as an afternoon snack or with a cup of tea. Most recipes call for granulated sugar, but we found that light brown sugar enhanced the coconut flavor. One cup of sweetened coconut was enough to give the cookies prominent coconut flavor while still allowing their buttery richness to shine through. To keep the texture light and crisp, we added just one egg, which was enough to hold the dough together. Forming these cookies was as easy as any other slice-and-bake cookie: We shaped the dough into a rectangular log, chilled it, and sliced the chilled log into thin cookies. To finish the cookies with their signature ridged top, we used a good, old-fashioned tool: a fork.

2 cups (10 ounces) all-purpose flour
½ teaspoon baking powder
¼ teaspoon baking soda
¼ teaspoon table salt
¼ teaspoon ground nutmeg
8 tablespoons unsalted butter, softened
1 cup packed (7 ounces) light brown sugar
1 large egg, room temperature
2 tablespoons milk
1 cup (3 ounces) sweetened shredded coconut

1. Whisk flour, baking powder, baking soda, salt, and nutmeg together in bowl. Using stand mixer fitted with paddle, beat butter and sugar on medium-high speed until pale and fluffy, about 2 minutes. Add egg and milk and beat until well combined. Reduce speed to low, add flour mixture and coconut, and mix until just incorporated.

2. Transfer dough to counter and, using your floured hands, roll dough into 15-inch log, then flatten top and sides to measure 3 inches by 1 inch. Wrap log tightly in plastic wrap and refrigerate until firm, at least 45 minutes or up to 3 days.

3. Adjust oven racks to upper-middle and lower-middle positions and heat oven to 350 degrees. Line 2 rimmed baking sheets with parchment paper.

4. Slice chilled dough into ¼-inch-thick rectangles and space them 1 inch apart on prepared sheets. Using floured fork, make crosswise indentations in dough slices. Bake until toasty brown, 15 to 18 minutes, switching and rotating sheets halfway through baking. Let cookies cool on sheets for 10 minutes, then transfer to wire rack. Let cookies cool completely before serving.

MOLDED COOKIES

MOLDED COOKIES BEGIN WITH A DOUGH that is slightly firmer than most so it can be shaped by hand into myriad forms. When an occasion calls for something a bit more refined than a basic drop or sliced cookie—which require little handling or artistry—molded cookies are your answer. These bite-size cookies may look fancy, but the dough is relatively simple to make; perhaps that's one reason they are a familiar sight at bake sales and on holiday tables. Creaming the butter and sugar is the typical mixing method for this type of cookie, but from there the dough can take many forms. Many start out shaped into a simple ball like a classic drop cookie before they are given a more intricate treatment—and sometimes a fanciful topping or filling—for a more festive, elegant affair.

KEY POINTS

Shape thumbprints with teaspoon measure

Require hand-shaping

Twice-baking is common

Thumbprints

As the cookie's name suggests, thumbprints are characterized by a hollowed-out center traditionally formed by pressing your thumb into individual balls of dough to form an indentation in the center which holds a filling—anything from a bright fruit jam to rich caramel—that offers a beautiful contrast to the crisp cookie surrounding it. We like to keep our thumbs out of thumbprints and use a teaspoon measure instead; its rounded underside creates the perfect-size divot. Sometimes we even reshape the indentation partway through baking, a trick that ensures enough space for a generous amount of filling. Creaming the butter and sugar is the most common mixing method for a dough with enough structure to handle the shaping and filling.

FORMING AND FILLING THUMBPRINTS

1. After baking cookies for 10 minutes, craters will have puffed up. Remove baking sheet from oven and use teaspoon measure to reshape original thumbprints.

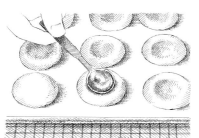

2. Snip small corner off zipper-lock bag filled with jam.

3. Carefully fill each indentation with about ½ teaspoon jam.

Blossoms

Whether or not you know their name, blossoms are a familiar presence on cookie trays all year long. These bite-size treats start out much like drop cookies—the dough is shaped into balls and baked. But once they are pulled from the oven they are crowned with their topping—commonly a Hershey's Kiss—and returned for a few more minutes of baking. While many recipes have you add the topping at the end of baking, we find that returning these treats to the oven to bake together briefly helps stabilize the exterior of the candy or confection, so the blossom components emerge united as one.

Rope Cookies

This style of molded cookie is fairly self explanatory: The dough is divided into portions and each portion is then rolled by hand into a long, thin rope. The rope can be formed into a variety of shapes such as a wreath, with the ends meeting up to form a circle. But this technique is also a great way to make quick work of portioning dough for recipes with a high yield of bite-size cookies: Once the ropes are rolled, you can simply cut each rope into individual pieces of dough rather than shape each piece by hand (like gnocchi!).

JAM THUMBPRINTS

Makes 48 cookies | 2 rimmed baking sheets

WHY THIS RECIPE WORKS With their jewel-like centers and rich, buttery, crisp cookies, jam thumbprints are a staple of bake sales and cookie swaps. Recipes traditionally call for plunging your thumb into balls of dough to make room for the filling, hence the name. Instead, we chose to use the bottom of a teaspoon measure to ensure even craters. When we added the jam to the indentations before baking, the centers became sticky and leathery; but jam added after baking was too loose. After a bit of trial and error, we discovered the key to success: reshaping the thumbprints halfway through baking before they were completely set. This meant we could fill them with a generous amount of jam, and adding the jam partway through baking resulted in a filling that was married to the cookie and set just enough. Any seedless jam can be used.

½ cup seedless jam
2¼ cups (11¼ ounces) all-purpose flour
½ teaspoon table salt
½ teaspoon baking soda
¼ teaspoon baking powder
12 tablespoons unsalted butter, softened
⅔ cup (4⅔ ounces) sugar
3 ounces cream cheese, softened
1 large egg
1½ teaspoons vanilla extract

1. Adjust oven rack to middle position and heat oven to 350 degrees. Line 2 rimmed baking sheets with parchment paper.

2. Fill small zipper-lock bag with jam and set aside. Whisk flour, salt, baking soda, and baking powder together in medium bowl. Using stand mixer fitted with paddle, beat butter and sugar on medium speed until fluffy, 3 to 6 minutes. Add cream cheese, egg, and vanilla and beat until combined, about 30 seconds. Reduce speed to low, slowly add flour mixture, and mix until incorporated.

3. Working with 1½ teaspoons dough at a time, roll into balls and space them 1½ inches apart on prepared sheets. Using greased rounded 1-teaspoon measure, make indentation in center of each dough ball.

4. Bake cookies, 1 sheet at a time, until just beginning to set and lightly browned around edges, about 10 minutes. Remove sheet from oven and gently reshape indentation in center of each cookie with greased rounded 1-teaspoon measure. Snip small corner off zipper-lock bag and carefully fill each indentation with about ½ teaspoon jam. Rotate sheet and continue to bake until lightly golden, 12 to 14 minutes. Let cookies cool on sheet for 10 minutes, then transfer to wire rack and let cool completely before serving.

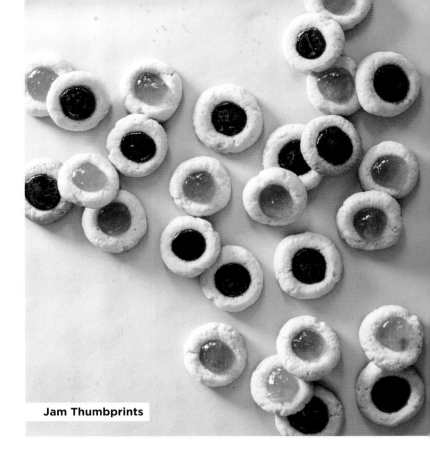

Jam Thumbprints

HAZELNUT LEMON CURD THUMBPRINTS

Makes 24 cookies | 2 rimmed baking sheets

WHY THIS RECIPE WORKS Jam thumbprints are appealing to kids and grownups alike: Who doesn't like a sweet surprise? But rarely do we see variations; we thought this category of cookie was ripe for a new, sophisticated interpretation. For the filling, we immediately thought of another fruity spread, one that's richer and a bit more refined than jam: lemon curd, a custard-like mixture made from eggs, sugar, butter, and, of course, lemon juice. A nut-based cookie seemed like an ideal pairing, and the warm, round flavor of hazelnuts provided a nice contrast to the tart lemon filling. We love homemade lemon curd, but it's a lot of work, especially when only ¼ cup is needed to fill all the cookies. Our favorite jarred lemon curd is Wilkin & Sons Tiptree Lemon Curd. Many other varieties of jarred lemon curd taste cloying, so purchase carefully.

1 cup (5 ounces) all-purpose flour
¾ cup hazelnuts, toasted and skinned
Pinch table salt
8 tablespoons unsalted butter, softened
⅓ cup (2⅓ ounces) granulated sugar
1 large egg yolk
¾ teaspoon vanilla extract
¼ cup lemon curd
Confectioners' sugar

1. Adjust oven racks to upper-middle and lower-middle positions and heat oven to 350 degrees. Line 2 rimmed baking sheets with parchment paper.

2. Process flour, hazelnuts, and salt in food processor until finely ground, about 45 seconds. Using stand mixer fitted with paddle, beat butter and granulated sugar on medium-high speed until pale and fluffy, 3 to 6 minutes. Add egg yolk and vanilla and beat until incorporated. Reduce speed to low, slowly add flour mixture, and mix until just combined.

3. Working with 1 tablespoon dough at a time, roll into balls and space them 2 inches apart on prepared sheets. Using greased rounded 1-teaspoon measure, make indentation in center of each dough ball.

4. Bake cookies until just beginning to set, about 10 minutes. Remove sheets from oven and gently reshape indentation in center of each cookie with greased rounded 1-teaspoon measure. Fill each indentation with ½ teaspoon lemon curd. Bake until cookies are just beginning to brown around edges, 8 to 10 minutes, switching and rotating sheets halfway through baking. Let cookies cool on sheets for 5 minutes, then transfer to wire rack and let cool completely. Dust with confectioners' sugar before serving.

Chocolate-Nut Thumbprints

CHOCOLATE-NUT THUMBPRINTS

Makes 48 cookies | 2 rimmed baking sheets

WHY THIS RECIPE WORKS Chocolate and nuts are a winning combination in any form; these cookies pack buttery toasted pecans into a rich cinnamon-scented dough that gets filled with a creamy chocolate ganache. Nut doughs tend to be crumbly, but the addition of egg yolks and a splash of heavy cream helped ours hold together. Processing the nuts until finely ground ensured that they incorporated easily into the dough. Rich chocolate ganache—here made from bittersweet chocolate and cream, with a small amount of corn syrup for a glossy sheen and touch of sweetness—dressed up the cookies and provided the perfect complement to their cinnamon-nut flavor.

  2 **cups pecans, toasted**
2½ **cups (12½ ounces) all-purpose flour**
 16 **tablespoons unsalted butter, cut into 16 pieces and softened**
  1 **cup (7 ounces) sugar**
  1 **teaspoon ground cinnamon**
  ¼ **teaspoon table salt**
  2 **tablespoons plus ½ cup heavy cream, divided**
  2 **large egg yolks**
  1 **teaspoon vanilla extract**
  6 **ounces bittersweet chocolate, chopped fine**
  2 **tablespoons corn syrup**

1. Adjust oven racks to upper-middle and lower-middle positions and heat oven to 375 degrees. Line 2 rimmed baking sheets with parchment paper. Process pecans in food processor until finely ground, about 30 seconds.

2. Using stand mixer fitted with paddle, mix flour, butter, sugar, cinnamon, salt, and pecans on low speed until crumbly, about 2 minutes. Add 2 tablespoons heavy cream, egg yolks, and vanilla and mix until dough forms cohesive mass.

3. Roll dough into 1¼-inch balls; space balls 1½ inches apart on prepared sheets. Using your wet thumb, make indentation in center of each ball. Bake for 10 minutes; remove sheets from oven and gently reshape indentation in center of each cookie with greased rounded 1-teaspoon measure. Switch and rotate baking sheets and continue to bake until just beginning to brown on edges, 8 to 10 minutes longer. Let cookies cool on sheets for 5 minutes, then transfer to wire rack and let cool completely.

4. Combine chocolate, corn syrup, and remaining ½ cup cream in saucepan over medium-low heat, stirring constantly until smooth; let cool for 1 hour. Fill indentation of each cookie with generous teaspoon chocolate mixture. Let chocolate set for at least 1 hour before serving.

PEANUT BLOSSOM COOKIES

Makes about 48 cookies | 2 rimmed baking sheets

WHY THIS RECIPE WORKS We love peanut blossoms, which are simply peanut butter cookies topped with a Hershey's Kiss, but we thought they could use a more robust peanut flavor. Adding more peanut butter didn't do the trick, and swapping chunky peanut butter for the creamy gave the cookies a craggy texture. We got the best flavor when we replaced a portion of the flour with finely ground roasted peanuts. Most recipes press the kisses into the cookies immediately after baking, but the warm cookies softened the kisses too much, and they took 4 hours to firm up again. Strangely, we found that adding the kisses during the last 2 minutes of baking helped them firm up more quickly. Why? It turns out that a little direct heat stabilizes and sets the exterior of the chocolate. Any Hershey's Kiss—dark, milk, white, or "Hugs"—works in this recipe.

> 1⅓ cups (6⅔ ounces) all-purpose flour, divided
> ½ cup salted dry-roasted peanuts
> ¼ teaspoon baking powder
> ¼ teaspoon baking soda
> ¼ teaspoon table salt
> 8 tablespoons unsalted butter, softened
> ⅓ cup packed (2⅓ ounces) dark brown sugar
> ⅓ cup (2⅓ ounces) granulated sugar
> ½ cup creamy peanut butter
> 1 large egg, room temperature
> 1 teaspoon vanilla extract
> 48–50 Hershey's Kisses, unwrapped

1. Process ⅔ cup flour and peanuts in food processor until peanuts are finely ground, about 15 seconds; transfer to bowl and whisk in baking powder, baking soda, salt, and remaining ⅔ cup flour.

2. Using stand mixer fitted with paddle, beat butter, brown sugar, and granulated sugar until fluffy, about 2 minutes. Add peanut butter and beat until combined. Add egg and vanilla and beat until combined. Reduce speed to low, add flour mixture in 2 additions, and mix until just combined. Cover bowl tightly with plastic wrap and refrigerate for 30 minutes.

3. Adjust oven rack to middle position and heat oven to 350 degrees. Line 2 rimmed baking sheets with parchment paper. Roll dough into 1-inch balls and space them 2 inches apart on prepared sheets. Bake, 1 sheet at a time, until cookies are just set and beginning to crack, 9 to 11 minutes. Working quickly, remove sheet from oven and place 1 candy in center of each cookie, pressing down firmly. Return sheet to oven and bake until cookies are light golden, about 2 minutes longer. Let cookies cool on sheet for 5 minutes, then transfer to wire rack and let cool completely before serving.

S'MORES BLOSSOM COOKIES

Makes 24 cookies | 2 rimmed baking sheets

WHY THIS RECIPE WORKS We wanted to package the nostalgic essence of s'mores into a neat blossom cookie. We made a butter cookie dough for the base and boosted its flavor by mixing in graham cracker crumbs. To really highlight the sweet whole-wheat flavor of the grahams and to add some crunch, we also rolled the balls of dough in more crushed graham crackers. A halved marshmallow sat neatly on top of the baked cookies; to get a brûlée on the marshmallows, we ran the baked and topped cookies under the broiler until the marshmallows developed a golden top. We topped each cookie with the recognizable Hershey's Kiss for chocolate flavor.

> 1¼ cups (6¼ ounces) all-purpose flour
> ½ teaspoon baking powder
> ¼ teaspoon baking soda
> ¼ teaspoon table salt
> 8 tablespoons unsalted butter, softened
> ½ cup (3½ ounces) sugar
> 8 whole graham crackers, crushed into
>   fine crumbs (1 cup), divided
> 1 large egg, room temperature
> 1 teaspoon vanilla extract
> 12 large marshmallows, halved crosswise
> 24 Hershey's Kisses, unwrapped

1. Adjust oven rack to middle position and heat oven to 350 degrees. Line 2 rimmed baking sheets with parchment paper. Whisk flour, baking powder, baking soda, and salt together in bowl.

2. Using stand mixer fitted with paddle, beat butter, sugar, and ½ cup graham cracker crumbs on medium-high speed until pale and fluffy, about 3 minutes. Add egg and vanilla and beat until incorporated. Reduce speed to low, slowly add flour mixture, and mix until just combined.

3. Spread remaining ½ cup graham cracker crumbs in shallow dish. Working with 1 tablespoon dough at a time, roll into balls, then toss in graham cracker crumbs to coat; space dough balls evenly on prepared sheets. Bake, 1 sheet at a time, until just set and beginning to crack on sides, 10 to 12 minutes. Let cookies cool on sheets for 5 minutes.

4. Adjust oven rack 10 inches from broiler element and heat broiler. Place 1 marshmallow half, cut side down, in center of each cookie. Broil cookies until marshmallows are deep golden brown, 30 to 45 seconds, rotating sheet halfway through broiling for even browning if needed. Transfer sheet to wire rack and immediately place 1 candy in center of each marshmallow, pressing down gently. Repeat with remaining cookies, marshmallows, and kisses. Let cookies cool completely before serving.

S'mores Blossom
Cookies

GIUGIULENI

Makes 48 cookies | 2 rimmed baking sheets

WHY THIS RECIPE WORKS Though less well-known in America than biscotti or angeletti, giugiuleni are a mainstay on Italian Christmas cookie trays. Featuring a coating of sesame seeds, these buttery cookies are sturdy, have a gentle crunch, and are subtly sweet, making them ideal for dipping into espresso. To make a cookie that was all about the flavor and crunch of the nutty sesame seeds, we started with a simple vanilla-scented dough. Instead of forming individual balls, we gave these cookies a unique shape by rolling the dough into a rope before cutting it into pieces, much like making gnocchi. To help the sesame seed coating stick to the cookies, we made a simple syrup in the microwave and dipped half of each dough piece into the syrup before pressing on the seeds.

    ½   cup sesame seeds
    2   tablespoons plus ⅓ cup (2⅓ ounces) granulated
        sugar, divided
    2   tablespoons water
    ⅓   cup packed (2⅓ ounces) brown sugar
    1   large egg plus 1 large yolk
    2   tablespoons milk
    ½   teaspoon vanilla extract
    2⅓ cups (11⅔ ounces) all-purpose flour
    2½ teaspoons baking powder
    ⅛   teaspoon table salt
    20 tablespoons (2½ sticks) unsalted butter, softened

1. Adjust oven racks to upper-middle and lower-middle positions and heat oven to 375 degrees. Line 2 rimmed baking sheets with parchment paper and grease parchment. Spread sesame seeds in shallow dish.

2. Combine 2 tablespoons granulated sugar and water in bowl and microwave until sugar is dissolved, about 1 minute; set aside. Whisk brown sugar, egg and yolk, milk, and vanilla together in bowl until frothy; set aside. Using stand mixer fitted with whisk attachment, mix flour, baking powder, salt, and remaining ⅓ cup granulated sugar on low speed until combined. Increase speed to medium, add butter, and mix until mixture resembles coarse cornmeal, 3 to 5 minutes. Add egg mixture and mix until dough just comes together, about 1 minute.

3. Using your floured hands, break off handful of dough and roll into ¾-inch-thick rope on lightly floured counter. Cut rope into 1½-inch lengths. Dip 1 side of lengths in sugar syrup, then in sesame seeds; space lengths 3 inches apart on prepared sheets, seed side up. Bake until lightly browned, 18 to 24 minutes, switching and rotating sheets halfway through baking. Let cookies cool on sheets for 5 minutes, then transfer to wire rack and let cool completely before serving. Repeat with remaining dough, syrup, and sesame seeds.

ALMOND-SPICE WREATHS

Makes 40 cookies | 2 rimmed baking sheets

WHY THIS RECIPE WORKS These light, flourless, nut-based cookies are shaped like beautiful wreaths. We made a chewy almond macaroon–like dough that, once chilled, was firm and malleable enough to form into ropes and shape into wreaths. For a unique wintry flavor profile, we added orange zest, ground coffee, and spices to the dough; we also folded in some marmalade at the end of mixing. After shaping the dough, we topped our wreaths with sliced almonds, dipping them in egg whites first so the almonds adhered. For shining accents, we pressed pieces of red and green maraschino cherries on top. Dusting the cookies with confectioners' sugar gave them a snowy coat.

COOKIES

    4   cups (18 ounces) almond flour
    2   tablespoons grated orange zest (2 oranges)
    1   tablespoon ground coffee
    1   teaspoon ground cinnamon
    1   teaspoon ground ginger
    ½   teaspoon ground cardamom
    ¼   teaspoon table salt
    3   large egg whites
    1½   cups (10½ ounces) granulated sugar
    2   teaspoons almond extract
    1   teaspoon vanilla extract
    3   tablespoons orange marmalade

TOPPING

    2   large egg whites
    2   cups sliced almonds
    40   maraschino cherries (red and green), quartered
         Confectioners' sugar

1. FOR THE COOKIES: Whisk almond flour, orange zest, coffee, cinnamon, ginger, cardamom, and salt together in bowl. Using stand mixer fitted with whisk attachment, whip egg whites on medium-low speed until foamy, about 1 minute. Increase speed to medium-high and whip whites to soft, billowy mounds, about 1 minute. Gradually add sugar and whip until glossy, soft peaks form, 2 to 3 minutes. Whip in almond extract and vanilla.

2. Fold almond flour mixture into whipped whites in 2 additions until few white streaks remain. Fold in marmalade until no white streaks remain. Transfer dough to counter and divide in half. Form each half into disk, wrap disks tightly in plastic wrap, and refrigerate until firm, at least 1 hour or up to 24 hours.

3. FOR THE TOPPING: Adjust oven racks to upper-middle and lower-middle positions and heat oven to 300 degrees. Line 2 rimmed baking sheets with parchment paper. Whisk egg whites in shallow dish until frothy. Spread almonds in second shallow dish.

4. Divide 1 disk of dough into 20 pieces. Roll each piece into 5-inch rope on lightly floured counter, shape into circle, and press ends together to seal. Dip 1 side of each wreath into egg whites, letting excess drip off, then press gently into almonds. Space, almond side up, evenly on prepared sheets. Press 4 cherry pieces into each wreath.

5. Bake cookies until firm and golden brown, 20 to 25 minutes, switching and rotating sheets halfway through baking. Let cookies cool on sheets for 5 minutes, then transfer to wire rack and let cool completely. Repeat with remaining dough, egg whites, almonds, and cherries. Dust with confectioners' sugar before serving.

PFEFFERNÜSSE

Makes 120 cookies | 2 rimmed baking sheets

WHY THIS RECIPE WORKS Pfeffernüsse (also known as peppernuts) are a traditional Christmas cookie with iterations found throughout Germany, the Netherlands, and Denmark. These spicy, bite-size cookies soften and develop flavor as they age. We wanted to tenderize this lean dough by incorporating butter so that we could enjoy Pfeffernüsse when we made them—no aging required. Despite their name, peppernuts don't call for nuts, but we found that adding a small amount of ground almonds tenderized the dough without adding too much richness. Blooming the spices in the butter boosted their flavor and their heat. Candied orange peel perfumed the cookies. Instead of the traditional, time-consuming method of rolling each individual cookie into small balls, we rolled the dough into logs and cut them into pieces before baking.

4 tablespoons unsalted butter
¾ teaspoon ground cardamom
½ teaspoon ground cinnamon
½ teaspoon ground allspice
¼ teaspoon pepper
⅓ cup molasses
¼ cup packed (1¾ ounces) light brown sugar
2 cups (10 ounces) all-purpose flour
¼ cup slivered almonds
¼ cup candied orange peel
½ teaspoon baking soda
½ teaspoon table salt
1 large egg
½ cup confectioners' sugar, sifted

1. Adjust oven racks to upper-middle and lower-middle positions and heat oven to 350 degrees. Line 2 rimmed baking sheets with parchment paper. Melt butter in 8-inch skillet over medium-low heat. Add cardamom, cinnamon, allspice, and pepper and cook for 15 seconds, stirring constantly; transfer to bowl and whisk in molasses and brown sugar to combine. Let butter mixture cool completely.

2. Process flour, almonds, orange peel, baking soda, and salt in food processor until finely ground, about 1 minute. Whisk egg into cooled butter mixture to combine. Stir in flour mixture until just incorporated. Transfer dough to counter. Form dough into disk, wrap disk tightly in plastic wrap, and refrigerate until firm, about 2 hours.

3. Divide dough into 10 equal pieces. Roll each piece into ½-inch-thick rope. Using bench scraper or sharp knife, cut ropes into 1-inch lengths and space them 1 inch apart on prepared sheets. Bake until just set and edges are lightly browned, 10 minutes, switching and rotating sheets halfway through baking. Let cookies cool on sheets for 5 minutes, then slide parchment onto wire rack and let cool completely. Repeat with remaining dough. Toss in confectioners' sugar to coat before serving.

Pfeffernüsse

ROLLED COOKIES

KEY POINTS

Chill dough before rolling

Roll dough to even thickness

Shape with cookie cutter

THE DOUGH FOR THIS TYPE OF COOKIE IS ROLLED THIN and stamped with a cookie cutter (or sometimes simply cut into shapes with a knife or pizza cutter). While cutout cookies aren't difficult to make, they do require a little more consideration to form than do those that are simply dropped onto a baking sheet or shaped into a log and sliced. Sometimes we roll the dough between two large sheets of parchment paper rather than on the counter; this eliminates the need for dusting the dough with an excessive amount of flour, which can result in dry cookies. This technique also minimizes sticking and makes it much easier to move the cookies to the baking sheet; you simply remove the top piece of parchment, stamp out the cookies, and then transfer them to the sheet with a thin offset spatula (which is much easier than trying to coax the cookies off the counter). Chilling the dough—typically after dividing and shaping the dough into disks—is key. This not only makes the dough much easier to work with but also ensures that your cookies will hold their shape when they're transferred to the baking sheet. Rolled cookies can range from thin and crisp like Speculoos (page 61) and Lemon Thins (page 60) to fine-crumbed with a shortbread texture like Lemon-Lavender Cookies (page 63) to slightly soft and chewy like Soft and Chewy Gingerbread Cookies (page 63) depending on the ingredients and mixing method used. But no matter the texture, their flat tops make them the perfect vehicle for festive additions such as a glaze or a sprinkling of sugar.

RESTING AND CHILLING THE DOUGH

Chilling the dough after mixing makes cookie rolling a much easier task for a couple of reasons. It prevents the butter from getting too warm and the dough from becoming too sticky. Also, a refrigerator rest allows the flour to hydrate and the gluten that was formed during mixing to relax, so the dough isn't too tough to roll out or doesn't retract upon rolling. Wrap your disks of dough tightly in plastic wrap and refrigerate the dough until it's firm yet malleable (we provide a time frame as a guideline in each recipe).

AVOIDING OVERBAKING

Thinly rolled cookies can go from perfectly baked to overbaked in a matter of minutes, so it's important to watch them closely—most cookies should show a slight resistance to the touch and start to become brown along the edges.

SCRAP-REDUCING STRATEGY

Once you've rolled out the dough, you want to make the most of it—we generally don't reroll the scraps more than once or twice as more rolling can make the dough tougher. Minimize scraps by cutting your cookie shapes close together, starting from the outside and working your way to the middle. When making large and small cookies, we like to alternate cutters as we stamp to use as much dough as possible.

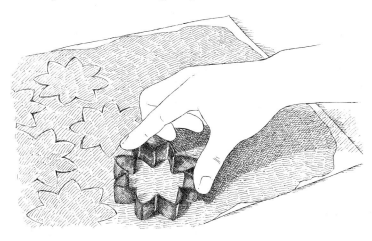

Speculoos

Lemon Thins

LEMON THINS

Makes about 40 cookies | 2 rimmed baking sheets

WHY THIS RECIPE WORKS Small and delicate, lemon thins had legions of fans in times past, and grocery store shelves, particularly in the South, were crowded with regional versions. We wanted to bring back these pleasantly crisp cookies, but when we tested existing recipes we found them to be too thick and soft or too crumbly or too chewy—and all of them were desperately short on lemon flavor. Texture was the first puzzle to solve, and we found the answer in an old test kitchen trick for making cookies lighter: Replacing a small amount of the flour with cornstarch made for incredibly tender yet crisp cookies. Still missing? Bold lemon flavor. A generous 2 tablespoons of juice along with a bit of pure lemon extract gave us the bright, sour flavor we sought. A light lemon glaze enforced the citrus flavor.

COOKIES

1½ cups (7½ ounces) all-purpose flour
 2 tablespoons cornstarch
 ¼ teaspoon table salt
 ¼ teaspoon baking powder
 ⅛ teaspoon baking soda
10 tablespoons unsalted butter, softened
 ½ cup (3½ ounces) granulated sugar
 2 tablespoons lemon juice
 1 large egg yolk
1½ teaspoons lemon extract

GLAZE

 1 cup (4 ounces) confectioners' sugar
 1 teaspoon grated lemon zest plus 7 teaspoons juice, plus extra juice if needed
    Pinch table salt

1. FOR THE COOKIES: Whisk flour, cornstarch, salt, baking powder, and baking soda together in bowl; set aside. Using stand mixer fitted with paddle, beat butter and sugar on medium-high speed until pale and fluffy, about 3 minutes. Add lemon juice, egg yolk, and lemon extract and beat until combined. Reduce speed to low and add flour mixture in 3 additions until just combined, scraping down bowl as needed. Transfer dough to counter and divide in half. Form each half into 5-inch disk, wrap disks tightly in plastic wrap, and refrigerate for at least 1 hour or up to 24 hours.

2. Adjust oven rack to middle position and heat oven to 325 degrees. Line 2 rimmed baking sheets with parchment paper. Remove 1 disk of dough from refrigerator and knead for 3 to 5 turns to make more pliable. On lightly floured counter, roll dough into 10-inch circle, ¼ inch thick.

3. Using 2-inch round cookie cutter, cut 14 or 15 rounds from dough. Reroll scraps up to 2 times and cut out remaining 5 or 6 rounds to yield 20 cookies. Space cookies 1 inch apart on 1 prepared sheet.

4. Bake cookies until edges are lightly browned, 12 to 14 minutes, rotating sheet halfway through baking. Let cookies cool on sheet for 5 minutes, then transfer to wire rack and let cool completely. Repeat with remaining dough.

5. FOR THE GLAZE: Whisk sugar, lemon zest and juice, and salt together in bowl. Working with 1 cookie at a time, dip top of cookie into glaze, then drag top lightly against rim of bowl to remove excess glaze. (If glaze thickens as it sits, add extra lemon juice as needed to maintain proper consistency.) Let glaze dry before serving, about 15 minutes.

SPECULOOS

Makes 32 cookies | 2 rimless baking sheets

WHY THIS RECIPE WORKS You might know speculoos from their familiar presence on countless flights. These much-loved Belgian cookies have a crisp, light, open-crumbed texture and a blend of caramelized sugar and warm spice flavors. To achieve the appropriate texture, we rolled the dough thin so it would bake up dry and crisp, and used only enough sugar to lightly sweeten the dough since sugar is hygroscopic and makes cookies moist. Adding baking powder along with the usual baking soda produced an open, airy crumb. For a subtle caramel taste, we chose turbinado sugar rather than traditional (but hard-to-find) Belgian brown sugar. A large amount of cinnamon along with small amounts of cardamom and cloves added complexity. Do not use cookie molds or an embossed rolling pin for the speculoos; they will not hold decorations.

1½ cups (7½ ounces) all-purpose flour
   5 teaspoons ground cinnamon
   1 teaspoon ground cardamom
   ¼ teaspoon ground cloves
   ¼ teaspoon baking powder
   ¼ teaspoon baking soda
   ¼ teaspoon table salt
   ¾ cup (6 ounces) turbinado sugar
   8 tablespoons unsalted butter, cut into
      ½-inch pieces and chilled
   1 large egg

1. Whisk flour, cinnamon, cardamom, cloves, baking powder, baking soda, and salt together in bowl. Using pencil and ruler, draw 10 by 12-inch rectangle in center of each of 2 large sheets of parchment paper, crisscrossing lines at corners. (Use crisscrosses to help line up top and bottom sheets as dough is rolled.)

2. Process sugar in food processor for 30 seconds (some grains will be smaller than granulated sugar; others will be larger). Add butter and process until uniform mass forms and no large pieces of butter are visible, about 30 seconds, scraping down sides of bowl as needed. Add egg and process until smooth and paste-like, about 10 seconds, scraping down sides of bowl as needed. Add flour mixture and process until no dry flour remains but mixture remains crumbly, about 30 seconds, scraping down sides of bowl as needed.

3. Transfer dough to bowl and knead gently with spatula until uniform and smooth, about 10 seconds. Place 1 piece of parchment on counter with pencil side facing down (you should be able to see rectangle through paper). Place dough in center of marked rectangle and press into 6 by 9-inch rectangle. Place second sheet of parchment over dough, with pencil side facing up, so dough is in center of marked rectangle. Using pencil marks as guide, use rolling pin and bench scraper to shape dough into 10 by 12-inch rectangle of even ⅜-inch thickness. Transfer dough with parchment to rimmed baking sheet. Refrigerate until dough is firm, at least 1½ hours (or freeze for 30 minutes). (Rolled dough can be wrapped in plastic wrap and refrigerated for up to 5 days.)

4. Adjust oven racks to upper-middle and lower-middle positions and heat oven to 300 degrees. Line 2 rimless baking sheets with parchment. Transfer chilled dough to counter. Gently peel off top layer of parchment from dough. Using fluted pastry wheel (or sharp knife or pizza cutter) and ruler, trim off rounded edges of dough that extend over marked edges of 10 by 12-inch rectangle. Cut dough lengthwise into 8 equal strips about 1¼ inches wide. Cut each strip crosswise into 4 equal pieces about 3 inches long. Transfer cookies to prepared sheets, spacing them at least ½ inch apart. Bake until cookies are lightly and evenly browned, 30 to 32 minutes, switching and rotating sheets halfway through baking. Transfer sheets to wire rack and let cookies cool completely before serving. (Cookies can be stored at room temperature for up to 3 weeks.)

Speculoos with Almonds

Once dough has been rolled into rectangle in step 3, gently peel off top layer of parchment. Sprinkle ½ cup sliced almonds evenly over dough. Using rolling pin, gently press almonds into dough. Return parchment to dough, flip dough over, and transfer with parchment to sheet. Proceed with recipe as directed.

Thin Chocolate-Mint Cookies

Lemon-Lavender Cookies

THIN CHOCOLATE-MINT COOKIES

Makes about 70 cookies | 2 rimmed baking sheets

WHY THIS RECIPE WORKS Thin Mints—the best-selling Girl Scout cookies with a crisp chocolate coating and cool mint flavor—are a favorite of children and adults alike. No longer wanting to count the days until the cookie season arrives, we decided to re-create them. To keep the mint flavor in check, we used peppermint oil in the chocolate coating only and omitted it from the cookie itself. Thin Mints get their crisp, short texture from palm kernel oil but we found that coconut oil, which is in the same family, did the trick. Baking the cookies until they were thoroughly dry ensured the proper crunch. For the shell, we turned to our easy microwave method for tempering chocolate, which yielded a chocolate coating that was every bit as attractive and crisp as one made by the traditional method.

COOKIES

- 1½ cups (7½ ounces) all-purpose flour
- ½ cup (1½ ounces) unsweetened cocoa powder
- ½ teaspoon table salt
- ¼ teaspoon baking powder
- ¼ teaspoon baking soda
- ½ cup refined coconut oil, chilled
- ¾ cup (5¼ ounces) sugar
- 2 tablespoons milk
- 1 large egg
- 1 teaspoon vanilla extract

CHOCOLATE COATING

- 1 pound semisweet chocolate (12 ounces chopped fine, 4 ounces grated)
- ⅛ teaspoon peppermint oil

1. FOR THE COOKIES: Whisk flour, cocoa, salt, baking powder, and baking soda together in bowl; set aside. Using stand mixer fitted with paddle, beat oil and sugar on medium-high speed until fluffy, about 2 minutes. Reduce speed to low; add milk, egg, and vanilla; and beat until combined, about 30 seconds. Slowly add flour mixture and beat until just combined, about 1 minute, scraping down bowl as needed. Divide dough in half. Form each half into 4-inch disk, wrap disks tightly in plastic wrap, and refrigerate until dough is firm yet malleable, about 45 minutes.

2. Adjust oven racks to upper-middle and lower-middle positions and heat oven to 350 degrees. Line 2 rimmed baking sheets with parchment paper. Working with 1 disk of dough at a time, roll into 11-inch circle, ⅛ inch thick, between 2 large sheets of lightly floured parchment paper. Remove top piece of parchment. Using 1¾-inch round cookie cutter, cut dough into rounds; space rounds ½ inch apart on prepared sheets. Gently reroll scraps up to 2 times, cut into rounds, and transfer to prepared sheets. Bake until cookies are very firm, 16 to 18 minutes, switching and rotating sheets halfway through baking. Let cookies cool on sheets for 5 minutes, then transfer to wire rack and let cool completely.

3. **FOR THE CHOCOLATE COATING:** Line baking sheet with parchment paper. Microwave finely chopped chocolate and oil in bowl at 50 percent power, stirring often, until about two-thirds melted, 2 to 4 minutes. (Melted chocolate should not be much warmer than body temperature; check by holding bowl in palm of your hand.) Add grated chocolate and stir until smooth, returning to microwave for no more than 5 seconds at a time to finish melting if necessary.

4. Working with 1 cookie at a time, place cookie on fork and dip bottom of cookie in chocolate. Using offset spatula, spread chocolate over top of cookie, creating thin coating. Transfer cookie to prepared baking sheet and repeat with remaining cookies. Let cookies sit until chocolate sets, about 15 minutes, before serving. (Cookies can be stored at room temperature for up to 2 weeks.)

lemon zest on low speed until combined. Add butter, 1 piece at a time, and mix until crumbly, 1 to 2 minutes. Add cream cheese and vanilla and beat until dough begins to form large clumps, about 30 seconds. Knead dough by hand, just until it forms cohesive mass. Divide dough in half. Form each half into 4-inch disk, wrap disks tightly in plastic wrap, and refrigerate for 30 minutes.

2. Adjust oven rack to middle position and heat oven to 375 degrees. Line 2 rimmed baking sheets with parchment paper. Roll each disk of dough ⅛ inch thick; refrigerate for 10 minutes.

3. Using 2½-inch cookie cutter, cut dough into shapes and space them 1½ inches apart on prepared sheets. Reroll scraps once, cut into shapes, and transfer to sheets. Sprinkle cookies evenly with lemon sugar. Bake cookies, 1 sheet at a time, until light golden brown, about 10 minutes, rotating sheet halfway through baking. Let cookies cool on sheet for 3 minutes, then transfer to wire rack and let cool completely before serving.

LEMON-LAVENDER COOKIES

Makes about 38 cookies | 2 rimmed baking sheets

WHY THIS RECIPE WORKS During the holidays, cookies spiced with cinnamon, nutmeg, anise, and ginger are common. But if your tastes tend to be on the more adventurous side, try these unique cookies for a refreshing change of pace. Lemon zest gives the cookies citrusy brightness, while dried lavender adds subtle floral notes. (The flowering lavender plant is actually a distant relative of mint, and the dried bluish-purple buds can be used very much like herbs.) A dusting of lemon sugar, made by mixing together granulated sugar and more lemon zest, gives the cookies flair. We find it important to thoroughly mince the dried lavender to release its flavor throughout the dough and to avoid crunchy bits in the cookies.

½ cup (3½ ounces) granulated sugar
1 tablespoon grated lemon zest, divided
2½ cups (12½ ounces) all-purpose flour
¾ cup (5¼ ounces) superfine sugar
1 teaspoon dried lavender, minced
¼ teaspoon table salt
16 tablespoons unsalted butter, cut into 16 pieces and softened
1 ounce cream cheese, softened
2 teaspoons vanilla extract

1. Stir granulated sugar and 2 teaspoons lemon zest in small bowl until combined; set aside. Using stand mixer fitted with paddle, mix flour, superfine sugar, lavender, salt, and remaining 1 teaspoon

SOFT AND CHEWY GINGERBREAD COOKIES

Makes about 20 cookies | 2 rimmed baking sheets

WHY THIS RECIPE WORKS These gingerbread cookies are nothing like the stale versions you punch a hole in and trim the Christmas tree with. While still flat enough to decorate, these cookies are soft and chewy and brimming with ginger and molasses flavors, not overwhelmed by dusty spices. For the proper chew, we needed more fat than most recipes use: 12 tablespoons of melted butter did the trick. Using a food processor made quick work of mixing the dough. We baked the cookies until they were just set around the edges and slightly puffed in the center; as they cooled, they settled into sublime chewiness. Depending on your cookie cutter dimensions, all of the cookies may not fit on the sheets and a second round of baking may be required. Try decorating these cookies with an icing (see page 42).

3 cups (15 ounces) all-purpose flour
¾ cup packed (5¼ ounces) dark brown sugar
1 tablespoon ground cinnamon
1 tablespoon ground ginger
¾ teaspoon baking soda
½ teaspoon ground cloves
½ teaspoon table salt
12 tablespoons unsalted butter, melted
¾ cup light molasses
2 tablespoons milk

TUTORIAL
Hungarian Kiffles

These cookie treasures neatly contain a golden apricot filling due to careful (but easy) shaping.

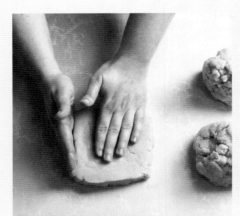

1. Divide dough into 3 pieces, form each piece into 5-inch square, wrap squares in plastic wrap, and refrigerate.

2. Roll 1 dough square into 12 by 9-inch rectangle on floured counter.

3. Cut dough into twelve 3-inch squares.

4. Place 1 heaping teaspoon filling onto center of each square.

5. Fold opposite corners over filling so they meet in center, enclosing filling completely.

6. Dust baked cookies with confectioners' sugar before serving.

1. Process flour, sugar, cinnamon, ginger, baking soda, cloves, and salt in food processor until combined, about 10 seconds. Add melted butter, molasses, and milk and process until soft dough forms and no streaks of flour remain, about 20 seconds, scraping down sides of bowl as needed.

2. Spray counter lightly with baking spray with flour, transfer dough to counter, and knead until dough forms cohesive ball, about 20 seconds. Divide dough in half. Form each half into 5-inch disk, wrap disks tightly in plastic wrap, and refrigerate for at least 1 hour or up to 24 hours.

3. Adjust oven racks to upper-middle and lower-middle positions and heat oven to 350 degrees. Line 2 rimmed baking sheets with parchment paper. Working with 1 disk of dough at a time, roll ¼ inch thick between 2 large sheets of parchment. (Keep second disk of dough refrigerated while rolling out first.) Remove top piece of parchment. Using 3½-inch cookie cutter, cut dough into shapes. Peel away scraps from around cookies and space shapes ¾ inch apart on prepared sheets. Repeat rolling and cutting steps with dough scraps up to 2 times.

4. Bake cookies until puffy and just set around edges, 9 to 11 minutes, switching and rotating sheets halfway through baking. Let cookies cool on sheets for 10 minutes, then transfer to wire rack and let cool completely before serving. (Cookies can be stored in wide, shallow airtight container, with sheet of parchment or waxed paper between each layer, at room temperature for up to 3 days.)

HUNGARIAN KIFFLES

Makes 36 cookies | rimmed baking sheet

WHY THIS RECIPE WORKS Like so many other fruit-filled sweets, these Hungarian cookies are a simple pairing of sticky-sweet filling and delicate crust. A combination of shortening and butter, along with sour cream and evaporated milk, made for an ultratender, slightly sweet dough. After rolling the dough out thin, we cut it into squares and placed a heaping teaspoon of filling—a tangy apricot "jam" that came together quickly in the food processor—in the middle of each piece. We then folded opposite corners over the filling so they met in the center; this ensured that the filling was completely enclosed. After baking, a dusting of powdered sugar was all they needed. You can use prunes instead of apricots in the filling, if desired. If the dough gets too soft or sticky to roll, return it to the refrigerator to firm up, and use plenty of flour on the counter and rolling pin.

1¼ cups (7½ ounces) dried apricots
1 cup water
1¼ cups (8¾ ounces) granulated sugar, divided
3¾ cups (18¾ ounces) all-purpose flour
1 tablespoon baking powder
1 teaspoon table salt
1 teaspoon grated lemon zest plus ½ teaspoon juice
½ cup sour cream
¼ cup evaporated milk
10 tablespoons vegetable shortening
8 tablespoons unsalted butter, softened
2 large egg yolks
Confectioners' sugar

1. Bring apricots and water to boil in medium saucepan over medium-high heat. Reduce heat to medium and simmer until water is mostly absorbed, about 5 minutes. Stir in ½ cup granulated sugar and cook until thickened, about 3 minutes. Process mixture in food processor until smooth, about 30 seconds.

2. Whisk flour, baking powder, salt, and lemon zest together in bowl. Whisk sour cream, evaporated milk, and lemon juice together in second bowl. Using stand mixer fitted with paddle, beat shortening, butter, and remaining ¾ cup granulated sugar on medium-high speed until fluffy, about 3 minutes. Add egg yolks and beat until combined. Reduce speed to low and add flour mixture in 4 additions, alternating with sour cream mixture in 3 additions. Divide dough into 3 pieces. Form each piece into 5-inch square, wrap squares tightly in plastic wrap, and refrigerate for 1 hour.

3. Adjust oven rack to middle position and heat oven to 325 degrees. Line rimmed baking sheet with parchment paper. Roll 1 dough square into 12 by 9-inch rectangle on floured counter. Cut dough into twelve 3-inch squares. Place 1 heaping teaspoon filling onto center of each square and fold opposite corners over filling so they meet in center, enclosing filling completely. Transfer squares to prepared sheet.

4. Bake until golden brown, 20 to 24 minutes, rotating sheet halfway through baking. Let cookies cool on sheet for 5 minutes, then transfer to wire rack. Repeat with remaining dough and filling. Let cookies cool completely and dust with confectioners' sugar before serving.

RUGELACH WITH RAISIN-WALNUT FILLING

Makes 32 rugelach | 2 rimmed baking sheets

WHY THIS RECIPE WORKS Part cookie, part pastry, rugelach are a traditional Jewish party snack. Their tight curls can contain a variety of bounteous sweet fillings, from nuts and jam to dried fruit and even chocolate. We started by adding more flour to the dough than most recipes call for, which helped make it more workable. A couple of tablespoons of sour cream in addition to the traditional cream cheese gave the cookies more tang and tenderized them further. For the filling, we settled on a combination of apricot preserves, raisins, and walnuts. Be sure to stop processing the dough when the mixture resembles moist crumbs. If the dough gathers into a cohesive mass around the blade of the food processor, you've overprocessed it. If at any point during the cutting and rolling of the crescents the sheet of dough softens and becomes hard to roll, slide it onto a baking sheet and freeze it until it is firm enough to handle. Feel free to substitute chopped pitted prunes, chopped dried apricots, or dried cranberries for the raisins in the filling.

DOUGH

- 2¼ cups (11¼ ounces) all-purpose flour
- 1½ tablespoons sugar
- ¼ teaspoon table salt
- 16 tablespoons unsalted butter, cut into ¼-inch pieces and chilled
- 8 ounces cream cheese, cut into ½-inch pieces and chilled
- 2 tablespoons sour cream

FILLING

- ⅔ cup apricot preserves
- 1 cup (7 ounces) sugar
- 1 tablespoon ground cinnamon
- 1 cup golden raisins, divided
- 2 cups walnuts, chopped fine

GLAZE

- 2 large egg yolks
- 2 tablespoons milk

1. FOR THE DOUGH: Pulse flour, sugar, and salt in food processor until combined, about 3 pulses. Add butter, cream cheese, and sour cream; pulse until dough comes together in small, uneven pebbles the size of cottage cheese curds, about 16 pulses. Transfer dough to counter, press into 9 by 6-inch log, and divide log into 4 equal pieces. Form each piece into 4½-inch disk. Place each disk between 2 sheets of plastic wrap and roll into 8½-inch circle. Stack dough circles, between parchment, on plate; freeze for 30 minutes.

2. FOR THE FILLING: Meanwhile, process apricot preserves in food processor until smooth, about 10 seconds. Combine sugar and cinnamon in small bowl; set aside. Line 2 rimmed baking sheets with parchment paper. Working with 1 dough circle at a time, remove dough from freezer and spread with 2½ tablespoons preserves. Sprinkle 2 tablespoons cinnamon sugar, ¼ cup raisins, and ½ cup walnuts over preserves and pat down gently with your fingers. Cut circle into 8 wedges. Roll each wedge into crescent shape; space crescents 2 inches apart on prepared sheets. Freeze crescents on sheets for 15 minutes.

3. FOR THE GLAZE: Adjust oven racks to upper-middle and lower-middle positions and heat oven to 375 degrees. Whisk egg yolks and milk in bowl. Brush crescents with glaze. Bake until rugelach are pale golden and slightly puffy, 21 to 23 minutes, switching and rotating sheets halfway through baking. Sprinkle each cookie with scant teaspoon cinnamon sugar. Transfer rugelach to wire rack and let cool completely before serving. (Rugelach can be stored at room temperature for up to 4 days.)

Chocolate-Raspberry Rugelach

Substitute ⅔ cup raspberry preserves for apricot preserves and substitute 1 cup mini semisweet chocolate chips for raisins.

Rugelach

TUTORIAL
Rugelach

A tender-flaky dough, a sweet filling, and a beautiful shape are all within reach with these rugelach steps.

1. Press dough into 9 by 6-inch log, and divide log into 4 equal pieces.

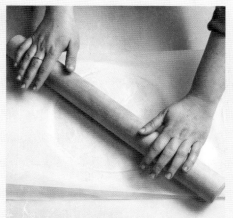

2. Form each piece into 4½-inch disk. Place each disk between 2 sheets of plastic wrap and roll into 8½-inch circle. Stack dough circles, between parchment, on plate; freeze for 30 minutes.

3. Working with 1 dough circle at a time, remove dough from freezer and spread with preserves. Sprinkle cinnamon sugar, raisins, and walnuts over preserves and pat down gently with your fingers.

4. Cut circle into 8 wedges.

5. Roll each wedge into crescent shape; space crescents 2 inches apart on prepared sheets. Freeze crescents on sheets for 15 minutes.

6. Brush crescents with glaze. Bake until rugelach are pale golden and slightly puffy, 21 to 23 minutes, switching and rotating sheets halfway through baking.

SANDWICH COOKIES

A GOOD SANDWICH COOKIE is all about balance, with a filling that provides contrasting flavor and texture to the cookies that contain it. The variations and combinations are endless—a filling might be rich and creamy or sweet and jamlike, while the cookies themselves could be crisp like shortbread or soft and cakey. But no matter the flavors and textures, sandwich cookies have much in common. For all cookies of this type, precisely portioning the dough and filling is one of the most important steps—we like to use a portion scoop or measuring spoon for these tasks. The filling should have a consistency substantial enough that it won't squish out the sides of the cookie with each bite, and it should help hold the cookies together. The cookies should be thin and flat or small and bite-size so that you can comfortably eat two of them sandwiched with filling. (One exception here would be the soft, cakelike whoopie pie, which is oversized and slightly domed by nature.) The temperature of each component plays an important role as well—a warm peanut butter filling makes the filling easy to sandwich, while a warm cookie can help the filling stick once cooled. Be sure to use a gentle hand when pressing the top cookie down so that the filling doesn't ooze out the sides.

FIXING UP FLAT STACKS

The cookie portion of most sandwich cookies should be relatively flat and thin so they are easy to fill and eat. There are a few ways to make sure your cookies are flat. As with cookies we like to decorate (see page 33), using a food processor and/or the reverse creaming method ensures you don't incorporate too much air at the mixing stage. Other sandwich cookie–specific techniques involve shaping.

Hand-Flatten This easy approach calls for simply flattening the mound of dough with your hand to a specified diameter.

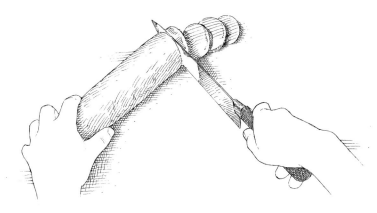

Slice and Bake Using the icebox cookie technique of shaping the dough into a log and then slicing it into rounds guarantees flat cookies of even thickness.

Linzer Sandwich Cookies

LINZER SANDWICH COOKIES

Makes about 24 sandwich cookies |
2 rimmed baking sheets

WHY THIS RECIPE WORKS Linzer cookies are a Christmas favorite based on the classic Austrian torte of the same name, which consists of a buttery, nutty dough spread with jam or preserves and topped with lattice strips (see page 436). For these cookies, the dough is thinner and thus more crisp. The top cookie sports a small cutout in the center, which exposes the jam. We opted for hazelnuts and upped the nuttiness by adding a hint of almond extract to the dough. We liked the bright flavor of raspberry jam. Chilled butter gave us dough that was easy to work with and resulted in crisp cookies that complemented the soft jam center. Using confectioners' sugar as the sole sweetener gave our cookies an extraordinarily tender texture and a fine crumb.

- ⅔ cup seedless raspberry jam
- ⅔ cup (2⅔ ounces) confectioners' sugar
- ½ cup hazelnuts, toasted and skinned
- 1 cup (5 ounces) all-purpose flour
- 6 tablespoons unsalted butter, cut into ½-inch pieces and chilled
- ¼ teaspoon table salt
- 1 large egg yolk
- 1 tablespoon heavy cream
- ½ teaspoon vanilla extract
- ¼ teaspoon almond extract

1. Simmer jam in small saucepan over medium heat, stirring frequently, until thickened and reduced to ½ cup, about 10 minutes; let cool completely, about 1 hour. Meanwhile, process sugar and hazelnuts in food processor until hazelnuts are finely ground, about 20 seconds. Add flour, butter, and salt and pulse until mixture resembles coarse meal, 15 to 20 pulses. Add egg yolk, cream, vanilla, and almond extract and process until dough forms ball, about 20 seconds. Transfer dough to counter. Form dough into disk, wrap disk tightly in plastic wrap, and refrigerate for 30 minutes.

2. Adjust oven racks to upper-middle and lower-middle positions and heat oven to 375 degrees. Line 2 rimmed baking sheets with parchment paper.

3. Roll dough ⅛ inch thick on counter. Using 2-inch fluted round cookie cutter, cut out rounds; space rounds ¾ inch apart on prepared sheets. Using smaller cutter, cut out centers of half of dough rounds. Gather and reroll scraps once. Bake until edges are lightly browned, 8 to 10 minutes, switching and rotating sheets halfway through baking. Let cookies cool on sheets for 5 minutes, then transfer to wire rack and let cool completely.

4. Spread bottom of each solid cookie with 1 teaspoon jam, then top with cutout cookie, pressing lightly to adhere. Let cookies set before serving, about 30 minutes.

**Peanut Butter
Sandwich Cookies**

PEANUT BUTTER SANDWICH COOKIES

Makes 24 sandwich cookies | **2 rimmed baking sheets**

WHY THIS RECIPE WORKS Our ideal peanut butter sandwich cookie is thin and crunchy with a smooth filling, and packed with peanut flavor. In addition to the obvious inclusion of peanut butter in the dough, we cut a portion of the flour with finely chopped peanuts, which boosted flavor dramatically. To make the cookies thin and crisp, we added milk; the increased moisture made a thinner dough that spread more during baking. Adding a full teaspoon of baking soda encouraged air bubbles within the dough to inflate so rapidly that they burst before the cookies set, leaving the cookies flat. Warming the peanut butter and butter for the filling in the microwave made the filling easy to spread and sandwich. Do not use unsalted peanut butter. Take care when processing the peanuts—you want to chop them, not turn them into a paste.

COOKIES
- 1¼ cups raw or dry-roasted peanuts, toasted and cooled
- ¾ cup (3¾ ounces) all-purpose flour
- 1 teaspoon baking soda
- ½ teaspoon table salt
- 3 tablespoons unsalted butter, melted
- ½ cup creamy peanut butter
- ½ cup (3½ ounces) granulated sugar

½ cup (3½ ounces) light brown sugar
3 tablespoons whole milk
1 large egg

FILLING
¾ cup creamy peanut butter
3 tablespoons unsalted butter
1 cup (4 ounces) confectioners' sugar

1. FOR THE COOKIES: Adjust oven racks to upper-middle and lower-middle positions and heat oven to 350 degrees. Line 2 rimmed baking sheets with parchment paper. Pulse peanuts in food processor until finely chopped, about 8 pulses. Whisk flour, baking soda, and salt together in bowl. Whisk melted butter, peanut butter, granulated sugar, brown sugar, milk, and egg together in second bowl. Using rubber spatula, stir flour mixture into peanut butter mixture until combined. Stir in chopped peanuts until evenly distributed.

2. Using 1-tablespoon measure or #60 scoop, drop 12 mounds evenly onto each prepared sheet. Using your dampened hand, press each mound until 2 inches in diameter.

3. Bake cookies until deep golden brown and firm to touch, 15 to 18 minutes, switching and rotating sheets halfway through baking. Let cookies cool on sheets for 5 minutes, then transfer to wire rack and let cool completely. Repeat with remaining dough.

4. FOR THE FILLING: Microwave peanut butter and butter until melted and warm, about 40 seconds. Using rubber spatula, stir in confectioners' sugar until combined.

5. Place 1 tablespoon (or #60 scoop) warm filling in center of bottom of half of cookies, then top with remaining cookies, pressing gently until filling spreads to edges. Let filling set for 1 hour before serving.

Peanut Butter Sandwich Cookies with Honey-Cinnamon Filling
Omit butter from filling. Stir 5 tablespoons honey and ½ teaspoon ground cinnamon into warm peanut butter before adding confectioners' sugar.

Peanut Butter Sandwich Cookies with Milk Chocolate Filling
Reduce peanut butter to ½ cup and omit butter from filling. Stir 6 ounces finely chopped milk chocolate into warm peanut butter until melted, microwaving for 10 seconds at a time if necessary, before adding confectioners' sugar.

BACI DI DAMA
Makes 32 sandwich cookies | 2 rimmed baking sheets

WHY THIS RECIPE WORKS Baci di dama, tiny chocolate-filled hazelnut cookies that translate as "lady's kisses," might just be the world's cutest cookie—until you try to make them. The fragile dough softens and crumbles, and the filling tends to ooze out the sides. Leaving bits of skin on the nuts firmed up the dough and added flavor and color. Portioning the dough usually requires scooping and weighing dozens of individual pieces, but we found a faster way. We pressed the dough into a baking pan, briefly froze it to firm it up, cut a "portion grid," and rolled each square into even balls. Neither ganache nor Nutella firmed up enough to fill the cookies. Warm melted chocolate became set and snappy but ran down the side. Letting the chocolate cool and thicken ensured that it didn't drip off. To skin the hazelnuts, gather the warm, toasted nuts in a dish towel and rub to remove some of the skins. A square-cornered metal baking pan works best for shaping the dough.

¾ cup hazelnuts, toasted and partially skinned
⅔ cup (3⅓ ounces) all-purpose flour
⅓ cup (2⅓ ounces) sugar
⅛ teaspoon table salt
6 tablespoons unsalted butter, cut into ½-inch pieces and chilled
2 ounces bittersweet chocolate, chopped

1. Adjust oven rack to middle position and heat oven to 325 degrees. Line 2 rimmed baking sheets with parchment paper. Line bottom of 8-inch square baking pan with parchment. Process hazelnuts, flour, sugar, and salt in food processor until hazelnuts are very finely ground, 20 to 25 seconds. Add butter and pulse until dough just comes together, 20 to 25 pulses.

2. Transfer dough to counter, knead briefly to form smooth ball, place in prepared pan, and press into even layer that covers bottom of pan. Freeze for 10 minutes. Run knife or bench scraper between dough and edge of pan to loosen. Transfer dough to counter and discard parchment. Cut dough into 64 squares (8 rows by 8 rows). Roll dough squares into balls and evenly space 32 dough balls on each prepared sheet. Bake, 1 sheet at a time, until cookies look dry and are fragrant (cookies will settle but not spread), about 20 minutes, rotating sheet halfway through baking. Transfer sheet to wire rack and let cookies cool completely.

3. Microwave chocolate in small bowl at 50 percent power, stirring every 20 seconds, until melted, 1 to 2 minutes. Allow chocolate to cool at room temperature until it is slightly thickened and registers 80 degrees, about 10 minutes. Invert half of cookies on each sheet. Using ¼-teaspoon measure, spoon chocolate onto flat surfaces of all inverted cookies. Top with remaining cookies, pressing lightly to adhere. Let chocolate set for at least 15 minutes before serving. (Cookies can be stored in airtight container at room temperature for up to 10 days.)

ALFAJORES DE MAICENA

Makes 24 sandwich cookies | rimmed baking sheet

WHY THIS RECIPE WORKS Beloved across Latin America, these buttery sandwich cookies are often filled with rich dulce de leche. While cornstarch in the dough leads to the characteristically crumbly, melt-in-the-mouth texture, we found that adding some flour created powdery-soft cookies with enough structure to hold together. Plenty of butter and a few egg yolks contributed additional tenderness and rich flavor. For the filling, we took a common shortcut and turned to the commercial kind. It's essential to buy the Nestlé La Lechera brand of canned dulce de leche, or the filling won't have the right consistency. Alfajores are fragile, so we've designed this recipe to make a few extra cookies in case some break. Coconut is a customary garnish, but you can also simply sift confectioners' sugar over the cookies before serving. Refrigerate any leftover dulce de leche for up to one month.

FILLING
- 2 (13.4-ounce) cans Nestlé La Lechera Dulce de Leche
- 1 teaspoon vanilla extract
- ¼ teaspoon table salt

COOKIES
- 1½ cups (6 ounces) cornstarch
- 1⅓ cups (6⅔ ounces) all-purpose flour
- 1 teaspoon baking powder
- ¼ teaspoon table salt
- 16 tablespoons unsalted butter, softened
- ½ cup (3½ ounces) sugar
- 3 large egg yolks
- 1 tablespoon brandy (optional)
- 1 teaspoon grated lemon zest
- 1 teaspoon vanilla extract
- 1 cup (3 ounces) unsweetened shredded coconut

1. FOR THE FILLING: Transfer dulce de leche to medium bowl. Stir in vanilla and salt until thoroughly incorporated. Cover and refrigerate until mixture is completely chilled, at least 2 hours.

2. FOR THE COOKIES: While filling chills, whisk cornstarch, flour, baking powder, and salt together in medium bowl. Using stand mixer fitted with paddle, beat butter and sugar on medium-high speed until pale and fluffy, 2 to 3 minutes. Add egg yolks; brandy, if using; lemon zest; and vanilla and beat until combined. Add cornstarch mixture; reduce speed to low; and mix until dough is smooth, scraping down bowl as needed.

3. Divide dough in half. Place 1 piece of dough in center of large sheet of parchment paper and press with your hand to ½-inch thickness. Place second large sheet of parchment over dough and roll dough ¼ inch thick. Using your flat hand on parchment, smooth out wrinkles on both sides. Transfer dough with parchment to rimmed baking sheet. Repeat pressing, rolling, and smoothing second piece of dough, then stack on top of first piece on sheet. Freeze until dough is firm, about 30 minutes.

4. Adjust oven racks to upper-middle and lower-middle positions and heat oven to 350 degrees. Transfer 1 piece of dough to counter. Peel off top layer of parchment and replace loosely. Flip dough and parchment. Peel away second piece of parchment and place on rimmed baking sheet. Using 2-inch round cutter, cut dough into rounds. Transfer rounds to prepared sheet, about ½ inch apart. Repeat with remaining dough and second rimmed baking sheet. Reroll, chill, and cut scraps until you have 26 rounds on each sheet.

5. Bake until tops are set but still pale and bottoms are light golden, 10 to 12 minutes, switching and rotating sheets halfway through baking. Let cookies cool on sheets for 5 minutes, then carefully transfer to wire rack and let cool completely.

6. To assemble, place half of cookies upside down on counter. Place about 2 teaspoons filling on each upside-down cookie.

Alfajores de Maicena

Hold 1 topped cookie on fingers of your hand. Place second, untopped cookie on top of filling, right side up, and press gently with fingers of your other hand until filling spreads to edges. Repeat with remaining cookies.

7. Place coconut in small bowl. Working with 1 cookie at a time, roll sides of cookies in coconut, pressing gently to help coconut adhere to exposed filling. Serve immediately or refrigerate in airtight container for up to 5 days. Allow refrigerated cookies to sit out at room temperature for 10 minutes before serving.

WHOOPIE PIES

Makes 6 sandwich cookies | 2 rimmed baking sheets

WHY THIS RECIPE WORKS Made up of two cookie-like chocolate cakes stuffed to the gills with fluffy marshmallow filling, the whoopie pie is a sweet indulgence. For the cake component, we drew inspiration from devil's food cake, creaming butter with sugar, adding eggs and buttermilk for tenderness, and using all-purpose flour and baking soda for the right amount of structure. For the chocolate flavor, we preferred the darker color and flavor that Dutch-processed cocoa provides. Replacing the granulated sugar with brown sugar deepened the flavor and added moisture. For the filling, we eschewed the traditional sugar and lard in favor of marshmallow crème, which we enriched with butter for a mixture that was fluffy yet firm. Don't be tempted to bake all the cakes on one baking sheet; the batter needs room to spread while it bakes.

CAKES

- 2 cups (10 ounces) all-purpose flour
- ½ cup (1½ ounces) Dutch-processed cocoa powder
- 1 teaspoon baking soda
- ½ teaspoon table salt
- 8 tablespoons unsalted butter, softened
- 1 cup packed (7 ounces) light brown sugar
- 1 large egg, room temperature
- 1 teaspoon vanilla extract
- 1 cup buttermilk

FILLING

- 12 tablespoons unsalted butter, softened
- 1¼ cups (5 ounces) confectioners' sugar
- 1½ teaspoons vanilla extract
- ⅛ teaspoon table salt
- 2½ cups marshmallow crème

1. FOR THE CAKES: Adjust oven racks to upper-middle and lower-middle positions and heat oven to 350 degrees. Line 2 rimmed baking sheets with parchment paper. Whisk flour, cocoa, baking soda, and salt together in bowl.

2. Using stand mixer fitted with paddle, beat butter and sugar on medium speed until pale and fluffy, about 3 minutes. Add egg and beat until incorporated, scraping down bowl as needed. Add vanilla and mix until incorporated. Reduce speed to low and add flour mixture in 3 additions, alternating with buttermilk in 2 additions. Give batter final stir by hand to ensure that no flour pockets remain. Using ⅓-cup dry measuring cup, scoop 6 mounds of batter onto each prepared sheet, spaced about 3 inches apart. Bake until centers spring back when lightly pressed, 15 to 18 minutes, switching and rotating sheets halfway through baking. Transfer sheets to wire rack and let cakes cool completely.

3. FOR THE FILLING: Using stand mixer fitted with paddle, beat butter and sugar on medium speed until fluffy, about 3 minutes. Beat in vanilla and salt. Add marshmallow crème and mix until combined, about 2 minutes. Refrigerate until slightly firm, about 30 minutes. (Filling can be refrigerated for up to 2 days.) Place ⅓ cup filling on bottom of half of cakes, then top with remaining cakes, pressing to spread filling to edge. Serve. (Whoopie pies can be refrigerated for up to 3 days.)

Whoopie Pies

BISCOTTI

THE FAMOUS ITALIAN COOKIES KNOWN AS BISCOTTI (which means "twice-baked") first appeared in the Roman empire as a dry food that provided easy nourishment on long journeys—and that was their sole purpose until the Renaissance when they reemerged in Tuscany and became the treasure they are today.

Biscotti—also called cantucci—are baked once as a single loaf and then again after that loaf is sliced into individual pieces. (The first baking actually cooks the dough, while the second baking makes the cookies crisp and dry.) These classic cookies should have plenty of crunch but they shouldn't be hard to eat. A modest amount of softened butter results in a perfectly balanced texture for biscotti that is neither too hard (made with no butter) nor too soft (made with ample butter)—one that can be dipped into your coffee (or Vin Santo) but doesn't need to be. Nuts such as almonds and hazelnuts are a common addition and serve a purpose beyond adding rich flavor and texture; when a portion of the nuts is finely ground and substituted for some of the flour, it interferes with gluten formation by getting in between pockets of gluten to create microscopic "fault lines" in the biscotti. The result is a hard cookie that still breaks apart easily when you take a bite. The treatment of eggs plays an important role as well: whipping them until doubled in volume before adding the other ingredients provides lightness and lift. You'll want a pencil and ruler when making these cookies—use them to create rectangles on your parchment paper for loaves of just the right size and thickness.

SHAPING AND BAKING BISCOTTI

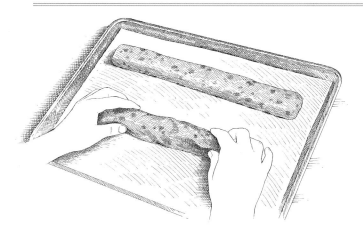

1. Using your floured hands, divided each dough half into 8 by 3-inch rectangle. Spray each loaf lightly with vegetable oil spray. Using rubber spatula lightly coated with oil spray, smooth tops and sides. Gently brush with egg white wash and bake.

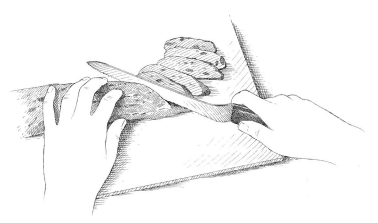

2. Let cool for 30 minutes, then use serrated knife to slice each loaf on slight bias into ½-inch-thick slices. Place biscotti on wire rack set in rimmed baking sheet and bake.

ITALIAN BAKED GOOD BOOSTER

Commonly used in Italian sweet breads such as panettone and pandoro, the Italian extract known as fiori di Sicilia has the citrusy and floral notes of orange peel, undergirded by a woodsy, vanilla-like aroma. Though the name translates as "flowers of Sicily," the exact formulation is proprietary. Our sample, purchased via mail order from the King Arthur Baking Company, smelled like an Italian bakery and tasted like a Creamsicle, though more complex.

This winning flavor combination makes an intriguing addition to dairy-rich desserts such as rice pudding (see page 180) or panna cotta (see 172); sweet, cheese-enriched items such as semolina and ricotta cake (see page 332), and a wide variety of other cookies. Though many sources recommend swapping out the vanilla in such recipes for an equal amount of fiori di Sicilia, we found the Italian extract more potent; however, its assertiveness mellows as it cooks. If you're baking your item until it's dry—biscotti (see page 76), for example—a one-to-one swap with vanilla is fine. But for items that remain moist, such as migliaccio di semolino, use only 75 percent as much fiori di Sicilia as vanilla. And for recipes in which vanilla is added only at the end, such as ice cream or panna cotta, use only half as much.

Almond Biscotti

ALMOND BISCOTTI

Makes 30 cookies | rimmed baking sheet

WHY THIS RECIPE WORKS Italians typically like their biscotti dry and hard, whereas Americans tend to favor a buttery, tender version. We wanted a cookie that fell in between, one that had plenty of crunch but wasn't tooth-breaking. Biscotti made with little (or no) fat were rocks, while doughs enriched with a full stick of butter baked up too soft. Four tablespoons of butter struck just the right balance, for a cookie that was both crunchy and tender. Whipping the eggs provided lift, and swapping some flour for ground almonds made the cookies more tender by breaking up the crumb and interrupting gluten development. The almonds will continue to toast during baking, so toast them just until they're fragrant.

1¼ cups whole almonds, lightly toasted, divided
1¾ cups (8¾ ounces) all-purpose flour
  2 teaspoons baking powder
  ¼ teaspoon table salt
  2 large eggs, plus 1 large white beaten with pinch table salt
  1 cup (7 ounces) sugar
  4 tablespoons unsalted butter, melted and cooled
1½ teaspoons almond extract
  ½ teaspoon vanilla extract
     Vegetable oil spray

1. Adjust oven rack to middle position and heat oven to 325 degrees. Using ruler and pencil, draw two 8 by 3-inch rectangles, spaced 4 inches apart, on piece of parchment paper. Grease rimmed baking sheet and place parchment on it, marked side down.

2. Pulse 1 cup almonds in food processor until coarsely chopped, 8 to 10 pulses; transfer to bowl and set aside. Process remaining ¼ cup almonds in now-empty food processor until finely ground, about 45 seconds. Add flour, baking powder, and salt; process to combine, about 15 seconds. Transfer flour mixture to second bowl. Process 2 eggs in now-empty food processor until lightened in color and almost doubled in volume, about 3 minutes. With processor running, slowly add sugar until thoroughly combined, about 15 seconds. Add melted butter, almond extract, and vanilla and process until combined, about 10 seconds. Transfer egg mixture to medium bowl. Sprinkle half of flour mixture over egg mixture and, using spatula, gently fold until just combined. Add remaining flour mixture and chopped almonds and gently fold until just combined.

3. Divide dough in half. Using your floured hands, form each half into 8 by 3-inch rectangle, using lines on parchment as guide. Spray each loaf lightly with oil spray. Using rubber spatula lightly coated with oil spray, smooth tops and sides of loaves. Gently brush tops of loaves with egg white beaten with salt.

TUTORIAL
Almond Biscotti

Twice the baking doesn't mean twice the difficulty. Make bakery biscotti at home.

1. Divide dough in half. Using your floured hands, form each half into 8 by 3-inch rectangle, using lines on parchment as guide.

2. Spray each loaf lightly with oil spray. Using rubber spatula lightly coated with oil spray, smooth tops and sides of rectangles.

3. Gently brush tops of rectangles with egg white wash.

4. Bake until loaves are set and beginning to crack on top, 25 to 30 minutes, rotating sheet halfway through baking.

5. Let loaves cool on baking sheet for 30 minutes. Transfer loaves to cutting board. Using serrated knife, slice each loaf on slight bias into ½-inch-thick slices.

6. Lay slices about ¼ inch apart on wire rack set in rimmed baking sheet. Bake until crisp on both sides, about 35 minutes, flipping slices halfway through baking.

**Chocolate-Hazelnut
Biscotti**

4. Bake until loaves are golden and just beginning to crack on top, 25 to 30 minutes, rotating sheet halfway through baking. Let loaves cool on sheet for 30 minutes, then transfer to cutting board. Using serrated knife, slice each loaf on slight bias into ½-inch-thick pieces. Set wire rack in rimmed baking sheet. Space slices, cut side down, about ¼ inch apart on prepared rack. Bake until crisp and golden brown on both sides, about 35 minutes, flipping slices halfway through baking. Let biscotti cool completely on wire rack before serving. (Biscotti can be stored at room temperature for up to 1 month.)

Anise Biscotti
Add 1½ teaspoons anise seeds to flour mixture in step 2. Substitute anise-flavored liqueur for almond extract.

Hazelnut-Rosemary-Orange Biscotti
Substitute lightly toasted and skinned hazelnuts for almonds. Add 2 tablespoons minced fresh rosemary to flour mixture in step 2. Substitute orange-flavored liqueur for almond extract and add 1 tablespoon grated orange zest to egg mixture with butter in step 2.

Pistachio-Spice Biscotti
Substitute shelled pistachios for almonds. Add 1 teaspoon ground cardamom, ½ teaspoon ground cloves, ½ teaspoon pepper, ¼ teaspoon ground cinnamon, and ¼ teaspoon ground ginger to flour mixture in step 2. Substitute 1 teaspoon water for almond extract. Increase vanilla to 1 teaspoon.

CHOCOLATE-HAZELNUT BISCOTTI

Makes 30 cookies | rimmed baking sheet

WHY THIS RECIPE WORKS Biscotti should be twice as nice if chocolate-flavored. But chocolate biscotti usually fall short in terms of flavor due to the extra time drying in the oven—and they're often as hard as jawbreakers. We wanted intensely chocolaty biscotti that didn't require hot coffee to soften. To get chocolate into the dough, we started with cocoa powder (plus some espresso powder) because it carries intense chocolate flavor and was easy to incorporate. For a nutty element, we chose complementary hazelnuts, which we lightly toasted. In addition, we ground some of the nuts to a fine meal; dispersed throughout the dough, they helped minimize gluten development and therefore that tough, hard texture. Before baking, we brushed the loaves with an egg white, which left a shiny, crackly sheen. These cookies were so rich in flavor, the typical chocolate dip was unnecessary.

1¼ cups hazelnuts, toasted and skinned, divided
1¼ cups (6¼ ounces) all-purpose flour
½ cup (1½ ounces) unsweetened cocoa powder
2 teaspoons baking powder
1 teaspoon instant espresso powder
¼ teaspoon table salt
2 large eggs, plus 1 large white beaten with pinch salt
1 cup (7 ounces) sugar
4 tablespoons unsalted butter, melted and cooled
½ teaspoon vanilla extract
Vegetable oil spray

1. Adjust oven rack to middle position and heat oven to 325 degrees. Using ruler and pencil, draw two 8 by 3-inch rectangles, spaced 4 inches apart, on piece of parchment paper. Grease rimmed baking sheet and place parchment on it, marked side down.

2. Pulse 1 cup hazelnuts in food processor until coarsely chopped, 8 to 10 pulses; transfer to bowl and set aside. Process remaining ¼ cup hazelnuts in now-empty processor until finely ground, about 45 seconds. Add flour, cocoa, baking powder, espresso powder, and salt and process until combined, about 15 seconds. Transfer flour mixture to second bowl.

3. Process 2 eggs in again-empty processor until lightened in color and almost doubled in volume, about 3 minutes. With processor running, slowly add sugar until thoroughly combined, about 15 seconds. Add melted butter and vanilla and process until combined, about 10 seconds. Transfer egg mixture to bowl. Sprinkle half of flour mixture over egg mixture and, using spatula, gently fold until just combined. Add remaining flour mixture and chopped hazelnuts and gently fold until just combined.

4. Divide dough in half. Using your floured hands, form each half into 8 by 3-inch rectangle, using lines on parchment as guide. Spray each loaf lightly with oil spray. Using rubber spatula lightly coated with oil spray, smooth tops and sides of rectangles. Gently brush tops of rectangles with egg white wash. Bake until loaves are set and beginning to crack on top, 25 to 30 minutes, rotating sheet halfway through baking.

5. Let loaves cool on baking sheet for 30 minutes. Transfer loaves to cutting board. Using serrated knife, slice each loaf on slight bias into ½-inch-thick slices. Lay slices cut side down, about ¼ inch apart on wire rack set in rimmed baking sheet. Bake until crisp on both sides, about 35 minutes, flipping slices halfway through baking. Let biscotti cool completely on wire rack, about 1 hour, before serving. (Biscotti can be stored at room temperature for up to 1 month.)

BROWNIES AND BLONDIES

Line pan with foil sling

Melt butter

Mix by hand

Cool completely before cutting

WHETHER IT'S PURE, RICH DECADENCE YOU CRAVE or a more complex affair featuring swirls of cream cheese or a blanket of gooey caramel, brownies are first and foremost about the chocolate. But brownies—and their counterpart, blondies—have universal appeal for reasons beyond their irresistible flavor and texture. Baked in a pan and then cut into tidy squares for serving, these sweet treats are not only delicious but also sturdy and portable, making them a great choice for bake sales, picnics, and potlucks. The texture of these classic bars is largely determined by the ingredients—the type of chocolate, the number of eggs (and whether extra yolks are added), and the amount of flour all play a role. But although the ingredients vary, the preparation for most brownies and blondies is similar: The butter is melted (typically right along with the chocolate for brownies) and the ingredients are simply mixed by hand. Sometimes we replace some of the butter with oil for just the right ratio of saturated to unsaturated fat—and satisfying chew.

Contrary to popular belief, blondies are not brownies without chocolate, nor are they chocolate chip cookies baked in a pan. Though the origins of both bars are murky, evidence suggests that the first brownie was actually (drumroll, please) a blondie. One of the first recipes for a confection dubbed a "brownie" appears in the 1896 edition of Fannie Farmer's *The Boston Cooking-School Cook Book* in reference to individual cakes flavored with molasses and baked in shallow tins; this was followed by a new version calling for chocolate in the 1906 edition. Over time, the name morphed into "blonde brownies," then "butterscotch brownies," and finally, decades later, simply "blondies," conferring upon this confection an identity all its own. With blondies and brownies of all kinds, it's important to avoid overbaking so they remain moist and tender. The hardest part of making these treats? Waiting for them to cool completely before cutting them and diving in.

WHICH BROWNIE ARE YOU?

We won't pick favorites, but you sure can. No matter what brownie texture you prefer, you can achieve it with our recipes.

Fudgy
- Melted butter
- Plenty of eggs
- Generous melted chocolate (in addition to cocoa powder)

Chewy
- 1:3 ratio of butter (a predominantly saturated fat) to vegetable oil (an unsaturated fat)
- More cocoa powder than melted chocolate

Cakey
- Cocoa powder and/or unsweetened chocolate
- Baking powder to lift and lighten the crumb

MAKING A FOIL SLING

For brownies, blondies, and other bar cookies, simply greasing a baking pan isn't enough. Sticky fillings can glue bars to the pans. It is hard to cut neat bars while they're still in the pan and inverting them would ruin their tops. A foil sling is a no-fuss way to extract bar cookies from the pan.

1. Line pan with 2 sheets of aluminum foil placed perpendicular to each other, with extra foil hanging over the edges of the pan. Push foil into corners, smoothing foil flush with pan.

2. Use foil handles to lift baked bars from pan.

MIXING BROWNIE AND BLONDIE BATTER

For the best-textured brownies and blondies, gently fold or stir in the flour and don't overmix. Properly mixed batter bakes into compact, tender brownies, while overmixed brownies bake up taller, tougher, and cakier. And what happens if you make brownies in a stand mixer? The effects of overmixing are even more noticeable, and the brownies taste less chocolaty. Mixing batter leads to gluten development. The overmixed brownies develop a strong gluten network that can trap the extra air created through fierce mixing.

Perfectly Mixed

Stirred Too Much

Mixed in a Stand Mixer

GETTING A SHINY TOP

Achieving a glossy, crackly top on a brownie can be an elusive goal, but we finally discovered the trick: The type of sweetener you use matters. You can achieve this sheen only with granulated sugar. Brown sugar forms crystals on the surface of a cooling brownie; when they reflect light, they create a matte surface. The pure sucrose in granulated sugar creates a glass-like, noncrystalline surface that produces a shiny effect. As for the crackly crust, its formation depends on sugar molecules rising to the surface of the batter and drying out during baking. Brown sugar has too much moisture; the surface can never dry enough to become crisp. The number of eggs you use in the recipe can also affect moisture.

Brownies Made with Brown Sugar

Brownies Made with White Sugar

KNOWING WHEN BROWNIES ARE DONE

Overbaked brownies are dry and chalky and the chocolate flavor is diminished. To determine doneness, insert a toothpick in the center of the brownies. If the brownies are perfectly baked, the toothpick should emerge with a few moist crumbs clinging to it. If it comes out clean, the brownies are overbaked.

FUDGY BROWNIES

Makes 36 brownies | 8-inch square baking pan

WHY THIS RECIPE WORKS For decadent brownies that would be a chocolate lover's dream, we used three forms of chocolate: unsweetened for intensity, cocoa powder for complexity, and bittersweet for moisture and well-rounded flavor. Melted butter was key to a fudgy texture, and three eggs contributed richness and structure. Granulated sugar gave the brownies a delicate, shiny, crackly top crust. We found it best to cut these brownies into small bites—a little goes a long way. Tasters preferred the more complex flavor of bittersweet chocolate over semisweet chocolate, but either type works well here, as does 5 ounces of bittersweet or semisweet chocolate chips in place of the bar chocolate.

5 ounces bittersweet or semisweet chocolate, chopped
2 ounces unsweetened chocolate, chopped
8 tablespoons unsalted butter, cut into 4 pieces
3 tablespoons unsweetened cocoa powder
1¼ cups (8¾ ounces) sugar
3 large eggs
2 teaspoons vanilla extract
½ teaspoon table salt
1 cup (5 ounces) all-purpose flour

1. Adjust oven rack to middle position and heat oven to 350 degrees. Make foil sling for 8-inch square baking pan by folding 2 long sheets of aluminum foil so each is 8 inches wide. Lay sheets of foil in pan perpendicular to each other, with extra foil hanging over edges of pan. Push foil into corners and up sides of pan, smoothing foil flush to pan. Grease foil.

2. Microwave bittersweet and unsweetened chocolates in bowl at 50 percent power for 2 minutes. Stir in butter and continue to microwave, stirring often, until melted. Whisk in cocoa and let mixture cool slightly.

3. Whisk sugar, eggs, vanilla, and salt in large bowl until combined. Whisk chocolate mixture into sugar mixture until smooth. Using rubber spatula, stir in flour until no dry streaks remain. Transfer batter to prepared pan and smooth top. Bake until toothpick inserted in center comes out with few moist crumbs attached, 35 to 40 minutes, rotating pan halfway through baking.

4. Let brownies cool completely in pan on wire rack, about 2 hours. Using foil overhang, remove brownies from pan. (Uncut brownies can be refrigerated for up to 3 days.) Cut into 36 pieces before serving.

Fudgy Triple-Chocolate Espresso Brownies
Whisk in 1½ tablespoons instant espresso powder or instant coffee powder along with cocoa in step 2.

Fudgy Brownies

GLUTEN-FREE FUDGY BROWNIES

Makes 16 brownies | 8-inch square baking pan

WHY THIS RECIPE WORKS While we couldn't go completely flourless (a naturally gluten-free solution) for these brownies if we wanted any structure, we did want to cut down on the amount of gluten-free flour blend we used for fudgy goodness. This gave the chocolate flavor too bitter an edge, however. We looked at the sources of chocolate we were using. Brownies made without cocoa lacked structure—it had to stay. Eliminating the unsweetened chocolate was a big step in the right direction, and switching the bittersweet out for semisweet chocolate eliminated the harsh flavor altogether. Not all brands of chocolate are processed in a gluten-free facility, so read labels carefully. Do not shortchange the batter's 30-minute rest or the brownies will taste gritty.

4 ounces (¾ cup plus 2 tablespoons) all-purpose gluten-free flour blend (see page 2)
½ teaspoon table salt
½ teaspoon xanthan gum (see page 2)
7 ounces semisweet chocolate, chopped coarse
8 tablespoons unsalted butter, cut into 8 pieces
3 tablespoons unsweetened cocoa powder
8¾ ounces (1¼ cups) sugar
3 large eggs
2 teaspoons vanilla extract

**Vegan Fudgy
Brownies**

VEGAN FUDGY BROWNIES

Makes 24 brownies | 13 by 9-inch baking pan

WHY THIS RECIPE WORKS Ultrachocolaty brownies typically take little work for an immensely satisfying reward. Could we make decadent brownies without butter and eggs? Happily, we found that we could. Neutral-flavored vegetable oil was a quick swap for the butter. We typically don't add chemical leavener to a fudgy brownie; however, we found that a small amount of baking powder gave our brownies lift and structure and eliminated the need to find a replacement for eggs. A combination of unsweetened chocolate and cocoa powder—bloomed in boiling water to unlock their flavor compounds—contributed intensity. Use organic sugar if you're a strict vegan. Not all chocolate chips are vegan, so check ingredient lists carefully. It's important to let the brownies cool thoroughly before cutting. Be sure to use a metal baking pan and not a glass baking dish in this recipe.

    2   cups (10 ounces) all-purpose flour
    1   teaspoon baking powder
    ¾   teaspoon table salt
    1   cup boiling water
    3   ounces unsweetened chocolate, chopped fine
    ¾   cup (2¼ ounces) unsweetened cocoa powder
    1½ teaspoons instant espresso powder (optional)
    2½ cups (17½ ounces) sugar
    ½   cup vegetable oil
    1   tablespoon vanilla extract
    ½   cup (3 ounces) bittersweet or semisweet chocolate chips

1. Make foil sling for 8-inch square baking pan by folding 2 long sheets of aluminum foil so each is 8 inches wide. Lay sheets of foil in pan perpendicular to each other, with extra foil hanging over edges of pan. Push foil into corners and up sides of pan, smoothing foil flush to pan. Spray with vegetable oil spray.

2. Whisk flour blend, salt, and xanthan gum together in bowl. Microwave chocolate, butter, and cocoa in bowl at 50 percent power, stirring often, until melted and smooth, 1 to 3 minutes; let mixture cool slightly.

3. Whisk sugar, eggs, and vanilla together in large bowl. Whisk in cooled chocolate mixture. Stir in flour mixture with rubber spatula and mix until well combined. Transfer batter to prepared pan and smooth top. Cover pan with plastic wrap and let batter rest for 30 minutes.

4. Adjust oven rack to middle position and heat oven to 350 degrees. Remove plastic and bake brownies until toothpick inserted in center comes out with few moist crumbs attached, 45 to 55 minutes, rotating pan halfway through baking.

5. Let brownies cool completely in pan on wire rack, about 2 hours. Using foil overhang, remove brownies from pan. Cut into 16 pieces before serving.

1. Adjust oven rack to lowest position and heat oven to 350 degrees. Make foil sling for 13 by 9-inch baking pan by folding 2 long sheets of aluminum foil; first sheet should be 13 inches wide and second sheet should be 9 inches wide. Lay sheets of foil in pan perpendicular to each other, with extra foil hanging over edges of pan. Push foil into corners and up sides of pan, smoothing foil flush to pan. Grease foil.

2. Whisk flour, baking powder, and salt together in bowl. Whisk boiling water; unsweetened chocolate; cocoa; and espresso powder, if using, in large bowl until well combined and chocolate is melted. Whisk in sugar, oil, and vanilla. Using rubber spatula, stir flour mixture into chocolate mixture until combined; fold in chocolate chips.

3. Scrape batter into prepared pan and smooth top. Bake until toothpick inserted halfway between edge and center comes out with few moist crumbs attached, 30 to 35 minutes, rotating pan halfway through baking.

4. Let brownies cool in pan on wire rack for 2 hours. Using foil overhang, remove brownies from pan. Return brownies to wire rack and let cool completely, about 1 hour. Cut into 24 pieces before serving. (Brownies can be stored at room temperature for up to 4 days.)

CHEWY BROWNIES

Makes 24 brownies | 13 by 9-inch baking pan

WHY THIS RECIPE WORKS While box-mix brownies may not offer superior chocolate flavor, there's no denying their chewy appeal. Determined to crack the code for chewy brownies, we discovered that the right proportions of fat were key. After many adjustments, we decided that an almost 1:3 ratio of saturated fat (butter) to unsaturated fat (vegetable oil) produced the chewiest brownies. Two whole eggs plus two extra yolks emulsified the batter. We whisked unsweetened cocoa and a little espresso powder into boiling water and then stirred in unsweetened chocolate. The heat unlocked the chocolate's flavor compounds, boosting its impact. If you use a glass baking dish instead of a metal baking pan, let the brownies cool for 10 minutes and then remove them promptly from the pan (otherwise, the superior heat retention of glass can lead to overbaking).

⅓ cup (1 ounce) Dutch-processed cocoa powder
1½ teaspoons instant espresso powder (optional)
½ cup plus 2 tablespoons boiling water
2 ounces unsweetened chocolate, chopped fine
½ cup plus 2 tablespoons vegetable oil
4 tablespoons unsalted butter, melted
2 large eggs plus 2 large yolks
2 teaspoons vanilla extract
2½ cups (17½ ounces) sugar
1¾ cups (8¾ ounces) all-purpose flour
¾ teaspoon table salt
6 ounces bittersweet chocolate, cut into ½-inch pieces

1. Adjust oven rack to lowest position and heat oven to 350 degrees. Make foil sling for 13 by 9-inch baking pan by folding 2 long sheets of aluminum foil; first sheet should be 13 inches wide and second sheet should be 9 inches wide. Lay sheets of foil in pan perpendicular to each other, with extra foil hanging over edges of pan. Push foil into corners and up sides of pan, smoothing foil flush to pan. Grease foil.

2. Whisk cocoa; espresso powder, if using; and boiling water in large bowl until smooth. Add unsweetened chocolate and whisk until chocolate is melted. Whisk in oil and melted butter. (Mixture may look curdled.) Whisk in eggs and yolks and vanilla until smooth and homogeneous. Whisk in sugar until fully incorporated. Using rubber spatula, stir in flour and salt until combined. Fold in chocolate pieces.

3. Transfer batter to prepared pan and smooth top. Bake until toothpick inserted halfway between edge and center comes out with few moist crumbs attached, 30 to 35 minutes, rotating pan halfway through baking. Let brownies cool in pan on wire rack for 1½ hours. Using foil overhang, remove brownies from pan. Transfer to wire rack and let cool completely, about 1 hour. Cut into 24 pieces before serving.

Chewy Brownies

Chewy Chocolate Frosted Brownies
After brownies have cooled in pan for 1 hour, microwave 1⅓ cup chocolate chips and 2 tablespoons vegetable oil in bowl at 50 percent power, stirring often, until chocolate is melted, 2 to 4 minutes. Let mixture cool until barely warm, about 5 minutes, then spread over brownies with spatula. Continue to let brownies cool until topping sets, 1 to 2 hours.

Chocolate-Mint Brownies
Omit bittersweet chocolate. Fold 4 ounces Andes Mints, cut into ½-inch pieces, into batter at end of step 2. Scatter 2 ounces Andes Mints, cut into ½-inch pieces, over top of batter before baking.

Nutella-Hazelnut Brownies
Omit bittersweet chocolate. Fold ⅓ cup toasted, skinned, and chopped hazelnuts into batter at end of step 2. Dollop ⅓ cup Nutella evenly over top of batter in pan. Using tip of paring knife, swirl Nutella into batter before baking.

Peanut Butter–Marshmallow Brownies
Omit bittersweet chocolate. Fold 1 cup peanut butter chips into batter at end of step 2. Dollop ½ cup marshmallow crème evenly over top of batter in pan. Using tip of paring knife, swirl marshmallow crème into batter before baking.

CREAM CHEESE BROWNIES

Makes 16 brownies | 8-inch square baking pan

WHY THIS RECIPE WORKS A good cream cheese brownie serves up a perfectly matched duet of velvety cheesecake and fudgy brownie, swirled together yet each maintaining its identity. Knowing that the cream cheese would add plenty of moisture, we started with a slightly cakey brownie. Mixed with just an egg and a bit of sugar, the cream cheese flavor in the filling was too muted; a half-cup of sour cream provided a refreshing tang that reinforced the flavor of the cream cheese. To compensate for the sour cream's extra moisture, we ditched the egg and stirred in a tablespoon of flour. For cream cheese in every bite, we spread most of the brownie batter in the pan and smoothed the cream cheese filling over it. Then, we dolloped the last bit of brownie batter on top and swirled everything together. To accurately test doneness, be sure to stick the toothpick through part of the brownie and not the cream cheese.

CREAM CHEESE FILLING

    4 ounces cream cheese, cut into 8 pieces
    ½ cup sour cream
    2 tablespoons sugar
    1 tablespoon all-purpose flour

BROWNIES

    ⅔ cup (3⅓ ounces) all-purpose flour
    ½ teaspoon baking powder
    ½ teaspoon table salt
    4 ounces unsweetened chocolate, chopped fine
    8 tablespoons unsalted butter
 1¼ cups (8¾ ounces) sugar
    2 large eggs
    1 teaspoon vanilla extract

1. Adjust oven rack to middle position and heat oven to 325 degrees. Make foil sling for 8-inch square baking pan by folding 2 long sheets of aluminum foil so each is 8 inches wide. Lay sheets of foil in pan perpendicular to each other, with extra foil hanging over edges of pan. Push foil into corners and up sides of pan, smoothing foil flush to pan. Grease foil.

2. **FOR THE CREAM CHEESE FILLING:** Microwave cream cheese in bowl until soft, 20 to 30 seconds. Whisk in sour cream, sugar, and flour.

3. **FOR THE BROWNIES:** Whisk flour, baking powder, and salt together in bowl. Microwave chocolate and butter in second bowl at 50 percent power, stirring often, until melted, 1 to 2 minutes. Whisk sugar, eggs, and vanilla together in third bowl. Whisk chocolate mixture into sugar mixture until incorporated. Using rubber spatula, fold in flour until combined.

4. Spread all but ½ cup brownie batter in even layer in prepared pan. Spread cream cheese mixture evenly over top. Microwave remaining brownie batter until warm and pourable, 10 to 20 seconds. Using spoon, dollop softened batter over cream cheese filling (6 to 8 dollops). Using butter knife, swirl brownie batter through cream cheese topping, making marbled pattern and leaving ½-inch border around edges.

5. Bake brownies until toothpick inserted in center comes out with few moist crumbs attached, 35 to 40 minutes, rotating pan halfway through baking.

6. Let brownies cool in pan on wire rack for 1 hour. Using foil overhang, remove brownies from pan. Transfer to wire rack and let cool completely, about 1 hour. Cut into 16 pieces before serving.

Cream Cheese Brownies

PEANUT BUTTER SWIRL BROWNIES

Makes 16 brownies | **8-inch square baking pan**

WHY THIS RECIPE WORKS We wanted a brownie reminiscent of everyone's favorite peanut butter cup, with swirls of peanut butter running throughout a chocolaty brownie base. We started with a basic chocolate brownie that comes together by hand. Dolloping large mounds of peanut butter over the batter before swirling it in resulted in unbalanced brownies; some bites were overloaded with sticky peanut butter while others contained no peanut butter at all. Smaller dollops distributed pockets of peanut butter throughout every brownie. If you store your peanut butter in the refrigerator, note that room-temperature peanut butter is much easier to work with.

> 8 tablespoons unsalted butter
> 3 ounces unsweetened chocolate, chopped coarse
> ⅔ cup (3⅓ ounces) all-purpose flour
> ½ teaspoon baking powder
> ¼ teaspoon table salt
> 1 cup (7 ounces) sugar
> 2 large eggs
> 1 teaspoon vanilla extract
> ⅓ cup creamy or chunky peanut butter

1. Adjust oven rack to middle position and heat oven to 350 degrees. Make foil sling for 8-inch square baking pan by folding 2 long sheets of aluminum foil so each is 8 inches wide. Lay sheets of foil in pan perpendicular to each other, with extra foil hanging over edges of pan. Push foil into corners and up sides of pan, smoothing foil flush to pan. Grease foil.

2. Microwave butter and chocolate in bowl at 50 percent power, stirring often, until melted, 1 to 3 minutes; let cool slightly.

3. Whisk flour, baking powder, and salt together in second bowl. Whisk sugar, eggs, and vanilla together in large bowl. Whisk chocolate mixture into sugar mixture until combined. Using rubber spatula, stir in flour mixture until just incorporated.

4. Transfer batter to prepared pan and smooth top. Using spoon, dollop small mounds of peanut butter over brownie batter. Using butter knife, swirl peanut butter through brownie batter. Bake until toothpick inserted in center comes out with few moist crumbs attached, 22 to 27 minutes, rotating pan halfway through baking.

5. Let brownies cool completely in pan on wire rack, about 2 hours. Using foil overhang, remove brownies from pan. Cut into 16 pieces before serving.

CHOCOLATE GANACHE– FILLED BROWNIES

Makes 12 brownies | **12-cup muffin tin**

WHY THIS RECIPE WORKS Brownies with rich chocolate ganache are the ultimate decadence, and a muffin-shaped brownie allows for a generous filling. We found that the best way to create space for the ganache was to press a shot glass into the just-baked brownies. A sprinkle of sea salt on the top sealed the deal. We suggest using parchment muffin liners to avoid the brownies sticking to the liners. We developed this recipe using Ghirardelli 60% Premium Baking Chips, but you can use semisweet chips, if you prefer. These brownies are best when made with a high-fat Dutch-processed cocoa powder such as Droste. It is important to press the indentations into the centers of the brownies 15 minutes after they come out of the oven.

BROWNIES
> ⅓ cup (2 ounces) bittersweet chocolate chips
> ⅓ cup (1 ounce) Dutch-processed cocoa powder
> ½ cup boiling water
> 2 cups (14 ounces) sugar
> ⅔ cup vegetable oil
> 2 large eggs
> 2 teaspoons vanilla extract
> 1⅓ cups (6⅔ ounces) all-purpose flour
> ¾ teaspoon table salt

GANACHE FILLING
> 1⅓ cups (8 ounces) bittersweet chocolate chips
> ½ cup heavy cream
> 1 teaspoon Maldon sea salt

1. **FOR THE BROWNIES:** Adjust oven rack to middle position and heat oven to 350 degrees. Line 12-cup muffin tin with parchment liners.

2. Place chocolate chips and cocoa in large bowl. Add boiling water and whisk until chocolate chips are fully melted. Whisk in sugar, oil, eggs, and vanilla until combined. Gently whisk in flour and salt until just incorporated.

3. Using ¼-cup dry measuring cup, portion batter into prepared muffin cups; evenly distribute any remaining batter among cups. Bake until toothpick inserted in center comes out with few moist crumbs attached, 40 to 45 minutes.

4. Let brownies cool in muffin tin on wire rack for 15 minutes. Spray base of 1¼-inch-diameter shot glass (or other object with similar diameter) with vegetable oil spray. Keeping brownies in muffin tin, press base of glass into center of each brownie, about 1 inch deep, respraying glass as needed. Remove brownies from muffin tin and let cool completely on rack, about 1 hour.

**Chocolate Ganache–
Filled Brownies**

5. FOR THE GANACHE FILLING: Microwave chocolate chips and cream in bowl at 50 percent power, stirring frequently with rubber spatula, until melted, 1 to 3 minutes. Distribute ganache evenly among indentations in brownies (about 1 heaping tablespoon each).

6. Let sit until ganache is set, about 4 hours. Sprinkle ganache evenly with salt. Serve. (Alternatively, brownies can be transferred to refrigerator and will set in about 1 ½ hours; let come to room temperature before serving.)

Peanut Butter Ganache–Filled Brownies
For ganache filling, substitute milk chocolate chips for bittersweet chocolate chips and creamy peanut butter for heavy cream; add ⅛ teaspoon table salt.

Salted Caramel–Filled Brownies
For ganache filling, substitute 10 ounces soft caramels for chocolate chips, reduce heavy cream to 2 tablespoons, and add ¼ teaspoon table salt. Increase microwaving time to 3 to 5 minutes.

BROWNED BUTTER BLONDIES
Makes 24 bars | 13 by 9-inch baking pan

WHY THIS RECIPE WORKS Blondies should be packed with butterscotch flavor, studded with nuts and chocolate, and have a satisfying chew. That chewy texture is thanks in part to melted butter; here we take blondies to the next level by browning the butter after melting it for nutty complexity. Brown sugar was a must for its underlying caramel notes, which highlighted the flavor of the browned butter. To keep the sweetness in check, we replaced a portion of the brown sugar with corn syrup. A full 2 tablespoons of vanilla brought even more complexity to the bars, and a generous amount of salt—we added it to the batter and also sprinkled some on top—brought all the flavors into focus. Chopped pecans and milk chocolate chips complemented the butterscotch flavor.

**Browned Butter
Blondies**

2¼	cups (11¼ ounces) all-purpose flour
1¼	teaspoons table salt
½	teaspoon baking powder
12	tablespoons unsalted butter
1¾	cups packed (12¼ ounces) light brown sugar
3	large eggs
½	cup corn syrup
2	tablespoons vanilla extract
1	cup pecans, toasted and chopped coarse
½	cup (3 ounces) milk chocolate chips
¼–½	teaspoon flake sea salt, crumbled (optional)

1. Adjust oven rack to middle position and heat oven to 350 degrees. Make foil sling for 13 by 9-inch baking pan by folding 2 long sheets of aluminum foil; first sheet should be 13 inches wide and second sheet should be 9 inches wide. Lay sheets of foil in pan perpendicular to each other, with extra foil hanging over edges of pan. Push foil into corners and up sides of pan, smoothing foil flush to pan. Grease foil.

2. Whisk flour, table salt, and baking powder together in medium bowl.

3. Melt butter in 10-inch skillet over medium-high heat, then continue to cook, swirling skillet constantly, until butter is dark golden brown and has nutty aroma, 1 to 3 minutes. Immediately transfer browned butter to large heatproof bowl.

4. Add sugar to hot butter and whisk until combined. Add eggs, corn syrup, and vanilla and whisk until smooth. Using rubber spatula, stir in flour mixture until fully incorporated. Stir in pecans and chocolate chips. Transfer batter to prepared pan; using spatula, spread batter into corners of pan and smooth surface. Sprinkle with sea salt, if using.

5. Bake until top is deep golden brown and springs back when lightly pressed, 35 to 40 minutes, rotating pan halfway through baking (blondies will firm as they cool). Let blondies cool completely in pan on wire rack, about 2 hours. Using foil overhang, remove blondies from pan. Cut into 24 pieces before serving. (Blondies can be wrapped tightly in plastic wrap and stored at room temperature for up to 5 days.)

CONGO BARS
Makes 36 bars | 13 by 9-inch baking pan
WHY THIS RECIPE WORKS A variation of the classic blondie, congo bars should be chewy (not cakey but not too dense), sweet but not cloying, and loaded with mix-ins. Many recipes for congo bars cream the butter, but this incorporated too much air and resulted in a cakey bar. The secret to bars with the ideal amount of chew was using melted butter. For sweetening, granulated sugar produced a flat-tasting bar but light brown sugar lent the perfect amount of dimension. When we combined the brown sugar with a substantial amount of vanilla extract and salt, the bars developed the rich butterscotch flavor we were after. The additions of chocolate chips for creamy richness, white chocolate chips for sweet milkiness, pecans for pleasant crunch, and coconut for toasted nuttiness produced the best congo bars yet. Be sure to check the bars early so you don't overbake them.

1½ cups (7½ ounces) all-purpose flour
  1 teaspoon baking powder
  ½ teaspoon table salt
1½ cups packed (10½ ounces) light brown sugar
 12 tablespoons unsalted butter, melted and cooled
  2 large eggs
1½ teaspoons vanilla extract
1½ cups (4½ ounces) unsweetened shredded coconut, toasted
  1 cup pecans or walnuts, toasted and chopped coarse
  ½ cup (3 ounces) semisweet chocolate chips
  ½ cup (3 ounces) white chocolate chips

1. Adjust oven rack to middle position and heat oven to 350 degrees. Make foil sling for 13 by 9-inch baking pan by folding 2 long sheets of aluminum foil; first sheet should be 13 inches wide and second sheet should be 9 inches wide. Lay sheets of foil in pan perpendicular to each other, with extra foil hanging over edges of pan. Push foil into corners and up sides of pan, smoothing foil flush to pan. Grease foil.

2. Whisk flour, baking powder, and salt together in bowl. Whisk sugar and melted butter in second bowl until combined. Whisk eggs and vanilla into sugar mixture until combined. Using rubber spatula, fold in flour mixture until just combined. Fold in coconut, pecans, semisweet chocolate chips, and white chocolate chips.

3. Transfer batter to prepared pan and smooth top. Bake until top is shiny and cracked and feels firm to touch, 22 to 25 minutes, rotating pan halfway through baking. Let bars cool completely in pan on wire rack, about 2 hours. Using foil overhang, remove bars from pan. Cut into 36 pieces before serving.

PEANUT BUTTER BLONDIES
Makes 24 bars | 13 by 9-inch baking pan
WHY THIS RECIPE WORKS The rich, nutty flavor of peanut butter is a perfect complement to the butterscotch notes of a blondie. But making a peanut butter blondie wasn't as simple as stirring some peanut butter into our classic blondie base—too much made our blondies dense and heavy from all the added fat. We maxed out at ½ cup of peanut butter, and even then we had to decrease the amount of butter. Chunky peanut butter packed double the peanut flavor of creamy and added welcome texture. Stirring some chopped peanuts into the batter gave our blondies good crunch, but it still wasn't enough. The surprise solution turned out to be peanut butter chips, which provided pockets of concentrated peanut butter flavor. If you store your peanut butter in the refrigerator, note that room temperature peanut butter will combine more easily with the batter.

1½ cups (7½ ounces) all-purpose flour
1 teaspoon baking powder
½ teaspoon table salt
1½ cups packed (10½ ounces) light brown sugar
8 tablespoons unsalted butter, melted and cooled
2 large eggs
4 teaspoons vanilla extract
½ cup chunky peanut butter
½ cup (3 ounces) peanut butter chips
¼ cup salted dry-roasted peanuts, chopped

1. Adjust oven rack to middle position and heat oven to 350 degrees. Make foil sling for 13 by 9-inch baking pan by folding 2 long sheets of aluminum foil; first sheet should be 13 inches wide and second sheet should be 9 inches wide. Lay sheets of foil in pan perpendicular to each other, with extra foil hanging over edges of pan. Push foil into corners and up sides of pan, smoothing foil flush to pan. Grease foil.

2. Whisk flour, baking powder, and salt together in bowl. Whisk sugar and melted butter in second bowl until combined. Whisk eggs and vanilla into sugar mixture until combined. Whisk in peanut butter until combined. Using rubber spatula, fold in flour mixture until just combined. Fold in peanut butter chips and peanuts.

3. Transfer batter to prepared pan and smooth top. Bake until toothpick inserted in center comes out with few moist crumbs attached, 30 to 35 minutes, rotating pan halfway through baking. Let blondies cool completely in pan on wire rack, about 2 hours. Using foil overhang, remove blondies from pan. Cut into 24 pieces before serving.

WHITE CHOCOLATE–RASPBERRY BLONDIES

Makes 16 bars | 8-inch square baking pan

WHY THIS RECIPE WORKS Bittersweet chocolate shouldn't have a monopoly on bar cookies. Here, white chocolate infuses these bars with a complex, buttery, caramelized flavor. The bars are satisfyingly chewy without being heavy. We used just enough white chocolate for a rich-tasting bar but not so much that it was cloyingly sweet. Juicy, bright raspberries are a perfect foil to the silky, mild sweetness of white chocolate, so we punctuated these bars with whole fresh berries. Tossing the raspberries with a little sugar before pressing them into the batter encouraged them to caramelize and tempered their tartness a bit. Baking these bars at a slightly higher temperature than most bar recipes call for—375 degrees instead of 350—resulted in beautifully browned edges that further enhanced the caramel notes. A final drizzle of white chocolate provided a beautiful finish.

1 cup (5 ounces) all-purpose flour
1 teaspoon baking powder
¼ teaspoon table salt
6 ounces white chocolate, divided
4 tablespoons unsalted butter, softened
½ cup (3½ ounces) plus 2 teaspoons sugar, divided
1 large egg
1 teaspoon vanilla extract
5 ounces (1 cup) raspberries

1. Adjust oven rack to middle position and heat oven to 375 degrees. Make foil sling for 8-inch square baking pan by folding 2 long sheets of aluminum foil so each is 8 inches wide. Lay sheets of foil in pan perpendicular to each other, with extra foil hanging over edges of pan. Push foil into corners and up sides of pan, smoothing foil flush to pan. Grease foil.

2. Whisk flour, baking powder, and salt together in bowl. Roughly chop 3 ounces chocolate and microwave in second bowl at 50 percent power, stirring often, until melted, about 1 minute. Chop remaining 3 ounces chocolate into ½-inch pieces.

3. Using stand mixer fitted with paddle, beat butter and ½ cup sugar on medium-high speed until pale and fluffy, about 3 minutes. Add egg and vanilla and beat until combined. Add melted chocolate and mix until incorporated, about 30 seconds. Reduce speed to low and slowly add flour mixture until combined, about 45 seconds. Stir in all but 2 tablespoons chopped chocolate.

4. Transfer batter to prepared pan and spread into even layer. Toss raspberries with remaining 2 teaspoons sugar to coat and gently press into batter, spacing evenly apart. Bake until edges are puffed and golden and toothpick inserted in center comes out with few moist crumbs attached, 25 to 35 minutes, rotating pan halfway through baking.

5. Let bars cool completely in pan on wire rack, about 2 hours. Using foil overhang, remove bars from pan. Microwave reserved 2 tablespoons chocolate in bowl at 50 percent power, stirring occasionally, until melted, about 45 seconds. Drizzle melted chocolate over bars. Cut into 16 pieces and let chocolate set, about 30 minutes, before serving.

White Chocolate–
Raspberry Blondies

BAR COOKIES

KEY POINTS

Line pan with foil sling

Grease foil well

Spread or press dough into pan

Use ruler to cut even squares

THE DOUGH FOR BAR COOKIES is baked in a large pan and then cut into individual portions; they don't really resemble "cookies" until after they are cut. Some have a stir-together simplicity and the dough is just pressed into the pan. Others feature distinct layers, with a tender but firm shortbread or cookie base that is parbaked before being topped with an intensely flavored filling such as gooey jam, creamy lemon curd, or sugary pecans (some have a buttery streusel topping as well).

With these gooey fillings and a high sugar content, bars can be nearly impossible to remove from a baking pan, no matter how well the pan is greased. We have a few tips for cutting perfect square or rectangular bars. The first is using a foil sling to lift the bars from the pan before cutting. Attempting to cut the bars while in the pan makes for uneven edges that can crumble; cutting outside of the pan makes even lines from edge to edge. And if you want your bars to be precise, don't just eyeball them before cutting; use a ruler to cut rows and columns at even intervals. For bars with creamy fillings, there's an easy trick for cutting clean squares without making a mess: Heat your knife under hot running water and then quickly dry the blade with a dish towel and slice. (You can repeat heating and drying the knife as needed.)

Pat-in-the-Pan Bars

This style of bar cookie is essentially nothing more than a cookie dough that gets pressed into a pan rather than shaped into individual balls before baking. They have a familiar, comforting appeal, and the ease with which they come together makes them among the simplest cookies to prepare. The butter is melted, which means you can just mix the ingredients together by hand. The batter is then spread into a pan—no shaping or layering required. Once they're cooled, all you need to do is cut them into squares (or in the case of our giant chocolate chip cookie on page 94, into wedges).

Three-Layer Bars

The appeal of layered bars is undeniable; they feature a contrast of flavors and textures, starting with a sturdy bottom crust that can easily support the upper layers. Sometimes this is achieved by parbaking the bottom crust alone to prevent it from becoming wet and soggy. Other times the entire pan can be assembled and baked in one go for ease. The filling could be anything from rich, creamy chocolate to a chewy, gooey combination of fruit and nuts. And the top layer typically adds some crunch or texture in the form of a buttery streusel.

JAM, JELLIES, AND PRESERVES

Fruity bar cookies often include a layer of jam. We also use jam to fill thumbprints and sandwich cookies. Is jam interchangeable with other fruit spreads? Jam is made from crushed or finely chopped fruit, which is cooked with pectin and sugar until the pieces of fruit are almost formless and the mixture is thickened. Preserves are similar, but they contain whole pieces or large chunks of fruit. Jam's good fruit flavor and relatively smooth texture make it our first choice for baking. Avoid jelly; it has a wan, overly sweet taste since it's made from just fruit juice, sugar, and pectin, so we reserve it for glazing desserts.

Shortbread-Crust Bars

This type of bar generally has two distinct layers—a buttery shortbread crust and the filling. In fact, they can look like miniature pies in bar form (see our Best Lemon Bars on page 98). But the filling for these cookies should be firmer than that for pie; whether it is smooth and creamy or chewy and studded with nuts, it needs to be able to hold its shape when sliced. To create that stability, we turn to a variety of techniques and ingredients such as precooking the filling for our lemon bars and using sweetened condensed milk in the filling of our Millionaire's Shortbread (page 99). Additionally, the relatively large surface area of the baking pan and plenty of time in the oven ensure the filling cooks through so that it is fully set.

MAKING A CRUST

For the perfect ratio of base to filling in each bite of a bar cookie, you'll want to be sure to build an even, level bottom crust. Sprinkle the crumb or flour mixture evenly over the pan bottom and press down firmly, using the flat bottom of a dry measuring cup.

Crumb-Crust Bars

Crumb crusts may be light and crisp or satisfyingly chewy and substantial—either way they are a cinch to prepare. Graham cracker crusts are perhaps the most well-known; at their most basic they are nothing more than graham cracker crumbs, melted butter, and a little sugar for a hint of sweetness, all mixed together and pressed into the pan before being baked to a light golden brown. Add to that some melted chocolate, corn syrup, and shredded coconut, as with Nanaimo Bars (page 103) and you have a much more decadent affair—and a crust that holds together with no baking required. No matter the style, crumb crusts are an ideal foil to a rich, creamy filling.

PARBAKING CRUMB CRUSTS

Parbaking the crust—that is, baking it before adding the other bar components—is a simple but important step. Baking the crust by itself until dry and golden brown ensures that it will stay crisp beneath a creamy or fruit filling.

CHOCOLATE CHIP SKILLET COOKIE

Serves 8 | 12-inch cast-iron skillet

WHY THIS RECIPE WORKS A cookie in a skillet? Unlike a traditional batch of cookies, this treatment doesn't require scooping, baking, and cooling multiple sheets of treats; instead, the whole thing bakes at once in a skillet. Plus, the hot bottom and tall sides of a cast-iron pan create a great crust. We cut back on the butter and chocolate chips in our usual cookie dough to ensure that the skillet cookie was crisp at the edges, baked through in the middle, and perfectly chewy. We increased the baking time to accommodate the giant size, but otherwise our skillet recipe was simpler and faster than baking regular cookies. We developed this recipe using a 12-inch cast-iron skillet; an ovensafe traditional or nonstick skillet can also be used. Top with ice cream, if desired.

    12 tablespoons unsalted butter, divided
    ¾ cup packed (5¼ ounces) dark brown sugar
    ½ cup (3½ ounces) granulated sugar
    2 teaspoons vanilla extract
    1 teaspoon table salt
    1 large egg plus 1 large yolk
    1¾ cups (8¾ ounces) all-purpose flour
    ½ teaspoon baking soda
    1 cup (6 ounces) semisweet chocolate chips

1. Adjust oven rack to upper-middle position and heat oven to 375 degrees. Melt 9 tablespoons butter in 12-inch cast-iron skillet over medium heat. Continue to cook, stirring constantly, until butter is dark golden brown and has nutty aroma and bubbling subsides, about 5 minutes; transfer to large bowl. Stir remaining 3 tablespoons butter into hot butter until completely melted.

2. Whisk brown sugar, granulated sugar, vanilla, and salt into melted butter until smooth. Whisk in egg and yolk until smooth, about 30 seconds. Let mixture sit for 3 minutes, then whisk for 30 seconds. Repeat process of resting and whisking 2 more times until mixture is thick, smooth, and shiny.

3. Whisk flour and baking soda together in separate bowl, then stir flour mixture into butter mixture until just combined, about 1 minute. Stir in chocolate chips, making sure no flour pockets remain.

4. Wipe skillet clean with paper towels. Transfer dough to now-empty skillet and press into even layer with spatula. Transfer skillet to oven and bake until cookie is golden brown and edges are set, about 20 minutes, rotating skillet halfway through baking. Using potholders, transfer skillet to wire rack and let cookie cool for 30 minutes. Being careful of hot skillet handle, slice cookie into wedges and serve.

MILK CHOCOLATE REVEL BARS

Makes 24 bars | 13 by 9-inch baking pan

WHY THIS RECIPE WORKS Chocolate revel bars are a nostalgic treat featuring a rich, dreamy chocolate filling sandwiched between an oatmeal cookie base and a crumbly topping. But making them can be a trying project, one that involves assembling and baking the dessert in stages. To streamline the process, we made our dough work double duty by using it to form both the sturdy base and the crumbly topping. A combination of oats and almonds gave these bars a simultaneously chewy and crunchy texture. For the creamy fudge filling, we used milk chocolate chips, which provided the familiar chocolaty sweetness we craved, and added sweetened condensed milk and butter for a sliceable, fudgy filling that was easy to incorporate. Best of all, these three-layered treats required only one trip to the oven. If all you can find is an 11.5-ounce bag of chocolate chips, that will be enough.

    3 cups (9 ounces) old-fashioned rolled oats
    2 cups (10 ounces) all-purpose flour
    1½ cups packed (10½ ounces) brown sugar
    1 cup raw whole almonds, chopped
    1 teaspoon baking soda
    1¼ teaspoons table salt, divided
    16 tablespoons unsalted butter, melted, plus
         2 tablespoons unsalted butter
    2 large eggs
    2 teaspoons vanilla extract
    2 cups (12 ounces) milk chocolate chips
    1 cup sweetened condensed milk

1. Adjust oven rack to middle position and heat oven to 350 degrees. Make foil sling for 13 by 9-inch baking pan by folding 2 long sheets of aluminum foil; first sheet should be 13 inches wide and second sheet should be 9 inches wide. Lay sheets of foil in pan perpendicular to each other, with extra foil hanging over edges of pan. Push foil into corners and up sides of pan, smoothing foil flush to pan. Grease foil.

2. Combine oats, flour, sugar, almonds, baking soda, and 1 teaspoon salt in large bowl. Whisk melted butter, eggs, and vanilla together in second bowl. Stir butter mixture into flour mixture until dough forms. Set aside 1½ cups dough for topping. Press remaining dough into even layer in bottom of prepared pan.

3. Microwave chocolate chips, condensed milk, remaining ¼ teaspoon salt, and remaining 2 tablespoons butter in bowl at 50 percent power, stirring occasionally, until melted and smooth, 2 to 4 minutes. (Mixture will resemble thick fudge.)

4. Transfer chocolate mixture to pan and spread evenly over crust to sides of pan. Crumble reserved dough and sprinkle pieces evenly over chocolate mixture. Bake until topping is golden brown, about 30 minutes, rotating pan halfway through baking. Let bars cool in pan on wire rack until set, about 6 hours. Using foil overhang, remove bars from pan. Cut into 24 pieces before serving.

Butterscotch Revel Bars
Substitute butterscotch chips for milk chocolate chips.

Dark Chocolate Revel Bars
Substitute bittersweet chocolate chips for milk chocolate chips.

RASPBERRY STREUSEL BARS

Makes 24 bars | 13 by 9-inch baking pan

WHY THIS RECIPE WORKS For the very best raspberry bars, we needed to strike just the right balance between bright fruit filling, tender shortbread crust, and crumbly topping. We started with a shortbread dough that served as both the crust and the base for our streusel. After pressing part of the mixture into the pan, we added oats, brown sugar, nuts, and a little extra butter to the rest and pinched it into clumps to create our topping. For a filling that stayed neatly sandwiched between the base and topping, we combined fresh raspberries with raspberry jam. A squeeze of lemon juice brightened the mix. Frozen raspberries can be substituted for fresh, but be sure to defrost them before using. Quick oats will work, but the bars will be less chewy and flavorful; do not use instant oats.

2½ cups (12½ ounces) all-purpose flour
⅔ cup (4⅔ ounces) granulated sugar
½ teaspoon table salt
18 tablespoons (2¼ sticks) unsalted butter, cut into 1-tablespoon pieces and softened, divided
½ cup (1½ ounces) old-fashioned rolled oats
½ cup pecans, toasted and chopped fine
¼ cup packed (1¾ ounces) light brown sugar
¾ cup raspberry jam
3¾ ounces (¾ cup) fresh raspberries
1 tablespoon lemon juice

1. Adjust oven rack to middle position and heat oven to 375 degrees. Make foil sling for 13 by 9-inch baking pan by folding 2 long sheets of aluminum foil; first sheet should be 13 inches wide and second sheet should be 9 inches wide. Lay sheets of foil in pan perpendicular to each other, with extra foil hanging over edges of pan. Push foil into corners and up sides of pan, smoothing foil flush to pan. Grease foil.

Chocolate Chip Skillet Cookie

Milk Chocolate Revel Bars

Raspberry Streusel Bars

Blueberry Streusel Bars
Thawed frozen blueberries will also work here.
Substitute blueberry jam and ¾ cup fresh blueberries for the raspberry jam and raspberries.

Cherry Streusel Bars
Measure the cherries while they are still frozen, and then transfer them to a paper towel–lined baking sheet to thaw. One 12-ounce jar of cherry preserves is more than enough preserves for this recipe.

Substitute 1 cup cherry preserves and 2 cups (9 ounces) frozen sweet cherries, thawed, for raspberry jam and raspberries. Decrease lemon juice to 2 teaspoons and add ¼ teaspoon almond extract and pinch salt to filling. Substitute ½ cup slivered almonds, chopped, for pecans.

2. Whisk flour, granulated sugar, and salt together in bowl of stand mixer. Fit mixer with paddle and beat in 16 tablespoons butter, 1 piece at a time, on medium-low speed until mixture resembles damp sand, 1 to 1½ minutes. Set aside 1¼ cups mixture in bowl for topping.

3. Sprinkle remaining flour mixture into prepared pan and press firmly into even layer. Bake until edges of crust begin to brown, 14 to 18 minutes, rotating pan halfway through baking. (Crust must still be hot when filling is added.)

4. Meanwhile, stir oats, pecans, and brown sugar into reserved topping mixture. Add remaining 2 tablespoons butter and pinch mixture between your fingers into clumps of streusel. Using fork, mash jam, raspberries, and lemon juice in small bowl until few berry pieces remain.

5. Spread berry mixture evenly over hot crust, then sprinkle with streusel. Bake until filling is bubbling and topping is deep golden brown, 22 to 25 minutes, rotating pan halfway through baking.

6. Let bars cool completely in pan on wire rack, about 2 hours. Using foil overhang, remove bars from pan. Cut into 24 pieces before serving. (Uncut bars can be frozen for up to 1 month; let wrapped bars thaw at room temperature for 4 hours before serving.)

GLUTEN-FREE GINGER-FIG STREUSEL BARS

Makes 16 bars | 8-inch square baking pan

WHY THIS RECIPE WORKS For a novel approach to fig bars, we introduced the bright, slightly spicy flavor of ginger and a crisp streusel topping. Without the gluten, the cookies' base couldn't support the filling and topping. Adding just ¼ teaspoon of xanthan gum gave the crust the structure it needed. For the streusel topping, we simply took a portion of our shortbread base mixture and added light brown sugar, walnuts, and oats. Fig preserves or spread provided just the right jammy consistency, and the addition of lemon juice, lemon zest, and crystallized ginger gave our bars the bright flavors we were seeking.

- 6 ounces (1⅓ cups) all-purpose gluten-free flour blend (see page 2)
- 2⅓ ounces (⅓ cup) granulated sugar
- ½ teaspoon ground ginger
- ¼ teaspoon table salt
- ¼ teaspoon xanthan gum (see page 2)
- 8 tablespoons unsalted butter, cut into ½-inch pieces and softened
- ⅓ cup walnuts, toasted and chopped fine
- ¼ cup gluten-free old-fashioned rolled oats
- 2 tablespoons packed light brown sugar
- ¾ cup fig preserves
- 1 tablespoon minced crystallized ginger
- ½ teaspoon grated lemon zest plus 2 teaspoons juice

TUTORIAL
Raspberry Streusel Bars

See how one dough makes two of three layers in these buttery, fruity bars.

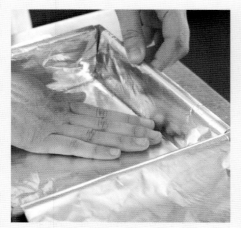

1. Fold 2 long sheets of aluminum foil; first sheet should be 13 inches wide and second sheet should be 9 inches wide. Lay sheets in pan perpendicular to each other. Push foil into corners and up sides of pan.

2. Set aside 1¼ cups flour mixture in bowl for topping.

3. Sprinkle remaining flour mixture into prepared pan and press firmly into even layer. Bake until edges of crust begin to brown, 14 to 18 minutes, rotating pan halfway through baking.

4. Meanwhile, stir oats, pecans, and brown sugar into reserved topping mixture. Add remaining 2 tablespoons butter and pinch mixture between your fingers into clumps of streusel.

5. Using fork, mash jam, raspberries, and lemon juice in small bowl until few berry pieces remain.

6. Spread berry mixture evenly over hot crust, then sprinkle with streusel. Bake until filling is bubbling and topping is deep golden brown, 22 to 25 minutes, rotating pan halfway through baking.

1. Adjust oven rack to middle position and heat oven to 375 degrees. Make foil sling for 8-inch square baking pan by folding 2 long sheets of aluminum foil so each is 8 inches wide. Lay sheets of foil in pan perpendicular to each other, with extra foil hanging over edges. Push foil into corners and up sides of pan, smoothing foil flush to pan. Grease foil.

2. Using stand mixer fitted with paddle, mix flour blend, granulated sugar, ground ginger, salt, and xanthan gum on low speed until combined, about 5 seconds. Add butter, 1 piece at a time, and beat until well combined, 2 to 3 minutes. (Add 1 to 2 tablespoons of water as needed if dough appears dry.) Set aside ½ cup mixture for topping. Press remaining mixture evenly into prepared pan using bottom of greased measuring cup. Bake until edges begin to brown, 14 to 18 minutes, rotating pan halfway through baking.

3. Meanwhile, mix walnuts, oats, and brown sugar into reserved dough. Combine preserves, crystallized ginger, and lemon zest and juice in separate bowl. Spread fig preserve mixture evenly over hot crust, then sprinkle with hazelnut-size clumps of oat topping. Bake until topping is golden brown and filling is bubbling, 22 to 25 minutes.

4. Let bars cool completely in pan on wire rack, 1 to 2 hours. Using foil overhang, remove bars from pan. Cut into 16 pieces before serving. (Bars can be refrigerated for up to 2 days; crust and streusel will soften.)

BEST LEMON BARS

Makes 12 bars | 8-inch square baking pan

WHY THIS RECIPE WORKS The sweet-tart taste of a good lemon bar captures the best of summer's bright flavors. To make our bars, we started at the bottom, with a pat-in-the-pan crust. Using melted butter allowed us to simply stir the crust together instead of using a food processor. For a truly crisp texture, we used granulated sugar instead of the usual confectioners' sugar and baked the crust until it was dark golden brown to ensure that it retained its crispness even after we topped it with the lemon filling. We cooked our filling on the stove to shorten the oven time and keep it from curdling when it baked. The combination of lemon juice and lemon zest provided complex flavor, and a couple of teaspoons of cream of tartar (tartaric acid) gave it a bright, lingering finish. Do not substitute bottled lemon juice for fresh here.

Best Lemon Bars

CRUST
- 1 cup (5 ounces) all-purpose flour
- ¼ cup (1¾ ounces) granulated sugar
- ½ teaspoon table salt
- 8 tablespoons unsalted butter, melted

FILLING
- 1 cup (7 ounces) granulated sugar
- 2 tablespoons all-purpose flour
- 2 teaspoons cream of tartar
- ¼ teaspoon table salt
- 3 large eggs plus 3 large yolks
- 2 teaspoons grated lemon zest plus ⅔ cup juice (4 lemons)
- 4 tablespoons unsalted butter, cut into 8 pieces
  Confectioners' sugar (optional)

1. FOR THE CRUST: Adjust oven rack to middle position and heat oven to 350 degrees. Make foil sling for 8-inch square baking pan by folding 2 long sheets of aluminum foil so each is 8 inches wide. Lay sheets of foil in pan perpendicular to each other, with extra foil hanging over edges of pan. Push foil into corners and up sides of pan, smoothing foil flush to pan.

2. Whisk flour, sugar, and salt together in bowl. Add melted butter and stir until combined. Transfer mixture to prepared pan and press into even layer over entire bottom of pan (do not wash bowl). Bake crust until dark golden brown, 19 to 24 minutes, rotating pan halfway through baking.

3. FOR THE FILLING: While crust bakes, whisk sugar, flour, cream of tartar, and salt together in now-empty bowl. Whisk in eggs and yolks until no streaks of egg remain. Whisk in lemon zest and juice. Transfer mixture to saucepan and cook over medium-low heat, stirring constantly, until mixture thickens and registers 160 degrees, 5 to 8 minutes. Off heat, stir in butter. Strain filling through fine-mesh strainer set over bowl.

4. Pour filling over hot crust and tilt pan to spread evenly. Bake until filling is set and barely jiggles when pan is shaken, 8 to 12 minutes. (Filling around perimeter may be slightly raised.) Let bars cool completely in pan on wire rack, at least 1½ hours. Using foil overhang, remove bars from pan. Cut into 12 pieces, wiping knife clean between cuts as necessary. (Lemon bars can be refrigerated for up to 2 days or frozen for up to 1 month; if frozen, thaw completely at room temperature before serving.) Dust bars with confectioners' sugar, if using, before serving.

MILLIONAIRE'S SHORTBREAD

Makes 40 bars | 13 by 9-inch baking pan

WHY THIS RECIPE WORKS Millionaire's shortbread is a fitting name for this impressively rich British cookie, which consists of a buttery shortbread base topped with a caramel-like layer, which is in turn topped with a layer of shiny chocolate. Sweetened condensed milk gives the caramel portion of this cookie a luxurious creaminess, but we found that its whey proteins sometimes caused the caramel sauce to break. Adding fresh cream solved the problem, as its proteins haven't been damaged by processing. Our easy method for tempering chocolate in the microwave resulted in a glossy, snappy top layer. For the right texture for the caramel filling, monitor the temperature with an instant-read thermometer.

CRUST
2½ cups (12½ ounces) all-purpose flour
½ cup (3½ ounces) granulated sugar
¾ teaspoon table salt
16 tablespoons unsalted butter, melted

FILLING
1 (14-ounce) can sweetened condensed milk
1 cup packed (7 ounces) brown sugar
½ cup heavy cream
½ cup corn syrup
8 tablespoons unsalted butter
½ teaspoon table salt

CHOCOLATE
8 ounces bittersweet chocolate (6 ounces chopped fine, 2 ounces grated)

Millionaire's Shortbread

1. FOR THE CRUST: Adjust oven rack to lower-middle position and heat oven to 350 degrees. Make foil sling for 13 by 9-inch baking pan by folding 2 long sheets of aluminum foil; first sheet should be 13 inches wide and second sheet should be 9 inches wide. Lay sheets of foil in pan perpendicular to each other, with extra foil hanging over edges of pan. Push foil into corners and up sides of pan, smoothing foil flush to pan.

2. Combine flour, sugar, and salt in medium bowl. Add melted butter and stir with rubber spatula until flour is evenly moistened. Crumble dough evenly over bottom of prepared pan. Using your fingertips and palm of your hand, press and smooth dough into even thickness. Using fork, pierce dough at 1-inch intervals. Bake until light golden brown and firm to touch, 25 to 30 minutes. Transfer pan to wire rack. Using sturdy metal spatula, press on entire surface of warm crust to compress (this will make finished bars easier to cut). Let crust cool until it is just warm, at least 20 minutes.

3. FOR THE FILLING: Stir all ingredients together in large, heavy-bottomed saucepan. Cook over medium heat, stirring frequently, until mixture registers between 236 and 239 degrees (temperature will fluctuate), 16 to 20 minutes.

4. Pour over crust and spread to even thickness (mixture will be very hot). Let cool completely, about 1½ hours.

5. FOR THE CHOCOLATE: Microwave finely chopped chocolate in bowl at 50 percent power, stirring often, until about two-thirds melted, 1 to 2 minutes. (Melted chocolate should not be much warmer than body temperature; check by holding bowl in palm of your hand.) Add grated chocolate and stir until smooth, returning to microwave for no more than 5 seconds at a time to finish melting if necessary. Spread evenly over filling. Refrigerate shortbread until chocolate is just set, about 10 minutes.

6. Using foil overhang, remove shortbread from pan. Using serrated knife and gentle sawing motion, cut shortbread in half crosswise to create two 6½ by 9-inch rectangles. Cut each rectangle in half to make four 3¼ by 9-inch strips. Cut each strip crosswise into 10 equal pieces, and serve. (Shortbread can be stored at room temperature, between layers of parchment, for up to 1 week.)

DREAM BARS

Makes 24 bars | 13 by 9-inch baking pan

WHY THIS RECIPE WORKS Whether you call them dream bars, magic bars, or seven-layer bars, these loaded confections have undeniable appeal. But often they contain far too many ingredients, making them too sweet. To revamp these bars, we nixed the superfluous—including chips of all kinds (from chocolate to white chocolate and butterscotch), toffee bits, and graham crackers—and chose only the most traditional ingredients: coconut and pecans. For the base, we mixed up a shortbread dough and deepened its toffee notes with brown sugar. After baking the base, we layered it with a pecan filling before adding the coconut topping. Soaking the shredded coconut in cream of coconut resulted in a rich, moist topping that caramelized beautifully. Try to spread the coconut mixture evenly over the pecan layer, but don't worry if it looks patchy.

CRUST

  2 cups (10 ounces) all-purpose flour
  ¾ cup packed (5¼ ounces) dark brown sugar
  ½ cup pecans
  ¼ teaspoon table salt
 10 tablespoons unsalted butter, cut into
    ½-inch pieces and chilled

TOPPING

1½ cups (4½ ounces) sweetened shredded coconut
  1 cup cream of coconut
  ¾ cup packed (5¼ ounces) dark brown sugar
  2 large eggs
  2 tablespoons all-purpose flour
1½ teaspoons baking powder
  1 teaspoon vanilla extract
  ½ teaspoon table salt
  1 cup pecans, toasted and chopped coarse

1. Adjust oven rack to middle position and heat oven to 350 degrees. Make foil sling for 13 by 9-inch baking pan by folding 2 long sheets of aluminum foil; first sheet should be 13 inches wide and second sheet should be 9 inches wide. Lay sheets of foil in pan perpendicular to each other, with extra foil hanging over edges of pan. Push foil into corners and up sides of pan, smoothing foil flush to pan. Grease foil.

2. FOR THE CRUST: Pulse flour, sugar, pecans, and salt in food processor until pecans are coarsely ground, about 10 pulses. Scatter butter over top and pulse until mixture resembles coarse meal, about 12 pulses. Transfer mixture to prepared pan and press firmly into even layer. Bake until golden brown, about 20 minutes. Let crust cool in pan on wire rack for 20 minutes.

3. FOR THE TOPPING: Combine coconut and cream of coconut in bowl. Whisk sugar, eggs, flour, baking powder, vanilla, and salt in second bowl until smooth. Stir in pecans, then spread filling over cooled crust. Dollop heaping tablespoons of coconut mixture over filling, then spread into even layer.

4. Bake until topping is deep golden brown, 35 to 40 minutes, rotating pan halfway through baking. Let bars cool completely in pan on wire rack, about 2 hours. Using foil overhang, remove bars from pan. Cut into 24 pieces before serving. (Bars can be refrigerated for up to 5 days.)

TURTLE BARS

Makes 24 bars | 13 by 9-inch baking pan

WHY THIS RECIPE WORKS To reimagine this classic candy as a bar cookie, we started with a chocolate shortbread base. For a caramel layer with sliceable chew, we cooked dulce de leche, butter, sugar, cream, and corn syrup, and then stirred in pecans. To the warm caramel we added chocolate chips, more pecans, and a sprinkle of salt. Use an instant-read thermometer to monitor the caramel; it is essential to cook the mixture to between 235 and 240 degrees in step 4 for it to set up properly. If you're using an electric stove, the mixture may take longer than 11 minutes to reach 235 degrees once it starts to boil. Using a large heavy-bottomed saucepan and stirring frequently will help ensure that the caramel doesn't scorch.

CRUST

1⅔ cups (8⅓ ounces) all-purpose flour
  ½ cup (3½ ounces) granulated sugar
  ⅓ cup (1 ounce) unsweetened cocoa powder
  ¾ teaspoon table salt
 12 tablespoons unsalted butter, melted

TOPPING

- 1 (13.4-ounce) can dulce de leche
- 1 cup packed (7 ounces) light brown sugar
- ½ cup heavy cream
- ½ cup light corn syrup
- 8 tablespoons unsalted butter
- ½ teaspoon table salt
- 2 cups coarsely chopped pecans, toasted, divided
- 1 cup (6 ounces) semisweet chocolate chips
- ½ teaspoon flake sea salt

1. Adjust oven rack to middle position and heat oven to 350 degrees. Make foil sling for 13 by 9-inch baking pan by folding 2 long sheets of aluminum foil; first sheet should be 13 inches wide and second sheet should be 9 inches wide. Lay sheets of foil in pan perpendicular to each other, with extra foil hanging over edges of pan. Push foil into corners and up sides of pan, smoothing foil flush to pan. Grease foil.

2. FOR THE CRUST: Combine flour, sugar, cocoa, and salt in bowl. Add melted butter and stir with rubber spatula until evenly moistened. Crumble dough over bottom of prepared pan. Press dough to even thickness using bottom of dry measuring cup. Using fork, poke dough all over, about 20 times. Bake until crust is fragrant and looks dry, 18 to 20 minutes. Transfer pan to wire rack. (Crust needn't cool completely before adding topping.)

3. FOR THE TOPPING: Combine dulce de leche, sugar, cream, corn syrup, butter, and table salt in large heavy-bottomed saucepan. Bring to boil over medium heat, 7 to 9 minutes, stirring frequently with rubber spatula.

4. Once boiling, continue to cook, stirring frequently to prevent scorching, until mixture registers between 235 and 240 degrees in several places, 9 to 11 minutes longer. (Mixture will be thick and bubbling vigorously.) Off heat, stir in 1½ cups pecans. Pour caramel mixture over crust and spread to even thickness. Sprinkle with chocolate chips and let sit until chocolate chips have softened, about 5 minutes.

5. Swirl softened chocolate chips through caramel mixture using butter knife. Sprinkle with remaining ½ cup pecans and flake sea salt. Let bars sit at room temperature until chocolate is set, at least 3 hours.

6. Using foil overhang, lift bars out of pan. (Caramel may stick to foil. Use paring knife to separate, if necessary.) Cut into 24 pieces before serving. (Bars can be stored at room temperature for up to 5 days.)

Turtle Bars

Strawberry Cheesecake Bars

Nanaimo Bars

STRAWBERRY CHEESECAKE BARS

Makes 24 bars | 13 by 9-inch baking pan

WHY THIS RECIPE WORKS Creamy cheesecake topped with glistening strawberries is popular for good reason: The bright, floral strawberries, with just a hint of acidity, help balance the cheesecake's richness. To capture the essence of strawberry cheesecake in a handheld bar, we started at the bottom with a classic graham cracker crust. We found that trying to add fresh strawberries, whether chopped or pureed, directly to the filling compromised the creamy texture of the cheesecake layer and prevented the bars from setting up correctly. Instead, we pureed the fresh berries and stirred them into a sweetened sour cream topping that we spread over the almost-done filling. After letting the bars cool and chilling them, we garnished each square with one strawberry slice. The result was perfect— strong strawberry flavor with no sacrifice of the cheesecake's signature creaminess.

CRUST

9 whole graham crackers, broken into pieces
½ cup (3½ ounces) sugar
¾ cup (3¾ ounces) all-purpose flour
¼ teaspoon table salt
8 tablespoons unsalted butter, melted

FILLING

1½ pounds cream cheese
1 cup (7 ounces) sugar
3 large eggs
2 teaspoons vanilla extract

TOPPING

6 ounces strawberries, hulled (1 heaping cup), plus 5 hulled strawberries, divided
½ cup (3½ ounces) plus 1 teaspoon sugar, divided
2 cups sour cream

1. Adjust oven rack to middle position and heat oven to 300 degrees. Make foil sling for 13 by 9-inch baking pan by folding 2 long sheets of aluminum foil; first sheet should be 13 inches wide and second sheet should be 9 inches wide. Lay sheets of foil in pan perpendicular to each other, with extra foil hanging over edges of pan. Push foil into corners and up sides of pan, smoothing foil flush to pan. Grease foil.

2. FOR THE CRUST: Process cracker pieces and sugar in food processor until finely ground, about 30 seconds. Add flour and salt and pulse to combine, about 2 pulses. Add melted butter and pulse until crumbs are evenly moistened, about 10 pulses.

3. Using your hands, press crumb mixture evenly into bottom of prepared pan. Using bottom of dry measuring cup, firmly pack crust into pan. Bake until fragrant and beginning to brown around edges, about 20 minutes. Let cool completely.

4. FOR THE FILLING: In clean, dry processor bowl, process cream cheese and sugar until smooth, about 3 minutes, scraping down sides of bowl as needed. With processor running, add eggs, one at a time, until just incorporated, about 30 seconds total. Scrape down sides of bowl. Add vanilla and process to combine, about 10 seconds. Pour cream cheese mixture over cooled crust. Bake until center is almost set but still jiggles slightly when pan is shaken, about 45 minutes.

5. FOR THE TOPPING: Meanwhile, in clean, dry processor bowl, process 6 ounces strawberries and ½ cup sugar until pureed, about 30 seconds. Stir strawberry puree and sour cream in bowl until combined.

6. Remove cheesecake from oven. Pour strawberry mixture over cheesecake (cheesecake layer should be completely covered). Return pan to oven and bake until topping is just set, about 15 minutes.

7. Let cheesecake cool completely in pan on wire rack, about 2 hours. Refrigerate until cold and set, at least 4 hours or up to 24 hours. Slice remaining 5 strawberries thin and gently toss with remaining 1 teaspoon sugar in bowl. Using foil overhang, lift cheesecake out of pan. Cut into 24 pieces. Garnish each piece with 1 strawberry slice before serving.

NANAIMO BARS

Makes 18 bars | 8-inch square baking pan

WHY THIS RECIPE WORKS These three-layer, no-bake bars are a Canadian favorite. We created a fudgy, chewy base by binding graham crackers, coconut, pecans, and cocoa powder with melted dark chocolate and corn syrup. The soft middle layer is traditionally made by creaming butter, confectioners' sugar, vanilla, and custard powder, an ingredient common in Canadian kitchens but not readily available stateside. Fortunately, we found that nonfat dry milk powder made an ideal replacement. A quick chocolate ganache slathered over the chilled filling helped these Nanaimo bars shine.

CRUST

½ cup (3 ounces) bittersweet chocolate chips
6 whole graham crackers, broken into 1-inch pieces
⅔ cup (2 ounces) sweetened shredded coconut
½ cup pecans, toasted
¼ cup (¾ ounce) unsweetened cocoa powder
⅛ teaspoon table salt
⅓ cup light corn syrup

FILLING

1¼ cups (5 ounces) confectioners' sugar
8 tablespoons unsalted butter, softened
¼ cup (¾ ounce) nonfat dry milk powder
⅛ teaspoon table salt
¼ cup heavy cream
2 teaspoons vanilla extract

TOPPING

⅔ cup (4 ounces) bittersweet chocolate chips
2 tablespoons unsalted butter
1 tablespoon light corn syrup

1. FOR THE CRUST: Make foil sling for 8-inch square baking pan by folding 2 long sheets of aluminum foil so each is 8 inches wide. Lay sheets of foil in pan perpendicular to each other, with extra foil hanging over edges of pan. Push foil into corners and up sides of pan, smoothing foil flush to pan. Grease foil.

2. Microwave chocolate chips in bowl at 50 percent power, stirring occasionally, until melted, 1 to 2 minutes. Process cracker pieces, coconut, pecans, cocoa, and salt in food processor until cracker pieces are finely ground, about 30 seconds. Add corn syrup and melted chocolate and pulse until combined, 8 to 10 pulses (mixture should hold together when pinched with your fingers). Transfer to prepared pan. Using bottom of greased measuring cup, press crumbs into even layer in bottom of pan. Refrigerate while making filling.

3. FOR THE FILLING: In clean, dry food processor, process sugar, butter, milk powder, and salt until smooth, about 30 seconds, scraping down sides of bowl as needed. Add cream and vanilla and process until fully combined, about 15 seconds. Spread filling evenly over crust. Cover pan with plastic wrap and refrigerate until filling is set and firm, about 2 hours.

4. FOR THE TOPPING: Microwave chocolate chips, butter, and corn syrup in bowl at 50 percent power, stirring occasionally, until melted and smooth, 1 to 2 minutes. Using offset spatula, spread chocolate mixture evenly over set filling. Refrigerate until topping is set, about 30 minutes.

5. Using foil overhang, remove bars from pan. Using chef's knife, trim outer ¼ inch of square to make neat edges (wipe knife clean with dish towel after each cut). Cut square into thirds to create 3 rectangles. Cut each rectangle crosswise into 6 equal pieces. Let bars sit at room temperature for 20 minutes before serving. (Bars can be refrigerated for up to 2 days.)

SPONGE CAKE COOKIES

KEY POINTS

Can be simply flavored or complex

Grease pans well

Whip eggs for light texture

THESE LIGHT, DELICATE CREATIONS really have more in common with an airy cake than a cookie, save for their miniature form. In fact, cake flour is often used because its low protein content delivers a delicate, fine crumb. This category of cookie can take many forms—it can be stacked and layered with jam for a real showstopper or simply baked in a molded pan for a more understated elegance. (If using a mold, you'll want to make sure you grease it thoroughly to ensure each petite cake releases cleanly.) Eggs play an especially important role in achieving the desired texture and appearance. The addition of an extra egg yolk can add moistness and richness without adding unnecessary liquid (which, in conjunction with the flour, produces gluten during mixing and can result in a tough crumb). Separating the eggs and whipping the whites can provide structure to a dough that will be piped onto the baking sheet—structure that is especially important in the absence of a leavener.

SHAPING LADYFINGERS

For our Ladyfingers (page 106) we deposit the batter onto the baking sheets with a piping bag for added flair. (While there are many different tips you can buy, most bags come with only the most basic one or two shapes.)

1. Holding pastry bag in 1 hand, fold top of pastry bag down about halfway. Insert ½-inch plain tip into point of bag and press securely in place.

2. Scrape batter into bag until bag is half full.

3. Pull up sides of bag, push down filling, and twist tightly. Push down on bag to squeeze the air out and push contents into tip.

4. Grip bag at base, twist, and squeeze to pipe batter into 3-inch by 1-inch strips, spacing them 1 inch apart on prepared sheets. If tip gets clogged during piping, move tip over bowl and apply more pressure to release blockage.

MADELEINES

Makes 24 cookies | **12-cookie madeleine mold**

WHY THIS RECIPE WORKS Madeleines are light, airy treats unlike any other cookie; they're sponge cakes in cookie form, with a beautiful ridged exterior formed by the shell-shaped tins in which they are baked. Despite their appeal, madeleines can be hard to find; fortunately, this French treat is easy to prepare at home. For madeleines with a light, tight crumb, we used downy-soft cake flour rather than all-purpose flour. To cool the baked madeleines without ruining their ridged exteriors, we let them sit in the greased molds for 10 minutes after baking to set their exteriors before transferring them to a wire rack. This way, the rack didn't imprint lines on our cookies as they cooled. This recipe calls for a 12-cookie madeleine mold; even if you have two molds, be sure to bake them one at a time.

    1 cup (4 ounces) cake flour
    ¼ teaspoon table salt
    2 large eggs plus 1 large yolk
    ½ cup (3½ ounces) sugar
    1 tablespoon vanilla extract
   10 tablespoons unsalted butter, melted and cooled

1. Adjust oven rack to middle position and heat oven to 375 degrees. Grease 12-cookie madeleine mold. Whisk flour and salt together in small bowl.

2. Using stand mixer fitted with paddle, beat eggs and yolk on medium-high speed until frothy, 3 to 5 minutes. Add sugar and vanilla and beat until very thick, 3 to 5 minutes. Using rubber spatula, gently fold in flour mixture, followed by melted butter.

3. Spoon half of batter into prepared mold, filling mold to rim. Bake until madeleines are golden and spring back when pressed lightly, about 10 minutes, rotating mold halfway through baking.

4. Let cookies cool in mold for 10 minutes. Remove madeleines from mold and transfer to wire rack. Repeat with remaining batter. Let madeleines cool completely before serving.

Almond Madeleines
Reduce vanilla to 2 teaspoons and add 1 teaspoon almond extract.

Chocolate Madeleines
Substitute ¼ cup sifted Dutch-processed cocoa for ¼ cup flour and add 2 teaspoons instant espresso powder to flour mixture in step 1.

Citrus Madeleines
Add 1 tablespoon grated lemon zest or orange zest with sugar and vanilla in step 2.

Rosewater Madeleines
Substitute 2 teaspoons rosewater for vanilla extract.

LADYFINGERS

Makes about 48 cookies | **2 rimmed baking sheets**

WHY THIS RECIPE WORKS For many, ladyfingers are known only as those hard packaged cookies that get soaked in espresso for tiramisu. But homemade ladyfingers have a lightly sweet flavor and soft texture that allow them to stand on their own. The key is creating a sponge cake–like batter that can be easily piped without deflating. To achieve this, we found that using all-purpose flour was a must for the batter to have enough structure to support the whipped egg whites. Adding a portion of the sugar once the egg whites reached very soft peaks ensured that we didn't overbeat them. Folding the whipped egg whites, yolks, and dry ingredients together at once kept the batter aerated. A light dusting of confectioners' sugar was enough to make these ladyfingers ready for dessert.

    ½ cup (3½ ounces) granulated sugar, divided
    ¼ cup (1 ounce) confectioners' sugar, divided
    4 large eggs, separated
    ⅛ teaspoon table salt
    1 teaspoon vanilla
    ¾ cup (3¾ ounces) all-purpose flour

1. Adjust oven racks to upper-middle and lower-middle positions and heat oven to 350 degrees. Line 2 rimmed baking sheets with parchment paper and spray with vegetable oil spray.

2. Whisk ¼ cup granulated sugar and 2 tablespoons confectioners' sugar together in small bowl. Using stand mixer fitted with whisk attachment, whip egg whites and salt on high speed until very soft peaks form (peaks should slowly lose their shape when whisk is removed), 30 to 45 seconds. Reduce speed to medium and gradually add sugar mixture. Increase speed to high and whip until glossy, stiff peaks form, about 30 seconds. Gently transfer whites to large bowl.

3. Fit stand mixer with paddle and beat egg yolks, vanilla, and remaining ¼ cup granulated sugar until thick and pale yellow, about 5 minutes. Pour yolk mixture on top of whites in bowl, then sift flour over top. Using rubber spatula, gently fold until combined.

4. Fill pastry bag fitted with ½-inch plain tip halfway with batter. Pipe batter into 3-inch by 1-inch strips, spacing them 1 inch apart on prepared sheets. Sift remaining 2 tablespoons confectioners' sugar over strips. Bake until edges are golden, 20 to 24 minutes, switching and rotating sheets halfway through baking. Let cookies cool on sheets for 5 minutes, then transfer to wire rack and let cool completely before serving.

ITALIAN RAINBOW COOKIES

Makes 60 cookies | 13 by 9-inch baking pan

WHY THIS RECIPE WORKS Rainbow cookies, Napoleon cookies, tricolor cookies, or Venetian cookies: Whatever you call them, these multilayered treats are part cake, part cookie, part confection, and unabashedly sweet. With their green, white, and red stripes, these Italian American cookies are meant to look like miniature Italian flags. Each colorful layer is made from an almond paste–enhanced sponge cake, for a sturdy, slightly dense confection that's easy to stack, slice, and eat in cookie form. For tricolored layers, we made one batter and separated it into thirds, adding food coloring to two of the portions. Once the layers had baked and cooled, we spread them with raspberry jam and stacked them. For a crowning touch, we spread a generous amount of melted chocolate over the surface. Running a fork through the chocolate in waves once it had set and thickened for a few minutes provided the final flourish.

Italian Rainbow Cookies

2 cups (8 ounces) cake flour
½ teaspoon baking powder
1½ cups (10½ ounces) sugar
8 ounces almond paste, cut into 1-inch pieces
7 large eggs
1 teaspoon vanilla extract
½ teaspoon table salt
8 tablespoons unsalted butter, melted and cooled slightly
⅛ teaspoon red food coloring
⅛ teaspoon green food coloring
⅔ cup seedless raspberry jam
1 cup (6 ounces) bittersweet chocolate chips

1. Adjust oven rack to middle position and heat oven to 350 degrees. Grease 13 by 9-inch baking pan. Make parchment paper sling by folding 1 long sheet of parchment 13 inches wide and laying across width of pan, with extra parchment hanging over edges of pan. Push parchment into corners and up sides of pan, smoothing parchment flush to pan. Grease parchment.

2. Combine flour and baking powder and sift into bowl; set aside. Process sugar and almond paste in food processor until combined, 20 to 30 seconds. Transfer sugar mixture to bowl of stand mixer; add eggs, vanilla, and salt. Fit mixer with whisk attachment and whip mixture on medium-high speed until pale and thickened, 5 to 7 minutes. Reduce speed to low and add melted butter. Slowly add flour mixture until just combined.

3. Transfer 2 cups batter to prepared pan and spread in even layer with offset spatula. Bake until top is set and edges are just starting to brown, 10 to 12 minutes. Let cool in pan for 5 minutes. Using parchment overhang, remove cake from pan and transfer to wire rack. Let cake and pan cool completely.

4. Divide remaining batter between 2 bowls. Stir red food coloring into first bowl and green food coloring into second bowl. Make new parchment sling for now-empty pan and repeat baking with each colored batter, letting pan cool after each batch.

5. Invert red layer onto cutting board and gently remove parchment. Spread ⅓ cup jam evenly over top. Invert plain layer onto red layer and gently remove parchment. Spread remaining ⅓ cup jam evenly over top. Invert green layer onto plain layer and gently remove parchment.

6. Microwave chocolate chips in bowl at 50 percent power, stirring occasionally, until melted, 2 to 4 minutes. Spread chocolate evenly over green layer. Let set for 2 minutes, then run fork in wavy pattern through chocolate. Let chocolate set, 1 to 2 hours. Using serrated knife, trim away edges. Cut lengthwise into 5 equal strips (about 1½ inches wide) and then crosswise into 12 equal strips (about 1 inch wide) before serving.

FLOURLESS
(AND ALMOST FLOURLESS)
COOKIES

Employ egg whites for structure

Use ground nuts

Manage sticky dough

FLOUR IS ARGUABLY ONE OF THE MOST IMPORTANT ingredients for just about any cookie; after all, it's responsible for giving most baked goods their structure. But eliminate the flour from cookies and you allow the flavors to really shine—think rich chocolate, nuts, and fragrant coconut—while also creating unique texture.

This type of cookie relies on egg whites to provide both structure and leavening, and there are a couple of different ways to incorporate them. For a cookie with satisfying chew, you can simply mix the egg whites right into the other ingredients. Whipping the whites with sugar until glossy, stiff peaks form will give you a cookie that's incredibly light and crisp. The biggest challenge with flourless (or mostly flourless) doughs is that they have a tendency to be wet and sticky, which makes sense given that you're removing the primary dry ingredient.

These recipes employ different tricks to make the doughs easier to work with. Letting the dough chill is one easy solution; this gives the remaining dry ingredients time to absorb excess moisture. Replacing granulated sugar with powdery fine confectioners' sugar or adding a little cornstarch creates a drier dough, as does treating chocolate as a dry ingredient by finely grating it rather than melting it.

BASLER BRUNSLI

Makes about 42 cookies | 2 rimmed baking sheets

WHY THIS RECIPE WORKS A holiday tradition in Switzerland, these delicately spiced chocolate cookies are soft and chewy. Containing no flour and naturally gluten-free, basler brunsli are loaded with chocolate and ground almonds and bound with just a couple of egg whites. To make our dough drier and easier to work with, we employed confectioners' sugar in place of much of the granulated sugar. We also treated the chocolate like a dry ingredient, grinding it in the food processor along with the others. Cocoa powder amped up the chocolate flavor without adding moisture. It's traditional to roll out the dough on a counter sprinkled with sugar, but this method prevented us from being able to reroll the scraps; instead we dunked each side of the cut cookies in a dish of sugar. Rechill the dough scraps if necessary before rerolling in step 4.

1¾ cups slivered almonds
1 cup (4 ounces) confectioners' sugar
4 ounces bittersweet chocolate, chopped
¼ cup (1¾ ounces) granulated sugar, plus
    ½ cup for coating
3 tablespoons unsweetened cocoa powder
1 teaspoon ground cinnamon
¼ teaspoon table salt
2 large egg whites
1 teaspoon vanilla extract

1. Adjust oven racks to upper-middle and lower-middle positions and heat oven to 325 degrees. Line 2 rimmed baking sheets with parchment paper.

2. Process almonds and confectioners' sugar in food processor until almonds are very finely ground, about 45 seconds. Add chocolate, ¼ cup granulated sugar, cocoa, cinnamon, and salt and process until chocolate is finely ground, about 30 seconds. Add egg whites and vanilla and pulse until dough forms, about 10 pulses.

3. Transfer dough to piece of parchment paper and knead gently to form smooth ball. Let dough sit until no longer sticky, about 10 minutes. Top with second piece of parchment and roll dough ¼ inch thick. Transfer dough, still between parchment, to refrigerator and let chill for 10 minutes.

4. Spread remaining ½ cup granulated sugar in shallow dish. Using 2-inch star cutter, cut dough into stars, gathering and rerolling scraps as necessary. Dip both sides of each star in granulated sugar to coat; space stars 1 inch apart on prepared sheets. Bake until puffed and cracked but centers are still soft, 13 to 15 minutes, switching and rotating sheets halfway through baking. Let cookies cool on sheets for 15 minutes, then transfer to wire rack and let cool completely before serving.

Triple-Coconut Macaroons

TRIPLE-COCONUT MACAROONS

Makes 48 cookies | 2 rimmed baking sheets

WHY THIS RECIPE WORKS Coconut macaroons are easy to find but usually quick to disappoint; we set out to make a great version, one with a chewy texture and plenty of coconut flavor. Recipes call for either sweetened or unsweetened shredded coconut; using all sweetened coconut led to an overly sticky cookie, while using only unsweetened created a bland-tasting one. So we used both, for a cookie with appealing texture and flavor. But what really set our macaroons apart was the addition of cream of coconut, which provided one more layer of big flavor. A few egg whites, plus some corn syrup, ensured that the macaroons held together and baked up moist and chewy. Be sure to use cream of coconut (such as Coco López) and not coconut milk. For larger macaroons, shape haystacks from a generous ¼ cup of batter and increase the baking time to 20 minutes.

1 cup cream of coconut
4 large egg whites
2 tablespoons light corn syrup
2 teaspoons vanilla extract
½ teaspoon table salt
3 cups (9 ounces) unsweetened shredded coconut
3 cups (9 ounces) sweetened shredded coconut

Almond Macaroons

1. Adjust oven racks to upper-middle and lower-middle positions and heat oven to 375 degrees. Line 2 rimmed baking sheets with parchment paper.

2. Whisk cream of coconut, egg whites, corn syrup, vanilla, and salt together in bowl; set aside. Toss unsweetened coconut and sweetened coconut together in large bowl, breaking up clumps with your fingertips. Pour cream of coconut mixture over coconut and mix until evenly moistened; transfer bowl to refrigerator for 15 minutes.

3. Drop 1-tablespoon mounds of dough onto prepared sheets, spacing them 1 inch apart. Using your moistened fingertips, form dough into loose haystacks. Bake until light golden brown, about 15 minutes, switching and rotating sheets halfway through baking.

4. Let cookies cool on sheets until slightly set, about 2 minutes, then transfer to wire rack and let cool completely before serving.

Chocolate-Dipped Triple-Coconut Macaroons

Let baked macaroons cool completely. Line 2 baking sheets with parchment paper. Chop 10 ounces semisweet chocolate. Microwave 8 ounces chocolate at 50 percent power, stirring occasionally, until melted, 2 to 4 minutes. Remove melted chocolate from microwave and stir in remaining 2 ounces chocolate until smooth. Holding macaroon by pointed top, dip bottom ½ inch up sides in chocolate, scrape off excess, and place macaroon on prepared baking sheet. Repeat with remaining macaroons. Refrigerate until chocolate sets, about 15 minutes, before serving.

ALMOND MACAROONS

Makes 24 cookies | 2 rimmed baking sheets

WHY THIS RECIPE WORKS Almond macaroons, commonly found in European-style bakeries, are flourless (and thus gluten-free) so they rely on egg whites for both structure and leavening. To start, we finely ground slivered almonds and sugar in a food processor. Then we added the egg whites and a little almond extract and processed the ingredients until the mixture formed a stiff but cohesive dough. To form macaroons into their traditional round shape, some recipes call for a pastry bag, but we simply rolled the dough into balls. We baked the macaroons at a relatively low temperature for cookies that were crunchy-chewy on the outside but still moist and soft on the inside. Be sure to line your baking sheets with parchment paper; the cookies will stick to unlined baking sheets and spread on greased ones.

3 cups (12 ounces) slivered almonds
1½ cups (10½ ounces) sugar
3 large egg whites
1 teaspoon almond extract

1. Adjust oven racks to upper-middle and lower-middle positions and heat oven to 325 degrees. Line 2 rimmed baking sheets with parchment paper.

2. Process almonds in food processor until finely ground, about 1 minute. Add sugar and process for 15 seconds longer. Add egg whites and almond extract and process just until paste forms. Scrape down bowl and continue to process until stiff but cohesive, malleable paste (similar in consistency to marzipan or pasta dough) forms, about 5 seconds longer. If mixture is crumbly or dry, add water by drops and process until proper consistency is reached.

3. Working with 2 tablespoons dough at a time, roll into balls and space them 1½ inches apart on prepared sheets. Bake until golden brown, 20 to 25 minutes, switching and rotating sheets halfway through baking. Transfer macaroons, still on parchment, to wire racks and let cool completely before serving.

Fudgy Almond Macaroons

These macaroons are done when they have cracked lightly across the top.

Decrease almonds to 1½ cups and add 1 cup Dutch-processed cocoa and ¼ teaspoon salt with sugar in step 2.

Lemon Almond Macaroons

Add 2 tablespoons grated lemon zest with sugar in step 2 and process 10 seconds longer.

Pine Nut–Crusted Almond Macaroons

Lightly beat 3 egg whites in small bowl. Spread 3 cups pine nuts in shallow dish. Dip each dough ball into beaten egg white, then roll in pine nuts, pressing lightly with your fingertips, before placing on prepared baking sheets. Flatten dough balls slightly with your fingers, making 1-inch-wide buttons.

WAFER COOKIES

Create thin, spreadable batter
Bake until golden brown
Handle baked cookies with care

WAFER COOKIES CAN BE AS SIMPLE AS GRAHAM CRACKERS or as fancy as lacy confections drizzled with chocolate. They are intended to be thin, light, and crisp so you'll notice that eggs—which help provide structure to baked goods—are absent from most of these cookies. The amount of flour plays an important role, as less flour creates a looser batter which is much easier to spread thin, while more flour is needed for doughs that are meant to be rolled out. Underbaking is not the goal here; you'll want to bake these delicate cookies until golden brown, which enhances both flavor and crispness. Some of the more intricate styles of wafer cookies are dipped in or drizzled with chocolate. For a chocolate coating that has an attractive sheen worthy of these elegant cookies, we use our foolproof method for tempering (typically a painstaking and finicky process of melting and cooling the chocolate to the optimal temperature range).

Parchment paper or a reusable baking mat is essential to prevent sticking with cookies this thin. Another invaluable tool? A small offset spatula. Often thought of as a cake-decorating tool, this small spatula features a blunt-edged, offset metal blade that can be used at various stages of the cookie-making process to create professional-looking cookies. It's perfect for spreading a thin batter into an even layer or for sliding under sticky dough or delicate cookies.

LACE COOKIES

Makes about 72 cookies | 2 rimmed baking sheets

WHY THIS RECIPE WORKS Made from a dropped batter that spreads and separates as it bakes into lacy, brittle, gossamer-thin wafers, lace cookies crunch when you bite into them and immediately melt in your mouth with the rich taste of butter and brown sugar. We eliminated eggs or any leavener from our recipe because they puffed the cookies. Humidity is the archenemy of lace cookies, so try to make them on a dry day. Otherwise, they will be chewy. If you have one, use a nonstick baking sheet liner. After cooling the cookies for 1 to 2 minutes, you can choose to shape them rather than keep them flat. To make a cigarette shape, place the cookie against the handle of a wooden spoon and roll the cookie over itself as quickly as possible. To form a tuile, lay the cookie over a rolling pin or a wine bottle set on its side so that the cookie forms a gentle curve. To form a cone, hold both sides of the cookie, wrap one side over the other, and overlap about an inch or so. To form a bowl (which you can fill with mousse or ice cream), lay the cookie over the bottom of a small bowl turned upside down and gently mold the cookie to follow the contour of the bowl.

- ¾ cup packed (5¼ ounces) dark brown sugar
- 8 tablespoons unsalted butter
- ½ cup light corn syrup
- 1 cup pecans or almonds, chopped fine
- 6 tablespoons (1¾ ounces) all-purpose flour
- 1 tablespoon heavy cream
- 1 teaspoon vanilla extract
- ¼ teaspoon table salt

1. Adjust oven rack to middle position and heat oven to 350 degrees. Line 2 rimmed baking sheets with parchment paper. Bring sugar, butter, and corn syrup just to boil in medium saucepan over medium heat, 5 to 6 minutes, stirring frequently. Off heat, mix in pecans, flour, cream, vanilla, and salt until smooth.

2. Drop 6 rounded teaspoons of batter 3 inches apart on each prepared sheet. Bake, 1 sheet at a time, until cookies spread thin and turn deep golden brown and bubbling has subsided, 6 to 7 minutes, rotating sheet halfway through baking. Let cookies cool and firm up slightly on sheet for 1 to 2 minutes, then transfer to wire rack. Let cool completely or shape as desired. Repeat with remaining batter. Serve.

Orange-Oatmeal Lace Cookies

Substitute 1 cup quick oats for pecans and add 1 tablespoon finely grated orange zest with vanilla.

Spiced Walnut Lace Cookies

Substitute 1 cup finely chopped walnuts for pecans and add ½ teaspoon each ground nutmeg and ground cinnamon and ¼ teaspoon each ground allspice, ground cloves, and ground ginger with vanilla.

Florentine Lace Cookies

FLORENTINE LACE COOKIES

Makes 24 cookies | 2 rimmed baking sheets

WHY THIS RECIPE WORKS By making a few tweaks to recipes that the pros use, we were able to create a streamlined recipe for these wafer-thin citrus-flavored almond cookies. Our main challenge was making the batter thin enough. Processing the almonds until they were coarsely ground gave the cookies a flatter profile, and upping the cream encouraged spread. For crispness and a delicate filigreed appearance, we used less flour so our cookies spread even thinner and we baked the cookies until they were deep golden brown from edge to edge. It's important to cook the cream mixture until it's thick and starting to brown at the edges; undercooked dough will be too runny to portion. Don't be concerned if some butter separates from the dough. For the most uniform cookies, make sure that your parchment paper lies flat.

- 2 cups slivered almonds
- ¾ cup heavy cream
- 4 tablespoons unsalted butter, cut into 4 pieces
- ½ cup (3½ ounces) sugar
- ¼ cup orange marmalade
- 3 tablespoons all-purpose flour
- 1 teaspoon vanilla extract
- ¼ teaspoon grated orange zest
- ¼ teaspoon table salt
- 4 ounces bittersweet chocolate, chopped fine

1. Adjust oven racks to upper-middle and lower-middle positions and heat oven to 350 degrees. Line 2 rimmed baking sheets with parchment paper. Process almonds in food processor until they resemble coarse sand, about 30 seconds.

2. Bring cream, butter, and sugar to boil in medium saucepan over medium-high heat. Cook, stirring frequently, until mixture begins to thicken, 5 to 6 minutes. Continue to cook, stirring constantly, until mixture begins to brown at edges and is thick enough to leave trail that doesn't immediately fill in when spatula is scraped along pan bottom, 1 to 2 minutes longer (it's OK if some darker speckles appear in mixture). Remove pan from heat and stir in almonds, marmalade, flour, vanilla, orange zest, and salt until combined.

3. Drop six 1-tablespoon portions of dough onto each prepared sheet, spaced at least 3½ inches apart. When cool enough to handle, use your dampened fingers to press each portion into 2½-inch circle.

4. Bake cookies until deep brown from edge to edge, 15 to 17 minutes, switching and rotating sheets halfway through baking. Transfer cookies, still on parchment, to wire racks. Repeat with remaining dough. Let cookies cool completely.

5. Microwave 3 ounces chocolate in bowl at 50 percent power, stirring frequently, until about two-thirds melted, 1 to 2 minutes. Remove bowl from microwave, add remaining 1 ounce chocolate, and stir until melted, returning to microwave for no more than 5 seconds at a time to complete melting if necessary. Transfer chocolate to small zipper-lock bag and snip off corner, making hole no larger than ¹⁄₁₆ inch.

6. Pipe zigzag of chocolate over each cookie on wire racks, distributing chocolate evenly among all cookies. Refrigerate until chocolate is set, about 30 minutes, before serving. (Cookies can be stored at cool room temperature for up to 4 days.)

TUILE CIGARS

Makes 28 cookies | 2 rimmed baking sheets

WHY THIS RECIPE WORKS Also called pirouettes, these delicate, lightly sweet cookies get their name from their rolled-up shape. We started by spreading small portions of the batter onto baking sheets; once they were baked, we quickly lifted an edge of the warm cookies with a metal spatula and used our fingers to roll them into a tight cigar. The rolling might take some practice at first, but the cookies

can be returned to the oven to resoften if needed. A dip in melted chocolate and finely chopped nuts gives the cigars party appeal. While we typically prefer to line our baking sheets with parchment paper, we found that the DeMarle Silpat Silicone Baking Mat worked best here, since it doesn't move when you spread the batter and it created a smoother bottom on the cookies. If you can't find a baking mat, lightly greased parchment secured to the baking sheets with vegetable oil spray will work.

¾ cup (3¾ ounces) all-purpose flour
1 tablespoon cornstarch
¼ teaspoon table salt
4 tablespoons unsalted butter, softened
½ cup (3½ ounces) sugar
3 large egg whites, room temperature
½ teaspoon vanilla extract
6 ounces milk, semisweet, or bittersweet chocolate, chopped (optional)
½ cup nuts, toasted and chopped fine (optional)

1. Adjust oven rack to middle position and heat oven to 350 degrees. Line 2 rimmed baking sheets with reusable baking mats. (Alternatively, lightly spray 2 baking sheets with vegetable oil spray, line with parchment paper, and lightly spray again.) Whisk flour, cornstarch, and salt together in small bowl.

2. Using stand mixer fitted with paddle, beat butter and sugar on medium-high speed until pale and fluffy, about 2 minutes. With mixer running, slowly add egg whites and vanilla and mix until well incorporated, scraping down bowl as needed. Reduce speed to low, add flour mixture, and mix until just combined.

3. Drop 2-teaspoon portions of batter onto prepared sheets, spaced at least 6 inches apart. Using small offset spatula, spread each into 5-inch circle of even thickness. Bake, 1 sheet at a time, until edges are golden brown, 5 to 7 minutes.

4. Working quickly, lift edge of each cookie with metal spatula and roll tightly into cigar shape; place seam side down on wire rack. If cookies become too stiff to roll, return to oven for 30 seconds to soften. Repeat with remaining batter. Let cookies cool completely.

5. Microwave chocolate, if using, at 50 percent power, stirring occasionally, until melted, 1 to 2 minutes. Dip about one-quarter of each cookie into chocolate, wiping away excess. Sprinkle evenly with nuts, if using; transfer to parchment-lined baking sheet; and let chocolate set, about 30 minutes, before serving.

TUTORIAL
Tuile Cigars
Learn how to shape such a delicate cookie into a sleek cylinder.

1. Drop 2-teaspoon portions of batter onto prepared sheets, spacing them at least 6 inches apart.

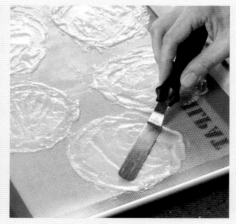

2. Using small offset spatula, spread each portion of batter into 5-inch circle of even thickness.

3. Bake, 1 sheet at a time, until edges are golden brown, 5 to 7 minutes. Working quickly, lift edge of each cookie with metal spatula.

4. Roll cookies tightly into cigar shape.

5. Place cigars seam side down on wire rack and let cool completely.

6. Dip about one-quarter of each cookie into melted chocolate, wiping away excess.

Graham Crackers

GRAHAM CRACKERS

Makes 48 crackers | 2 rimmed baking sheets

WHY THIS RECIPE WORKS Homemade graham crackers boast a warmer, rounder wheaty graham flavor and heartier texture than store-bought versions. Our first step was to use twice as much coarse whole-wheat graham flour as white flour. A combination of molasses and granulated sugar contributed caramel flavor and crispness. For flat crackers with an open, striated crumb, we mixed the dough like pie dough, pulsing chilled butter into the flour. Remove the crackers from the oven when they are golden and firm around the edges so they are crisp but not dried out. Graham flour is sold at well-stocked supermarkets and health food stores. Labeling may vary: Both Bob's Red Mill Whole Wheat Graham Flour and Arrowhead Mills Stone-Ground Whole Wheat Flour work well.

1½ cups (8¼ ounces) graham flour
¾ cup (3¾ ounces) all-purpose flour
½ cup (3½ ounces) sugar
1 teaspoon baking powder
1 teaspoon baking soda
½ teaspoon table salt
¼ teaspoon ground cinnamon
8 tablespoons unsalted butter, cut into ½-inch pieces and chilled
5 tablespoons water
2 tablespoons molasses
1 teaspoon vanilla extract

1. Adjust oven racks to upper-middle and lower-middle positions and heat oven to 375 degrees. Process graham flour, all-purpose flour, sugar, baking powder, baking soda, salt, and cinnamon in food processor until combined, about 3 seconds. Add butter and process until mixture resembles coarse cornmeal, about 15 seconds. Add water, molasses, and vanilla and process until dough comes together, about 20 seconds.

2. Transfer dough to counter and divide into 4 equal pieces. Working with 1 piece of dough at a time (keep remaining pieces covered with plastic wrap), roll into 11 by 8-inch rectangle, ⅛ inch thick, between 2 large sheets of parchment paper. Remove top piece of parchment and trim dough into tidy 10 by 7½-inch rectangle with knife, then score into twelve 2½-inch squares. Prick each square several times with fork.

3. Slide 2 pieces of rolled-out and scored dough, still on parchment, onto separate rimmed baking sheets. Bake until golden brown and edges are firm, about 15 minutes, switching and rotating sheets halfway through baking. Slide baked crackers, still on parchment, onto wire rack. Repeat with remaining 2 pieces of rolled-out dough. Let crackers cool completely. Transfer cooled crackers, still on parchment, to cutting board and carefully cut apart along scored lines. Serve. (Graham crackers can be stored at room temperature for up to 2 weeks.)

FAIRY GINGERBREAD

Makes 60 cookies | 2 rimless baking sheets

WHY THIS RECIPE WORKS With no eggs, no leavener, and batter spread paper-thin on a rimless baking sheet, fairy gingerbread is unlike ordinary gingerbread. The cookies we tried melted in our mouths—but they were also bland. For bolder flavor, we not only increased the ground ginger called for in most recipes but we also toasted it. Fresh grated ginger added another layer of spice. While these old-fashioned cookies traditionally lack leavener, a little baking soda helped them retain their airy crispness after baking. Use baking sheets that measure at least 15 by 12 inches. Don't be disconcerted by the scant amount of batter: You really are going to spread the batter very thin. Use the edges of the parchment paper as your guide, covering the entire surface thinly and evenly. For easier grating, freeze a 2-inch piece of peeled ginger for 30 minutes and then use a rasp-style grater.

1½ teaspoons ground ginger
¾ cup plus 2 tablespoons (4⅜ ounces) all-purpose flour
½ teaspoon baking soda
¼ teaspoon table salt
5 tablespoons unsalted butter, softened
9 tablespoons packed (4 ounces) light brown sugar
4 teaspoons grated fresh ginger
¾ teaspoon vanilla extract
¼ cup whole milk, room temperature

1. Adjust oven racks to upper-middle and lower-middle positions and heat oven to 325 degrees. Spray 2 rimless baking sheets (or inverted rimmed baking sheets) with vegetable oil spray and cover each with 15 by 12-inch sheet parchment paper. Heat ground ginger in small skillet over medium heat until fragrant, about 1 minute. Combine flour, baking soda, salt, and toasted ginger in medium bowl.

2. Using stand mixer fitted with paddle, beat butter and sugar on medium-high speed until light and fluffy, about 2 minutes. Add fresh ginger and vanilla and mix until incorporated. Reduce speed to low and add flour mixture in 3 additions, alternating with milk in 2 additions; scrape down bowl as needed.

3. Evenly spread ¾ cup batter to cover parchment on each prepared sheet (batter will be very thin). Bake until deep golden brown, 16 to 20 minutes, switching and rotating sheets halfway through baking. Immediately score cookies into 3 by 2-inch rectangles. Let cool completely, about 20 minutes. Using tip of paring knife, separate cookies along score marks and serve.

fruit desserts

THE WORLD OF FRUIT-CENTRIC DESSERTS includes an array of seemingly humble recipes that make the fruit the star. They can be as pure as roasted fruit glazed with a sweet syrup or topped with a rich sauce. Often, the dessert is a baked affair: Sweetened fruit or fruit filling is paired with a buttery crisp or biscuit topping. Many fruit desserts are beloved American classics, such as homey, comforting apple crisp and summery strawberry shortcake. Others, such as sonker, Texas-style cobbler, and bananas Foster, have a specific regional connection.

Fruit appears in pies, tarts, and cakes in this book but this section is of simple, unarguably fruit-centric desserts. And as with many simple desserts, success depends on both technique and the best ingredients. Fruit quality is paramount. Proper storage and handling are also important because many fruits are delicate and highly perishable; don't let them become soft and spoil before you have a chance to use them! This sounds obvious, but when it comes to fresh fruit, buying at the height of its growing season—and buying locally grown varieties whenever possible—will make a huge difference in the quality of your fruit dessert. Sure, you can buy blueberries or raspberries year-round, but they are not as good as those you will find in your market in the summer months. The rock-hard peaches you can find in the supermarket in April will likely be mealy and may or may not ripen after you bring them home; they are absolutely no match for the fresh and fragrant summer peaches you can buy in July. If you want to make a peach cobbler before peach season, it is probably better to use a recipe designed to work with frozen peaches.

Fruit Dessert Equipment Corner

There is little specialty equipment needed to make simple fruit desserts, but there are a few things that will make your job easier since prepping the fruit will demand the bulk of your time.

Food Processor

A food processor makes quick work of making dough for shortcake or cobbler biscuits and toppings for crisps and crumbles. Trust us: It's a great investment for your kitchen. You'll use it for countless other recipes—desserts through-out this book and savory items too. Look for a bowl that has a capacity of at least 11 cups. With a powerful motor, responsive pulsing action, sharp blades, and a simple design, the **Cuisinart Custom 14 Cup Food Processor** ($169) aced our tests.

Baking Dish

This versatile dish is ideal for crisps and cobblers, with plenty of space to contain a bubbling fruit filling and topping. Look for Pyrex. It's sturdy and dishwasher-safe, and the thick tempered glass retains plenty of heat to ensure deep, even browning. Also, because it's glass, it is naturally scratch-resistant, which means you can cut and serve straight from the pan. You'll frequently use a 13 x 9-inch pan. (Note that Pyrex is not broiler-safe; if a recipe requires use of the broiler, we recommend Mrs. Anderson's Baking Lasagna Pan with Handle ($36.96.)

Skillet

A good skillet is essential for the preparation of a wide variety of desserts, from pan-roasted pears and baked apples to fruit crisps and bananas Foster. Because many recipes start on the stovetop and then move to the oven to finish, you'll want a skillet that is ovensafe. Our favorite traditional skillet is the **All-Clad D3 Stainless Steel 12″ Fry Pan with Lid** ($119.95).

Pastry Brush

We use a pastry brush to paint shortcake biscuits with an egg wash before baking, to brush fruit with oil before grilling, and to evenly coat peaches with a honey glaze. With a thick head of uniformly sized bristles, the **Winco Flat Pastry and Basting Brush, 1½ Inch** ($6.93) picks up plenty of liquid and is agile.

Apple Corer

With the right tool you can peel, core, and slice an apple in one fell swoop. We love **VKP Brands Johnny Apple Peeler, Suction Base, Stainless Steel Blades, Red** ($23.38). This sturdy, classic cast-iron device let us quickly prep apples, whether they were perfectly round or lopsided, small or oversize. It took just about 15 seconds to put an apple on the prongs; peel, core, and slice it; and discard the core.

Cherry Pitter

You can pit cherries by hand, but a cherry pitter can save lots of time. The **Leifheit Cherry Pitter "Cherry-mat"** ($29.99) is incredibly fast and effective. Its small dowel creates relatively petite holes, too, leaving more cherry.

Fruit Peeler

The tiny serrations of a fruit peeler lift away tomato and peach skins without damaging the delicate flesh. If you hate to blanch and shock these fruits in order to peel them by hand, a good peeler with a razor-sharp blade is worth the investment. Our favorite is the **Messermeister Serrated Swivel Peeler** ($5.50).

OUR CONTROVERSIAL GLOSSARY OF FRUIT DESSERTS

The next best thing to the taste of a crumble, grunt, or sonker is its quirky (and argued-over) moniker. Each of these desserts is composed of fruit and a sweetened topping, the latter of which can be anything from a pastry or biscuit dough to a pancake-like batter to a streusel—and the definitions often vary by region. Here's a handful of our favorites and their defining characteristics.

Betty	Sweetened fruit baked with layers of bread crumbs and butter
Buckle	Thick cake batter poured over fruit
Cobbler*	Biscuit dough dolloped over fruit to resemble cobblestones
Crisp/Crumble	Fruit baked under a crunchy, streusel-like topping. Crisps often contain oats; crumbles are often oat-free
Slump/Grunt	Fruit cooked beneath dollops of soft dumpling dough that "slump" under heat
Pandowdy	Pie dough or bread that is pressed into fruit as it bakes
Sonker	Syrupy cooked fruit baked under a pancake batter

* "Cobbler" is perhaps the most controversial name. In some corners of the United States, a cobbler can be a double-crust rectangular pie. In others, it's a buckle.

RIPENING FRUIT

Fruits fall into two categories: climacteric fruits (such as apples, apricots, bananas, blueberries, cantaloupes, figs, kiwis, mangos, nectarines, papayas, peaches, pears, and plums), which can ripen off the parent plant, and nonclimacteric fruits (including cherries, pineapples, citrus fruits, grapes, raspberries, and strawberries), which cannot. The difference lies in their responses to ethylene gas, which occurs naturally in plants. For climacteric fruits, once the amount of ethylene reaches a certain threshold, there is accelerated use of oxygen and release of carbon dioxide and enzymatic actions that lead to softening and the conversion of starches into sugar. Storing unripe climacteric fruits in a paper bag with a ripe fruit can help speed ripening because the bag traps some ethylene, concentrating

it in the air around the fruit. Nonclimacteric fruits produce very little ethylene after they are harvested and they usually don't convert their starches to sugars, so they should be ripe when you purchase them.

WASHING FRUIT

There's no need to buy a fruit and vegetable wash to clean your fruit. A spray bottle filled with 3 parts water and 1 part distilled white vinegar works just as well to clean smooth-surfaced produce such as apples and pears: Just spray and rinse. In our tests, this method removed 98 percent of surface bacteria. For delicate fruits like berries, fill a bowl with 3 parts water and 1 part vinegar and add the fruit. Drain, rinse with tap water, and pat dry with paper towels. You can also spin berries dry in a paper towel–lined salad spinner. It is good practice to wash produce that has inedible rinds and peels, such as melons, because cutting into a contaminated peel can drag pathogens inside.

COMMON DESSERT FRUITS

When the star of a recipe is the fruit, it pays to use the right variety and to take care when buying and preparing it. We don't cover every fruit in this section, but we've highlighted the ones we use most often when making fruit desserts.

BERRIES

Fresh berries of any kind require special handling to preserve their delicate texture and flavor. It is best to take them out of the containers in which they were purchased, especially if they've been packed in the cardboard containers found at most farm stands. Don't wash berries until you are going to use them.

Blueberries

There are two types of fresh blueberries: tiny field-grown berries such as the wild Maine blueberries available for a few weeks in the summer, and the larger berries you'll see year-round.

Frozen blueberries, which are picked when fully ripe and immediately individually quick-frozen, make a good stand-in for fresh in many recipes, and they cost far less than fresh. In fact, a blueberry dessert made out of season will taste better (and be much cheaper) if you use frozen berries. That said, be sure to use a recipe that has been tested using frozen blueberries and that includes instructions on how they should be handled.

Raspberries

Look for berries that are bright red, plump, and juicy and free of signs of mold. Inspect the packaging for dark stains, which indicate that some of the berries have been crushed.

Raspberries are usually sold in small, flat containers that keep the berries separate, but if you are buying them in a larger container at a farm stand, lay them out on a plate lined with paper towels for storage in the refrigerator. They are delicate and highly perishable, so you should use them soon after you buy them.

Strawberries

Look for strawberries that have a bright sheen and that are fragrant, red through to the center, and firm. Larger strawberries are less flavorful and sometimes hollow in the middle, so look for medium strawberries. If buying packaged berries, inspect the packaging to be sure that the berries are free of mold and that those on the bottom are not crushed.

Strawberries will not continue to ripen after you bring them home, so don't buy them if they are yellow around the stem.

Frozen strawberries (usually individually quick-frozen) are widely available. In our testing we found that brand does make a difference and that some had off-flavors. Our favorite brand is Cascadian Farm Frozen Premium Organic Strawberries.

APPLES

Choosing the best apple varieties for fruit desserts is the key to success. Typically, a combination of tart and sweet varieties works best. Apart from flavor differences, some turn mushy in the oven while others hold their shape. In general, more acidic, or tart, apples—Cortland, Empire, Granny Smith—hold their shape. Sweet varieties such as Golden Delicious, Braeburn, and Jonagold will soften more than tart ones but still retain their shape. McIntosh apples, although tart and great eaten fresh, fall apart and become very watery when baked. Since apples are not prone to chilling injury, they can be stored anywhere in the fridge.

Hulling Strawberries

Here are two methods we use for hulling strawberries depending on what tools we have on hand.

A. Use serrated tip of grapefruit spoon to cut around leafy stem and remove white core and stem.

B. Alternatively, push plastic straw through bottom of berry and up through leafy steam end to remove core as well as leafy top.

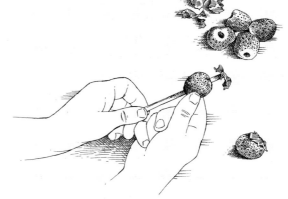

Washing Berries

1. Place berries in large bowl of clean water and bob them about gently with your hands.

2. Line salad spinner with layers of paper towels and carefully disperse berries. Spin gently until berries are dry, about 20 seconds.

Preventing Apple Blowouts

While developing our recipe for Baked Apples (page 134), we couldn't ignore a persistent problem: apples that "blew out" and collapsed in the oven. To find out if removing the skin would solve the issue, we prepared batches of baked Granny Smith apples with both the skin on and the skin off. To our surprise, all the skin-off apples held their shape, without a single blowout. Within the skin-on batch, half of the apples collapsed. In nature, the peel protects an apple; in the oven, it traps moisture that's been transformed into steam. As the steam attempts to escape, its outward pressure ruptures cells and eventually bursts through the apple's skin, causing blowouts. Removing all the skin allows the steam to escape without damaging the fruit's structure. We peel off apple skin for most recipes.

PEARS

Pears will continue to ripen after they have been harvested —in fact they ripen best off the tree. Ripening on the branch causes them to develop deposits of lignin and cellulose called "stone cells" that make the flesh gritty. Purchase firm pears and let them ripen at room temperature for a few days to ensure the best quality. Pears ripen from the inside out, so checking at the neck—the fruit's narrowest point—will give the earliest indication that the pear has started to ripen. Ripening can be accelerated by putting them in a paper bag with a banana. But check them frequently; they go from just right to mush in a matter of hours. Here are common varieties.

Anjou

With their light yellow-green hue, Anjou pears are creamy, tender, and incredibly juicy when ripe. They can be eaten out of hand and are also great for roasting, as the hot oven concentrates their mild flavor.

Bartlett

Often a darker green when underripe, these pears turn a beautiful greenish-yellow when ready to eat. Their sweet, flowery flavor becomes more powerful when they are roasted or baked.

Coring Apples

With a Corer

1. Cut small slice from top and bottom of apple.

2. Holding apple steady on bottom side, push corer through, then cut apple according to recipe. (This is even easier with our winning device; see page 120.)

Without a Corer

Cut sides of apple squarely away from core, then cut each piece of apple according to recipe.

Coring Pears

1. Using melon baller, cut around central core of halved peeled pear with circular motion and remove core.

2. Draw melon baller from central core to top of pear, removing interior stem.

3. Remove blossom end.

Bosc

Easily recognized for their dull, brownish skin, Bosc pears stay sweet and complex once cooked. Bosc pears develop sweetness earlier in the ripening process than other pears, so firm, slightly underripe ones already have plenty of flavor. They're also firmer when ripe, so they hold their shape better than other varieties.

STONE FRUIT

Peaches, nectarines, and plums are generally classified as clingstone, freestone, or semifreestone, terms that refer to how firmly the pit attaches to the flesh of the fruit. Freestone fruits are easier to deal with and when it comes to peaches, nectarines, and apricots, they're common at the grocery store. Common plum varieties are red, black, and Italian prune plums. Peaches and nectarines come in yellow and white; yellow peaches and nectarines are more acidic but tend to mellow as they soften, while white are prized for their very sweet taste. We like yellow specimens better for desserts. Yellow fruit's sturdier flesh holds up to baking; white fruit can taste overly sweet.

Store stone fruits at room temperature unless they are fully ripe and you are trying to extend their shelf life—refrigerating stone fruits can make them mealy.

CHERRIES

Ruby-hued sour cherries are a favorite choice for pies and cobblers because their soft, juicy flesh and bright, classic cherry flavor hold up in the oven, but they're rarely available in supermarkets. Because the season for fresh sour cherries is so fleeting, we often turn to sour Morello cherries in a jar, which have a deep ruby-red color, tart flavor, and plump and meaty texture. Bing (or Rainier) sweet cherries are more available in the supermarket; their sweet, dense flesh can be a challenge when baking but we work around it. Buy cherries with firm, plump, unwrinkled, and unblemished flesh. Store them in the refrigerator in a zipper-lock bag, and do not wash them until you are ready to use them.

Peeling Peaches

When peaches are baked in a dessert, their delicate skin can easily turn leathery in the oven. Here's how we remove the skin in the test kitchen.

1. Using paring knife, score small X at base of each peach.

2. Lower peaches into boiling water with slotted skimmer. Cover and blanch until skins loosen, about 2 minutes.

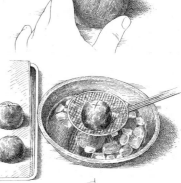

3. Using slotted skimmer, remove peaches to ice water and let stand to stop cooking, about 1 minute.

4. Use paring knife to remove strips of loosened peel, starting at X on base of each peach.

Pitting Cherries Without a Pitter

Cherry pitters make pitting cherries quick and simple. But since not everyone owns such a tool, we looked for an alternative.

Our favorite method involves an empty wine bottle and a drinking straw. Simply sit the cherry on the open top of the bottle and use the straw to push the pit through. The bottle will catch the pits and juices, making cleanup easy as pie.

PINEAPPLES

We prefer Costa Rican–grown pineapples, also labeled "extra-sweet" or "gold." They are consistently honey-sweet in comparison with acidic Hawaiian pineapples, which have greenish (not yellow) skin. Pineapple will not become sweeter once picked, so purchase golden, fragrant fruit that gives slightly when pressed. You can also tell if a pineapple is ripe by tugging at a leaf in the center of the fruit. If the leaf releases with little effort, the pineapple is ripe. Avoid pineapple with dried-out leaves and a fermented aroma, as these indicate that the fruit is overripe. Unpeeled pineapple should be stored at room temperature.

MANGOS

Native to Southeast Asia, mangos have sweet, floral, and silky-smooth flesh that clings to a large, flat pit. Mangos are very fragrant when ripe and should yield to gentle pressure. Store mangos on the counter; they will ripen at room temperature.

Cutting Up a Pineapple

1. Trim off bottom and top of pineapple so it sits flat on counter.

2. Rest pineapple on trimmed bottom and cut off skin in thin strips from top to bottom, using sharp paring, chef's, or serrated knife.

3. Quarter pineapple lengthwise, then cut tough core from each quarter. Slice pineapple according to recipe.

Cutting Up a Mango

1. Cut thin slice from 1 end of mango so it sits flat on counter.

2. Resting mango on trimmed end, cut off skin in thin strips from top to bottom.

3. Cut down along each side of flat pit to remove flesh.

4. Trim around pit to remove any remaining flesh. Chop or slice according to recipe.

SIMPLY FRUIT

KEY POINTS

Simmer firm fruit

Pour hot syrup over delicate fruit

IN-SEASON FRUIT CAN BE AN ELEGANT DESSERT. It's delicious baked with toppings (see page 140) or into a pie. But fruit doesn't need to be baked at all to be beautiful. There are simple presentations—poaching, roasting—that really put an emphasis on the specimens themselves. Poaching gently cooks fruit in liquid and allows the fruit to retain its shape and texture and infuses it with flavor. The result is a tender, intact piece of fruit draped in a glossy coating of sauce. When poaching firmer fruit, like pears, it's usually necessary to simmer the fruit in the poaching liquid before allowing it to cool in a reduced, syrupy version of the liquid. This slow cooking and cooling permits the fruit (ripe but firm) to soften gently and absorb maximum flavor from the syrup. For more delicate fruit, you can simply make the syrup first and then pour the hot syrup over the fruit so it doesn't turn to mush. Poaching liquid can be infused with a variety of flavorings.

When fruit is roasted, something magical is achieved. Without a crust or a crumble to shield the fruit from the heat of the oven, its exterior caramelizes into a rich, nutty foil to the subtly sweet interior. (Caramelization describes the chemical reactions that take place when any sugar is heated to the point that its molecules begin to break apart and generate hundreds of new flavor, color, and aroma compounds.) Ripe but still firm fruit is ideal—rock-hard fruit will never fully soften or release much juice. A two-stage cooking process, often from stovetop browning to cooking through in the oven, yields tender, beautifully caramelized fruit. The juices left in the pan make the ideal base for a glossy sauce or glaze.

These are simply fruit desserts; plate them with simple vanilla ice cream, yogurt, whipped cream, or tangy crème fraîche.

WHITE WINE–POACHED PEARS WITH LEMON AND HERBS

Serves 6 to 8 | large saucepan

WHY THIS RECIPE WORKS This French classic features just-ripe pears poached gently in wine and then chilled; the result is meltingly tender shapely fruit infused with flavor. Bartlett and Bosc pears, with their honeyed sweetness and clean curves, were ideal. Poaching the fruit in white wine resulted in a nuanced flavor that tasters loved, especially when we enhanced it with some lemon, mint, and thyme. After poaching the pear halves, we removed them from the pot and reduced the liquid to a syrupy consistency before pouring it back over the fruit. Letting the pears cool in the syrup prevented them from drying out and allowed them to absorb some of the syrup, giving them a candied translucency and making them plump, sweet, and pleasantly spiced. Select pears that yield slightly when pressed. Use a medium-bodied dry white wine such as Sauvignon Blanc or Chardonnay here.

- 1 vanilla bean
- 1 (750-ml) bottle dry white wine
- ¾ cup (5¼ ounces) sugar
- 6 (2-inch) strips lemon zest
- 5 sprigs fresh mint
- 3 sprigs fresh thyme
- ½ cinnamon stick
- ⅛ teaspoon table salt
- 6 ripe but firm Bosc or Bartlett pears (8 ounces each), peeled, halved, and cored

1. Cut vanilla bean in half lengthwise. Using tip of paring knife, scrape out seeds. Bring wine, sugar, lemon zest, mint sprigs, thyme sprigs, cinnamon stick, salt, and vanilla seeds and pod to boil in large saucepan over high heat and cook, stirring occasionally, until sugar has dissolved, about 5 minutes.

2. Add pears and return to boil. Reduce heat to medium-low, cover, and simmer until pears are tender and toothpick slips easily in and out of pears, 10 to 20 minutes, gently turning pears over every 5 minutes.

3. Using slotted spoon, transfer pears to shallow casserole dish. Bring syrup to simmer over medium heat and cook, stirring occasionally, until slightly thickened and measures 1¼ to 1½ cups, about 15 minutes. Strain syrup through fine-mesh strainer over pears; discard solids. Let pears cool to room temperature, then cover and refrigerate until well chilled, at least 2 hours or up to 3 days. Serve.

White Wine-Poached Pears with Lemon and Herbs

Poached Rhubarb with Balsamic, Caraway, and Labneh

Poaching rhubarb, a vegetable that becomes soft fast, benefits from a more careful poaching procedure than other fruits. Try our pseudo sous-vide method.

1. Gently lower bag of rhubarb into water, allowing remaining air bubbles to rise to top of bag.

2. Reopen 1 corner of zipper, release remaining air pockets, and seal bag fully. Clip top corner of bag to side of pot, making sure rhubarb is fully submerged.

3. Cook until rhubarb can be pierced easily with paring knife, 30 to 40 minutes. Carefully transfer bag to ice bath; chill for 10 minutes.

4. Snip off 1 corner of zipper-lock bag to create small hole; drain liquid through hole into 10-inch skillet. Whisk in remaining sugar and vinegar and bring to simmer over medium-high heat.

5. Reduce heat to low and cook, swirling pan occasionally, until mixture is thick and reduced to ⅓ cup, 13 to 15 minutes. Let syrup cool for 20 minutes.

6. Open bag and transfer rhubarb to bowl. Stir 2 teaspoons syrup and caraway seeds into rhubarb. Divide rhubarb evenly among labneh.

POACHED RHUBARB WITH BALSAMIC, CARAWAY, AND LABNEH

Serves 4 to 6 | Dutch oven

WHY THIS RECIPE WORKS Perfectly poached rhubarb should be tender but intact, with just a hint of crispness. But rhubarb is a tricky thing: It's notorious for going from crunchy and raw to blown-out mush in a matter of minutes. While many vegetables are held together by sturdy cellulose, the walls of rhubarb cells are a delicate construction of pectin, which weakens and dissolves when heated, releasing the pressure and turning the stalk to goo. That's fine for pie fillings and jams but not poached fruit. To get our dream texture, we mimicked a sous vide machine on our stovetop, keeping the rhubarb at a steady temperature until it finished slowly cooking through with no blowouts. We flavored the tart rhubarb boldly and paired it with rich, tangy labneh.

RHUBARB

    2   stalks rhubarb, cut into ½-inch pieces
    ½   cup (3½ ounces) plus 3 tablespoons and
        1 teaspoon sugar, divided
    2   tablespoons plus 2 cups water, divided
    ½   ounce lemon zest strips
    6   fresh thyme sprigs
    ¼   teaspoon kosher salt
    3   cups ice
    4   teaspoons balsamic vinegar

LABNEH CREAM

    ½   cup plus 2 tablespoons heavy cream
    3   tablespoons sugar
    ¼   teaspoon kosher salt
    ⅔   cup labneh or full-fat Greek yogurt
    2   teaspoons caraway seeds, toasted
    1   tablespoon fresh basil leaves, torn into ¼-inch pieces

1. FOR THE RHUBARB: Heat 4 quarts water in Dutch oven over medium heat to 145 degrees; cover and turn heat to low.

2. Toss rhubarb, ½ cup sugar, 2 tablespoons water, lemon zest, thyme, and salt in medium bowl to combine. Transfer rhubarb and liquid to 1-quart zipper-lock bag. Press out as much air as possible from bag and seal. Gently lower bag into water, allowing remaining air bubbles to rise to top of bag (do not let go of bag). Reopen 1 corner of zipper, release remaining air pockets, and seal bag fully. Clip top corner of bag to side of pot, making sure rhubarb is fully submerged. Cook until rhubarb can be pierced easily with paring knife, 30 to 40 minutes, adjusting heat as necessary to maintain temperature between 140 and 145 degrees. Meanwhile, combine ice and remaining 2 cups water in large bowl. Using tongs, carefully remove bag from water bath and transfer to ice bath; chill for 10 minutes.

3. Snip off 1 corner of zipper-lock bag to create small hole; drain liquid through hole into 10-inch skillet. Whisk in remaining 3 tablespoons and 1 teaspoon sugar and vinegar and bring to simmer over medium-high heat. Reduce heat to low and cook, swirling pan occasionally, until mixture is thick and reduced to ⅓ cup, 13 to 15 minutes. Transfer syrup to small bowl and let cool at room temperature for 20 minutes. (If syrup is too thick at room temperature to easily drizzle from a spoon, adjust consistency with 1 to 2 teaspoons water.) Meanwhile, open bag and transfer rhubarb to medium bowl; discard lemon zest strips and thyme sprigs. (Rhubarb and syrup can be refrigerated separately in airtight containers for up to 2 days.)

4. FOR THE LABNEH CREAM: Whisk cream, sugar, and salt in large bowl until frothy, about 30 seconds. Whisk in labneh until mixture is smooth and holds its shape, about 1 minute longer.

5. Stir 2 teaspoons syrup and caraway seeds into rhubarb. Divide labneh mixture evenly among bowls and make divot in center with spoon. Divide rhubarb evenly among bowls, dolloping it into divots. Drizzle with extra syrup and sprinkle with basil. Serve.

PEACHES AND CHERRIES POACHED IN SPICED WINE

Serves 6 | small saucepan

WHY THIS RECIPE WORKS Poaching sweet cherries and floral peaches in a red wine syrup allows their beautiful shape and texture to remain intact while improving their tenderness and enhancing their flavor. We found that a 2:1 ratio of wine to sugar resulted in a glossy syrup that nicely coated the fruit. We boiled the syrup to dissolve the sugar and then poured the hot syrup over the fruit, allowing it to cook gently. To infuse the fruit with flavor as it cooled in the wine syrup, we added half a cinnamon stick and a couple of whole cloves to the mix. Select peaches that yield slightly when pressed.

    1   pound ripe but firm peaches, peeled, halved,
        pitted, and sliced ¼ inch thick
    1   pound fresh sweet cherries, pitted and halved
    ½   cinnamon stick
    2   whole cloves
    2   cups dry red wine
    1   cup (7 ounces) sugar

Combine peaches, cherries, cinnamon stick, and cloves in large bowl. Bring red wine and sugar to boil in small saucepan over high heat and cook, stirring occasionally, until sugar has dissolved, about 5 minutes. Pour syrup over fruit, cover, and let cool to room temperature. Discard cinnamon stick and cloves. Serve.

Roasted Pears with Dried Apricots and Pistachios

ROASTED PEARS WITH DRIED APRICOTS AND PISTACHIOS

Serves 4 to 6 | 12-inch ovensafe skillet

WHY THIS RECIPE WORKS Pears are an excellent fruit to roast because their shape and texture hold up well. After peeling and halving the pears, we cooked them in butter on the stovetop to evaporate some of their juices and concentrate their flavor; this also jump-started caramelization. We moved the pears to the oven to turn their flesh tender and brown. We then put the exuded juices to use in a quick pan sauce. We deglazed the pan with dry white wine and added the complementary flavors of dried apricots and cardamom; a little lemon added a nice burst of citrus. Select pears that yield slightly when pressed. We prefer Bosc pears in this recipe, but Comice and Bartlett pears will also work.

2½ tablespoons unsalted butter, divided
4 ripe but firm Bosc pears (6 to 7 ounces each), peeled, halved, and cored
1¼ cups dry white wine
½ cup dried apricots, quartered
⅓ cup (2⅓ ounces) sugar
¼ teaspoon ground cardamom
⅛ teaspoon table salt
1 teaspoon lemon juice
⅓ cup shelled pistachios, toasted and chopped

1. Adjust oven rack to middle position and heat oven to 450 degrees. Melt 1½ tablespoons butter in 12-inch ovensafe skillet over medium-high heat. Place pear halves, cut side down, in skillet. Cook, without moving, until pears are just beginning to brown, 3 to 5 minutes.

2. Transfer skillet to oven and roast for 15 minutes. Flip pears and continue to roast until fork easily pierces fruit, 10 to 15 minutes. Remove skillet from oven (skillet handle will be hot).

3. Transfer pears to serving dish. Being careful of hot skillet handle, return skillet to medium-high heat and add wine, apricots, sugar, cardamom, salt, and remaining 1 tablespoon butter. Bring to vigorous simmer, whisking to scrape up any browned bits. Cook until sauce is reduced and has consistency of maple syrup, 7 to 10 minutes. Off heat, stir in lemon juice. Pour sauce over pears, sprinkle with pistachios, and serve.

Roasted Pears with Golden Raisins and Hazelnuts
Omit cinnamon. Substitute golden raisins for apricots and skinned hazelnuts for pistachios. Stir 1 teaspoon grated fresh ginger into sauce with lemon juice.

ROASTED APPLES WITH DRIED FIGS AND WALNUTS

Serves 4 to 6 | 12-inch ovensafe skillet

WHY THIS RECIPE WORKS Apples are one of the most popular fruits for dessert but they don't require pastry casings or sweet toppings to be good. Roasting transforms apples into a sophisticated dessert. After roasting, we used the juices to build a lush sauce, reducing it with some red wine and stirring in dried figs and sugar for extra texture and sweetness. A sprinkling of toasted walnuts added a little crunch. We recommend Gala apples for this recipe, but Fuji will also work. A low-tannin wine such as Pinot Noir works well.

2½ tablespoons unsalted butter, divided
  4 Gala apples (6 to 7 ounces each), peeled, halved, and cored
1¼ cups red wine
  ½ cup dried Black Mission figs, stemmed and quartered
  ⅓ cup (2⅓ ounces) sugar
  ¾ teaspoon pepper
  ⅛ teaspoon table salt
  1 teaspoon lemon juice
  ⅓ cup walnuts, toasted and chopped

1. Adjust oven rack to middle position and heat oven to 450 degrees. Melt 1½ tablespoons butter in 12-inch ovensafe skillet over medium-high heat. Place apple halves, cut side down, in skillet. Cook, without moving apples, until they are just beginning to brown, 3 to 5 minutes.

2. Transfer skillet to oven and roast for 15 minutes. Flip apples and continue to roast until fork easily pierces fruit, 10 to 15 minutes. Remove skillet from oven (skillet handle will be hot).

3. Transfer apples to serving dish. Being careful of hot skillet handle, return skillet to medium-high heat and add wine, figs, sugar, pepper, salt, and remaining 1 tablespoon butter. Bring to vigorous simmer, whisking to scrape up any browned bits. Cook until sauce is reduced and has consistency of maple syrup, 7 to 10 minutes. Off heat, stir in lemon juice. Pour sauce over apples, sprinkle with walnuts, and serve.

Roasted Apples with Dried Figs and Walnuts

ROASTED APPLES WITH CRANBERRIES AND PECANS

Serves 4 to 6 | 12-inch ovensafe skillet

WHY THIS RECIPE WORKS These roasted apples get the luxe treatment. A finish of cream and brandy creates a caramel-sauce coating with intense richness and apple flavor. We prefer apple brandy but regular brandy also provides a nice flavor.

1½ tablespoons unsalted butter
  4 Gala apples (6 to 7 ounces each), peeled, halved, and cored
  ¾ cup apple cider
  ½ cup dried cranberries
  ½ cup (3½ ounces) sugar
  ½ cup heavy cream
  ¼ cup apple brandy
  ¼ teaspoon table salt
  ⅓ cup pecans, toasted and chopped

1. Adjust oven rack to middle position and heat oven to 450 degrees. Melt butter in 12-inch ovensafe skillet over medium-high heat. Place apple halves, cut side down, in skillet. Cook, without moving apples, until they are just beginning to brown, 3 to 5 minutes.

2. Transfer skillet to oven and roast for 15 minutes. Flip apples and continue to roast until fork easily pierces fruit, 10 to 15 minutes. Remove skillet from oven (skillet handle will be hot).

3. Transfer apples to serving dish. Being careful of hot skillet handle, return skillet to medium-high heat and add cider and cranberries. Bring to vigorous simmer, whisking to scrape up any browned bits. Cook until sauce has reduced by half, 3 to 5 minutes. Using slotted spoon, transfer cranberries to platter with apples.

4. Stir sugar into cider and continue to cook, stirring frequently, until deep golden brown and surface is covered with tiny bubbles, 1 to 2 minutes. Remove pan from heat; carefully pour cream and brandy into caramel mixture and swirl to incorporate (mixture will bubble and steam); let bubbling subside. Return pan to heat and continue to cook until thickened and syrupy, 1 to 2 minutes. Remove from heat and whisk in salt.

5. Pour sauce over apples, sprinkle with pecans, and serve.

ROASTED PLUMS WITH DRIED CHERRIES AND ALMONDS

Serves 4 to 6 | 12-inch ovensafe skillet

WHY THIS RECIPE WORKS Roasted plums develop a richly caramelized exterior and earthy, winey flavor that are incredibly appealing, making them an unexpected and easy dessert. To help the plums retain their shape, we kept the skins on and simply halved and pitted them. When we browned the halves on the stovetop, we banished some moisture. The oven phase roasted them and created deeper browning. Reducing the juices in the pan with white wine created a flavorful sauce. A handful of dried cherries added a burst of tartness and tender chew, while toasted almonds provided a crunchy garnish. This recipe works equally well with red or black plums.

2½ tablespoons unsalted butter, divided
4 ripe but firm plums (4 to 6 ounces each),
    halved and pitted
1¼ cups dry white wine
½ cup dried cherries
⅓ cup (2⅓ ounces) sugar
¼ teaspoon ground cinnamon
⅛ teaspoon table salt
1 teaspoon lemon juice
⅓ cup sliced almonds, toasted

1. Adjust oven rack to middle position and heat oven to 450 degrees. Melt 1½ tablespoons butter in 12-inch ovensafe skillet over medium-high heat. Place plum halves, cut side down, in skillet. Cook, without moving plums, until they are just beginning to brown, about 3 minutes.

2. Transfer skillet to oven and roast for 5 minutes. Flip plums and continue to roast until fork easily pierces fruit, about 5 minutes. Remove skillet from oven (skillet handle will be hot).

3. Transfer plums to serving dish. Being careful of hot skillet handle, return skillet to medium-high heat and add wine, cherries, sugar, cinnamon, salt, and remaining 1 tablespoon butter. Bring to vigorous simmer, whisking to scrape up any browned bits. Cook until sauce is reduced and has consistency of maple syrup, 7 to 10 minutes. Off heat, stir in lemon juice. Pour sauce over plums, sprinkle with almonds, and serve.

RUM-GLAZED ROASTED PINEAPPLE

Serves 8 | 12-inch ovensafe skillet

WHY THIS RECIPE WORKS This roasted dish features the tropical combination of sweet pineapple and a rum glaze. To caramelize the pineapple, we sliced it into broad wedges and started them in butter on the stovetop. Once the wedges were slightly browned on the first side, we moved the skillet to the oven to finish roasting the fruit. We deglazed the pan with rum and then added sugar, vanilla, and a touch of butter for even more richness before reducing it to a syrupy consistency. A little extra rum stirred in at the end reinforced the sauce's flavor. Toasted macadamia nuts offered a crunchy, buttery finish.

2 tablespoons unsalted butter, divided
1 pineapple, peeled, cored, and cut lengthwise into 8 wedges
1 cup plus 2 teaspoons light or dark rum, divided
½ cup packed (3½ ounces) light brown sugar
½ teaspoon vanilla extract
⅛ teaspoon table salt
⅓ cup macadamia nuts, toasted and chopped

1. Adjust oven rack to middle position and heat oven to 450 degrees. Melt 1 tablespoon butter in 12-inch ovensafe skillet over medium heat. Arrange pineapple wedges cut side down in skillet and cook, without moving pineapple, until just beginning to brown, 3 to 5 minutes.

2. Transfer skillet to oven and roast until pineapple is softened, about 12 minutes. Flip pineapple and continue to roast until golden brown on second side and fork slips easily in and out of pineapple, 15 to 20 minutes. Remove skillet from oven (skillet handle will be hot).

3. Transfer pineapple to serving dish. Being careful of hot skillet handle, add 1 cup rum, sugar, vanilla, salt, and remaining 1 tablespoon butter to skillet and let warm through. Bring to simmer over medium-high heat, and cook, stirring often, until sauce is thickened and measures about ½ cup, about 4 minutes. Off heat, stir in remaining 2 teaspoons rum. Drizzle pineapple with sauce, sprinkle with macadamia nuts, and serve.

ROASTED ORANGES IN SPICED SYRUP

Serves 6 | 13 by 9-inch baking dish

WHY THIS RECIPE WORKS Light and fragrant, glazed oranges finish off a large meal nicely. Our method capitalizes on the caramelized flavor of roasted oranges. Slicing the oranges into thick rounds meant exposing more of the fruit to the oven's heat, which allowed the flavor to concentrate. To avoid drying out the fruit during roasting, we arranged the slices in a shallow pool of caramel syrup in a baking dish. Our syrupy sauce—a simple reduction of sugar and water—came together easily on the stovetop, and steeping a cinnamon stick and cloves in it gave the sweet sauce spicy warmth. Adding fresh orange juice to the sauce reinforced the citrus flavor. We roasted the oranges for 20 minutes, just until they were appealingly soft and tender.

7 oranges (6 whole, 1 juiced to yield ½ cup)
¾ cup (5¼ ounces) sugar
½ cup water
2 whole cloves
1 cinnamon stick

1. Adjust oven rack to middle position and heat oven to 450 degrees. Cut away peel and pith from oranges, then slice crosswise into ½-inch-thick rounds. Arrange oranges evenly in 13 by 9-inch baking dish, overlapping rounds as needed.

2. Combine sugar, water, cloves, and cinnamon stick in medium saucepan. Bring to boil over medium-high heat and cook, without stirring, until mixture is amber colored, 8 to 10 minutes. Reduce heat to low and continue to cook, swirling saucepan occasionally, until dark amber, 2 to 5 minutes. (Caramel will register 350 degrees.)

3. Off heat, carefully stir in orange juice (mixture will bubble and steam). Return saucepan to medium heat and cook, stirring frequently, until caramel dissolves completely into orange juice and turns syrupy, about 2 minutes.

4. Pour syrup and spices over orange slices. Roast until syrup is bubbling and oranges are slightly wilted, 18 to 20 minutes. Transfer dish to wire rack and let cool slightly. Discard cloves and cinnamon stick. Serve warm or at room temperature.

Rum-Glazed Roasted Pineapple

Roasted Oranges in Spiced Syrup

ROASTED FIGS WITH BALSAMIC GLAZE AND MASCARPONE

Serves 6 | 12-inch ovensafe skillet

WHY THIS RECIPE WORKS We turned simple roasted figs into an elegant dessert by infusing them with the complex sweetness of balsamic vinegar and the floral notes of honey. Reducing the vinegar on the stovetop turned it viscous and syrupy, and adding honey to it softened the flavors. Roasting figs on their own can yield dry, scorched fruit, so instead we roasted them in the balsamic glaze. As the figs roasted, they lent their natural sweetness to the surrounding syrup. We created an easy topping of honeyed mascarpone cheese flavored with lemon zest. A final sprinkle of toasted pistachios added a crunch. For more information on figs, see page 363.

½ cup balsamic vinegar
¼ cup honey, divided
1 tablespoon unsalted butter
1½ pounds fresh figs, stemmed and halved
4 ounces (½ cup) mascarpone cheese
½ teaspoon grated lemon zest
⅓ cup shelled pistachios, toasted and chopped

1. Adjust oven rack to middle position and heat oven to 450 degrees. Bring vinegar, 3 tablespoons honey, and butter to simmer in 12-inch ovensafe skillet over medium-high heat and cook until reduced to ⅓ cup, about 3 minutes. Off heat, add figs and toss to coat. Transfer skillet to oven and roast until figs are tender, 8 to 10 minutes.

2. Remove skillet from oven (skillet handle will be hot) and let figs rest for 5 minutes. Combine mascarpone, lemon zest, and remaining 1 tablespoon honey in bowl. Divide figs among individual bowls. Dollop with mascarpone mixture, drizzle with balsamic syrup, and sprinkle with pistachios. Serve.

BAKED APPLES

Serves 6 | 12-inch ovensafe nonstick skillet

WHY THIS RECIPE WORKS Fresh apples stuffed with dried fruit, nuts, and spices and baked until tender make a dessert that's simultaneously cozy and sophisticated. Granny Smiths, with their firm flesh and tart, fruity flavor, were the best apples for the job. Peeling the apples after cutting off the top allowed steam to escape and the apples to retain their tender-firm texture. A melon baller helped us scoop out a spacious cavity for the filling. After capping the filled apples, we basted them as they baked with a cider and maple syrup sauce so they emerged lightly glazed and full of flavor.

7 large Granny Smith apples (8 ounces each), divided
6 tablespoons unsalted butter, softened, divided
⅓ cup dried cranberries, chopped coarse
⅓ cup pecans, toasted and chopped coarse
¼ cup packed (1¾ ounces) brown sugar
3 tablespoons old-fashioned rolled oats
1 teaspoon finely grated orange zest
½ teaspoon ground cinnamon
Pinch table salt
⅓ cup maple syrup
⅓ cup plus 2 tablespoons apple cider, divided

1. Adjust oven rack to middle position and heat oven to 375 degrees. Peel, core, and cut 1 apple into ¼-inch dice. Combine diced apple, 5 tablespoons butter, cranberries, pecans, sugar, oats, orange zest, cinnamon, and salt in bowl; set aside.

2. Shave thin slice off bottom (blossom end) of remaining 6 apples to allow them to sit flat. Cut top ½ inch off stem end of apples and reserve. Peel apples and use melon baller or small measuring spoon to remove 1½-inch-diameter core, being careful not to cut through bottom of apples.

3. Melt remaining 1 tablespoon butter in 12-inch ovensafe nonstick skillet over medium heat. Add apples, stem side down, and cook until cut surface is golden brown, about 3 minutes. Flip apples, reduce heat to low, and spoon filling inside, mounding excess filling over cavities; top with reserved apple caps. Add maple syrup and ⅓ cup cider to skillet. Transfer skillet to oven and bake until skewer inserted into apples meets little resistance, 35 to 40 minutes, basting every 10 minutes with maple syrup mixture in pan. Remove skillet from oven (skillet handle will be hot).

4. Transfer apples to serving platter. Being careful of hot skillet handle, stir up to 2 tablespoons of remaining cider into sauce in skillet to adjust consistency. Pour sauce over apples and serve.

Baked Apples with Dried Apricots and Almonds
Substitute coarsely chopped dried apricots for cranberries, coarsely chopped toasted almonds for pecans, and 1 teaspoon vanilla extract for cinnamon.

Baked Apples with Dried Figs and Macadamia Nuts
Substitute coarsely chopped dried figs for cranberries, coarsely chopped toasted macadamia nuts for pecans, lemon zest for orange zest, and ¼ teaspoon ground ginger for cinnamon.

Baked Apples with Raisins and Walnuts
Substitute coarsely chopped raisins for cranberries, coarsely chopped toasted walnuts for pecans, lemon zest for orange zest, and ¼ teaspoon ground nutmeg for cinnamon.

TUTORIAL
Baked Apples

Properly filling and capping the cavity makes for luscious baked apples.

1. Shave thin slice off bottom (blossom end) of 6 apples. Cut top ½ inch off stem end of apples and reserve.

2. Peel apples and use melon baller or small measuring spoon to remove 1½-inch-diameter core, being careful not to cut through bottom of apples.

3. Melt 1 tablespoon butter in 12-inch ovensafe nonstick skillet over medium heat. Add apples and cook until cut surface is golden brown, about 3 minutes.

4. Flip apples, reduce heat to low, and spoon filling inside, mounding excess filling over cavities; top with reserved apple caps.

5. Add maple syrup and ⅓ cup cider to skillet.

6. Transfer skillet to oven and bake until skewer inserted into apples meets little resistance, 35 to 40 minutes, basting every 10 minutes with mixture in pan.

Bananas Foster

1. Combine butter, sugar, cinnamon stick, lemon zest, and 1 tablespoon rum in 12-inch skillet. Cook over medium-high heat, stirring constantly, until sugar dissolves and mixture has thickened, about 2 minutes.

2. Reduce heat to medium and add bananas to pan, spooning some sauce over each quarter. Cook until bananas are glossy and golden on bottom, about 1 ½ minutes. Flip bananas; continue to cook until very soft but not mushy or falling apart, about 1 ½ minutes longer.

3. Off heat, add remaining 3 tablespoons rum and allow rum to warm slightly, about 5 seconds. Wave lit fireplace match or wooden skewer over pan until rum ignites, shaking pan to distribute flame over entire pan. After flames subside, 15 to 30 seconds, discard cinnamon stick and lemon zest. Divide ice cream among serving bowls and top with bananas and sauce. Serve.

BANANAS FOSTER

Serves 4 | 12-inch skillet

WHY THIS RECIPE WORKS Invented during the 1950s at Brennan's, one of New Orleans's most storied restaurants, bananas Foster is composed of bananas caramelized in a butterscotch sauce, flambéed with liquor, and usually paired with scoops of vanilla ice cream. Though the type of liquor can vary, we strongly preferred rum. Recipes call for anywhere from a scant 1 tablespoon to a whopping 2 cups; we determined that 1 tablespoon per serving imparted a robust rum taste without overwhelming the other ingredients. We added a little rum to the sauce and used the rest to flambé the bananas. As for the bananas, we cooked them in the sauce until soft, flipping them over halfway through cooking so they turned out tender.

 4 tablespoons unsalted butter
 ½ cup packed (3 ½ ounces) dark brown sugar
 1 (3-inch) cinnamon stick
 1 (2-inch) strip lemon zest
 ¼ cup dark rum, divided
 2 large, firm, ripe bananas, peeled, halved crosswise, then halved lengthwise
 1 pint vanilla ice cream

CHILLED MAPLE-GLAZED ORANGES

Serves 6 | 12-inch nonstick skillet

WHY THIS RECIPE WORKS Most recipes for glazed or macerated oranges are cloyingly sweet and lack complexity. For a complex and intensely fragrant dessert, we thought that the caramel notes of maple syrup might provide the perfect counterpoint to the bright, juicy oranges. We started by macerating sliced oranges in a cooked maple caramel and then poaching them in the oven. But poaching rendered the oranges mushy and soft. Instead, we decided to sear the orange halves before slicing them; we then used the fond to flavor the maple caramel and added some cloves for a subtle spicy note. Charring the peels and steeping them in the sauce gave the caramel a potent orange flavor, bittersweet undertones, and a vibrant complexity that was hard to resist. A sprinkle of pine nuts brought just enough textural contrast. You can substitute Cara Cara or blood oranges for the navel oranges in this recipe, though the sugar content will vary slightly.

 7 navel oranges (6 whole, scrubbed and dried, 1 juiced to yield ⅓ cup juice)
 1 tablespoon unsalted butter, divided
 6 tablespoons maple syrup
 4 whole cloves
 ¼ teaspoon table salt
 ¼ cup pine nuts, toasted

1. Using vegetable peeler, remove twenty 2-inch strips orange zest from whole oranges, avoiding pith. Using paring knife, cut away remaining peel and pith from oranges and cut each orange in half lengthwise.

2. Melt 1½ teaspoons butter in 12-inch nonstick skillet over medium-high heat. Add peels and cook, stirring occasionally, until well browned, 3 to 5 minutes. Transfer peels to small bowl. Melt remaining 1½ teaspoons butter in now-empty skillet over medium heat. Add orange halves, curved side down, and cook until dark golden brown, 3 to 5 minutes. Transfer oranges to cutting board and cut crosswise into ½-inch-thick slices; transfer to large bowl.

3. Add maple syrup to now-empty skillet and bring to boil over medium heat. Reduce heat to medium-low and cook until mixture thickens and registers 270 degrees, 3 to 4 minutes (syrup will smell slightly burnt). Off heat, carefully stir in browned peels, orange juice, cloves, and salt. Return skillet to medium-low heat and cook, swirling occasionally, until mixture thickens slightly and registers 220 degrees, about 2 minutes.

4. Strain mixture through fine-mesh strainer into bowl with orange slices. Add some of peels and cloves from strainer to oranges and stir gently to combine. Cover with plastic wrap and refrigerate, stirring occasionally, for at least 2 hours or up to 2 days.

5. To serve, portion oranges and syrup into serving bowls, discarding peels and cloves. Sprinkle with pine nuts and serve.

Caramelized Pears with Blue Cheese and Black Pepper–Caramel Sauce

CARAMELIZED PEARS WITH BLUE CHEESE AND BLACK PEPPER–CARAMEL SAUCE

Serves 6 | 12-inch nonstick skillet

WHY THIS RECIPE WORKS A new take on the classic pairing of sweet, ripe pears and pungent blue cheese, this dessert unites the duo with a rich caramel sauce. We brought water and sugar to a boil in a skillet and then added the halved and cored pears to cook in the browning caramel. Some cream transformed the sticky sugar syrup into a smooth sauce that clung lightly to the pears, and a bit of black pepper and salt balanced the flavors. For an attractive presentation, we arranged the pears on a serving platter with wedges of blue cheese and drizzled them with the sauce. Any variety of pear can be used as long as it is firm. We recommend using a strong blue cheese such as Stilton to complement the sweetness of the pears.

⅓ cup water
⅔ cup (4⅔ ounces) sugar
3 firm pears, halved and cored
⅔ cup heavy cream
¼ teaspoon black peppercorns, roughly crushed
3 ounces strong blue cheese, cut into 6 wedges

1. Pour water into 12-inch nonstick skillet, then pour sugar into center of skillet, being careful not to let it hit sides of skillet. Bring to boil over high heat, stirring occasionally, until sugar is fully dissolved and liquid is bubbling. Add pears to skillet, cut sides down; cover, reduce heat to medium-high, and cook until pears are almost tender and paring knife inserted into center meets slight resistance, 13 to 15 minutes.

2. Uncover, reduce heat to medium, and cook until sauce is golden brown and cut sides of pears are beginning to brown, 3 to 5 minutes. Pour cream around pears and cook, shaking skillet, until sauce is smooth and deep caramel in color and cut sides of pears are golden brown, 3 to 5 minutes.

3. Off heat, transfer pears, cut sides up, to wire rack set in rimmed baking sheet and let cool slightly. Add peppercorns to sauce in skillet and season with salt to taste. Transfer to small bowl.

4. Carefully (pears will still be hot) arrange pears, cut sides up, and blue cheese on serving platter. Lightly drizzle pears and blue cheese with caramel sauce. Serve immediately, passing remaining caramel sauce separately.

TUTORIAL
Chilled Maple-Glazed Oranges

Learn how to get deep caramel flavor in these steps to chilled maple oranges.

1. Melt 1½ teaspoons butter in 12-inch nonstick skillet over medium-high heat. Add peels and cook, stirring occasionally, until well browned, 3 to 5 minutes. Transfer peels to small bowl.

2. Melt remaining 1½ teaspoons butter in skillet over medium heat. Add orange halves, curved side down, and cook until dark golden brown, 3 to 5 minutes.

3. Transfer oranges to cutting board and cut crosswise into ½-inch-thick slices; transfer to large bowl.

4. Add maple syrup to skillet and bring to boil over medium heat. Reduce heat to medium-low and cook until mixture thickens and registers 270 degrees, 3 to 4 minutes (syrup will smell slightly burnt).

5. Off heat, carefully stir in peels, orange juice, cloves, and salt. Cook over medium-low heat, swirling occasionally, until mixture thickens slightly and registers 220 degrees, about 2 minutes.

6. Strain mixture through fine-mesh strainer into bowl with orange slices. Add some of peels and cloves from strainer to oranges and stir gently to combine.

STRAWBERRY-RHUBARB COMPOTE WITH ICE CREAM

Serves 6 | 12-inch nonstick skillet

WHY THIS RECIPE WORKS A compote transforms summer fruit into the simplest of desserts: a lightly sweet topping for ice cream (it's also good on Greek yogurt or ricotta cheese). Gentle cooking releases the fruit's juices without breaking it down into jam. For our compote we chose the classic pairing of strawberries and rhubarb. After cooking the rhubarb briefly we added the berries off the heat, which prevented an overly soft compote, as did transferring the compote to a bowl to cool.

- ½ vanilla bean
- 6 tablespoons honey
- ¼ cup water
-   Pinch table salt
- 8 ounces rhubarb, peeled and cut into 1-inch lengths
- 20 ounces strawberries, hulled and quartered (4 cups)
- 1 tablespoon unsalted butter
- 3 cups vanilla ice cream or frozen yogurt
- 1 tablespoon minced fresh mint

1. Cut vanilla bean in half lengthwise. Using tip of paring knife, scrape out seeds and reserve bean. Bring vanilla seeds and bean, honey, water, and salt to simmer in 12-inch nonstick skillet over medium heat. Stir in rhubarb and cook until it begins to soften and sauce thickens slightly, 4 to 6 minutes.

2. Off heat, gently stir in strawberries and butter until butter has melted. Discard vanilla bean, transfer compote to bowl, and let cool to room temperature, 10 to 15 minutes. (Compote can be refrigerated for up to 1 day; return to room temperature before serving.)

3. Scoop ice cream into serving bowls and top each with about ½ cup of compote. Sprinkle with mint and serve immediately.

PLUM-BLACKBERRY COMPOTE

Serves 6 | 12-inch nonstick skillet

Try to buy plums of similar ripeness so that they cook evenly. To prevent the compote from overcooking, be sure to transfer it to a bowl to cool.

- ½ vanilla bean
- 6 tablespoons water
- ¼ cup honey
-   Pinch table salt
- 1½ pounds plums, pitted, sliced ⅓ inch thick, then halved crosswise
- 10 ounces (2 cups) blackberries
- 1 tablespoon unsalted butter
- 3 cups vanilla ice cream or frozen yogurt
- 1 tablespoon minced fresh mint

1. Cut vanilla bean in half lengthwise. Using tip of paring knife, scrape out seeds and reserve bean. Bring vanilla seeds and bean, water, honey, and salt to simmer in 12-inch nonstick skillet over medium heat. Stir in plums and cook until they begin to soften and sauce thickens slightly, 5 to 7 minutes.

2. Stir in blackberries and continue to cook until they begin to soften, about 1 minute. Off heat, stir in butter until melted. Discard vanilla bean, transfer compote to bowl, and let cool to room temperature, 10 to 15 minutes. (Compote can be refrigerated for up to 1 day; return to room temperature before serving.)

3. Scoop ice cream into serving bowls and top each with about ½ cup of compote. Sprinkle with mint and serve immediately.

APRICOT SPOON SWEETS

Makes 4 cups | Dutch oven

WHY THIS RECIPE WORKS The serving of "spoon sweets" in Greece and parts of the Middle East is a long-standing ritual. A special jar of fruit with a spoon hanging from its neck appears whenever visitors arrive. Each visitor takes a spoonful of the sweet fruit straight from the jar. We wanted a recipe for this welcoming treat using apricots. While traditionally an all-honey syrup is used to preserve the fruit, it's very sweet. We settled on a syrup made of water, sugar, and honey; once the syrup was reduced, we added the apricots and lemon juice and simmered them briefly to achieve the perfect texture for the fruit. The acidity of the lemon juice balanced the sweetness of the syrup and also helped to prevent the apricots from oxidizing, or turning brown. Select apricots that yield slightly when pressed.

- 1½ cups (10½ ounces) sugar
- 1 cup honey
- ¾ cup water
- 1½ pounds ripe but firm apricots, pitted and cut into ½-inch wedges
- 2 tablespoons lemon juice

1. Bring sugar, honey, and water to boil in Dutch oven over high heat and cook, stirring occasionally, until syrup measures 2 cups, about 10 minutes.

2. Add apricots and lemon juice and return to boil. Reduce heat to medium-low and simmer, stirring occasionally, until apricots soften and release their juice, about 5 minutes. Remove pot from heat and let cool completely.

3. Transfer apricots and syrup to airtight container and refrigerate for 24 hours before serving. (Fruit can be refrigerated for up to 1 week.)

TOPPED AND BAKED FRUIT

THESE HOMEY, COMFORTING FRUIT DESSERTS feature two distinct components: lightly sweetened fruit and a batter or dough that transforms into a crisp topping, biscuit, or cake when baked, offering a rich, buttery counterpoint to the tender, juicy fruit. Whereas poaching or roasting fruit is a relatively quick process, baked fruit desserts generally call for lower temps and longer cooking times. This allows the fruit to slowly soften and release its juices to form a coating sauce of sorts, which aids in a cohesive filling. Many of these desserts bake like a casserole, but starting the fruit in a skillet on the stovetop can help reduce the juices more quickly into a thick, glossy sauce. Then, the even, all-encompassing heat of the oven allows the fruit filling to cook gently until juicy and bubbling. Most of these desserts are simple to prepare, and although some work best with fresh fruit, many do just as well with the frozen variety, allowing you to enjoy these satisfying desserts any time of year. From familiar crumbles, cobblers, and shortcakes to the intriguingly named sonkers and Bettys, you're sure to find a fruit dessert you enjoy. And whether you use the stovetop or oven, fresh in-season fruit or frozen, we think you'll find that a scoop of ice cream or a dollop of whipped cream always adds the perfect finishing touch.

KEY POINTS

Fruit variety is important

Lemon juice enhances filling

Precooking fruit keeps pastry crisp

Let cool before serving to thicken

Dumplings

Featuring tender fruit encased in a rich pastry, fruit dumplings are an old-fashioned favorite. Our dumplings are either baked in or served with a luxurious sauce. The dough should be sturdy enough to stand up to the sauce as well as the moisture released by the fruit—but sturdy doesn't have to mean tough. The key to dumplings that have plenty of structure but are still light and tender is an ample amount of baking powder.

LIGHT AND LEAVENED

While pie dough is one popular choice for dumplings, we've found that something moist and leavened, like the biscuit dough for our apple dumplings and the baking soda–lifted pastry for our peach dumplings, better absorbs the dessert's liquid for an intact dessert and dough that doesn't rip.

Pie Dough

Biscuit Dough

TWO ROTTEN APPLES

When cooking such a large piece of fruit in our dumplings, we found that some apple varieties didn't cook through quickly enough, while others turned to mush within the pastry. It's essential to pick the right apple and prep it correctly.

Heatstroke
McIntosh apples can't take the heat. They turn into applesauce before the pastry is baked.

Extra Crunch
Whole apples are barely cooked when the pastry is done. We use halved Golden Delicious.

Crisps and Crumbles

A crisp or crumble is one of the simplest ways to make a baked dessert with fresh fruit. Both start with a layer of tender, lightly sweetened fruit, which, when baked, bubbles up appealingly around the edges of a crisp, crunchy, streusel-like topping. The topping for both typically features a combination of flour, sugar, and butter, as well as nuts for the rich crunch. A crisp topping, however, also contains oats for a lighter, looser texture. (You may encounter dessert recipes that stray from these definitions, and that's OK.) For a well-made crumble or crisp, regardless of the type of fruit you're using, it's important to keep the topping from becoming soggy. The first step is to eliminate some of the juice from the filling, either by letting the fruit macerate or by partially cooking the filling so the liquid has a chance to reduce before the topping is added. Chilling or parbaking the topping before adding it to the filling also helps ensure a crisp or crumble that lives up to its name.

COMBINING FRUITS

While there's absolutely nothing wrong with sticking to a single fruit in a crumble or crisp, pairing two or more fruits together offers a range of flavors, textures, and colors for a unique dessert. Here are a few of our favorite combinations. They blend sweet with tart and floral with earthy and also take into account the rate at which fruits break down in the oven.

- Strawberries and rhubarb
- Apples and cranberries or raspberries
- Any combination of blackberries, raspberries, blueberries, and strawberries
- Peaches and raspberries or blueberries
- Nectarines and blackberries
- Plums and cherries
- Pears and cranberries

PUTTING THE "CRISP" IN FRUIT CRISP

There are a few steps you can take to ensure that a crisp topping lives up to its name.

1. ELIMINATE MOISTURE Fruit exudes a lot of liquid, so it's important to remove some of that moisture before adding the topping; otherwise, it will be soggy and soft rather than crisp. You can do this by tossing the fruit with sugar and letting the juice drain, or by parbaking the filling, which allows the juices to reduce and evaporate.

2. COMBINE OATS AND NUTS A mixture of chewy oats and crunchy nuts, bound together with flour, sugar, and butter, creates a substantial—but not dense—topping that stays atop the fruit filling and bakes to buttery crisp perfection.

3. ADD WATER TO THE TOPPING For our Gluten-Free Apple Crisp (page 147), we found that adding a little water to the topping helped it clump together.

DON'T DIVE IN TOO SOON

Waiting at least 45 minutes before digging into a crumble is hard but worth it. As the dessert cools, the fruit's pectin molecules (which dissolve in the fruit's water during cooking) form a gel that immobilizes the water, resulting in a nicely set filling. Cut into the crumble before that gel has firmed and the filling runs out like hot soup, as below.

Bettys

A Betty is a retro dessert that uses fruit and bread in a totally simple yet genius way. Somewhat similar to a crisp, it features bread crumbs enriched with butter and sugar. But what's unique about the Betty is that this mixture forms not only a topping but a bottom layer as well. The bread crumbs on the bottom soften as they absorb the fruit's flavor-packed juices, while the crumbs on top crisp to a beautiful golden brown.

ONE MIXTURE, TWO TEXTURES

Both of our Bettys use bread crumbs in two different ways: Our Apple-Blackberry Betty (page 152) layers the buttered, lightly sweetened bread crumbs beneath the filling, where they plump and caramelize as they capture the exuded fruit juices, and on top, for a layer that crisps to golden-brown perfection. Our Peach Betty (page 153) also features a top layer of crispy bread crumbs, but here the remaining crumbs are mixed right into the filling where they soften as they absorb the peaches' ample juices, an appropriate method for this quick stovetop-to-oven Betty.

Cobblers and Grunts

The combination of crisp, golden biscuits atop a bubbling mixture of tender, juicy fruit is always enticing when made with fresh, height-of-the-season fruit. Plus, cobblers are easy to make: Drop biscuits and a simple fruit filling take just a little time. For a filling with the proper texture, juicy fruit is best; blueberries, blackberries, peaches, nectarines, strawberries, and sour cherries all work well. One problem that plagues cobblers is gummy biscuits. To fix this, we parbake the biscuits as well as the filling; this way, the fruit and biscuits don't spend enough time mingled together for the biscuits to become soggy underneath. The oddly named dessert known as a grunt is similar to cobbler, although the dough is steamed rather than baked on top of the cooked fruit filling.

TIPS FOR MAKING ANY FRUIT & BISCUIT COBBLER

Cobblers, with their simple fruit fillings and stir-together drop biscuits, are easy to make—especially if you keep these tips and tricks in mind.

ADD LEMON TO THE FILLING Lemon enhances the fruit's flavor and balances the sweetness in virtually any fruit dessert.

MIX BISCUITS AT THE LAST MINUTE Wait until just before baking to mix the premeasured wet and dry biscuit ingredients. This ensures that the leaveners (which are activated by liquid) will be at full strength, contributing to a light and fluffy topping.

JUST DROP THE BISCUITS Many traditional biscuit recipes call for cutting cold fat (butter or shortening) into the flour before adding the liquid. Drop biscuits are easier: Just stir all the ingredients together, drop, and bake.

PRO BAKER'S TRICK When portioning dough with a measuring cup, greasing the cup first makes for an easy release. We like to grease measuring cups with vegetable oil spray, but an even smear of vegetable oil or butter works, too.

BAKE THE FRUIT AND BISCUITS SEPARATELY In general we like to bake the fruit filling and biscuit topping separately before combining the two; this ensures a perfectly cooked filling and crisp—rather than gummy or doughy—biscuits.

BAKE ON A RIMMED BAKING SHEET Cobbler filling can bubble over and make a mess of your oven. Baking the cobbler on a rimmed baking sheet prevents this.

Batter Bakes

The defining characteristic of this type of fruit dessert is the pancake-like batter, which bakes into a tender cake. The cake mingles with a sweet, juicy fruit filling for a homey, comforting treat. Sonkers and Texas-style cobblers are two examples of this style. The key is to use plenty of fat in the form of butter; because fat floats, incorporating a generous amount of butter into the batter ensures that it will float toward the top rather than sink toward the bottom, buried under the stewed fruit. The result is cake with irresistibly crisp edges and a lightly golden crust.

OVEN-STEWING

To prevent the batter for our sonker (see page 158) from sinking into the filling, we take two steps. One is to stew the fruit in the baking dish (bake at a moderate temperature with a little water until bubbling) before adding the topping. Stewed berries give the batter a uniform, level surface on which to bake (eliminating crevices of raw batter), and their heat helps bake the batter from underneath. We also add a little bit of cornstarch; this thickens the fruit's juices a bit and helps the filling withstand the batter's weight without sacrificing too much moisture.

PEACH DUMPLINGS

Serves 6 to 8 | 8-inch square baking pan

WHY THIS RECIPE WORKS Old-fashioned peach dumplings were made by wrapping peach halves or slices in tender pastry dough and baking or boiling them in a sweetened syrup. To make a modern version, we started with two large ripe peaches cut into wedges (frozen sliced peaches worked just as well). Adding baking powder to the dough kept it light and fluffy, even while it simmered in syrup. And blending a couple of peach slices and ½ cup of concentrated peach preserves into the sauce amplified the peach flavors and made it thicker and more luscious. We developed this recipe using a metal baking pan. If using a glass or ceramic baking dish, increase the baking time by 10 minutes in step 6.

DOUGH

- 1½ cups (7½ ounces) all-purpose flour
- 1 tablespoon sugar
- 2 teaspoons baking powder
- ¾ teaspoon table salt
- ½ cup whole milk
- 2 tablespoons unsalted butter, melted

Peach Dumplings

PEACHES AND SAUCE

- 2 large fresh peaches, peeled, halved, pitted, and each half cut into 4 equal wedges, or 10 ounces frozen sliced peaches, divided
- ¾ cup water
- 6 tablespoons unsalted butter, cut into 6 pieces
- ⅓ cup (2⅓ ounces) plus 1 teaspoon sugar, divided Pinch table salt
- ½ cup peach preserves
- 1 tablespoon lemon juice
- ¼ teaspoon ground cinnamon

1. FOR THE DOUGH: Adjust oven rack to middle position and heat oven to 350 degrees. Combine flour, sugar, baking powder, and salt in large bowl. Combine milk and melted butter in second bowl (butter may form clumps). Using rubber spatula, stir milk mixture into flour mixture until just incorporated. Turn out dough onto lightly floured counter and knead until no streaks of flour remain, about 1 minute. Return dough to large bowl, cover with plastic wrap, and set aside.

2. FOR THE PEACHES AND SAUCE: Set aside 12 peach slices. (If using frozen peaches, select 12 largest slices and freeze until ready to use.)

3. Combine water, butter, ⅓ cup sugar, salt, and remaining 4 peach slices in medium saucepan. Bring to simmer over medium-high heat and cook, stirring occasionally, until butter is melted and sugar is dissolved (and frozen peaches are thawed). Remove from heat and let cool for 5 minutes. Transfer peach mixture to blender, add peach preserves and lemon juice, and process until smooth, about 30 seconds. Set aside peach sauce.

4. Roll dough into 12-inch square, about ⅛ inch thick. Using pizza cutter or chef's knife, trim away and discard outer ½-inch edges of dough to make neat square. Cut dough in half. Working with 1 dough half at a time, cut crosswise into 3 equal rectangles, then cut each rectangle diagonally to create triangles. Repeat with second dough half. (You should have 12 triangles.)

5. Working with 1 dough triangle at a time, place 1 reserved peach slice on wide end of triangle. Roll dough around peach slice and transfer dumpling, seam side down, to 8-inch square baking pan. Repeat with remaining dough triangles and peach slices, staggering dumplings in 3 rows of 4 (dumplings will touch; this is OK).

6. Pour peach sauce over dumplings in pan. Combine cinnamon and remaining 1 teaspoon sugar in small bowl. Sprinkle dumplings with cinnamon sugar. Bake until dumplings are golden on top and syrup is bubbling in center of pan, about 45 minutes. Let cool for 10 minutes before serving.

TUTORIAL
Peach Dumplings

Learn how to get peaches in their blankets so they bake into sweet, golden dumplings.

1. Using pizza cutter or chef's knife, trim away and discard outer ½-inch edges of dough to make neat square. Cut dough in half.

2. Working with 1 dough half at a time, cut crosswise into 3 equal rectangles.

3. Cut each rectangle diagonally to create triangles. Repeat with second dough half. (You should have 12 triangles.)

4. Working with 1 dough triangle at a time, place 1 reserved peach slice on wide end of triangle.

5. Roll dough around peach slice and transfer dumpling, seam side down, to 8-inch square baking pan.

6. Repeat with remaining dough triangles and peach slices, staggering dumplings in 3 rows of 4 (dumplings will touch; this is OK).

Baked Apple Dumplings

BAKED APPLE DUMPLINGS

Serves 8 | rimmed baking sheet

WHY THIS RECIPE WORKS Apple dumplings are a homespun combination of warm pastry, a soft-baked apple, raisins, butter, and cinnamon, but often the apples turn too soft or are unevenly baked. The pastry can also turn gummy from the apples' juices. We found that biscuit dough was easier to work with than pie dough and did a great job of absorbing the liquid from the apples without getting mushy. Rather than baking the dumplings in syrup as some recipes instruct, we served our sauce on the side, which preserved the dumplings' texture. Use a melon baller or a metal teaspoon measure to core the apples. We like to serve the dumplings warm with vanilla ice cream and our Cider Sauce (recipe follows). Other moderately firm apples, such as Braeburns or Galas, can be used in this recipe.

DOUGH
2½ cups (12½ ounces) all-purpose flour
3 tablespoons sugar
2 teaspoons baking powder
¾ teaspoon table salt
10 tablespoons unsalted butter, cut into ½-inch pieces and chilled
5 tablespoons vegetable shortening, cut into ½-inch pieces and chilled
¾ cup buttermilk, chilled

APPLE DUMPLINGS
6 tablespoons (2⅔ ounces) sugar
1 teaspoon ground cinnamon
3 tablespoons unsalted butter, softened
3 tablespoons golden raisins, chopped
4 Golden Delicious apples
2 egg whites, lightly beaten

1. FOR THE DOUGH: Process flour, sugar, baking powder, and salt in food processor until combined, about 15 seconds. Scatter butter and shortening over flour mixture and pulse until mixture resembles wet sand, about 10 pulses; transfer to bowl. Stir in buttermilk until dough forms. Turn out onto lightly floured counter and knead briefly until dough is cohesive. Press dough into 8 by 4-inch rectangle. Cut in half, wrap each half tightly in plastic wrap, and refrigerate until firm, about 1 hour.

2. FOR THE APPLE DUMPLINGS: Adjust oven rack to middle position and heat oven to 425 degrees. Combine sugar and cinnamon in small bowl. In second bowl, combine butter, raisins, and 3 tablespoons cinnamon sugar. Peel apples and halve through equator. Remove core and pack butter mixture into each apple half.

3. On lightly floured counter, roll each dough half into 12-inch square. Cut each into four 6-inch squares. Lightly brush edges of 1 dough square with egg whites and place 1 apple half, cut side up, in center. Gather dough 1 corner at a time on top of apple, crimping edges to seal. Repeat with remaining dough squares and apple halves. Using paring knife, cut vent hole in top of each dumpling.

4. Line rimmed baking sheet with parchment paper. Arrange dumplings on prepared sheet, brush tops with egg whites, and sprinkle with remaining cinnamon sugar. Bake until dough is golden brown and juices are bubbling, 20 to 25 minutes. Let cool on sheet for 10 minutes. Serve.

CIDER SAUCE
Makes about 1½ cups
To make this sauce ahead, refrigerate the reduced cider mixture for up to two days. To serve, return the mixture to a simmer and whisk in the butter and lemon juice off the heat.

1 cup apple cider
1 cup water
1 cup sugar
½ teaspoon ground cinnamon
2 tablespoons unsalted butter
1 tablespoon lemon juice

Bring cider, water, sugar, and cinnamon to simmer in saucepan and cook over medium-high heat until thickened and reduced to 1½ cups, about 15 minutes. Off heat, whisk in butter and lemon juice. Serve.

Apple Crumble

1. Adjust oven racks to upper-middle and lowest positions and heat oven to 400 degrees. Toss apples, 2 tablespoons sugar, lemon juice, ½ teaspoon salt, and cinnamon together in large bowl. Transfer to 8-inch square baking pan with at least 2-inch sides and press into even layer. Cover pan tightly with aluminum foil and place on rimmed baking sheet. Transfer sheet to oven and bake on lower rack for 35 minutes.

2. While apples bake, whisk flour, almonds, remaining ½ cup sugar, and remaining ½ teaspoon salt in medium bowl until combined. Add melted butter, vanilla, and water and stir with spatula until clumps form and no dry flour remains.

3. Remove sheet from oven and smooth top of apples with spatula. If apples have not collapsed enough to leave at least ¼ inch of space below rim of pan, replace foil, return sheet to oven, and continue to bake 5 to 15 minutes longer.

4. Scatter topping evenly over apples, breaking up any clumps larger than a marble. Transfer sheet to upper rack and bake until topping is evenly browned and filling is just bubbling at edges, 25 to 35 minutes. Transfer pan to wire rack and let cool for at least 45 minutes before serving.

APPLE CRUMBLE

Serves 6 to 8 | 8-inch square baking pan

WHY THIS RECIPE WORKS Making an apple crumble that tastes primarily of apples starts with plenty of fruit. We baked 4 pounds of apples in a covered pan before applying the topping, which allowed the apples to collapse into a thick layer of filling. Adding nuts to the streusel loosened its consistency so that it didn't bake up dense. Applying the topping midway through baking minimized its exposure to the juicy fruit, preventing it from becoming soggy. We like Golden Delicious apples here, but you can use Braeburn or Honeycrisp apples (or a mix of all three). You should have 4 pounds of apples before peeling and coring. Dark brown sugar gives the topping a deeper color. Do not use a glass baking dish here.

- 4 pounds Golden Delicious apples, peeled, cored, and cut into ¾-inch pieces
- 2 tablespoons packed plus ½ cup packed (3½ ounces) dark brown sugar, divided
- 2 tablespoons lemon juice
- 1 teaspoon table salt, divided
- ¾ teaspoon ground cinnamon
- 1 cup (5 ounces) all-purpose flour
- ½ cup sliced almonds, chopped fine
- 6 tablespoons unsalted butter, melted
- 2 teaspoons vanilla extract
- 2 teaspoons water

GLUTEN-FREE APPLE CRISP

Serves 6 | 8-inch square baking dish

WHY THIS RECIPE WORKS Thinking that a fruit crisp would be easy to make gluten-free since only the topping contains flour, we started by simply swapping out the all-purpose flour for a gluten-free blend. But the flour blend's low protein content caused the topping to resist holding together. Recognizing that using less flour would work to our advantage, we added more oats and nuts, toasting them and then finely grinding nearly half of them to a flourlike consistency. In the end, we needed just ⅓ cup of flour blend. Because the apples needed more time in the oven than the topping, we parbaked the filling. Some of the Golden Delicious apples broke down and created a saucy filling. The baked crisp can be kept at room temperature for up to 4 hours; rewarm in the oven.

TOPPING
- ¾ cup (2¼ ounces) gluten-free old-fashioned rolled oats
- ¾ cup sliced almonds
- 1½ ounces (⅓ cup) all-purpose gluten-free flour blend (see page 2)
- 1¾ ounces (¼ cup packed) brown sugar
- 2 tablespoons granulated sugar
- 2 teaspoons vanilla extract
- 1 teaspoon water
- ⅛ teaspoon table salt
- 6 tablespoons unsalted butter, cut into 6 pieces and softened

FILLING

4 teaspoons lemon juice
¾ teaspoon cornstarch
6 Golden Delicious apples (8 ounces each), 5 peeled
  and cut into ½-inch cubes, 1 peeled and grated
2⅓ ounces (⅓ cup) granulated sugar
  Pinch table salt
  Pinch ground cinnamon
  Pinch ground nutmeg

1. FOR THE TOPPING: Adjust oven rack to middle position and heat oven to 400 degrees. Place oats and nuts in 2 piles on parchment paper–lined baking sheet, and bake until lightly toasted, 3 to 5 minutes. Remove from oven and let cool completely.

2. Pulse ½ cup oats, flour blend, brown sugar, granulated sugar, vanilla, water, and salt in food processor until combined, about 5 pulses. Sprinkle butter and half of almonds over top and process until mixture clumps together into large, crumbly balls, about 30 seconds, stopping halfway through to scrape down bowl. Sprinkle remaining almonds and remaining ¼ cup oats over mixture and combine with 2 quick pulses. Transfer mixture to bowl.

3. FOR THE FILLING: Whisk lemon juice and cornstarch in large bowl until cornstarch is dissolved. Stir in apples, sugar, salt, cinnamon, and nutmeg. Transfer mixture to 8-inch square baking dish, cover tightly with aluminum foil, and bake for 20 minutes.

4. Remove baking dish from oven, uncover, and stir filling well. Pinch topping into grape-size pieces (with some smaller loose bits) and sprinkle over filling. Bake until topping is well browned and fruit is tender and bubbling around edges, 20 to 25 minutes, rotating dish halfway through baking. Let crisp cool on wire rack until warm, about 15 minutes. Serve.

SKILLET APPLE CRISP

Serves 6 to 8 | 12-inch ovensafe skillet

WHY THIS RECIPE WORKS A skillet can bring out the best in apples; its shallow, flared shape encourages evaporation and browning. We added some apple cider, which we reduced to a syrupy consistency for intense fruity depth. Brown sugar, oats, and pecans gave our topping complexity and satisfying texture. Once topped, we slid our skillet crisp into the oven for a quick browning and to finish cooking the apples. If your skillet is not ovensafe, prepare the recipe through step 3 and then transfer the filling to a 13 by 9-inch baking dish. Top the filling as directed and bake for an additional 5 minutes. We like Golden Delicious apples for this recipe, but any sweet, crisp apple such as Honeycrisp or Braeburn can be substituted. Do not use Granny Smith apples in this recipe. While old-fashioned oats are preferable in this recipe, quick-cooking oats can be substituted.

TOPPING

¾ cup (3¾ ounces) all-purpose flour
¾ cup pecans, chopped fine
¾ cup (2¼ ounces) old-fashioned oats
½ cup packed (3½ ounces) light brown sugar
¼ cup (1¾ ounces) granulated sugar
½ teaspoon ground cinnamon
½ teaspoon table salt
8 tablespoons unsalted butter, melted

FILLING

3 pounds Golden Delicious apples (about 7 medium), peeled,
  cored, halved, and cut into ½-inch-thick wedges
¼ cup (1¾ ounces) granulated sugar
¼ teaspoon ground cinnamon (optional)
1 cup apple cider
2 teaspoons lemon juice
2 tablespoons unsalted butter

1. FOR THE TOPPING: Adjust oven rack to middle position and heat oven to 450 degrees. Combine flour, pecans, oats, brown sugar, granulated sugar, cinnamon, and salt in medium bowl. Stir in melted butter until mixture is thoroughly moistened and crumbly. Set aside.

2. FOR THE FILLING: Toss apples; sugar; and cinnamon, if using, together in large bowl; set aside. Bring cider to simmer in 12-inch ovensafe skillet over medium heat; cook until reduced to ½ cup, about 5 minutes. Transfer reduced cider to bowl or liquid measuring cup; stir in lemon juice and set aside.

3. Melt butter in now-empty skillet over medium heat. Add apple mixture and cook, stirring frequently, until apples are beginning to soften and become translucent, 12 to 14 minutes. (Do not fully cook apples.) Off heat, gently stir in cider mixture until apples are coated.

4. Sprinkle topping evenly over fruit, breaking up any large chunks. Place skillet on baking sheet and bake until fruit is tender and topping is deep golden brown, 15 to 20 minutes. Let cool on wire rack until warm, at least 15 minutes. Serve.

Skillet Apple Crisp with Maple and Bacon

Cook 6 slices bacon, cut into ¼-inch pieces, in 12-inch skillet over medium heat, stirring frequently, until crisp, 5 to 7 minutes. Using slotted spoon, transfer bacon to paper towel–lined plate. Pour off fat from skillet and discard. (Do not wash skillet.) Stir bacon into topping mixture after adding butter. Omit sugar and cinnamon from filling. Toss apples with ⅓ cup maple syrup in step 2 and proceed as directed.

Skillet Apple Crisp with Raspberries and Almonds
Substitute slivered almonds for pecans. Add ⅛ teaspoon almond extract to reduced cider with lemon juice in step 2. Stir 5 ounces raspberries into apple mixture along with reduced cider in step 3.

Skillet Apple Crisp with Vanilla and Cardamom
Substitute ½ cup shelled pistachios and ¼ cup walnuts for pecans. Substitute ½ teaspoon ground cardamom for cinnamon in filling and add seeds from 1 vanilla bean to apple, sugar, and cardamom mixture.

PEAR CRISP WITH MISO AND ALMONDS

Serves 6 | 10-inch ovensafe skillet

WHY THIS RECIPE WORKS In this unique twist on pear crisp, a little bit of white miso—a fermented soybean paste—brings incredible depth and complexity to the crunchy topping. The warm filling of juicy pears is lavishly draped in a gooey caramel-like blanket and then topped with a luxurious crust of rich, salty-sweet miso-almond crumble. Bosc pears that were just shy of ripe worked best here because they retained their shape after baking. Dried cherries, lemon zest and juice, almond extract, and chopped sliced almonds complemented the sweet floral flavor of the pears. Be sure to use white (shiro) miso—which is relatively mellow and sweet—in this recipe. If you can't find it, you can substitute ½ teaspoon of table salt. Dried cranberries can be substituted for the cherries.

TOPPING
- ¾ cup (3¾ ounces) all-purpose flour
- ½ cup panko bread crumbs
- ⅓ cup sliced almonds, toasted and chopped coarse
- ¼ cup packed (1¾ ounces) light brown sugar
- 1 teaspoon grated lemon zest
- ¼ teaspoon ground cinnamon
- 6 tablespoons unsalted butter, melted
- 1 tablespoon white miso
- ¼ teaspoon almond extract

FILLING
- 2 pounds slightly underripe Bosc pears, peeled, quartered lengthwise, cored, and sliced crosswise ½ inch thick
- ¾ cup packed (5¼ ounces) light brown sugar
- ⅓ cup dried cherries
- ¼ cup heavy cream
- 1 tablespoon cornstarch
- 1 tablespoon lemon juice
- ¼ teaspoon table salt
- 2 tablespoons unsalted butter

Pear Crisp with Miso and Almonds

1. **FOR THE TOPPING:** Adjust oven rack to middle position and heat oven to 375 degrees. Whisk flour, panko, almonds, sugar, lemon zest, and cinnamon together in bowl. Whisk melted butter, miso, and almond extract in second bowl until miso is dissolved. Stir butter mixture into flour mixture until no dry spots of flour remain and mixture forms clumps. Refrigerate until ready to use (topping can be covered and refrigerated for up to 24 hours).

2. **FOR THE FILLING:** Toss pears, sugar, cherries, cream, cornstarch, lemon juice, and salt in large bowl until thoroughly combined. Melt butter in 10-inch ovensafe skillet over medium-high heat. Add pear mixture and cook, stirring frequently, until pears have released enough liquid to be mostly submerged and juices have thickened and turned glossy, 6 to 8 minutes. Off heat, stir to ensure cherries are evenly distributed.

3. Squeeze topping into large clumps with your hands. Crumble topping into pea-size pieces over filling. Bake until topping is browned and filling is bubbling around sides of skillet, 20 to 25 minutes. Let cool for 15 minutes. Serve.

Strawberry-Rhubarb Crisp

STRAWBERRY-RHUBARB CRISP

Serves 6 | 10-inch ovensafe skillet

WHY THIS RECIPE WORKS The pairing of sweet strawberries and tart rhubarb is a classic for good reason; we wanted to bring them together in a crisp that lived up to its name. Since the amount of liquid that strawberries and rhubarb exude can vary, we cooked them on the stovetop with some brown sugar and cornstarch to coax out excess liquid. Once the filling had just the right jammy consistency, we covered it with an easy stir-together topping and baked it until golden brown. If using frozen strawberries, there's no need to thaw them completely; you can chop them as soon as they're soft enough. If using frozen strawberries and frozen rhubarb, you may need to increase the stovetop cooking time by up to 4 minutes. Depending on the amount of trimming required, you may need to buy more than 1 pound of rhubarb to ensure that you end up with 3½ cups. Serve with vanilla ice cream.

TOPPING

- ¾ cup (3¾ ounces) all-purpose flour
- ½ cup panko bread crumbs
- ¼ cup packed (1¾ ounces) light brown sugar
- ½ teaspoon table salt
- ¼ teaspoon ground cinnamon
- 6 tablespoons unsalted butter, melted

FILLING

- 1 pound fresh rhubarb, trimmed and cut into ½-inch pieces, or frozen rhubarb, thawed and cut into ½-inch pieces (3½ cups)
- 12 ounces fresh strawberries, hulled and chopped coarse, or frozen strawberries, thawed and chopped coarse (2 cups)
- 1¼ cups packed (8¾ ounces) light brown sugar
- 2 tablespoons cornstarch
- ⅛ teaspoon table salt

1. **FOR THE TOPPING:** Whisk flour, panko, sugar, salt, and cinnamon together in bowl. Add melted butter and stir until no dry spots of flour remain and mixture forms clumps. Refrigerate until ready to use.

2. **FOR THE FILLING:** Adjust oven rack to middle position and heat oven to 375 degrees. Toss all ingredients in large bowl until thoroughly combined. Transfer to 10-inch ovensafe skillet. Cook over medium-high heat, stirring frequently, until fruit has released enough liquid to be mostly submerged, rhubarb is just beginning to break down, and juices have thickened, about 8 minutes. Remove skillet from heat.

3. Squeeze topping into large clumps with your hands. Crumble topping into pea-size pieces and sprinkle evenly over filling. Bake until topping is browned and filling is bubbling around sides of skillet, about 20 minutes. Let cool for 15 minutes. Serve.

SUMMER BLUEBERRY CRISP

Serves 6 | 12-inch ovensafe skillet

WHY THIS RECIPE WORKS Many blueberry crisps are plagued by soupy fillings that turn their crunchy toppings into mush. We wanted to allow the blueberries to shine without drowning the streusel topping. Cornstarch thickened the filling without muting the berry flavor. For an extra-chunky streusel that would stay crunchy on top of the berries, we pulsed flour, butter, brown sugar, and oats in the food processor until large crumbles formed. After 30 minutes in the oven, our crisp emerged browned and bubbling, the streusel still crisp atop the juicy, deep purple filling. Do not substitute quick or instant oats in this recipe. In step 2, do not press the topping into the berry mixture or it may sink and become soggy. Frozen berries do not work in this recipe because they shed too much liquid.

½ cup (3½ ounces) granulated sugar
4 teaspoons cornstarch
¼ teaspoon table salt, divided
25 ounces (5 cups) blueberries
⅔ cup (3⅓ ounces) all-purpose flour
½ cup (1½ ounces) old-fashioned rolled oats
⅓ cup packed (2⅓ ounces) light brown sugar
½ teaspoon ground cinnamon
6 tablespoons unsalted butter, cut into 6 pieces and chilled

1. Adjust oven rack to lower-middle position and heat oven to 375 degrees. Whisk granulated sugar, cornstarch, and ⅛ teaspoon salt together in large bowl. Add blueberries to bowl and toss to coat. Transfer to 8-inch square baking dish.

2. Pulse flour, oats, brown sugar, cinnamon, and remaining ⅛ teaspoon salt in food processor until combined, about 5 pulses. Scatter butter over top and pulse until dime-size clumps form, about 15 pulses. Transfer topping to bowl and pinch together any powdery parts. Sprinkle topping evenly over blueberries.

3. Bake until filling is bubbling around edges and topping is golden brown, about 30 minutes, rotating dish halfway through baking. Transfer dish to wire rack and let cool for at least 30 minutes before serving. (Cooled crisp can be wrapped in plastic wrap and refrigerated for up to 24 hours. Let crisp sit at room temperature for 30 minutes before serving.)

VEGAN PEACH CRUMBLE

Serves 4 to 6 | 8-inch square baking dish

WHY THIS RECIPE WORKS Peaches are certainly juicier than apples, but they can also vary quite a bit more than apples in terms of juiciness and sweetness. To get a great peach crumble every time with fickle peaches, we let peeled, sliced peaches macerate in sugar for half an hour before draining them and measuring out the amount of peach juice that would be added back to the filling: always ¼ cup. This both concentrated the peaches' flavor and controlled their moisture content. To ensure that the crumble topping would stay crisp on top of the delicate peaches, we parbaked it separately first (while the peaches were macerating) and then added it to the fruit in the baking dish to bake until browned and bubbling. We recommend fresh peaches in this recipe. If you are a strict vegan, use organic sugar.

FILLING
3½ pounds ripe but firm peaches, peeled, pitted, and cut into ¾-inch-thick wedges
⅓ cup (2⅓ ounces) granulated sugar
1 tablespoon lemon juice
1¼ teaspoons cornstarch
Pinch table salt
Pinch ground cinnamon
Pinch ground nutmeg

TOPPING
1 cup (5 ounces) all-purpose flour
¼ cup (1¾ ounces) granulated sugar
¼ cup packed (1¾ ounces) brown sugar
2 teaspoons vanilla extract
⅛ teaspoon table salt
6 tablespoons refined coconut oil or unsalted butter, melted
½ cup sliced almonds, divided
1 tablespoon water

1. Adjust oven racks to lower-middle and upper-middle positions and heat oven to 350 degrees. Line rimmed baking sheet with parchment paper.

2. **FOR THE FILLING:** Gently toss peaches and sugar together in large bowl and let sit for 30 minutes, tossing occasionally. Drain peaches in colander set over large bowl. Whisk ¼ cup drained peach juice, lemon juice, cornstarch, salt, cinnamon, and nutmeg together in small bowl; discard excess peach juice. Toss juice mixture with peaches and transfer to 8-inch square baking dish.

3. **FOR THE TOPPING:** While peaches are macerating, pulse flour, granulated sugar, brown sugar, vanilla, and salt in food processor until combined, about 5 pulses. Add melted oil, ¼ cup almonds, and water and process until combined, about 30 seconds, scraping down sides of bowl as needed. Add remaining ¼ cup almonds and pulse until combined, about 2 pulses. Transfer mixture to prepared sheet, pinch into rough ½-inch chunks with some smaller, loose bits, and spread into even layer. Bake on upper rack until lightly browned and firm, 15 to 19 minutes.

4. Sprinkle topping evenly over peaches and spread into even layer with spatula, packing down lightly and breaking up any very large pieces. Place dish on lower rack and increase oven temperature to 375 degrees. Bake until topping is well browned and juices are bubbling around edges, 20 to 30 minutes. Let cool for at least 45 minutes before serving.

NO-BAKE CHERRY CRUMBLE

Serves 6 | 10-inch nonstick skillet

WHY THIS RECIPE WORKS Most fruit crisps are baked in the oven, but we wanted a summer cherry dessert that didn't require us to turn on the oven at all. After testing various methods, we found that the best was actually the easiest: After browning a topping of almonds, sugar, flour, and butter in a skillet on the stovetop, we use the same pan to cook the filling. We cooked pitted sweet cherries with sugar, lemon juice, and almond and vanilla extracts. Some cornstarch thickened the filling to a syrupy consistency, and dried cherries soaked up excess moisture while adding texture and more cherry flavor.

TOPPING
¾ cup sliced almonds, divided
⅔ cup (3⅓ ounces) all-purpose flour
¼ cup packed (1¾ ounces) light brown sugar
¼ cup (1¾ ounces) granulated sugar
½ teaspoon vanilla extract
¼ teaspoon ground cinnamon
¼ teaspoon table salt
6 tablespoons unsalted butter, melted

FILLING
⅓ cup (2⅓ ounces) granulated sugar, divided
1 tablespoon cornstarch
2 pounds fresh sweet cherries, pitted and halved
1 tablespoon lemon juice
1 teaspoon vanilla extract
½ teaspoon table salt
¼ teaspoon almond extract
⅔ cup dried cherries

1. FOR THE TOPPING: Finely chop ¼ cup almonds. Combine chopped almonds, flour, brown sugar, granulated sugar, vanilla, cinnamon, and salt in bowl. Stir in melted butter until mixture resembles wet sand and no dry flour remains.

2. Toast remaining ½ cup almonds in 10-inch nonstick skillet over medium-low heat until just beginning to brown, about 4 minutes. Add flour mixture and cook, stirring constantly, until lightly browned, 6 to 8 minutes; transfer to plate to cool. Wipe skillet clean with paper towels.

3. FOR THE FILLING: Combine 2 tablespoons sugar and cornstarch in small bowl; set aside. Combine fresh cherries, lemon juice, vanilla, salt, almond extract, and remaining sugar in now-empty skillet. Cover and cook over medium heat until cherries release their juice, about 7 minutes, stirring halfway through cooking. Uncover, stir in dried cherries, and simmer until cherries are very tender, about 3 minutes.

4. Stir in cornstarch mixture and simmer, stirring constantly, until thickened, 1 to 3 minutes. Off heat, distribute topping evenly over filling. Return skillet to medium-low heat and cook until filling is bubbling around edges, about 3 minutes. Let cool off heat for at least 30 minutes before serving.

APPLE-BLACKBERRY BETTY

Serves 6 to 8 | 8-inch square baking dish

WHY THIS RECIPE WORKS An apple Betty features a filling with lightly sweetened bread crumbs both above and below the apples. Two tablespoons of water mixed into the apples created steam to jump-start cooking. Bread crumbs mixed with butter and brown sugar and pressed into the bottom of the dish absorbed excess moisture from the apples, while those on the top crisped and browned. You can substitute another soft, enriched bread such as challah or brioche for the sandwich bread. For the apples, feel free to substitute a sweet variety and a tart variety of your choice. You can substitute raspberries or blueberries for the blackberries. It's fine to use frozen berries (or simply omit them). We like the flavor of nutmeg here, but substitute ½ teaspoon of ground cinnamon if you prefer it. Serve with vanilla ice cream, if desired.

10 ounces (about 7 slices) hearty white sandwich bread, cut into 1-inch pieces
½ cup packed (3½ ounces) plus ⅓ cup packed (2⅓ ounces) light brown sugar, divided
¾ teaspoon table salt, divided
6 tablespoons unsalted butter, melted
1½ pounds Golden Delicious apples, peeled, cored, and cut into ½-inch pieces
1 pound Granny Smith apples, peeled, cored, and cut into ½-inch pieces
2 tablespoons water
1 teaspoon vanilla extract
¼ teaspoon ground nutmeg
3¾ ounces (¾ cup) blackberries, berries larger than ¾ inch cut in half crosswise

1. Adjust oven racks to upper-middle and lower-middle positions and heat oven to 375 degrees. Pulse bread in food processor until coarsely ground, about 15 pulses. Add ½ cup sugar and ½ teaspoon salt and pulse to combine, about 5 pulses. Drizzle

with melted butter and pulse until evenly distributed, about 5 pulses. Scatter 2½ cups bread crumb mixture in 8-inch square baking dish. Press gently to create even layer.

2. Combine apples, water, vanilla, nutmeg, remaining ⅓ cup sugar, and remaining ¼ teaspoon salt in bowl. Pile apple mixture atop bread crumb mixture in dish and spread and press into even layer. Sprinkle blackberries over apples (dish will be very full). Distribute remaining bread crumb mixture evenly over blackberries, and press lightly to form uniform layer. Cover tightly with aluminum foil. (Uncooked Betty can be refrigerated for up to 2 days.) Place on rimmed baking sheet and bake on lower rack until apples are soft, 1 hour to 1 hour 10 minutes.

3. Remove foil and transfer dish to upper rack. Bake until crumbs on top are crisp and well browned, about 15 minutes. Transfer to wire rack and let cool for at least 20 minutes before serving.

No-Bake Cherry Crumble

PEACH BETTY

Serves 6 | 12-inch nonstick ovensafe skillet

WHY THIS RECIPE WORKS Betty is a homey dessert made by layering sliced fruit and fresh bread crumbs in a deep dish and baking them until the fruit is tender and the crumb topping is crisp. For our recipe, we opted for a skillet, which we used to precook the peaches. This step both deepened their flavor and evaporated their juices, preventing a soupy Betty. Adding melted butter to fresh bread crumbs made for a topping that wasn't quite crisp; cold butter created a fluffy, super-crisp topping. A little lemon juice brightened up the Betty, while a bit of vanilla extract brought out the flavor of the peaches. Merely coating the cooked peaches with bread crumbs and sliding the skillet into the oven left us with a sodden coating; instead, we mixed a portion of the bread crumbs in with the fruit to sop up some of the juices that hadn't evaporated.

Apple-Blackberry Betty

TOPPING
- 4 slices hearty white sandwich bread, torn into pieces
- 5 tablespoons unsalted butter, cut into ½-inch pieces and chilled
- 1 tablespoon granulated sugar
- ¼ teaspoon ground cinnamon

PEACH FILLING
- 2 tablespoons unsalted butter
- 3½ pounds peaches, peeled, halved, pitted, and cut into ½-inch wedges
- ⅓ cup (2⅓ ounces) granulated sugar
- ⅓ cup packed (2⅓ ounces) light brown sugar
- 1 tablespoon lemon juice
- 1 teaspoon vanilla extract
- ⅛ teaspoon table salt

1. **FOR THE TOPPING:** Adjust oven rack to middle position and heat oven to 400 degrees. Pulse bread and butter in food processor until coarsely ground, about 15 pulses. Set aside. Combine sugar and cinnamon in small bowl.

2. **FOR THE PEACH FILLING:** Melt butter in 12-inch nonstick ovensafe skillet over medium-high heat. Cook peaches, stirring occasionally, until they begin to caramelize, 8 to 12 minutes. Off heat, stir in 1 cup crumb mixture, granulated sugar, brown sugar, lemon juice, vanilla, and salt.

3. Top peach mixture with remaining crumbs. Sprinkle with cinnamon sugar and bake until topping is golden brown and juices are bubbling, 20 to 25 minutes. Let cool for 10 minutes. Serve warm.

Peach Betty

SOUR CHERRY COBBLER
Serves 12 | 13 by 9-inch baking dish

WHY THIS RECIPE WORKS The tart, bracing flavor and plump texture of sour cherries make them an ideal pairing with the tender, golden biscuits of a cobbler. Since sour cherries have such a short season (they are typically available for only a few weeks in the summer and regionally at that), we looked to an alternative so we could make a cherry cobbler whenever we wanted. Jarred Morello cherries have a deep ruby red hue, tart flavor, and pleasantly chewy texture that fit the bill. What's more, they are packed in a sugar syrup, which added welcome flavor to our cobbler filling. Replacing some of the cherry juice with red wine provided complexity and prevented the filling from being overly sweet, while some cinnamon and a bit of almond extract rounded out the flavors. Topped with a fleet of rustic drop biscuits, this was a cherry cobbler we could enjoy any time of year. Use less sugar if you prefer a cobbler on the tart side, more if you prefer a sweeter cobbler.

TOPPING
- 2 cups (10 ounces) all-purpose flour
- ½ cup (3½ ounces) sugar, divided
- ½ teaspoon baking powder
- ½ teaspoon baking soda
- ½ teaspoon salt
- 6 tablespoons unsalted butter, cut into ½-inch pieces and chilled
- 1 cup buttermilk

FILLING
- 4 (24-ounce) jars sour cherries, drained, 2 cups syrup reserved
- ¾–1 cup (5¼ to 7 ounces) sugar
- 3 tablespoons plus 1 teaspoon cornstarch
  Pinch salt

Sour Cherry Cobbler

1 cup dry red wine
1 cinnamon stick
¼ teaspoon almond extract

1. Adjust oven rack to middle position and heat oven to 425 degrees. Line rimmed baking sheet with parchment paper. Line second rimmed baking sheet with aluminum foil.

2. **FOR THE TOPPING:** Pulse flour, 6 tablespoons sugar, baking powder, baking soda, and salt in food processor until combined, about 3 pulses. Scatter butter pieces over top and pulse until mixture resembles coarse meal, about 15 pulses. Transfer mixture to large bowl; add buttermilk and stir until combined.

3. Using greased ¼-cup measure, scoop out and drop 12 mounds of dough onto prepared baking sheet, spacing 1½ inches apart. Sprinkle remaining 2 tablespoons sugar evenly over top of biscuits and bake until lightly browned, about 15 minutes, rotating baking sheet halfway through baking. (Do not turn oven off.)

4. **FOR THE FILLING:** Meanwhile, arrange cherries in even layer in 13 by 9-inch baking dish. Combine sugar, cornstarch, and salt in medium saucepan. Stir in reserved cherry juice and wine and add cinnamon stick; bring mixture to simmer over medium-high heat, stirring frequently, until mixture thickens, about 5 minutes. Remove cinnamon stick, stir in almond extract, and pour hot liquid over cherries.

5. Arrange hot biscuits in 3 rows of 4 biscuits over warm filling. Place baking dish on foil-lined baking sheet and bake until filling is bubbling and biscuits are deep golden brown, about 10 minutes. Transfer baking dish to wire rack and let cool for 10 minutes; serve warm.

SKILLET PEACH COBBLER
Serves 6 to 8 | 12-inch ovensafe nonstick skillet
WHY THIS RECIPE WORKS We wanted a juicy peach cobbler that avoided a watery filling and soggy topping. To achieve this, we used a skillet to sauté the peaches in butter and sugar to release their juices and concentrate flavor; we then continued to cook them down until the liquid was reduced. Withholding some of the peaches and adding them just before baking prevented a mushy filling. We also made the biscuits sturdy enough to stand up to the fruit by mixing melted butter rather than cold butter into the dry ingredients. The biscuits are modest in size, and you can bake them right on the cobbler. You can substitute 4 pounds of frozen sliced peaches for the fresh; there is no need to defrost them. Start step 2 when the peaches are almost done. A serrated peeler makes quick work of peeling fresh peaches.

FILLING
4 tablespoons unsalted butter
5 pounds peaches, peeled, halved, pitted, and cut into ½-inch wedges, divided
6 tablespoons (2⅔ ounces) sugar
⅛ teaspoon table salt
1 tablespoon lemon juice
1½ teaspoons cornstarch

TOPPING
1½ cups (7½ ounces) all-purpose flour
6 tablespoons (2⅔ ounces) sugar, divided
1½ teaspoons baking powder
¼ teaspoon baking soda
¼ teaspoon table salt
¾ cup buttermilk
4 tablespoons unsalted butter, melted and cooled
1 teaspoon ground cinnamon

1. **FOR THE FILLING:** Adjust oven rack to middle position and heat oven to 425 degrees. Melt butter in 12-inch ovensafe nonstick skillet over medium-high heat. Add two-thirds of peaches, sugar, and salt and cook, covered, until peaches release their juices, about 5 minutes. Remove lid and simmer until all liquid has evaporated and peaches begin to caramelize, 15 to 20 minutes. Add remaining peaches and cook until heated through, about 5 minutes. Whisk lemon juice and cornstarch in small bowl, then stir into peach mixture. Cover skillet and set aside off heat.

2. **FOR THE TOPPING:** Meanwhile, whisk flour, 5 tablespoons sugar, baking powder, baking soda, and salt in medium bowl. Stir in buttermilk and melted butter until dough forms. Turn dough out onto lightly floured work surface and knead briefly until smooth, about 30 seconds.

3. Combine remaining 1 tablespoon sugar and cinnamon. Break dough into rough 1-inch pieces and space them about ½ inch apart on top of hot peach mixture. Sprinkle with cinnamon sugar and bake until topping is golden brown and filling is thickened, 18 to 22 minutes. Let cool on wire rack for 10 minutes. Serve.

BLUEBERRY COBBLER
Serves 8 | 9-inch deep-dish pie plate
WHY THIS RECIPE WORKS We wanted a cobbler that put the blueberry flavor front and center, with a light, tender biscuit topping that could hold its own against the fruit filling. We started by preparing a filling using 6 cups of fresh berries and just enough sugar to sweeten them. Cornstarch worked well to thicken the fruit's juices. Parbaking the biscuit topping ensured that the biscuits wouldn't become soggy once placed on top of the fruit, and precooking the fruit filling meant all we had to do

was set the parbaked biscuits on the hot filling and bake them together for 15 minutes until bubbly. Taste the fruit before adding sugar; use less if it is very sweet, more if it is tart. Do not let the biscuit batter sit for longer than 5 minutes or so before baking.

TOPPING

1½ cups (7½ ounces) all-purpose flour
¼ cup (1¾ ounces) plus 2 teaspoons sugar, divided
1½ teaspoons baking powder
¼ teaspoon baking soda
¼ teaspoon table salt
¾ cup buttermilk, chilled
6 tablespoons unsalted butter, melted and hot
⅛ teaspoon ground cinnamon

FILLING

⅓–⅔ cup (2⅓ to 4⅔ ounces) sugar
4 teaspoons cornstarch
30 ounces (6 cups) blueberries
1 tablespoon lemon juice
½ teaspoon ground cinnamon

1. FOR THE TOPPING: Adjust oven rack to middle position and heat oven to 400 degrees. Line rimmed baking sheet with parchment paper. Whisk flour, ¼ cup sugar, baking powder, baking soda, and salt together in large bowl.

2. In separate bowl, stir buttermilk and melted butter together until butter forms small clumps. Using rubber spatula, stir buttermilk mixture into flour mixture until just incorporated and dough pulls away from sides of bowl.

3. Using greased ¼-cup measure, scoop out and drop 8 mounds of dough onto prepared baking sheet, spaced about 1½ inches apart. Combine remaining 2 teaspoons sugar with cinnamon, then sprinkle over biscuits. Bake biscuits until puffed and lightly browned on bottom, about 10 minutes, rotating sheet halfway through baking. Remove parbaked biscuits from oven; set aside.

4. FOR THE FILLING: Whisk sugar and cornstarch together in large bowl. Add blueberries, lemon juice, and cinnamon and toss gently to combine. Transfer fruit mixture to 9-inch deep-dish pie plate, cover with aluminum foil, and place on foil-lined rimmed baking sheet. Bake until filling is hot and berries have released their juice, 40 to 50 minutes.

5. Remove fruit from oven, uncover, and stir gently. Arrange parbaked biscuits over top, squeezing them slightly as needed to fit into dish. Bake cobbler until biscuits are golden brown and fruit is bubbling, about 15 minutes. Transfer to wire rack and let cool for 15 minutes before serving.

GLUTEN-FREE BLUEBERRY COBBLER WITH CORNMEAL BISCUITS

Serves 8 | 9-inch deep-dish pie plate

WHY THIS RECIPE WORKS For our gluten-free blueberry cobbler we settled on rustic cornmeal drop biscuits instead of traditional biscuits. Equal cup amounts of cornmeal and all-purpose gluten-free flour blend created a sturdy biscuit that held up to the fruit filling. For leaveners, we used both baking soda and baking powder to give our biscuits the lift and sturdiness they needed to hold their shape, as well as to keep them from being too dense. As with our traditional cobblers, we found that baking the filling and biscuits separately, then combining them just before serving, gave us a perfectly cooked filling and tender biscuits. Be ready to serve the cobbler as soon as it comes out of the oven; the bottom of the biscuits will become quite soggy if allowed to sit on top of the warm fruit for too long.

BISCUITS

5 ounces (1 cup) cornmeal
4½ ounces (1 cup) all-purpose gluten-free flour blend (see page 2)
3 tablespoons sugar, divided
2 teaspoons baking powder
¼ teaspoon baking soda
½ teaspoon table salt
¼ teaspoon xanthan gum (see page 2)
8 tablespoons unsalted butter, cut into ¼-inch pieces and chilled
¾ cup buttermilk, chilled

FILLING

2⅓ ounces (⅓ cup) sugar
4 teaspoons cornstarch
¼ teaspoon table salt
30 ounces (6 cups) blueberries
1½ teaspoons grated lemon zest plus 1 tablespoon juice

1. FOR THE BISCUITS: Adjust oven rack to upper-middle and lower-middle positions and heat oven to 375 degrees. Line baking sheet with parchment paper. Pulse cornmeal, flour blend, 2 tablespoons sugar, baking powder, baking soda, salt, and xanthan gum in food processor until combined, about 5 pulses. Scatter butter pieces over top and pulse until mixture resembles coarse cornmeal with a few slightly larger butter lumps, about 10 pulses.

2. Transfer cornmeal mixture to medium bowl, add buttermilk, and stir with fork until dough gathers into moist clumps. Using greased ¼-cup dry measure, scoop out and drop eight 2¼-inch-wide mounds of dough onto prepared sheet, spaced about 1 inch apart. (Do not make biscuits wider or they won't all fit in pie plate when baked.)

TUTORIAL
Blueberry Cobbler

It's worth parbaking the biscuits for this cobbler—it means no soggy biscuit bottoms and perfectly stewed fruit.

1. Using greased ¼-cup measure, scoop out and drop 8 mounds of biscuit dough onto baking sheet, spaced about 1½ inches apart.

2. Bake biscuits until puffed and lightly browned on bottom, about 10 minutes, rotating sheet halfway through baking. Remove parbaked biscuits from oven.

3. Transfer blueberry mixture to 9-inch pie plate, cover with aluminum foil, and place on foil-lined rimmed baking sheet.

4. Bake until filling is hot and berries have released their juice, 40 to 50 minutes. Remove fruit from oven, uncover, and stir gently.

5. Arrange parbaked biscuits over top, squeezing them slightly as needed to fit into dish.

6 . Bake cobbler until biscuits are golden brown and fruit is bubbling, about 15 minutes. Transfer to wire rack and let cool for 15 minutes before serving.

3. Sprinkle remaining 1 tablespoon sugar over biscuits and bake on upper rack until biscuits are puffed and lightly browned, 25 to 30 minutes, rotating sheet halfway through baking. Let biscuits cool on wire rack. (Cooled biscuits can be held at room temperature in zipper-lock bag for up to 2 hours.)

4. FOR THE FILLING: Stir sugar, cornstarch, and salt together in large bowl. Gently stir in blueberries and lemon zest and juice until evenly combined. Transfer to 9-inch deep-dish pie plate, cover with aluminum foil, and place on foil-lined rimmed baking sheet. Bake on lower rack until blueberries are beginning to burst and juices are bubbling around edge, 40 to 50 minutes, stirring halfway through baking.

5. Uncover blueberries and stir gently. Arrange biscuits on top of fruit and continue to bake until biscuits have warmed through, about 5 minutes. Serve immediately.

BLUEBERRY GRUNT

Serves 12 | Dutch oven

WHY THIS RECIPE WORKS This old-fashioned fruit dessert boasts sweetened stewed berries covered with drop biscuit dough. A Dutch oven was the perfect vessel; the heavy bottom prevented the fruit from burning, and the heavy lid held in steam nicely. To avoid washed-out fruit and a soggy topping, we cooked down half of the berries until jammy and then stirred in the remaining berries to maintain fresh fruit flavor. A little bit of cornstarch further thickened the filling. We placed a dish towel under the lid during cooking to absorb condensation that would turn the biscuits soggy. A sprinkling of cinnamon sugar over the finished biscuits provided sweet crunch. Do not use frozen blueberries here, as they will make the filling watery.

FILLING
2½ pounds (8 cups) blueberries, divided
 ½ cup (3½ ounces) sugar
 2 tablespoons water
 1 teaspoon grated lemon zest plus 1 tablespoon juice
 ½ teaspoon ground cinnamon
 1 teaspoon cornstarch

TOPPING
 ¾ cup buttermilk
 6 tablespoons unsalted butter, melted and cooled slightly
 1 teaspoon vanilla extract
2¼ cups (11¼ ounces) all-purpose flour
 ½ cup (3½ ounces) sugar, divided
1½ teaspoons baking powder
 ½ teaspoon baking soda
 ½ teaspoon table salt
 ½ teaspoon ground cinnamon

1. FOR THE FILLING: Cook 4 cups blueberries, sugar, water, lemon zest, and cinnamon in Dutch oven over medium-high heat, stirring occasionally, until mixture is thick and jam-like, 10 to 12 minutes. Whisk lemon juice and cornstarch in small bowl until combined, then stir into blueberry mixture. Add remaining 4 cups blueberries and cook until heated through, about 1 minute. Remove pot from heat and cover to keep warm.

2. FOR THE TOPPING: Combine buttermilk, melted butter, and vanilla in 2-cup liquid measuring cup. Whisk flour, 6 tablespoons sugar, baking powder, baking soda, and salt together in large bowl. Slowly stir buttermilk mixture into flour mixture until dough forms.

3. Using small ice cream scoop or 2 large spoons, spoon golf ball–size dough pieces on top of warm berry mixture (you should have 14 pieces). Wrap lid of Dutch oven with clean dish towel (keeping towel away from heat source) and cover pot. Simmer gently until biscuits have doubled in size and toothpick inserted in center comes out clean, 16 to 22 minutes.

4. Combine cinnamon and remaining 2 tablespoons sugar in bowl. Remove lid and sprinkle biscuit topping with cinnamon sugar. Serve immediately.

LAZY STRAWBERRY SONKER

Serves 6 | 8-inch square baking dish

WHY THIS RECIPE WORKS Sonker is a juicy, fruit-filled deep-dish dessert rarely found outside Surry County, North Carolina. A subset of recipes dub themselves "lazy" sonkers, in which the fruit is cooked into a sweet stew and topped with a batter that bakes into a distinct, lightly crisp layer of cake. For our version, we tossed strawberries with sugar, salt, water, and cornstarch and then baked them until they bubbled and thickened. We then poured the batter over the filling and returned it to the oven, where the hot filling baked the batter from underneath into a tender-yet-crisp raft of cake. If you're using frozen strawberries in this recipe, there's no need to let them thaw. In steps 2 and 3, be sure to stir the strawberry filling as directed, scraping the bottom of the dish to incorporate the cornstarch so that it evenly and thoroughly thickens the mixture. In step 3, add the butter to the batter while it is still hot so it remains pourable, and be sure to mix the batter only right before pouring it over the filling.

 2 pounds fresh strawberries, hulled (6½ cups)
 1 cup (7 ounces) sugar, divided
 ½ teaspoon table salt, divided
 ¼ cup water
 3 tablespoons cornstarch
 1 cup (5 ounces) all-purpose flour

Lazy Strawberry Sonker

Lazy Peach Sonker

Substitute 2 ½ pounds peaches, peeled, halved, pitted, and cut into ½-inch-thick wedges, for strawberries.

TEXAS-STYLE BLUEBERRY COBBLER

Serves 8 to 10 | 13 by 9-inch baking dish

WHY THIS RECIPE WORKS In the Hill Country region of Texas, cobblers feature a thick, pancake-like batter that forms a craggy surface studded with fruit. Melting some of the butter in the baking pan before pouring in the batter creates rich, deliciously crisp edges. Lemon brightens blueberry desserts, so we pulsed sugar and lemon zest in a food processor and mashed some of the citrusy sugar with blueberries to add some light acidity while also breaking down the berries. Once the assembled cobbler went into the oven, the batter rose and the fruit sank, creating the signature pocketed surface. Keep a close eye on the butter as it melts in the oven so that it doesn't scorch. Place the hot baking dish with butter on a wire rack after removing it from the oven. Avoid untreated aluminum pans here. If using frozen blueberries, thaw them first.

- 4 tablespoons unsalted butter, cut into 4 pieces, plus 8 tablespoons melted and cooled
- 1 ½ cups (10 ½ ounces) sugar, divided
- 1 ½ teaspoons grated lemon zest
- 15 ounces (3 cups) blueberries
- 1 ½ cups (7 ½ ounces) all-purpose flour
- 2 ½ teaspoons baking powder
- ¾ teaspoon table salt
- 1 ½ cups milk

1. Adjust oven rack to upper-middle position and heat oven to 350 degrees. Place 4 tablespoons cut-up butter in 13 by 9-inch baking dish and transfer to oven. Heat until butter is melted, 8 to 10 minutes.

2. Meanwhile, pulse ¼ cup sugar and lemon zest in food processor until combined, about 5 pulses; set aside. Using potato masher, mash blueberries and 1 tablespoon lemon sugar together in bowl until berries are coarsely mashed.

3. Combine flour, baking powder, salt, and remaining 1 ¼ cups sugar in large bowl. Whisk in milk and 8 tablespoons melted, cooled butter until smooth. Remove baking dish from oven, transfer to wire rack, and pour batter into prepared pan.

4. Dollop mashed blueberry mixture evenly over batter, sprinkle with remaining lemon sugar, and bake until golden brown and edges are crisp, 45 to 50 minutes, rotating pan halfway through baking. Let cobbler cool on wire rack for 30 minutes. Serve warm.

- 1 teaspoon baking powder
- ½ cup whole milk
- 8 tablespoons unsalted butter, melted and hot
- ¼ teaspoon vanilla extract

1. Adjust oven rack to middle position and heat oven to 350 degrees. Line rimmed baking sheet with parchment paper. Combine strawberries, ¼ cup sugar, and ¼ teaspoon salt in bowl. Whisk water and cornstarch together in second bowl; add to strawberry mixture and toss until strawberries are evenly coated.

2. Transfer strawberry mixture to 8-inch square baking dish and place dish on prepared sheet. Bake until filling is bubbling around sides of dish, 35 to 40 minutes, stirring and scraping bottom of dish with rubber spatula halfway through baking.

3. Remove sheet from oven and stir filling, being sure to scrape bottom and corners of dish with rubber spatula. Whisk flour, baking powder, remaining ¾ cup sugar, and remaining ¼ teaspoon salt together in bowl. Whisk in milk, melted butter, and vanilla until smooth. Pour batter evenly over filling.

4. Bake until surface is golden brown and toothpick inserted in center comes out with no crumbs attached, 35 to 40 minutes, rotating dish halfway through baking. Let sonker cool on wire rack for 15 minutes. Serve.

Lazy Strawberry Sonker

SHORTCAKES

WHILE SOME FOLKS LIKE TO SPOON JUICY, sweetened fruit over pound cake, sponge cake, or even angel food cake, our idea of shortcake definitely involves a biscuit. While shortcakes are a simple dessert with three distinct components—the fruit and biscuits, plus whipped cream—it's important to take care with each part to ensure shortcakes live up to their promise.

Macerating and crushing a portion of the fruit encourages the fruit to release its juices and gives the filling just the right texture. Rich-tasting homemade biscuits are also key, and our recipes incorporate both a stick of butter for richness and an egg for tenderness (you'll see coconut oil in our vegan short-cakes). Some drop biscuits can turn out dense and compact, without the flakiness and lightness we want in a biscuit. To create light and flaky drop biscuits, we sometimes add melted butter to cold buttermilk. When combined with the cold butter-milk, the butter forms clumps. As those clumps of butter melt during baking, the water in the butter evaporates and creates steam, which lightens the biscuits.

With a sprinkling of sugar before baking, the shortcakes emerge from the oven browned, tender, and ready to serve as a bed for the juicy fruit. Properly whipped cream is the crowning glory for this summertime favorite.

While shortcakes are best served warm, most cooled cakes can be stored in a zipper-lock bag at room temperature for 24 hours. They will lose some of their crispness, but you can bring it back by warming them in a 300-degree oven for 10 minutes.

STRAWBERRY SHORTCAKES

Serves 6 to 8 | rimmed baking sheet

WHY THIS RECIPE WORKS Strawberry shortcake is a must-have summer dessert. We wanted a juicy strawberry filling that would stay put in between our biscuits. The solution? We chose the ripest berries we could find (for the best flavor), and then mashed some of them into a chunky sauce and sliced the rest. Left to sit for a bit with a little sugar, the berry mixture macerated, exuding even more flavorful juice, making for a thick, chunky filling that soaked into, and didn't slip off, our tender biscuits. This recipe will yield six biscuits, and scraps can be gathered and patted out to yield another biscuit or two; these, though, will not be as tender as the first.

2½ pounds strawberries, hulled (8 cups), divided
½ cup (3½ ounces) plus 3 tablespoons sugar, divided
2 cups (10 ounces) all-purpose flour
1 tablespoon baking powder
½ teaspoon table salt
8 tablespoons unsalted butter, cut into ½-inch pieces and chilled
⅔ cup half-and-half
1 large egg plus 1 large egg white, lightly beaten
1 recipe Whipped Cream (page 548)

1. Crush 3 cups strawberries with potato masher. Slice remaining berries and stir into crushed berries with 6 tablespoons sugar. Let sit at room temperature, stirring occasionally, until fruit begins to release its juices, about 30 minutes or up to 2 hours.

2. Meanwhile, adjust oven rack to lower-middle position and heat oven to 425 degrees. Line rimmed baking sheet with parchment paper. Pulse flour, baking powder, salt, and 3 tablespoons sugar in food processor until combined. Scatter butter pieces over top and pulse until mixture resembles coarse cornmeal, about 15 pulses. Transfer to large bowl.

3. In separate bowl, whisk half-and-half and egg together. Add half-and-half mixture to flour mixture and stir with rubber spatula until large clumps form. Turn mixture onto lightly floured counter and knead lightly until dough comes together.

4. Using your fingertips, pat dough into 9 by 6-inch rectangle about 1 inch thick. Cut out 6 biscuits using floured 2¾-inch biscuit cutter. Pat remaining dough into 1-inch thick piece and cut out 2 more biscuits. Place biscuits on baking sheet, spaced 1 inch apart.

5. Brush top of biscuits with egg white and sprinkle with remaining 2 tablespoons sugar. Bake biscuits until golden brown, 12 to 14 minutes. Let biscuits cool on baking sheet for about 10 minutes. (Biscuits can be stored at room temperature for up to 3 days or frozen for up to 1 month; to serve, refresh in 350-degree oven for 3 to 5 minutes, or 7 to 10 minutes for frozen biscuits.)

6. Split each biscuit in half and place bottoms on individual serving plates. Spoon portion of berries over each bottom, then top with dollop of whipped cream. Cap with biscuit tops and serve immediately.

PEACH SHORTCAKES

Serves 6 | rimmed baking sheet

WHY THIS RECIPE WORKS If you're lucky enough to have ripe farm-stand peaches, making peach shortcake is not challenging. But try making shortcake with hard, mealy peaches and you'll end up with a flavorless filling and a dry, crumbly biscuit. For a peach shortcake recipe that would work with any peach, regardless of quality, we found that macerating sliced peaches (as with strawberries) didn't adequately moisten and sweeten the fruit. Microwaving some of the peaches with peach schnapps until they were tender, and then mashing them to create a jam that we added to the remaining uncooked peaches, gave the fruit the moisture and sweetness we were looking for. Orange juice or orange liqueur can be used in place of the peach schnapps.

FRUIT
2 pounds peaches, peeled, halved, pitted, and cut into ¼-inch-thick wedges, divided
6 tablespoons (2⅔ ounces) sugar, divided
2 tablespoons peach schnapps

BISCUITS
2 cups (10 ounces) all-purpose flour
2 teaspoons baking powder
2 tablespoons sugar, divided
¾ teaspoon table salt
⅔ cup cold buttermilk
1 large egg
8 tablespoons unsalted butter, melted and hot
1 recipe Whipped Cream (page 548)

1. **FOR THE FRUIT:** Gently toss three-quarters of peaches with ¼ cup sugar in large bowl and let sit at room temperature for 30 minutes. In separate bowl, microwave remaining peaches, remaining 2 tablespoons sugar, and schnapps until bubbling, 1 to 1½ minutes, stirring twice during cooking. Using potato masher, crush microwaved peaches into coarse pulp, then let cool at room temperature for 30 minutes.

2. **FOR THE BISCUITS:** Meanwhile, adjust oven rack to middle position and heat oven to 475 degrees. Line rimmed baking sheet with parchment paper. Whisk flour, baking powder, 1 tablespoon sugar, and salt in large bowl.

3. Whisk buttermilk and egg in bowl until combined. Stir in hot melted butter until butter forms small clumps. Using rubber spatula, stir buttermilk mixture into flour mixture until just incorporated and dough pulls away from sides of bowl.

4. Using greased ⅓-cup dry measure, scoop out and drop 6 mounds of dough onto prepared sheet, spaced about 1½ inches apart. Sprinkle with remaining 1 tablespoon sugar. Bake until tops are golden brown and crisp, about 15 minutes, rotating baking sheet halfway through baking. Let biscuits cool on sheet for 15 minutes. (Biscuits can be stored at room temperature for up to 1 day.)

5. Split each biscuit in half and place bottoms on individual serving plates. Spoon portion of mashed fruit over each bottom, followed by peach slices and any exuded juices. Top with dollop of whipped cream, cap with biscuit tops, and dollop with remaining whipped cream. Serve immediately.

Peach Shortcakes

BROWN SUGAR–BERRY SHORTCAKES

Serves 6 | rimmed baking sheet

WHY THIS RECIPE WORKS Replacing the usual granulated sugar in both the fruit and the biscuits with brown sugar added complexity and an appealing caramel note to these shortcakes. Including sour cream in our biscuit a lent a unique tanginess and tender crumb. We mashed some of the berries with the sugar to release their juices but kept most of them whole for tartness and texture. Finally, we incorporated brown sugar and sour cream into the whipped topping. Depending on the sweetness of your berries, you may need more or less sugar.

FRUIT

23 ounces (4½ cups) blackberries, blueberries, and raspberries
8 ounces strawberries, hulled (1½ cups)
4–6 tablespoons packed (1¾ to 2⅔ ounces) light brown sugar

SHORTCAKES

2 cups (10 ounces) all-purpose flour
3 tablespoons packed light brown sugar
1 tablespoon baking powder
½ teaspoon table salt
8 tablespoons unsalted butter, cut into ½-inch pieces and chilled, plus 2 tablespoons melted
1 large egg
½ cup sour cream
2 tablespoons granulated sugar

BROWN SUGAR CREAM TOPPING

1 cup heavy cream
¼ cup sour cream
¼ cup packed (1¾ ounces) light brown sugar

1. **FOR THE FRUIT:** Combine berries and strawberries in large bowl. Measure 2 cups mixed berries and place in medium bowl. Add sugar to medium bowl and mash berry mixture with potato masher until combined. Fold mashed berry mixture into remaining 4 cups mixed berries and let sit at room temperature until sugar has dissolved and berry mixture is juicy, about 30 minutes.

2. **FOR THE SHORTCAKES:** Adjust oven rack to upper-middle position and heat oven to 375 degrees. Line rimmed baking sheet with parchment paper. Pulse flour, brown sugar, baking powder, and salt in food processor until no lumps of sugar remain, about 15 pulses. Scatter chilled butter pieces over top and pulse until mixture resembles coarse meal, about 7 pulses. Transfer to large bowl.

3. Whisk egg and sour cream together in small bowl. Stir into flour mixture with rubber spatula until large clumps form. Using your hands, knead lightly until dough comes together and no dry flecks of flour remain.

4. Using large (#10) ice cream scoop, scoop 6 dough rounds onto baking sheet. Brush tops with melted butter and sprinkle with granulated sugar. Bake until golden brown, 25 to 30 minutes, rotating baking sheet halfway through baking. Let shortcakes cool on baking sheet for 10 minutes. (Cooled shortcakes can be wrapped tightly in plastic wrap and stored at room temperature for up to 24 hours.)

5. **FOR THE TOPPING:** Using stand mixer fitted with whisk attachment, whip cream, sour cream, and sugar on medium-low speed until

foamy, about 1 minute. Increase speed to high and whip until stiff peaks form, 1 to 3 minutes. Use serrated knife to split each shortcake in half and place bottom pieces on individual plates. Spoon equal portion of berry mixture over shortcake bottoms, top fruit with whipped cream, and cap whipped cream with shortcake tops. Serve.

VEGAN STRAWBERRY SHORTCAKES

Serves 8 | 2 rimmed baking sheets

WHY THIS RECIPE WORKS Strawberry shortcake is a three-part dessert, and only one—the fruit filling—is vegan. For the biscuits, we melted and cooled coconut oil before adding it to cold plant-based milk. The oil acted similarly to butter, instantly solidifying into clumps that made for tender biscuits. Some lemon juice added a buttermilk-style tang. Coconut milk whipped perfectly into velvety billows. You will need to chill the unopened cans of coconut milk for at least 24 hours before use. If you are a strict vegan, use organic sugar.

STRAWBERRIES

2 pounds strawberries, hulled and quartered (6⅓ cups), divided
6 tablespoons (2⅔ ounces) granulated sugar

SHORTCAKES

2 cups (10 ounces) all-purpose flour
2 tablespoons granulated sugar
2 teaspoons baking powder
½ teaspoon baking soda
½ teaspoon table salt
1 cup plant-based milk, chilled
½ cup refined coconut oil, melted and cooled slightly
1 tablespoon lemon juice
1 tablespoon turbinado sugar

1 recipe Coconut Whipped Cream (recipe follows)

1. FOR THE STRAWBERRIES: Using potato masher, mash one-third of strawberries with sugar in bowl. Stir in remaining strawberries, cover, and let sit while making shortcakes, at least 30 minutes or up to 2 hours.

2. FOR THE SHORTCAKES: Adjust oven rack to middle position and heat oven to 475 degrees. Set rimmed baking sheet in second baking sheet and line with parchment paper. Whisk flour, granulated sugar, baking powder, baking soda, and salt together in large bowl. Whisk milk, melted oil, and lemon juice together (oil will clump) in second bowl. Stir milk mixture into flour mixture until just incorporated.

3. Using greased ⅓-cup dry measuring cup, drop level scoops of batter 1½ inches apart on prepared sheet. Sprinkle evenly with

**Brown Sugar–
Berry Shortcakes**

turbinado sugar. Bake until tops are golden, 12 to 14 minutes, rotating sheet halfway through baking. Transfer biscuits to wire rack and let cool completely, about 30 minutes.

4. Split each biscuit in half and place bottoms on individual plates. Using slotted spoon, portion strawberries over biscuit bottoms, then top with dollop of coconut whipped cream. Cap with shortcake tops and serve immediately.

COCONUT WHIPPED CREAM

Makes about 2 cups
The cream from canned coconut milk easily whips into delicately flavored soft-peaked billows.

4 (14-ounce) cans coconut milk
2 tablespoons granulated sugar
2 teaspoons vanilla extract

Refrigerate unopened cans of coconut milk for at least 24 hours to ensure that 2 distinct layers form. Skim top layer of cream from each can and measure out 2 cups of cream (save any extra cream and milky liquid for another use). Using stand mixer fitted with whisk attachment, whip coconut cream, sugar, and vanilla on low speed until well combined, about 30 seconds. Increase speed to high and whip until mixture thickens and soft peaks form, about 2 minutes. (Coconut whipped cream can be refrigerated for up to 4 days.)

creamy spoon desserts

RICH, CREAMY DESSERTS—the soft, silky kind meant to be eaten with a spoon—are found in one form or another all over the world: Sweetened grain puddings are popular throughout the Middle East, panna cotta is an Italian classic, flan is a favorite in both Spain and parts of Latin America, and tapioca pudding is a distinctly American tradition. They range from elegant restaurant classics such as individual crème brûlées to comforting favorites that are meant to be shared—think banana pudding layered with vanilla wafers and plenty of whipped cream. This category of desserts includes those that are smooth and creamy throughout like chocolate pots de crème, as well as ones that are much more substantial with a range of contrasting flavors and textures, such as a rustic bread pudding.

Some of these desserts, such as soufflés, have a reputation for being finicky and often cause a certain amount of anxiety. This makes sense: If it's something you've enjoyed only in a restaurant, it's bound to have an aura of mystery attached. And while it's true that many egg-based desserts such as custards, mousses, and puddings require precise temperatures or timing to turn out just right, over the years we've learned how to simplify and streamline many of these techniques for more foolproof results. (And as it turns out, soufflés aren't nearly as fragile and tenuous as you've probably been led to believe.)

Whether homey or refined, spoon desserts look as good as they taste. They can be dressed up with billows of whipped cream, topped with glistening berries, drizzled with honey, and garnished with crisp candied nuts. Many of them are prepared in dishes as elegant as the desserts themselves—petite fluted ramekins showcase individual creamy custards, while large glass trifle dishes expose the beauty of these multilayered affairs. Perhaps one of the most appealing aspects of these desserts is that most of them can—and in many cases should—be made ahead. That makes them ideal for an upscale dinner party or even a casual gathering where you don't want to leave all the preparation to the last minute.

Spoon Desserts Equipment Corner

Fine-Mesh Strainer

Fine-mesh strainers are great for sifting flour or powdered sugar as well as straining puddings, custards, and sauces to ensure a silky-smooth consistency. Our favorite strainer, the **5.5-cup Rösle Fine-Mesh Strainer, Round Handle, 7.9 inches, 20 cm** ($45), isn't cheap, but it's built to last. Its very fine mesh consistently turned out some of the smoothest custards and sleekest purees. Its wide, flat hook made it sit stably on all sorts of cookware, and its metal grip made it comfortable to hold.

Roasting Pan

For any dessert that requires a water bath—think crème brûlée and flan—a roasting pan is an essential piece of equipment. It should be large and sturdy, heat evenly, and have easy-to-grip handles. Our favorite is the **Cuisinart MultiClad Pro Stainless 16″ Roasting Pan with Rack** ($129.95).

Ramekins

Ramekins—small round baking dishes—are the classic choice for several spoon desserts and other individually portioned desserts. (They stand in ably for a mini prep bowl or a salt cellar as well.) We prefer thick, heavy ceramic ramekins with classic straight sides. **Le Creuset Stackable Ramekins** ($16 for one ramekin), our favorites, were the heaviest and thickest in the bunch. Everything we cooked in them emerged evenly baked and they're stackable—but they're also expensive. HIC Soufflé Ramekins ($22.52 for a set of six) are our best buy; they don't bake quite as evenly and don't stack, but they work well and are a great value.

Soufflé Dish

A round, straight-sided ceramic soufflé dish elegantly launches a soufflé—that's its raison d'être. Soufflés rose reliably in each of the four classic soufflé dishes we tested. Differences came down to two factors: the actual (versus stated) capacity of each dish and the thickness of each dish's walls. With its straight, not-too-thin but not-too-thick sides and just the right capacity to hold the batter with a little room to spare, our favorite, the **HIC 64 Ounce Soufflé dish** ($15.12), produced evenly cooked soufflés that rose high and did us proud.

Instant-Read Thermometer

When it comes to sweet tasks, thermometers aren't just for candy making. They also take the temperature of a pastry cream, fruit curd, or caramel (check the temperature in various locations since it varies a bit from place to place in the pot) and judge the doneness of custard-based desserts. A digital instant-read thermometer—rather than a slow-registering stick candy thermometer—will provide you with an accurate reading almost immediately; this is especially important with egg-based fillings, which can quickly overcook into a curdled mess. Thermometers with long probes easily reach into deep pots. The **ThermoWorks Thermapen ONE** ($105) has every bell and whistle.

Tongs

With their curved shape and rubber grips, jar lifters are ideal for removing ramekins of custard from their water bath (we like the **Ball Secure-Grip Jar Lifter,** $10.99). But if you don't have one, here's an alternative: Wrapping rubber bands around each of a tongs' pincers helps them get a secure hold on a ramekin.

GETTING TO KNOW THICKENERS

Achieving the right consistency in a sauce, custard, pie, or jam takes a little knowledge—and some help from these common thickeners.

ALL-PURPOSE FLOUR: STRUCTURE-BUILDING STANDBY
Flour can thicken a substance alone, as part of a slurry (a paste of water and a starch), or in conjunction with a fat. In either of the latter two cases, combine them with liquid gradually and whisk them in well before the mixture boils, when the flour's starches cause the mixture to thicken.

CORNSTARCH: PUDDING AND CUSTARD STABILIZER
Because cornstarch is a pure starch, it is a more effective thickener than flour (which is only 75 percent starch). But cornstarch-thickened sauces break down more quickly than flour-thickened ones, so be sure to follow the cooking times for recipes thickened with cornstarch and to reduce the heat once the dish has thickened (cornstarch must come to a boil or near-boil for its thickening power to kick in). Cornstarch is our go-to thickener for puddings such as Butterscotch Pudding (page 179) as well as our Pastry Cream (page 186); mix it with cold liquid before heating it to prevent clumping.

BUTTER: SMOOTH FINISHER The ultimate sauce finisher, butter contributes a glossy sheen, richness, flavor, and thickening to custards like Lemon Curd (page 188). But in order to achieve the right body, it's important to add butter off the heat. Because butter is an emulsion that can be broken by high temperatures, at around 160 degrees your nicely thickened sauce will lose its body.

EGG YOLKS: CURD, NOT CURDLED Rich custards such as Crème Anglaise (page 187) rely on egg yolks to achieve a creamy texture. Temperature is key to their thickening ability: If the yolks get too hot, their proteins coagulate and lose water, leaving you with a curdled, watery sauce. The takeaway? Don't boil custards thickened with egg yolks; you'll know that your custard has thickened when a spatula leaves a clear trail in the pan.

PECTIN: SURE JELLED Commercial pectin begins with apple or citrus extract and is chemically processed to produce a dry, powdered substance. Unlike gelatin, regular pectin requires the presence of sugar and acid in order to gel (that's why there's special pectin for low-sugar jams and preserves); you'll find it in fruit pies such as Fresh Strawberry Pie (page 411).

TAPIOCA: FRUIT PIE ENHANCER Tapioca starch comes from the tropical root vegetable cassava, also called manioc or yuca. This neutral-tasting thickener dissolves easily during baking or cooking and can be an asset in some fruit pies—it preserves rather than dampens fresh fruit flavor—and of course Creamy Tapioca Pudding (page 182). Minute Tapioca is our favorite brand.

GELATIN: GOOD FORM We use this pure protein in a variety of ways in the test kitchen, but it's essential for setting and stabilizing desserts such as Classic Panna Cotta (page 172) and Strawberry Mousse (page 204). Basically, gelatin is used to turn liquids into solids, resulting in a soft but set texture. While gelatin is sold both as thin sheets and in powdered form, we use powdered versions in our recipes. Both forms must be hydrated in cold water before being melted and incorporated (for more information on gelatin, see page 171).

FOR CREAMY CUSTARDS, GO STIR CRAZY

While developing our recipe for Butterscotch Pudding (see page 179), we noticed that some batches turned out slightly grainy, while others were silky smooth. The problem, we were surprised to learn, wasn't undissolved cornstarch: It was the butter. Once the pudding cooled and the fat solidified, any bits that hadn't been thoroughly broken down came across as grainy on the tongue. Vigorously whisking the pudding—or any custard with a generous amount of butter—breaks down the fat into tiny droplets that are too small to detect once the mixture cools. (It's the same principle as emulsifying a vinaigrette: Thoroughly whisking in the oil ensures that the fat breaks down into tiny droplets that don't "break" the dressing.)

KNOWING WHEN PUDDINGS AND CUSTARDS ARE DONE

Egg-based puddings and custards can curdle if cooked beyond 185 degrees. We take crème anglaise off the heat when the mixture registers 175 to 180 degrees. When making the base for ice cream (see page 536) we make sure to push the temperature to 180 degrees for maximum thickness. Baked custards, such as flan and crème brûlée, should jiggle (but not slosh) when gently shaken. This will occur between 170 and 175 degrees.

SHOULD YOU USE HOT OR COLD WATER FOR WATER BATHS?

The success of many custard recipes (crème brûlée, flan, even cheesecake) depends on baking in a water bath, which allows these delicate desserts to cook more evenly: Because the water never reaches a temperature higher than that of boiling water, or 212 degrees, the water further slows down cooking in these desserts.

We've always called for adding boiling water to the roasting pan for the bath, but we decided to see if this was really necessary. We baked three batches each of crème brûlée (prepared in 4-ounce ramekins) and cheesecake (prepared in a 9-inch springform pan), with three different starting temperatures for the water bath. In the baths that started with boiling water, not only did both desserts cook the fastest but these samples had a smoother, more uniform texture. The desserts baked in baths that started with ice water did not cook uniformly; the bottom half was perfectly done while the top half was overcooked. The results weren't as extreme with baths that started with room-temperature water, but the desserts were still unevenly baked and not satisfactory.

The reason is this: The temperature of boiling water is much closer to the temperature of the oven, which means that the lower portion sitting in the bath and the upper exposed portion start in environments of similar temperature and thus cook evenly. Meanwhile, it will take a bath started with cold or room-temperature water a period of time to heat up, thus slowing the cooking of the submerged portion.

**Beet Panna Cotta
with Candied Black
Sesame Seeds**

GELATINS

GELATIN HAS LONG BEEN USED to impart a silken, delicate texture to desserts such as panna cotta and some mousses. In contrast to other thickening agents, gelatin begins to melt at body temperature, contributing to a luxuriously smooth, soft-yet-set consistency. A pure protein, gelatin changes a liquid into a semisolid state by trapping water and slowing its movement; essentially, it has a stabilizing effect.

There are two methods for blooming powdered gelatin. The most common is to sprinkle it in an even layer on a dish of cold liquid—typically water or some form of dairy—where it slowly hydrates. The other approach, called "bulking," is done by whisking the gelatin together with sugar (or another dry ingredient) before mixing it into the liquid. The sugar helps separate the gelatin granules so that they remain independent while they disperse throughout the watery liquid and can hydrate thoroughly and evenly. The mixture is heated to dissolve the gelatin and then poured into dishes and chilled. As the mixture cools, it sets into a solid gel. The right ratio of gelatin to liquid is essential for the dessert to form just enough structure to hold its shape and develop a silky, luxurious texture. With no baking required and time in the refrigerator being essential, these cool, creamy treats are the ideal make-ahead dessert.

KEY POINTS

Bloom gelatin

Chill for adequate time

ALL ABOUT GELATIN

What It Is Gelatin is made by boiling collagen-rich animal bones and connective tissues in water to unravel the collagen into long protein strands. The gelatin is then extracted from the liquid and dried to create granules (powder).

How It Works Achieving properly gelled gelatin is a two-step process. First, it must be bloomed, or hydrated, in cool water. The cool water penetrates slowly through each granule of gelatin, ensuring that it hydrates fully and dissolves. (If you skip blooming and add gelatin directly to hot water, the surface of each granule will rapidly hydrate and stick to its neighbors in clumps, while the interiors of the granules remain unhydrated and undissolved.)

The second step to properly gelled gelatin is heating, which causes the protein molecules to dissolve so that the mixture is fluid. Then, as the mixture cools to about body temperature, the strands tangle together, forming a mesh that slows the flow of the liquid, thickening it. Finally, after enough time has elapsed, that mesh is sturdy enough to stop the liquid from flowing altogether, turning it into a solid gel.

UNMOLDING PANNA COTTA

Many recipes recommend dipping the ramekins in hot water to help release the panna cotta, but we found this method ineffective. The walls of the ramekins are too thick to transfer enough heat to loosen the dessert. Here is a better way. (Make sure that the serving plates are cool before umolding the panna cotta onto them.)

1. Run paring knife around inside edge of ramekin to loosen panna cotta.

2. Cover ramekin with serving plate and invert panna cotta onto plate, jiggling ramekin if necessary.

VEGETARIAN GELATIN SUBSTITUTES

While traditional gelatin is derived from animal collagen, unflavored vegetarian gelatin substitutes mainly come from vegetable gums and seaweed extracts.

Agar agar, like gelatin, thickens recipes. It's a complex polysaccharide (carbohydrate) made from red seaweed, so it's OK for vegetarians to eat. Unlike more consistent gelatin, agar agar comes in flakes or powder and may vary in strength from brand to brand. We tested the Eden brand of agar agar sea vegetable flakes (the only one carried by our local supermarkets; natural foods stores typically carry several brands) and found that ¾ teaspoon of the flakes firmed a cup of water to the same consistency as a level teaspoon of gelatin did.

But while agar agar thickens liquids at about the same ratios as gelatin, it requires more liquid and more time to dissolve. To fully dissolve the agar agar, we needed to soak the flakes in the water for 10 minutes, then boil the mixture for another 10 minutes. Note that agar agar won't thicken cream or milk-based liquids.

We found another gelatin substitute, Natural Desserts Unflavored Jel Dessert, at a natural foods store. Once again, we weren't surprised to find that substituting this thickening agent in existing recipes calling for gelatin isn't a simple swap. The vegetarian substitute must be boiled to become activated, it must be added to the other ingredients immediately afterward, and it doesn't work in highly acidic environments. As a starting point for adapting an existing recipe, increase the Natural Desserts product to 1½ times the amount of gelatin called for.

CLASSIC PANNA COTTA

Serves 8 | eight 5-ounce ramekins

WHY THIS RECIPE WORKS Panna cotta is a classic Italian dessert in which sweetened cream and a little milk are thickened with gelatin. It should have the texture of a light custard—barely set when chilled. The amount of gelatin proved critical; we used a light hand, adding just enough to make the dessert firm enough to unmold. Because gelatin sets more quickly at cold temperatures, we minimized the amount of heat by softening the gelatin in cold milk and then heating it very briefly until it was melted. We gradually added vanilla-infused cream to the gelatin mixture and stirred everything over an ice bath to incorporate the gelatin. A vanilla bean gives the panna cotta the deepest flavor, but 2 teaspoons of vanilla extract can be used instead. Serve with lightly sweetened berries.

2¾ teaspoons unflavored gelatin
1 cup cold whole milk
3 cups cold heavy cream
1 vanilla bean
6 tablespoons (2⅔ ounces) sugar
Pinch table salt

1. Sprinkle gelatin over milk in medium saucepan and let sit until gelatin softens, about 5 minutes. Meanwhile, place cream in large measuring cup. Cut vanilla bean in half lengthwise. Using tip of paring knife, scrape out vanilla seeds. Add vanilla bean and seeds to cream. Set eight 5-ounce ramekins on rimmed baking sheet. Fill large bowl halfway with ice and water.

2. Heat milk and gelatin mixture over high heat, stirring constantly, until gelatin is dissolved and mixture registers 135 degrees, about 1½ minutes. Off heat, stir in sugar and salt until dissolved, about 1 minute.

3. Stirring constantly, slowly strain cream through fine-mesh strainer into milk mixture. Transfer mixture to clean bowl and set over bowl of ice water. Stir mixture often until slightly thickened and mixture registers 50 degrees, about 10 minutes. Strain mixture through fine-mesh strainer into second large liquid measuring cup, then distribute evenly among ramekins.

4. Cover baking sheet with plastic wrap, making sure that plastic does not touch surface of panna cottas. Refrigerate until custards are just set (mixture should wobble when shaken gently), at least 4 hours or up to 24 hours. (If unmolding, run paring knife around inside edge of each ramekin to loosen panna cotta. Cover ramekin with serving plate and invert; set plate on counter and gently shake ramekin to release panna cotta.) Serve.

Lemon Panna Cotta
Add four 2-inch strips lemon zest, cut into thin strips, to cream with vanilla bean. Add ¼ cup lemon juice (2 lemons) to strained cream mixture before dividing among serving dishes.

BUTTERMILK-VANILLA PANNA COTTA WITH BERRIES AND HONEY

Serves 8 | eight 5-ounce ramekins

WHY THIS RECIPE WORKS Buttermilk's tangy edge adds depth and moderates the richness of the heavy cream in this unique, flavorful panna cotta. We made this simple dessert even easier by skipping the traditional step of sprinkling gelatin over cold water to bloom it before dissolving it in hot cream. Instead, we whisked together the gelatin, sugar, and salt and then whisked in cold heavy cream. Dispersed by the sugar and salt, the gelatin granules had plenty of space to absorb water from the cream. Bringing the mixture to 150 degrees ensured that the gelatin fully dissolved and the floral notes of the vanilla bean infused into the cream. To prevent curdling, we let the mixture cool to 110 degrees before adding the buttermilk. A drizzle of honey and a few ripe summer berries made a simple, elegant garnish.

½ cup (3½ ounces) sugar
2 teaspoons unflavored gelatin
Pinch table salt
2 cups heavy cream
1 vanilla bean
2 cups buttermilk
Honey
Fresh raspberries and/or blackberries

1. Whisk sugar, gelatin, and salt in small saucepan until very well combined. Whisk in cream and let sit for 5 minutes. Cut vanilla bean in half lengthwise. Using tip of paring knife, scrape out seeds. Add bean and seeds to cream mixture. Cook over medium heat, stirring occasionally, until mixture registers 150 to 160 degrees, about 5 minutes. Remove from heat and let mixture cool to 105 to 110 degrees, about 15 minutes. Strain cream mixture through fine-mesh strainer into medium bowl, pressing on solids to extract as much liquid as possible. Gently whisk in buttermilk.

2. Set eight 5-ounce ramekins on rimmed baking sheet. Divide buttermilk mixture evenly among ramekins. Cover sheet in plastic wrap, making sure that plastic does not touch surface of panna cottas. Refrigerate for at least 6 hours or up to 3 days.

3. Working with 1 panna cotta at a time, insert paring knife between panna cotta and side of ramekin. Gently run knife around inside edge of ramekin to loosen panna cotta. Cover ramekin with serving plate and invert; set plate on counter and gently shake ramekin, if necessary, to release panna cotta. Drizzle each panna cotta with honey, then top with 3 to 5 berries and serve.

Pink Peppercorn-Pomegranate Panna Cotta

1. Bring heavy cream and peppercorns to simmer in medium saucepan over medium heat. Transfer to bowl, cover, and let sit until flavors meld, about 10 minutes.

2. Meanwhile, pour pomegranate juice into clean medium saucepan. Sprinkle surface evenly with gelatin and let sit until gelatin softens, about 5 minutes. Fill large bowl halfway with ice and water. Set six 5-ounce ramekins on rimmed baking sheet.

3. Heat juice and gelatin mixture over high heat, stirring constantly, until gelatin is dissolved and mixture registers 135 degrees, 1 to 2 minutes. Off heat, whisk in sugar and salt until dissolved, about 1 minute. Stirring constantly, slowly add cream mixture. Transfer mixture to now-empty bowl and set over prepared ice water bath. Stir mixture often until slightly thickened and mixture registers 50 degrees, about 20 minutes. Strain mixture through fine-mesh strainer into 4-cup liquid measuring cup, then divide evenly among ramekins. Cover baking sheet with plastic wrap, making sure that plastic does not touch surface of panna cottas. Refrigerate until panna cottas are just set (mixture should wobble when shaken gently), at least 4 hours or up to 12 hours.

4. Working with 1 panna cotta at a time, insert paring knife between panna cotta and side of ramekin. Gently run knife around inside edge of ramekin to loosen panna cotta. Cover ramekin with serving plate and invert; set plate on counter and gently shake ramekin, if necessary, to release panna cotta. Sprinkle with pomegranate seeds, white chocolate shavings, and sea salt. Serve.

PINK PEPPERCORN-POMEGRANATE PANNA COTTA

Serves 6 | six 5-ounce ramekins

WHY THIS RECIPE WORKS Pink peppercorns (not true pepper) are by far the fruitiest and most floral of peppercorn varieties, so they take well to dessert. The clean dairy flavor of creamy panna cotta was a lovely canvas for the subtle pungency of pink pepper. To balance the spiciness and richness, we incorporated pomegranate juice into the base, which provided not only complementary fruitiness but also smashing color. A garnish of pomegranate seeds and shaved white chocolate was a rich adornment, while a touch of coarse finishing salt brought all the flavors to life. If you'd like to make the panna cotta a day ahead, reduce the amount of gelatin by ½ teaspoon and chill the filled ramekins for at least 18 hours or up to 24 hours.

  2 cups heavy cream
  3 tablespoons pink peppercorns, cracked
  1 cup pomegranate juice
  2 teaspoons unflavored gelatin
  3 tablespoons sugar
  ⅛ teaspoon table salt
  ½ cup pomegranate seeds
    Shaved white chocolate
    Flake sea salt

BEET PANNA COTTA WITH CANDIED BLACK SESAME SEEDS

Serves 6 | six 5-ounce ramekins

WHY THIS RECIPE WORKS We wanted to showcase the natural sweetness of beets by making them the feature ingredient in a unique twist on panna cotta. We first processed beets to a pulp in the food processor and then squeezed the pulp through cheesecloth to release the beet juice. We substituted that beet juice for some of the dairy in the panna cotta base, which we gently heated with a small amount of sugar and gelatin. We added buttermilk for a little tang and then portioned the panna cotta mixture into ramekins and chilled it to set the gelatin. For a crunchy garnish, we took the leftover beet pulp and dried it in the oven before tossing it with candied black sesame seeds and flaky sea salt. The finished dessert had a beautiful silky texture and subtle sweetness from the beets, which paired perfectly with the smoky caramel notes of the sesame brittle.

PANNA COTTA

1½ pounds red beets (2 large beets), rinsed, peeled, and cut into 1-inch pieces
2 teaspoons unflavored gelatin
1 cup plus 2 tablespoons heavy cream
¼ cup (1¾ ounces) sugar
¼ teaspoon kosher salt
¾ cup buttermilk

BLACK SESAME BRITTLE

2 tablespoons black sesame seeds
1 tablespoon sugar
1 teaspoon honey
   Flake sea salt

1. FOR THE PANNA COTTA: Line fine-mesh strainer with 3 layers of cheesecloth, leaving 6 inches overhang on all sides, and set over medium bowl. Process beets in food processor for 30 seconds. Stop processor, scrape down sides of bowl, then continue processing until beets form pulpy paste, 30 to 60 seconds longer. Transfer beet paste to prepared strainer and allow beet juice to drain into bowl. Gather overhanging cheesecloth and squeeze beets to release as much juice as possible (you should have about 1 cup juice).

Optional but highly recommended: Adjust oven rack to middle position and heat oven to 200 degrees. Line rimmed baking sheet with parchment paper. Spread beet pulp in even layer on prepared sheet and transfer to oven. Bake until dry and crunchy, 1 to 1½ hours. Transfer ¼ cup beet crumbs to small bowl; set aside. Remaining beet crumbs can be transferred to airtight container and stored at room temperature for up to 1 week. (Try the extra beet crumbs sprinkled on salads or hummus.)

2. Transfer ¾ cup beet juice to medium saucepan. Transfer remaining ¼ cup beet juice to small bowl. Sprinkle gelatin evenly over surface of beet juice in bowl; let stand for 10 minutes to hydrate gelatin.

3. Add cream, sugar, and salt to beet juice in saucepan and whisk to combine. Cook over medium-low heat, whisking frequently to dissolve sugar, until mixture registers 140 degrees, about 5 minutes. Add beet juice–gelatin mixture to saucepan, whisking to dissolve gelatin and break up any clumps, and continue cooking until mixture registers 150 degrees, 1 to 2 minutes longer. Remove saucepan from heat and strain mixture through fine-mesh strainer into large measuring cup or pitcher.

4. Let panna cotta base cool to 105 degrees. Add buttermilk and whisk to combine. Set six 5-ounce ramekins or bowls on baking sheet. Divide base evenly among ramekins. Cover sheet in plastic wrap, making sure that plastic does not touch surface of panna cottas. Refrigerate until just set (mixture should wobble when shaken gently), at least 4 hours or up to 24 hours.

5. FOR THE BLACK SESAME BRITTLE: Line rimmed baking sheet with reusable silicone pan liner. Combine sesame seeds, sugar, and honey in small skillet. Cook over medium heat, stirring constantly with rubber spatula, until mixture has sandy texture, 1 to 2 minutes. Continue to cook, stirring frequently, until sugar melts and caramelizes, 1 to 2 minutes longer. Off heat, stir mixture until seeds are evenly coated and then quickly transfer to prepared sheet. Spread into thin, even layer and let cool at room temperature until sugar hardens, 5 to 10 minutes. (Sesame brittle can be stored in airtight container for up to 1 week.)

6. Using your hands, break sesame brittle into ¼-inch pieces. Combine brittle and ¾ teaspoon flake sea salt. (If you made optional beet crumbs, combine brittle, beet crumbs, and 1 teaspoon flake sea salt.) Sprinkle top of each panna cotta evenly with sesame brittle and serve.

LEMON BISQUE

Serves 12 | 13 by 9-inch baking dish

WHY THIS RECIPE WORKS This old-fashioned dessert has nothing to do with soup: It's actually a fluffy lemony pudding sandwiched between thin layers of graham cracker crumbs that's a welcome finish to any meal. Be sure to refrigerate the evaporated milk for at least 8 hours so it's cold enough to whip properly. Use a food processor to grind the graham crackers.

¾ cup (5¼ ounces) sugar
1 (3-ounce) package lemon-flavored gelatin
1 cup boiling water
1 tablespoon grated lemon zest plus ¼ cup juice (2 lemons)
8 whole graham crackers, ground (1 cup)
1 (12-ounce) can evaporated milk, chilled

1. Dissolve sugar and gelatin in boiling water in bowl. Stir in lemon zest and juice. Refrigerate until mixture is thickened but not completely set, about 1½ hours.

2. Grease 13 by 9-inch baking dish with vegetable oil spray and coat with ½ cup ground crackers. Using stand mixer fitted with whisk attachment, whip evaporated milk on medium-high speed until stiff peaks form, about 5 minutes. Transfer mixture to large bowl. Using clean, dry mixer bowl and whisk attachment, whip chilled gelatin mixture on medium-high speed until thickened and light lemon-colored, about 4 minutes.

3. Using large spatula, fold gelatin mixture into whipped evaporated milk until no yellow streaks remain. Transfer mixture to prepared dish and smooth top. Sprinkle remaining ½ cup ground crackers evenly over top. Cover and refrigerate until fully chilled and set, at least 4 hours or up to 24 hours. Serve.

TUTORIAL
Beet Panna Cotta

Learn how to make panna cotta with a punch of pink—and real earthy beet flavor.

1. Process beets in food processor for 30 seconds. Continue processing until beets form pulpy paste, 30 to 60 seconds longer. Transfer beet paste to prepared strainer.

2. Allow beet juice to drain into bowl. Gather overhanging cheesecloth and squeeze beets to release as much juice as possible (you should have about 1 cup juice).

3. Transfer ¾ cup beet juice to medium saucepan. Add cream, sugar, and salt and whisk to combine. Cook over medium-low heat, whisking frequently, until mixture registers 140 degrees, about 5 minutes.

4. Add beet juice–gelatin mixture to saucepan, whisking to dissolve gelatin and break up any clumps, and continue cooking until mixture registers 150 degrees, 1 to 2 minutes longer.

5. Remove saucepan from heat and strain mixture through fine-mesh strainer into large measuring cup or pitcher.

6. Let panna cotta base cool to 105 degrees. Add buttermilk and whisk to combine. Divide base evenly among bowls.

PUDDINGS

Thicken with cornstarch

Use more milk than cream

Press parchment on surface before chilling to prevent skin

Serve with whipped cream

PUDDING IS A HOMEY, NOSTALGIC DESSERT that appeals to kids and adults alike. It can stand on its own or be incorporated into layered desserts—such as Banana Pudding (page 180) or Tiramisu (page 183)—as a cool, creamy contrast to other elements. From classic vanilla and chocolate varieties to old-fashioned favorites such as tapioca, these cool, soft, and creamy treats are pure comfort.

But nostalgia alone isn't enough to make a dessert worthwhile; for a pudding to be truly great it needs to have just the right texture and a flavor that lives up to its name. While the process of preparing pudding varies, most recipes follow a similar path. It starts with heating milk, half-and-half, or cream with sugar in a saucepan. Next a thickener is added, and often egg yolks. The egg yolks are gently warmed in a process called tempering, which calls for slowly stirring a portion of the heated dairy into the yolks to prevent them from curdling. (However, we have found that tempering isn't always strictly necessary; you'll learn why.) This mixture is then simmered; once thickened, it gets poured through a fine-mesh strainer, which eliminates any lumps for a perfectly smooth pudding. Finally, parchment is pressed against the surface to prevent a skin from forming and the pudding is chilled until set. We love how a light, airy dollop of whipped cream on top of a serving contrasts the denser pudding below.

TEMPER TANTRUM

The traditional approach to preparing custards, puddings, and sauces, which rely on eggs for thickening power, requires tempering the eggs. The technique calls for heating the dairy, whisking a portion into the eggs (to which any sugar has usually been added), and then adding this mixture back to the pan with the rest of the hot dairy before cooking the mixture to the final temperature. Conventional cooking wisdom says that tempering prevents the eggs from seizing up into tight curds by allowing them to warm up gradually. But we have found this isn't the case. Tempering doesn't work because of the gradual heating of the yolks; it works because the addition of liquid dilutes the uncooked egg proteins, making it harder for them to link up and form firm clumps when heated.

The real benefit of tempering is that it reduces the amount of constant stirring necessary since the dairy is already heated by the time the eggs go into the pot, which jump-starts cooking. That said, it does require some back-and-forth and multiple bowls. If you forgo tempering and choose to put everything in the pot at the same time, just make sure to stir constantly from the outset to prevent the eggs from forming clumps.

PEELING THE SKIN

A thin, dry "skin" forms on the surface of puddings because as the mixture is heated, two things happen: Water evaporates, and proteins and sugar become more concentrated. Together, this results in a dry barrier on the liquid's surface. You can prevent the skin from forming during cooking by stirring, but what about afterward? The most common method is to press parchment paper onto the surface, which prevents evaporation. But this approach can be messy and fussy if you're dealing with individual portions in cups or ramekins.

We came up with a simpler way: After cooking, simply let the mixture cool until a skin forms, about 20 minutes, and then pour it through a fine-mesh strainer into a large bowl. Portion it, and then refrigerate the portions, uncovered, until cool. Cover the cooled portions with plastic wrap (no need to press it onto the surface of the pudding) until serving time. We found that this technique will work equally well on puddings and custards.

water proteins

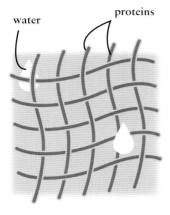

Undiluted Eggs
Proteins link up,
forming clumps.

Diluted Eggs
Liquid gets in the way of
the proteins, making it harder
for them to form bonds.

Classic Vanilla Pudding

2. Meanwhile, whisk cornstarch and remaining ¼ cup milk in large bowl until no lumps remain, about 15 seconds. Whisk in egg yolks until fully incorporated, about 30 seconds.

3. When milk mixture comes to simmer, remove from heat and, whisking constantly, very slowly add hot milk mixture to yolk mixture to temper.

4. Return milk-yolk mixture to saucepan. Return saucepan to medium heat and cook, whisking constantly, until pudding is thickened and registers 175 to 180 degrees in several places, about 1 minute. Off heat, whisk in butter and vanilla.

5. Strain pudding through fine-mesh strainer into clean bowl. Press lightly greased parchment paper against surface of pudding. Refrigerate until cold and set, at least 3 hours. Whisk pudding until smooth just before serving.

CREAMY CHOCOLATE PUDDING

Serves 6 | large saucepan

WHY THIS RECIPE WORKS While we fondly recall enjoying chocolate pudding in childhood, the reality is that most chocolate puddings fail to impress our grown-up palates with their lackluster chocolate flavor, overwhelming sweetness, and grainy texture. We were surprised to learn that graininess is caused by too much cocoa butter rather than by too many cocoa solids. Using a moderate amount of bittersweet chocolate in combination with unsweetened cocoa and espresso powder gave us potent chocolate flavor with a supremely smooth texture. For thickening, cornstarch proved the right choice, and using mostly milk, along with half a cup of heavy cream and three egg yolks, ensured a silky, smooth texture. We prefer this recipe made with 60 percent bittersweet chocolate; using a chocolate with a higher cacao percentage will result in a thicker pudding. One or 2 percent low-fat milk may be substituted for the whole milk with a small sacrifice in richness. Do not substitute skim milk.

CLASSIC VANILLA PUDDING

Serves 4 | large saucepan

WHY THIS RECIPE WORKS Vanilla pudding is clean and classic, never flashy, and elegant in its simplicity. Our version is lusciously creamy with just the right texture—thanks to the tempered eggs. Stirring in a bit of cornstarch helps to thicken the mixture more quickly. For optimal creaminess, we chose whole milk. Puddings made with half-and-half or cream were just too rich, which obscured the vanilla flavor. We found that extract gave a stronger flavor than vanilla bean in this pudding. A little bit of butter, stirred in at the end with the vanilla extract, added just a touch more richness and gave the finished pudding a beautiful sheen. Straining the pudding before refrigerating it for a few hours ensured a perfectly silky texture.

2¾ cups whole milk, divided
½   cup (3½ ounces) sugar
¼   teaspoon table salt
¼   cup (1 ounce) cornstarch
3   large egg yolks
2   tablespoons unsalted butter, chilled
1   tablespoon vanilla extract

1. Heat 2½ cups milk, sugar, and salt in large saucepan over medium heat until simmering, stirring occasionally to dissolve sugar.

2   teaspoons vanilla extract
½   teaspoon instant espresso powder
½   cup (3½ ounces) sugar
3   tablespoons unsweetened cocoa powder
2   tablespoons cornstarch
¼   teaspoon table salt
½   cup heavy cream
3   large egg yolks
2½ cups whole milk
5   tablespoons unsalted butter, cut into 8 pieces
4   ounces bittersweet chocolate, chopped fine

1. Stir vanilla and espresso powder together in bowl; set aside. Whisk sugar, cocoa, cornstarch, and salt together in large saucepan. Whisk in cream and egg yolks until fully incorporated, making sure to scrape corners of saucepan. Whisk in milk until incorporated.

2. Place saucepan over medium heat; cook, whisking constantly, until mixture is thickened and bubbling over entire surface, 5 to 8 minutes. Cook for 30 seconds longer, remove from heat, add butter and chocolate, and whisk until melted and fully incorporated. Whisk in vanilla mixture.

3. Strain pudding through fine-mesh strainer into clean bowl. Press lightly greased parchment paper against surface of pudding. Refrigerate for at least 4 hours or up to 2 days. Serve.

Creamy Chocolate Pudding with Cinnamon and Chipotle
Add ½ teaspoon cinnamon, ¼ teaspoon chipotle chile powder, and pinch cayenne pepper to saucepan along with cocoa powder.

INSTANT CHOCOLATE PUDDING

Serves 4 | **large saucepan**
WHY THIS RECIPE WORKS Boxed instant pudding has just one thing going for it: speed. We wanted a quick chocolate pudding that actually tasted good. Straining the pudding before chilling is typically a key step in the pudding-making process; this eliminates any bits of egg for a perfectly smooth texture. Ditching the eggs entirely allowed us to skip this tedious task. The right ratio of cornstarch to milk thickened our pudding to the proper consistency. For further convenience we swapped semisweet bar chocolate for milk chocolate chips—not only was there no chopping required, but the mild, creamy milk chocolate prevented the pudding from being overly rich and thick. Some vanilla extract and a dash of salt cut the sweetness and enhanced the chocolate flavor.

¼ cup packed (1¾ ounces) light brown sugar
3 tablespoons Dutch-processed cocoa powder
3 tablespoons cornstarch
¼ teaspoon table salt
2¾ cups whole milk
¼ cup heavy cream
1 cup (6 ounces) milk chocolate chips
½ teaspoon vanilla extract

1. Combine sugar, cocoa, cornstarch, and salt in large saucepan. Whisk milk and cream into sugar mixture until smooth. Add chocolate chips and bring to simmer over medium heat, whisking occasionally. Reduce heat to medium-low and cook, whisking constantly, until thickened and large bubbles appear at surface, 2 to 3 minutes. Remove saucepan from heat and stir in vanilla.

2. Transfer pudding to large bowl and press lightly greased parchment paper against surface of pudding. Refrigerate until cold, at least 4 hours. Serve. (Pudding can be refrigerated in airtight container for up to 3 days. Whisk pudding before serving.)

Instant Chocolate-Almond Pudding
Substitute almond extract for vanilla. Sprinkle with ½ cup toasted sliced almonds before serving.

BUTTERSCOTCH PUDDING

Serves 8 | **large saucepan**
WHY THIS RECIPE WORKS With its incredibly rich, nuanced, bittersweet flavor, from-scratch butterscotch pudding is worlds away from the dull, sweet kind you get from an instant mix. But making butterscotch pudding can be temperamental: A custard is combined with homemade caramel, and the usual approach of boiling it from start to finish is tricky in a blink-and-you've-burned-it way. Our method is forgiving: Boil the caramel to jump-start it, then reduce the heat and gently simmer it until it reaches the right temperature. Most recipes have you temper the yolks and cornstarch, add everything to the dairy in the pot, and stir away. We swapped this fussy method in favor of pouring the boiling caramel directly over the thickening agents. When taking the temperature of the caramel in step 1, tilt the saucepan and move the thermometer back and forth to equalize hot and cool spots.

12 tablespoons unsalted butter, cut into ½-inch pieces
½ cup (3½ ounces) granulated sugar
½ cup packed (3½ ounces) dark brown sugar
¼ cup water
2 tablespoons light corn syrup
1 teaspoon lemon juice
¾ teaspoon table salt
1 cup heavy cream, divided
2¼ cups whole milk, divided
4 large egg yolks
¼ cup cornstarch
2 teaspoons vanilla extract
1 teaspoon dark rum

1. Bring butter, granulated sugar, brown sugar, water, corn syrup, lemon juice, and salt to boil in large saucepan over medium heat, stirring occasionally to dissolve sugar and melt butter. Once mixture is at full rolling boil, cook, stirring occasionally, for 5 minutes (caramel should register about 240 degrees). Immediately reduce heat to medium-low and gently simmer (caramel should maintain steady stream of lazy bubbles—if not, adjust heat accordingly), stirring frequently, until mixture is color of dark peanut butter, 12 to 16 minutes (caramel should register about 300 degrees and have slight burnt smell).

2. Remove saucepan from heat; carefully pour ¼ cup cream into caramel mixture and swirl to incorporate (mixture will bubble and steam); let bubbling subside. Whisk vigorously and scrape corners of saucepan until mixture is completely smooth, at least 30 seconds. Return saucepan to medium heat and gradually whisk in remaining ¾ cup cream until smooth. Whisk in 2 cups milk until mixture is smooth, scraping corners and edges of saucepan to remove any remaining bits of caramel.

3. Microwave remaining ¼ cup milk until simmering, 30 to 45 seconds. Whisk egg yolks and cornstarch in large bowl until smooth. Gradually whisk in hot milk until smooth; set aside.

4. Return saucepan to medium-high heat and bring mixture to full rolling boil, whisking frequently. Once mixture is boiling rapidly and beginning to climb toward top of saucepan, working quickly, immediately pour into bowl with yolk mixture in 1 motion (do not add gradually). Whisk thoroughly for 10 to 15 seconds (mixture will thicken after a few seconds). Whisk in vanilla and rum.

5. Press lightly greased parchment paper against surface of pudding. Cover and refrigerate until fully set, at least 3 hours or up to 3 days. Whisk pudding until smooth just before serving.

OLD-FASHIONED RICE PUDDING

Serves 4 to 6 | large saucepan

WHY THIS RECIPE WORKS Recipes for rice pudding vary dramatically, calling for different types of rice, different liquids, and different techniques. We found that a simple stovetop method of combining everything and gently simmering it all, uncovered, until the rice was tender worked best. Not only was this easy, but the finished pudding also had the creamiest texture. Long-grain rice proved far better than short-grained, which turned inedibly stodgy once it cooled. For the liquid, the richer flavor of cream or half-and-half didn't suit this simple pudding; we liked milk, which reduced and sweetened as the pudding cooked. We reserved ½ cup of the milk to help loosen the pudding before serving. Two percent low-fat milk may be substituted for the whole milk with a small sacrifice in richness; do not substitute 1 percent low-fat or skim milk.

    6   cups whole milk, divided
    ½   cup (3½ ounces) sugar
    ½   teaspoon table salt
    ½   cup long-grain white rice
    2   teaspoons vanilla extract

1. Combine 5½ cups milk, sugar, and salt in large saucepan and bring to boil over medium-high heat.

2. Stir in rice and reduce heat to low. Cook, adjusting heat to maintain gentle simmer and stirring occasionally to prevent scorching, until rice is soft and pudding has thickened to consistency of yogurt, 50 minutes to 1 hour. Stir in vanilla.

3. Transfer pudding to large bowl and let cool completely, about 2 hours, or let cool and refrigerate until cold, about 2 hours longer. Just before serving, stir in remaining ½ cup milk.

Cinnamon-Raisin Rice Pudding

In step 1, add 1 cinnamon stick to milk mixture. Combine ⅓ cup raisins and ⅓ cup water in bowl; cover and microwave for 1 minute. Let sit until softened, about 5 minutes; drain. Stir raisins into cooked rice pudding as it cools in step 3. Discard cinnamon stick.

BANANA PUDDING

Serves 12 | 3½-quart trifle dish

WHY THIS RECIPE WORKS All too often, banana pudding is nothing more than vanilla pudding layered with slices of banana. We think banana belongs in the pudding itself. Roasting bananas intensified their flavor and helped break them down so we could incorporate them easily directly into the creamy pudding. The pudding should be refrigerated for at least 8 hours before serving so that the cookies have a chance to soften and the flavors to blend. It can be stored for up to two days. If your food processor bowl holds less than 11 cups, puree the pudding, the roasted bananas, and the lemon juice in batches in step 3, transferring the batches to a large bowl to combine. We call for a 3½-quart trifle dish for this recipe; however, a 4-quart bowl can be used in its place. Garnish the pudding with extra wafers, if desired.

PUDDING

    7   slightly underripe large bananas (3 unpeeled, 4 peeled)
    1½ cups (10½ ounces) sugar, divided
    8   large egg yolks
    6   tablespoons cornstarch
    6   cups half-and-half
    ½   teaspoon table salt
    3   tablespoons unsalted butter
    1   tablespoon vanilla extract
    3   tablespoons lemon juice, divided
    1   (12-ounce) box vanilla wafers, divided

TOPPING

    1   cup heavy cream, chilled
    1   tablespoon sugar
    ½   teaspoon vanilla extract

TUTORIAL
Butterscotch Pudding

Once you've mastered pudding you can flavor it, here daringly, with deep, rich butterscotch. What isn't daring? Our simple approach.

1. Bring butter, granulated sugar, brown sugar, water, corn syrup, lemon juice, and salt to boil in large saucepan over medium heat, stirring occasionally. Cook, stirring occasionally, for 5 minutes (caramel should register about 240 degrees).

2. Off heat, carefully pour ¼ cup cream into caramel mixture and swirl to incorporate; let bubbling subside. Whisk vigorously and scrape corners of saucepan until mixture is completely smooth, at least 30 seconds.

3. Return saucepan to medium heat and gradually whisk in remaining ¾ cup cream until smooth. Whisk in 2 cups milk until mixture is smooth, scraping corners and edges of saucepan to remove any remaining bits of caramel.

4. Return saucepan to medium-high heat, whisking frequently. Once mixture is boiling rapidly and beginning to climb toward top of saucepan, immediately pour into bowl with yolk mixture in 1 motion (do not add gradually).

5. Whisk thoroughly for 10 to 15 seconds (mixture will thicken after a few seconds). Whisk in vanilla and rum.

6. Spray piece of parchment paper with vegetable oil spray and press directly against surface of pudding. Cover and refrigerate until fully set, at least 3 hours or up to 3 days.

Banana Pudding

5. FOR THE TOPPING: Using stand mixer fitted with whisk attachment, whip cream, sugar, and vanilla on medium-low speed until foamy, about 1 minute. Increase speed to high and whip until stiff peaks form, 1 to 3 minutes. (Whipped topping can be refrigerated for up to 4 hours.) Top pudding with whipped topping before serving.

Peanutty Banana Pudding

Sandwich 2 wafers around 1 banana slice and ½ teaspoon creamy peanut butter in step 4; repeat with remaining wafers (you'll need ½ cup peanut butter total). Assemble by alternating layers of pudding and wafer-banana sandwiches, ending with pudding. Sprinkle ¼ cup chopped salted dry-roasted peanuts over whipped cream–topped pudding before serving.

Toasted Coconut Banana Pudding

Substitute 1 (16-ounce) can coconut milk for 2 cups half-and-half in step 2. Sprinkle ¼ cup toasted sweetened shredded coconut over whipped cream–topped pudding before serving.

1. FOR THE PUDDING: Adjust oven rack to upper-middle position and heat oven to 325 degrees. Place unpeeled bananas on baking sheet and bake until skins are completely black, about 20 minutes. Let cool for 5 minutes, then peel.

2. Meanwhile, whisk ½ cup sugar, egg yolks, and cornstarch in medium bowl until smooth. Bring half-and-half, salt, and remaining 1 cup sugar to simmer in large saucepan over medium heat. Whisk ½ cup half-and-half mixture into yolk mixture to temper. Slowly whisk tempered yolk mixture into saucepan. Cook, whisking constantly, until mixture is thick and large bubbles appear on surface, about 2 minutes. Off heat, stir in butter and vanilla.

3. Transfer pudding to food processor. Add 2 tablespoons lemon juice and roasted bananas and process until smooth, about 15 seconds. Transfer to large bowl and press lightly greased parchment paper against surface of pudding. Refrigerate until slightly cooled, about 45 minutes.

4. Slice peeled bananas ¼ inch thick and toss with remaining 1 tablespoon lemon juice in bowl. Spoon one-quarter of pudding into 3-quart trifle dish and top with layer of wafers, layer of sliced bananas, and another layer of wafers. Repeat layering twice, ending with pudding. Press lightly greased parchment against surface of pudding and refrigerate until wafers have softened, at least 8 hours or up to 2 days.

CREAMY TAPIOCA PUDDING

Serves 4 | medium saucepan

WHY THIS RECIPE WORKS Many recipes for tapioca pudding have intricate directions that fail to produce anything special. Happily, we had the best luck with the easiest method: We combined all the ingredients and let them sit to soften the tapioca, brought the mixture to a boil, and then stirred, stirred, stirred. That's it—the pudding thickened as it cooled. For richness, we added an egg plus a yolk and lightened the entire mixture with whipped cream. This recipe uses Minute tapioca (also labeled "quick-cooking") and cooks in a fraction of the time of traditional pearl tapioca; do not substitute traditional pearl tapioca here.

2½ cups whole milk
1 large egg plus 1 large yolk, lightly beaten
¼ cup (1¾ ounces) plus 1 tablespoon granulated sugar, divided
1 tablespoon packed light brown sugar
¼ teaspoon table salt
¼ cup Minute tapioca
1 teaspoon vanilla extract
½ cup heavy cream, chilled

1. Combine milk, egg and yolk, ¼ cup granulated sugar, brown sugar, salt, and tapioca in medium saucepan and let sit for 5 minutes. Bring mixture to boil over medium heat, then reduce heat and simmer, stirring constantly, for 2 minutes.

2. Off heat, stir in vanilla and scrape pudding into medium bowl. Press lightly greased parchment paper against surface of pudding and refrigerate until set, at least 1 hour or up to 2 days.

3. Using stand mixer fitted with whisk attachment, whip cream and remaining 1 tablespoon granulated sugar together on medium-low speed until foamy, about 1 minute. Increase speed to high and whip until stiff peaks form, 1 to 3 minutes. Gently fold half of whipped cream into pudding. Serve, garnishing with remaining whipped cream.

TIRAMISU

Serves 10 to 12 | 13 by 9-inch baking dish

WHY THIS RECIPE WORKS With its boozy, coffee-soaked ladyfingers and sweet, creamy filling, it's no wonder tiramisu is Italian for "pick me up." We briefly moistened the ladyfingers in a mixture of coffee, espresso powder, and more rum. We prefer a tiramisu with a pronounced rum flavor; for a less potent rum flavor, reduce the amount of rum in the coffee mixture. Brandy or whiskey can be substituted for the rum. Don't let the mascarpone warm to room temperature before whipping. Dried ladyfingers are also called savoiardi; you will need between 42 and 60, depending on their size and the brand.

2½ cups strong brewed coffee, room temperature
1½ tablespoons instant espresso powder
9 tablespoons dark rum, divided
6 large egg yolks
⅔ cup (4⅔ ounces) sugar
¼ teaspoon table salt
1½ pounds (3 cups) mascarpone cheese, chilled
¾ cup heavy cream, chilled
14 ounces dried ladyfingers
3½ tablespoons unsweetened cocoa powder
¼ cup grated semisweet or bittersweet chocolate (optional)

1. Whisk coffee, espresso powder, and 5 tablespoons rum in wide bowl or baking dish until espresso dissolves.

2. Using stand mixer fitted with whisk attachment, mix egg yolks at low speed until just combined. Add sugar and salt and mix at medium-high speed until pale yellow, 1½ to 2 minutes, scraping down sides of bowl as needed. Reduce speed to medium, add remaining ¼ cup rum, and mix at medium speed until just combined, 20 to 30 seconds; scrape bowl. Add mascarpone and mix until no lumps remain, 30 to 45 seconds, scraping down bowl as needed. Transfer mixture to large bowl.

3. In now-empty mixer bowl (no need to clean mixer bowl), whip cream on medium-low speed until foamy, about 1 minute. Increase speed to high and whip until stiff peaks form, 1 to 3 minutes. Using rubber spatula, fold one-third of whipped cream into mascarpone mixture to lighten, then gently fold in remaining whipped cream until no white streaks remain.

4. Working with 1 ladyfinger at a time, drop half of ladyfingers into coffee mixture, roll, remove, and transfer to 13 by 9-inch baking dish. (Do not submerge ladyfingers in coffee mixture; entire process should take no longer than 2 to 3 seconds for each cookie.) Arrange soaked cookies in single layer in baking dish, breaking or trimming ladyfingers as needed to fit neatly into dish.

5. Spread half of mascarpone mixture over ladyfingers, spreading it to sides and into corners of dish, and smooth top. Place 2 tablespoons cocoa in fine-mesh strainer and dust cocoa over mascarpone. Repeat with remaining ladyfingers, mascarpone, and 1½ tablespoons cocoa to make second layer. Clean edges of dish, cover with plastic wrap, and refrigerate until set, at least 6 hours or up to 24 hours. Before serving, sprinkle with grated chocolate, if using.

SEMOLINA PUDDING WITH ALMONDS AND DATES

Serves 6 to 8 | large saucepan

WHY THIS RECIPE WORKS Aromatic sweetened milk puddings are popular throughout the Middle East. We decided to infuse ours with cardamom and saffron. Toasted semolina flour, which is made from durum wheat, thickened the pudding nicely and gave it a pleasantly coarse texture;. Almonds brought a nutty crunch, and dates offered a contrasting honeyed sweetness. Traditional recipes often call for chilling the pudding, but we like it warm.

1 tablespoon extra-virgin olive oil
¾ cup fine semolina flour
4½ cups whole milk, plus extra as needed
½ cup (3½ ounces) sugar
½ teaspoon ground cardamom
⅛ teaspoon saffron threads, crumbled
⅛ teaspoon table salt
½ cup slivered almonds, toasted and chopped
3 ounces pitted dates, sliced thin (½ cup)

1. Heat oil in 12-inch skillet over medium heat until shimmering. Add semolina and cook, stirring occasionally, until fragrant, 3 to 5 minutes; transfer to bowl.

2. Bring milk, sugar, cardamom, saffron, and salt to simmer in large saucepan over medium heat. Whisking constantly, slowly add semolina, 1 tablespoon at a time, and cook until mixture thickens slightly and begins to bubble, about 3 minutes. Remove saucepan from heat, cover, and let pudding rest for 30 minutes.

3. Stir pudding to loosen and adjust consistency with extra warm milk as needed. Sprinkle individual portions with almonds and dates before serving.

CUSTARDS

Can be a sauce, spread, filling, or stand-alone dessert

Temper or dilute eggs with liquid to avoid curdling

Use temperature as a guide to doneness

RICHER AND MORE PLUSH THAN PUDDING, creamy custard desserts have a quiet, confident elegance. They take a few forms, from pourable dessert sauces like Crème Anglaise (page 187) and spreads like Lemon Curd (page 188) to classic individual desserts like Crème Caramel (page 193) and custard-layered trifles. At their most basic, all custards are cooked mixtures of eggs and dairy in which the eggs are largely the source of proteins and the dairy largely the source of water. When the proteins are heated, they link up and form a matrix that traps the water, giving the custard structure.

The exact texture of a custard mainly depends on the ratio of eggs to dairy: The more the proteins are diluted with water (from the dairy), the looser the custard's consistency will be. The temperature to which the custard is cooked can also determine the firmness of the set. And cooking egg custards requires careful control of temperatures. When exposed to too much heat, the egg proteins will form stronger bonds with the surrounding proteins, making clumps and separating from the liquid surrounding them. This is called curdling. To minimize this risk, we use gentle heat when preparing custards. For those that are prepared on the stovetop, we temper the eggs, or heat them very gently by mixing them with a small amount of hot liquid, in order to slow the rate of cooking (see page 177 for more information). Some custards are started on the stove and finished in the oven; for those that are baked, a low oven mitigates the heat differential between the exterior and the interior. It also slows down the rate of cooking, thereby increasing the window of time when a dessert is perfectly cooked. In addition to a low-temperature oven, we sometimes bake delicate egg-based desserts in a water bath (see page 327 for more information).

CUSTARD KEYS

While there are exceptions, these are the basics steps for preparing most classic custards like Lemon Curd (page 188) and Classic Crème Brûlée (page 191).

Heat dairy (or other liquid) and sugar The mixture is brought to a simmer or boil on the stovetop to heat.

Add eggs This often involves tempering, or adding a small amount of the heated dairy to the eggs to gently warm them before adding them to the rest of the dairy.

Strain custard The custard is poured through a fine-mesh strainer to remove any lumps and ensure a completely smooth, silky custard.

Bake If the custard will be baked, it goes into the oven once it's portioned into dishes.

Take temperature Once the custard reaches 170 to 180 degrees, it will be just barely set and ready to come out of the oven. (If the custard is being cooked entirely on the stovetop, this will happen before straining.)

Let chill Chilling the custard for a few hours allows it to finish setting up.

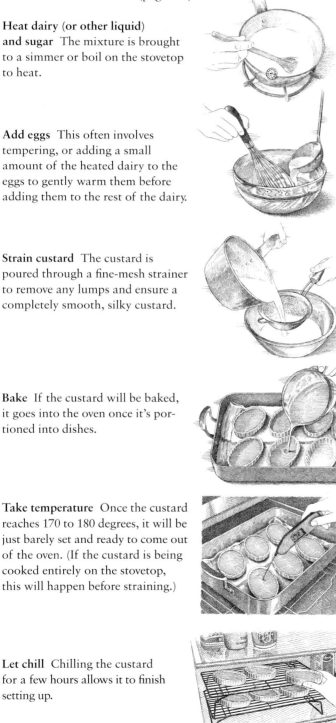

HOW TO FIX BROKEN CUSTARD

When custards such as Crème Anglaise (page 187) are heated, they turn thick and creamy as milk and egg proteins unfurl and bond with each other. However, if they are overheated, too many bonds form and the proteins clump. Fortunately, there's an easy fix: A quick buzz with an immersion blender effectively breaks down the clumps, restoring a perfectly creamy texture.

If you notice lumps beginning to form in a custard, immediately pour it out of the hot pot into a bowl and pulse it with a hand-held blender in 5-second intervals until it is nearly smooth. This can take from 15 to 45 seconds, depending on how big the lumps are. Be careful not to overprocess or you can wind up with irreparably thin, watery custard. Don't use a blender or food processor; they incorporate too much air and will leave the mixture frothy, not creamy. After blending, pour the liquid through a fine-mesh strainer to remove any remaining lumps and continue with your recipe.

CANNED MILK PRODUCTS

The advent of canned milk in Latin America in the late 1800s helped make flan, which was introduced by Spanish conquistadores 300 years earlier, even more popular. When refrigeration became widespread and shelf-stable milk was no longer as necessary, the practice of using the canned stuff stuck. And with good reason: Evaporated and sweetened condensed milks give flan a distinctively thick, luxurious texture and caramelized notes.

Evaporated and condensed milk both begin the same way: by heating milk in a vacuum so that 60 percent or more of the water evaporates. The resulting thick liquid is then either given a high temperature treatment to sterilize it, making evaporated milk, or sweetened to preserve it, making condensed milk. Both evaporated and condensed milk have about twice the concentration of fat and protein as regular whole milk; because of this, they can sometimes create an overly tight structure when combined with egg proteins in a custard, resulting in a stiff, almost rubbery consistency. Our solution? Add ½ cup of fresh milk, which loosens the texture without adding much protein of its own or diluting dairy flavor.

Learning Mother Custards

Many custards, as defined in this chapter, are table desserts themselves—all they need is a spoon. But learning to make basic sauces, spreads, and fillings is an incredibly useful skill because it transfers to all those table desserts. These custards are used for cakes, tarts, pastries, and more and are referenced throughout this book.

PASTRY CREAM

Pastry cream is a classic French vanilla custard and it's the key ingredient in desserts such as Fresh Fruit Tart (page 427), which get their identity from their filling. Most recipes for pastry cream follow the same process—heat some milk, temper the egg yolks with the hot milk, and cook the mixture until thickened. We prefer to use half-and-half or whole milk because it adds a nice richness without tasting too heavy. We have also found that adding a little cornstarch makes the method more foolproof—it ensures that the sauce will thicken up nicely and helps prevent the eggs from curdling as they cook.

PASTRY CREAM
Makes 2 cups

You can substitute 1½ teaspoons vanilla extract for the vanilla bean; stir the extract into the pastry cream with the butter in step 4.

- ½ vanilla bean
- 2 cups half-and-half
- ½ cup (3½ ounces) sugar, divided
- Pinch table salt
- 5 large egg yolks
- 3 tablespoons cornstarch
- 4 tablespoons unsalted butter, cut into 4 pieces

1. Cut vanilla bean in half lengthwise. Using tip of paring knife, scrape out seeds. Bring vanilla bean and seeds, half-and-half, 6 tablespoons sugar, and salt to simmer in medium saucepan over medium-high heat, stirring occasionally.

2. Meanwhile, whisk egg yolks, cornstarch, and remaining 2 tablespoons sugar in bowl until smooth.

3. Whisk about 1 cup half-and-half mixture into yolk mixture to temper. Slowly whisk tempered egg mixture into remaining half-and-half mixture. Reduce heat to medium and continue to cook, whisking constantly, until pastry cream is thickened and few bubbles burst on surface, about 30 seconds.

4. Off heat, remove vanilla bean and whisk in butter. Transfer pastry cream to bowl and press plastic wrap directly on surface. Refrigerate until cold and set, at least 3 hours or up to 2 days.

Almond Pastry Cream
Omit vanilla bean. Add ¾ teaspoon almond extract with butter in step 4.

Mocha Pastry Cream
Omit vanilla bean. Add 1 teaspoon instant espresso powder or instant coffee powder to half-and-half in step 1.

Pastry Cream Patience
Pastry cream is an anomaly among custards. Although overheating a typical custard can lead to curdling, it's vital to bring pastry cream almost to a boil. Doing so sets the eggs and activates the starch, thereby ensuring a proper consistency.

As a typical custard heats, the egg proteins unravel and intertwine, eventually forming cross-links that can result in coagulation, or curdling. Why is pastry cream different? Because it contains a fair amount of starch (flour or cornstarch), which affects texture in two ways. First, the starch interferes with the cross-linking of egg proteins, thus preventing coagulation. Second, pastry cream must be heated to a temperature high enough to destroy the amylase enzyme present in egg yolks, which would otherwise break down the starch and make the pastry cream runny.

The takeaway: For pastry cream that will be thick, not soupy, once it cools, make sure to heat it sufficiently. When it's hot enough, three or four bubbles will burst on the surface, its temperature will read 200 degrees on an instant-read thermometer, and it will appear thick and glossy.

Making Pastry Cream

1. Bring half-and-half, 6 tablespoons sugar, vanilla bean, vanilla seeds, and salt to simmer in medium saucepan over medium-high heat, stirring occasionally.

2. Meanwhile, whisk egg yolks, cornstarch, and remaining 2 tablespoons sugar in bowl until smooth.

3. Whisk about 1 cup half-and-half mixture into yolk mixture to temper.

4. Slowly whisk tempered egg mixture into remaining half-and-half mixture.

5. Reduce heat to medium and continue to cook, whisking constantly, until pastry cream is thickened and few bubbles burst on surface, about 30 seconds.

6. Off heat, remove vanilla bean and whisk in butter. Transfer pastry cream to bowl and press plastic wrap directly on surface. Refrigerate to chill.

CRÈME ANGLAISE

Crème anglaise is a luxurious pourable custard typically served at cool room temperature or chilled. This versatile sauce is a great way to enhance fresh fruit, cakes, tarts, and many other desserts. It's also the base of creamy baked desserts such as Classic Crème Brûlée (page 191). Crème anglaise relies on the thickening power of egg yolks when they are heated. Straining the cooked mixture provides insurance that this sauce will be silky smooth.

CRÈME ANGLAISE
Makes about 1½ cups
We prefer the complex flavor of a vanilla bean here, but 1 teaspoon of vanilla extract can be used instead; if using vanilla extract, skip the steeping stage in step 1 and stir the extract into the sauce after straining it in step 3.

- ½ vanilla bean
- 1½ cups whole milk
- Pinch table salt
- 4 large egg yolks
- ¼ cup (1¾ ounces) sugar

1. Cut vanilla bean in half lengthwise. Using tip of paring knife, scrape out seeds. Bring vanilla bean and seeds, milk, and salt to simmer in medium saucepan over medium-high heat, stirring occasionally. Remove from heat, cover, and let steep for 20 minutes.

2. Whisk egg yolks and sugar in large bowl until smooth. Whisking constantly, very slowly add hot milk mixture to yolk mixture to temper. Return milk-yolk mixture to saucepan and cook over low heat, stirring constantly with rubber spatula, until sauce thickens slightly and registers 175 to 180 degrees, 5 to 7 minutes.

3. Strain sauce through fine-mesh strainer set over clean bowl; discard vanilla bean. Cover and refrigerate until cool, about 45 minutes. (Sauce can be refrigerated, with plastic wrap pressed directly on surface, for up to 3 days.)

Coffee Crème Anglaise
Add 1½ teaspoons instant espresso powder to saucepan with vanilla bean and seeds.

Earl Grey Crème Anglaise
Substitute 1 Earl Grey tea bag for vanilla bean. Remove tea bag after steeping in step 1.

Orange Crème Anglaise
Substitute 2 (3-inch) strips orange zest for vanilla bean. Stir 1 tablespoon Grand Marnier into finished sauce after straining.

When Is Crème Anglaise Ready?

An instant-read thermometer is the most reliable way to judge when crème anglaise has reached the proper temperature of 175 to 180 degrees. But you can also judge the progress of a custard sauce by its thickness. Dip a wooden spoon into the custard and run your finger across the back. (Yes, this old-fashioned method really does work.)

Not Yet When its temperature is between 165 and 170 degrees, the custard will still be thin, and a line drawn on the back of the spoon will not hold.

Ready When its temperature is between 175 and 180 degrees, the custard will coat the spoon, and the line will maintain neat edges.

Too Far When its temperature goes above 180 degrees, small chunks will become visible in the curdled custard.

LEMON CURD

Lemon curd is a custard-style mixture made from eggs, sugar, butter, and lemon juice. Although it does not contain milk or cream, the eggs are gently and carefully combined with hot liquid, in this case lemon juice, just as they are in other stove-top custards. The juice is the key to the creamy, silky texture of this recipe, despite the high amount of eggs to the relatively small amount of liquid—the same proportion of eggs to cream would typically scramble. The strength of the acid in the juice explains why. The acid changes the way the egg proteins behave, making them less likely to curdle and more likely to form a creamy, soft gel. Lemon curd can top cut biscuits and fill or top cakes (try a dollop on our Olive Oil Cake on page 285).

LEMON CURD
Makes 2 cups

¾ cup lemon juice (4 lemons)
1¼ cups (8¾ ounces) sugar
⅛ teaspoon table salt
3 large eggs plus 5 large yolks
6 tablespoons unsalted butter, cut into
  ½-inch pieces and frozen

1. Cook lemon juice, sugar, and salt in medium saucepan over medium-high heat, stirring occasionally, until sugar dissolves and mixture is hot (do not boil), about 1 minute.

2. Whisk eggs and yolks in large bowl until combined, then, whisking constantly, very slowly add hot lemon mixture to egg mixture to temper. Return mixture to saucepan and cook over medium-low heat, stirring constantly, until mixture is thickened and registers 170 to 175 degrees.

3. Off heat, stir in frozen butter until melted and incorporated. Strain curd through fine-mesh strainer into bowl and press plastic wrap directly against surface. Refrigerate until curd is firm and spreadable, at least 1½ hours. (Curd can be refrigerated for at least 1½ hours or up to 3 days.)

Making Lemon Curd

1. Cook lemon juice, sugar, and salt in medium saucepan over medium-high heat, stirring occasionally, until sugar dissolves and mixture is hot, about 1 minute.

2. Whisk eggs and yolks in large bowl until combined, then, whisking constantly, very slowly add hot lemon mixture to egg mixture to temper.

3. Return mixture to saucepan and cook over medium-low heat, stirring constantly, until mixture is thickened and registers 170 to 175 degrees.

4. Off heat, stir in frozen butter until melted and incorporated.

5. Strain curd through fine-mesh strainer into bowl and press plastic wrap directly against surface. Refrigerate to chill.

Why Eggs in Lemon Curd Don't Curdle

How does such a high proportion of eggs in the presence of a relatively small amount of liquid produce the creamy, silken texture of lemon curd, while the same proportion of eggs and cream would simply scramble?

The difference has to do with acid content. Egg proteins are tangled bundles of amino acids. Each bundle carries a similar electrical charge, which causes them to repel one another. Applying heat causes the bundles to unravel, at which point they are inclined to pull together and form a clump. In the process of clumping, the amino acid molecules squeeze out any liquid that comes between them. This is known as curdling. Introducing an acid to the egg proteins can increase their electrical charges. Consequently, when the proteins are heated and unwind, they are even more strongly repelled by one another and are inclined to interact more with the liquid. This produces what we know as a gel, the effect that we pleasantly experienced with our lemon curd ("curd" is a misnomer in this case). Thus the lemon juice, while encouraging an egg to cook and form a solid, keeps the solid moist and creamy.

POTS DE CRÈME

Serves 8 | eight 5- to 7-ounce ramekins

WHY THIS RECIPE WORKS Classic pots de crème are incredibly silky and pack an intense hit of chocolate. These petite chocolate custards are usually baked but we took an unconventional user-friendly approach that resulted in ultrarich results: We cooked the custard on the stovetop, whisking it until it was thickened and reached a doneness temperature of 175 to 180 degrees for a dessert with the right body. Then we poured the cooked custard into ramekins and chilled them. We skipped over semisweet chocolate, which was too mild for our dark chocolate dreams. Bittersweet chocolate, and lots of it—50 percent more than most recipes—gave our custards the rich flavor we sought and thickened the mix. We prefer pots de crème made with 60 percent cacao bittersweet chocolate, but 70 percent bittersweet chocolate can also be used—you will need to reduce the amount of chocolate to 8 ounces.

10 ounces bittersweet chocolate, chopped fine
1 tablespoon vanilla extract
1 tablespoon water
½ teaspoon instant espresso powder
5 large egg yolks
5 tablespoons (2¼ ounces) sugar
¼ teaspoon table salt
1½ cups heavy cream
¾ cup half-and-half
Whipped Cream (page 548)
Cocoa powder and/or chocolate shavings (optional)

1. Place chocolate in bowl and set fine-mesh strainer over top. Combine vanilla, water, and espresso powder in second bowl.

2. Whisk egg yolks, sugar, and salt in third bowl until combined. Whisk in cream and half-and-half. Transfer cream mixture to medium saucepan and cook over medium-low heat, stirring constantly and scraping bottom of pot with wooden spoon, until thickened and silky and registers 175 to 180 degrees, 8 to 12 minutes. (Do not let custard overcook or simmer.)

3. Immediately pour custard through fine-mesh strainer over chocolate. Let mixture stand to melt chocolate, about 5 minutes. Add espresso mixture and whisk until smooth. Divide chocolate custard evenly among eight 5- to 7-ounce ramekins. Gently tap ramekins against counter to remove air bubbles.

4. Let pots de crème cool completely, then cover with plastic wrap and refrigerate until chilled, at least 4 hours or up to 3 days. (Before serving, let pots de crème stand at room temperature for 20 to 30 minutes.)

5. Dollop each pot de crème with about 2 tablespoons whipped cream and garnish with cocoa and/or chocolate shavings, if using. Serve.

Milk Chocolate Pots de Crème
Milk chocolate behaves differently in this recipe than bittersweet chocolate, and more of it must be used to ensure that the custard sets.

Substitute 12 ounces milk chocolate for bittersweet chocolate and reduce sugar in pots de crème to 2 tablespoons.

Pots de Crème

CLASSIC CRÈME BRÛLÉE

Serves 6 | six 5-ounce ramekins or shallow dishes

WHY THIS RECIPE WORKS Crème brûlée is all about the contrast between the crisp sugar crust and the silky custard underneath. For the smoothest, richest custard, we used a lot of egg yolks as well as heavy cream. Sugar, a vanilla bean, and a pinch of salt were the only additions. We baked the custard in a low-to-moderate oven (300 degrees) in a waterbath to 170 to 175 degrees for gentle baking and a delicate set. A propane or butane torch along with an even sprinkling of turbinado sugar are the keys to a perfect caramelized sugar crust. Separate the eggs and whisk the yolks after the cream has finished steeping; if left to sit, the surface of the yolks will dry and form a film. While we prefer turbinado or Demerara sugar for the caramelized sugar crust, regular granulated sugar will work, too, but use only 1 teaspoon for each ramekin. Once the sugar on top is brûléed, serve within 30 minutes or the crust will soften.

- 1 vanilla bean
- 3 cups heavy cream, divided
- ½ cup (3½ ounces) granulated sugar
- Pinch table salt
- 9 large egg yolks
- 9 teaspoons turbinado sugar or Demerara sugar

1. Adjust oven rack to lower-middle position and heat oven to 300 degrees. Cut vanilla bean in half lengthwise. Using tip of paring knife, scrape out seeds. Combine vanilla bean and seeds, 2 cups cream, granulated sugar, and salt in medium saucepan. Bring mixture to boil over medium heat, stirring occasionally to dissolve sugar. Off heat, cover and let steep for 15 minutes.

2. Stir remaining 1 cup cream into cream mixture. Whisk egg yolks in large bowl until uniform. Whisk about 1 cup cream mixture into yolks, then repeat with 1 cup more cream mixture. Whisk in remaining cream mixture until thoroughly combined. Strain mixture through fine-mesh strainer into 8-cup liquid measuring cup, discarding solids.

3. Meanwhile, place dish towel in bottom of large baking dish or roasting pan. Set six 4- or 5-ounce ramekins (or shallow fluted dishes) on towel. Bring kettle of water to boil.

4. Divide cream mixture evenly among ramekins. Set baking dish on oven rack. Taking care not to splash water into ramekins, pour enough boiling water into dish to reach two-thirds up sides of ramekins. Bake until centers of custards are just barely set and register 170 to 175 degrees, 25 to 35 minutes depending on ramekin type, checking temperature 5 minutes early.

5. Transfer ramekins to wire rack and let custards cool completely, about 2 hours. Set ramekins on rimmed baking sheet, cover tightly with plastic wrap, and refrigerate until cold, about 4 hours.

6. Uncover ramekins and gently blot tops dry with paper towels. Sprinkle each with 1 to 1½ teaspoons turbinado sugar (depending on ramekin type). Tilt and tap each ramekin to distribute sugar evenly, then dump out excess sugar and wipe rims of ramekins clean. Caramelize sugar with torch until deep golden brown, continually sweeping flame about 2 inches above ramekin. Serve.

Orange Blossom Crème Brûlée

Add 2 teaspoons orange blossom water to strained custard before portioning into ramekins.

Tea-Infused Crème Brûlée

Substitute 10 Irish Breakfast tea bags, tied together, for vanilla bean; after steeping tea in cream, squeeze bags with tongs or press into fine-mesh strainer to extract all liquid. Whisk 1 teaspoon vanilla extract into yolks before adding cream mixture.

**Classic
Crème Brûlée**

**Chocolate–Peanut
Butter Crème Brûlée**

CHOCOLATE–PEANUT BUTTER CRÈME BRÛLÉE

Serves 8 | **eight 5- to 7-ounce ramekins**

WHY THIS RECIPE WORKS We love the creaminess and textural contrasts of crème brûlée, but we reinvented this classic French dessert by giving it a very American chocolate-peanut profile. We added ¼ cup of creamy peanut butter to our custard base in addition to 4 ounces of bittersweet chocolate, which made the custard chocolaty without adversely affecting the texture or obscuring the peanut butter flavor. We replaced a portion of the cream with milk to prevent the custard from becoming overly rich from the added fat from the chocolate and peanut butter. We doubled down on the crunch for this new spin, topping the caramelized sugar with toasty, sweet-salty candied peanuts. Use peanuts in the Candied Nuts.

2¾ cups heavy cream, divided
½ cup (3½ ounces) granulated sugar
4 ounces bittersweet chocolate, chopped fine
¼ cup creamy peanut butter
1 cup whole milk
10 large egg yolks
3 tablespoons turbinado sugar or Demerara sugar
1 recipe Candied Nuts (page 551)

1. Adjust oven rack to lower-middle position and heat oven to 300 degrees. Place dish towel in bottom of large baking dish or roasting pan. Set eight 5- to 7-ounce ramekins (or shallow fluted dishes) on towel. Bring kettle of water to boil.

2. Combine 2 cups cream and granulated sugar in medium saucepan. Bring mixture to boil over medium heat, stirring occasionally to dissolve sugar. Off heat, whisk in chocolate and peanut butter until melted and smooth. Stir in remaining ¾ cup heavy cream and milk. Meanwhile, whisk egg yolks in large bowl until uniform. Whisk about 1 cup chocolate mixture into yolks; repeat with 1 cup more chocolate mixture. Whisk in remaining chocolate mixture until thoroughly combined. Strain custard through fine-mesh strainer into 4-cup liquid measuring cup; discard solids. Divide custard evenly among ramekins.

3. Set baking dish on oven rack. Taking care not to splash water into ramekins, pour enough boiling water into dish to reach two-thirds up sides of ramekins. Bake until centers of custards are just barely set and register 170 to 175 degrees, 25 to 35 minutes depending on ramekin type, checking temperature 5 minutes early. Transfer ramekins to wire rack and let cool completely, about 2 hours. Set ramekins on baking sheet, cover tightly with plastic wrap, and refrigerate until cold, at least 4 hours or up to 3 days.

4. Uncover ramekins and gently blot tops dry with paper towels. Sprinkle each with 1 to 1½ teaspoons turbinado sugar (depending on ramekin type). Tilt and tap each ramekin to distribute sugar evenly, then dump out excess sugar and wipe rims of ramekins clean. Caramelize sugar with torch until deep golden brown, continually sweeping flame about 2 inches above ramekin. Rechill custards for 30 minutes. Sprinkle with candied peanuts before serving.

CRÈME CARAMEL

Serves 8 | eight 5- to 7-ounce ramekins

WHY THIS RECIPE WORKS This classic French dessert is a simple baked custard, but what makes it really stand out is the caramel sauce that enrobes it. Three whole eggs and two yolks resulted in a texture that was firm but not rubbery. Light cream and milk for the dairy component provided the proper amount of richness. The caramel came together quickly; we simply dissolved sugar in water and cooked the mixture until caramel-colored. You can vary the amount of sugar in the custard to suit your taste. We prefer the full ⅔ cup, but you can reduce that amount to as little as ½ cup to create a greater contrast between the custard and the caramel.

CARAMEL
⅓ cup water
2 tablespoons light corn syrup
¼ teaspoon lemon juice
1 cup (7 ounces) sugar

CUSTARD
1½ cups whole milk
1½ cups light cream
3 large eggs, plus 2 large yolks
⅔ cup (4⅔ ounces) sugar
1½ teaspoons vanilla extract
Pinch table salt

1. FOR THE CARAMEL: Combine water, corn syrup, and lemon juice in 2- to 3-quart saucepan. Pour sugar into center of saucepan, taking care not to let sugar granules touch sides of pan. Gently stir with clean spatula to moisten sugar thoroughly. Bring to boil over medium-high heat and cook, without stirring, until sugar is completely dissolved and liquid is clear, 6 to 10 minutes. Reduce heat to medium-low and continue to cook (swirling occasionally) until caramel darkens to honey color, 4 to 5 minutes longer. Remove pan immediately from heat and, working

quickly but carefully (caramel is above 300 degrees and will burn if it touches your skin), pour portion of caramel into each of eight ungreased 5- to 7-ounce ramekins. Allow caramel to cool and harden, about 15 minutes. (Ramekins can be covered and refrigerated for up to 2 days; return to room temperature.)

2. FOR THE CUSTARD: Adjust oven rack to middle position and heat oven to 350 degrees. Heat milk and cream in medium saucepan over medium heat, stirring occasionally, until steam appears and/or mixture registers 160 degrees, 6 to 8 minutes; remove from heat. Meanwhile, gently whisk whole eggs, egg yolks, and sugar in large bowl until just combined. Off heat, gently whisk warm milk mixture, vanilla, and salt into eggs until just combined but not at all foamy. Strain mixture through fine-mesh strainer into large measuring cup; set aside.

3. Bring kettle of water to boil. Place kitchen towel in bottom of roasting pan. Arrange ramekins on towel, making sure they do not touch. Divide reserved custard mixture among ramekins and carefully place roasting pan on oven rack. Carefully pour boiling water into pan until water reaches halfway up sides of ramekins; cover entire pan loosely with aluminum foil. Bake until paring knife inserted halfway between center and edge of custards comes out clean, 35 to 40 minutes. Transfer custards to wire rack and let cool to room temperature. (Custards can be covered with plastic wrap and refrigerated for up to 2 days.)

4. Working with 1 custard at a time, insert paring knife between custard and side of ramekin. Gently run knife around inside edge of ramekin to loosen custard. Cover ramekin with serving plate and invert; set plate on counter and gently shake ramekin, if necessary, to release custard. Serve.

Espresso Crème Caramel
Crush the espresso beans lightly with the bottom of a skillet.

Heat ½ cup lightly crushed espresso beans with milk and cream mixture until steam appears and mixture registers 160 degrees, 6 to 8 minutes. Off heat, cover and let steep until coffee flavor has infused milk and cream, about 15 minutes. Strain mixture through fine-mesh strainer and proceed as directed, discarding crushed espresso beans. Reduce vanilla extract to 1 teaspoon.

FLAN

Serves 8 to 10 | loaf pan

WHY THIS RECIPE WORKS You may notice a similarity between flan and Crème Caramel (page 193), as they both feature a layer of caramel. But this Latin style of baked custard is far richer, with a texture somewhere between those of cheesecake and pudding. It gets its thick, luxurious texture and caramelized, toffee-like flavor from a combination of evaporated and sweetened condensed milk. Adding a small amount of fresh milk ensured the custard was densely creamy rather than stiff. This recipe should be made at least one day before serving. We recommend an 8½ by 4½-inch loaf pan for this recipe. If your pan is 9 by 5 inches, begin checking for doneness after 1 hour. You may substitute 2 percent milk for the whole milk, but do not use skim milk. Serve the flan on a platter with a raised rim to contain the liquid caramel.

⅔ cup (4⅔ ounces) sugar
2 large eggs plus 5 large yolks
1 (14-ounce) can sweetened condensed milk
1 (12-ounce) can evaporated milk
½ cup whole milk
1½ tablespoons vanilla extract
½ teaspoon table salt

1. Stir sugar and ¼ cup water in medium saucepan until sugar is completely moistened. Bring to boil over medium-high heat, 3 to 5 minutes, and cook, without stirring, until mixture begins to turn golden, 1 to 2 minutes. Gently swirling pan, continue to cook until sugar is color of peanut butter, 1 to 2 minutes longer. Off heat, swirl pan until sugar is reddish-amber and fragrant, 15 to 20 seconds. Carefully swirl in 2 tablespoons warm tap water until incorporated; mixture will bubble and steam. Pour caramel into 8½ by 4½-inch loaf pan; do not scrape out saucepan. Set loaf pan aside.

2. Adjust oven rack to middle position and heat oven to 300 degrees. Line bottom of 13 by 9-inch baking pan with dish towel, folding towel to fit smoothly, and set aside. Bring 2 quarts water to boil. Whisk eggs and yolks in large bowl until combined. Add condensed milk, evaporated milk, whole milk, vanilla, and salt and whisk until incorporated. Strain mixture through fine-mesh strainer into prepared loaf pan.

3. Cover loaf pan tightly with aluminum foil and place in prepared baking pan. Place baking pan in oven and carefully pour all of boiling water into pan. Bake until center of custard jiggles slightly when shaken and custard registers 180 degrees, 1¼ to 1½ hours. Remove foil and leave custard in water bath until loaf pan has cooled completely. Remove loaf pan from water bath, wrap tightly with plastic wrap, and chill overnight or for up to 4 days.

4. To unmold, slide paring knife around inside edges of pan. Cover pan with serving platter and invert; set platter on counter. When flan is released, remove loaf pan. Using rubber spatula, scrape residual caramel onto flan. Slice and serve. (Leftover flan may be covered loosely with plastic wrap and refrigerated for up to 4 days.)

Coffee Flan

Whisk 4 teaspoons instant espresso powder into egg-milk mixture in step 2 until dissolved.

Orange-Cardamom Flan

Whisk 2 tablespoons orange zest and ¼ teaspoon ground cardamom into egg-milk mixture in step 2 before straining.

INDIVIDUAL FRESH BERRY GRATINS

Serves 4 | 4 shallow 6-ounce gratin dishes

WHY THIS RECIPE WORKS Zabaglione is an ethereal Italian custard flavored with wine and often accompanied by fresh berries. We liked a light, crisp white wine rather than the traditional Marsala here, but the decreased sugar made our custard runny so we folded in some whipped cream. Briefly running the custards under the broiler produced warm, succulent berries and a golden-brown crust. You will need four shallow 6-ounce broiler-safe gratin dishes, but a broiler-safe pie plate or gratin dish can be used instead. Make sure to cook the egg mixture in a glass bowl over water that is barely simmering. Do not use frozen berries for this recipe. To prevent scorching, pay close attention to the gratins when broiling. Use a medium-bodied dry white wine such as Sauvignon Blanc or Chardonnay in this recipe.

BERRY MIXTURE

11 ounces (2¼ cups) blackberries, blueberries, and/or raspberries
4 ounces strawberries, hulled and halved lengthwise if small or quartered if large (¾ cup)
2 teaspoons granulated sugar
Pinch table salt

ZABAGLIONE

3 large egg yolks
3 tablespoons granulated sugar, divided
3 tablespoons dry white wine
2 teaspoons packed light brown sugar
3 tablespoons heavy cream, chilled

1. **FOR THE BERRY MIXTURE:** Line rimmed baking sheet with aluminum foil. Toss berries, strawberries, sugar, and salt together in bowl. Divide berry mixture evenly among 4 shallow 6-ounce gratin dishes and place on prepared sheet; set aside.

2. **FOR THE ZABAGLIONE:** Whisk egg yolks, 2 tablespoons plus 1 teaspoon granulated sugar, and wine in medium bowl until sugar has dissolved, about 1 minute. Set bowl over saucepan of barely simmering water and cook, whisking constantly, until mixture is frothy. Continue to cook, whisking constantly, until mixture is slightly thickened, creamy, and glossy, 5 to 10 minutes (mixture will form loose mounds when dripped from whisk). Remove bowl from saucepan and whisk constantly for 30 seconds to cool slightly. Transfer bowl to refrigerator and chill until egg mixture is completely cool, about 10 minutes.

3. Meanwhile, adjust oven rack 6 inches from broiler element and heat broiler. Combine brown sugar and remaining 2 teaspoons granulated sugar in bowl.

4. Whisk heavy cream in large bowl until it holds soft peaks, 30 to 90 seconds. Using rubber spatula, gently fold whipped cream into cooled egg mixture. Spoon zabaglione over berries. Sprinkle sugar mixture evenly on top. Let sit until sugar dissolves, about 10 minutes. Broil gratins until sugar is bubbly and caramelized, 1 to 4 minutes. Serve immediately.

Flan

PEACH ZABAGLIONE GRATIN

Serves 4 to 6 | 1½-quart gratin dish

WHY THIS RECIPE WORKS For a twist on the classic zabaglione with berries, we made this one a "peaches and cream," with peach flavor incorporated into the custard. We kept the peaches simple, macerating them in sugar, Marsala wine, a little vanilla, and salt. We then added egg yolks to the sweetened, wine-infused liquid from the peaches and prepared the custard. After spooning the zabaglione over the peaches, we used a broiler (or blowtorch) to toast the top. For the best results, use in-season, ripe peaches here. Don't use cooking Marsala in this recipe—use a drinking-quality Marsala instead. Other sweet wines such as moscato and port can be used. Make sure to cook the egg mixture in a glass bowl over water that is barely simmering.

1½ pounds ripe peaches, halved, pitted, and cut into ¾-inch wedges
 ½ cup (3½ ounces) sugar
 ¼ cup sweet Marsala
 1 teaspoon vanilla extract
 ¼ teaspoon table salt
 4 large egg yolks

Peach Zabaglione Gratin

1. Gently toss peaches, sugar, Marsala, vanilla, and salt together in bowl. Let sit for 30 minutes, stirring occasionally. Set colander in medium bowl. Transfer peach mixture to colander and let drain for 2 minutes; reserve accumulated peach liquid.

2. Remove colander from bowl and whisk egg yolks into accumulated peach liquid. Set bowl with egg yolk mixture over large saucepan with 1 inch of barely simmering water (water should not touch bottom of bowl). Cook, whisking constantly, until zabaglione is thickened to point where ribbons sit on top of mixture when drizzled from whisk and mixture registers 165 to 170 degrees, 10 to 15 minutes for metal bowl or about 20 minutes for glass bowl. Arrange peaches in single layer in shallow 1½-quart gratin dish. Spoon zabaglione over peaches to cover completely.

3A. FOR A BROILER: Adjust oven rack 6 inches from broiler element and heat broiler. Broil until top is well browned, 30 to 60 seconds.

3B. FOR A BLOWTORCH: Ignite torch and continuously sweep flame above zabaglione until well browned, about 2 minutes.

4. Serve immediately.

Lemon Snow

LEMON SNOW
Serves 8 to 10 | small saucepan

WHY THIS RECIPE WORKS We thought lemon "snow"—a retro dessert featuring a chilled lemon foam topped with a cream sauce—deserved reviving. A combination of lemon zest and juice gave the snow a bright, pleasantly tart bite. We whisked the zest and juice into dissolved gelatin and whipped this mixture with egg whites, creating a light, creamy foam that resembled fresh snowdrifts. We enriched the custard sauce with butter. If you're concerned about eating raw egg whites, use pasteurized shell eggs. For an accurate measurement of boiling water, bring a kettle of water to a boil and then measure out the desired amount.

LEMON SNOW
- ¼ cup cold water
- 2 teaspoons unflavored gelatin
- 1 cup boiling water
- 1 cup (7 ounces) sugar
- 1 teaspoon grated lemon zest plus ⅓ cup juice (2 lemons)
  Pinch table salt
- 3 large egg whites

CUSTARD SAUCE
- 3 large egg yolks
- ¼ cup (1¾ ounces) sugar
  Pinch table salt
- 1¼ cups whole milk
- 1 tablespoon unsalted butter
- 1¼ teaspoons vanilla extract

1. FOR THE LEMON SNOW: Place cold water in medium bowl. Sprinkle gelatin over water and let sit until gelatin softens, about 5 minutes. Whisk boiling water into mixture until gelatin dissolves. Whisk sugar, lemon zest and juice, and salt into gelatin mixture until dissolved. Cover with plastic wrap and refrigerate until cool and slightly gelatinous, about 2 hours.

2. Combine egg whites and gelatin mixture in bowl of stand mixer fitted with whisk attachment. Whip on medium-low speed until foamy, about 1 minute. Increase speed to medium-high and whip until soft peaks form, 11 to 14 minutes. Scrape lemon snow into bowl, or divide among dessert glasses, and refrigerate until set, about 2 hours.

3. FOR THE CUSTARD SAUCE: Whisk egg yolks, sugar, and salt in bowl until combined. Bring milk to boil in small saucepan. Slowly stir milk into yolk mixture with wooden spoon. Return milk-yolk mixture to pot, reduce heat to low, and cook, stirring constantly, until sauce is slightly thickened and registers 175 to 180 degrees, 2 to 4 minutes. Pour through fine-mesh strainer into 2-cup liquid measuring cup. Stir in butter and vanilla until incorporated. Refrigerate until cool and serve with lemon snow.

TUTORIAL
Peach Zabaglione

The zabaglione for this dessert uses exuded peach juices to become extra-peachy in this refined "peaches-and-cream" dessert.

1. Transfer peach-marsala mixture to colander and let drain for 2 minutes; reserve accumulated peach liquid.

2. Remove colander from bowl and whisk egg yolks into accumulated peach liquid.

3. Set bowl with egg yolk mixture over large saucepan with 1 inch of barely simmering water (water should not touch bottom of bowl). Cook, whisking constantly.

4. Cook until zabaglione is thickened to point where ribbons sit on top of mixture when drizzled from whisk and mixture registers 165 to 170 degrees, about 20 minutes.

5. Arrange peaches in single layer in shallow 1½-quart gratin dish. Spoon zabaglione over peaches to cover completely.

6. If using blowtorch, ignite torch and continuously sweep flame above zabaglione until well browned, about 2 minutes.

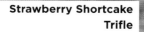

Strawberry Shortcake Trifle

STRAWBERRY SHORTCAKE TRIFLE

Serves 12 | 3½-quart trifle dish

WHY THIS RECIPE WORKS We wanted strawberries to be the star of our trifle, so to get the most out of them, we tossed them with a bit of sugar and let them sit for a spell, intensifying their sweetness and creating a lightly sugared syrup. For a festive, grown-up vibe, we added orange liqueur to the syrup. Inspired by strawberry shortcake, we opted to use fluffy, tender biscuits in place of the typical cake component. To construct the trifle, we layered pieces of the biscuits followed by some of the strawberries and their syrup. Next came a healthy dose of vanilla pastry cream followed by some whipped cream. After repeating those layers twice, we decorated the top with sliced strawberries. We call for a 3½-quart trifle dish for this recipe; however, a 4-quart bowl can be used in its place.

CUSTARD

- 2 cups whole milk
- ½ cup (3½ ounces) sugar, divided
- Pinch table salt
- 5 large egg yolks
- 3 tablespoons cornstarch
- 4 tablespoons unsalted butter, cut into 4 pieces and chilled
- 1½ teaspoons vanilla extract

BISCUITS

- 2 cups (10 ounces) all-purpose flour
- 2 teaspoons baking powder
- ½ teaspoon baking soda
- 1 teaspoon sugar
- ¾ teaspoon table salt
- ½ cup whole milk, chilled
- ½ cup heavy cream, chilled
- 8 tablespoons unsalted butter, melted

STRAWBERRIES

- 3 pounds strawberries
- ½ cup (3½ ounces) sugar
- ¼ cup Grand Marnier
- Pinch table salt

WHIPPED CREAM

- 1½ cups heavy cream, chilled
- 2 tablespoons sugar
- ½ teaspoon vanilla extract

1. **FOR THE CUSTARD:** Combine milk, 6 tablespoons sugar, and salt in medium saucepan and bring to simmer over medium heat, stirring occasionally to dissolve sugar. Meanwhile, whisk egg yolks, cornstarch, and remaining 2 tablespoons sugar in medium bowl until mixture is pale yellow and thick, about 1 minute.

2. Gradually whisk half of milk mixture into yolk mixture to temper. Return milk-yolk mixture to saucepan. Return to simmer over medium heat and cook, whisking constantly, until mixture is thickened and 3 or 4 bubbles burst on surface, about 3 minutes. Off heat, whisk in butter and vanilla. Transfer mixture to clean bowl, press greased parchment paper directly onto surface, and refrigerate until set, at least 3 hours.

3. **FOR THE BISCUITS:** Meanwhile, adjust oven rack to middle position and heat oven to 450 degrees. Line baking sheet with parchment. Whisk flour, baking powder, baking soda, sugar, and salt together in large bowl. Stir milk, cream, and melted butter together in small bowl (butter will form clumps).

4. Add dairy mixture to flour mixture and stir with rubber spatula until just combined. Using greased ¼-cup dry measuring cup, drop 12 scant scoops of batter 1½ inches apart on prepared sheet. Bake until biscuit tops are golden brown, about 12 minutes, rotating sheet halfway through baking. Transfer biscuits to wire rack and let cool completely, about 20 minutes.

5. **FOR THE STRAWBERRIES:** Set aside 6 strawberries. Hull remaining strawberries and cut into ½-inch pieces. Combine cut strawberries, sugar, Grand Marnier, and salt in large bowl. Let sit at room temperature for 30 minutes.

6. **FOR THE WHIPPED CREAM:** Using stand mixer fitted with whisk attachment, whip cream, sugar, and vanilla on low speed until foamy, about 1 minute. Increase speed to high and whip until stiff peaks form, 1 to 3 minutes. Refrigerate until ready to use.

7. Drain strawberries in colander set in bowl, reserving all juice. Whisk chilled custard to recombine. Break 4 biscuits into 1-inch pieces and arrange on bottom of 3½-quart trifle dish. Pour one-third of reserved strawberry juice over biscuits. Top with one-third of strawberries, followed by one-third of custard. Spread 1 cup whipped cream evenly over custard. Repeat layers twice. Cover dish with plastic wrap and refrigerate for at least 1 hour or up to 24 hours. Hull reserved strawberries and slice thin, then shingle in center of trifle. Serve.

MOUSSES

KEY POINTS

Whole eggs increase
creamy richness

Carefully fold in whipped eggs

Stabilize fruit mousse with gelatin

MOUSSE MAKES AN IDEAL END TO A MEAL and is perfect for entertaining: It doesn't require turning on the oven, it looks elegant once it's portioned into bowls and dressed up with a simple garnish, and it's entirely make-ahead. It's also a dessert of many textures. It can be dense and rich or fluffy and ethereal, but we generally prefer a mousse that falls somewhere in the middle—one that is creamy yet light so we can enjoy more than a couple of spoonfuls. Dairy and eggs are the cornerstones of most conventional mousses, but we have also found ways to create an entirely vegan mousse by employing ingredients such as aquafaba (the viscous liquid in a can of chickpeas that has a keen ability to whip to stiff peaks just like egg whites) and rich, creamy avocado. Whipped cream or beaten egg whites are typically responsible for lift and structure, although gelatin is also sometimes added for extra stability. Egg yolks contribute richness and a silky consistency but they can also mask the flavor of lighter versions. The key factor in most mousse recipes is the star ingredient. Ripe, juicy berries can make a mousse loose and runny, while dark, decadent chocolate can lead to an overly dense or chalky texture, so each requires its own brand of troubleshooting and treatment.

FIGURING OUT FOLDING

The goal of folding is to incorporate delicate, airy ingredients such as whipped cream or beaten egg whites into heavy, dense ingredients such as egg yolks, custard, or chocolate without deflating the whipped mixture. We like to start the process by lightening the heavier ingredients with one-quarter or one-third of the whipped mixture. A balloon whisk is ideal for the task: Its tines cut into and loosen the heavier mixture, allowing the whipped mixture to be integrated more readily. Next, the remaining whipped mixture can be easily incorporated into the lightened mixture. For this round of folding, we preserve the airiness of the dessert by using a rubber spatula, which is gentler than a whisk.

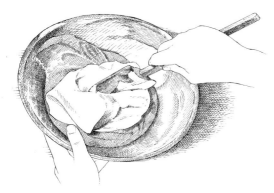

1. Cut through center of 2 mixtures down to bottom of bowl.

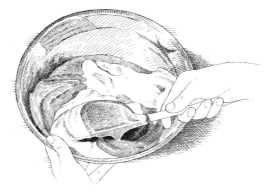

2. Pull spatula toward you, scraping along bottom and up side of bowl.

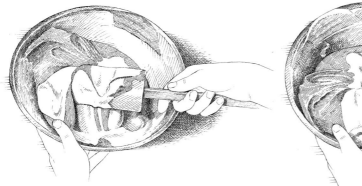

3. Once spatula is out of mixture, rotate it so any mixture clinging to blade falls back onto surface.

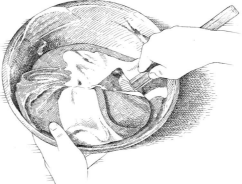

4. Spin bowl quarter turn and repeat until mixture is just incorporated.

CHOCOLATE MOUSSE

Serves 6 to 8 | 6 to 8 ramekins

WHY THIS RECIPE WORKS We were after an airy and light mousse with rich dark-chocolate flavor. We melted a hefty 12 ounces of bittersweet chocolate chips with water (rather than cream or butter, which dulled the flavor). Folding in whipped whole eggs made for a mousse that was fluffy yet lusciously creamy. Deflating the eggs a little while folding was OK, but it was important to use a large bowl and scrape the bottom to incorporate everything thoroughly (see page 201). Refrigerating the mousse for at least 6 hours gave it just the right amount of structure. To bring the eggs to room temperature quickly, place the whole, uncracked eggs in a bowl of warm water for 15 minutes. We developed this recipe using Ghirardelli 60% Premium Baking Chips. We call for individual serving glasses or ramekins, but this mousse can also be chilled in a large serving dish. Just increase the chilling time to at least 8 hours.

- 8 large eggs, room temperature
- 2 tablespoons sugar
- 2 cups (12 ounces) bittersweet chocolate chips
- ¼ cup water
- 1 recipe Whipped Cream (page 548)

1. Using stand mixer fitted with whisk attachment, whip eggs on medium speed until foamy, about 1 minute. Add sugar, increase speed to high, and whip until tripled in volume and ribbons form on top of mixture when dribbled from whisk, 5 to 7 minutes. Set aside.

2. Microwave chocolate and water in large bowl at 50 percent power, stirring occasionally with rubber spatula, until chocolate is melted, about 2 minutes.

3. Whisk one-third of egg mixture into chocolate mixture until fully combined. Using clean rubber spatula, gently fold in remaining egg mixture, making sure to scrape up any chocolate from bottom of bowl, until no streaks remain.

4. Portion mousse evenly into 6 to 8 ramekins or serving dishes. Cover with plastic wrap and refrigerate for at least 6 hours or up to 2 days.

5. Top mousse with whipped cream. Serve.

WHITE CHOCOLATE MOUSSE WITH RASPBERRY SAUCE

Serves 4 | 4 ramekins

WHY THIS RECIPE WORKS For a creamy white chocolate mousse, we started with 12 ounces of finely chopped white chocolate. Since white chocolate is especially prone to scorching, we melted it gently in a double boiler with egg yolks and water. Folding in cream whipped to soft peaks made for a mousse that was fluffy yet lusciously creamy. Allowing the mousse to set by refrigerating it for at least 8 hours gave the dessert just the right amount of structure: It melted in the mouth but still held its shape on a spoon. A stir-together, sweet-tart raspberry sauce balanced the richness of the white chocolate mousse. We prefer bar chocolate from brands such as Ghirardelli or Callebaut for this recipe. We use a glass bowl for the double boiler because glass conducts heat more evenly and gently than metal. Top the mousse with our Candied Nuts (page 551) (we like pistachios here), if desired.

- 12 ounces white chocolate, chopped fine
- 3 large egg yolks
- 1 cup heavy cream, chilled
- 5 ounces (1 cup) frozen raspberries
- 4 teaspoons sugar
- 4 teaspoons lime juice

1. Stir chocolate, egg yolks, and 2 tablespoons water together in medium glass bowl with rubber spatula. Set bowl over large saucepan of barely simmering water (water should not touch bottom of bowl) and cook, stirring and scraping sides of bowl constantly, until chocolate is just melted. (Once chocolate begins to melt, remove bowl from heat every 10 to 15 seconds so yolks don't overcook.)

2. Using stand mixer fitted with whisk attachment, whip cream on medium-low speed until foamy, about 1 minute. Increase speed to high and whip until soft peaks form, 1 to 2 minutes.

3. Gently whisk one-third of whipped cream into chocolate mixture until fully combined. Gently fold in remaining whipped cream with rubber spatula, making sure to scrape up any chocolate mixture from bottom of bowl, until no streaks remain.

4. Portion mousse evenly into 4 ramekins or serving dishes. Cover with plastic wrap and refrigerate for at least 8 hours or up to 2 days.

5. About 1 hour before serving, combine raspberries, sugar, and lime juice in bowl. Let sit at room temperature until raspberries defrost; stir periodically to combine. (Raspberry sauce can be made simultaneously with mousse and allowed to thaw in refrigerator.)

6. Spoon raspberry sauce over mousse. Serve.

CARAMELIZED WHITE CHOCOLATE MOUSSE

Serves 6 | 10-inch ovensafe nonstick skillet

WHY THIS RECIPE WORKS White chocolate has a relatively mild, sweet, milky vanilla flavor; but by applying heat to white chocolate, its plentiful sugars and milk solids caramelize and it becomes a different confection entirely—bold, less sweet, and rich with butterscotch notes. To caramelize the chocolate, we roasted it in a relatively low oven, stirring all along the way for even cooking, until the color resembled peanut butter and the texture became dry and crumbly. We whisked water into the caramelized chocolate and cooked it on the stovetop just until the chocolate was mostly smooth again; any remaining small lumps were easily strained out. Folding whipped egg whites and whipped cream into the chocolate and egg yolks gave the creamy mousse a light, buoyant texture. We like serving the mousse with berries; their tartness balances the sweetness. If the interior of your nonstick skillet is very dark, start checking the caramelized white chocolate for doneness 5 minutes earlier.

8 ounces white chocolate, chopped
5 tablespoons water
2 large eggs, separated
⅛ teaspoon table salt
1 cup heavy cream, chilled

1. Adjust oven rack to middle position and heat oven to 300 degrees. Place chocolate in 10-inch ovensafe nonstick skillet. Transfer skillet to oven and bake until chocolate is melted, about 10 minutes. Stir chocolate and spread into even layer. Continue to bake, stirring and spreading into even layer every 10 minutes, until golden brown, 30 to 35 minutes. (Chocolate will become dry and crumbly as it bakes.)

2. Transfer skillet to stovetop and set over medium-low heat. Being careful of hot skillet handle, add water to chocolate and cook, whisking constantly, until mixture is fully combined and mostly smooth, about 2 minutes. Strain chocolate mixture through fine-mesh strainer into large bowl, pressing on solids to extract as much chocolate mixture as possible; discard solids. Let cool until just warmer than room temperature, about 10 minutes. Whisk in egg yolks and salt until fully combined.

White Chocolate Mousse with Raspberry Sauce

Caramelized White Chocolate Mousse

Strawberry Mousse

3. Using stand mixer fitted with whisk attachment, whip egg whites on medium-low speed until foamy, about 1 minute. Increase speed to medium-high and whip until soft peaks form, about 1 minute. Using whisk, stir about one-quarter of whipped egg whites into chocolate mixture to lighten it. Using rubber spatula, gently fold in remaining egg whites until a few white streaks remain.

4. Return now-empty bowl to mixer and whip cream on medium-low speed until foamy, about 1 minute. Increase speed to high and whip until soft peaks form, about 1 minute. Using rubber spatula, fold whipped cream into mousse until no white streaks remain. Portion mousse evenly into 6 ramekins or serving dishes. Cover with plastic wrap and refrigerate until set and firm, at least 2 hours or up to 24 hours. Serve.

STRAWBERRY MOUSSE

Serves 4 to 6 | 4 to 6 ramekins

WHY THIS RECIPE WORKS There are few things better than a juicy, sweet strawberry fresh from the market. We wanted to highlight these jewels of early summer in a mousse with a creamy yet firm texture and amped-up strawberry flavor. We used a mix of cream cheese and cream as our base, and we processed the berries into small pieces and macerated them with sugar and a little salt to draw out their juice. We then reduced the released liquid to a syrup before adding it to the mousse, which standardized the amount of moisture in the dessert and also concentrated the berry flavor. Fully pureeing the juiced berries contributed bright, fresh berry flavor. In step 1, be careful not to overprocess the berries. For more-complex berry flavor, replace the 3 tablespoons of raw strawberry juice in step 2 with strawberry or raspberry liqueur.

  2 pounds strawberries, hulled (6½ cups), divided
  ½ cup (3½ ounces) sugar, divided
     Pinch table salt
1¾ teaspoons unflavored gelatin
  4 ounces cream cheese, cut into 8 pieces and softened
  ½ cup heavy cream, chilled

1. Dice enough strawberries into ¼-inch pieces to measure 1 cup; refrigerate until ready to serve. Pulse remaining strawberries in food processor in 2 batches until most pieces are ¼ to ½ inch thick (some larger pieces are fine), 6 to 10 pulses. Transfer strawberries to bowl and toss with ¼ cup sugar and salt. (Do not clean processor.) Cover bowl and let sit, stirring occasionally, for 45 minutes.

2. Drain processed strawberries in fine-mesh strainer set over bowl (you should have about ⅔ cup juice). Measure out 3 tablespoons juice into small bowl, sprinkle gelatin over juice, and let sit until gelatin softens, about 5 minutes. Transfer remaining juice to small saucepan and cook over medium-high heat until reduced to 3 tablespoons, about 10 minutes. Off heat, whisk in softened gelatin mixture until gelatin dissolves. Whisk in cream cheese until smooth, then transfer to large bowl.

3. While juice is reducing, return strawberries to now-empty processor and process until smooth, 15 to 20 seconds. Strain puree through fine-mesh strainer into medium bowl, pressing on solids to remove seeds (you should have about 1⅔ cups puree). Discard any solids in strainer. Add strawberry puree to juice-gelatin mixture and whisk until incorporated.

4. Using stand mixer fitted with whisk, whip cream on medium-low speed until foamy, about 1 minute. Increase speed to high and whip until soft peaks form, 1 to 3 minutes. Gradually add remaining ¼ cup sugar and whip until stiff peaks form, 1 to 2 minutes. Whisk whipped cream into strawberry mixture until no white streaks remain. Portion mousse evenly into 4 to 6 ramekins or serving dishes and chill for at least 4 hours or up to 2 days. (If chilled longer than 6 hours, let mousse sit at room temperature for 10 minutes before serving.) Serve, garnishing with reserved diced strawberries.

Strawberry Mousse with Frozen Strawberries
Substitute 1½ pounds (5¼ cups) of thawed frozen strawberries for fresh strawberries. Skip step 1 (do not process berries). Proceed with the recipe, adding the ½ cup of sugar and the salt to the whipped cream in step 4.

LEMON YOGURT MOUSSE WITH BLUEBERRY SAUCE

Serves 6 | 6 ramekins

WHY THIS RECIPE WORKS A creamy, refreshing, and slightly tangy chilled lemon mousse is a perfect way to highlight the ubiquitous citrus fruit. Greek yogurt, with its thick texture and tangy flavor, made a good base for our mousse. Unflavored gelatin and whipped egg whites held the mousse together without weighing it down. A combination of lemon zest and juice gave us well-rounded, bold citrus flavor. A vibrant berry sauce complemented the bright citrus flavor of the mousse. You can substitute 1 cup of frozen blueberries for the fresh berries. Do not substitute low-fat or nonfat Greek yogurt in this recipe.

BLUEBERRY SAUCE
- 4 ounces (¾ cup) blueberries
- 2 tablespoons sugar
- 2 tablespoons water
- Pinch table salt

MOUSSE
- ¾ teaspoon unflavored gelatin
- 3 tablespoons water
- ½ cup whole Greek yogurt
- ¼ cup heavy cream
- 1½ teaspoons grated lemon zest plus 3 tablespoons juice
- 1 teaspoon vanilla extract
- ⅛ teaspoon table salt
- 3 large egg whites
- ¼ teaspoon cream of tartar
- 6 tablespoons (2⅔ ounces) sugar

1. **FOR THE BLUEBERRY SAUCE:** Bring blueberries, sugar, water, and salt to simmer in medium saucepan over medium heat. Cook, stirring occasionally, until sugar has dissolved and fruit is heated through, 2 to 4 minutes.

2. Transfer mixture to blender and process until smooth, about 20 seconds. Strain puree through fine-mesh strainer, pressing on solids to extract as much puree as possible (you should have about ½ cup). Spoon sauce evenly into six 4-ounce ramekins and refrigerate until chilled, about 20 minutes.

3. **FOR THE MOUSSE:** Sprinkle gelatin over water in bowl and let sit until gelatin softens, about 5 minutes. In separate bowl, whisk yogurt, heavy cream, lemon zest and juice, vanilla, and salt together until smooth.

4. Whisk egg whites, cream of tartar, and sugar together in bowl of stand mixer. Set bowl over saucepan of barely simmering water and cook, whisking constantly, until mixture has tripled in volume and registers about 160 degrees, 5 to 10 minutes. Off heat, quickly whisk in hydrated gelatin until dissolved. Transfer bowl to stand mixer fitted with whisk attachment and whip on medium-high speed until stiff, shiny peaks form, 4 to 6 minutes. Add yogurt mixture and continue to whip until just combined, 30 to 60 seconds.

5. Portion mousse evenly into 6 chilled ramekins, cover tightly with plastic wrap, and refrigerate until chilled and set, 6 to 8 hours. Serve chilled.

Lemon Yogurt Mousse with Raspberry Sauce
Substitute 1 cup fresh or frozen raspberries for blueberries.

Lemon Yogurt Mousse with Strawberry Sauce
Substitute 1 cup halved fresh or frozen strawberries for blueberries and reduce amount of water to 2 teaspoons.

FOOLS

Use whipped cream instead
of custard

Cook some fruit

Incorporate some tartness

A FOOL IS A QUICK DESSERT that just happens to have a quaint and quirky name. It was brought to America by British colonists in the 1700s, and traditional recipes call for gently heating milk, cream, sugar, and egg yolks until thickened and then folding in cooked fruit once the custard has cooled. The resulting dessert has a deep, fruity flavor and a silken creaminess. But while fool-making tradition dictates that the cream be mixed into the fruit, we find that arranging the fruit and cream in layers produces a more interesting—and visually pleasing—result. (That being said, we do sometimes like to fold a fruit puree into the cream before layering it with the fruit for a colorful and flavorful infusion.) Modern recipes typically skip making a custard and use whipped cream instead. We find that whipped cream works well in some fools—such as our tropical twist with pineapple and mango—but in others it is a bit too light and airy. For those we like to make the whipped cream a little more custard-like with the addition of rich, tangy sour cream.

Berry Fools

BERRY FOOLS

Serves 6 | small saucepan

WHY THIS RECIPE WORKS For an updated spin on this old-fashioned dessert, we thickened the fruit puree with gelatin and incorporated both sour cream and heavy cream for just the right touch of richness and tanginess. Whole berries layered with this fruit-infused whipped cream made for a beautiful presentation, and a topping of crushed sweet wheat crackers contributed nutty flavor and a subtle crunch. You may substitute frozen fruit for fresh, but there will be a slight compromise in texture. If using frozen fruit, reduce the amount of sugar in the puree by 1 tablespoon. The thickened fruit puree can be made up to 4 hours in advance; just be sure to whisk it well in step 4 to break up any clumps. We like the granular texture and nutty flavor of Carr's Whole Wheat Crackers, but graham crackers or gingersnaps will also work in this recipe.

- 2 pounds strawberries, hulled (6 cups), divided
- 12 ounces (2¼ cups) raspberries, divided
- ¾ cup (5¼ ounces) sugar, divided
- 2 teaspoons unflavored powdered gelatin
- 1 cup heavy cream
- ¼ cup sour cream
- ½ teaspoon vanilla extract
- 4 Carr's Whole Wheat Crackers, crushed fine (¼ cup)
- 6 sprigs fresh mint (optional)

1. Process 3 cups strawberries, 1 cup raspberries, and ½ cup sugar in food processor until mixture is completely smooth, about 1 minute. Strain berry puree through fine-mesh strainer into 4-cup liquid measuring cup (you should have 2½ cups puree; reserve any excess for another use). Transfer ½ cup puree to small bowl and sprinkle gelatin over top; stir until gelatin is incorporated and let stand for at least 5 minutes. Heat remaining 2 cups puree in small saucepan over medium heat until it begins to bubble, 4 to 6 minutes. Remove pan from heat and stir in gelatin mixture until dissolved. Transfer gelatin-puree mixture to medium bowl, cover with plastic wrap, and refrigerate until cold, about 2 hours.

2. Meanwhile, chop remaining strawberries into rough ¼-inch pieces. Toss strawberries, remaining raspberries, and 2 tablespoons sugar together in medium bowl. Set aside for 1 hour.

3. Place cream, sour cream, vanilla, and remaining 2 tablespoons sugar in chilled bowl of stand mixer fitted with paddle. Beat on low speed until bubbles form, about 30 seconds. Increase speed to medium and continue to beat until paddle leaves trail, about 30 seconds. Increase speed to high; continue to beat until mixture has nearly doubled in volume and holds stiff peaks, about 30 seconds. Transfer ⅓ cup whipped cream mixture to small bowl and set aside.

4. Remove thickened berry puree from refrigerator and whisk until smooth. With mixer running at medium speed, slowly add two-thirds of puree to whipped cream mixture; mix until incorporated, about 15 seconds. Using spatula, gently fold in remaining thickened puree, leaving streaks of puree.

5. Transfer uncooked berries to fine-mesh strainer; shake strainer gently to remove any excess berry juice. Divide two-thirds of berries evenly among 6 tall parfait or sundae glasses. Divide creamy berry mixture evenly among glasses, followed by remaining uncooked berries. Top each glass with reserved plain whipped cream mixture. Sprinkle with crushed crackers and garnish with mint sprigs, if using. Serve immediately.

PINEAPPLE-MANGO FOOLS

Serves 8 | 12-inch skillet

WHY THIS RECIPE WORKS To allow the fruit flavor to shine in this tropical spin on the dessert known as a fool, we caramelized the pineapple and mango in a skillet to concentrate their flavor; flambéing some rum in the pan gave the mixture complexity without any harshness from the alcohol. Pulsing the mixture a few times in a food processor gave it just the right texture—not completely smooth, but not overly chunky either. Thai basil and lime juice offered nuanced, sophisticated flavor. We added a small amount of honey to our whipped cream for complementary sweetness, and we topped the layered desserts with toasted macadamia nuts for crunch and buttery, nutty flavor. If you can't find Thai basil, regular basil will work. Before flambéing, be sure to roll up long shirtsleeves, tie back long hair, and turn off the exhaust fan and any lit burners.

- 2 tablespoons unsalted butter
- 1 pineapple, peeled, cored, and cut into ½-inch pieces (4 cups)
- 1 mango, peeled, pitted, and cut into ½-inch pieces
- ¼ teaspoon table salt
- ¼ cup dark rum
- 2 tablespoons shredded fresh Thai basil
- 2 teaspoons lime juice
- 2 cups heavy cream
- 2 tablespoons honey
- ½ cup macadamia nuts, toasted and chopped

1. Melt butter in 12-inch skillet over medium-high heat. Add pineapple, mango, and salt and cook, stirring occasionally, until golden brown, 15 to 20 minutes. Off heat, add rum and let warm through, about 5 seconds. Wave lit match over pan until rum ignites, then shake pan to distribute flames. When flames subside, scrape up any browned bits and transfer to large bowl. Refrigerate until chilled, about 45 minutes.

2. Pulse chilled pineapple mixture in food processor until finely chopped and no pieces larger than ¼ inch remain, about 5 pulses. Transfer to bowl and stir in basil and lime juice.

3. Using stand mixer fitted with whisk attachment, whip cream and honey on medium-low speed until foamy, about 1 minute. Increase speed to high and whip until soft peaks form, 1 to 3 minutes. Spoon ¼ cup pineapple mixture into bottoms of eight 8-ounce glasses or jars, then top evenly with ¼ cup whipped cream. Spoon remaining pineapple mixture into glasses and dollop remaining whipped cream over top. Sprinkle with macadamia nuts and serve immediately.

CRANBERRY-RASPBERRY FOOLS

Serves 8 | medium saucepan

WHY THIS RECIPE WORKS This no-bake, no-fuss berry fool adds bold, brash cranberries to the mix. The cranberries' tart flavor is the perfect foil to the rich whipped cream and sweet raspberries. We pureed both the cranberries and raspberries with orange juice and sugar and then pressed this mixture through a fine-mesh strainer to ensure that our cranberry-raspberry fools would be silky smooth. Gently folding this puree into the whipped cream gave our fools the proper light and fluffy consistency.

 1 pound (4 cups) fresh or frozen cranberries
10 ounces (2 cups) fresh or frozen raspberries
 ½ cup orange juice
 1 cup (7 ounces) plus 2 tablespoons sugar, divided
    Pinch table salt
 3 cups heavy cream, chilled, divided

1. Bring cranberries, raspberries, orange juice, 1 cup sugar, and salt to boil in medium saucepan over medium-high heat. Reduce heat to medium and simmer until cranberries are softened and mixture becomes jammy, about 15 minutes. Puree in blender or food processor until smooth, then press through fine-mesh strainer into medium bowl. Set aside to cool to room temperature.

2. In electric mixer, beat 2 cups cream to stiff peaks. Gently fold into cooled cranberry mixture until no streaks remain. Spoon mixture into eight 6- to 8-ounce serving dishes.

3. When ready to serve, beat remaining 1 cup cream and remaining 2 tablespoons sugar to stiff peaks. Dollop cream onto fools. Serve.

Pineapple-Mango Fools

Cranberry–Raspberry Fools

SOUFFLÉS

Use egg whites and yolks

Use minuscule amounts of flour

Leave headspace between batter and lip of dish

Test doneness with two spoons

Should be barely set but not soupy

THE IDEAL SOUFFLÉ HAS A DRAMATIC RISE above its dish; a crusty exterior cloaking an airy but substantial outer layer; and a rich, loose center that is not completely set. It also bursts with the pure flavor of the main ingredient in every bite. There's a pervasive myth that soufflés are fragile and fraught with disaster, ready to collapse with the slightest disturbance. But soufflés are neither complicated nor finicky; there is usually some room for modification, and achieving the ideal soufflé sometimes means making adjustments like dialing back on flour and butter (which can mute flavor) and adding more of the star ingredients (like chocolate). And while many recipes call for whipping the egg whites to stiff peaks and gently folding them into the base mixture for maximum volume, sometimes you want a soufflé with a bit less airiness. Beating the egg whites to stiff peaks and then combining them vigorously with the other ingredients whips out just enough air from the whites to break down some of their structure, resulting in a perfectly risen soufflé with ideal consistency.

We have found that the typical but fussy step of greasing a parchment collar and securing it around the lip of the dish to prevent oven overflow isn't necessary; instead, you can simply leave an inch of headspace between the top of the batter and the lip of the dish. For a foolproof way to tell if your soufflé is done, take two large spoons, pull open the top of the soufflé, and peek inside. The center should be barely set. If it still looks soupy, return it to the oven. This in no way harms the soufflé. After all, a soufflé is not a balloon; it's a matrix of very fine bubbles. No tool can pop enough of them to cause it to fall.

SHOOT BELOW THE RIM

Soufflé recipes traditionally require attaching a greased parchment collar around the lip of the soufflé dish. Extending the collar several inches above the dish keeps the soufflé contained so that it rises up rather than spills over. But we found that the old-fashioned approach isn't necessary. The key is giving the fluid batter enough room to set up before it rises above the dish's lip. It takes about 20 minutes for the batter to reach the rim, at which point it's set and will continue to rise up, rather than spill over. Leaving 1 inch of space between the batter and the rim gives the batter room to set. Because soufflé dishes vary a bit in capacity, you may not need all the batter in a recipe, so discard any left over after filling your dish to the proper level.

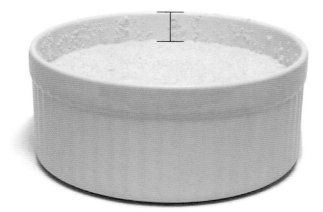

Batter poured shy of the top rim will rise high.

SLAMMING THE DOOR

Baked desserts rise as tiny air bubbles in the batter expand in the heat of the oven. To find out if slamming the door shut would interrupt the process enough to spell disaster, we mixed batters for muffins, yellow cake, angel food cake, and soufflé and loaded them into hot ovens. Just before each item reached its maximum height, we opened the oven door all the way and gave it a hard slam. The sturdy muffins emerged unharmed, as did the yellow cake. Even the notoriously fragile angel food cake and the soufflé survived the vigorous slamming. Why? A properly developed foam—whether powered by baking soda, baking powder, or beaten egg whites—is pretty resilient. While very rough handling (dropping a half-baked cake, for example) can make it collapse, there's no need to worry about slamming doors.

CHOCOLATE SOUFFLÉ

Serves 6 to 8 | 2-quart soufflé dish

WHY THIS RECIPE WORKS The essence of a great chocolate soufflé lies in the balancing act among the chocolate, egg whites, egg yolks, and butter. Soufflés are often made with a base of béchamel; however, the milk in this sauce can mute the flavor of the chocolate. This version removes all the flour and milk, using significantly more chocolate and reducing the butter. Creating an egg-foam base by beating the yolks with sugar until thick and folding that into our chocolate-butter mixture resulted in a soufflé with plenty of volume. Beating the egg whites to stiff peaks contributed more lift.

- 4 tablespoons unsalted butter, cut into ½-inch pieces, plus 1 tablespoon, softened, for dish
- ⅓ cup (2⅓ ounces) sugar, plus 1 tablespoon for dish
- 8 ounces bittersweet or semisweet chocolate, chopped coarse
- 1 tablespoon orange-flavored liqueur, such as Grand Marnier
- ½ teaspoon vanilla extract
- ⅛ teaspoon table salt
- 6 large eggs, separated, plus 2 large whites
- ¼ teaspoon cream of tartar

1. Adjust oven rack to lower-middle position and heat oven to 375 degrees. Grease 2-quart soufflé dish with softened butter, then coat dish evenly with 1 tablespoon sugar; refrigerate until ready to use.

2. Melt chocolate and remaining 4 tablespoons butter in medium heatproof bowl set over saucepan filled with 1 inch barely simmering water, making sure that water does not touch bottom of bowl and stirring mixture occasionally until smooth. Stir in liqueur, vanilla, and salt; set aside.

3. Using stand mixer fitted with paddle, beat egg yolks and remaining ⅓ cup sugar on medium speed until thick and pale yellow, about 3 minutes. Fold into chocolate mixture.

4. Using clean, dry mixer bowl and whisk attachment, whip egg whites and cream of tartar on medium-low speed until foamy, about 1 minute. Increase speed to medium-high and whip until stiff peaks form, 3 to 4 minutes. Using rubber spatula, vigorously stir one-quarter of whipped whites into chocolate mixture. Gently fold in remaining whites until just incorporated. Transfer mixture to prepared dish. (To prevent soufflé from overflowing, leave at least 1 inch of space between top of batter and rim of dish; discard excess batter). Bake until fragrant, fully risen, and exterior is set but interior is still a bit loose and creamy but not soupy, about 25 minutes. (To check doneness, use 2 large spoons to gently pull open top and peek inside.) Serve immediately.

Mocha Soufflé

Add 1 tablespoon instant espresso powder dissolved in 1 tablespoon hot water with liqueur in step 2.

Chocolate Soufflé

SKILLET LEMON SOUFFLÉ

Serves 6 | 10-inch ovensafe skillet

WHY THIS RECIPE WORKS Hoping to place soufflés in the realm of everyday cooking, we decided to find out if we could make one in a skillet. We added a little flour to a simple base of whipped egg yolks to keep the soufflé creamy rather than foamy. (Lemon soufflé lacks the fat of chocolate soufflé.) Lemon juice and zest provided bright flavor that shined through the eggy base. We folded in beaten egg whites and poured the mixture into a buttered skillet. After a few minutes on the stovetop, the soufflé was just set around the edges and on the bottom, so we moved the skillet to the oven to finish. A few minutes later our soufflé was puffed, golden on top, and creamy in the middle. Don't open the oven door during the first 7 minutes of baking, but do check the soufflé regularly for doneness during the final few minutes in the oven. Using a 10-inch traditional (not nonstick) skillet is essential to getting the right texture and height in the soufflé.

TUTORIAL
Chocolate Soufflé

Think chocolate soufflé is a dessert Mount Everest? Think again. See how soufflé reaches achievable heights.

1. Grease 2-quart soufflé dish with softened butter, then coat dish evenly with 1 tablespoon sugar; refrigerate until ready to use.

2. Beat egg yolks and remaining sugar on medium speed until thick and pale yellow, about 3 minutes. Fold into chocolate mixture.

3. Whip egg whites and cream of tartar to stiff peaks. Using rubber spatula, vigorously stir one-quarter of whipped whites into chocolate mixture.

4. Gently fold in remaining whites until just incorporated.

5. Transfer mixture to prepared dish.

6. Bake until fragrant, fully risen, and exterior is set but interior is still a bit loose and creamy but not soupy, about 25 minutes. (To check doneness, use 2 large spoons to gently pull open top and peek inside.)

Skillet Lemon Soufflé

5 large eggs, separated
¼ teaspoon cream of tartar
⅔ cup (4⅔ ounces) granulated sugar, divided
⅛ teaspoon table salt
1 teaspoon grated lemon zest plus ⅓ cup juice (2 lemons)
2 tablespoons unbleached all-purpose flour
1 tablespoon unsalted butter
Confectioners' sugar, for dusting

1. Adjust oven rack to middle position and heat oven to 375 degrees. Using stand mixer fitted with whisk attachment, whip egg whites and cream of tartar together on medium-low speed until foamy, about 1 minute. Gradually add ⅓ cup granulated sugar and salt, then increase mixer speed to medium-high, and continue to whip until stiff peaks form, 3 to 4 minutes. Gently transfer whites to clean bowl and set aside.

2. Whip egg yolks and remaining ⅓ cup granulated sugar on medium-high speed until pale and thick, about 1 minute. Whip in lemon zest and juice and flour until incorporated, about 30 seconds. Fold one-quarter of whipped egg whites into yolk mixture until almost no white streaks remain. Gently fold in remaining egg whites until just incorporated.

3. Melt butter in 10-inch ovensafe skillet over medium-low heat. Swirl pan to coat it evenly with melted butter, then gently scrape soufflé batter into skillet and cook until edges begin to set and bubble slightly, about 2 minutes.

4. Transfer skillet to oven and bake soufflé until puffed, center jiggles slightly when shaken, and surface is golden, 7 to 11 minutes. Using potholder (skillet handle will be hot), remove skillet from oven. Dust soufflé with confectioners' sugar and serve immediately.

INDIVIDUAL CHILLED LEMON SOUFFLÉS

Serves 8 | eight 5- to 7-ounce ramekins

WHY THIS RECIPE WORKS A chilled lemon soufflé is a refreshing dessert featuring delightful marriages of cream and foam, sweet and sour, high lemony notes and rich custard. We started with a custard base of milk, egg yolks, and sugar, adding a little cornstarch to prevent the yolks from curdling. To this we added lemon juice and zest and gelatin (so the mixture would set up while chilling). Folding whipped cream and beaten egg whites into the custard gave us a satisfying but light custard with bright lemon flavor. Pouring the batter into individual ramekins made for an elegant presentation. For the best texture, serve the soufflés after 1½ hours of chilling. They may be chilled for up to 6 hours; though the texture will stiffen slightly because of the gelatin, they will taste just as good.

Fallen Chocolate Cakes

2 teaspoons unflavored gelatin
2½ teaspoons grated lemon zest plus ½ cup juice (3 lemons)
1 cup whole milk
¾ cup (5¼ ounces) sugar, divided
2 large eggs, separated, plus 3 large whites, room temperature
¼ teaspoon cornstarch
Pinch cream of tartar
¾ cup heavy cream
Mint leaves, raspberries, confectioners' sugar, or finely chopped pistachios (optional)

1. Sprinkle gelatin over lemon juice in small bowl and set aside.

2. Heat milk and ½ cup sugar in medium saucepan over medium-low heat, stirring occasionally, until steaming and sugar is dissolved, about 5 minutes. Meanwhile, whisk egg yolks, cornstarch, and 2 tablespoons sugar in medium bowl until pale yellow and thickened. Whisking constantly, gradually add hot milk mixture to yolks. Return milk-egg mixture to saucepan and cook, stirring constantly, over medium-low heat until foam has dissipated to thin layer and mixture thickens to consistency of heavy cream and registers 185 degrees, about 4 minutes. Pour mixture through fine-mesh strainer set over medium bowl; stir in lemon juice mixture and zest. Set bowl with custard in large bowl of ice water; stir occasionally to cool.

3. While custard mixture is chilling, use stand mixer fitted with whip attachment to whip egg whites and cream of tartar on medium speed until foamy, about 1 minute. Increase speed to medium-high; gradually add remaining 2 tablespoons sugar and continue to whip until soft peaks form, 1 to 3 minutes. Do not overwhip. Remove bowl containing custard mixture from ice water bath; gently whisk in about one-third of egg whites, then fold in remaining whites with large rubber spatula until almost no white streaks remain.

4. Whip cream in now-empty mixer on medium-high speed until soft peaks form when beater is lifted, 2 to 3 minutes. Fold cream into custard and egg-white mixture until no white streaks remain.

5. Divide mixture evenly among eight 5- to 7-ounce ramekins. Chill until set but not stiff, about 1½ hours. Garnish, if desired, and serve.

Individual Chilled Lemon Soufflés with White Chocolate
The white chocolate in this variation subdues the lemony kick.

Add 2 ounces chopped white chocolate to the warm custard before adding lemon juice mixture and the zest in step 2. Stir until melted and fully incorporated.

FALLEN CHOCOLATE CAKES
Serves 8 | eight 5- to 7-ounce ramekins
WHY THIS RECIPE WORKS Fallen chocolate cake, also known as molten chocolate cake, is superlatively decadent, with its undercooked center that pours seductively out of a mound of rich chocolate cake. We wanted to turn this restaurant-menu standard into a practical recipe for home cooks. Rather than beating the egg whites and yolks separately, we found that beating the eggs with sugar to a foam and then folding them into melted chocolate delivered cakes with the rich, moist texture we wanted. A mere 2 tablespoons of flour did an able job of holding the soufflé-like cakes together. Finally, we wanted to ensure that these decadent desserts would arrive at the table hot and still molten; happily, we found that we could prepare the batter ahead of time and refrigerate the filled ramekins until ready to bake. You can substitute bittersweet chocolate for the semisweet; the flavor will be slightly more intense.

Unsweetened cocoa powder, for ramekins
8 ounces semisweet chocolate, chopped
8 tablespoons unsalted butter, cut into 8 pieces
4 large eggs plus 1 large yolk, room temperature
½ cup (3½ ounces) granulated sugar
1 teaspoon vanilla extract
¼ teaspoon table salt
2 tablespoons all-purpose flour
Confectioners' sugar

1. Adjust oven rack to middle position and heat oven to 400 degrees. Grease eight 5- to 7-ounce ramekins and dust with cocoa. Arrange ramekins on rimmed baking sheet. Microwave chocolate and butter in large bowl at 50 percent power, stirring occasionally, until melted and smooth, 2 to 4 minutes; set aside.

2. Using stand mixer fitted with whisk attachment, whip eggs, yolk, granulated sugar, vanilla, and salt on high speed until eggs are pale yellow and have nearly tripled in volume. (Egg foam will form ribbon that sits on top of mixture for 5 seconds when dribbled from whisk.) Scrape egg mixture over chocolate mixture, then sprinkle flour on top. Using rubber spatula, gently fold egg mixture and flour into chocolate until mixture is uniformly colored.

3. Divide batter evenly among prepared ramekins. (Unbaked cakes can be refrigerated for up to 8 hours. Return to room temperature for 30 minutes before baking.) Bake until cakes have puffed about ½ inch above rims of ramekins, have thin crust on top, and jiggle slightly at center when ramekins are shaken very gently, 12 to 13 minutes. Run thin knife around edges of ramekins to loosen cakes. Invert each ramekin onto plate and let sit until cakes release themselves from ramekins, about 1 minute. Lift off ramekins, dust with confectioners' sugar, and serve.

BREAD PUDDINGS

Use challah

Toast bread to dry

Use egg yolks only for flavor and texture

Soak adequately

IN ITS ORIGINAL FORM, bread pudding was a humble dish whose main virtue was ingenuity: A leftover loaf of bread on its way to becoming a brick was softened with milk, sweetened with sugar, baked, and so reborn as a warm, custardy confection. Bread pudding even survived during the Civil War: Soldiers on both sides of the line made their own versions by boiling cracker crumbs, sugar, raisins, and water in tin cups over an open fire.

Fast forward to present day and a basic recipe typically begins with soaking stale bread in a rich custard of egg yolks, heavy cream, and sugar before baking the pudding. A relatively low oven temperature and using only the egg yolks help prevent the pudding from curdling. Using just yolks also helps the pudding set, for a silky custard with no trace of egginess. (One exception is our unique Berry Pudding, which uses no eggs and in fact isn't baked at all.) One of the biggest variables—and challenges—is the bread itself. The type of bread used makes a huge difference in the texture of the finished pudding; a crusty French bread will obviously produce vastly different results than an airy Italian loaf. And while most recipes keep with tradition and call for stale bread, we have found that it's much better to "stale" the bread yourself by lightly toasting it. Toasted bread works even better than stale bread at soaking up custard, ensuring a silky texture.

STALING VERSUS TOASTING

Many recipes that call for stale bread give you two options: using naturally staled, day-old bread, or bread that is "quick staled" by drying in a low oven. Does it matter which technique you use? To find out, we staled bread in two ways: unwrapped on the counter for three days and in a 225-degree oven for about 35 minutes. We then used it to make bread pudding. The recipes made with oven-dried bread had a fresher taste and a superior structure compared to the naturally staled bread, which turned gummy once combined with other ingredients.

As bread stales naturally, its starch molecules recrystallize in a process called retrogradation, causing the bread to become hard and crumbly, but not necessarily dry. The naturally staled bread was still too moist to produce optimal results. Staling bread quickly in the oven, on the other hand, mostly hardens bread through the removal of moisture, not through retrogradation (which works best at cooler temperatures), ultimately leading to a drier—and better—structure.

BEST BREAD

We tried pudding with a wide variety of breads to determine the best in the basket. We cubed up the bread varieties, combined them with a custard, and baked. As expected, the results were as varied as the breads themselves. The pudding made with French bread was too coarse and rustic. The airy Italian loaf disintegrated into the custard, leaving zero distinction between bread and pudding. Meanwhile, the croissant pudding was too buttery and rich to eat a serving. Plain sandwich breads were serviceable but not extraordinary. For the most comforting pudding, use challah. This soft, braided loaf swelled nicely, absorbing liquid without disintegrating, and its deep gold crust retained a satisfying chew. Best of all, its faint sweetness and rich buttery flavor aligned perfectly with the fundamental flavors of the pudding.

TESTING BREAD PUDDING FOR DONENESS

Bread pudding is as much about eggs and custard as it is about bread, so determining the proper doneness is important. To test the pudding, place bread pudding on baking sheet and bake on upper rack until custard has just set, pressing center of pudding with finger reveals no runny liquid, and pudding registers 170 degrees, 45 to 50 minutes.

CLASSIC BREAD PUDDING

Serves 8 to 10 | 13 by 9-inch baking dish

WHY THIS RECIPE WORKS Contemporary versions of this humble dish vary in texture, from mushy, sweetened porridge to chewy cousins of overcooked holiday stuffing. For us, bread pudding done right means a moist, creamy (but not eggy) interior and a crisp top crust. We cut the bread—we liked challah for its rich flavor—into cubes, lightly toasted them, and soaked them in custard before baking. The custard was creamy and smooth, but not as set as we wanted. Adding more eggs but using just the yolks gave us a luscious, silky custard with no trace of egginess. For a crackly crust, we dotted the top of the pudding with additional toasted bread cubes, which we brushed with butter and sprinkled with sugar. If you cannot find challah, a firm high-quality sandwich bread such as Arnold Country Classics White or Pepperidge Farm Farmhouse Hearty White may be substituted.

Classic Bread Pudding

2 tablespoons packed light brown sugar
¾ cup (5¼ ounces) plus 1 tablespoon granulated sugar, divided
1 (14-ounce) loaf challah bread, cut into ¾-inch cubes (about 10 cups)
9 large egg yolks
4 teaspoons vanilla extract
¾ teaspoon table salt
2½ cups heavy cream
2½ cups milk
2 tablespoons unsalted butter, melted

1. Adjust oven racks to middle and lower-middle positions and heat oven to 325 degrees. Combine brown sugar and 1 tablespoon granulated sugar in small bowl; set aside.

2. Spread bread cubes in single layer on 2 rimmed baking sheets. Bake, tossing occasionally, until just dry, about 15 minutes, switching sheets halfway through baking. Let bread cubes cool for about 15 minutes; set aside 2 cups.

3. Whisk egg yolks, vanilla, salt, and remaining ¾ cup sugar together in large bowl. Whisk in cream and milk until combined. Add remaining 8 cups cooled bread cubes and toss to coat. Transfer mixture to 13 by 9-inch baking dish and let stand, occasionally pressing bread cubes into custard, until cubes are thoroughly saturated, about 30 minutes.

4. Spread reserved bread cubes evenly over top of soaked bread mixture and gently press into custard. Using pastry brush, dab melted butter over top of unsoaked bread pieces. Sprinkle brown sugar mixture evenly over top. Place bread pudding on rimmed baking sheet and bake on upper rack until custard has just set, pressing center of pudding with your finger reveals no runny liquid, and pudding registers 170 degrees, 45 to 50 minutes. Transfer to wire rack and let cool until pudding is set and just warm, about 45 minutes. Serve.

Pecan Bread Pudding with Bourbon and Orange
Add ⅔ cup chopped toasted pecans, 1 tablespoon all-purpose flour, and 1 tablespoon softened butter to brown sugar mixture in step 1 and mix until crumbly. Add 1 tablespoon bourbon and 2 teaspoons finely grated orange zest to egg yolk mixture in step 3.

Rum Raisin Bread Pudding with Cinnamon
Combine ⅔ cup golden raisins and 5 teaspoons dark rum in small bowl. Microwave until hot, about 20 seconds; set aside to cool, about 15 minutes. Add ⅛ teaspoon ground cinnamon to sugar mixture in step 1 and stir cooled raisin mixture into custard in step 3.

BERRY PUDDING

Serves 6 | 8½ by 4½-inch loaf pan

WHY THIS RECIPE WORKS To make this traditional British dessert, a pudding mold—or often simply a bowl or other pan—is lined snugly with crustless bread, filled with lightly sweetened and cooked berries, and topped with a bread "lid." The pudding is compressed with weights before it's inverted and unmolded. For our version, we used four different kinds of berries, and we cooked only a portion of them in order to retain the freshness of the fruit. To avoid a soggy pudding, we drained the berries and used the sweet juices to moisten the bread. Rich, eggy challah was the best choice for this dessert, and "staling" it in the oven made it even sturdier. To prevent the pudding from slumping, we thickened the filling with a combination of unflavored gelatin and apricot preserves. Fill in any gaps in pudding crusts with toast trimmings.

    8 (¼-inch-thick) slices challah, crusts removed
   12 ounces strawberries, hulled and chopped (2 cups)
    8 ounces blackberries, halved (1½ cups)
    8 ounces (1½ cups) blueberries
    5 ounces (1 cup) raspberries
    ½ cup (3½ ounces) granulated sugar
    1 teaspoon unflavored gelatin
    2 tablespoons cold water
    ½ cup (5½ ounces) apricot preserves
    1 cup heavy cream, chilled
    1 tablespoon confectioners' sugar

1. Adjust oven rack to middle position and heat oven to 350 degrees. Line 8 ½ by 4½-inch loaf pan with plastic wrap, pushing plastic into corners and up sides of pan and allowing excess to overhang long sides. Make cardboard cutout just large enough to fit inside pan.

2. Place challah on wire rack set in rimmed baking sheet. Bake until dry, about 10 minutes, flipping challah and rotating sheet halfway through baking. Let challah cool completely.

3. Combine strawberries, blackberries, blueberries, and raspberries in bowl. Transfer half of mixture to medium saucepan, add granulated sugar, and bring to simmer over medium-low heat, stirring occasionally. Reduce heat to low and continue to cook until berries release their juices and raspberries begin to break down, about 5 minutes. Off heat, stir in remaining berries. After 2 minutes, strain berries through fine-mesh strainer set over medium bowl for 10 minutes, stirring berries once halfway through straining (do not press on berries). Reserve berry juice. (You should have ¾ to 1 cup.)

Berry Pudding

**Chocolate Bread
Pudding**

4. Sprinkle gelatin over water in bowl and let sit until gelatin softens, about 5 minutes. Microwave until mixture is bubbling around edges and gelatin dissolves, about 30 seconds. Whisk preserves and gelatin mixture together in large bowl. Fold in strained berries.

5. Trim 4 slices of challah to fit snugly side by side in bottom of loaf pan (you may have extra challah). Dip slices in reserved berry juice until saturated, about 30 seconds per side, then place in bottom of pan. Spoon berry mixture over challah. Trim remaining 4 slices of challah to fit snugly side by side on top of berries (you may have extra challah). Dip slices in reserved berry juice until saturated, about 30 seconds per side, then place on top of berries. Cover pan loosely with plastic and place in 13 by 9-inch baking dish. Place cardboard cutout on top of pudding. Top with 3 soup cans to weigh down pudding. Refrigerate pudding for at least 8 hours or up to 24 hours.

6. Using stand mixer fitted with whisk attachment, whip cream and confectioners' sugar on medium-low speed until foamy, about 1 minute. Increase speed to high and whip until soft peaks form, 1 to 3 minutes. Transfer to serving bowl. Remove cans, cardboard, and plastic from top of pudding. Loosen pudding by pulling up on edges of plastic. Place inverted platter over top of loaf pan and flip platter and pan upside down to unmold pudding. Discard plastic. Slice pudding with serrated knife and serve with whipped cream.

CHOCOLATE BREAD PUDDING

Serves 12 | 13 by 9-inch baking dish

WHY THIS RECIPE WORKS Bread pudding—with its rich, custardy base and pieces of bread that are at once crispy, chewy, and soft—is immensely satisfying. We knew that adding chocolate to the mix would be a winning proposition. A combination of cocoa powder and melted chocolate was key, and we preferred the richness of semisweet chocolate. Rich challah suited the chocolate base better than delicate sandwich bread, but we ran into a problem: The melted chocolate made the base too thick to fully soak into the bread. The solution was allowing the bread to soak in a warm mixture of cream, milk, cocoa, espresso powder, and sugar before adding the custard of melted chocolate, egg yolks, sugar, and cream. A generous drizzle of chocolate sauce provided the finishing touch.

1 (1-pound) loaf challah, cut into ½-inch cubes
4 cups heavy cream, divided
2 cups whole milk
½ cup (1½ ounces) unsweetened cocoa powder
1 tablespoon instant espresso powder
1 cup (7 ounces) sugar, divided
8 ounces semisweet chocolate, chopped
10 large egg yolks

1. Adjust oven rack to middle position and heat oven to 300 degrees. Toast challah cubes on rimmed baking sheet, stirring occasionally, until golden and crisp, about 30 minutes. Transfer to large bowl.

2. Increase oven temperature to 325 degrees. Grease 13 by 9-inch baking pan. Heat 1½ cups cream, milk, cocoa, espresso powder, and ½ cup sugar in small saucepan over medium-high heat, stirring occasionally, until steaming and sugar has completely dissolved. Pour warm cream mixture over toasted challah and let stand, tossing occasionally, until liquid has been absorbed, about 10 minutes.

3. Meanwhile, bring 1 cup cream to simmer in now-empty saucepan over medium-high heat. Remove from heat, add chocolate to hot cream, and stir until chocolate has melted and mixture is smooth. Transfer 1 cup chocolate mixture to bowl and let cool for 5 minutes (cover pan and set aside remaining chocolate mixture). Whisk egg yolks, remaining 1½ cups cream, and remaining ½ cup sugar into chocolate mixture in bowl until combined.

4. Transfer soaked challah mixture to prepared pan, distributing it evenly over bottom of pan. Pour chocolate custard mixture evenly over challah mixture. Bake until custard is just set and surface of pudding is slightly crisp, about 45 minutes, rotating pan halfway through baking. Transfer to wire rack and let cool for 30 minutes.

5. Warm reserved chocolate mixture over low heat, then pour over pudding. Serve. (Leftover bread pudding can be wrapped in plastic wrap and refrigerated for up to 3 days; reheat individual portions in microwave.)

PART 04

cakes

CAKES ARE THE ANYTIME DESSERT. Celebratory layer cakes are sure to bring smiles to a birthday party, while snack cakes and rustic fruit-topped cakes are everyday treats that perk up a sluggish afternoon or end a school day on a sweet note. Coffee cakes offer an excuse to eat cake for breakfast, and petite cupcakes easily satisfy a solo craving. Just like the occasions on which they're eaten, cakes vary greatly in terms of flavor, texture, and appearance. They can be tall, multilayer affairs reserved for special occasions such as Coconut Layer Cake (page 249). They can be incredibly light with a simple flavor profile such as Angel Food Cake (page 286), or dense, rich, and decadent like Flourless Chocolate Cake (page 317).

Feelings about cake can run deep and are often linked to specific memories, family history, or simple flavor preferences. Maybe for you, the ultimate cake is the one you had on your birthday every year, perhaps a yellow layer cake with billows of chocolate frosting. Some, such as yule logs, have a clear connection to a holiday while others have strong seasonal ties—a tender cake bursting with ripe peaches begs to be enjoyed outdoors on a summer evening, while a pumpkin snack cake captures the flavors of fall. Or maybe your fondness isn't tied to anything specific at all: The casual comfort of a slice of rich pound cake is enticing any day of the year.

As with other baked goods, the way in which you combine the ingredients dictates the texture of the cake and its crumb; learn the difference between creaming, reverse creaming, and ribboning in this section and when it's best to use each technique. There are cakes with a stir-together simplicity for the novice baker or one who wants a simple route to cake on a weekday. And there are yeasted, pastry-style cakes for experienced bakers. You'll see warm, rich chocolate affairs and cool, creamy ice cream cakes. There are classics such as Carrot Sheet Cake (page 263) for the traditionalist and more unique creations like Blackberry-Mascarpone Lemon Cake (page 252) for those looking for some modern inspiration.

Cake Equipment Corner

There are certain pieces of equipment that make cake baking easier (and more accurate). These are the basic tools you'll need and the specialty items you'll want.

Other items that are important for cakes in particular are a digital scale and rimmed baking sheets.

MIXING CAKES

Stand Mixer

A stand mixer, with its hands-free operation, numerous attachments, and strong mixing arm, is a worthwhile investment if you plan on baking cakes regularly. Heft matters, as does a strong motor that doesn't give out when whipping for a long period of time. Our favorite stand mixer is the **KitchenAid Pro Line Series 7 Quart Stand Mixer** ($549.95). Our best buy is the KitchenAid Classic Plus Series 4.5 Quart Tilt-Head Stand Mixer ($229.99).

Whisk

We tested 10 slim, tapered French-style models and skinny balloon whisks, as they're best at getting into corners. For an all-purpose whisk, we like 10 moderately thin wires. Our favorite, with its grippy handle and lightweight frame for whipping, was the **OXO Good Grips 11" Balloon Whisk** ($9.99).

Rubber Spatula

You'll want the no-nonsense **Rubbermaid Professional 13.5" High-Heat Scraper** ($14.50) and the **Di Oro Living Seamless Silicone Spatula—Large** ($10.97). The large head on the Rubbermaid spatula makes it easy to properly fold ingredients; the Di Oro Living spatula is a good multipurpose tool.

CAKE PANS

Round (8- and 9-inch)

We had two requirements for a cake pan: sides that are at least two inches tall and a light color. Why? Tall sides reduce the risk of batter rising up over the edge of the pan, while a light finish produces evenly baked, taller, and more level cakes with a tender crust. (By contrast, a darker pan produces a darker cake, as dark-colored pans absorb heat more efficiently than light-colored ones. Darker pans also made cakes that were distinctly domed.) We highly recommend the solidly built **Nordic Ware Naturals Nonstick Round Cake Pan in 8-inch** ($13.50) and **9-inch** ($14.32) sizes.

Square (8-inch)

Our winning pan, **All-Clad Pro-Release NonStick Bakeware 8 inch Square Cake Pan** ($31.64), evenly baked brownies and browned cakes. With a nonstick coating, it released baked goods easily. It has a molded, not folded, construction, so cleanup was a breeze. Distinct, wide handles made it easy for us to maneuver the pan in and out of the oven. The pan retained only minor scratches from cutting—they were far less noticeable than in other pans in our lineup. Keep in mind that this pan has tapered edges, so we don't recommend using it to bake layer cakes.

13 by 9-inch Baking Pan

The **Williams-Sonoma Goldtouch Nonstick Rectangular Cake Pan, 9" x 13"** ($32.95) produced the most evenly cooked, professional-looking baked goods of all the baking pans we tested.

Loaf Pan

Cakes baked in our winning loaf pan, the **USA Pan Loaf Pan, 1-lb Volume** ($14.95), were narrow and tall with crisp corners and even golden color. Note that loaf pan size really matters; all of our recipes were developed in this 8½ by 4½-inch pan. If your pan measures 9 by 5 inches, another common size, you'll need to check for doneness earlier than the recipe indicates; otherwise, the cake will bake up dry. Cakes baked in a 9 by 5-inch pan will be shorter and flatter than those baked in our winner.

Muffin Tin

Because dark muffin tins conduct heat faster, the sides of cupcakes and muffins baked in these set quickly, leaving the rest of the batter to rise upward, which sometimes resulted in oddly conical or bulbous shapes. In addition to a light interior, we like a muffin tin with a large rim, which makes it easy to move around. Our favorite is the **OXO Good Grips Non-Stick Pro 12-Cup Muffin Pan** ($24.99).

Bundt Pan

The most important attribute of a Bundt pan is its ability to cleanly release a cake from its decorative ridges. But our winner had even more features we liked. The roomy **Nordic Ware Anniversary Bundt Pan** ($30.99) has large handles, making it easy to grip, maneuver, and flip. It also has the deepest, most well-defined ridges and produced the most eye-catching cakes. For more information on Bundt pans, see page 289.

Tube Pan

It's essential to buy a tube pan with a removable bottom; otherwise, extracting the cake from the pan is nearly impossible. The **Chicago Metallic 2-Piece Angel Food Cake Pan with Feet** ($17.99) is a perfect specimen, yielding tall, evenly browned cakes. It has a non-stick surface, and feet on its rim to elevate the cake while it cools.

Springform Pan

Bottom line: A completely leakproof springform pan doesn't exist. But there are design elements that make some much better than the rest. We like the **Williams-Sonoma Goldtouch Springform Pan, 9"** ($49.95) and the **Nordic Ware 9" Leakproof Springform Pan** ($16.22): Both have wide rimmed bases for maneuverability and leak-catching, and they each produced evenly browned cheesecakes that were easy to release.

Cake Equipment Corner

ASSEMBLING CAKES

Cardboard Rounds

Cardboard rounds—which you can buy online or in craft stores—are simple but immensely helpful: They're great for moving cake layers, building cakes, lifting and transporting cakes, and serving cakes.

Offset Spatula

For frosting a cake, there's no better tool than an offset spatula. The long, narrow blade on the **OXO Good Grips Bent Icing Knife** ($9.99) is ideal for scooping and spreading frosting, and it bends like a stairstep where it meets the handle for better leverage. The 6.5-inch blade is sturdy but nimble and very comfortable in hand.

Piping Sets

Floppy cloth pastry bags can stain or hold on to smells. Canvas bags tend to be too stiff. We prefer disposable plastic bags; they're easy to handle for neat cake decorating and effortless to clean. In addition, we consider six different tips essential to cover a range of decorating needs: #4 round, #12 round, #70 round, #103 petal, #2D large closed star, and #1M open star. You'll also want four couplers—plastic nozzles that adhere the tip to the bag. We like Wilton supplies.

Cake Carrier

We like to store and transport cakes in the **Progressive Collapsible Cupcake and Cake Carrier** ($29.95). It has comfortable handles and a sturdy locking system, as well as a collapsible design for easier storage. It can fit either 9-inch round or square layer cakes, or up to 24 cupcakes (with an included insert).

Cake Stand

While you can frost and decorate cakes on any surface, it's much easier to get smooth coatings on a rotating cake stand. The **Winco Revolving Cake Decorating Stand** ($29.98) provides excellent visibility and comfort. It rotates quickly and smoothly, and it has three shallow circles etched onto its surface for cake centering.

INGREDIENT ALCHEMY

Basic pantry ingredients can be mixed and measured in countless ways to yield an incredible array of cakes with a variety of flavors and textures, from light, moist, and tender to dense, rich, and indulgent—and everything in between.

Butter: A Key Cake Ingredient

The temperature of butter affects the texture of finished cakes. We soften butter for creaming so it's malleable enough to be whipped but firm enough to retain air, which provides structure and leavening for cakes like Red Velvet Layer Cake (page 237). If the butter is too soft, it can't hold air bubbles and the cake will be flat and dense. With reverse creaming, softened butter coats the flour particles for an ultratender texture, as in our Classic White Layer Cake (page 234).

Some recipes, such as Genoise Sponge Cake (page 281), get enough lift and a fluffy crumb from the whipped eggs in the recipe; in these instances we use melted butter, which is more easily incorporated. And when we desire a rustic crumb, as with our Applesauce Snack Cake (page 255), we simply stir in the melted butter.

Egg Temperature

For good measure, many of our cake recipes call for room-temperature eggs, but for most recipes the differences between a cake made with cold eggs and one made with room-temperature eggs are fairly minimal: When we made our Fluffy Yellow Layer Cake (page 233) with cold eggs rather than room-temperature eggs, the cake took 5 extra minutes to bake and the crumb was slightly less fine and even. That said, the cold-egg cake was acceptable.

However, letting eggs come to room temperature is critical in finicky cakes, such as Angel Food Cake (page 286), Chiffon Cake (page 284), and Pound Cake (page 302), which rely on air incorporated into the beaten eggs as a primary means of leavening. In these cases, we found that cold eggs didn't whip nearly as well as room-temperature eggs and the cakes didn't rise properly and were too dense.

Different Dairies; Different Cakes

Milk thins out batters and contributes to a cakey crumb as the liquid generates steam in the oven. We most often use whole milk in our cake recipes; the fat in whole milk tenderizes the crumb and can weaken gluten just enough for a cake that has structure but isn't tough and chewy.

Buttermilk can add a tangy flavor to cakes, but its inclusion is often more about texture: As an acidic ingredient, buttermilk tenderizes. When an acidic ingredient is used, baking soda is typically the leavener of choice; the two interact for extra fluffiness.

Yogurt and sour cream, both acidic, produce similar results to buttermilk, but sour cream can make for an even more tender cake, as it's higher in fat than low-fat buttermilk and thus has two tenderizing properties.

Two Leaveners Are (Sometimes) Better Than One

Using both baking powder and baking soda in a cake recipe rather than just baking powder can give you better control over rise and over the alkalinity of the batter. If a batter with baking powder is highly acidic, we'll add baking soda as well for extra support so that the baking powder isn't neutralized and deactivated. The baking soda will make the batter more alkaline. Alkaline batters brown more and have a weaker gluten structure so they bake up with a more tender, porous crumb. So while baking powder alone is sufficient for leavening, the addition of baking soda can lighten a cake's crumb and create better browning.

Preparing Cake Pans

If you're serving a cake right out of the pan, the pan usually needs only to be greased and floured. But if you want to remove the cake from the pan, you'll need to line it; otherwise, the cake could stick and break into pieces as you attempt to remove it. Some exceptions: High-fat pound cakes, curved Bundt cakes, cheesecakes, and, most important, chiffon and angel food cakes (these need to stick to the sides of the pan in order to maintain their delicate rise).

1. Place cake pan on sheet of parchment and trace around bottom of pan. Cut out parchment circle.

2. Evenly spray bottom and sides of pan with vegetable oil spray or rub with butter.

3. Fit parchment into pan, grease the parchment, and then sprinkle with several tablespoons of flour. Shake and rotate pan to coat it evenly, and shake out excess.

CAKE MIXING METHODS

Most cakes share the same basic ingredients; it's the way those ingredients are combined that makes all the difference in the style and crumb of the final product. Here's a look at the major cake mixing methods.

Creaming

Creaming is a fundamental technique that helps cakes rise: The tiny pockets of air created during the process expand from the leavener in the recipe. Creaming creates a fluffy crumb and a cake with good height.

THE RESULT	GOOD FOR
• Fluffy, somewhat open crumb	• Bundt cakes
• Tall rise	• Everyday cakes
	• Some layer cakes

Reverse Creaming

The process of reverse creaming starts with combining all of the dry ingredients, after which softened butter is incorporated, followed by any liquid ingredients. The butter coats the flour particles, minimizing gluten development for a tender, fine crumb. Since the butter isn't beaten with sugar, less air is incorporated, which translates to less rise and a sturdier cake.

THE RESULT	GOOD FOR
• Ultratender but sturdy structure; resists crumbling	• Layer cakes
• Fine, velvety crumb	• Coffee cakes with heavy toppings
• Even rise	• Filled cupcakes

Creaming versus Reverse Creaming

One technique isn't better than the other, but each results in a unique texture and shape. A creamed cake layer will have a higher rise with a domed top. A cake made with reverse creaming will have a flat top and a finer crumb—perfect for stacking and frosting.

Creaming   **Reverse Creaming**

Whipped Whites

Whipped egg whites are often thought of as another form of leavening, and this is basically true. But it's not the egg itself that grows the cake, it's air. As egg whites are whipped, their proteins loosen and stretch, capturing and trapping air inside a fluffy foam that gives cakes lift.

THE RESULT
- Light texture
- Airy, springy crumb

GOOD FOR
- Angel food cakes
- Jelly roll cakes
- Some pound-style cakes

Ribboning

Whipping whole eggs with sugar until they double in volume is another mixing method that can act as leavener for a cake that's light yet still rich in flavor. The term "ribboning" refers to the ribbon-like strands that form between the whisk and batter when whipped. Sometimes the eggs and sugar are heated together before whipping, creating a more viscous mixture. This leads to a more stable foam and, in turn, a loftier, sturdier cake.

THE RESULT
- Light and fluffy but substantial texture
- Rich flavor

GOOD FOR
- Genoise cakes
- Sponge cakes that require the structure to stand up to a filling
- Chocolate cakes that need help with lift

The Quick-Bread Method

This method is the easiest of all the mixing methods: The wet ingredients are stirred into to the dry ingredients until just combined. This technique doesn't introduce extra air into the batter; the result is a cake with a rustic crumb.

THE RESULT
- Coarse crumb
- Sturdy structure

GOOD FOR
- Upside-down cakes
- Snack cakes

When's the Cake Done?

The amount of time it will take for a cake to bake depends on many factors, such as the temperature of the oven and the depth of the batter. But don't rely on the recipe's time alone: A near foolproof way to test doneness is with the classic toothpick test. Most butter cakes are finished baking when a toothpick inserted in the center of the cake comes out clean. For moister chocolate cakes the toothpick should come out with a few crumbs attached to ensure the cake isn't dry.

Perfectly Baked Chocolate Cake   Underbaked Chocolate Cake

COOLING WITH CARE

Some delicate cakes, like Angel Food Cake (page 286), need to cool completely in the pan before being turned out. Others, such as cheesecakes, need time to set up before being released from the springform pan. And some cakes, such as Jelly Roll Cake (page 285), need to be manipulated while warm and have to be removed from the pan immediately. But the majority of cakes need just a little cooling time in the pan—about 10 minutes—to set up, after which they should be removed from the pan so that the residual heat doesn't overbake them. Cool cakes on a wire cooling rack where air can circulate around them. After removing a cake from a pan, be sure to remove the parchment before reinverting the cake right side up. If you're storing cooled cake layers at room temperature before building your layer cake, wrap them well in plastic wrap. If you opt to freeze them, wrap them in plastic followed by a layer of aluminum foil. You can freeze layers for up to one month; defrost wrapped cakes at room temperature.

LAYER CAKES

NO BIRTHDAY PARTY IS COMPLETE WITHOUT a frosted layer cake, but these recipes are a reminder that the cake itself is cause for celebration. Two- and three-layer cakes generally feature relatively thick cake layers, each baked in its own pan, with frosting between the layers as well as on the top and sides. Taller cakes, impressive showstoppers of four layers, usually involve slicing cake layers in half horizontally to create more, thinner ones (we'll show you how), but sometimes we find it easiest to bake thin layers of cake in batches.

No matter how towering the cake at hand, there are some universal steps for ensuring layer cake success, such as dividing the batter evenly between the pans so the layers cook at the same rate and have the same height. But other key factors, such as the type of flour and the mixing method, depend on the desired outcome. Cake flour, which has a low protein content, will deliver cake layers with a delicate, fine crumb, whereas all-purpose flour is used when we need a cake with more structure (as we do when melted chocolate or another dense, heavy ingredient is added to the batter). Creaming the butter and sugar will create a fluffy crumb and layers with good height (we use it for our Red Velvet Layer Cake on page 237), but sometimes another approach is best: For Classic White Layer Cake (page 234), reverse creaming gives us a sturdy cake with an ultrafine, downy crumb, and a technique known as ribboning gives our Old-Fashioned Chocolate Layer Cake (page 234) the proper structure to stack and tenderness.

We include lots of frostings to experiment pairing with cakes, but for some cakes, the frosting requires careful consideration. For the tallest cakes, it must be easy to spread yet have enough structure to support the weight of the cake's many layers.

KEY POINTS

Bake in light-colored pans

Grease pans and line with parchment

Evenly divide batter among pans

Level cake with serrated knife if it domes

Line cake platter with parchment strips to avoid mess

LAYER UP

Sometimes our cakes are simple two-layer affairs—one layer per cake pan—and sometimes they reach greater heights. If we're making a four-layer cake, it usually means we're slicing standard layers in half. The task seems daunting, but if you follow these instructions, you'll achieve thin, even layers without stress.

1. Measure height of the cake. Using paring knife, mark midpoint at several places around sides of the cake.

2. Using marks as guide, score entire circumference of cake with long serrated knife.

3. Following scored lines, run knife around cake several times, cutting inward. Once knife is inside cake, use back-and-forth motion.

4. Once knife cuts through cake, separate layers and gently insert your fingers between them. Lift top layer and place it on counter.

NAKED CAKES

An increasingly popular style of sky-high layer cake is the naked cake—layer cakes with sheer coatings or completely bare sides. At once elegant and rustic, these cakes showcase the juxtaposition of layer and filling to beautiful effect. We like the technique of scraping frosting along the sides of the cake—just enough to give the cake a thin veil but not so much that you can't see the stacked layers. We use this technique in our Blackberry-Mascarpone Lemon Cake (page 252) and our Cranberry-Orange Olive Oil Cake (page 250). You'll want to be a bit more graceful in your filling of the cakes, as it will show through the sides.

1. After filling cake, spread 1½ cups frosting over top. Spread remaining frosting evenly over sides of cake to cover with thin coat of frosting.

2. Run edge of offset spatula around cake sides to create sheer veil of frosting.

COOL LAYERS

It's essential that the cake layers be fully cooled before applying the frosting; nearly all frostings contain butter, which means that if the frosting comes in contact with a cake that's warmer than room temperature, it will melt and reveal spotty patches of cake, and lose its volume. It can take 2 hours to fully cool cake layers.

Frosted When Cool   **Frosted When Warm**

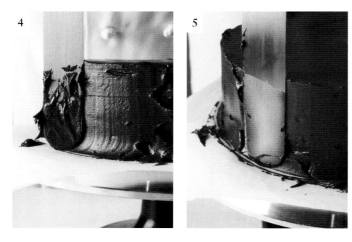

FROSTING A LAYER CAKE

These steps are for a two-layer cake but the technique is transferable to more layers. For frosting recipes, see pages 240–246.

1. Keep the Platter Clean
Cover the edges of the cake stand or platter with 4 strips of parchment paper. The strips ensure that extra frosting doesn't end up on the platter. Once the cake is frosted, you can slide out and discard the parchment for a neat presentation.

2. Frost the First Layer
You may want to anchor your cake by dolloping a small amount of frosting in the center of the cake stand and then placing a cake layer on top. Our layers come from the oven nice and level, but if your layers do dome, use a serrated knife to gently remove the domed portion from each cake layer. (Brush the crumbs off the cake since they can mar the frosting.) Dollop the correct portion of frosting in the center of the cake layer. Using an offset spatula, spread the frosting evenly from the center to the edge of the cake. (The recipe may instruct you to leave a border.)

3. Frost the Top
Place the second layer on top, making sure it's aligned with the first layer. As you place the top layer, don't push down on it or you risk squeezing the frosting out the sides of the cake, but do press gently to make sure it adheres. Spread frosting evenly over the top layer, pushing it over the edge of the cake.

4. Frost the Sides
Gather several tablespoons of frosting with the tip of an offset spatula. Gently smear frosting onto the sides of the cake. Repeat until the sides are covered. If you spread a large amount of frosting on the sides, you risk getting crumbs in the frosting or causing the layers to shift. Clean off the spatula as needed.

5. Smooth It Out
Gently run the edge of the spatula around the sides of the cake to smooth out bumps and tidy areas where the frosting on the top and sides merge. You can run the edge of the spatula over the top of the cake to give it a smooth look, too. Remove the strips of parchment before serving.

FLUFFY YELLOW LAYER CAKE

Serves 10 to 12 | two 9-inch round cake pans

WHY THIS RECIPE WORKS When we think of birthday cake, the first thing that comes to mind is yellow cake covered in billowy chocolate frosting. But many recipes turn out dry, heavy, or cottony rounds rather than rich, buttery, tender cake. Our first step toward an ultralight texture was to skip the traditional creaming method (for more information on creaming, see page 228) and adopt a chiffon cake technique—using whipped egg whites to get high volume and a light texture. This gave us a fluffy cake that was still sturdy enough to support a substantial frosting. A combination of butter and vegetable oil gave our cake layers a buttery-rich flavor while ensuring that they remained incredibly moist. Substituting buttermilk for milk produced a downy, fine crumb.

Fluffy Yellow Layer Cake

2½ cups (10 ounces) cake flour
1¼ teaspoons baking powder
¼ teaspoon baking soda
¾ teaspoon table salt
1¾ cups (12¼ ounces) sugar, divided
1 cup buttermilk, room temperature
10 tablespoons unsalted butter, melted and cooled
3 large eggs, separated, plus 3 large yolks, room temperature
3 tablespoons vegetable oil
2 teaspoons vanilla extract
Pinch cream of tartar
5 cups Chocolate Frosting (page 241)

1. Adjust oven rack to middle position and heat oven to 350 degrees. Grease two 9-inch round cake pans, line with parchment paper, grease parchment, and flour pans. Whisk flour, baking powder, baking soda, salt, and 1½ cups sugar together in bowl. Whisk buttermilk, melted butter, egg yolks, oil, and vanilla together in second bowl.

2. Using stand mixer fitted with whisk attachment, whip egg whites and cream of tartar on medium-low speed until foamy, about 1 minute. Increase speed to medium-high and whip whites to soft billowy mounds, about 1 minute. Gradually add remaining ¼ cup sugar and whip until glossy, stiff peaks form, 2 to 3 minutes; transfer to third bowl.

3. Add flour mixture to now-empty mixer bowl and mix on low speed, gradually adding buttermilk mixture and mixing until almost incorporated (a few streaks of dry flour will remain), about 15 seconds. Scrape down bowl, then mix on medium-low speed until smooth and fully incorporated, 10 to 15 seconds.

4. Using rubber spatula, stir one-third of whites into batter. Gently fold remaining whites into batter until no white streaks remain. Divide batter evenly between prepared pans and smooth tops with rubber spatula. Gently tap pans on counter to settle batter. Bake until toothpick inserted in center comes out clean, 20 to 22 minutes, switching and rotating pans halfway through baking. Let cakes cool in pans on wire rack for 10 minutes. Remove cakes from pans, discarding parchment, and let cool completely on rack, about 2 hours. (Cake layers can be stored at room temperature for up to 24 hours or frozen for up to 1 month; defrost at room temperature.)

5. Line edges of cake platter with 4 strips of parchment paper to keep platter clean. Place 1 cake layer on platter. Spread 1½ cups frosting evenly over top, right to edge of cake. Top with second cake layer, press lightly to adhere, then spread remaining frosting evenly over top and sides of cake. Carefully remove parchment strips before serving.

CLASSIC WHITE LAYER CAKE

Serves 10 to 12 | two 9-inch round cake pans

WHY THIS RECIPE WORKS Elegant white cake is simply a butter cake made with whipped egg whites instead of whole eggs for a soft, fine crumb. Unfortunately, most white cakes emerge from the oven dry, cottony, and riddled with small holes. Tackling the texture problem, we mixed the cake using the reverse creaming method—adding the butter to the dry ingredients so that it coated the flour particles for an ultratender crumb. As for the large air pockets, we suspected that the stiffly beaten whites were the culprit. So instead, we simply mixed the whites with the milk and beat them in. This cake was fine, free of holes, and delightfully tall and light.

  1 cup whole milk, room temperature
  6 large egg whites, room temperature
  1 teaspoon vanilla extract
  2¼ cups (9 ounces) cake flour
  1¾ cups (12¼ ounces) sugar
  4 teaspoons baking powder
  1 teaspoon table salt
  12 tablespoons unsalted butter, cut into 12 pieces and softened
  5 cups Vanilla Frosting (page 241)

1. Adjust oven rack to middle position and heat oven to 350 degrees. Grease two 9-inch round cake pans, line with parchment paper, grease parchment, and flour pans. Whisk milk, egg whites, and vanilla together in bowl.

2. Using stand mixer fitted with paddle, mix flour, sugar, baking powder, and salt on low speed until combined. Add butter, 1 piece at a time, and mix until only pea-size pieces remain, about 1 minute. Add all but ½ cup milk mixture, increase speed to medium-high, and beat until light and fluffy, about 1 minute. Reduce speed to medium-low, add remaining ½ cup milk mixture, and beat until incorporated, about 30 seconds (batter may look curdled). Give batter final stir by hand.

3. Divide batter evenly between prepared pans and smooth tops with rubber spatula. Gently tap pans on counter to settle batter. Bake until toothpick inserted in center comes out with few crumbs attached, 23 to 25 minutes, switching and rotating pans halfway through baking. Let cakes cool in pans on wire rack for 10 minutes. Remove cakes from pans, discarding parchment, and let cool completely on rack, about 2 hours. (Cake layers can be stored at room temperature for up to 24 hours or frozen for up to 1 month; defrost at room temperature.)

4. Line edges of cake platter with 4 strips of parchment paper to keep platter clean. Place 1 cake layer on platter. Spread 1½ cups frosting evenly over top, right to edge of cake. Top with second cake layer, press lightly to adhere, then spread remaining frosting evenly over top and sides of cake. Carefully remove parchment strips before serving.

OLD-FASHIONED CHOCOLATE LAYER CAKE

Serves 10 to 12 | two 9-inch round cake pans

WHY THIS RECIPE WORKS Over the years, chocolate cakes have become denser, richer, and squatter. We wanted a more traditional chocolate layer cake with a tender, airy, open crumb. To start, we turned to an old-fashioned technique called ribboning, in which eggs are whipped with sugar until they double in volume before the butter, dry ingredients, and milk are added. This process of aerating the eggs gave our cake height, structure, and remarkable tenderness. For a moist cake with rich chocolate flavor, we once again looked to historical sources, which suggested using buttermilk instead of milk and making a "pudding" with a mixture of chocolate, water, and sugar. The results were just what we were looking for. Do not substitute natural cocoa powder for the Dutch-processed cocoa powder. We recommend using milk chocolate for the Chocolate Frosting (page 241).

  4 ounces unsweetened chocolate, chopped coarse
  ½ cup hot water
  ¼ cup (¾ ounce) Dutch-processed cocoa powder
  1¾ cups (12¼ ounces) sugar, divided
  1¾ cups (8¾ ounces) all-purpose flour
  1½ teaspoons baking soda
  1 teaspoon table salt
  1 cup buttermilk
  2 teaspoons vanilla extract
  4 large eggs plus 2 large yolks, room temperature
  12 tablespoons unsalted butter, cut into 12 pieces and softened
  5 cups Chocolate Frosting (page 241)

1. Adjust oven rack to middle position and heat oven to 350 degrees. Grease two 9-inch round cake pans, line with parchment paper, grease parchment, and flour pans.

2. Combine chocolate, hot water, and cocoa in medium heatproof bowl set over saucepan filled with 1 inch barely simmering water, making sure that water does not touch bottom of bowl and stirring with heat-resistant rubber spatula until chocolate is melted, about 2 minutes. Add ½ cup sugar to chocolate mixture and stir until thick and glossy, 1 to 2 minutes. Remove bowl from heat; set aside to cool.

3. Whisk flour, baking soda, and salt together in medium bowl. Combine buttermilk and vanilla in second bowl. Using stand mixer fitted with whisk attachment, whip eggs and yolks on medium-low speed until combined, about 10 seconds. Add remaining 1¼ cups sugar, increase speed to high, and whip until light and fluffy, 2 to 3 minutes. Fit stand mixer with paddle. Add cooled chocolate mixture to egg mixture and mix on medium speed until thoroughly combined, 30 to 45 seconds,

TUTORIAL

Old-Fashioned Chocolate Layer Cake

This old-fashioned cake required an old-fashioned mixing technique. Learn how we use "ribboning" to create the fluffy but richly chocolate cake we desired.

1. Combine chocolate, hot water, and cocoa in heatproof bowl set over saucepan filled with 1 inch barely simmering water, stirring with spatula until chocolate is melted, about 2 minutes.

2. Add ½ cup sugar to chocolate mixture and stir until thick and glossy, 1 to 2 minutes. Remove bowl from heat; set aside to cool.

3. Whip eggs and yolks on medium-low speed until combined, about 10 seconds. Add remaining 1 ¼ cups sugar, increase speed to high, and whip until light and fluffy, 2 to 3 minutes.

4. Fit stand mixer with paddle. Add cooled chocolate mixture to egg mixture and mix on medium speed until thoroughly combined, 30 to 45 seconds, scraping down bowl as needed.

5. Add butter, 1 piece at a time, mixing for about 10 seconds after each addition.

6. Add flour mixture in 3 additions, alternating with buttermilk mixture in 2 additions, mixing until incorporated after each addition (about 15 seconds) and scraping down bowl as needed.

scraping down bowl as needed. Add butter, 1 piece at a time, mixing for about 10 seconds after each addition. Add flour mixture in 3 additions, alternating with buttermilk mixture in 2 additions, mixing until incorporated after each addition (about 15 seconds) and scraping down bowl as needed. Reduce speed to medium-low and mix until batter is thoroughly combined, about 15 seconds. Give batter final stir by hand.

4. Divide batter evenly between prepared pans and smooth tops with rubber spatula. Bake until toothpick inserted in center comes out with few moist crumbs attached, 25 to 30 minutes, switching and rotating pans halfway through baking. Let cakes cool in pans on wire rack for 10 minutes. Remove cakes from pans, discarding parchment, and let cool completely on rack, about 2 hours. (Cake layers can be stored at room temperature for up to 24 hours or frozen for up to 1 month; defrost at room temperature.)

5. Line edges of cake platter with 4 strips of parchment paper to keep platter clean. Place 1 cake layer on platter. Spread 1½ cups frosting evenly over top, right to edge of cake. Top with second cake layer, press lightly to adhere, then spread remaining frosting evenly over top and sides of cake. Carefully remove parchment strips before serving.

**Devil's Food
Layer Cake**

DEVIL'S FOOD LAYER CAKE

Serves 10 to 12 | two 9-inch round cake pans

WHY THIS RECIPE WORKS The name of this cake refers to its color, which is very dark—almost black. Unfortunately, the flavor often fails to match the rich hue. For an intensely chocolate devil's food cake, we used a combination of unsweetened chocolate and Dutch-processed cocoa powder (which is less acidic than natural cocoa and enhances browning). Mixing the chocolate and cocoa with hot water, rather than milk, ensured a strong presence. Brown sugar and some espresso powder further underscored the deep chocolate notes. The chocolaty impact of this dark-as-night cake was clear as day. Sweet, marshmallowy seven-minute frosting tempers the cake's darkness. For an accurate measurement of boiling water, bring a full kettle of water to a boil and then measure out the desired amount. Do not substitute natural cocoa powder for the Dutch-processed cocoa powder.

½ cup (1½ ounces) Dutch-processed cocoa powder, plus extra for pan
1½ cups (7½ ounces) all-purpose flour
1 teaspoon baking soda
½ teaspoon baking powder
¼ teaspoon table salt
1¼ cups boiling water

4 ounces unsweetened chocolate, chopped
1 teaspoon instant espresso powder or instant coffee powder
10 tablespoons unsalted butter, cut into 10 pieces and softened
1½ cups packed (10½ ounces) light brown sugar
3 large eggs, room temperature
½ cup sour cream, room temperature
1 teaspoon vanilla extract
5 cups Seven-Minute Frosting (page 244)

1. Adjust oven rack to middle position and heat oven to 350 degrees. Grease two 9-inch round cake pans, then dust with cocoa powder and line bottoms with parchment paper.

2. Whisk flour, baking soda, baking powder, and salt together in bowl. Whisk boiling water, chocolate, espresso powder, and cocoa in second bowl until smooth.

3. Using stand mixer fitted with paddle, beat butter and sugar on medium-high speed until pale and fluffy, about 3 minutes. Add eggs, one at a time, and beat until combined, about 30 seconds. Beat in sour cream and vanilla until incorporated. Reduce speed to low and add flour mixture in 3 additions, alternating with chocolate mixture in 2 additions, scraping down bowl as needed. Give batter final stir by hand.

4. Divide batter evenly between prepared pans and smooth tops with rubber spatula. Gently tap pans on counter to settle batter. Bake until toothpick inserted in center comes out with few crumbs attached, 18 to 22 minutes, switching and rotating pans halfway through baking. Let cakes cool in pans on wire rack for 10 minutes. Remove cakes from pans, discarding parchment, and let cool completely on rack, about 2 hours. (Cake layers can be stored at room temperature for up to 24 hours or frozen for up to 1 month; defrost at room temperature.)

5. Line edges of cake platter with 4 strips of parchment paper to keep platter clean. Place 1 cake layer on platter. Spread 1½ cups frosting evenly over top, right to edge of cake. Top with second cake layer, press lightly to adhere, then spread remaining frosting evenly over top and sides of cake. Carefully remove parchment strips before serving.

Red Velvet Layer Cake

RED VELVET LAYER CAKE

Serves 10 to 12 | two 9-inch round cake pans

WHY THIS RECIPE WORKS Although it's perhaps best known for its shocking bright color, red velvet layer cake is more than just a novelty: Its tender, light, and moist texture is also a hallmark of the cake. For the ideal red velvet cake, we discovered that two ingredients were essential: buttermilk and vinegar. This combination of liquids reacted with the baking soda in our recipe to create a fine, tender crumb. We also found that the type of cocoa powder we used was important. Unlike Dutch-processed cocoa, natural cocoa powder is acidic; so in addition to providing a light chocolate flavor to the cake, natural cocoa further enhanced the cake's light and airy texture. (In fact, the ruddy color of the original red velvet cake didn't come from dye but from the reaction of the natural cocoa and the buttermilk and vinegar.) Do not substitute Dutch-processed cocoa powder for the natural cocoa powder.

2¼ cups (11¼ ounces) all-purpose flour
1½ teaspoons baking soda
 Pinch table salt
1 cup buttermilk
2 large eggs
1 tablespoon distilled white vinegar
1 teaspoon vanilla extract
2 tablespoons natural unsweetened cocoa powder
2 tablespoons (1 ounce) red food coloring
12 tablespoons unsalted butter, cut into 12 pieces and softened
1½ cups (10½ ounces) sugar
5 cups Cream Cheese Frosting (page 243)

1. Adjust oven rack to middle position and heat oven to 350 degrees. Grease two 9-inch round cake pans, line with parchment paper, grease parchment, and flour pans. Whisk

flour, baking soda, and salt together in bowl. Whisk buttermilk, eggs, vinegar, and vanilla together in second bowl. Mix cocoa and red food coloring in third bowl until smooth paste forms.

2. Using stand mixer fitted with paddle, beat butter and sugar on medium-high speed until pale and fluffy, about 3 minutes. Reduce speed to low and add flour mixture in 3 additions, alternating with buttermilk mixture in 2 additions, scraping down bowl as needed. Beat in cocoa mixture until batter is uniform. Give batter final stir by hand.

3. Divide batter evenly between prepared pans and smooth tops with rubber spatula. Gently tap pans on counter to settle batter. Bake until toothpick inserted in center comes out clean, about 25 minutes, switching and rotating pans halfway through baking. Let cakes cool in pans on wire rack for 10 minutes. Remove cakes from pans, discarding parchment, and let cool completely on rack, about 2 hours. (Cake layers can be stored at room temperature for up to 24 hours or frozen for up to 1 month; defrost at room temperature.)

4. Line edges of cake platter with 4 strips of parchment paper to keep platter clean. Place 1 cake layer on platter. Spread 1½ cups frosting evenly over top, right to edge of cake. Top with second cake layer, press lightly to adhere, then spread remaining frosting evenly over top and sides of cake. Carefully remove parchment strips before serving.

GLUTEN-FREE CHOCOLATE LAYER CAKE

Serves 10 to 12 | two 9-inch round cake pans

WHY THIS RECIPE WORKS Everyone loves (and deserves!) a rich chocolate cake, but too often the gluten-free translation is less than appealing; our initial survey of recipes turned out dense, brick-like cakes. We wanted a recipe for truly great gluten-free cake. A combination of cocoa powder and bittersweet chocolate provided the best chocolate flavor, but the rich bar chocolate weighed down our cake. Swapping out the traditional butter for oil lightened our cake. A combination of ingredients—baking powder, baking soda, and xanthan gum—was necessary for leavening these rich layers. The soda helped keep the cake tender, while the powder gave it lift; xanthan gum contributed the structure typically provided by gluten. It's essential to weigh the flour. Once it's frosted, serve the cake within a few hours.

**Gluten-Free
Chocolate Layer Cake**

1 cup vegetable oil
6 ounces bittersweet chocolate, chopped
2 ounces (⅔ cup) unsweetened cocoa powder
7 ounces (1¼ cups) all-purpose gluten-free flour blend (see page 2)
1½ teaspoons baking powder
1 teaspoon baking soda
1 teaspoon xanthan gum (see page 2)
1 teaspoon salt
4 large eggs
2 teaspoons vanilla extract
10½ ounces (1½ cups) sugar
1 cup whole milk
5 cups Chocolate Buttercream (page 242)

1. Adjust oven rack to lower-middle position and heat oven to 350 degrees. Grease two 9-inch round cake pans, line bottoms with parchment paper, and grease parchment.

2. Microwave oil, chocolate, and cocoa in bowl at 50 percent power, stirring occasionally, until melted, about 2 minutes. Whisk mixture until smooth, then set aside to cool slightly. Whisk flour blend, baking powder, baking soda, xanthan gum, and salt together in second bowl.

3. Whisk eggs and vanilla together in large bowl. Whisk in sugar until well combined. Whisk in cooled chocolate mixture and milk until combined. Whisk in flour blend mixture until batter is thoroughly combined and smooth. Divide batter evenly between prepared pans and smooth tops with rubber spatula. Bake until toothpick inserted in center comes out clean, 30 to 32 minutes, switching and rotating pans halfway through baking.

4. Let cakes cool in pans on wire rack for 10 minutes. Run thin knife around edge of cake pans. Remove cakes from pans, discarding parchment, and let cool completely on rack, about 1½ hours. (Cake layers can be stored at room temperature for up to 24 hours.)

5. Line edges of cake platter with 4 strips of parchment paper to keep platter clean. Place 1 cake layer on platter. Spread 1½ cups frosting evenly over top, right to edge of cake. Top with second cake layer, press lightly to adhere, then spread remaining frosting evenly over top and sides of cake. Carefully remove parchment strips before serving.

VEGAN YELLOW LAYER CAKE

Serves 10 to 12 | two 9-inch round cake pans

WHY THIS RECIPE WORKS Our vegan yellow layer cake stands tall for any celebration. But nailing the recipe was a big challenge. After all, none of the ingredients that give yellow cake structure or lightness are vegan. And with yellow cake, off-flavors have nowhere to hide. Replacing the eggs would be no small feat. Eggs provide cakes with lift and structure, and most of the common substitutes we tried left us with heavy cakes. Then, after lots of testing, we landed on aquafaba; the liquid found in canned chickpeas, whipped to stiff peaks like egg whites and folded into the batter, acted as the perfect stand-in, trapping tiny air bubbles for a classic fluffy crumb. To enhance fluffiness more, we baked the cake in a hot oven—400 degrees—to boost oven spring (the rise that baked goods experience when they first hit the oven). And a lengthy baking time of 25 to 30 minutes helped dry out the layers so there was no pastiness. Using oat milk further promoted browning thanks to its sugar content. If you are a strict vegan, use organic sugar.

- 1¾ cups unsweetened oat milk, room temperature
- ½ cup coconut oil, melted and cooled
- 1½ tablespoons vanilla extract
- 5 tablespoons aquafaba
- 1 teaspoon cream of tartar
- 4 cups (16 ounces) cake flour
- 1¾ cups (12¼ ounces) sugar
- 1 tablespoon baking powder
- 1 teaspoon salt
- 4 cups Creamy Vegan Chocolate Frosting (page 246)

1. Adjust oven rack to middle position and heat oven to 400 degrees. Grease two 9-inch round cake pans, line with parchment paper, and grease parchment.

2. Whisk oat milk, melted oil, and vanilla together in bowl. Using stand mixer fitted with whisk attachment, whip aquafaba and cream of tartar on high speed until stiff foam that clings to whisk forms, 3 to 9 minutes; transfer to clean bowl.

3. Add flour, sugar, baking powder, and salt to now-empty mixer bowl and mix on low speed until well combined, about 1 minute. Gradually add milk mixture and continue to mix until just incorporated, about 15 seconds. Scrape down bowl and whisk attachment, then continue to whip on medium-low speed until smooth and fully incorporated, 10 to 15 seconds.

4. Using rubber spatula, stir one-third of whipped aquafaba into batter to lighten, then gently fold in remaining aquafaba until no white streaks remain. Divide batter evenly between prepared pans. Bake until cakes are set and spring back when pressed lightly, 25 to 30 minutes, switching and rotating pans halfway through baking. Let cakes cool in pans on wire rack for 10 minutes. Remove cakes from pans, discarding parchment, and let cool completely on rack, about 2 hours.

5. Line edges of cake platter with 4 strips of parchment paper to keep platter clean. Place 1 cake layer on platter. Spread 1½ cups frosting evenly over top, right to edge of cake. Top with second cake layer, press lightly to adhere, then spread remaining frosting evenly over top and sides of cake. Carefully remove parchment strips before serving.

Vegan Yellow Layer Cake

Frostings and Frosting Cakes

Frosting is more than just sweetened butter. In the following pages, you'll find our collection of frostings you can use to fill and coat cakes with two or more layers, sheet cakes, and cupcakes. We provide different yields of frosting to accommodate each type of cake. For tips on frosting a cake, check out page 232.

FROSTING VARIETIES

American Buttercream
What we'd simply call frosting, American buttercream is a timeless fluffy combination of butter and sugar. Confectioners' sugar is the best choice because it thickens the frosting, eliminating the need for eggs, and—owing to its superfine texture—provides stability without the grit. We add a little heavy cream for an ultracreamy consistency you can't get from butter and sugar alone. This is typically the sweetest frosting option. Our Vanilla Frosting (page 241) is an American buttercream.

Swiss Meringue Buttercream
This buttercream is less sweet than most frostings, and it's also one of the easiest buttercreams to make. It starts with a cooked egg-white meringue, to which you gradually add softened butter—and lots of it—until the mixture becomes light and fluffy. Its ultrasatiny texture makes it an elegant and decadent option. Our Chocolate Buttercream (page 242) is a Swiss meringue buttercream.

French Buttercream
French buttercream is richer than Swiss meringue buttercream because its egg base is egg yolks rather than whites. Pouring a hot sugar syrup over the yolks ensures that they are cooked to a safe temperature. Then, as with a Swiss meringue buttercream, a generous amount of softened butter is whipped in. Our luxurious Vanilla Buttercream (page 245) is a French meringue buttercream.

German Buttercream
German buttercream starts out like American buttercream—butter is beaten until light and fluffy—but then an egg-based pastry cream is added. The custard contributes a super-creamy texture for a soft, light buttercream that, while rich, isn't overwhelming. We fill layers of our Chocolate-Espresso Dacquoise (page 480) with a German buttercream.

Seven-Minute Frosting
If you like marshmallows or meringues, you'll love seven-minute frosting. This frosting is playful, simple, and sweet; and since it doesn't contain butter, it isn't very rich. Although the egg white base requires cooking, the frosting is easy to prepare, taking just 7 minutes to whip up (hence the name). The sticky frosting looks particularly nice in swirls and billows.

Ganache
Ganache is simply a decadent, truffle-like mixture of melted chocolate and cream. Depending on the amount of cream used, ganache can be a pourable glaze, a fudgy filling, or a whipped frosting (like our Chocolate Ganache Frosting on page 242), making it a versatile option.

Whipped Cream
Whipped cream is all that's needed for rustic cakes or those that are particularly rich. When whipped cream is being used in place of frosting, we prefer to make it in the food processor (see page 243). It's dense, creamy, and perfect for spreading over cakes. And because the smaller air bubbles created by the food processor are more stable than the bigger bubbles created by a stand mixer, we've found that processed cream keeps its thick, dense texture for two full weeks.

VANILLA FROSTING

Makes 5 cups, enough for two-layer cake

American buttercream frostings such as this and our Chocolate Frosting are basically regular old frostings—a timeless fluffy combination of butter and sugar. We cut the butter into pieces and let them soften—but not too much, or the frosting will be greasy. Many recipes for vanilla frosting call for milk; we prefer heavy cream, which gives the frosting a silky quality. For colored frosting, stir in drops of food coloring at the end, but be sure to use a light hand—a little goes a long way.

   1 pound (4 sticks) unsalted butter, each
      stick cut into quarters and softened
   ¼ cup heavy cream
   1 tablespoon vanilla extract
   ¼ teaspoon table salt
   4 cups (16 ounces) confectioners' sugar

1. Using stand mixer fitted with paddle, beat butter, cream, vanilla, and salt on medium-high speed until smooth, about 1 minute. Reduce speed to medium-low, slowly add sugar, and beat until incorporated and smooth, about 4 minutes.

2. Increase speed to medium-high and beat until frosting is light and fluffy, about 5 minutes. (Frosting can be refrigerated for up to 3 days; let soften at room temperature, about 2 hours, then rewhip on medium speed until smooth, 2 to 5 minutes.)

To make 3 cups, enough for cupcakes or sheet cake:
Reduce butter to 20 tablespoons (2½ sticks), reduce cream to 2 tablespoons, reduce vanilla to 2 teaspoons, reduce salt to ⅛ teaspoon, and reduce confectioners' sugar to 2½ cups (10 ounces).

To make 6 cups, enough for three-layer cake: Increase butter to 1¼ pounds (5 sticks), increase vanilla to 4 teaspoons, and increase confectioners' sugar to 5 cups (1¼ pounds).

Coffee Frosting

For 5 cups frosting: Add 3 tablespoons instant espresso powder or instant coffee powder to mixer with butter.

For 3 cups frosting: Add 1½ tablespoons instant espresso powder or instant coffee powder to mixer with butter.

For 6 cups frosting: Add ¼ cup instant espresso powder or instant coffee powder to mixer with butter.

Orange Frosting

For 5 cups frosting: Add 1 tablespoon grated orange zest and 2 tablespoons juice to mixer with butter.

For 3 cups frosting: Add 1½ teaspoons grated orange zest and 1 tablespoon juice to mixer with butter.

For 6 cups frosting: Add 1½ tablespoons grated orange zest and 2½ tablespoons juice to mixer with butter.

CHOCOLATE FROSTING

Makes 5 cups, enough for two-layer cake

We combined a hefty amount of cocoa powder with melted chocolate to give this frosting deep flavor. Using both confectioners' sugar and corn syrup made it smooth and glossy. To keep the frosting from separating and turning greasy, we turned to the food processor: The machine eliminated risk of over-beating, as it blended the ingredients quickly without melting the butter or incorporating too much air. The result was a thick, fluffy foolproof frosting that spread like a dream. Bittersweet, semisweet, or milk chocolate can be used.

   30 tablespoons (3¾ sticks) unsalted butter, softened
   1½ cups (6 ounces) confectioners' sugar
    1 cup (3 ounces) Dutch-processed cocoa powder
    ⅛ teaspoon table salt
    1 cup light corn syrup
   1½ teaspoons vanilla extract
   12 ounces chocolate, melted and cooled

Process butter, sugar, cocoa, and salt in food processor until smooth, about 30 seconds, scraping down sides of bowl as needed. Add corn syrup and vanilla and process until just combined, 5 to 10 seconds. Scrape down sides of bowl, then add chocolate and process until smooth and creamy, 10 to 15 seconds. (Frosting can be kept at room temperature for up to 3 hours or refrigerated for up to 3 days; if refrigerated, let stand at room temperature for 1 hour and stir before using.)

To make 3 cups, enough for cupcakes or sheet cake: Reduce butter to 20 tablespoons (2½ sticks), reduce confectioners' sugar to 1 cup (4 ounces), reduce cocoa powder to ¾ cup (2¼ ounces), reduce corn syrup to ¾ cup, reduce vanilla to 1 teaspoon, and reduce chocolate to 8 ounces.

To make 6 cups, enough for three-layer cake: Increase butter to 1¼ pounds (5 sticks), increase confectioners' sugar to 2 cups (8 ounces), increase cocoa powder to 1½ cups (4½ ounces), and increase chocolate to 1 pound.

CHOCOLATE BUTTERCREAM

Makes 5 cups, enough for two-layer cake

When we want a more refined chocolate frosting, we opt for a cooked buttercream of the Swiss meringue variety in which egg whites and granulated sugar are heated over a double boiler and then whipped with knobs of softened butter. This creamy chocolate frosting is the perfect crowning touch for any of our chocolate cakes. The melted chocolate should be cooled to between 85 and 100 degrees before being added to the frosting.

    1   cup (7 ounces) sugar
    5   large egg whites
    ⅛   teaspoon table salt
    28 tablespoons (3½ sticks) unsalted butter, cut into
        28 pieces and softened
    14 ounces bittersweet chocolate, melted and cooled
    1¼ teaspoons vanilla extract

1. Combine sugar, egg whites, and salt in bowl of stand mixer. Set bowl over saucepan filled with 1 inch of barely simmering water, making sure that water does not touch bottom of bowl. Cook, whisking constantly, until mixture registers 150 degrees, about 3 minutes.

2. Remove bowl from heat and transfer to stand mixer fitted with whisk attachment. Whip warm egg mixture on medium speed until it has consistency of shaving cream and has cooled slightly, about 5 minutes. Add butter, 1 piece at a time, and whip until smooth and creamy, about 2 minutes. (Frosting may look curdled after half of butter has been added; it will smooth out with additional butter.)

3. Add chocolate and vanilla and mix until combined. Increase speed to medium-high and whip until light and fluffy, about 30 seconds, scraping down bowl as needed. If frosting seems too soft after adding chocolate, chill it briefly in refrigerator, then rewhip until creamy. (Frosting can be refrigerated for up to 24 hours; warm frosting briefly in microwave until just slightly softened, 5 to 10 seconds, then stir until creamy.)

To make 3 cups, enough for cupcakes or sheet cake: Reduce sugar to ½ cup (3½ ounces), reduce egg whites to 3, reduce butter to 16 tablespoons, and reduce chocolate to 8 ounces.

To make 6 cups, enough for three-layer cake: Increase egg whites to 6, increase salt to ¼ teaspoon, increase butter to 1 pound (4 sticks), increase chocolate to 1 pound, and increase vanilla to 1½ teaspoons.

Malted Milk Chocolate Buttercream

For 5 cups frosting: Substitute milk chocolate for bittersweet chocolate. Add ⅓ cup malted milk powder to frosting with chocolate in step 3.

For 3 cups frosting: Substitute milk chocolate for bittersweet chocolate. Add ¼ cup malted milk powder to frosting with chocolate in step 3.

For 6 cups frosting: Substitute milk chocolate for bittersweet chocolate. Add ½ cup malted milk powder to frosting with chocolate in step 3.

Peanut Butter Buttercream

For 5 cups frosting: Substitute 1 cup creamy peanut butter for chocolate. Garnish with ½ cup chopped peanuts.

For 3 cups frosting: Substitute ⅔ cup creamy peanut butter for chocolate. Garnish with ½ cup chopped peanuts.

For 6 cups frosting: Substitute 1⅓ cups creamy peanut butter for chocolate. Garnish with ½ cup chopped peanuts.

CHOCOLATE GANACHE FROSTING

Makes 5 cups, enough for two-layer cake

The richest chocolate frosting is also the easiest to make. When we want an intense topping, we go with ganache, made simply from heavy cream and semisweet chocolate.

    1   pound semisweet chocolate, chopped
    2   cups heavy cream

1. Place chocolate in large heatproof bowl. Bring cream to boil in small saucepan. Pour boiling cream over chocolate, and let sit, covered, for 5 minutes. Whisk mixture until smooth, then cover with plastic wrap and refrigerate until cool and slightly firm, about 1 hour.

2. Using stand mixer fitted with whisk attachment, whip cooled chocolate mixture on medium speed until fluffy and mousse-like and soft peaks form, about 2 minutes.

To make 3 cups, enough for cupcakes or sheet cake: Reduce chocolate to 10 ounces and reduce heavy cream to 1¼ cups.

To make 6 cups, enough for three-layer cake: Increase chocolate to 1¼ pounds and increase heavy cream to 2½ cups. Increase chilling time in step 1 to about 2 hours.

PEANUT BUTTER FROSTING

Makes 5 cups, enough for two-layer cake

This peanut butter frosting is just sweet enough, with undeniable peanut flavor. The butter and heavy cream contributed to a smooth and creamy texture that wasn't greasy. We mixed the cream with the butter and peanut butter before adding the sugar; this helped lighten the butter. Do not use crunchy, old-fashioned, or natural peanut butter in this recipe.

22 tablespoons (2¾ sticks) unsalted butter, cut into 22 pieces and softened
1⅓ cups creamy peanut butter
3 tablespoons heavy cream
2 teaspoons vanilla extract
⅛ teaspoon table salt
2 cups (8 ounces) confectioners' sugar

1. Using stand mixer fitted with paddle, beat butter, peanut butter, cream, vanilla, and salt on medium-high speed until smooth, about 1 minute. Reduce speed to medium-low, slowly add sugar, and beat until incorporated and smooth, about 4 minutes.

2. Increase speed to medium-high and beat until frosting is light and fluffy, about 5 minutes. (Frosting can be refrigerated for up to 3 days; let soften at room temperature, about 2 hours, then rewhip on medium speed until smooth, 2 to 5 minutes.)

To make 3 cups, enough for cupcakes or sheet cake: Reduce butter to 12 tablespoons, reduce peanut butter to ¾ cup, reduce cream to 1½ tablespoons, reduce vanilla to 1½ teaspoons, and reduce confectioners' sugar to 1¼ cups (5 ounces).

To make 6 cups, enough for three-layer cake: Increase butter to 24 tablespoons (3 sticks), increase peanut butter to 1½ cups, and increase confectioners' sugar to 2½ cups (10 ounces).

CREAM CHEESE FROSTING

Makes 5 cups, enough for two-layer cake

We enriched our cream cheese frosting with sour cream for extra tang. Slowly adding the confectioners' sugar to the other ingredients at a low speed and then turning up the speed gave us more control over the texture, ultimately producing a light, fluffy frosting. Do not use low-fat or fat-free cream cheese. This frosting has a soft, loose texture; it won't work with a three-layer cake. If the frosting becomes too soft to work with, let it chill in the refrigerator until firm.

1¼ pounds cream cheese, softened
12 tablespoons unsalted butter, cut into 12 pieces and softened
2 tablespoons sour cream
2 teaspoons vanilla extract
¼ teaspoon table salt
2½ cups (10 ounces) confectioners' sugar

1. Using stand mixer fitted with paddle, beat cream cheese, butter, sour cream, vanilla, and salt on medium-high speed until smooth, about 2 minutes. Reduce speed to medium-low, slowly add sugar, and beat until incorporated and smooth, about 4 minutes.

2. Increase speed to medium-high and beat until frosting is light and fluffy, about 4 minutes. (Frosting can be refrigerated for up to 3 days; let soften at room temperature, about 1 hour, then rewhip on medium speed until smooth, about 2 minutes.)

To make 3 cups, enough for cupcakes or sheet cake: Reduce cream cheese to 12 ounces, reduce butter to 6 tablespoons, reduce sour cream to 1½ tablespoons, reduce vanilla to 1 teaspoon, and reduce confectioners' sugar to 1½ cups (6 ounces).

Whipped Cream Frosting

Need a simple frosting that takes barely a minute to make? Whip some cream, sugar, and vanilla in a food processor. Whereas whipping cream in a stand mixer produces light, billowy peaks, the sharp, fast-moving blades of a food processor can't add as much air. Instead, they produce a dense, creamy consistency that works well as a quick, spreadable topping for snack cakes, angel food and chiffon cakes, and cupcakes. It's also very effective when piped through a pastry bag to make decorative edging. Even better, because the smaller air bubbles created by the food processor are more stable than the bigger bubbles created by a stand mixer, we found that the processed cream kept its thick, dense texture for two full weeks.

HONEY CREAM CHEESE FROSTING

Makes 5 cups, enough for two-layer cake

Honey pairs nicely with the tang of cream cheese, giving this frosting a distinct yet nuanced, well-rounded flavor profile. Do not use low-fat or fat-free cream cheese or the frosting will have a soupy consistency. If the frosting becomes too soft to work with, let it chill in the refrigerator until firm.

- 1¼ pounds cream cheese, softened
- 12 tablespoons unsalted butter, cut into 12 pieces and softened
- 1 tablespoon vanilla extract
- ¼ teaspoon table salt
- ⅔ cup honey

1. Using stand mixer fitted with whisk attachment, whip cream cheese, butter, vanilla, and salt on medium-high speed until smooth, about 2 minutes.

2. Reduce speed to medium-low, add honey, and whip until smooth, about 2 minutes. Increase speed to medium-high and whip until frosting is light and fluffy, 3 to 5 minutes. (Frosting can be refrigerated for up to 3 days; let soften at room temperature, about 1 hour, then rewhip on medium speed until smooth, about 2 minutes.)

To make 3 cups, enough for cupcakes or sheet cake: Reduce cream cheese to 12 ounces, reduce butter to 8 tablespoons, reduce vanilla to 2 teaspoons, reduce salt to ⅛ teaspoon, and reduce honey to 6 tablespoons.

To make 6 cups, enough for three-layer cake: Increase cream cheese to 1½ pounds, increase butter to 16 tablespoons, increase vanilla to 4 teaspoons, and increase honey to ¾ cup.

Maple Cream Cheese Frosting

Substitute maple syrup for honey.

SEVEN-MINUTE FROSTING

Makes 5 cups, enough for two-layer cake

This quick frosting is the one for you if you like marshmallows or meringues. It's playful, simple, and sweet; and since it doesn't contain any butter, it isn't very rich. Taking its name from the time it takes to beat the frosting over simmering water, our easy recipe is the perfect finishing touch to any cake or cupcake. The trick to producing a thick, glossy frosting was to cook a combination of egg whites, sugar, and corn syrup gently over a pan of simmering water before whipping the mixture until cooled and stiff peaks formed. This frosting should be spread on thick and then swept into big, billowy swirls using the back of a spoon.

- 1½ cups (10½ ounces) sugar
- 2 large egg whites
- 6 tablespoons cold water
- 1½ tablespoons light corn syrup
- ¼ teaspoon cream of tartar
  Pinch table salt
- 1 teaspoon vanilla extract

1. Combine sugar, egg whites, cold water, corn syrup, cream of tartar, and salt in bowl of stand mixer. Set bowl over saucepan filled with 1 inch barely simmering water, making sure that water does not touch bottom of bowl. Cook, whisking constantly, until mixture registers 160 degrees, 5 to 10 minutes.

2. Remove bowl from heat and transfer to stand mixer fitted with whisk attachment. Whip warm egg white mixture on medium speed until soft peaks form, about 5 minutes. Add vanilla, increase speed to medium-high, and continue to whip until mixture has cooled completely and stiff peaks form, 5 to 7 minutes. Use immediately.

To make 3 cups, enough for cupcakes or sheet cake: Reduce sugar to 1 cup (7 ounces), reduce water to ¼ cup, reduce corn syrup to 1 tablespoon, reduce cream of tartar to ⅛ teaspoon, reduce vanilla to ½ teaspoon.

To make 6 cups, enough for three-layer cake: Increase sugar to 1¾ cups (12¼ ounces), increase egg whites to 3, increase water to 7 tablespoons, increase corn syrup to 5 teaspoons, and increase vanilla to 1¼ teaspoons.

VANILLA BUTTERCREAM
Makes 5 cups, enough for two-layer cake

Classic French buttercreams rely on sugar alone for the sweetener, but we discovered that substituting corn syrup for some of the sugar gave our buttercream a more fluid—yet stable—consistency. The addition of corn syrup also made it easier to melt the sugar. Some recipes call for whole eggs, but we preferred the richer texture that resulted from using only yolks. It was essential to heat the sugar syrup while the yolks were whipping; adding the syrup while hot ensured that the egg yolks reached a safe temperature. We whipped the yolk-syrup mixture not just to aerate it, but also to cool it off before we added the softened butter; this prevented the butter from melting into pools of grease. Be sure to pour the syrup into the eggs slowly to avoid scrambling the eggs. Do not use a handheld mixer. For colored frosting, stir in drops of food coloring at the end; a little goes a long way. This buttercream has a natural pale yellow color, but if stored in the refrigerator the buttercream will darken slightly over time.

    7   large egg yolks
    ¾   cup (5¼ ounces) sugar
    ⅔   cup light corn syrup
    2½   teaspoons vanilla extract
    ⅛   teaspoon table salt
    1⅛   pounds (4½ sticks) unsalted butter, each
         stick cut into quarters and softened

1. Using stand mixer fitted with whisk attachment, whip egg yolks on medium speed until slightly thickened and pale yellow, 4 to 6 minutes.

2. Meanwhile, bring sugar and corn syrup to boil in small saucepan over medium heat, stirring occasionally to dissolve sugar, about 3 minutes. Without letting hot sugar mixture cool off, reduce speed to low and slowly pour hot sugar syrup into whipped egg yolks without hitting sides of bowl or whisk. Increase speed to medium-high and whip until mixture is light and fluffy and bowl is no longer warm, 5 to 10 minutes.

3. Reduce speed to medium-low and add vanilla and salt. Add butter, 1 piece at a time, and whip until completely incorporated, about 2 minutes. Increase speed to medium-high and whip until buttercream is smooth and silky, about 2 minutes. If mixture looks curdled, wrap hot, wet dish towel around bowl and continue to whip until smooth, 1 to 2 minutes. (Buttercream can be refrigerated for up to 3 days; let soften at room temperature, about 2 hours, then rewhip on medium speed until smooth, about 2 minutes.)

To make 3 cups, enough for cupcakes or sheet cake: Reduce egg yolks to 3, reduce sugar to ½ cup (3½ ounces), reduce corn syrup to ⅓ cup, reduce vanilla to 1½ teaspoons, reduce salt to pinch, and reduce butter to 20 tablespoons (2½ sticks).

To make 6 cups, enough for three-layer cake: Increase egg yolks to 8, increase sugar to 1 cup (7 ounces), increase corn syrup to ¾ cup, increase vanilla to 1 tablespoon, increase salt to ¼ teaspoon, and increase butter to 1¼ pounds (5 sticks).

MIRACLE FROSTING
Makes 5 cups, enough for two-layer cake

True to its name, this old-fashioned cooked frosting magically transforms from a paste into a fluffy, creamy frosting as you beat it. Most recipes call for cooking the flour and milk together until a thick paste forms, and then creaming the butter and sugar before beating the two mixtures together. But this technique left little lumps of flour suspended in the icing. Adding the sugar to the flour and cooking it with the milk solved the problem. To firm the icing and make it more spreadable, we adjusted the ratio of milk to flour and substituted cornstarch for a small amount of the flour.

    1½   cups (10½ ounces) sugar
    ¼   cup (1¼ ounces) all-purpose flour
    3   tablespoons cornstarch
    ½   teaspoon table salt
    1½   cups milk
    24   tablespoons (3 sticks) unsalted butter, softened
    2   teaspoons vanilla extract

1. Whisk sugar, flour, cornstarch, and salt together in medium saucepan. Slowly whisk in milk until smooth. Cook over medium heat, whisking constantly and scraping corners of saucepan, until mixture boils and is very thick, 4 to 8 minutes. Transfer mixture to wide bowl and let cool completely, about 2 hours.

2. Using stand mixer fitted with paddle, beat butter on medium-high speed until light and fluffy, about 5 minutes. Reduce speed to medium, add cooled milk mixture and vanilla, and mix until combined, scraping down sides of bowl as needed. Increase speed to medium-high and beat until frosting is light and fluffy, 3 to 5 minutes.

To make 3 cups, enough for cupcakes or sheet cake: Reduce sugar to ¾ cup (5¼ ounces), reduce flour to 2½ tablespoons, reduce cornstarch to 5 teaspoons, reduce salt to ¼ teaspoon, reduce milk to ¾ cup, reduce butter to 14 tablespoons, and reduce vanilla to 1¼ teaspoons.

To make 6 cups, enough for three-layer cake: Increase sugar to 1¾ cups (12¼ ounces), increase flour to 5 tablespoons (1½ ounces), increase cornstarch to 3 tablespoons plus 2 teaspoons, increase milk to 1¾ cups, increase butter to 30 tablespoons (3¾ sticks), and increase vanilla to 1 tablespoon.

Miracle Coffee Frosting

For 5 cups frosting: Add 2 tablespoons instant espresso powder to flour mixture in step 1.

For 3 cups frosting: Add 5 teaspoons instant espresso powder to flour mixture in step 1.

For 6 cups frosting: Add 2½ tablespoons instant espresso powder to flour mixture in step 1.

Miracle Milk Chocolate Frosting

For 5 cups frosting: Add 5 tablespoons Dutch-processed cocoa powder to flour mixture in step 1 and add 3¾ ounces melted and cooled semisweet chocolate to light and fluffy frosting in step 2 and beat until incorporated, about 30 seconds.

For 3 cups frosting: Add 3 tablespoons Dutch-processed cocoa powder to flour mixture in step 1 and add 2¼ ounces melted and cooled semisweet chocolate to light and fluffy frosting in step 2 and beat until incorporated, about 30 seconds.

For 6 cups frosting: Add 6 tablespoons Dutch-processed cocoa powder to flour mixture in step 1 and add 4½ ounces melted and cooled semisweet chocolate to light and fluffy frosting in step 2 and beat until incorporated, about 30 seconds.

CREAMY VEGAN CHOCOLATE FROSTING

Makes 4 cups, enough for two-layer cake

For a rich, billowy vegan chocolate frosting, we began by melting semisweet chocolate with coconut milk. For an even richer frosting, we discarded the milky liquid from the cans of coconut milk and used just the layer of cream. Chilling the cans of milk overnight helped separate the cream from the milk. We whipped the thick mixture into a light, mousse-like frosting. This frosting was downright decadent, but it separated a bit. Using chocolate chips instead of bar chocolate was our fix. Chocolate chips contain emulsifying agents, which stabilized the mixture. Not all semisweet chocolate chips are vegan, so check ingredient lists carefully.

  3 (14-ounce) cans coconut milk
3⅓ cups (1¼ pounds) semisweet chocolate chips
  ¼ teaspoon table salt

1. Refrigerate unopened cans of coconut milk for at least 24 hours to ensure that 2 distinct layers form. Skim cream layer from each can and measure out 1½ cups cream (save any extra cream for another use and discard milky liquid).

2. Microwave coconut cream, chocolate chips, and salt in bowl at 50 percent power, whisking occasionally, until melted and smooth, 2 to 4 minutes; transfer to bowl of stand mixer. Press plastic wrap directly on surface of chocolate mixture and refrigerate until cooled completely and texture resembles firm cream cheese, about 3 hours, stirring halfway through chilling. (If mixture has chilled for longer and is very stiff, let stand at room temperature until softened but still cool.) Using stand mixer fitted with whisk attachment, whip at high speed until fluffy, mousse-like soft peaks form, 2 to 4 minutes, scraping down bowl halfway through whipping.

To make 2 cups, enough for cupcakes: Use 2 cans of coconut milk to obtain ¾ cup cream. Reduce chocolate chips to 1⅔ cups (10 ounces) and salt to ⅛ teaspoon.

WORKING WITH BUTTERCREAM

We love our basic Vanilla Frosting (page 241): Softened butter and confectioners' sugar are beaten together and a little cream is added. It's simple and sweet and works on most cakes. But there's a world beyond this American frosting to explore. This tutorial for Vanilla Buttercream (page 245) will give you the confidence to try your hand at a classic buttercream, which is made with melted sugar and egg yolks for an ultrasilky texture. (For more information on frosting varieties, see page 240.)

1. WHIP THE EGG YOLKS: Using a stand mixer fitted with the whisk attachment, whip the egg yolks on medium speed until they're slightly thickened and pale yellow, 4 to 6 minutes. You must whip the yolks until they're thick and pale before you pour the sugar mixture into the mixing bowl or it won't come together properly.

2. COOK THE SUGAR AND CORN SYRUP: Bring the sugar and corn syrup to a boil in a small saucepan over medium heat, stirring occasionally to dissolve the sugar, about 3 minutes. You want to heat the sugar syrup at the same time the yolks are whipping so the hot syrup will be ready once the yolks are done. The corn syrup gives the buttercream a fluid but stable consistency.

3. SLOWLY ADD THE HOT SYRUP: With the mixer on low speed, pour the hot sugar syrup into the whipped egg yolks. Pouring the hot syrup into the egg yolks gently raises their temperature to a safe level. If you dump the syrup into the bowl all at once you can scramble the eggs. Aim to pour the syrup into the bowl so that it avoids both the whisk and the sides (where it can seize).

4. WHIP THE MIXTURE UNTIL COOL: Increase the mixer speed to medium-high and whip the mixture until it's light and fluffy and the bowl is no longer warm, 5 to 10 minutes. Whipping aerates the yolk mixture and makes it easier to add the butter in the next step.

5. BEAT IN THE SOFTENED BUTTER: Reduce the mixer speed to medium-low and add the vanilla and salt. Gradually add the softened butter until it's completely incorporated. Cold butter will clump up and you will have to overbeat the frosting to smooth it back out.

6. WHIP THE FROSTING UNTIL SILKY: Increase the mixer speed to medium-high and whip the buttercream until it's smooth and silky. If the finished frosting looks curdled, the butter was probably too cold. Wrap a hot wet towel around the bowl and whip until smooth.

CARROT LAYER CAKE

Serves 12 to 16 | rimmed baking sheet

WHY THIS RECIPE WORKS We wanted a sleek, stacked, dressed-up version of carrot cake with thin layers of light cake and a rich cream cheese frosting. We baked our cake in a rimmed baking sheet, sliced it into four pieces, and stacked them. Adding a little baking soda to the batter helped the carrots break down and soften. Buttermilk powder provided extra tang to our cream cheese frosting and thickened it to just the right consistency. Shred the carrots on the large holes of a box grater or in a food processor fitted with the shredding disk. To ensure the proper consistency for the frosting, use cold cream cheese. If your baked cake is of an uneven thickness, adjust the orientation of the layers as they are stacked to produce a level cake. Assembling this cake on a cardboard cake rectangle trimmed to an 8 by 6-inch rectangle makes it easy to pick it up and press the pecans onto the sides.

CAKE

1¾ cups (8¾ ounces) all-purpose flour
2 teaspoons baking powder
1 teaspoon baking soda
1½ teaspoons ground cinnamon
¾ teaspoon ground nutmeg
½ teaspoon table salt
¼ teaspoon ground cloves
1¼ cups packed (8¾ ounces) light brown sugar
¾ cup vegetable oil
3 large eggs
1 teaspoon vanilla extract
2⅔ cups shredded carrots (4 carrots)
⅔ cup dried currants

FROSTING AND NUTS

16 tablespoons unsalted butter, softened
3 cups (12 ounces) confectioners' sugar
⅓ cup (1 ounce) buttermilk powder
2 teaspoons vanilla extract
¼ teaspoon table salt
12 ounces cream cheese, cut into 12 equal pieces and chilled
2 cups pecans, toasted and chopped coarse

1. FOR THE CAKE: Adjust oven rack to middle position and heat oven to 350 degrees. Grease 18 by 13-inch rimmed baking sheet, line with parchment paper, and grease parchment.

2. Whisk flour, baking powder, baking soda, cinnamon, nutmeg, salt, and cloves together in large bowl. Whisk sugar, oil, eggs, and vanilla in second large bowl until mixture is smooth. Stir in carrots and currants. Add flour mixture and fold with rubber spatula until mixture is just combined.

Carrot Layer Cake

3. Transfer batter to prepared sheet and smooth top with offset spatula. Bake until center is firm to touch, 15 to 18 minutes, rotating sheet halfway through baking. Let cake cool in pan on wire rack for 5 minutes. Invert cake onto rack (do not remove parchment), then reinvert onto second rack. Let cake cool completely, about 30 minutes.

4. FOR THE FROSTING AND NUTS: Using stand mixer fitted with paddle, beat butter, sugar, buttermilk powder, vanilla, and salt on low speed until smooth, about 2 minutes, scraping down bowl as needed. Increase speed to medium-low, add cream cheese, 1 piece at a time, and mix until smooth, about 2 minutes.

5. Transfer cooled cake to cutting board, parchment side down. Using sharp chef's knife, cut cake and parchment in half crosswise, then lengthwise, making 4 equal rectangles, about 8 by 6 inches each.

6. Place 1 cake layer, parchment side up, on 8 by 6-inch cardboard rectangle and carefully remove parchment. Spread ⅔ cup frosting evenly over top, right to edge of cake. Repeat with 2 more cake layers, pressing lightly to adhere and spreading ⅔ cup frosting evenly over each layer. Top with remaining cake layer and spread 1 cup frosting evenly over top. Spread remaining frosting evenly over sides of cake. (It's fine if some crumbs show through frosting on sides, but if you go back to smooth top of cake, be sure that spatula is free of crumbs.)

7. Hold cake with your hand and gently press pecans onto sides with your other hand. Refrigerate for at least 1 hour. Transfer cake to platter and serve. (Cake can be refrigerated for up to 24 hours; bring to room temperature before serving.)

COCONUT LAYER CAKE

Serves 10 to 12 | two 9-inch round cake pans

WHY THIS RECIPE WORKS The ideal coconut cake is perfumed inside and out with the subtle essence of coconut. We wanted a four-layer affair featuring moist, tender cake with a delicate, yielding crumb and silky frosting covered with a deep drift of downy coconut. For the cake layers, we preferred a rich and moist butter cake made with low-protein cake flour for a supertender crumb. Using cream of coconut and coconut extract in the cake delivered full, well-rounded coconut flavor. For a light yet rich frosting we chose an egg white–based buttercream that we flavored with more coconut extract and cream of coconut. A woolly coating of toasted shredded coconut provided textural interest and delivered a final dose of flavor. Be sure to use cream of coconut (such as Coco López) and not coconut milk here. One 15-ounce can of cream of coconut is enough for both the cake and the frosting.

CAKE
    1 large egg plus 5 large whites
    ¾ cup cream of coconut
    ¼ cup water
    1 teaspoon coconut extract
    1 teaspoon vanilla extract
 2¼ cups (9 ounces) cake flour
    1 cup (7 ounces) sugar
    1 tablespoon baking powder
    ¾ teaspoon table salt
   12 tablespoons unsalted butter, cut into 12 pieces and softened
    2 cups (6 ounces) sweetened shredded coconut

FROSTING
    4 large egg whites
    1 cup (7 ounces) sugar
      Pinch table salt
    1 pound (4 sticks) unsalted butter, each stick cut into 6 pieces and softened
    ¼ cup cream of coconut
    1 teaspoon coconut extract
    1 teaspoon vanilla extract

1. FOR THE CAKE: Adjust oven rack to lower-middle position and heat oven to 325 degrees. Grease two 9-inch round cake pans, line with parchment paper, grease parchment, and flour pans. Whisk egg and whites together in 4-cup liquid measuring cup. Whisk in cream of coconut, water, coconut extract, and vanilla.

2. Using stand mixer fitted with paddle, mix flour, sugar, baking powder, and salt on low speed until combined. Add butter, 1 piece at a time, until only pea-size pieces remain, about 1 minute. Add half of egg mixture, increase speed to medium-high, and beat until light and fluffy, about 1 minute. Reduce speed to medium-low, add remaining egg mixture, and beat until incorporated, about 30 seconds. Give batter final stir by hand.

3. Divide batter evenly between prepared pans and smooth tops with rubber spatula. Gently tap pans on counter to settle batter. Bake until toothpick inserted in center comes out clean, about 30 minutes, switching and rotating pans halfway through baking.

4. Let cakes cool in pans on wire rack for 10 minutes. Remove cakes from pans, discarding parchment, and let cool completely on rack, about 2 hours. (Cake layers can be stored at room temperature for up to 24 hours or frozen for up to 1 month; defrost cakes at room temperature.) Meanwhile, spread shredded coconut on rimmed baking sheet and toast in oven until shreds are mix of golden brown and white, 15 to 20 minutes, stirring 2 or 3 times; let cool.

5. FOR THE FROSTING: Combine egg whites, sugar, and salt in bowl of stand mixer and set over medium saucepan filled with 1 inch barely simmering water, making sure that water does not touch bottom of bowl. Cook, whisking constantly, until mixture is opaque and registers 120 degrees, about 2 minutes.

6. Remove bowl from heat and transfer to stand mixer fitted with whisk attachment. Whip egg white mixture on high speed until glossy, sticky, and barely warm (80 degrees), about 7 minutes. Reduce speed to medium-high and whip in butter, 1 piece at a time, followed by cream of coconut, coconut extract, and vanilla, scraping down bowl as needed. Continue to whip until combined, about 1 minute.

7. Using long serrated knife, cut 1 horizontal line around sides of each layer; then, following scored lines, cut each layer into 2 even layers.

8. Line edges of cake platter with 4 strips of parchment to keep platter clean. Place 1 cake layer on platter. Spread ¾ cup frosting evenly over top, right to edge of cake. Repeat with 2 more cake layers, pressing lightly to adhere and spreading ¾ cup frosting evenly over each layer. Top with remaining cake layer and spread remaining frosting evenly over top and sides of cake. Sprinkle top of cake evenly with toasted coconut, then gently press remaining toasted coconut onto sides. Carefully remove parchment strips before serving. (Cake can be refrigerated for up to 24 hours; bring to room temperature before serving.)

CRANBERRY-ORANGE OLIVE OIL CAKE

Serves 10 to 12 | three 9-inch round cake pans

WHY THIS RECIPE WORKS This elegant cake featuring layers of contrasting flavors—tart cranberry, fruity olive oil, and silky vanilla buttercream—brings the magic of a snowy evening to the dinner table. The jewel-like sugared cranberries and rosemary sprigs give it a wintry feel. For a supermoist cake full of citrusy flavor, we added orange zest and Grand Marnier to the batter and brushed the cake with a Grand Marnier soaking syrup. Cranberry curd made a fresh, bright filling that was creamy but firm enough to remain in a distinct layer in the cake. Instead of frosting the sides of our cake, we merely scraped them with a thin veil of our frosting so the lovely, sophisticated layers peeked through. You will need cake pans with at least 2-inch-tall sides for this recipe. For the best results, use a good-quality extra-virgin olive oil. You needn't thaw the cranberries before using them.

CRANBERRY CURD
- 12 ounces (3 cups) frozen cranberries
- 1 cup (7 ounces) granulated sugar
- 2 teaspoons grated orange zest plus ¼ cup juice
- ¼ teaspoon table salt
- 2 large eggs plus 2 large yolks
- 8 tablespoons unsalted butter, cut into ½-inch pieces and chilled

CAKE
- 2⅔ cups (13⅓ ounces) all-purpose flour
- 1½ teaspoons baking powder
- 1¼ teaspoons table salt
- 4 large eggs plus 1 large yolk
- 2 cups (14 ounces) plus 2 tablespoons granulated sugar, divided
- 1 tablespoon grated orange zest
- 1⅓ cups extra-virgin olive oil
- 1 cup plus 2 tablespoons milk
- ½ cup Grand Marnier or other orange liqueur, divided

GARNISH
- 1¾ cups (12¼ ounces) granulated sugar, divided
- 2 (3- to 4-inch-long) fresh rosemary sprigs
- 10 ounces (2½ cups) frozen cranberries

BUTTERCREAM
- 20 tablespoons (2½ sticks) unsalted butter, softened
- 2½ cups (10 ounces) confectioners' sugar
- ⅛ teaspoon table salt
- 2 tablespoons heavy cream
- 2 teaspoons vanilla extract

Cranberry-Orange Olive Oil Cake

1. FOR THE CRANBERRY CURD: Cook cranberries, sugar, orange zest and juice, and salt in medium saucepan over medium-low heat, mashing occasionally with potato masher, until cranberries have mostly broken down and mixture measures 1¼ cups, 10 to 12 minutes. Strain cranberry mixture through fine-mesh strainer into bowl, pressing on solids with rubber spatula to extract as much puree as possible. Discard solids.

2. Whisk eggs and yolks into cranberry mixture in bowl. Return mixture to saucepan and cook over medium-low heat, stirring constantly with rubber spatula, until mixture is thickened and registers 175 degrees in multiple spots, 5 to 7 minutes.

3. Off heat, stir in butter until incorporated. Transfer curd to bowl, press piece of plastic wrap directly onto surface of curd, and refrigerate for at least 3 hours. (Curd can be refrigerated for up to 3 days.)

4. FOR THE CAKE: Adjust oven rack to middle position and heat oven to 350 degrees. Grease three 9-inch round cake pans, line with parchment paper, grease parchment, and flour pans. Whisk flour, baking powder, and salt together in bowl.

5. Using stand mixer fitted with whisk attachment, whip eggs and yolk on medium speed until foamy, about 1 minute. Add 2 cups sugar and orange zest, increase speed to high, and whip until mixture is fluffy and pale yellow, about 3 minutes.

Cranberry-Orange Olive Oil Cake

This cake has a lot of delicious (and sparkling, festive) components. We break down how to build it so it's easy.

1. Bring 1 cup water and 1 cup granulated sugar to boil in medium saucepan over high heat; cook, stirring constantly, until sugar dissolves, about 3 minutes. Off heat, dip rosemary sprigs in sugar syrup, then roll in sugar in dish. Transfer to plate.

2. Stir cranberries into syrup and let syrup cool completely, about 30 minutes. Drain cranberries and, working in 3 batches, roll cranberries in sugar in dish and transfer to large plate. Let stand at room temperature to dry, about 1 hour.

3. Fill pastry bag fitted with ½-inch-wide straight tip with 1 cup buttercream. Using half of buttercream, pipe ½-inch-high ring of buttercream around top perimeter of cake layer. Spread half of cranberry curd evenly inside buttercream ring.

4. Place second cake layer on top, pressing lightly to adhere. Pipe another ring of buttercream around cake layer with buttercream left in bag. Spread remaining curd inside ring. Top with remaining cake layer, pressing lightly to adhere.

5. Spread ¾ cup buttercream evenly over top of cake. Spread remaining buttercream evenly over sides of cake to cover with thin coating. Run edge of offset spatula around cake sides to create sheer veil of buttercream so cake beneath is visible.

6. Sprinkle ½ cup cranberries around bottom of cake. Pile remaining cranberries on top of 1 side of cake in half-moon shape. Place rosemary sprigs at base of cranberries.

6. Reduce speed to medium and, with mixer running, slowly pour in oil. Mix until oil is fully incorporated, about 1 minute. Reduce speed to low, add half of flour mixture, and mix until incorporated, about 1 minute, scraping down bowl as needed. Add milk and ¼ cup Grand Marnier and mix until combined, about 30 seconds. Add remaining flour mixture and mix until just incorporated, about 1 minute.

7. Divide batter evenly among prepared pans and smooth tops with rubber spatula. Bake until cake is deep golden brown and toothpick inserted in center comes out with few crumbs attached, 40 to 45 minutes. Transfer pans to wire rack and let cool for 15 minutes. Loosen cakes from pans with paring knife, then invert onto greased wire rack and discard parchment. Invert cakes again and let cool completely on rack, about 1½ hours.

8. Bring ¼ cup water, remaining 2 tablespoons sugar, and remaining ¼ cup Grand Marnier to boil in small saucepan over medium heat; cook until sugar dissolves, about 3 minutes. Let cool completely, about 30 minutes. Once cooled, brush top and sides of cake layers with syrup.

9. FOR THE GARNISH: Place ¾ cup sugar in shallow dish; set aside. Bring 1 cup water and remaining 1 cup granulated sugar to boil in medium saucepan over high heat; cook, stirring constantly, until sugar dissolves, about 3 minutes. Off heat, dip rosemary sprigs in sugar syrup, then roll in sugar in dish. Transfer to plate.

10. Stir cranberries into syrup and let syrup cool completely, about 30 minutes. (Cranberries in syrup can be refrigerated for up to 24 hours.) Drain cranberries in fine-mesh strainer; discard syrup. Working in 3 batches, roll cranberries in sugar in dish and transfer to large plate. Let stand at room temperature to dry, about 1 hour.

11. FOR THE BUTTERCREAM: Using stand mixer fitted with whisk attachment, whip butter on medium-high speed until smooth, about 20 seconds. Add sugar and salt and mix on medium-low speed until most of sugar is moistened, about 45 seconds. Scrape down bowl. Add cream and vanilla and whip on medium-high speed until light and fluffy, about 4 minutes, scraping down bowl as needed.

12. Fill pastry bag fitted with a ½-inch-wide straight tip with 1 cup buttercream. Place 1 cake layer on cake turntable. Using half of buttercream, pipe ½-inch-high ring of buttercream around top perimeter of cake layer. Spread half of cranberry curd (about 1 scant cup) evenly inside buttercream ring.

13. Place second cake layer on top, pressing lightly to adhere. Pipe another ½-inch-high ring of buttercream around top perimeter of cake layer with remaining buttercream in pastry bag. Spread remaining cranberry curd evenly inside buttercream ring. Top with remaining cake layer, pressing lightly to adhere. Refrigerate to allow buttercream to firm up, about 30 minutes.

14. Spread ¾ cup buttercream evenly over top of cake. Spread remaining buttercream evenly over sides of cake to cover with thin coat of buttercream. Run edge of offset spatula around cake sides to create sheer veil of buttercream so cake beneath is visible. Sprinkle ½ cup cranberries around bottom of cake. Pile remaining cranberries on top of 1 side of cake in half-moon shape. Place rosemary sprigs at base of cranberries. Serve.

BLACKBERRY-MASCARPONE LEMON CAKE

Serves 12 to 16 | two 8-inch round cake pans

WHY THIS RECIPE WORKS This showstopping cake is strikingly beautiful, impressively tall, and features layers of contrasting flavors and textures: tart lemon, sweet blackberries, and a silky mascarpone whipped cream. Lemon chiffon cake was the perfect base; it has a light fluffy texture but enough structure to stand four layers tall. Replacing half of the mascarpone with tangy cream cheese helped stabilize the frosting and ensured a creamy texture. We whipped the two cheeses with sugar until just light and fluffy before folding in gelatin-enhanced whipped

Blackberry-Mascarpone Lemon Cake

cream for structure. The addition of a vibrant homemade blackberry jam to the frosting made it as beautiful as it was delicious. For a modern, elegant finish, we merely scraped the sides of the cake with a thin veil of our frosting so the lovely layers peeked through. Be sure to let the cake pans cool completely before repeating with more batter.

BLACKBERRY JAM

1 pound (3¼ cups) blackberries, plus extra for garnish
1 cup (7 ounces) granulated sugar

CAKE

2½ cups (10 ounces) cake flour, divided
2 cups (14 ounces) granulated sugar, divided
1 tablespoon baking powder, divided
½ teaspoon table salt, divided
10 large eggs (4 whole, 6 separated), room temperature, divided
12 tablespoons unsalted butter, melted and cooled, divided
¼ cup water, divided
2 teaspoons grated lemon zest plus ¼ cup juice (2 lemons), divided
4 teaspoons vanilla extract, divided

MASCARPONE FROSTING

1 teaspoon unflavored gelatin
2 tablespoons water
8 ounces (1 cup) mascarpone cheese, room temperature
8 ounces cream cheese, softened
¼ cup (1 ounce) confectioners' sugar
1 teaspoon vanilla extract
⅛ teaspoon table salt
2 cups heavy cream, chilled

1. FOR THE BLACKBERRY JAM: Process blackberries in food processor until smooth, about 1 minute; transfer to large saucepan. Stir sugar into blackberries and bring to boil over medium-high heat. Boil mixture, stirring often and adjusting heat as needed, until thickened and measures 1½ cups, 15 to 20 minutes. Transfer jam to bowl and let cool completely. (Jam can be refrigerated for up to 1 week; stir to loosen and bring to room temperature before using.)

2. FOR THE CAKE: Adjust oven rack to lower-middle position and heat oven to 325 degrees. Lightly grease two 8-inch round cake pans, line with parchment paper, grease parchment, and flour pans. Whisk 1¼ cups flour, ¾ cup sugar, 1½ teaspoons baking powder, and ¼ teaspoon salt together in large bowl. Whisk in 2 eggs and 3 yolks, 6 tablespoons melted butter, 2 tablespoons water, 1 teaspoon lemon zest and 2 tablespoons juice, and 2 teaspoons vanilla until smooth.

3. Using stand mixer fitted with whisk attachment, whip 3 egg whites on medium-low speed until foamy, about 1 minute. Increase speed to medium-high and whip whites to soft, billowy mounds, about 1 minute. Gradually add ¼ cup sugar and whip until glossy, soft peaks form, 1 to 2 minutes. Whisk one-third of whites into batter to lighten. Using rubber spatula, gently fold remaining whites into batter in 2 batches until no white streaks remain.

4. Divide batter evenly between prepared pans and smooth tops with rubber spatula. Bake until toothpick inserted in center comes out clean, 30 to 40 minutes, switching and rotating pans halfway through baking.

5. Let cakes cool in pans on wire rack for 10 minutes. Remove cakes from pans, discarding parchment, and let cool completely on rack, about 2 hours. Repeat steps 2 through 5 with remaining cake ingredients to make 2 more cake layers.

6. FOR THE MASCARPONE FROSTING: Sprinkle gelatin over water in bowl and let sit until gelatin softens, about 5 minutes. Microwave mixture in 5-second increments until gelatin is dissolved and liquefied.

7. Using clean, dry mixer bowl and whisk attachment, whip mascarpone, cream cheese, sugar, vanilla, and salt on medium speed until light and fluffy, about 30 seconds, scraping down bowl as needed; transfer to large bowl. Using clean, dry mixer bowl and whisk attachment, whip cream on medium-low speed until foamy, about 1 minute. Increase speed to high and whip until soft peaks just begin to form, about 1 minute, scraping down bowl as needed. Slowly pour in gelatin mixture, and continue to beat until stiff peaks form, about 1 minute. Using rubber spatula, stir one-third of whipped cream into mascarpone mixture to lighten; gently fold remaining whipped cream into mixture in 2 batches. Stir room-temperature blackberry jam to loosen, then gently fold jam into mascarpone mixture until combined. Refrigerate frosting for at least 20 minutes or up to 24 hours before using.

8. Line edges of cake platter with 4 strips of parchment to keep platter clean and place small dab of frosting in center of platter to anchor cake. Place 1 cake layer on platter. Spread 1 cup frosting evenly over top, right to edge of cake. Repeat with 2 more cake layers, pressing lightly to adhere and spreading 1 cup frosting evenly over each layer. Top with remaining cake layer and spread 1½ cups frosting evenly over top. Spread remaining frosting evenly over sides of cake to cover with thin coat of frosting. Run edge of offset spatula around cake sides to create sheer veil of frosting. (Cake sides should still be visible.) Refrigerate cake for 20 minutes. Garnish with blackberries and carefully remove parchment strips before serving. (Cake can be refrigerated for up to 24 hours; bring to room temperature before serving.)

SNACK CAKES

Use melted butter or oil

Stir together batter

Don't overbake

YOU DON'T NEED A SPECIAL OCCASION to make a snack cake: These one-layer, informal affairs are meant to be cut into squares and added to a lunchbox or enjoyed as an afternoon snack. They have a sturdy yet tender texture thanks to their stir-together simplicity; most use the quick-bread method of mixing in which the dry and wet ingredients are mixed separately and then combined—no mixers or food processors required. This technique doesn't introduce extra air into the batter and the result is a cake with a loose, rustic crumb. We frequently use oil or a combination of oil and butter for the fat, which ensures an incredibly moist cake (our Easy Chocolate Snack Cake on page 257 relies on mayonnaise for the oil). Most snack cakes need no adornment other than perhaps a simple dusting of confectioners' sugar or dollop of whipped cream. These cakes are appealingly easy, making them a great option for beginner bakers or for anyone wanting to enjoy a fuss-free treat on short notice.

APPLESAUCE SNACK CAKE

Serves 9 | 8-inch square baking pan

WHY THIS RECIPE WORKS Applesauce snack cake is generally a square cake with a loose, rustic crumb that might be enjoyed after school and is moist and tender; we wanted it to actually taste like apples. We used the simple quick-bread method, mixing the wet ingredients separately and then gently adding the dry ingredients by hand. More applesauce made for a gummy cake, and fresh apples added too much moisture. An apple cider reduction, however, contributed a pleasing sweetness and a slight tang without excess moisture. And dried apples—plumped in the cider—gave our cake even more apple flavor. This cake is very moist, so it's best to err on the side of overbaked when testing its doneness. We prefer the rich flavor of cider for this recipe, but apple juice can be substituted.

    1   cup apple cider
    ¾   cup dried apples, cut into ½-inch pieces
    1   cup unsweetened applesauce, room temperature
    ⅔   cup (4⅔ ounces) sugar
    ½   teaspoon ground cinnamon
    ¼   teaspoon ground nutmeg
    ⅛   teaspoon ground cloves
    1½ cups (7½ ounces) all-purpose flour
    1   teaspoon baking soda
    1   large egg, room temperature
    ½   teaspoon table salt
    8   tablespoons unsalted butter, melted and cooled
    1   teaspoon vanilla extract

1. Adjust oven rack to middle position and heat oven to 325 degrees. Make foil sling for 8-inch square baking pan by folding 2 long sheets of aluminum foil so each is 8 inches wide. Lay sheets of foil in pan perpendicular to each other, with extra foil hanging over edges of pan. Push foil into corners and up sides of pan, smoothing foil flush to pan.

2. Combine cider and dried apples in small saucepan and simmer over medium heat until liquid evaporates and mixture appears dry, about 15 minutes. Let mixture cool completely, then process with applesauce in food processor until smooth, 20 to 30 seconds.

3. Whisk sugar, cinnamon, nutmeg, and cloves together in bowl; set aside 2 tablespoons mixture for topping. Whisk flour and baking soda together in second bowl.

4. Whisk egg and salt together in large bowl. Whisk in sugar mixture until well combined and light-colored, about 20 seconds. Whisk in melted butter in 3 additions, whisking after each addition until incorporated. Whisk in applesauce mixture and vanilla. Using rubber spatula, fold in flour mixture until just combined.

5. Transfer batter to prepared pan and smooth top with rubber spatula. Gently tap pan on counter to settle batter. Sprinkle reserved sugar mixture evenly over top. Bake until toothpick inserted in center comes out clean, 35 to 40 minutes, rotating pan halfway through baking. Let cake cool completely in pan on wire rack, 1 to 2 hours. Using foil overhang, lift cake from pan. Serve. (Cake can be stored at room temperature for up to 2 days.)

Applesauce Snack Cake with Oat-Nut Streusel
Add 2 tablespoons brown sugar, ⅓ cup chopped pecans or walnuts, and ⅓ cup old-fashioned rolled oats or quick oats to sugar mixture set aside for topping, then add 2 tablespoons softened unsalted butter and pinch with your fingers to incorporate and form mixture into hazelnut-size clumps.

Ginger-Cardamom Applesauce Snack Cake
Substitute ½ teaspoon ground ginger and ¼ teaspoon ground cardamom for cinnamon, nutmeg, and cloves. Add 1 tablespoon finely chopped crystallized ginger to sugar mixture set aside for topping.

Applesauce Snack Cake

PUMPKIN-CHOCOLATE SNACK CAKE

Serves 16 | 8-inch square baking pan

WHY THIS RECIPE WORKS Sweet pumpkin puree incorporated into a basic snack cake batter results in a moist and flavorful snack cake that can be whipped up in under an hour. Using the quick-bread method, we stirred together the dry and wet ingredients separately before mixing the two together until just combined. This helped avoid an overmixed, tough cake. Pumpkin pie spice added warm autumnal flavor, and mini chocolate chips punctuated each bite with pops of melty richness. We prefer mini chocolate chips here, but you can substitute standard-size semisweet chocolate chips, if desired. One 15-ounce can of pumpkin puree is more than enough for this recipe. You can transfer the leftover pumpkin to a zipper-lock bag and freeze it for up to a month.

1 cup (5 ounces) all-purpose flour
1 tablespoon pumpkin pie spice
1 teaspoon baking powder
½ teaspoon baking soda
¼ teaspoon table salt
1 cup canned unsweetened pumpkin puree
1 cup (7 ounces) sugar
½ cup vegetable oil
2 large eggs
½ cup (3 ounces) mini semisweet chocolate chips

1. Adjust oven rack to middle position and heat oven to 350 degrees. Grease and flour 8-inch square baking pan. Whisk flour, pumpkin pie spice, baking powder, baking soda, and salt together in large bowl. Whisk pumpkin, sugar, oil, and eggs together in second bowl.

2. Stir pumpkin mixture into flour mixture until just combined. Stir in chocolate chips until just incorporated. Transfer batter to prepared pan and smooth top with rubber spatula. Bake until paring knife inserted in center comes out clean, about 35 minutes.

3. Let cake cool in pan on wire rack for 20 minutes. Remove cake from pan and let cool completely on rack, about 1 hour. Serve. (Cake can be stored at room temperature for up to 2 days.)

Pumpkin-Chocolate Snack Cake

CLASSIC GINGERBREAD CAKE

Serves 16 | 8-inch square baking pan

WHY THIS RECIPE WORKS Gingerbread cake should be moist and spicy through and through. Ground ginger and grated fresh ginger, with additional heat from cinnamon and black pepper, ensured our gingerbread tasted like ginger. Dark stout added bittersweet flavor, and replacing butter with vegetable oil allowed the ginger flavor to shine. To keep our gingerbread from sinking in the middle—a problem with most recipes—we incorporated the baking soda with the wet ingredients and vigorously mixed some of the batter to strengthen it. If you're sensitive to spice, decrease the amount of ground ginger to 1 tablespoon. Guinness Draught is our favorite stout. Serve the gingerbread plain or with Whipped Cream (page 548).

¾ cup stout
½ teaspoon baking soda
¾ cup packed (5¼ ounces) light brown sugar
⅔ cup molasses
¼ cup (1¾ ounces) granulated sugar
1½ cups (7½ ounces) all-purpose flour
2 tablespoons ground ginger
½ teaspoon baking powder
½ teaspoon table salt
¼ teaspoon ground cinnamon
¼ teaspoon pepper
2 large eggs
⅓ cup vegetable oil
1 tablespoon finely grated fresh ginger

1. Adjust oven rack to middle position and heat oven to 350 degrees. Grease and flour 8-inch square baking pan.

2. Bring stout to boil in medium saucepan over medium heat, stirring occasionally. Off heat, stir in baking soda (mixture will foam vigorously). When foaming subsides, stir in brown sugar, molasses, and granulated sugar until dissolved; set aside. Whisk flour, ground ginger, baking powder, salt, cinnamon, and pepper together in large bowl; set aside.

3. Transfer stout mixture to second large bowl. Whisk in eggs, oil, and fresh ginger until combined. Whisk stout-egg mixture into flour mixture in 3 additions, stirring vigorously until completely smooth after each addition.

4. Transfer batter to prepared pan and gently tap on counter to release air bubbles. Bake until top of cake is just firm to touch and toothpick inserted in center comes out clean, 35 to 45 minutes, rotating pan halfway through baking. Let cake cool in pan on wire rack, about 1½ hours. Cut into 2-inch squares and serve warm or at room temperature. (Leftover cake can be wrapped in plastic wrap and stored at room temperature for up to 2 days.)

EASY CHOCOLATE SNACK CAKE

Serves 9 | 8-inch square baking pan

WHY THIS RECIPE WORKS We wanted a simple-to-make chocolate cake that would please all ages and palates with an undeniable but not overly rich chocolate presence perfect for snacking. Blooming unsweetened cocoa powder in coffee intensified its flavor, and we supplemented the cocoa with a small amount of bittersweet chocolate. Many recipes for chocolate snack cake call for mayonnaise only—no additional eggs—for richness and moisture. We liked a cake made with mayo, but we found that also adding an egg to the batter gave it moisture, as well as a pleasantly springy texture that we loved. If you want to take the cake out of the pan, grease the pan, line with parchment paper, grease the parchment, and then flour the pan. We like to dust this simple all-purpose cake with confectioners' sugar, but it can also be served plain or dressed up for dessert with Whipped Cream (page 548).

1½ cups (7½ ounces) all-purpose flour
1 cup (7 ounces) sugar
½ teaspoon baking soda
¼ teaspoon table salt
⅔ cup mayonnaise
1 large egg
2 teaspoons vanilla extract
½ cup (1½ ounces) Dutch-processed cocoa powder
2 ounces bittersweet chocolate, chopped fine
1 cup hot brewed coffee
Confectioners' sugar (optional)

1. Adjust oven rack to middle position and heat oven to 350 degrees. Grease and flour 8-inch square baking pan. Whisk flour, sugar, baking soda, and salt together in large bowl. Whisk mayonnaise, egg, and vanilla together in second bowl.

2. Combine cocoa and chocolate in third bowl, pour hot coffee over top, and whisk until smooth; let cool slightly. Whisk in mayonnaise mixture until combined. Stir chocolate mixture into flour mixture until combined.

3. Transfer batter to prepared pan and smooth top with rubber spatula. Gently tap pan on counter to settle batter. Bake until toothpick inserted in center comes out with few crumbs attached, 30 to 35 minutes, rotating pan halfway through baking. Let cake cool completely in pan on wire rack, 1 to 2 hours. Dust with confectioners' sugar, if using, before serving.

SHEET CAKES

NOT EVERY OCCASION CALLS FOR A LAYERED AFFAIR.
Classic sheet cakes, baked in a large rectangular pan and then frosted, are impressive in scale yet simpler in construction than their layered counterparts. Sheet cakes serve a crowd, making them an ideal choice for birthday parties, potlucks, and cookouts. These cakes can be served straight from the pan or turned out and frosted on all sides for a more finished look, and their generous surface area is ideal for decorating or crafting a celebratory message (see page 260 for information on writing with icing). These are all favorites, from yellow and chocolate varieties sure to please kids of all ages to milky, caramelly Tres Leches Cake (page 264).

KEY POINTS

Don't underbake

Cool cake completely in pan

Take care when slicing in metal pan

DETERMINING DONENESS

The toothpick test is the gold standard for determining the doneness of most cakes, and sheet cakes are no different. However, with sheet cakes it's important to also use any other cues given in the recipe; because of the cake's large surface area, it may take a few tests to determine doneness. Use the baking times as a guide and refer to visual cues to determine doneness. A toothpick inserted in the center of the cake should come out with a few crumbs attached (unless otherwise stated in the recipe), and the cake should spring back when pressed lightly.

Underdone Cake

Perfectly Baked Cake

REMOVING A SHEET CAKE FROM THE PAN

Sheet cakes are all about ease, so most of the time we simply frost them and then serve them right from the pan. But some situations call for a more elegant presentation, in which case you may want to turn out the cake. Because of its large surface area, removing a sheet cake from the pan isn't as easy as removing a round cake layer. Below are our tricks. (Make sure to line the bottom of the pan with parchment in addition to greasing and flouring it if you choose to remove the cake from the pan.)

1. Run paring knife around edge of cooled cake to loosen it. (Be careful not to scratch bottom of baking pan.)

2. Gently flip cake out of pan onto wire rack.

3. Peel parchment paper off bottom of cake and invert large platter over cake.

4. Holding both rack and platter firmly, gently flip cake right side up onto the platter.

Writing On a Cake

Writing a festive message on a sheet cake is easy because there's a lot of space to work with. Here are a few tricks. First, skip the writing glazes and gels at the supermarket. We tested those that are sold in small tubes and those sold in aerosol cans, but we found both were awkward to use and neither tasted very good. (In addition, the glazes often didn't set up well.) Instead, make your own simple icing for writing (recipe follows).

To write out your message, first make sure the top of the cake is level and evenly frosted. Use a very small pastry bag fitted with a round tip, which allows for sure control. Before writing on the cake, practice on a piece of parchment paper (roughly the same size as the cake) to get yourself accustomed to the icing, the size and style of your letters, and the overall spacing of your message. You can use your free hand to steady your writing hand for a smooth, even script.

ICING FOR WRITING
Makes about ⅔ cup

This recipe makes plenty of icing for both practice and the actual cake. If you find the icing stiff and difficult to pipe, return it to the bowl and add additional water, a little at a time, to loosen. If the icing is too thin and runny, return it to the bowl and add more confectioners' sugar, a little at a time, to stiffen.

1½ cups (6 ounces) confectioners' sugar
 2 tablespoons unsalted butter, melted and cooled
    Water, as needed
    Food coloring (optional)

1. Mix sugar, melted butter, and 1 tablespoon water in small bowl with rubber spatula to make smooth paste. Add more water, 1 teaspoon at a time, until icing is very smooth and creamy (similar to room-temperature peanut butter).

2. Stir in drops of food coloring, if using, 1 drop at a time, until you achieve desired color. (Icing can be stored in piping bag at room temperature for up to 3 hours. For longer storage, refrigerate icing in covered container for up to 3 days.)

Chocolate Icing for Writing

Whisk 2 tablespoons unsweetened cocoa powder into sugar before adding butter. Add 2 tablespoons water with butter, then continue to add water as needed to adjust icing's consistency.

YELLOW SHEET CAKE

Serves 12 to 15 | 13 by 9-inch baking pan

WHY THIS RECIPE WORKS For a tender cake with a fine, plush texture, we started by using bleached cake flour. Its altered starch is more absorbent than the starch in unbleached flour, so it can accommodate more liquid, sugar, and fat (we use butter for flavor and vegetable oil for moistness) without collapsing under the extra weight. Reverse creaming incorporated only a small amount of air, resulting in a superfine texture. Use a metal baking pan for this recipe; a glass baking dish will cause the edges of the cake to overbake as it cools. It's important to use bleached cake flour here; substituting unbleached cake flour or a combination of all-purpose flour and cornstarch will cause the cake to fall. To ensure the proper texture, weigh the flour.

    4 large eggs plus 2 large yolks
   ½ cup buttermilk
    1 tablespoon vanilla extract
2¼ cups (9 ounces) bleached cake flour
1¾ cups (12¼ ounces) sugar
1¼ teaspoons baking powder
   ¼ teaspoon baking soda
   ½ teaspoon table salt
    8 tablespoons unsalted butter, softened
   ½ cup vegetable oil
    3 cups Chocolate Frosting (page 241)

1. Adjust oven rack to middle position and heat oven to 350 degrees. Grease and flour 13 by 9-inch baking pan. Combine eggs and yolks, buttermilk, and vanilla in 2-cup liquid measuring cup and whisk with fork until smooth.

2. Combine flour, sugar, baking powder, baking soda, and salt in bowl of stand mixer fitted with paddle. Mix on low speed until combined, about 20 seconds. Add butter and oil and mix on low speed until combined, about 30 seconds. Increase speed to medium and beat until lightened, about 1 minute. Reduce speed to low and, with mixer running, slowly add egg mixture. When mixture is fully incorporated, stop mixer and scrape down bowl and paddle thoroughly. Beat on medium-high speed until batter is pale, smooth, and thick, about 3 minutes. Transfer batter to prepared pan and smooth top. Tap pan firmly on counter 5 times to release any large air bubbles.

3. Bake until toothpick inserted in center comes out with few crumbs attached, 28 to 32 minutes. Let cake cool completely in pan on wire rack, about 2 hours. Frost cake. Refrigerate until frosting is set, about 20 minutes, before serving.

Yellow Sheet Cake

CHOCOLATE SHEET CAKE

Serves 12 to 15 | 13 by 9-inch baking pan

WHY THIS RECIPE WORKS For a chocolate sheet cake that boasted deep chocolate flavor and color, we used a combination of Dutch-processed cocoa and melted bittersweet chocolate; the cocoa offered pure, assertive chocolate flavor while the bittersweet chocolate contributed complexity as well as the right amount of fat and sugar. We knew we wanted a milk chocolate ganache frosting to offset the intense flavor of the cake; to make our ganache thicker, richer, and creamier than the norm, we added plenty of softened butter to the warm chocolate-cream mixture. Once the frosting was assembled, we refrigerated it to cool it quickly so that it would spread nicely, and then gave it a quick whisk to smooth it out and lighten its texture. Do not substitute natural cocoa powder for the Dutch-processed cocoa powder. If you want to take the cake out of the pan, grease the pan, line with parchment paper, grease the parchment, and then flour the pan.

Chocolate Sheet Cake

CAKE

1½ cups (10½ ounces) sugar
1¼ cups (6¼ ounces) all-purpose flour
½ teaspoon baking soda
½ teaspoon table salt
1 cup whole milk
8 ounces bittersweet chocolate, chopped fine
¾ cup (2¼ ounces) Dutch-processed cocoa powder
⅔ cup vegetable oil
4 large eggs
1 teaspoon vanilla extract

FROSTING

1 pound milk chocolate, chopped
⅔ cup heavy cream
16 tablespoons unsalted butter, cut into 16 pieces and softened

1. FOR THE CAKE: Adjust oven rack to middle position and heat oven to 325 degrees. Grease 13 by 9-inch baking pan. Whisk sugar, flour, baking soda, and salt together in bowl; set aside.

2. Combine milk, chocolate, and cocoa in large saucepan. Place saucepan over low heat and cook, whisking frequently, until chocolate is melted and mixture is smooth. Remove from heat and let cool slightly, about 5 minutes. Whisk oil, eggs, and vanilla into chocolate mixture (mixture may initially look curdled) until smooth and homogeneous. Add sugar mixture and whisk until combined, making sure to scrape corners of saucepan.

3. Transfer batter to prepared pan. Bake until firm in center when lightly pressed and toothpick inserted in center comes out with few crumbs attached, 30 to 35 minutes, rotating pan halfway through baking. Let cake cool completely in pan on wire rack, 1 to 2 hours.

4. FOR THE FROSTING: While cake is baking, combine chocolate and cream in large heatproof bowl set over saucepan filled with 1 inch barely simmering water, making sure that water does not touch bottom of bowl. Whisk mixture occasionally until chocolate is uniformly smooth and glossy, 10 to 15 minutes. Remove bowl from saucepan. Add butter, whisking once or twice to break up pieces. Let mixture stand for 5 minutes to finish melting butter, then whisk until completely smooth. Refrigerate frosting, without stirring, until cooled and thickened, 30 minutes to 1 hour.

5. Once cool, whisk frosting until smooth. (Whisked frosting will lighten in color slightly and should hold its shape on whisk.) Spread frosting evenly over top of cake. Serve. (Leftover cake can be refrigerated for up to 2 days.)

CARROT SHEET CAKE

Serves 12 to 15 | 13 by 9-inch baking pan

WHY THIS RECIPE WORKS We wanted an incredibly tasty carrot cake that was easier, faster, and more moist than ever. Shredding the carrots and making the cream cheese frosting in a food processor made quick work of these otherwise tedious steps. A couple of easy but uncommon techniques ensured an ultramoist and superflavorful cake. First, we plumped and softened golden raisins in fragrant orange juice before stirring them into the batter. Then, we soaked the still-hot, just-baked cake in a stir-together buttermilk syrup, both moistening the cake and layering in brightness that balanced the sweetness of the cake while enhancing the tanginess of the cream cheese frosting. Shred the carrots in a food processor fitted with the shredding disk or on the large holes of a box grater. One pound of carrots is about six medium carrots and will yield about 12 ounces of shredded carrots after peeling and trimming.

Carrot Sheet Cake

CAKE

- 1 cup golden raisins
- ¼ cup orange juice
- 2½ cups (12½ ounces) all-purpose flour
- 1 tablespoon pumpkin pie spice
- 2 teaspoons baking powder
- 1 teaspoon baking soda
- ¾ teaspoon table salt
- 1½ cups packed (10½ ounces) light brown sugar
- 1¼ cups vegetable oil
- 4 large eggs
- 1 tablespoon vanilla extract
- 1 pound carrots, peeled and shredded (3 cups)
- 1 cup (4 ounces) confectioners' sugar
- ⅔ cup buttermilk

FROSTING

- 12 ounces cream cheese, softened
- 2 cups (8 ounces) confectioners' sugar
- 8 tablespoons unsalted butter, softened
- 1 teaspoon vanilla extract
- ⅛ teaspoon table salt
- 1 cup pecans, toasted and chopped (optional)

1. FOR THE CAKE: Adjust oven rack to middle position and heat oven to 350 degrees. Grease 13 by 9-inch baking pan. Combine raisins and orange juice in small bowl. Microwave, covered, until hot, about 1 minute. Let stand, covered, until raisins are soft, about 5 minutes.

2. Whisk flour, pumpkin pie spice, baking powder, baking soda, and salt together in medium bowl; set aside. Whisk brown sugar, oil, eggs, and vanilla in large bowl until smooth; stir in carrots and raisin mixture. Stir in flour mixture with rubber spatula until just combined.

3. Transfer batter to prepared pan and smooth top with rubber spatula. Bake until toothpick inserted in center of cake comes out clean, 33 to 38 minutes, rotating pan halfway through baking. Transfer pan to wire rack.

4. Immediately whisk confectioners' sugar and buttermilk together until smooth. Brush buttermilk syrup evenly over entire surface of hot cake (use all of syrup). Let cake cool completely in pan on wire rack, about 3 hours.

5. FOR THE FROSTING: Process cream cheese, sugar, butter, vanilla, and salt in food processor until smooth, about 30 seconds, scraping down sides of bowl with rubber spatula as needed. Spread frosting evenly over surface of cake, leaving ½-inch border. Sprinkle frosting evenly with pecans, if using. Serve. (Cake can be refrigerated for up to 2 days.)

Carrot-Ginger Sheet Cake with Cardamom

Substitute 1 teaspoon ground cinnamon and 1 teaspoon ground cardamom for pumpkin pie spice. Stir in 1½ tablespoons grated fresh ginger with carrots and raisin mixture in step 2. Sprinkle 2 tablespoons finely chopped crystallized ginger over top of frosted cake with pecans in step 5.

Tres Leches Cake

TRES LECHES CAKE

Serves 12 to 15 | 13 by 9-inch baking pan

WHY THIS RECIPE WORKS Tres leches is a light, sweet sponge cake soaked with a mixture of "three milks" (heavy cream, evaporated milk, and sweetened condensed milk). Making a great one requires a careful balancing act: The cake should be moist, but not mushy, and the clean dairy flavor of the milks should be clear and sweet, but not sickeningly so. For a sponge cake that would be sturdy enough to hold up to the milk mixture, we used whipped whole eggs instead of the usual egg whites. Although some recipes use equal amounts of each milk for the soak, we found that cutting back on the cream produced a thicker mixture that didn't oversaturate the cake. Cooking the condensed milk in the microwave until it was thickened and straw-colored before mixing it with the other milks gave each bite of cake a hint of caramel flavor. The cake is best frosted with its fluffy whipped topping just before serving.

MILK MIXTURE
- 1 (14-ounce) can sweetened condensed milk
- 1 (12-ounce) can evaporated milk
- 1 cup heavy cream
- 1 teaspoon vanilla extract

CAKE
- 2 cups (10 ounces) all-purpose flour
- 2 teaspoons baking powder
- 1 teaspoon table salt
- ½ teaspoon ground cinnamon
- 8 tablespoons unsalted butter
- 1 cup whole milk
- 4 large eggs, room temperature
- 2 cups (14 ounces) sugar
- 2 teaspoons vanilla extract

TOPPING
- 1 cup heavy cream
- 3 tablespoons corn syrup
- 1 teaspoon vanilla extract

1. FOR THE MILK MIXTURE: Pour condensed milk into large bowl. Microwave, covered, at 10 percent power, stirring every 3 to 5 minutes until milk is slightly darkened and thickened, 9 to 15 minutes. Slowly whisk in evaporated milk, cream, and vanilla until incorporated. Let mixture cool completely.

2. FOR THE CAKE: Adjust oven rack to middle position and heat oven to 325 degrees. Grease and flour 13 by 9-inch baking pan. Whisk flour, baking powder, salt, and cinnamon together in bowl. Heat butter and milk in small saucepan over low heat until butter is melted; remove from heat and set aside.

Texas Sheet Cake

3. Using stand mixer fitted with whisk attachment, whip eggs on medium speed until foamy, about 30 seconds. Slowly add sugar and continue to whip until fully incorporated, 5 to 10 seconds. Increase speed to medium-high and whip until mixture is thick and glossy, 5 to 7 minutes. Reduce speed to low, add butter mixture and vanilla, and mix until combined, about 15 seconds. Add flour mixture in 3 additions, mixing on medium speed after each addition and scraping down bowl as needed, until flour is fully incorporated, about 30 seconds. Transfer batter to prepared pan. Bake until toothpick inserted in center comes out clean, 30 to 35 minutes, rotating pan halfway through baking. Let cake cool in pan on wire rack for 10 minutes.

4. Using skewer, poke holes at ½-inch intervals in top of cake. Slowly pour milk mixture over cake. Let sit at room temperature for 15 minutes, then refrigerate, uncovered, for at least 3 hours or up to 24 hours.

5. FOR THE TOPPING: Thirty minutes before serving, remove cake from refrigerator. Using stand mixer fitted with whisk attachment, whip cream, corn syrup, and vanilla on medium-low speed until foamy, about 1 minute. Increase speed to high and whip until soft peaks form, 1 to 3 minutes. Spread topping evenly over top of cake. Serve.

TEXAS SHEET CAKE

Serves 12 to 15 | **rimmed baking sheet**

WHY THIS RECIPE WORKS Texas sheet cake is no ordinary sheet cake: It's a sheet pan–size, pecan-topped chocolate cake with three distinct layers of chocolaty goodness. A diverse range of textures is created when the chocolate icing is poured over the hot cake. Once the cake has cooled, there's a fudgy middle layer where the icing and hot cake have melded. For the cake, a combination of butter and vegetable oil produced a dense, brownie-like texture, while cocoa powder and melted semisweet chocolate yielded a cake that was ultrachocolaty yet still moist and dense. The icing was the final element, and getting its texture right was key—replacing milk with heavy cream gave it more body, while adding corn syrup produced a lustrous finish. For the signature fudge-like layer between the icing and cake, we spread the warm icing over the cake straight out of the oven and let it soak into the hot cake.

CAKE
  2 cups (10 ounces) all-purpose flour
  2 cups (14 ounces) granulated sugar
  ½ teaspoon baking soda
  ½ teaspoon table salt
  2 large eggs plus 2 large yolks
  ¼ cup sour cream
  2 teaspoons vanilla extract
  8 ounces semisweet chocolate, chopped
  ¾ cup vegetable oil
  ¾ cup water
  ½ cup (1½ ounces) unsweetened cocoa powder
  4 tablespoons unsalted butter

ICING
  8 tablespoons unsalted butter
  ½ cup heavy cream
  ½ cup (1½ ounces) unsweetened cocoa powder
  1 tablespoon light corn syrup
  3 cups (12 ounces) confectioners' sugar
  1 tablespoon vanilla extract
  1 cup pecans, toasted and chopped

1. FOR THE CAKE: Adjust oven rack to middle position and heat oven to 350 degrees. Grease 18 by 13-inch rimmed baking sheet. Whisk flour, sugar, baking soda, and salt together in large bowl. Whisk eggs and yolks, sour cream, and vanilla in second bowl until smooth.

2. Heat chocolate, oil, water, cocoa, and butter in large saucepan over medium heat, stirring occasionally, until smooth, 3 to 5 minutes. Whisk chocolate mixture into flour mixture until incorporated. Whisk egg mixture into batter. Transfer batter to prepared sheet. Bake until toothpick inserted in center comes out clean, 18 to 20 minutes, rotating sheet halfway through baking. Transfer sheet to wire rack.

3. FOR THE ICING: About 5 minutes before cake is done baking, heat butter, cream, cocoa, and corn syrup in large saucepan over medium heat, stirring occasionally, until smooth, about 4 minutes. Off heat, whisk in sugar and vanilla. Spread warm icing evenly over hot cake and sprinkle with pecans. Let cake cool completely in pan on wire rack, about 1 hour, then refrigerate until icing is set, about 1 hour longer. Serve.

CUPCAKES

KEY POINTS

Evenly divide batter among
muffin cups

Cool cupcakes in tins for 10 minutes,
then finish cooling on wire rack

Let cool completely before frosting

SOME THINGS ARE BETTER when you don't have to share,
including (or especially!) dessert. The cupcake concept—a
dainty, portion-controlled, out-of-hand snack universally
recognized from childhood birthday parties—is an answer to
that. Culinary historians argue about the word "cupcake." Some
think it comes from a centuries-old practice of baking individual
little cakes in teacups, while others believe the word refers to
the late 19th-century shift in American kitchens from measuring
by weight to measuring by cups. Whatever the word's linguistic
journey, we love cupcakes in any form. While the most celebratory
versions may be crowned with frosting and sprinkles, other
individual little cakes—such as French Financiers on page 275—
are more refined, and their simplicity allows the nuances of
flavor and texture to shine. But if cupcake appeal is all about
getting the best attributes of cake in a portable package, the
irony is that most (even those from highly specialized bakeries)
can't deliver the goods. That's because cupcakes aren't always
simply pint-size versions of their larger cake counterparts; the
tender crumb of a cake that's ideal when eaten with a fork may
become a crumbly mess when eaten out of hand. Determining
the proper ratio of ingredients and mixing method are key to
creating a cupcake with the right structure.

PORTIONING BATTER

Spring-loaded ice cream scoops aren't our favorite for ice cream, but we found a better use for them: portioning cupcake batter. Our foolproof way for filling muffin tins is to portion ⅓ cup of the batter into each cup and then circle back and evenly add the remaining batter with a spoon. A #12 ice cream scoop (which holds ⅓ cup batter) makes it easy to portion batter without making a mess around the edges of the pan. Spray the scoop with vegetable oil spray so the batter slides off.

CUPCAKES TO GO

Toting a single cupcake for a take-along snack sounds like a good idea—until you're faced with squished cake and frosting. To safely transport a cupcake, lay the lid of a clean pint-size deli container upside down and place your cupcake on it. Invert the container, slip it over the cupcake and down onto the lid, and seal it shut, thus creating a safe shell around the cupcake.

Frosted

Frosted cupcakes are a birthday party staple. But all too often, the cake part of a cupcake seems like an afterthought—nothing more than a vehicle for mounds of frosting. The cupcake itself should be able to stand on its own, with a moist, tender (but not crumbly) crumb that appeals to kids and adults alike. Just the right amount of creamy, not-too-sweet frosting offers the perfect contrast to the tender cake.

Decorating Cupcakes

There are countless ways to decorate a cupcake. We simply spread cupcakes with frosting for an easy and classically elegant look. For a fancier display, we pipe frosting with a pastry bag fitted with a large star tip to create intricate swirls.

FLAT TOP WITH COATED SIDES

1. Place 2 to 3 tablespoons of frosting on each cupcake, forming thick layer. Using small offset spatula, spread to create a flat top.

2. Using spatula, smooth frosting so it's flush with edges of cupcake. Reflatten top as necessary.

3. Place topping such as chopped nuts on plate. Holding cupcake at its base, gently roll outer edges of frosting in topping.

PIPED AND TOPPED

1. Place frosting in pastry bag fitted with ½-inch plain or star tip. Starting at outside edge and working inward, pipe frosting into spiral.

2. Sprinkle lightly with topping, if desired.

MAKING CUPCAKES SPARKLE

When you want to add your own special touch to freshly frosted cupcakes, you can draw designs (see our recipe for Icing for Writing on page 260), but there's another way to give your cupcakes flair. Try this easy method for creating fun sprinkle shapes.

Press a simply shaped cookie cutter into smooth frosting on a cupcake. Using the cookie cutter outline as a guide, fill the shape with sprinkles, colored sugar, or another confection of a contrasting color. Carefully remove the cookie cutter, leaving behind a festive decoration.

Filled

At first glance, these cupcakes may be indistinguishable from classic frosted versions. But one bite and you're sure to be pleasantly surprised at the rich, creamy filling within. Whether it's rich pastry cream, gooey salted caramel, or a decadent chocolate ganache, it's important that the cupcake have enough structure to support the filling. Even so, we have found that injecting it into the cupcake results in a crumbly mess. A much better approach is to cut a cone out of the top, spoon the filling in, and then replace the top before frosting the cupcake as usual.

FILLING CUPCAKES

1. Insert tip of paring knife at 45-degree angle about ¼ inch from edge of cupcake and cut cone from top of cupcake.

2. Slice off all but top ¼ inch from each cone, leaving small disk of cake.

3. Place 2 tablespoons filling inside each cupcake and place tops on filling.

Tea Cakes

Tea cakes are just what their name implies: Without a thick coating of frosting or a rich, decadent filling, these individual cakes are ideal as a sweet treat with a cup of afternoon tea or coffee. They come together quickly, and while some are drizzled with a delicate glaze, others call for no adornment at all. The relative simplicity of these cakes allows the contrast between tender, buttery, chewy interior and fine, crisp exterior to take center stage. Note that for some tea cakes (such as Financiers on page 275) you'll need a mini muffin tin—the petite size of these two-bite cakes offers the perfect ratio of crisp crust to chewy crumb.

Mug Cakes

Cupcakes that are actually prepared in a cup—or mug, to be specific—are perhaps the easiest cakes of all. "Baked" in the microwave, mug cakes offer a near-instant dessert for two that you can enjoy whenever the mood strikes. Because they come together so quickly, paying attention to the details is key. Using a moderate amount of fat helps prevent too much steam from causing excessive rise—and overflow—while operating at 50 percent power slows the cooking process so that the gluten develops more slowly, resulting in cakes that are tender and light. We developed our recipes in a full-size, 1200-watt microwave. If you're using a compact microwave with 800 watts or fewer, increase the cooking time to 90 seconds for each interval. For either size microwave, reset to 50 percent power at each stage of cooking. Use a mug that holds at least 12 ounces, or the batter will overflow.

YELLOW CUPCAKES

Makes 12 cupcakes | muffin tin

WHY THIS RECIPE WORKS We wanted a rich and tender yellow cupcake that would be delicious on its own merit without needing to hide under a mound of frosting. We started with a simple ingredient list: all-purpose flour (cake flour produced too fine a crumb), a combination of a whole egg and two yolks (fewer whites meant richer flavor), sugar, butter, and sour cream (for tangy richness). Surprisingly, the easiest mixing technique—simply throwing everything into the mixer together—gave us the best cupcakes of the bunch. Why? One possible answer is that egg yolks contain emulsifiers, and with three in this recipe, there was enough to hold the fat and liquid together even when mixed in such a haphazard fashion. The cupcakes that emerged from the oven were buttery, tender, and lightly golden.

Strawberry Cupcakes

1½ cups (7½ ounces) all-purpose flour
 1 cup (7 ounces) sugar
1½ teaspoons baking powder
 ½ teaspoon table salt
 8 tablespoons unsalted butter,
    cut into 8 pieces and softened
 ½ cup sour cream
 1 large egg plus 2 large yolks
1½ teaspoons vanilla extract
 3 cups Vanilla Buttercream (page 245)

1. Adjust oven rack to middle position and heat oven to 350 degrees. Line 12-cup muffin tin with paper or foil liners.

2. Using stand mixer fitted with paddle, mix flour, sugar, baking powder, and salt on low speed until combined. Increase speed to medium, add butter, sour cream, egg and yolks, and vanilla, and beat until smooth and satiny, about 30 seconds. Scrape down bowl with rubber spatula and stir by hand until smooth and no flour pockets remain.

3. Divide batter evenly among prepared muffin cups. Bake until tops are light golden and toothpick inserted in center comes out clean, 20 to 24 minutes, rotating muffin tin halfway through baking.

4. Let cupcakes cool in muffin tin on wire rack for 15 minutes. Remove cupcakes from muffin tin and let cool completely on rack, about 30 minutes. (Unfrosted cupcakes can be stored at room temperature for up to 24 hours.) Spread or pipe frosting evenly on cupcakes. Serve.

STRAWBERRY CUPCAKES

Makes 12 cupcakes | muffin tin

WHY THIS RECIPE WORKS We were amazed to discover how many recipes for strawberry cupcakes rely on a packet of strawberry-flavored Jell-O for the flavor base. We resolved to use real berries. We put together a quick cake base and added chopped frozen strawberries (which are of reliable quality year-round) to the batter, but they disrupted the fine crumb of the cake and left behind mushy pockets. For our next round of testing, we pressed the liquid out of the strawberries and added just the juice to the batter. This time our cakes had good flavor, but the texture was still mushy. Reducing the liquid on the stovetop was the solution: This concentrated the strawberry flavor beautifully and eliminated the excess moisture. We added the strawberry solids left behind from straining to our frosting for another dose of strawberry flavor.

1⅛ cups (4½ ounces) cake flour
 2 teaspoons baking powder
 ½ teaspoon table salt
10 ounces (2 cups) frozen whole strawberries
 6 tablespoons whole milk
 2 large eggs
 2 teaspoons vanilla extract
 6 tablespoons unsalted butter, softened
 7 tablespoons (3 ounces) sugar
 3 cups Honey Cream Cheese Frosting (page 244)

1. Adjust oven rack to middle position and heat oven to 350 degrees. Line 12-cup muffin tin with paper or foil liners. Whisk flour, baking powder, and salt together in bowl. Microwave strawberries in covered bowl until softened and very juicy, about 4 minutes.

2. Transfer strawberries to fine-mesh strainer set over small saucepan and press firmly with rubber spatula to extract as much liquid as possible; set aside solids for frosting. Boil strained strawberry juice over medium-high heat, stirring occasionally, until syrupy and measures ¼ cup, about 8 minutes. Transfer juice to bowl and let cool for 5 minutes. Whisk in milk until combined, followed by eggs and vanilla.

3. Using stand mixer fitted with paddle, beat butter and sugar on medium-high speed until pale and fluffy, about 3 minutes. Slowly add juice mixture and beat until well combined, about 1 minute, scraping down bowl as needed (mixture will look soupy). Reduce speed to low, add flour mixture, and mix until combined, about 1 minute. Give batter final stir by hand.

4. Divide batter evenly among prepared muffin cups. Bake until toothpick inserted in center comes out with few crumbs attached, 15 to 20 minutes, rotating muffin tin halfway through baking.

5. Let cupcakes cool in muffin tin on wire rack for 10 minutes. Remove cupcakes from muffin tin and let cool completely on rack, about 1 hour. (Unfrosted cupcakes can be stored at room temperature for up to 3 days.) Stir reserved strawberry solids into frosting until combined. Spread or pipe frosting evenly on cupcakes. Serve.

GLUTEN-FREE BIRTHDAY CUPCAKES

Makes 12 Cupcakes | **muffin tin**

WHY THIS RECIPE WORKS Using the easiest mixing method (combining everything in a bowl) was the right direction for a gluten-free cupcake—it resulted in a compact cupcake that wasn't overly crumbly. We used oil instead of melted butter to make sure the fat emulsified within this gluten-free batter. Our cupcakes were doming, and while we couldn't remove the baking soda (it helped with browning and tenderness), we found we could reduce the amount of baking powder substantially. Adding some melted white chocolate for this not-chocolate cake boosted the richness without making the cakes greasy, so the butter flavor wasn't missed.

  4 ounces white chocolate, chopped
  6 tablespoons vegetable oil
6½ ounces (¾ cup plus ⅔ cup) all-purpose
     gluten-free flour blend (see page 2)
  1 teaspoon baking powder

⅛ teaspoon baking soda
½ teaspoon xanthan gum
½ teaspoon salt
  2 large eggs
  2 teaspoons vanilla extract
3½ ounces (½ cup) sugar
⅓ cup sour cream
  3 cups Vanilla Frosting (page 241)

1. Adjust oven rack to middle position and heat oven to 325 degrees. Line 12-cup muffin tin with paper or foil liners.

2. Microwave white chocolate and oil in bowl at 50 percent power, stirring occasionally, until melted, about 2 minutes. Whisk mixture until smooth, then set aside to cool slightly. Whisk flour blend, baking powder, baking soda, xanthan gum, and salt together in second bowl.

3. Whisk eggs and vanilla together in large bowl. Whisk in sugar until well combined. Whisk in cooled chocolate mixture and sour cream until combined. Whisk in flour blend mixture until batter is thoroughly combined and smooth.

4. Divide batter evenly among prepared muffin cups. Bake until cupcakes are set on top and spring back when pressed lightly, 20 to 22 minutes, rotating muffin tin halfway through baking. Let cupcakes cool in muffin tin on wire rack for 10 minutes. Remove cupcakes from muffin tin and let cool completely, about 1 hour. (Unfrosted cupcakes can be stored at room temperature for up to 24 hours.) Spread or pipe frosting evenly on cupcakes. Serve.

VEGAN DARK CHOCOLATE CUPCAKES

Makes 12 cupcakes | **muffin tin**

WHY THIS RECIPE WORKS Great dark chocolate cupcakes need to be rich and tender with deep flavor, and these vegan cupcakes fit the bill. We started by folding whipped aquafaba (see page 497)—the liquid from canned chickpeas—stabilized with cream of tartar, into our batter. This helped us achieve a light, fluffy crumb. Next we focused on complex chocolate flavor. But when we added enough bittersweet chocolate to satisfy our cravings, the cupcakes took on a chalky texture; reducing the bittersweet chocolate and adding ½ cup of cocoa powder kept our cupcakes tender. Not all brands of bittersweet chocolate are vegan, so check ingredient lists carefully. If you are a strict vegan, use organic sugar. Do not use natural cocoa powder in this recipe; it gives the cupcakes a rubbery, spongy texture. These cupcakes are best served the day they are made.

1⅓ cups (6⅔ ounces) all-purpose flour
1 cup (7 ounces) sugar
¾ teaspoon baking powder
¼ teaspoon baking soda
½ teaspoon table salt
1 cup water
½ cup (1½ ounces) Dutch-processed cocoa powder
1 ounce bittersweet chocolate, chopped
¼ cup coconut oil
¾ teaspoon vanilla extract
¼ cup aquafaba
1 teaspoon cream of tartar
1 recipe Creamy Vegan Chocolate Frosting (page 246)

1. Adjust oven rack to middle position and heat oven to 400 degrees. Line 12-cup muffin tin with paper or foil liners. Whisk flour, sugar, baking powder, baking soda, and salt together in large bowl.

2. Microwave water, cocoa, chocolate, oil, and vanilla in second bowl at 50 percent power, whisking occasionally, until melted and smooth, about 2 minutes; let cool slightly.

3. Meanwhile, using stand mixer fitted with whisk attachment, whip aquafaba and cream of tartar on high speed until stiff foam that clings to whisk forms, 3 to 9 minutes. Using rubber spatula, stir chocolate mixture into flour mixture until batter is thoroughly combined and smooth (batter will be thick). Stir one-third of whipped aquafaba into batter to lighten, then gently fold in remaining aquafaba until no white streaks remain.

4. Divide batter evenly among prepared muffin cups. Bake until tops are set and spring back when pressed lightly, 16 to 20 minutes, rotating muffin tin halfway through baking.

5. Let cupcakes cool in muffin tin for 10 minutes, then transfer to wire rack and let cool completely, about 1 hour. Spread frosting evenly over cupcakes. Serve.

ULTIMATE CHOCOLATE CUPCAKES WITH GANACHE FILLING

Makes 12 cupcakes | muffin tin

WHY THIS RECIPE WORKS All too often, cupcakes that are packed with enough chocolate to be worthy of their name usually suffer in term of structure and fall apart into a crumbly mess. We were loath to compromise the chocolate's intensity, so instead we tried fortifying the structure of the cupcakes, substituting higher-protein bread flour for all-purpose flour, which yielded a cupcake that was markedly less crumbly yet not tough. Mixing

bittersweet chocolate and some cocoa powder with hot coffee intensified their flavors, and replacing the butter with neutral-flavored vegetable oil allowed the chocolate flavor to dominate. Just a couple teaspoons of distilled white vinegar helped activate the baking soda without throwing off our carefully constructed ratio of ingredients. For a final bit of decadence we spooned ganache onto the cupcakes, which sank to the middle for a truffle-like center. Though we highly recommend the ganache filling, you can omit it for a more traditional cupcake.

FILLING
2 ounces bittersweet chocolate, chopped fine
¼ cup heavy cream
1 tablespoon confectioners' sugar

CUPCAKES
3 ounces bittersweet chocolate, chopped fine
⅓ cup (1 ounce) unsweetened cocoa powder
¾ cup brewed coffee, hot
¾ cup (4⅛ ounces) bread flour
¾ cup (5¼ ounces) granulated sugar
½ teaspoon table salt
½ teaspoon baking soda
6 tablespoons vegetable oil
2 large eggs
2 teaspoons distilled white vinegar
1 teaspoon vanilla extract
3 cups Chocolate Buttercream (page 242)

1. **FOR THE FILLING:** Microwave chocolate, cream, and sugar in bowl at 50 percent power until mixture is warm to touch, about 30 seconds. Whisk until smooth, then transfer bowl to refrigerator and let sit until filling is just chilled, no longer than 30 minutes.

2. **FOR THE CUPCAKES:** Adjust oven rack to middle position and heat oven to 350 degrees. Line 12-cup muffin tin with paper or foil liners. Place chocolate and cocoa in large heatproof bowl. Pour hot coffee over mixture and let sit, covered, for 5 minutes. Whisk chocolate mixture gently until smooth, then transfer to refrigerator and let cool completely, about 20 minutes.

3. Whisk flour, sugar, salt, and baking soda together in bowl. Whisk oil, eggs, vinegar, and vanilla into cooled chocolate mixture until smooth. Add flour mixture and whisk until smooth.

4. Divide batter evenly among prepared muffin cups. Place 1 slightly rounded teaspoon filling on top of each portion of batter. Bake cupcakes until set and just firm to touch, 17 to 19 minutes, rotating muffin tin halfway through baking. Let cupcakes cool in muffin tin on wire rack for 10 minutes. Remove cupcakes from muffin tin and let cool completely on rack, about 1 hour. (Unfrosted cupcakes can be stored at room temperature for up to 24 hours.) Spread or pipe frosting evenly on cupcakes. Serve.

CHOCOLATE CREAM CUPCAKES

Makes 12 cupcakes | muffin tin

WHY THIS RECIPE WORKS Cream-filled Hostess cupcakes conjure memories of lunch box envy. But we knew this iconic cupcake could stand some improvement—starting with the weak chocolate flavor. For the cake, we found that blooming cocoa powder in boiling water intensified its flavor, and semisweet chips and espresso powder added further complexity. We wanted the filling to be substantial enough that it wouldn't dribble out. Combining marshmallow crème—and some butter for richness—with a little gelatin gave us a creamy filling that stayed put. Injecting the filling into the cupcakes caused them to crumble and tear, so we cut inverted cones from the tops of the cupcakes instead. For an accurate measurement of boiling water, bring a full kettle of water to a boil and then measure out the desired amount.

CUPCAKES

- 1 cup (5 ounces) all-purpose flour
- ½ teaspoon baking soda
- ¼ teaspoon table salt
- ½ cup boiling water
- ⅓ cup (1 ounce) unsweetened cocoa powder
- ⅓ cup (2 ounces) semisweet chocolate chips
- 1 tablespoon instant espresso powder
- ¾ cup (5¼ ounces) sugar
- ½ cup sour cream
- ½ cup vegetable oil
- 2 large eggs
- 1 teaspoon vanilla extract

FILLING

- ¾ teaspoon unflavored gelatin
- 3 tablespoons water
- 4 tablespoons unsalted butter, softened
- 1 teaspoon vanilla extract
  Pinch table salt
- 1¼ cups marshmallow crème

GLAZE

- ½ cup (3 ounces) semisweet chocolate chips
- 3 tablespoons unsalted butter

1. FOR THE CUPCAKES: Adjust oven rack to middle position and heat oven to 325 degrees. Grease and flour 12-cup muffin tin.

2. Whisk flour, baking soda, and salt together in bowl. Whisk boiling water, cocoa, chocolate chips, and espresso powder in large bowl until smooth. Whisk sugar, sour cream, oil, eggs, and vanilla into cocoa mixture until combined. Whisk in flour mixture until just incorporated. Divide batter evenly among prepared muffin cups. Bake until toothpick inserted in center

Chocolate Cream Cupcakes

comes out with few crumbs attached, 18 to 22 minutes, rotating muffin tin halfway through baking. Let cupcakes cool in muffin tin on wire rack for 10 minutes. Remove cupcakes from muffin tin and let cool completely on rack, about 1 hour.

3. FOR THE FILLING: Sprinkle gelatin over water in large bowl and let sit until gelatin softens, about 5 minutes. Microwave until mixture is bubbling around edges and gelatin dissolves, about 30 seconds. Whisk in butter, vanilla, and salt until combined. Let mixture cool until just warm to touch, about 5 minutes, then whisk in marshmallow crème until smooth. Refrigerate filling until set, about 30 minutes. Transfer ⅓ cup filling to pastry bag fitted with small plain tip; set aside remaining mixture for filling cupcakes.

4. FOR THE GLAZE: Microwave chocolate chips and butter in small bowl at 50 percent power, stirring occasionally, until melted and smooth, 1 to 2 minutes. Let glaze cool completely, about 10 minutes.

5. Insert tip of paring knife at 45-degree angle ¼ inch from edge of each cupcake and cut cone from top of cupcake. Slice off bottom ½ inch from each cone and discard. Place 1 tablespoon filling inside each cupcake and place tops on filling, pressing to adhere. Spread each cupcake with 2 teaspoons cooled glaze and let sit for 10 minutes. Using pastry bag, pipe curlicues across tops of glazed cupcakes. Serve. (Cupcakes can be stored at room temperature for up to 2 days.)

SALTED CARAMEL CUPCAKES

Makes 12 cupcakes | muffin tin

WHY THIS RECIPE WORKS We wanted to create a cupcake that highlighted the pairing of savory salt and sweet caramel, one that would be dressed up enough for any celebration. We started by giving our cupcakes a core of salted caramel sauce, adding some extra butter to help it set up and prevent oozing. Since we were already preparing a homemade caramel sauce for the cupcakes, we decided to add it to our vanilla frosting as well for a double hit of caramel flavor. We piped the frosting into swirls before drizzling it with more caramel sauce and sprinkling it with sea salt for an eye-catching topping. When taking the temperature of the caramel in steps 3 and 4, remove the pot from the heat and tilt the pan to one side. Use your thermometer to stir the caramel back and forth to equalize hot and cool spots, which will help ensure an accurate reading.

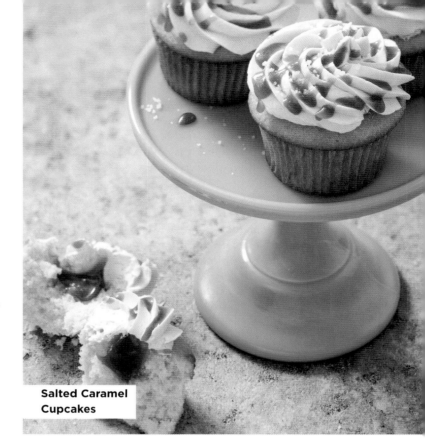

Salted Caramel Cupcakes

CUPCAKES

- 1¾ cups (8¾ ounces) all-purpose flour
- 1 cup (7 ounces) granulated sugar
- 1½ teaspoons baking powder
- ¾ teaspoon table salt
- 12 tablespoons unsalted butter, cut into 12 pieces and softened
- 3 large eggs
- ¾ cup milk
- 1½ teaspoons vanilla extract

SALTED CARAMEL SAUCE

- ⅔ cup (4⅔ ounces) granulated sugar
- 2 tablespoons light corn syrup
- 2 tablespoons water
- ½ cup heavy cream
- 4 tablespoons unsalted butter, cut into 4 pieces
- ½ teaspoon vanilla extract
- ½ teaspoon table salt

FROSTING

- 20 tablespoons (2½ sticks) unsalted butter, cut into 10 pieces and softened
- 2 tablespoons heavy cream
- 2 teaspoons vanilla extract
- ⅛ teaspoon table salt
- 2½ cups (10 ounces) confectioners' sugar

  Flake sea salt

1. FOR THE CUPCAKES: Adjust oven rack to middle position and heat oven to 350 degrees. Line 12-cup muffin tin with paper or foil liners. Using stand mixer fitted with paddle, mix flour, sugar, baking powder, and salt on low speed until combined. Add butter, 1 piece at a time, and mix until mixture resembles coarse sand, about 1 minute. Add eggs, one at a time, and mix until combined. Add milk and vanilla, increase speed to medium, and mix until light, fluffy, and no lumps remain, about 3 minutes.

2. Divide batter evenly among prepared muffin cups. Bake until toothpick inserted in center comes out clean, 18 to 20 minutes, rotating muffin tin halfway through baking. Let cupcakes cool in muffin tin on wire rack for 10 minutes. Remove cupcakes from muffin tin and let cool completely on rack, about 1 hour. (Cupcakes can be refrigerated for up to 2 days; bring to room temperature before continuing with recipe.)

3. FOR THE SALTED CARAMEL SAUCE: Combine sugar, corn syrup, and water in small saucepan. Bring to boil over medium-high heat and cook, without stirring, until mixture is light amber colored, 4 to 6 minutes. Reduce heat to low and continue to cook, swirling saucepan occasionally, until mixture is medium amber and registers 355 to 360 degrees, about 1 minute longer.

4. Off heat, carefully stir in cream, butter, vanilla, and salt (mixture will bubble and steam). Return saucepan to medium heat and cook, stirring frequently, until smooth and caramel reaches 240 to 245 degrees, 2 to 4 minutes. Remove from heat and allow bubbles to subside. Carefully measure ¼ cup caramel into heatproof liquid measuring cup and set aside for frosting. Transfer remaining caramel to heatproof bowl and let both cool until just warm to touch, 15 to 20 minutes.

5. While caramel is cooling, use paring knife to cut out cone-shaped wedge from top of each cupcake, about 1 inch from cupcake edge and 1 inch deep into center of cupcake. Discard cones. Fill each cupcake with 2 teaspoons warm caramel sauce; set aside remaining caramel for frosting.

6. **FOR THE FROSTING:** Using stand mixer fitted with paddle, beat butter, cream, vanilla, and salt on medium-high speed until smooth, about 1 minutes. Reduce speed to medium-low, slowly add sugar, and beat until incorporated and smooth, about 4 minutes. Increase speed to medium-high and beat until frosting is light and fluffy, about 5 minutes. Stop mixer and add ¼ cup caramel to bowl. Beat on medium-high speed until fully incorporated, about 2 minutes.

7. Spread or pipe frosting evenly on cupcakes, drizzle with remaining caramel sauce (rewarming sauce as needed to keep fluid), and sprinkle with flake sea salt. Serve. (Cupcakes can be stored at room temperature for up to 4 hours before serving.)

Financiers

FINANCIERS

Makes 24 cakes | mini muffin tin

WHY THIS RECIPE WORKS For financiers with complex almond flavor and contrasting textures, we started by stirring together almond flour, sugar—granulated, for a pleasantly coarse texture—all-purpose flour, and egg whites. Once these ingredients were whisked together, it was just a matter of stirring in nutty browned butter and baking the cakes. Because egg whites can vary in size, measuring the whites by weight or volume is essential. Baking spray with flour ensures that the cakes bake up with appropriately flat tops; we don't recommend substituting vegetable oil spray in this recipe. You can adorn the top of the batter with slivered almonds before baking if desired. To enjoy the crisp edges of the cakes, eat them on the day they're baked; store leftovers in an airtight container at room temperature for up to three days.

  5 tablespoons unsalted butter
  ¾ cup (3 ounces) finely ground almond flour
  ½ cup plus 1 tablespoon (4 ounces) sugar
  2 tablespoons all-purpose flour
  ⅛ teaspoon table salt
  ⅓ cup (3 ounces) egg whites (3 to 4 large eggs)

1. Adjust oven rack to middle position and heat oven to 375 degrees. Generously spray 24-cup mini-muffin tin with baking spray with flour. Melt butter in 10-inch skillet over medium-high heat. Cook, stirring and scraping skillet constantly with rubber spatula, until milk solids are dark golden brown and butter has nutty aroma, 1 to 3 minutes. Immediately transfer butter to heatproof bowl.

2. Whisk almond flour, sugar, all-purpose flour, and salt together in second bowl. Add egg whites. Using rubber spatula, stir until combined, mashing any lumps against side of bowl until mixture is smooth. Stir in butter until incorporated. Distribute batter evenly among prepared muffin cups (cups will be about half full).

3. Bake until edges are well browned and tops are golden, about 14 minutes, rotating muffin tin halfway through baking. Remove tin from oven and immediately invert wire rack on top of tin. Invert rack and tin; carefully remove tin. Turn cakes right side up and let cool for at least 20 minutes before serving.

Chocolate Chunk Financiers
Place one ½-inch dark chocolate chunk on top of each cake (do not press into batter) before baking.

Pistachio Financiers
Substitute ¾ cup (3 ounces) shelled untoasted pistachios for the almond flour. Process pistachios and all-purpose flour in food processor until finely ground, about 1 minute, scraping down sides of bowl twice during processing.

Plum Financiers
Pit 1 small firm plum and cut into 6 wedges. Slice each wedge crosswise ¼ inch thick. Shingle 2 slices on top of each cake (do not press into batter) before baking.

LAVENDER TEA CAKES WITH VANILLA BEAN GLAZE

Makes 12 tea cakes | muffin tin

WHY THIS RECIPE WORKS With tender, buttery interiors and fine, crisp exteriors, these lavender-infused tea cakes are a sophisticated treat. Our starting point was a simple butter cake, and we found that increasing the butter and replacing the milk with buttermilk gave us rich yet delicate cakes. For petite cakes that didn't dome, we baked them in a muffin tin and carefully adjusted the leaveners and batter amounts. To keep the cakes from sticking and to ensure an attractive, crackly exterior, we brushed the pan with butter and sugar. After baking, we inverted the cakes so that their flat bottoms became the tops. We then spread each cake with a glaze made from vanilla bean, confectioners' sugar, and milk. For a special touch, decorate with candied violets. To coarsely grind dried lavender, pound the dried flowers in a mortar and pestle or pulse several times in a spice grinder.

CAKES

- ⅔ cup (4⅔ ounces) granulated sugar, plus 2 tablespoons for pan, divided
- 6 tablespoons unsalted butter, cut into 6 pieces and softened, plus 2 tablespoons melted, for pan
- 1 cup (5 ounces) all-purpose flour
- ½ teaspoon table salt
- ½ teaspoon baking powder
- ¼ teaspoon baking soda
- ¼ cup buttermilk, room temperature
- 1½ teaspoons dried lavender, coarsely ground
- 1 teaspoon vanilla extract
- 2 large eggs, room temperature

GLAZE

- 1 vanilla bean
- 1¾ cups (7 ounces) confectioners' sugar
- 2–4 tablespoons milk

1. FOR THE CAKES: Adjust oven rack to lower-middle position and heat oven to 325 degrees. Whisk 2 tablespoons sugar and melted butter together in bowl. Brush 12-cup muffin tin with butter-sugar mixture.

2. Whisk flour, salt, baking powder, and baking soda together in bowl. Whisk buttermilk, lavender, and vanilla together in small bowl. Using stand mixer fitted with paddle, beat butter and remaining ⅔ cup sugar on medium-high speed until pale and fluffy, about 3 minutes. Add eggs, one at a time, and beat until combined. Reduce speed to low and add flour mixture in 3 additions, alternating with buttermilk mixture in 2 additions, scraping down bowl as needed. Increase speed to medium-high and beat until completely smooth, about 30 seconds. Give batter final stir by hand.

3. Divide batter evenly among prepared muffin cups and smooth tops. Bake until golden brown and toothpick inserted in center comes out clean, about 15 minutes, rotating muffin tin halfway through baking.

4. Let cakes cool in muffin tin on wire rack for 10 minutes. Invert muffin tin over wire rack and gently tap pan several times to help cakes release. Let cakes cool completely on rack, bottom side up, about 30 minutes. (Unglazed cakes can be stored at room temperature for up to 24 hours.)

5. FOR THE GLAZE: Cut vanilla bean in half lengthwise. Using tip of paring knife, scrape out seeds. Whisk vanilla seeds, sugar, and 2 tablespoons milk in bowl until smooth. Gradually add remaining 2 tablespoons milk as needed, teaspoon by teaspoon, until glaze is thick but pourable. Spoon glaze over top of each cooled cake, letting some drip down sides. Let glaze set for 10 minutes before serving.

MOLTEN CHOCOLATE MICROWAVE MUG CAKES

Makes 2 mug cakes | two 12-ounce coffee mugs

WHY THIS RECIPE WORKS Individual molten chocolate cakes are refined, but we wanted a faster way to satisfy the craving for decadent, fudgy cake and warm chocolate filling. The idea of mug cakes cooked in the microwave was alluring, but these cakes are frequently rubbery and bland—and tend to explode over the brim. Supplementing bittersweet chocolate with cocoa powder, which produces less steam, decreased the chance of an overflow. For a light, tender crumb, we microwaved the cakes gently at 50 percent power, stirring the batter halfway through to ensure even cooking. For the gooey, molten center, we dropped chocolate into each cake.

- 4 tablespoons unsalted butter
- 1 ounce bittersweet chocolate, chopped, plus 1 ounce broken into 4 equal pieces
- ¼ cup (1¾ ounces) sugar
- 2 large eggs
- 2 tablespoons unsweetened cocoa powder
- 1 teaspoon vanilla extract
- ¼ teaspoon table salt
- ¼ cup (1¼ ounces) all-purpose flour
- ½ teaspoon baking powder

1. Microwave butter and chopped chocolate in large bowl at 50 percent power, stirring often, until melted, about 1 minute. Whisk sugar, eggs, cocoa, vanilla, and salt into chocolate mixture until smooth. In separate bowl, combine flour and baking powder. Whisk flour mixture into chocolate mixture until combined. Divide batter evenly between two 12-ounce coffee mugs.

2. Place mugs on opposite sides of microwave turntable. Microwave at 50 percent power for 45 seconds. Stir batter and microwave at 50 percent power for 45 seconds (batter will rise to just below rim of mug).

3. Press 2 chocolate pieces into center of each cake until chocolate is flush with top of cake. Microwave at 50 percent power for 30 seconds to 1 minute (chocolate pieces should be melted and cake should be slightly wet around edges of mug and somewhat drier toward center). Let cakes sit for 2 minutes before serving.

Molten Mocha Microwave Mug Cakes
Add 1 tablespoon instant espresso powder along with sugar to chocolate mixture in step 1.

Lavender Tea Cakes with Vanilla Bean Glaze

LEMON POPPY SEED MUG CAKE

Serves 1 | one 12-ounce coffee mug

WHY THIS RECIPE WORKS Mug cakes aren't just an excuse to eat gooey, decadent chocolate—the technique can apply to even the lightest and fluffiest of cakes. And they're perfect any time of day when you're trying to satisfy a solo craving. We created a simple cake batter full of lemon zest and juice, with an egg contributing a lovely yellow hue and a few spoonfuls of poppy seeds adding pleasing texture and contrasting color. We mixed everything in the single mug we cooked in. After less than 2 minutes in the microwave, we had a soft, pillowy, lemon cake, just waiting for a topping of whipped cream and/or blueberry compote.

3 tablespoons all-purpose flour
2 tablespoons sugar
2 teaspoons poppy seeds (optional)
1½ teaspoons grated lemon zest plus 2 teaspoons juice
¼ teaspoon baking powder
⅛ teaspoon table salt
2 tablespoons unsalted butter, cut into 2 pieces
1 large egg
½ teaspoon vanilla extract

1. Whisk flour; sugar; poppy seeds, if using; lemon zest; baking powder; and salt together in bowl; set aside. Microwave butter in 12-ounce mug at 50 percent power, stirring often, until melted, 1 to 2 minutes. Add flour mixture, egg, vanilla, and lemon juice and mix until smooth and well combined (being sure to scrape corners of mug).

2. Microwave cake batter at 50 percent power until cake has doubled in size and is firm, but top is just wet to the touch, 1 minute 30 seconds to 2 minutes (cake may rise above edge of mug but will not overflow). Let cake rest for 2 minutes. Serve.

Lemon Poppy Seed Mug Cake

SPONGE CAKES

Fold batter gently to avoid deflating

Only spray cake pan when recipe calls for it

Use tube pan with feet

SPONGE CAKES ARE SOMETHING MAGICAL: They have an impossibly light, airy structure yet are sturdy enough to handle rich fillings, creamy toppings, and juicy fruit with ease. These cakes—which include angel food, genoise, and chiffon—are all "foam" cakes. That is, they depend on eggs (whole or separated) beaten to a foam to provide lift and structure. But although they all use eggs for structure, they differ in two ways: whether fat (butter, milk, or oil) is added and whether the foam is made from whole eggs, egg whites, or a combination. The leanest of the foam cakes is angel food, which is made only with egg whites. A genoise is made by whipping whole eggs and uses a moderate amount of melted butter, while a chiffon cake calls for beating whole eggs and/or yolks together and then folding in whipped egg whites; it also typically incorporates some oil for richness.

FOLDING FACTS

One key to maximizing airiness in cake batters is minimizing the number of strokes used to fold in the dry ingredients.

Sift It Sifting the dry ingredients over the foam and folding them into it in batches helps prevent clumps of flour that need aggressive mixing.

Go Bowling Transferring the egg foam from the narrow mixer bowl to a wide, shallow bowl makes the folding process more efficient.

BE GENTLE

A comparison of two genoise cakes illustrates what happens if the batter deflates while folding (left). Gently folding the batter will help avoid this problem and give you a tender, airy crumb (right) with a structure capable of absorbing flavored syrups, fruit juices, or liqueurs.

Bad Cake   **Good Cake**

Genoise

Genoise is a type of sponge cake that has a rich flavor from whole eggs and melted butter. Its light yet sturdy structure and rich buttery flavor make it ideal for layering into a gorgeous creation: Rounds of genoise pair well with everything from tart raspberry jam and bright lemon curd to sour cherries and sweet, juicy berries—and, of course, plenty of lightly sweetened whipped cream. Like any sponge, a genoise should have an airy, springy texture thanks to properly whipped eggs. To make sure the egg foam remains fully aerated, we heat the egg-sugar mixture so that all of the sugar dissolves; this makes for a more viscous mixture that is more stable and less likely to deflate.

ABSORPTION ABILITIES

The structure of a genoise cake comes from abundant egg proteins that unwind and link with each other when the eggs are whipped and form a strong mesh once baked. When this mesh encounters moisture—from juicy berries, a layer of jam, or a flavorful syrup—it isn't affected and the water just fills in any gaps in the network. The upshot? Unlike a butter cake, which practically dissolves when soaked with juice, genoise holds its shape and doesn't crumble apart. That's why we use genoise cake as the base for our Refined Strawberry Shortcake (page 281).

Super Soaker
Genoise absorbs juice and holds together.

Crumbles Under Pressure
Butter cake doesn't have the structure to hold up.

Angel Food Cake

Angel food cake is tall and perfectly shaped, with a snowy white, tender crumb. Unlike most other cakes, angel food cake uses no oil or butter—you don't even grease the pan. It doesn't call for baking soda or baking powder, either, relying solely on beaten egg whites for its dramatic height. There's a good reason angel food cakes—and some chiffon cakes—are baked in tube pans, and it's not just aesthetics. These specialty vessels actually help delicate cakes rise. Because egg foam–based cakes contain very little flour, and therefore very little structure-building gluten, the batter needs something to cling to as it bakes, or it will collapse. Enter the tube pan's tall sides: As the egg foam heats up, it will climb up the sides (and conical center) of the pan.

HANGING OUT

To ensure that angel and chiffon cakes have the lightest, fluffiest texture, you'll want to let them cool upside down; if you cool the cake right side up, it will fall flat under its own weight and have a rubbery texture. You can invert it over a large metal kitchen funnel but it's just as easy to grab something you likely already have: a heavy-bottomed bottle (like an empty wine bottle).

Chiffon

Chiffon cake is something of a cross between angel food cake and pound cake. Like angel food cake, chiffon cake gets its dramatic height and light, fluffy texture from whipped egg whites. Like pound cake, it contains plentiful fat (from egg yolks and oil) to make it rich and tender, plus baking powder to help it rise.

NOT SO STIFF PEAKS

Many recipes for chiffon cake call for egg whites beaten to "very stiff" peaks. In test after test, we found that very stiff whites are impossible to incorporate into the batter. Instead, we beat the whites to slightly softer peaks ("until just stiff and glossy") and then give them added support with sugar and/or cream of tartar.

Blotchy Cake
Because very stiff whites couldn't be uniformly incorporated, the cake has holes and intermittent patches of egg white.

CHIFFON CAKE GET OUT

Like angel food cake, chiffon cake is baked in an ungreased pan. Why? The beaten egg whites need to cling to the pan to rise. If the pan were greased, they couldn't. Here's how to remove a chiffon cake from the pan.

1. When cake is cool, turn pan right side up and run flexible knife around tube and outer edge.

2. Use tube to pull cake out of pan and set it on inverted baking pan. Cut bottom free.

3. Invert cake onto serving plate and gently twist tube to remove.

CUTTING PARCHMENT PAPER FOR TUBE PANS

Instead of a simple round of parchment, tube pans, naturally, require a parchment "doughnut" to accommodate the tube. This is an important step for cakes like angel food, where you can't grease the pan (it will inhibit the cake's rise).

1. Cut a square of parchment paper slightly bigger than the size of the bottom of the tube pan.

2. Form the paper into a large triangle by folding the top left corner over to meet the bottom right corner.

3. Fold the top right corner over the bottom left corner.

4. Continue to make a smaller triangle by folding the bottom right corner over the bottom left corner.

5. Hold the folded piece of parchment over the tube pan, with the pointed end in the center of the pan. Using scissors, trim both the pointed edge and outside edge so that the parchment just fits inside the pan.

6. Unfold the parchment and lay it over the bottom of the tube pan.

GENOISE SPONGE CAKE

Serves 10 to 12 | two 9-inch round cake pans

WHY THIS RECIPE WORKS Genoise-style sponge cakes are a study in contrasts. They are light but have good structure (making them ideal for layering with fruit or cream fillings); they're elegant even when unadorned; and unlike other egg-aerated cakes (such as chiffon and angel food), they contain both whole eggs and melted butter for rich flavor. But with no chemical leaveners, the cake can be dense, flat, and rubbery if the eggs aren't perfectly aerated. To ensure the ideal texture, we followed a few key steps. First, fully dissolving the sugar in the eggs by heating the mixture over simmering water made for a more viscous mixture that was extremely capable of holding air. Next, transferring the egg mixture to a wide, shallow bowl made folding more efficient, which also helped the batter retain air. Finally, lightening the melted butter by combining it with some of the egg foam made it easier to incorporate.

  4 tablespoons unsalted butter, melted and cooled slightly
  1 teaspoon vanilla extract
  ½ teaspoon grated lemon zest
  1¼ cups (5 ounces) cake flour
  ¼ teaspoon table salt
  5 large eggs
  ¾ cup (5¼ ounces) granulated sugar
  ⅔ cup raspberry jam
    Confectioners' sugar

1. Adjust oven rack to middle position and heat oven to 350 degrees. Spray two 9-inch round cake pans with baking spray with flour, line with parchment paper, and spray parchment with baking spray with flour. Combine melted butter, vanilla, and lemon zest in bowl. Whisk flour and salt together in second bowl.

2. Combine eggs and granulated sugar in bowl of stand mixer; place bowl over medium saucepan filled with 2 inches simmering water, making sure that water does not touch bottom of bowl. Whisking constantly, heat until sugar is dissolved and mixture registers 115 to 120 degrees, about 3 minutes.

3. Transfer bowl to stand mixer fitted with whisk attachment. Whip on high speed until eggs are pale yellow and have tripled in volume, about 5 minutes. (Egg foam will form ribbon that sits on top of mixture for 5 seconds when dribbled from whisk.) Measure out ¾ cup egg foam, whisk into butter mixture until well combined, and set aside.

4. Transfer remaining egg foam to large, wide bowl and sift one-third of flour mixture over egg foam in even layer. Using rubber spatula, gently fold batter 6 to 8 times until small streaks of flour remain. Repeat folding 6 to 8 times with half of remaining flour mixture. Sift remaining flour mixture over batter and gently fold 10 to 12 times until flour is completely incorporated.

5. Pour butter mixture over batter in even layer. Gently fold until just incorporated, taking care not to deflate batter. Divide batter evenly between prepared pans. Bake until centers of cakes are set and bounce back when gently pressed and toothpick inserted in center comes out clean, 13 to 16 minutes. Remove cakes from pans, discarding parchment, and let cool completely on wire rack, about 2 hours.

6. Place 1 cake layer on platter. Spread jam evenly over top. Top with second cake layer and press lightly to adhere. Dust with confectioners' sugar before serving.

REFINED STRAWBERRY SHORTCAKE

Serves 8 to 10 | two 9-inch round cake pans

WHY THIS RECIPE WORKS We liked the idea of transforming strawberry shortcake into a whole cake with an elegant presentation. We decided on a genoise sponge cake, which gets its structure from egg proteins—rather than the weaker gluten proteins a butter cake depends on—making it sturdy enough to support a juicy berry topping without breaking down. Cutting a circle out of one of the cake layers gave us an inset portion to fill with a fresh strawberry filling, and macerating the berries with sugar and a little lemon juice gave them a glossy, vibrant appearance. We thickened some of the juice with cornstarch and then tossed it with the berries for a more cohesive filling. Brushing the remaining juice over the cake before adding the berries ensured that it was evenly moistened. Cool the melted butter only slightly, to between 95 and 110 degrees.

STRAWBERRIES
  2 pounds strawberries, hulled and sliced lengthwise ¼ inch thick (6 cups)
  ¼ cup (1¾ ounces) granulated sugar
  2 teaspoons lemon juice
    Pinch table salt
  ½ teaspoon cornstarch

CAKE
  4 tablespoons unsalted butter, melted and cooled slightly
  1 teaspoon vanilla extract
  ½ teaspoon grated lemon zest
  1¼ cups (5 ounces) cake flour
  ¼ teaspoon table salt
  5 large eggs
  ¾ cup (5¼ ounces) granulated sugar

WHIPPED CREAM
  1 cup heavy cream, chilled
  ⅓ cup crème fraîche
  3 tablespoons confectioners' sugar, plus extra for dusting

1. **FOR THE STRAWBERRIES:** Toss strawberries with sugar, lemon juice, and salt in large bowl. Set aside for at least 1½ hours or up to 3 hours.

2. **FOR THE CAKE:** Adjust oven rack to middle position and heat oven to 350 degrees. Spray two 9-inch round cake pans with baking spray with flour, line with parchment paper, and spray parchment with baking spray with flour. Combine melted butter, vanilla, and lemon zest in bowl. Whisk flour and salt together in second bowl.

3. Combine eggs and sugar in bowl of stand mixer; place bowl over saucepan filled with 2 inches simmering water, making sure that water does not touch bottom of bowl. Whisking constantly, heat until sugar is dissolved and mixture registers 115 to 120 degrees, about 3 minutes.

4. Transfer bowl to stand mixer fitted with whisk attachment. Whip on high speed until eggs are pale yellow and have tripled in volume, about 5 minutes. (Egg foam will form ribbon that sits on top of mixture for 5 seconds when dribbled from whisk.) Measure out ¾ cup egg foam, whisk into butter mixture until combined, and set aside.

5. Transfer remaining egg foam to large, wide bowl and sift one-third of flour mixture over egg foam in even layer. Using rubber spatula, gently fold batter 6 to 8 times until small streaks of flour remain. Repeat folding 6 to 8 times with half of remaining flour mixture. Sift remaining flour mixture over batter and gently fold 10 to 12 times until flour is completely incorporated.

6. Pour butter mixture over batter in even layer. Gently fold until just incorporated, taking care not to deflate batter. Divide batter evenly between prepared pans.

7. Bake until center of cakes are set and bounce back when gently pressed and toothpick inserted in center comes out clean, 13 to 16 minutes. Remove cakes from pans, discarding parchment, and let cool completely on wire rack, about 2 hours.

8. Drain berries in fine-mesh strainer set over bowl. Measure out 2 tablespoons juice into small bowl (reserve remaining juice in bowl) and stir in cornstarch until well combined. Microwave, stirring every 10 seconds, until mixture is very thick and translucent, 30 to 45 seconds. Set aside.

9. Place 1 cake layer right side up on platter. Place second layer upside down on cutting board. Using paring knife, cut circle from center of cake on board, leaving 1-inch-wide ring of cake. (Reserve circle for another use.) Place upside-down cake ring on top of layer on platter. Using pastry brush, brush all of unthickened strawberry juice onto bottom cake layer and inner sides of cake ring. Gently combine berries and reserved thickened juice in now-empty bowl. Spoon berry mixture into cake ring, forming even layer.

10. **FOR THE WHIPPED CREAM:** Using stand mixer fitted with whisk attachment, whip cream and crème fraîche on low speed until foamy, about 1 minute. Add sugar, increase speed to medium-high, and whip until soft peaks form, about 2 minutes. Dollop 2 tablespoons whipped cream onto center of cake. Transfer remaining whipped cream to serving bowl. Dust cake ring with confectioners' sugar. Serve, passing extra whipped cream separately.

BLACK FOREST CAKE

Serves 10 to 12 | 9-inch springform pan

WHY THIS RECIPE WORKS In Germany, Black Forest cake is an architectural masterpiece that sandwiches layers of chocolate cake with marinated cherries and thick drifts of sweetened whipped cream. To create our own version of this impressive dessert we started with a light yet sturdy chocolate genoise, which provided the perfect base on which to layer the other elements. For whipped cream with enough structure to hold up under the weight of this towering cake, we simmered some of the cream with cornstarch before whipping it with the rest of the cream. Jarred sour cherries tasted great and were even better when galvanized by a generous amount of kirsch. The cake's trademark garnish of chocolate shavings and whole cherries gave the cake a stunning crown. If you can't find jarred sour cherries, you can substitute high-quality canned cherries. Be sure to whip the cream only until soft peaks start to form.

CAKE
¾ cup (3¾ ounces) all-purpose flour
¼ cup (¾ ounce) unsweetened cocoa powder
½ teaspoon table salt
6 large eggs
1 cup (7 ounces) sugar
1 teaspoon vanilla extract
4 tablespoons unsalted butter, melted

CHERRIES
2 cups jarred sour cherries in light syrup, drained with 1 cup syrup reserved, divided
½ cup (3½ ounces) sugar
½ cup kirsch or other cherry-flavored liqueur

WHIPPED CREAM
¼ cup (1¾ ounces) sugar
1 tablespoon cornstarch
3 cups heavy cream, chilled, divided
1½ teaspoons vanilla extract

Shaved semisweet chocolate

1. **FOR THE CAKE:** Adjust oven rack to middle position and heat oven to 350 degrees. Line bottom of 9-inch springform pan with parchment paper (do not grease). Sift flour, cocoa, and salt onto large piece of parchment; set aside.

2. Combine eggs and sugar in bowl of stand mixer; place bowl over saucepan filled with 2 inches simmering water, making sure that water does not touch bottom of bowl. Whisking constantly, heat until sugar is dissolved and mixture registers 115 to 120 degrees, about 3 minutes. Transfer bowl to stand mixer fitted with whisk attachment. Whip on high speed until eggs are pale yellow and have tripled in volume, about 5 minutes. (Egg foam will form ribbon that sits on top of mixture for 5 seconds when dribbled from whisk.) Whip in vanilla, about 5 seconds. Transfer 1 cup egg foam to medium bowl and whisk in reserved melted butter until combined; set aside.

3. Grab both ends of parchment containing flour-cocoa mixture. With mixer running on low speed, slowly sprinkle flour-cocoa mixture into whipped egg mixture and mix until barely incorporated. Add melted butter mixture to bowl and mix gently to incorporate, being careful not to deflate batter.

4. Transfer batter to pan and smooth top with offset spatula. Bake until center of cake is set and bounces back when gently pressed, about 35 minutes, rotating pan halfway through baking. Let cake cool in pan on wire rack for 10 minutes. Remove cake from pan, discarding parchment, and let cool completely on wire rack, about 2 hours. Using long serrated knife, cut 2 horizontal lines around sides of cake; then, following scored lines, cut cake into 3 even layers. (Cake can be wrapped tightly in plastic wrap and stored at room temperature for up to 2 days, refrigerated for up to 5 days, or frozen for up to 2 months.)

5. **FOR THE CHERRIES:** Reserve 8 prettiest cherries for garnish in small bowl. Slice remaining cherries in half and place in second bowl. Bring reserved cherry syrup and sugar to simmer in medium saucepan over medium heat and cook until syrup is thickened and measures about ½ cup, 8 to 10 minutes. Off heat, stir in kirsch. Toss 1 tablespoon syrup with cherries reserved for garnish. Toss 3 tablespoons more syrup with halved cherries.

6. Poke top of cake layers thoroughly with wooden skewer and brush with remaining syrup.

7. **FOR THE WHIPPED CREAM:** Whisk sugar and cornstarch together in small saucepan and slowly whisk in ½ cup cream. Bring mixture to simmer over medium heat, whisking constantly, until mixture thickens, 2 to 3 minutes. Let mixture cool completely, about 30 minutes.

Black Forest Cake

Chiffon Cake

8. Using stand mixer fitted with whisk attachment, whip remaining 2½ cups cream and vanilla on low speed until frothy, about 30 seconds. Increase speed to medium and continue to whip until mixture begins to thicken, about 30 seconds. Slowly add cooled sugar mixture and continue to whip until soft peaks form, about 1 minute.

9. Line edges of cake platter with 4 strips of parchment paper to keep platter clean. Place 1 cake layer on platter. Spread ½ cup whipped cream over top, right to edge of cake, then cover with half of sliced cherries. Repeat with 1 more cake layer, ½ cup more whipped cream, and remaining sliced cherries. Top with remaining cake layer, pressing lightly to adhere. Spread remaining whipped cream evenly over top and sides of cake.

10. Refrigerate cake so it absorbs soaking syrup, at least 2 hours or up to 24 hours. Before serving, let cake sit at room temperature for 30 minutes to 1 hour, then gently press shaved chocolate into sides of cake. Evenly space 8 small piles shaved chocolate around top of cake and top each with cherry. Carefully remove parchment strips before serving.

CHIFFON CAKE

Serves 12 | 16-cup tube pan

WHY THIS RECIPE WORKS Chiffon cake has the airy height of angel food cake with the richness of pound cake, but classic recipes aren't always perfect. For this particular cake, we found that sifting the dry ingredients was unnecessary so we eliminated this common step. We also perfected the method for beating our egg whites—slowly adding sugar once the eggs had been beaten to soft peaks and then continuing to beat them until just stiff and glossy—to avoid little pockets of cooked egg whites.

  5 large eggs, separated
  1 teaspoon cream of tartar
1½ cups (10½ ounces) sugar, divided
1⅓ cups (5⅓ ounces) cake flour
  2 teaspoons baking powder
  ½ teaspoon table salt
  ¾ cup water
  ½ cup vegetable oil
  1 tablespoon vanilla extract

1. Adjust oven rack to lower-middle position and heat oven to 325 degrees. Using stand mixer fitted with whisk, whip egg whites and cream of tartar on medium-high speed until soft peaks form, about 2 minutes. With mixer running, slowly add 2 tablespoons sugar and whip until just stiff and glossy, about 1 minute; set aside.

Olive Oil Cake

2. Combine flour, baking powder, salt, and remaining sugar in large bowl. Whisk water, oil, egg yolks, and vanilla in medium bowl until smooth. Whisk wet mixture into flour mixture until smooth. Whisk one-third whipped egg whites into batter, then gently fold in remaining whites, 1 scoop at a time, until well combined. Scrape mixture into 16-cup ungreased tube pan.

3. Bake until skewer inserted into center comes out clean and cracks in cake appear dry, 55 minutes to 1 hour 5 minutes. Let cool, inverted, to room temperature, about 3 hours. To unmold, turn pan right side up and run flexible knife around tube and outer edge. Use tube to pull cake out of pan and set it on inverted baking pan. Cut bottom free. Invert cake onto serving plate and gently twist tube to remove. Serve.

Orange Chiffon Cake

Reduce total sugar to 1¼ cups. Replace water with ¾ cup orange juice and add 1 tablespoon grated orange zest along with vanilla in step 2. For glaze, whisk 3 tablespoons orange juice, 2 tablespoons softened cream cheese, and ½ teaspoon grated orange zest in medium bowl until smooth. Add 1½ cups confectioners' sugar and whisk until smooth. Pour glaze over cooled cake. Let glaze set for 15 minutes. Serve.

OLIVE OIL CAKE

Serves 8 to 10 | 9-inch springform pan

WHY THIS RECIPE WORKS We wanted our olive oil cake to have a light, fine-textured, and plush crumb, with a subtle but noticeable olive oil flavor. Whipping the sugar with the whole eggs, rather than just the whites, produced a fine texture that was airy but sturdy enough to support the olive oil–rich batter. To emphasize the defining flavor, we opted for a good-quality extra-virgin olive oil and supplemented its fruitiness with a tiny bit of lemon zest. A crackly sugar topping added a touch of sweetness and sophistication. For the best flavor, use a fresh, high-quality extra-virgin olive oil. If your springform pan is prone to leaking, place a rimmed baking sheet on the oven floor to catch any drips.

1¾ cups (8¾ ounces) all-purpose flour
  1 teaspoon baking powder
¾ teaspoon table salt
  3 large eggs
1¼ cups (8¾ ounces) plus 2 tablespoons sugar, divided
¼ teaspoon grated lemon zest
¾ cup extra-virgin olive oil
¾ cup milk

1. Adjust oven rack to middle position and heat oven to 350 degrees. Grease 9-inch springform pan. Whisk flour, baking powder, and salt together in bowl.

2. Using stand mixer fitted with whisk attachment, whip eggs on medium speed until foamy, about 1 minute. Add 1¼ cups sugar and lemon zest, increase speed to high, and whip until mixture is fluffy and pale yellow, about 3 minutes. Reduce speed to medium and, with mixer running, slowly pour in oil. Mix until oil is fully incorporated, about 1 minute. Add half of flour mixture and mix on low speed until incorporated, about 1 minute, scraping down bowl as needed. Add milk and mix until combined, about 30 seconds. Add remaining flour mixture and mix until just incorporated, about 1 minute, scraping down bowl as needed.

3. Transfer batter to prepared pan; sprinkle remaining 2 tablespoons sugar over entire surface. Bake until cake is deep golden brown and toothpick inserted in center comes out with few crumbs attached, 40 to 45 minutes. Transfer pan to wire rack and let cool for 15 minutes. Remove side of pan and let cake cool completely, about 1½ hours. Cut into wedges and serve. (Leftover cake can be stored at room temperature for up to 1 day.)

JELLY ROLL CAKE

Serves 8 to 10 | rimmed baking sheet

WHY THIS RECIPE WORKS Many recipes for filled, rolled sponge cakes yield cakes that are far too fragile. The secret to a flexible cake that doesn't crack is to use plenty of eggs. Whipping the eggs until they were thick enhanced their structure-building abilities. While the cake was still hot, we rolled it into a spiral and allowed it to sit for 15 minutes before unrolling it and adding the filling. This early roll gave the cake memory so it stayed snug once rolled again with the jam. To avoid deflating the batter, hold the bowl as close to the baking sheet as possible, using a rubber spatula to gently push the batter into the sheet. Make sure not to overbake the cake, which can cause cracking once rolled. You will need at least a 20 by 15-inch smooth dish towel for this recipe. While raspberry jam is traditional, you can use another flavor. Serve with Whipped Cream (page 548), if desired.

¾ cup (3¾ ounces) all-purpose flour
  1 teaspoon baking powder
¼ teaspoon table salt
  5 large eggs, room temperature
¾ cup (5¼ ounces) granulated sugar
½ teaspoon vanilla extract
    Confectioners' sugar
⅔ cup seedless jam

1. Adjust oven rack to lower-middle position and heat oven to 350 degrees. Grease 18 by 13-inch rimmed baking sheet, line with parchment paper, grease parchment, and flour sheet. Whisk flour, baking powder, and salt together in bowl; set aside.

2. Using stand mixer fitted with whisk attachment, whip eggs at medium-high speed and gradually add granulated sugar and then vanilla, about 1 minute. Continue to whip mixture until very thick and voluminous, 4 to 8 minutes. Sift flour mixture over egg mixture; using rubber spatula, gently fold batter until just incorporated.

3. Pour batter into prepared sheet with rubber spatula and spread into even layer with offset spatula. Bake until cake is firm and springs back when touched, 12 to 17 minutes, rotating baking sheet halfway through baking. Lay clean dish towel on counter and dust with confectioners' sugar.

4. Immediately run thin knife around edge of baking sheet to loosen cake, then flip hot cake out onto towel, discarding parchment. Starting from short side, roll cake and towel snugly into log. Let cake cool, seam side down, for 15 minutes.

5. Gently unroll cake. Spread jam evenly over cake, leaving ½-inch border along edges. Reroll cake gently but snugly around jam, leaving towel behind as you roll. Trim ends of cake, transfer cake to platter, and let cake cool completely, about 30 minutes. Dust with confectioners' sugar before serving.

Angel Food Cake

ANGEL FOOD CAKE

Serves 12 | 16-cup tube pan

WHY THIS RECIPE WORKS Angel food cake is downy-soft and incredibly light—with the right balance of ingredients and the proper technique. We created a stable egg white base by starting the whites at medium-low speed until frothy and then increasing the speed to medium-high to form soft, billowy mounds. A delicate touch was required when incorporating the flour, which we sifted over the batter and gently folded in. We strongly recommend using a tube pan with a removable bottom. If your tube pan does not have a removable bottom, you will need to line it with parchment (see page 280). Do not grease the pan; greasing prevents the cake from climbing up and clinging to the sides as it bakes, and a greased pan will produce a disappointingly short cake. Serve this cake as is or dust with confectioners' sugar.

¾ cup (3 ounces) cake flour
1½ cups (10½ ounces) sugar, divided
12 large egg whites, room temperature
1 teaspoon cream of tartar
¼ teaspoon table salt
1½ teaspoons vanilla extract
1½ teaspoons lemon juice
½ teaspoon almond extract

1. Adjust oven rack to lower-middle position and heat oven to 325 degrees. Line 16-cup tube pan with parchment paper but do not grease. Whisk flour and ¾ cup sugar together in bowl.

2. Using stand mixer fitted with whisk attachment, whip egg whites, cream of tartar, and salt on medium-low speed until foamy, about 1 minute. Increase speed to medium-high and whip to soft, billowy mounds, about 1 minute. Gradually add remaining ¾ cup sugar and whip until soft, glossy peaks form, 1 to 2 minutes. Add vanilla, lemon juice, and almond extract and beat until just blended.

3. Sift flour mixture over egg whites, about 3 tablespoons at a time, gently folding mixture into whites after each addition with large rubber spatula.

4. Gently transfer batter to prepared pan and smooth top with rubber spatula. Bake until golden brown and top springs back when pressed firmly, 50 minutes to 1 hour, rotating pan halfway through baking.

5. If pan has prongs around rim for elevating cake, invert pan on them. If not, invert pan over neck of bottle or funnel so that air can circulate all around it. Let cake cool completely in pan, 2 to 3 hours.

6. Run thin knife around edge of pan to loosen cake, then gently tap pan upside down on counter to release cake. Peel off parchment and turn cake right side up onto platter. Serve. (Cake can be stored at room temperature for up to 2 days or refrigerated for up to 4 days.)

CHOCOLATE-ORANGE ANGEL FOOD CAKE

Serves 12 | 16-cup tube pan

WHY THIS RECIPE WORKS For an elegant upgrade to angel food cake, we incorporated the classic combination of chocolate and orange. Simply mixing in chopped bittersweet chocolate was a failure: The chunks of chocolate disrupted the ultradelicate structure of the egg white–leavened cake. Finely grated chocolate was easier to distribute evenly throughout the batter. Orange zest added fragrance, while a splash of orange liqueur amped up the citrus flavor further. We strongly recommend using a tube pan with a removable bottom, but a pan without one can be lined with parchment paper (see page 280). (If your tube pan has a removable bottom, you do not need to line it with parchment.) Do not grease the pan; greasing prevents the cake from climbing up and clinging to the sides as it bakes, and a greased pan will produce a disappointingly short cake. Finely grating the chocolate is key here; use either a Microplane grater or the fine holes of a box grater.

Chocolate-Orange Angel Food Cake

¾ cup (3 ounces) cake flour
1½ cups (10½ ounces) sugar, divided
12 large egg whites, room temperature
1 teaspoon cream of tartar
¼ teaspoon table salt
1 tablespoon Grand Marnier
2 teaspoons grated orange zest
½ teaspoon vanilla extract
2 ounces bittersweet chocolate, finely grated

1. Adjust oven rack to lower-middle position and heat oven to 325 degrees. Line 16-cup tube pan with parchment paper but do not grease. Whisk flour and ¾ cup sugar together in bowl; set aside.

2. Using stand mixer fitted with whisk attachment, whip egg whites, cream of tartar, and salt on medium-low speed until foamy, about 1 minute. Increase speed to medium-high and whip to soft, billowy mounds, about 1 minute. Gradually add remaining ¾ cup sugar and whip until soft, glossy peaks form, 1 to 2 minutes. Add Grand Marnier, orange zest, and vanilla and whip until just blended.

3. Sift flour mixture over whites, about 3 tablespoons at a time, gently folding mixture into whites after each addition with large rubber spatula. Gently fold in chocolate.

4. Gently transfer batter to prepared pan and smooth top with rubber spatula. Bake until golden brown and top springs back when pressed firmly, 50 minutes to 1 hour, rotating pan halfway through baking.

5. If pan has prongs around rim for elevating cake, invert pan on them. If not, invert pan over neck of bottle or funnel so that air can circulate all around it. Let cake cool completely in pan, 2 to 3 hours.

6. Run thin knife around edge of pan to loosen cake, then gently tap pan upside down on counter to release cake. Peel off parchment and turn cake right side up onto platter. Serve. (Cake can be stored at room temperature for up to 2 days or refrigerated for up to 4 days.)

BUNDT CAKES

Grease nooks and ridges of pan
Use skewer to test doneness
Let cool for 3 hours before slicing

BUNDT CAKES HAVE A UNIQUE, BEAUTIFUL PRESENCE thanks to the pan in which they're baked. The Bundt pan came to prominence in America after World War II and is modeled on a classic German pan, called the kugelhopf, which is used to bake a yeasted bread. Bundt pans are tall with decorative ridges or fluting, and they produce a cake with impressive height and a graceful, undulating ring shape. With its elegant form, this cake doesn't require complicated finishing techniques or fancy embellishments: A dusting of confectioners' sugar or a drizzling with a simple glaze and the cake is ready to serve. This unfussy quality makes Bundt cakes perfect vehicles for showcasing simple flavors such as honey, citrus, or chocolate. Other than the uniquely shaped, heavyweight pan, what makes a Bundt cake a Bundt cake? While there are no absolutes, most Bundt cakes are mixed using the standard technique of creaming butter and sugar; they're typically richer than a sheet or sponge cake, and have a buttery flavor and tight, even crumb that's not quite as dense as a pound cake. Though it creates an aesthetically unique cake, the central hole in a Bundt pan is really a practical innovation. It tunnels through the center of the cake, providing faster and more even heat distribution so that dense batters bake uniformly from edge to edge.

BUNDTS OF ALL KINDS

A Bundt pan is a special tube pan with decorative ridges or fluting. We love the beautiful, traditional appearance of cakes baked in our favorite pan, the Nordic Ware Anniversary Bundt Pan (for more information on our winning Bundt pan, see page 225). But Nordic Ware also makes a number of other Bundt pan shapes that we had fun experimenting with in the kitchen. We particularly like the 75th Anniversary Braided, Jubilee, and Vintage Star Bundt pans. The only differences? They don't have the helpful handles found on the anniversary Bundt. And these pans are smaller, holding about 10 or 12 cups of batter, so they won't accommodate every recipe. We've noted in individual recipes if they work in these pans. Since their designs are intricate, be sure to grease the pan properly so the cakes come out with ease.

75th Anniversary Braided Bundt Pan

Jubilee Bundt Pan

Vintage Star Bundt Pan

PREPARING A BUNDT PAN

A Bundt pan makes an attractive cake only if you can get it out in one piece. A generous spray of baking spray with flour does the job for most properly baked cakes (underbaked cakes will stick) except for chocolate. These moist cakes stuck when we simply greased the pan, but if we introduced flour they retained a white coating. Our foolproof solution? Make a paste from 1 tablespoon melted butter and 1 tablespoon cocoa powder and apply it with a pastry brush. This thoroughly coats the surface of the pan, including all the nooks and crannies.

STORING AND FREEZING

The shape of these cakes isn't all they have in common: They also take well to storage. Most cakes, even glazed ones, can be wrapped in plastic wrap or stored in an airtight container at room temperature for as long as two to four days, depending on the recipe. For long-term storage, the freezer sometimes works better than the refrigerator, which can make some cakes stale. To freeze, wrap the cooled cake in plastic wrap, then in aluminum foil, and freeze for up to one month. If you do plan on freezing your cake, avoid glazing until it's defrosted. To defrost a frozen cake, thaw it completely at room temperature (do not unwrap), about 4 hours. (Thawing the cake while still wrapped ensures a nice, firm crust.)

HONEY CAKE

Serves 12 | 12-cup nonstick Bundt pan

WHY THIS RECIPE WORKS Honey cake is a staple at dinners celebrating Rosh Hashanah, and serves as a symbol of the sweet year ahead. Just ¼ cup of oil and some applesauce kept this cake moist but not greasy. Orange juice boosted the power of the baking soda, ensuring a light cake. For the honey to make its presence known, we used a whopping 1¾ cups; lowering the oven temperature prevented the sweet cake from burning. Use unsweetened applesauce. If you plan to make this cake ahead of time, hold off on glazing it until 30 minutes before serving. You can bake this cake in a decorative 10-cup Bundt pan; place a baking sheet under the Bundt pan.

CAKE

2½ cups (12½ ounces) all-purpose flour
1¼ teaspoons table salt
  1 teaspoon baking powder
  ½ teaspoon baking soda
  ½ cup water
  4 large eggs
  6 tablespoons unsweetened applesauce
  ¼ cup vegetable oil
  ¼ cup orange juice
  1 teaspoon vanilla extract
1¾ cups honey

GLAZE

  1 cup (4 ounces) confectioners' sugar
1½ tablespoons water
  1 teaspoon vanilla extract
     Pinch table salt

1. FOR THE CAKE: Adjust oven rack to middle position and heat oven to 325 degrees. Spray 12-cup nonstick Bundt pan heavily with baking spray with flour. Whisk flour, salt, baking powder, and baking soda together in large bowl. Whisk water, eggs, applesauce, oil, orange juice, and vanilla in second bowl until combined. Whisk honey into egg mixture until incorporated.

2. Whisk honey mixture into flour mixture until combined. Transfer batter to prepared pan. Bake until skewer inserted in center comes out clean, 45 to 55 minutes, rotating pan halfway through baking.

3. Let cake cool in pan on wire rack for 30 minutes. Using small spatula, loosen cake from sides of pan, invert onto rack set in rimmed baking sheet, and remove pan. Let cake cool completely, about 3 hours. (Cake can be wrapped in plastic wrap and stored at room temperature for up to 3 days.)

4. FOR THE GLAZE: Whisk sugar, water, vanilla, and salt together in bowl. Drizzle glaze over cooled cake and let set until dry, about 30 minutes, before serving.

Chocolate Sour Cream Bundt Cake

CHOCOLATE SOUR CREAM BUNDT CAKE

Serves 12 | 12-cup nonstick Bundt pan

WHY THIS RECIPE WORKS We wanted a chocolate Bundt cake that would taste every bit as good as it looks, with a fine crumb, moist texture, and rich chocolate flavor. To achieve this, we used both bittersweet chocolate and cocoa powder, dissolving them in boiling water to bloom their flavor. Brown sugar and sour cream provided moisture and a subtle tang. We prefer natural cocoa here; Dutch-processed cocoa will result in a compromised rise. For an accurate measurement of boiling water, bring a full kettle of water to a boil and then measure out the desired amount. You can bake this cake in a decorative 10-cup Bundt pan; place a baking sheet under the Bundt pan. We like to serve this cake with raspberries and/or Tangy Whipped Cream (page 548).

  ¾ cup (2¼ ounces) natural unsweetened cocoa powder, plus 1 tablespoon for pan
 12 tablespoons unsalted butter, cut into 12 pieces and softened, plus 1 tablespoon, melted, for pan
  6 ounces bittersweet chocolate, chopped
  1 teaspoon instant espresso powder (optional)
  ¾ cup boiling water
  1 cup sour cream, room temperature
1¾ cups (8¾ ounces) all-purpose flour
  1 teaspoon table salt

1 teaspoon baking soda
2 cups packed (14 ounces) light brown sugar
1 tablespoon vanilla extract
5 large eggs, room temperature
  Confectioners' sugar (optional)

1. Adjust oven rack to lower-middle position and heat oven to 350 degrees. Mix 1 tablespoon cocoa and melted butter into paste. Using pastry brush, thoroughly coat interior of 12-cup nonstick Bundt pan.

2. Combine chocolate; espresso powder, if using; and remaining ¾ cup cocoa in bowl. Pour boiling water over mixture and let sit, covered, for 5 minutes. Whisk mixture gently until smooth. Let cool completely, then whisk in sour cream. Whisk flour, salt, and baking soda together in second bowl.

3. Using stand mixer fitted with paddle, beat softened butter, brown sugar, and vanilla on medium-high speed until pale and fluffy, about 3 minutes. Add eggs, one at a time, and beat until combined. Reduce speed to low and add flour mixture in 3 additions, alternating with chocolate–sour cream mixture in 2 additions, scraping down bowl as needed. Give batter final stir by hand.

4. Transfer batter to prepared pan and smooth top with rubber spatula. Bake until skewer inserted in center comes out with few crumbs attached, 45 to 50 minutes, rotating pan halfway through baking. Let cake cool in pan on wire rack for 10 minutes. Invert cake onto rack, remove pan, and let cool completely, about 3 hours. Dust with confectioners' sugar, if using, before serving. (Cake can be stored at room temperature for up to 24 hours.)

MARBLED BLUEBERRY BUNDT CAKE

Serves 12 | 12-cup nonstick Bundt pan

WHY THIS RECIPE WORKS Blueberry Bundt cake is a summertime favorite, but cultivated blueberries can be oversized and bland, wreaking havoc in a cake. The berries refuse to stay suspended in the batter and burst into soggy pockets when baked. We solved these problems by pureeing the fruit, seasoning it with sugar and lemon, and bumping up its natural pectin content with low-sugar pectin for a thickened, fresh-tasting filling. We swirled our filling throughout the cake for an attractive marbled appearance and bright blueberry flavor in every bite. Spray the pan well in step 1 to prevent sticking. For fruit pectin we recommend both Sure-Jell for Less or No Sugar Needed Recipes and Ball RealFruit Low or No-Sugar Needed Pectin. If using frozen berries, thaw them before blending in step 3. This cake can be served plain or with Whipped Cream (page 548).

Marbled Blueberry Bundt Cake

CAKE
    3 cups (15 ounces) all-purpose flour
1½ teaspoons baking powder
    ¾ teaspoon baking soda
    1 teaspoon table salt
    ½ teaspoon ground cinnamon
    ¾ cup buttermilk
    2 teaspoons grated lemon zest plus 3 tablespoons juice
    2 teaspoons vanilla extract
    3 large eggs plus 1 large yolk, room temperature
   18 tablespoons (2¼ sticks) unsalted butter, cut into 18 pieces and softened
    2 cups (14 ounces) sugar

FILLING
    ¾ cup (5¼ ounces) sugar
    3 tablespoons low- or no-sugar-needed fruit pectin
      Pinch table salt
   10 ounces (2 cups) fresh or thawed frozen blueberries
    1 teaspoon grated lemon zest plus 1 tablespoon juice

1. FOR THE CAKE: Adjust oven rack to lower-middle position and heat oven to 325 degrees. Spray 12-cup nonstick Bundt pan generously with baking spray with flour. Whisk flour, baking powder, baking soda, salt, and cinnamon together in large bowl. Whisk buttermilk, lemon zest and juice, and vanilla together in second bowl. Gently whisk eggs and yolk in third bowl to combine.

TUTORIAL
Marbled Blueberry Bundt Cake
We take the marbling of this thick batter seriously for a beautiful, berry-ful Bundt.

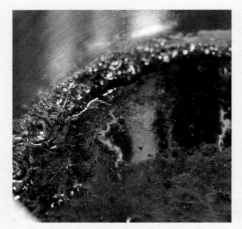

1. Heat sugar-blueberry mixture over medium heat until just simmering, about 3 minutes, stirring frequently to dissolve sugar and pectin.

2. Add remaining puree and lemon juice to cooled mixture and whisk to combine. Let sit until slightly set, about 8 minutes.

3. Spoon half of batter into prepared pan and smooth top with rubber spatula. Using back of spoon, create ½-inch-deep channel in center of batter.

4. Spoon half of filling into channel.

5. Using butter knife or small offset spatula, thoroughly swirl filling into batter (there should be no large pockets of filling remaining).

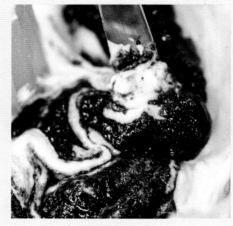

6. Repeat swirling step with remaining batter and filling.

2. Using stand mixer fitted with paddle, beat butter and sugar on medium-high speed until pale and fluffy, about 3 minutes, scraping down bowl as needed. Reduce speed to medium and beat in half of eggs until incorporated, about 15 seconds. Repeat with remaining eggs, scraping down bowl after incorporating. Reduce speed to low and add one-third of flour mixture, followed by half of buttermilk mixture, mixing until just incorporated after each addition, about 5 seconds. Repeat using half of remaining flour mixture and all of remaining buttermilk mixture. Scrape down bowl, add remaining flour mixture, and mix at medium-low speed until batter is thoroughly combined, about 15 seconds. Remove bowl from mixer and fold batter once or twice with rubber spatula to incorporate any remaining flour. Cover bowl with plastic wrap and set aside while preparing filling (batter will inflate a bit).

3. FOR THE FILLING: Whisk sugar, pectin, and salt together in small saucepan. Process blueberries in blender until mostly smooth, about 1 minute. Transfer ¼ cup blueberry puree and lemon zest to saucepan with sugar mixture and stir to thoroughly combine. Heat sugar-blueberry mixture over medium heat until just simmering, about 3 minutes, stirring frequently to dissolve sugar and pectin. Transfer mixture to bowl and let cool for 5 minutes. Add remaining puree and lemon juice to cooled mixture and whisk to combine. Let sit until slightly set, about 8 minutes.

4. Spoon half of batter into prepared pan and smooth top with rubber spatula. Using back of spoon, create ½-inch-deep channel in center of batter. Spoon half of filling into channel. Using butter knife or small offset spatula, thoroughly swirl filling into batter (there should be no large pockets of filling remaining). Repeat swirling step with remaining batter and filling.

5. Bake until top is golden brown and skewer inserted in center comes out clean, 1 hour to 1 hour 10 minutes, rotating pan halfway through baking. Let cake cool in pan on wire rack for 10 minutes. Invert cake onto rack, remove pan, and let cool for at least 3 hours before serving. (Cake can be stored at room temperature for up to 24 hours.)

SAFFRON-ORANGE BUNDT CAKE

Serves 12 | 12-cup nonstick Bundt pan

WHY THIS RECIPE WORKS The floral, earthy notes of saffron offer a unique and sophisticated twist to classic Bundt cake. Blooming the saffron in hot water released its flavor and aroma, but we were disappointed to find the cake lacked the bright yellow color. Adding more saffron was overpowering, so we turned to turmeric; just ⅛ teaspoon turned the cake a sunny yellow without adding flavor. For the orange, we used both zest and juice in the cake as well as in the glaze for an unmistakable presence. You can bake this cake in a decorative 10-cup Bundt

pan; place a baking sheet under the Bundt pan. The cake has a light, fluffy texture when eaten the day it is baked, but if well wrapped and held at room temperature overnight its texture becomes denser—like that of pound cake.

CAKE
- 1 tablespoon boiling water
- ½ teaspoon saffron threads, crumbled
- ⅛ teaspoon ground turmeric
- ¾ cup buttermilk
- 4 teaspoons grated orange zest plus 2 tablespoons juice
- 1 teaspoon vanilla extract
- 3 cups (15 ounces) all-purpose flour
- 1 teaspoon table salt
- 1 teaspoon baking powder
- ½ teaspoon baking soda
- 18 tablespoons (2¼ sticks) unsalted butter, cut into 18 pieces and softened
- 2 cups (14 ounces) granulated sugar
- 3 large eggs plus 1 large yolk

GLAZE
- 2 cups (8 ounces) confectioners' sugar
- 1 teaspoon grated orange zest plus 2–4 tablespoons juice

1. FOR THE CAKE: Adjust oven rack to lower-middle position and heat oven to 350 degrees. Spray 12-cup nonstick Bundt pan with baking spray with flour. Combine boiling water, saffron, and turmeric in 2-cup liquid measuring cup and let steep for 15 minutes. Whisk in buttermilk, orange zest and juice, and vanilla until combined.

2. Whisk flour, salt, baking powder, and baking soda together in bowl. Using stand mixer fitted with paddle, beat butter and sugar on medium-high speed until pale and fluffy, about 3 minutes. Add eggs and yolk, one at a time, and beat until combined. Reduce speed to low and add flour mixture in 3 additions, alternating with saffron mixture in 2 additions, scraping down bowl as needed. Give batter final stir by hand.

3. Transfer batter to prepared pan and smooth top with rubber spatula. Bake until top is golden and skewer inserted in center comes out clean, 50 to 55 minutes, rotating pan halfway through baking. Let cake cool in pan on wire rack set in rimmed baking sheet for 10 minutes. Invert cake onto rack, remove pan, and let cool completely, at least 3 hours. (Unglazed cake can be stored at room temperature for up to 24 hours.)

4. FOR THE GLAZE: Whisk sugar, orange zest, and 2 tablespoons juice in bowl until smooth. Gradually add remaining 2 tablespoons orange juice as needed, teaspoon by teaspoon, until glaze is thick but still pourable. Drizzle glaze over cooled cake and let set for 10 minute before serving.

COFFEE CAKES

Rich butter cake base

Must have structure to support
fillings or toppings

Baked in cake or tube pans

THE CUSTOM OF SIPPING A HOT BEVERAGE while enjoying a sweet cake or bread goes back to 17th-century Europe when German, Dutch, and Scandinavian cooks were habitual pastry makers and coffee was fast becoming part of the daily routine. Eventually, the practice spread to the United States, and today, three types of coffee cake are common: the yeasted kind, featuring a sweet cheese and/or fruit filling; the rich sour cream Bundt version that shows off elegant bands of crumb filling when sliced; and the streusel-topped type, with a nutty crunch highlighting a moist cake. For timing and ease, we are particularly drawn to the latter two styles, which call for the use of chemical leaveners to lift the dense batter; this means no waiting for the dough to rise. The cake portion is moist—neither too light and fluffy nor too dense—and enriched with eggs, butter, and sometimes sour cream. The streusel might be used as both a filling and a topping and offers an inviting contrast to the tender cake; it can be nothing more than a simple mix of flour, sugar, and butter, but it often features nuts for richness and crunch. With just the right hit of sweetness, this is a snack cake you can enjoy any time of day.

BASIC CINNAMON COFFEE CAKE

Serves 9 | 8-inch square baking pan

WHY THIS RECIPE WORKS Coffee cake as we know it today is a crumbly, sweet treat with layers of streusel. Unlike yeast-leavened breakfast pastries, this chemically leavened coffee cake comes together quickly—and it's so easy that you could pass the recipe to the kids. Measuring out the batter for the bottom layer of this square cake was essential for keeping the filling from sinking to the bottom of the pan. For a soft, sweet cinnamon swirl in the center and hearty crumbles on top, we used the streusel mixture for both but omitted the flour and butter in the filling portion to avoid a grainy interior. We developed this recipe using a metal baking pan. If using a glass or ceramic baking dish, increase the baking time to 55 minutes and let the cake cool for 45 minutes before cutting it. We prefer dark brown sugar in this recipe, but you can use light brown sugar instead.

FILLING AND STREUSEL
¾ cup packed (5 ¼ ounces) dark brown sugar
1 tablespoon ground cinnamon
½ teaspoon table salt
½ cup (2 ½ ounces) all-purpose flour
4 tablespoons unsalted butter, melted

CAKE
2 ¼ cups (11 ¼ ounces) all-purpose flour
1 ¼ cups (8 ¾ ounces) granulated sugar
1 ¼ teaspoons baking powder
½ teaspoon baking soda
¾ teaspoon table salt
1 cup whole milk
12 tablespoons unsalted butter, melted
1 large egg plus 1 large yolk, lightly beaten
2 teaspoons vanilla extract

1. FOR THE FILLING AND STREUSEL: Adjust oven rack to middle position and heat oven to 350 degrees. Spray 8-inch square baking pan with vegetable oil spray. Combine brown sugar, cinnamon, and salt in medium bowl. Reserve ¼ cup packed brown sugar mixture for filling. Stir flour into remaining brown sugar mixture. Add melted butter and mix until no dry spots remain and mixture forms clumps; set aside streusel.

2. FOR THE CAKE: Whisk flour, granulated sugar, baking powder, baking soda, and salt together in large bowl. Stir in milk, melted butter, egg and yolk, and vanilla until just combined. Pour 2 ¼ cups batter into prepared pan and spread into even layer. Sprinkle reserved brown sugar mixture evenly over batter. Dollop remaining batter evenly over filling and spread to edges of pan with offset spatula. Crumble streusel into pea-size crumbs evenly over top layer of batter.

Basic Cinnamon Coffee Cake

3. Bake until center of cake is set and toothpick inserted in center comes out with few moist crumbs attached, 45 to 50 minutes. Let cake cool in pan on wire rack for 30 minutes. Cut into squares and serve warm, or let cool completely before cutting and serving. (Cake can be stored at room temperature for up to 3 days.)

Basic Ginger-Nutmeg Coffee Cake
Add 2 teaspoons ground ginger and ¼ teaspoon ground nutmeg to flour mixture in step 2.

Basic Orange-Cardamom Coffee Cake
Add 1 tablespoon grated orange zest and 1 teaspoon ground cardamom to flour mixture in step 2.

SOUR CREAM COFFEE CAKE

Serves 12 to 16 | 16-cup tube pan

WHY THIS RECIPE WORKS Consisting of little more than flat, dry yellow cake topped with hard, pellet-like crumbs and nary a cinnamon swirl in sight, store-bought versions of coffee cake are a far cry from our sour cream version. Sour cream adds some extra decadence, moisture, and density to coffee cake that we love. Another thing we love: generous crisp, crunchy, melt-in-your-mouth streusel, not just on the top but also inside. Using all-purpose flour and four eggs in our batter gave the cake, which we baked tall in a tube pan, good structure. Using the reverse creaming method ensured a velvety, tight crumb. For the ultimate streusel, we combined brown sugar, plenty of cinnamon, and cold butter for the inner swirls. Then we added pecans to a portion and showered the top of the cake.

STREUSEL

¾ cup (3¾ ounces) all-purpose flour
¾ cup (5¼ ounces) granulated sugar
½ cup packed (3½ ounces) dark brown sugar, divided
2 tablespoons ground cinnamon
1 cup pecans, chopped
2 tablespoons unsalted butter, cut into 2 pieces and chilled

CAKE

1½ cups sour cream, divided
4 large eggs
1 tablespoon vanilla extract
2¼ cups (11¼ ounces) all-purpose flour
1¼ cups (8¾ ounces) granulated sugar
1 tablespoon baking powder
¾ teaspoon baking soda
¾ teaspoon table salt
12 tablespoons unsalted butter, cut into ½-inch cubes and softened

1. FOR THE STREUSEL: Process flour, granulated sugar, ¼ cup brown sugar, and cinnamon in food processor until combined, about 15 seconds. Transfer 1¼ cups flour-sugar mixture to bowl and stir in remaining ¼ cup brown sugar; set aside for filling. Add pecans and butter to processor and pulse until mixture resembles coarse meal, about 10 pulses; set aside for topping.

2. FOR THE CAKE: Adjust oven rack to lowest position and heat oven to 350 degrees. Grease and flour 16-cup tube pan. Whisk 1 cup sour cream, eggs, and vanilla together in bowl.

3. Using stand mixer fitted with paddle, mix flour, sugar, baking powder, baking soda, and salt on low speed until combined. Add butter and remaining ½ cup sour cream and mix until dry ingredients are moistened and mixture resembles wet sand with few large butter pieces remaining, about 1½ minutes. Increase speed to medium and beat until batter comes together, about 10 seconds, scraping down bowl with rubber spatula. Reduce speed to medium-low and gradually add egg mixture in 3 additions, beating for 20 seconds and scraping down bowl after each addition. Increase speed to medium-high and beat until batter is light and fluffy, about 1 minute.

4. Spread 2 cups batter in prepared pan and smooth top with rubber spatula. Sprinkle evenly with ¾ cup streusel filling. Repeat with another 2 cups batter and remaining ¾ cup streusel filling. Spread remaining batter over filling, then sprinkle with streusel topping.

Sour Cream Coffee Cake

5. Bake until cake feels firm and skewer inserted in center comes out clean, 50 minutes to 1 hour, rotating pan halfway through baking. Let cake cool in pan on wire rack for 30 minutes. Remove cake from pan and let cool completely on rack, about 2 hours. Serve. (Cake can be wrapped in aluminum foil and stored at room temperature for up to 5 days.)

Apricot-Almond Sour Cream Coffee Cake
Substitute 1 cup slivered almonds for pecans and ½ teaspoon almond extract for vanilla extract. Spoon six 2-teaspoon mounds apricot jam over bottom layer of batter before sprinkling with streusel and another six 2-teaspoon mounds jam over middle layer of batter before sprinkling with streusel.

Lemon-Blueberry Sour Cream Coffee Cake
Toss 1 cup frozen blueberries with 1 teaspoon grated lemon zest in small bowl. Sprinkle ½ cup blueberries over bottom layer of batter before sprinkling with streusel and remaining ½ cup blueberries over middle layer of batter before sprinkling with streusel.

Sour Cream Coffee Cake with Chocolate Chips
Sprinkle ½ cup chocolate chips over bottom layer of batter before sprinkling with streusel and another ½ cup chocolate chips over middle layer of batter before sprinkling with streusel.

PEACH COFFEE CAKE

Serves 8 | 9-inch springform pan

WHY THIS RECIPE WORKS The addition of fruit gives this coffee cake a unique edge. We aimed for strong peach presence. We added peach preserves to the batter along with a dash of almond extract, which we found complemented and intensified the peach flavor. To rid our cake of the pesky gummy layer that formed beneath the peaches, we tossed the peach slices with sugar and let them sit before arranging them on the batter. This helped pull out the extra moisture that was gumming up the works. If you have anything less than peak-of-the-season fresh peaches, it's probably best to opt for frozen peaches.

PEACHES
- 2 peaches, halved, pitted, and cut into ½-inch wedges, or 12 ounces frozen sliced peaches, thawed
- 2 tablespoons granulated sugar
- ¼ teaspoon table salt

TOPPING
- ½ cup (2½ ounces) all-purpose flour
- ¼ cup packed (1¾ ounces) brown sugar
- ½ teaspoon ground cinnamon
- ⅛ teaspoon table salt
- 3 tablespoons unsalted butter, melted

CAKE
- 1½ cups (7½ ounces) all-purpose flour
- ¾ cup (5¼ ounces) granulated sugar
- 2 teaspoons baking powder
- 1 teaspoon table salt
- ½ cup sour cream
- 2 large eggs
- 4 tablespoons unsalted butter, melted
- 1½ teaspoons vanilla extract
- ¼ teaspoon almond extract
- ½ cup peach preserves

1. FOR THE PEACHES: Toss peaches, sugar, and salt together in bowl. Let sit at room temperature until peaches exude juice, about 30 minutes. Drain peaches in colander set over bowl; reserve 2 tablespoons juice.

2. Adjust oven rack to middle position and heat oven to 350 degrees. Grease 9-inch springform pan.

3. FOR THE TOPPING: Stir flour, sugar, cinnamon, and salt together in bowl. Stir in melted butter until clumps form. Set aside.

Peach Coffee Cake

4. FOR THE CAKE: Whisk flour, sugar, baking powder, and salt together in bowl. Whisk sour cream, eggs, melted butter, vanilla, almond extract, and reserved peach juice together in large bowl. Add flour mixture to sour cream mixture and stir until just combined (batter will be quite thick). Stir preserves into batter until just combined (some chunks of preserves may be visible; this is OK).

5. Transfer batter to prepared pan and spread into even layer. Arrange peaches in concentric circles over batter, overlapping slightly as needed. Sprinkle topping over peaches.

6. Bake until topping is golden brown and toothpick inserted in center of cake comes out with few crumbs attached, 45 to 50 minutes, rotating pan halfway through baking. Transfer pan to wire rack and let cool completely, about 2 hours. Run thin knife between cake and side of pan; remove side of pan. Cut into wedges and serve.

New York-Style Crumb Cake

NEW YORK–STYLE CRUMB CAKE

Serves 9 | 8-inch square baking pan

WHY THIS RECIPE WORKS The original crumb cake was brought to New York by German immigrants; sadly, most people know only the store-bought variety. We wanted a recipe closer to the original, with just the right balance between tender yellow cake and thick, lightly spiced crumb topping. Starting with the cake, we reduced the amount of butter so the richness wouldn't be overwhelming. To compensate for the drier cake, we added buttermilk and removed an egg white to avoid a rubbery texture. For a soft, cookie-like crumb topping, we mixed sugar with melted butter and cake flour; broken into substantial pieces, this dough-like topping held together during baking and created a thick layer of moist crumbs with golden edges. Do not substitute all-purpose flour for the cake flour. When topping the cake, take care not to push the crumbs into the batter. This recipe can be easily doubled and baked in a 13 by 9-inch baking pan; increase the baking time to about 45 minutes.

CRUMB TOPPING

- 8 tablespoons unsalted butter, melted and warm
- ⅓ cup (2⅓ ounces) granulated sugar
- ⅓ cup packed (2⅓ ounces) dark brown sugar
- ¾ teaspoon ground cinnamon
- ⅛ teaspoon table salt
- 1¾ cups (7 ounces) cake flour

CAKE

- 1¼ cups (5 ounces) cake flour
- ½ cup (3½ ounces) granulated sugar
- ¼ teaspoon baking soda
- ¼ teaspoon table salt
- 6 tablespoons unsalted butter, cut into 6 pieces and softened
- ⅓ cup buttermilk
- 1 large egg plus 1 large yolk
- 1 teaspoon vanilla extract
   Confectioners' sugar

1. Adjust oven rack to upper-middle position and heat oven to 325 degrees. Make foil sling for 8-inch square baking pan by folding 2 long sheets of aluminum foil so each is 8 inches wide. Lay sheets of foil in pan perpendicular to each other, with extra foil hanging over edges of pan. Push foil into corners and up sides of pan, smoothing foil flush to pan.

2. **FOR THE CRUMB TOPPING:** Whisk melted butter, granulated sugar, brown sugar, cinnamon, and salt in bowl until combined. Add flour and stir with rubber spatula or wooden spoon until mixture resembles thick, cohesive dough; set aside and let cool completely, 10 to 15 minutes.

3. **FOR THE CAKE:** Using stand mixer fitted with paddle, mix flour, granulated sugar, baking soda, and salt on low speed until combined. Add butter, 1 piece at a time, and mix until mixture resembles moist crumbs, with no visible butter chunks remaining, 1 to 2 minutes. Add buttermilk, egg and yolk, and vanilla, increase speed to medium-high, and beat until light and fluffy, about 1 minute, scraping down bowl as needed.

4. Transfer batter to prepared pan. Using rubber spatula, spread batter into even layer. Using your hands, roll pieces of crumb-topping dough between your thumb and forefinger into large pea-size pieces. Spread pieces, breaking up any large chunks, in even layer over batter, beginning with edges and working toward center. Bake until crumbs are golden and toothpick inserted in center of cake comes out clean, 35 to 40 minutes, rotating pan halfway through baking. Let cake cool in pan on wire rack for at least 30 minutes. Using foil overhang, lift cake from pan. Dust with confectioners' sugar before serving. (Leftover cake can be refrigerated for up to 2 days; bring to room temperature before serving.)

CREAM CHEESE COFFEE CAKE

Serves 12 to 16 | 16-cup tube pan

WHY THIS RECIPE WORKS Cream cheese–filled coffee cake is a brunch dream but often the cake surrounding this tangy core is bland, or the cream cheese sinks to the bottom. Rich sour cream contributed moisture to our cake as well as a subtle tang that enhanced our cream cheese swirl. For the filling, we settled on a base mixture of softened cream cheese and sugar and then added lemon juice to cut the richness and a hint of vanilla extract for depth. Incorporating a small amount of the cake batter into the cheese ensured our filling wasn't grainy. The filling not only stayed creamy, but it fused to the cake during baking; this eliminated any gaps and guaranteed perfect swirls of filling. Sliced almonds, sugar, and lemon zest formed a glistening, crackly crust on top of our rich, moist cake.

TOPPING

- ¼ cup (1¾ ounces) sugar
- 1½ teaspoons grated lemon zest
- ½ cup sliced almonds

CAKE

- 2¼ cups (11¼ ounces) all-purpose flour
- 1⅛ teaspoons baking powder
- 1⅛ teaspoons baking soda
- 1 teaspoon table salt
- 10 tablespoons unsalted butter, cut into 10 pieces and softened
- 1⅛ cups (7¾ ounces) plus 5 tablespoons (2¼ ounces) sugar, divided
- 1 tablespoon grated lemon zest plus 4 teaspoons juice
- 4 large eggs
- 5 teaspoons vanilla extract, divided
- 1¼ cups sour cream
- 8 ounces cream cheese, softened

1. Adjust oven rack to middle position and heat oven to 350 degrees. Spray 16-cup tube pan with vegetable oil spray.

2. **FOR THE TOPPING:** Stir sugar and lemon zest in small bowl until combined and sugar is moistened. Stir in almonds; set aside.

3. **FOR THE CAKE:** Whisk flour, baking powder, baking soda, and salt together in bowl; set aside. Using stand mixer fitted with paddle, beat butter, 1⅛ cups sugar, and lemon zest on medium-high speed until pale and fluffy, about 3 minutes. Add eggs, one at a time, and beat until combined. Add 4 teaspoons vanilla and mix to combine. Reduce speed to low and add flour mixture in 3 additions, alternating with sour cream in 2 additions, scraping down bowl as needed. Give batter final stir by hand.

Cream Cheese Coffee Cake

4. Set aside 1¼ cups batter. Using rubber spatula, spread remaining batter in prepared pan and smooth top. Return now-empty bowl to mixer and beat cream cheese, lemon juice, remaining 5 tablespoons sugar, and remaining 1 teaspoon vanilla on medium speed until smooth and slightly lightened, about 1 minute. Add ¼ cup reserved batter and mix until incorporated. Spoon cream cheese mixture evenly over batter, keeping filling about 1 inch from edges of pan; smooth top. Spread remaining 1 cup reserved batter over filling and smooth top. Using butter knife or offset spatula, gently swirl filling into batter using figure-8 motion, being careful not to drag filling to bottom or edges of pan. Gently tap pan on counter to release air bubbles. Sprinkle topping evenly over batter, pressing gently to adhere.

5. Bake until top is golden and just firm and skewer inserted in center of cake comes out clean (skewer will be wet if inserted in cream cheese filling), 45 to 50 minutes, rotating pan halfway through baking. Remove pan from oven and firmly tap on counter 2 or 3 times (top of cake may sink slightly). Let cake cool in pan on wire rack for 1 hour. Remove cake from pan and let cool completely on rack, about 1½ hours. Serve. (Leftover cake can be refrigerated for up to 2 days; bring to room temperature before serving.)

POUND CAKES

Use 8½ by 4½-inch loaf pan
for tall slices

Overmixing results in tough cake

Tap pan on counter to settle batter

Stores well at room temperature
or frozen

A SLICE OF TRULY EXCELLENT POUND CAKE can transform an ordinary snacking moment into one that's sublime. Satisfyingly dense yet tender, buttery, and rich, these everyday cakes are endlessly versatile and adapt well to a multitude of flavorings: For generations, cooks have dressed up pound cake batter with sour cream, cream cheese, chocolate, and brown sugar and served warm slices slathered with salted butter or topped with fresh berries. They can be glazed but are rarely frosted.

Pound cake recipes date back to the 18th century and originally called for a pound each of flour, sugar, butter, and eggs—hence the name. Most classic recipes require ingredients at a precise temperature and a mixing method that's finicky. Why? Because there's no milk in a pound cake, you have to rely on the butter and eggs to form a proper emulsion. If the eggs are too cold or the butter is too warm, you end up with a curdled batter and a dense, heavy cake. Modern recipes have been tweaked to produce more consistent, foolproof results. For one, a small amount of baking powder is sometimes added to help achieve a slightly lighter texture, higher rise, and more consistent crumb (historically eggs were the only ingredient in pound cake that gave it lift). And in some recipes, we use hot, melted butter and a food processor: The fast-moving blade of the processor, in conjunction with the hot butter, emulsifies the liquid ingredients quickly and consistently.

LOAF PAN SIZES

Loaf pans can vary in size by more than an inch, which translates to dramatic differences in the final size and shape of the baked loaf. The pound cakes in this chapter have been designed to work with our favorite pan, the USA Pan Loaf Pan, which measures 8½ by 4½ inches. If you use a larger pan (9 by 5 is common), the cake will look squatter and skimpier when sliced. (There's more room in the pan for the batter to spread out.) The cake, however, will taste the same—just make sure to check for doneness 5 minutes earlier than specified in the recipe to avoid overbaking, as the larger surface area means the cake will bake faster. To accurately measure the size of your loaf pan, measure the top of the pan from inside edge to inside edge, not the bottom.

Baked in 9 by 5-inch loaf pan

Baked in 8½ by 4½-inch loaf pan

POUND CAKE ON TAP

When it comes to cake baking, some old-time advice is more folklore than fact (our favorite: don't slam doors, jump, or yell in the kitchen when a cake is in the oven), but we've wondered if lightly rapping the pound cake batter actually does anything. The theory is that mixing thick pound cake batter creates air bubbles that remain trapped, leaving the baked cake dotted with holes. We baked two pound cakes, tapped and untapped. The cake that hadn't been tapped was indeed dotted with holes, while the cake we'd tapped against the counter had a neat, even crumb.

Untapped Batter
Trapped air bubbles in the thick batter cause holes in the finished cake.

Tapped Batter
For a neat, even crumb, tap the batter-filled pan on the counter before baking the cake.

POUND CAKE

Serves 8 | 8½ by 4½-inch loaf pan

WHY THIS RECIPE WORKS A rich, golden pound cake is a must in any baker's repertoire. But classic pound cake recipes tend to be very particular, requiring ingredients at certain temperatures as well as finicky mixing methods. In our search for a simple, foolproof pound cake recipe, we uncovered two key elements: hot melted (rather than softened) butter and a food processor. The combination of the fast-moving blade of the processor and the hot melted butter emulsified the liquid ingredients quickly before they had a chance to curdle. Sifting the dry ingredients over our emulsified egg mixture in three additions, and whisking them in after each addition, allowed us to incorporate the dry ingredients easily and ensured that no pockets of flour marred our finished cake.

- 1½   cups (6 ounces) cake flour
- 1   teaspoon baking powder
- ½   teaspoon table salt
- 1¼   cups (8¾ ounces) sugar
- 4   large eggs, room temperature
- 1½   teaspoons vanilla extract
- 16   tablespoons unsalted butter, melted and hot

1. Adjust oven rack to middle position and heat oven to 350 degrees. Grease and flour 8½ by 4½-inch loaf pan. Whisk flour, baking powder, and salt together in bowl.

2. Process sugar, eggs, and vanilla in food processor until combined, about 10 seconds. With processor running, add hot melted butter in steady stream until incorporated. Transfer to large bowl.

3. Sift flour mixture over egg mixture in 3 additions, whisking to combine after each addition until few streaks of flour remain. Continue to whisk batter gently until almost no lumps remain (do not overmix).

4. Transfer batter to prepared pan and smooth top with rubber spatula. Gently tap pan on counter to settle batter. Bake until toothpick inserted in center comes out with few crumbs attached, 50 minutes to 1 hour, rotating pan halfway through baking.

5. Let cake cool in pan on wire rack for 10 minutes. Run thin knife around edge of pan, remove cake from pan, and let cool completely on rack, about 2 hours. Serve. (Cake can be stored at room temperature for up to 3 days or frozen for up to 1 month; defrost cake at room temperature.)

Almond Pound Cake

Add 1 teaspoon almond extract and ¼ cup slivered almonds to food processor with sugar, eggs, and vanilla. Sprinkle 2 tablespoons slivered almonds over cake before baking.

Ginger Pound Cake

Add 3 tablespoons minced crystallized ginger, 1½ teaspoons ground ginger, and ½ teaspoon ground mace to food processor with sugar, eggs, and vanilla.

Lemon Pound Cake

Add 2 tablespoons grated lemon zest (2 lemons) and 2 teaspoons juice to food processor with sugar, eggs, and vanilla.

Orange Pound Cake

Add 1 tablespoon grated orange zest and 1 tablespoon juice to food processor with sugar, eggs, and vanilla.

CHOCOLATE POUND CAKE

Serves 8 | 8½ by 4½-inch loaf pan

WHY THIS RECIPE WORKS Adding chocolate to pound cake can mar the cake's finely tuned texture. We wanted to retool classic pound cake to make it ultrachocolaty without compromising its hallmark velvety-soft crumb. We started by blooming cocoa powder in the microwave with butter and bittersweet chocolate for a rich, chocolaty base. When we added this mixture to the other liquid ingredients in the food processor, the fast-moving blades emulsified everything before it had a chance to curdle. Cake flour was imperative to make this cake tender and fine-crumbed. This cake is delicious on its own, but we also like to glaze it with All-Purpose Chocolate Glaze (page 549) or top slices with a scoop of ice cream and fresh berries.

- 16   tablespoons unsalted butter
- ¾   cup (2¼ ounces) unsweetened cocoa powder
- 2   ounces bittersweet chocolate, chopped fine
- 1   cup (4 ounces) cake flour
- ½   teaspoon table salt
- ¼   teaspoon baking powder
- 1¼   cups (8¾ ounces) sugar
- 4   large eggs, room temperature
- 1½   teaspoons vanilla extract

1. Adjust oven rack to middle position and heat oven to 325 degrees. Grease and flour 8½ by 4½-inch loaf pan. Microwave butter, cocoa, and chocolate in bowl at 50 percent power, stirring occasionally, until melted and smooth; let cool slightly.

2. Whisk flour, salt, and baking powder together in second bowl. Process sugar, eggs, and vanilla in food processor until combined, about 10 seconds, scraping down sides of bowl as needed. Add chocolate mixture and process until incorporated, about 10 seconds; transfer to large bowl.

TUTORIAL
Pound Cake

When pound cake is perfect, it's really something special. Learn these foolproof steps to make the best.

1. Process sugar, eggs, and vanilla in food processor until combined, about 10 seconds.

2. With processor running, add hot melted butter in steady stream until incorporated. Transfer to large bowl.

3. Sift flour mixture over egg mixture in 3 additions, whisking to combine after each addition until few streaks of flour remain.

4. Continue to whisk batter gently until almost no lumps remain (do not overmix).

5. Transfer batter to prepared pan and smooth top with rubber spatula. Gently tap pan on counter to settle batter.

6. Bake until toothpick inserted in center comes out with few crumbs attached, 50 minutes to 1 hour, rotating pan halfway through baking.

3. Sift flour mixture over egg mixture in 3 additions, whisking to combine after each addition until few streaks of flour remain. Continue to whisk batter gently until almost no lumps remain (do not overmix).

4. Transfer batter to prepared pan, smooth top with rubber spatula, and gently tap pan on counter to settle batter. Bake until toothpick inserted in center comes out with few moist crumbs attached, 1 hour 5 minutes to 1¼ hours, rotating pan halfway through baking.

5. Let cake cool in pan on wire rack for 10 minutes. Run thin knife around edge of pan, remove cake from pan, and let cool completely on rack, about 2 hours. Serve.

RASPBERRY SWIRL POUND CAKE

Serves 8 | 8½ by 4½-inch loaf pan

WHY THIS RECIPE WORKS We wanted to incorporate the flavor of sweet-tart raspberries into tender, rich pound cake. Adding a generous spoonful of vibrant lemon zest helped balance and round out the rich batter. A simple raspberry filling swirled into the cake gave it the fresh fruit element we sought and provided ribbons of juicy textural contrast and a lovely ruby color throughout. Cooking the berries briefly with sugar and just enough cornstarch to thicken the sauce ensured that the surrounding cake wouldn't become soggy. We prefer to use frozen raspberries for this recipe because they are more consistently sweet than fresh. If you have access to very good fresh berries, use them instead.

RASPBERRY FILLING
- 1 teaspoon cornstarch
- 1 teaspoon water
- 8 ounces (about 1⅔ cups) frozen raspberries
- ¼ cup (1¾ ounces) sugar
- ¼ teaspoon table salt

POUND CAKE
- 5 large eggs, room temperature
- 2 teaspoons vanilla extract
- 1¾ cups (8¾ ounces) all-purpose flour
- ¾ teaspoon table salt
- ½ teaspoon baking powder
- ⅓ cup sour cream
- 2 tablespoons milk
- 14 tablespoons unsalted butter, softened but still cool
- 1¼ cups (8¾ ounces) sugar
- 1 tablespoon grated lemon zest

1. **FOR THE RASPBERRY FILLING:** Stir cornstarch and water together in bowl; set aside. Cook raspberries, sugar, and salt in small saucepan over medium heat, stirring occasionally, until slightly thickened and mixture measures 1 scant cup, 8 to 10 minutes.

2. Stir cornstarch mixture to recombine, then stir into raspberry sauce. Cook until thickened, about 1 minute. Transfer filling to bowl and refrigerate, uncovered, until no longer warm, about 1 hour. (Filling can be covered and refrigerated for up to 2 days.)

3. **FOR THE POUND CAKE:** Adjust oven rack to lower-middle position and heat oven to 300 degrees. Grease and flour 8½ by 4½-inch loaf pan. Whisk eggs and vanilla together in 2-cup liquid measuring cup. Whisk flour, salt, and baking powder together in bowl. Whisk sour cream and milk together in second bowl.

4. Using stand mixer fitted with paddle, beat butter, sugar, and lemon zest on medium-high speed until pale and fluffy, 5 to 7 minutes, scraping down bowl as needed.

5. Reduce speed to medium and gradually add egg mixture in slow, steady stream. Scrape down bowl and continue to mix on medium speed until uniform, about 1 minute longer (batter may look slightly curdled).

6. Reduce speed to low and add flour mixture in 3 additions, alternating with sour cream mixture in 2 additions, scraping down bowl as needed. Give batter final stir by hand.

7. Transfer half of batter (about 2 cups) to prepared pan. Stir raspberry filling to loosen. Spoon half of raspberry filling over length of batter in pan, leaving ½ inch border. Using butter knife, thoroughly swirl filling throughout batter, taking care to not leave any big deposits of filling in center or along sides of pan.

8. Transfer remaining batter to pan and repeat spooning and swirling with remaining raspberry filling. Tap pan on counter twice to release air bubbles.

9. Bake until toothpick inserted 1 inch to side of split in center of cake comes out clean (very top center of cake may seem underdone; this is OK), 1½ hours to 1 hour 40 minutes, rotating pan halfway through baking.

10. Run thin knife around edges of pan. Let cake cool in pan on wire rack for 15 minutes. Remove cake from pan and let cool completely on rack, about 2 hours. Slice and serve. (Cake can be stored at room temperature for up to 3 days or frozen for up to 1 month; defrost cake at room temperature.)

CREAM CHEESE POUND CAKE

Serves 12 | 12-cup nonstick Bundt pan

WHY THIS RECIPE WORKS While classic pound cake is baked in a loaf pan, cream cheese versions are typically prepared in a Bundt pan for a big and beautiful presentation. Simply mixing cream cheese into the batter resulted in a cake with a heavy, coarse crumb, so we removed the leavener; this cut down on the cake's lift for a velvety, tight crumb. A couple extra egg yolks made our cake supremely moist and tender. Baking our cake in a low oven took a little longer, but it produced a perfect golden-brown crust and a moist, tender interior. We prefer whole milk in this recipe, but any percentage fat will work. You can bake this cake in a decorative 10-cup Bundt pan (for more information, see page 289); place a baking sheet under the Bundt pan. We like to serve this rich cake with sweet-tart Strawberry-Rhubarb Compote (page 139).

    3 cups (12 ounces) cake flour
    1 teaspoon table salt
    4 large eggs plus 2 large yolks, room temperature
    ¼ cup milk
    2 teaspoons vanilla extract
   24 tablespoons (3 sticks) unsalted butter, softened
    6 ounces cream cheese, softened
    3 cups (21 ounces) sugar

1. Adjust oven rack to middle position and heat oven to 300 degrees. Spray 12-cup nonstick Bundt pan with baking spray with flour. Whisk flour and salt together in bowl. Whisk eggs and yolks, milk, and vanilla together in 2-cup liquid measuring cup.

2. Using stand mixer fitted with paddle, beat butter, cream cheese, and sugar on medium-high speed until pale and fluffy, about 3 minutes. Reduce speed to low and very slowly add egg mixture, mixing until incorporated (batter may look slightly curdled). Add flour mixture in 3 additions, scraping down bowl as needed. Give batter final stir by hand.

3. Transfer batter to prepared pan. Gently tap pan on counter to release air bubbles. Bake until skewer inserted in center comes out clean, 1 hour 20 minutes to 1½ hours, rotating pan halfway through baking. Let cake cool in pan on wire rack for 15 minutes. Invert cake onto rack, remove pan, and let cool completely, about 2 hours. Serve. (Cake can be stored at room temperature for up to 3 days or frozen for up to 1 month; defrost cake at room temperature.)

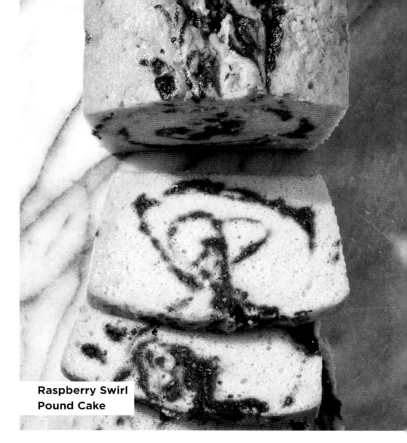

Raspberry Swirl Pound Cake

Cream Cheese Pound Cake

FRUIT CAKES

TORTES, BUCKLES, AND UPSIDE-DOWN CAKES: These desserts showcase fruit in a big way. To be sure, fruit features in a variety of cakes in this book—mashed bananas are stirred into a snack cake, a jamlike filling is swirled throughout a pound cake, and strawberries are spooned into the middle of a refined shortcake. But these rustic fruit cakes stand apart in that the fruit is truly the star of the show. Berries folded right into the batter; chunks of fresh peaches suspended in a rich, tender crumb; a caramelized layer of sweet-tart rhubarb melded with a plush, sturdy cake: In each flavor-packed, satisfying cake, the fruit is a cohesive yet distinct component. Most are simple to put together, requiring nothing more than a whisk and spatula, or perhaps a quick blitz in the food processor. This ease, along with the beautiful contrast of buttery, tender cake and bright, glistening jewel-toned fruit, gives these desserts an informal elegance that makes them ideal for casual entertaining.

KEY POINTS

Fortify crumb with ground nuts

Eliminate excess juice where possible

Mix with quick-bread method for coarser crumb

Precook fruit to pack more in

Rustic Fruit Cakes

The biggest challenge of these charming cakes lies in creating a tender yet sturdy crumb that can support the substantial pieces of juicy fruit. Some, such as Rustic Plum Cake (page 310) replace a portion of the flour with ground nuts; this gives the cake's crumb just enough structure to help keep the pieces of fruit from sinking. And in our Summer Peach Cake (page 308) we toss the peaches with panko breadcrumbs, which absorb excess moisture and keep the peaches suspended in the batter. Gently cooking the fruit is one way to eliminate excess moisture and prevent a soggy filling (it also serves to intensify the flavor of the fruit).

FORGING FRUIT FLAVOR

Even the most beautiful specimens can taste wan when suspended in batter. The test kitchen has a number of fruit-specific tricks to make them taste their best when baked.

Precook the Fruit
Roasting the peaches in our Summer Peach Cake (page 308) caramelizes their sugars and concentrates their sweet-tart flavor. For our Rustic Plum Cake (page 310), we reduce a little jam and brandy to a syrup in a skillet and sauté the plums, cut side down, in the mixture until they release their juice; the plums become intensely flavored without being overcooked.

Flavor the Batter
We use the whole fruit to get citrus flavor in every bite of our Clementine Cake (page 308), microwaving the fruit until soft and processing it with all the other cake ingredients into a smooth batter.

Choose the Right Varieties
Bosc pears have dense flesh and hold their shape best after baking into our Pear-Walnut Upside-Down Cake (page 314). Italian prune plums are less watery and more concentrated in flavor than other plum varieties for an exquisite plum cake (page 310).

Use the Juice
The juice that the plums in Rustic Plum Cake (page 310) release reduces to become a serving sauce; pineapple juice added to the caramel for Pineapple Upside-Down Cake (page 313) amplifies the pineapple flavor missing in other pineapple upside-down cakes.

Buckles

A buckle—cousin to crumble, crisp, and coffee cake—consists of a thick cake batter mixed with chopped fruit or berries and baked under a crunchy streusel topping, with the substance of the dessert being the fruit rather than the cake. Friendly and rustic, it's been a favorite of New England home cooks for hundreds of years. And the curious name? The cake, burdened as it is with fruit and streusel topping, is said to buckle on the surface as it bakes.

Upside-Down Cake

"Pineapple" and "upside-down cake" are practically synonymous. But long before the introduction of canned pineapple in the early 1900s sparked a craze for pineapple in baked goods, upside-down cakes were made with a variety of seasonal fruit. The ideal fruit upside-down cake features a glistening caramelized topping and fruit resting on a flavorful, tender butter cake. The proportions and textures of the base, the fruit, and the topping marry well, providing the perfect balance of fruit and cake in each bite. The basic technique is straightforward: Pour melted butter and brown sugar into a pan or skillet, add sliced fruit, spread cake batter over the fruit, and bake. The slices caramelize on the bottom of the pan, revealing a layer of burnished amber fruit when the cake is turned out.

QUICK-BREAD CAKE

To achieve the pleasantly coarse crumb characteristic of a good upside-down cake, we forgo the usual method of creaming the butter and sugar and use the quick-bread method instead. Creaming produces a tender cake that tends to buckle under the weight of the fruit (and that's a different cake). The quick-bread method, in which the butter is melted and the liquid and dry ingredients are mixed separately before being combined, introduces less air and creates a sturdier crumb much better suited to supporting the fruit.

CLEMENTINE CAKE

Serves 8 | 9-inch springform pan

WHY THIS RECIPE WORKS To achieve the maximum amount of bright, floral clementine flavor for this citrusy cake, we put clementines both inside and on top. For the batter, we relied on the standard creaming method but added clementines that we had softened in the microwave and pureed. While the cake was baking, we quickly candied some sliced clementines in a sugar solution. A showstopping white glaze set off the bright orange candied fruit slices. Look for clementines that are about 2 inches in diameter (about 1¾ ounces each). Use a mandoline to get consistent slices of clementine to arrange on top of the cake; you can also use a chef's knife. We found it easier to slice the clementines when they were cold.

CAKE

- 9 ounces clementines, unpeeled, stemmed (5 clementines)
- 2¼ cups (7½ ounces) sliced blanched almonds, toasted
- 1 cup (5 ounces) all-purpose flour
- 1¼ teaspoons baking powder
- ¼ teaspoon table salt
- 10 tablespoons unsalted butter, cut into 10 pieces and softened
- 1½ cups (10½ ounces) granulated sugar
- 5 large eggs

CANDIED CLEMENTINES

- 4 clementines, unpeeled, stemmed
- 1 cup water
- 1 cup (7 ounces) granulated sugar
- ⅛ teaspoon table salt

GLAZE

- 2 cups (8 ounces) confectioners' sugar
- 2½ tablespoons water, plus extra as needed
  Pinch table salt

1. FOR THE CAKE: Adjust oven rack to middle position and heat oven to 325 degrees. Spray 9-inch springform pan with vegetable oil spray, line bottom with parchment paper, and grease parchment. Microwave clementines in covered bowl until softened and some juice is released, about 3 minutes. Discard juice and let clementines cool for 10 minutes.

2. Process almonds, flour, baking powder, and salt in food processor until almonds are finely ground, about 30 seconds; transfer to second bowl. Add clementines to now-empty processor and process until smooth, about 1 minute, scraping down sides of bowl as needed.

3. Using stand mixer fitted with paddle, beat butter and sugar on medium-high speed until pale and fluffy, about 3 minutes. Add eggs, one at a time, and beat until combined, scraping down bowl as needed. Add clementine puree and beat until incorporated, about 30 seconds.

4. Reduce speed to low and add almond mixture in 3 additions until just combined, scraping down bowl as needed. Using rubber spatula, give batter final stir by hand. Transfer batter to prepared pan and smooth top. Bake until toothpick inserted in center comes out clean, 55 minutes to 1 hour. Let cake cool completely in pan on wire rack, about 2 hours.

5. FOR THE CANDIED CLEMENTINES: While cake cools, line baking sheet with triple layer of paper towels. Slice clementines ¼ inch thick perpendicular to stem; discard rounded ends. Bring water, sugar, and salt to simmer in small saucepan over medium heat and cook until sugar has dissolved, about 1 minute. Add clementines and cook until softened, about 6 minutes. Using tongs, transfer clementines to prepared sheet and let cool for at least 30 minutes, flipping halfway through cooling to blot away excess moisture.

6. FOR THE GLAZE: Whisk sugar, water, and salt in bowl until smooth. Adjust consistency with extra water as needed, ½ teaspoon at a time, until glaze has consistency of thick craft glue and leaves visible trail in bowl when drizzled from whisk.

7. Carefully run paring knife around cake and remove side of pan. Using thin metal spatula, lift cake from pan bottom; discard parchment and transfer cake to serving platter. Pour glaze over cake and smooth top with offset spatula, allowing some glaze to drip down sides. Let sit for 1 hour to set.

8. Just before serving, select 8 uniform candied clementine slices (you will have more than 8 slices; reserve extra slices for another use) and blot away excess moisture with additional paper towels. Arrange slices around top edge of cake, evenly spaced. Serve. (Cake can be stored at room temperature for up to 2 days.)

SUMMER PEACH CAKE

Serves 8 to 10 | 9-inch springform pan

WHY THIS RECIPE WORKS Add ripe peaches to cake and problems abound: All the juice makes for a soggy cake and their delicate flavor gets lost. Roasting the peaches—and tossing them with peach schnapps—concentrated their flavor and expelled moisture. However, the peaches became swathed in a flavorful but gooey film when cooked. We coated our roasted peaches in panko bread crumbs, which absorbed the film; the crumbs then dissolved into the cake. Peach slices and a sprinkling of almond sugar gave the cake a beautiful finish. To crush the panko, place the crumbs in a zipper-lock bag and smash with a rolling pin. Orange liqueur can be substituted for the schnapps. If using farm-fresh peaches, omit the schnapps.

TUTORIAL
Clementine Cake

This cake is unusually fruity. That's because it calls for a puree of whole clementines (in addition to candied ones on top). Clementine cake, indeed.

1. Microwave clementines in covered bowl until softened and some juice is released, about 3 minutes. Discard juice and let clementines cool for 10 minutes.

2. Add clementines to empty processor and process until smooth, about 1 minute, scraping down sides of bowl as needed. Add clementine puree to batter and beat until incorporated, about 30 seconds.

3. While cake is cooking, slice clementines ¼ inch thick perpendicular to stem; discard rounded ends.

4. Bring water, sugar, and salt to simmer in small saucepan over medium heat and cook until sugar has dissolved, about 1 minute. Add clementines and cook until softened, about 6 minutes.

5. Using tongs, transfer clementines to prepared sheet and let cool for at least 30 minutes, flipping halfway through cooling to blot away excess moisture.

6. Just before serving, select 8 uniform candied clementine slices and blot away excess moisture with additional paper towels. Arrange slices around top edge of glazed cake, evenly spaced.

PEACHES

2½ pounds peaches, peeled, halved, pitted, and cut into ½-inch wedges, divided
5 tablespoons peach schnapps, divided
4 teaspoons lemon juice, divided
3 tablespoons granulated sugar, divided

CAKE

1 cup (5 ounces) all-purpose flour
1¼ teaspoons baking powder
¾ teaspoon table salt
½ cup packed (3½ ounces) light brown sugar
⅓ cup (2⅓ ounces) plus 3 tablespoons granulated sugar, divided
2 large eggs, room temperature
8 tablespoons unsalted butter, melted and cooled
¼ cup sour cream
1½ teaspoons vanilla extract
⅜ teaspoon almond extract, divided
⅓ cup panko bread crumbs, crushed fine

1. FOR THE PEACHES: Adjust oven rack to middle position and heat oven to 425 degrees. Line rimmed baking sheet with aluminum foil and spray with vegetable oil spray. Grease and flour 9-inch springform pan. Gently toss 24 peach wedges with 2 tablespoons schnapps, 2 teaspoons lemon juice, and 1 tablespoon sugar in bowl; set aside.

2. Cut remaining peach wedges crosswise into 3 chunks and gently toss with remaining 3 tablespoons schnapps, 2 teaspoons lemon juice, and 2 tablespoons sugar in second bowl. Spread peach chunks onto prepared baking sheet and bake until exuded juices begin to thicken and caramelize at edges of pan, 20 to 25 minutes. Let peaches cool completely on pan, about 30 minutes. Reduce oven temperature to 350 degrees.

3. FOR THE CAKE: Whisk flour, baking powder, and salt together in bowl. Whisk brown sugar, ⅓ cup granulated sugar, and eggs in large bowl until thick and thoroughly combined, about 45 seconds. Slowly whisk in melted butter until combined. Whisk in sour cream, vanilla, and ¼ teaspoon almond extract until combined. Add flour mixture and whisk until just combined.

4. Pour half of batter into prepared pan and spread to pan edges with rubber spatula. Sprinkle crushed panko over roasted peaches and toss gently to combine. Arrange peaches evenly in pan and press gently into batter. Gently spread remaining batter over peaches, smooth top, and arrange reserved peaches attractively over top, also placing wedges in center. Combine remaining 3 tablespoons granulated sugar and remaining ⅛ teaspoon almond extract in bowl; sprinkle over top.

5. Bake cake until golden brown and toothpick inserted in center comes out clean, 50 minutes to 1 hour, rotating pan halfway through baking. Let cake cool in pan on wire rack for 5 minutes.

Run thin knife around edge of pan to loosen cake, then remove sides of pan. Let cake cool completely on rack, 2 to 3 hours. Slide thin metal spatula between cake bottom and pan bottom to loosen, then slide cake onto platter. Serve.

RUSTIC PLUM CAKE

Serves 8 to 10 | 9-inch springform pan

WHY THIS RECIPE WORKS For our plum cake, we replaced some of the all-purpose flour with homemade almond flour, which created a moist cake that was sturdy enough to hold the plums aloft. Poaching the plums in brandy and red currant jelly heightened their flavor and kept them moist. This recipe works best with Italian prune plums. If substituting regular plums, use an equal weight, cut them into eighths, and stir them a few times while cooking in step 1. Don't use canned plums. Don't add the leftover plum cooking liquid to the cake before baking; reserve it and serve with the finished cake. The cake can be served warm or at room temperature; if serving warm, remove the sides of the pan after letting the cake cool for 30 minutes. Serve this cake with Whipped Cream (page 548), if desired.

3 tablespoons brandy
2 tablespoons red currant jelly or seedless raspberry jam
1 pound Italian prune plums, halved and pitted
¾ cup (5¼ ounces) granulated sugar
⅓ cup slivered almonds
¾ cup (3¾ ounces) all-purpose flour
½ teaspoon baking powder
¼ teaspoon table salt
6 tablespoons unsalted butter, cut into 6 pieces and softened
1 large egg plus 1 large yolk, room temperature
1 teaspoon vanilla extract
¼ teaspoon almond extract (optional)
   Confectioners' sugar (optional)

1. Cook brandy and jelly in 10-inch nonstick skillet over medium heat until thick and syrupy, 2 to 3 minutes. Remove skillet from heat and add plums, cut side down. Return skillet to medium heat and cook, shaking pan to prevent plums from sticking, until plums release their juices and liquid reduces to thick syrup, about 5 minutes. Let plums cool in skillet for 20 minutes.

2. Adjust oven rack to middle position and heat oven to 350 degrees. Grease and flour 9-inch springform pan. Process granulated sugar and almonds in food processor until nuts are finely ground, about 1 minute. Add flour, baking powder, and salt and pulse to combine, about 5 pulses. Add butter and pulse until mixture resembles coarse sand, about 10 pulses. Add egg and yolk; vanilla; and almond extract, if using, and process until smooth, about 5 seconds, scraping down sides of bowl as needed (batter will be very thick and heavy).

Rustic Plum Cake

CAKE

1½ cups (9 ounces) dried apricots (1 cup chopped fine,
    ½ cup halved crosswise)
¼ cup dark rum
1 cup dried cherries
1 cup (5 ounces) all-purpose flour
1¼ teaspoons baking powder
¾ teaspoon table salt
½ cup packed (3½ ounces) light brown sugar
⅓ cup (2⅓ ounces) granulated sugar
2 large eggs, room temperature
8 tablespoons unsalted butter, melted and cooled
1½ teaspoons vanilla extract
1 teaspoon grated lemon zest
1 teaspoon grated orange zest
¾ cup walnuts, toasted and chopped

SOAK AND GLAZE

⅓ cup dark rum
2 tablespoons orange juice
2 tablespoons apricot jam

3. Transfer batter to prepared pan and smooth top with rubber spatula. Stir plums to coat with syrup. Arrange plum halves, skin side down, evenly over surface of batter (reserve leftover syrup). Bake until golden and toothpick inserted in center comes out with few crumbs attached, 40 to 50 minutes, rotating pan halfway through baking. Run thin knife around edge of pan to loosen cake. Let cake cool completely in pan on wire rack, about 2 hours. Remove sides of pan and dust cake with confectioners' sugar, if using. Slide thin metal spatula between cake bottom and pan bottom to loosen, then slide cake onto platter. Serve with reserved plum syrup.

MODERN FRUITCAKE

Serves 10 to 12 | 8-inch round cake pan

WHY THIS RECIPE WORKS Fruitcake is often dense, dry, and laden with artificial candied fruit. We wanted a refined take. To replace the neon glacé fruits, we landed on tart dried cherries and sweet apricots; as the pieces of fruit cooked in the cake they turned translucent, giving them a naturally glacéed effect. We made a sturdy batter that supported 2 cups of fruit as well as ¾ cup of walnuts. A small amount of rum in the batter along with a rum and orange juice soak gave the cake a subtly boozy flavor. We laid halved pieces of dried apricots around the bottom of the pan so that the finished cake had a festive fruit crown, and we finished it with a simple apricot glaze.

1. FOR THE CAKE: Adjust oven rack to middle position and heat oven to 350 degrees. Grease 8-inch round cake pan, line with parchment paper, grease parchment, and flour pan. Arrange halved apricots cut side down, perpendicular to pan edge, in tightly packed ring around bottom of pan. Microwave rum in bowl until steaming, about 30 seconds; stir in chopped apricots and cherries and let sit for 20 minutes, stirring once halfway through cooling.

2. Whisk flour, baking powder, and salt together in bowl. Whisk brown sugar, granulated sugar, and eggs in large bowl until thoroughly combined and thick, about 45 seconds. Slowly whisk in melted butter until combined. Whisk in vanilla, lemon zest, and orange zest. Gently whisk in flour mixture until just combined. Using rubber spatula, fold in rum-soaked fruits and walnuts.

3. Pour batter into prepared pan and smooth top with rubber spatula. Bake until deep golden brown and skewer inserted in center comes out clean, 55 minutes to 1 hour 5 minutes, rotating pan halfway through baking. Let cake cool in pan on wire rack for 5 minutes. Run thin knife around edge of pan to loosen cake, invert cake onto wire rack set in rimmed baking sheet, and remove pan.

4. FOR THE SOAK AND GLAZE: Microwave rum and orange juice in bowl until steaming, about 30 seconds. Measure out 2 tablespoons rum mixture and whisk with apricot jam; strain through fine-mesh strainer into bowl, discarding solids, and set aside. Using skewer, poke 15 to 20 holes over cake. Brush warm cake with remaining rum–orange juice mixture and let cool completely, at least 3 hours. Brush apricot glaze over cake and let sit for 10 minutes. Serve. (Cooled cake and glaze can be wrapped tightly in plastic wrap, separately, and stored at room temperature for up to 1 week. Brush with glaze just before serving.)

MIXED BERRY BUCKLE

Serves 8 | 9-inch round cake pan

WHY THIS RECIPE WORKS A buckle—cousin to crumble, crisp, and coffee cake—consists of a thick cake batter mixed with chopped fruit and baked under a crunchy streusel topping. We wanted our version to showcase fresh, seasonal berries at their peak ripeness. Tossing the berries with sugar brought out their natural sweetness. When baked, the dense, buttery cake suspended the berries, creating a luscious, summery dessert. We prefer the flavor of fresh mixed berries here, but you can also use a single variety of berries as long as the total amount still equals 15 ounces (3 cups). If using all fresh blueberries, omit the ¼ cup sugar for tossing the berries in step 4; blueberries are sweet enough on their own. You can also use 15 ounces (3 cups) of frozen mixed berries that have been thawed, drained for 30 minutes in a colander, and then patted dry with paper towels.

STREUSEL

- 1 cup (5 ounces) all-purpose flour
- ½ cup packed (3½ ounces) light brown sugar
- 6 tablespoons unsalted butter, melted
- ½ teaspoon table salt

CAKE

- ½ cup whole milk
- 2 large eggs
- 4 tablespoons unsalted butter, melted
- 1 teaspoon vanilla extract
- 1 cup (5 ounces) all-purpose flour
- ½ cup (3½ ounces) granulated sugar, divided
- 1½ teaspoons baking powder
- 1 teaspoon grated lemon zest
- ½ teaspoon table salt
- 5 ounces (1 cup) blackberries, cut in half crosswise
- 5 ounces (1 cup) blueberries
- 5 ounces (1 cup) raspberries, cut in half crosswise

1. FOR THE STREUSEL: Stir all ingredients in bowl until no dry spots remain and mixture forms clumps. Refrigerate until streusel is firm, at least 10 minutes. Keep refrigerated until ready to use.

2. FOR THE CAKE: Adjust oven rack to middle position and heat oven to 350 degrees. Grease 9-inch round cake pan, line with parchment paper, grease parchment, and flour pan.

3. Whisk milk, eggs, melted butter, and vanilla in bowl until well combined. Whisk flour, ¼ cup sugar, baking powder, lemon zest, and salt together in large bowl. Stir milk mixture into flour mixture until just combined.

4. Toss blackberries, blueberries, and raspberries with remaining ¼ cup sugar in separate bowl until coated. Using rubber spatula, gently fold half of berry mixture into batter until evenly

Mixed Berry Buckle

distributed. Transfer batter to prepared pan and spread to edges of pan with spatula. Sprinkle remaining half of berry mixture evenly over top.

5. Break streusel into pea-size crumbs and distribute evenly over berries. Bake until top of buckle is golden brown and toothpick inserted in center comes out clean, about 50 minutes, rotating pan halfway through baking. Let buckle cool in pan on wire rack for 2 hours.

6. Run paring knife around edges of pan to release buckle from pan. Place inverted plate on top of pan (do not use plate or platter on which you intend to serve buckle). Invert buckle, remove pan, and discard parchment. Reinvert buckle onto serving platter. Cut into wedges and serve.

INDIVIDUAL BLACKBERRY-WALNUT BUCKLES

Serves 8 | eight 6-ounce ramekins

WHY THIS RECIPE WORKS We wanted to up the elegance of this rustic dessert by reimagining the buckle in miniature form. Replacing some of the flour in our batter with ground nuts provided richness and a substantial flavor boost, and we found that different nuts paired well with specific fruits; we particularly liked blackberry with walnut, cherry with almond, and raspberry with pistachio. Since we already had the food processor out for grinding the nuts, we decided to make the rest of the batter right in the processor, reserving the berries to fold in at the end. Rather than obscuring our smaller-scale buckles with a heavy streusel topping, we simply topped each ramekin with a sprinkling of nuts. Do not substitute frozen berries here. Serve warm with vanilla ice cream or Whipped Cream (page 548).

½ cup walnuts, chopped coarse, divided
4 tablespoons unsalted butter, softened
¾ cup (5¼ ounces) sugar
¼ teaspoon table salt
2 large eggs
⅓ cup heavy cream
1 teaspoon vanilla extract
¾ cup (3¾ ounces) all-purpose flour
½ teaspoon baking powder
15 ounces (3 cups) blackberries

1. Adjust oven rack to middle position and heat oven to 375 degrees. Lightly spray eight 6-ounce ramekins with vegetable oil spray; set aside. Toast ¼ cup walnuts in dry 8-inch skillet over medium heat until lightly browned and fragrant, 3 to 4 minutes; let cool completely.

2. Process toasted walnuts, butter, sugar, and salt in food processor until finely ground, 10 to 15 seconds. With processor running, add eggs, cream, and vanilla and continue to process until smooth, about 5 seconds. Add flour and baking powder and pulse until just incorporated, about 5 pulses.

3. Transfer batter to large bowl. Using rubber spatula, gently fold in blackberries. Divide batter evenly among prepared ramekins and sprinkle top of each buckle with remaining ¼ cup walnuts.

4. Bake buckles on rimmed baking sheet until golden and cake begins to pull away from sides of ramekins, 25 to 35 minutes. Let cool completely on wire rack, about 45 minutes. Serve.

Cherry-Almond Buckles
You can substitute fresh pitted sweet cherries or canned sweet cherries in syrup for the frozen cherries; make sure they have been rinsed and patted dry.

Substitute sliced or slivered almonds for walnuts; almond extract for vanilla extract; and 3 cups frozen sweet cherries, thawed, drained, and patted dry, for blackberries.

Raspberry-Pistachio Buckles
Don't use frozen raspberries in this recipe; they're too mushy.

Substitute pistachios for walnuts and raspberries for blackberries.

PINEAPPLE UPSIDE-DOWN CAKE

Serves 8 | 9-inch round cake pan
WHY THIS RECIPE WORKS For a showstopping update on this beautiful retro cake, we started with fresh pineapple instead of canned and used round cutters to make our own rings in order to preserve the classic look. Simmering the rings in a mixture of pineapple juice and brown sugar tenderized them and drove off some of their excess moisture to prevent a soggy cake. After transferring the softened rings to the cake pan, we cooked down the juice-sugar mixture and added butter to make a luscious pineapple caramel sauce. Doubling the typical amount of caramel ensured a beautifully glossy cake top and allowed us to brush some onto the other side of the cake. You will need a 3¼-inch round cutter and a 1¼-inch round cutter or apple corer to make the pineapple rings. If you prefer, you can substitute 2 additional tablespoons of pineapple juice for the rum in step 5.

1 pineapple, peeled
1½ cups packed (10½ ounces) light brown sugar
1 cup plus 2 tablespoons pineapple juice, divided
7 maraschino cherries, stemmed and patted dry
12 tablespoons unsalted butter, cut into 12 pieces, plus 8 tablespoons melted
1 teaspoon table salt, divided
2 tablespoons dark rum
1½ cups (7½ ounces) all-purpose flour
1 teaspoon baking powder
1 cup (7 ounces) granulated sugar
½ cup whole milk
2 large eggs
1 teaspoon vanilla extract

1. Adjust oven rack to middle position and heat oven to 350 degrees. Grease 9-inch round cake pan, line with parchment paper, and grease parchment.

2. Cut seven ½-inch-thick crosswise slices from pineapple. (Reserve remaining pineapple for another use.) Using 3¼-inch round cutter, cut slices into neat rounds; discard trimmings. Using 1¼-inch round cutter or apple corer, remove core from pineapple slices to create rings; discard core pieces.

3. Combine brown sugar and 1 cup pineapple juice in 12-inch skillet. Add pineapple rings to skillet in single layer. Bring to boil over medium-high heat and cook until rings have softened, about 10 minutes, flipping rings halfway through cooking. Transfer rings to prepared pan, placing 1 ring in center of pan and arranging remaining 6 rings around circumference of pan (rings will fit snugly in pan without overlapping). Place cherries in centers of rings.

4. Return brown sugar mixture to boil over medium-high heat and cook, stirring frequently, until rubber spatula dragged across bottom of skillet leaves trail that fills in slowly, bubbles increase in size, and mixture registers 260 degrees, 3 to 6 minutes. Carefully stir in 12 tablespoons butter and ½ teaspoon salt until butter is melted (caramel may look separated at first). Return mixture to boil and cook until frothy and uniform in texture, about 1 minute. Let caramel cool off heat for 5 minutes.

5. Transfer caramel to 4-cup liquid measuring cup. Pour ¾ cup caramel evenly over pineapple rings, gently shaking pan to distribute. Whisk rum and remaining 2 tablespoons pineapple juice into remaining caramel; set aside.

6. Whisk flour, baking powder, and remaining ½ teaspoon salt together in bowl. Whisk granulated sugar, milk, eggs, and vanilla in large bowl until smooth, about 1 minute. Whisk 8 tablespoons melted butter into milk mixture until combined. Whisk flour mixture into milk mixture until no dry flour remains.

7. Transfer batter to prepared pan and smooth top with rubber spatula. Bake until light golden brown and toothpick inserted in center comes out clean, 50 minutes to 1 hour.

8. Transfer pan to wire rack. Immediately run paring knife between cake and sides of pan. Using toothpick, poke about 80 holes evenly over cake. Microwave reserved caramel mixture until warm, about 1 minute. Brush cake with ½ cup reserved caramel mixture. Let cake cool in pan for 25 minutes. Carefully invert cake onto serving plate. Brush top of cake with remaining reserved caramel mixture as desired. Serve warm or at room temperature, passing any remaining caramel mixture separately.

PEAR-WALNUT UPSIDE-DOWN CAKE

Serves 8 to 10 | 9-inch round cake pan

WHY THIS RECIPE WORKS Despite its title as the queen of fruit, the regal pear doesn't get enough attention in desserts. We thought it was time to explore pear upside-down cake, which would be a perfect way to showcase pears' subtle floral flavor and graceful curved shape. We tried every variety of pear at the store and found that Bosc pears, with their dense flesh, held their shape best after baking. Unlike hardier fruits, delicate pears could be sliced into wedges and baked raw; the slices softened up just enough once baked without falling apart. Instead of the sweet yellow cake base typical of upside-down cakes, we made a walnut-based cake, which was light yet sturdy, earthy-tasting and less sweet, and visually attractive. Serve with crème fraîche, lightly sweetened whipped cream, or our Tangy Whipped Cream (page 548).

TOPPING

4 tablespoons unsalted butter, melted
½ cup packed (3½ ounces) dark brown sugar
2 teaspoons cornstarch
⅛ teaspoon table salt
3 ripe but firm Bosc pears (8 ounces each)

CAKE

1 cup walnuts, toasted
½ cup (2½ ounces) all-purpose flour
½ teaspoon table salt
¼ teaspoon baking powder
⅛ teaspoon baking soda
3 large eggs
1 cup (7 ounces) sugar
4 tablespoons unsalted butter, melted
¼ cup vegetable oil

1. FOR THE TOPPING: Adjust oven rack to middle position and heat oven to 300 degrees. Grease 9-inch round cake pan and line with parchment paper. Pour melted butter over bottom of pan and swirl to evenly coat. Combine sugar, cornstarch, and salt in small bowl and sprinkle evenly over melted butter.

2. Peel, halve, and core pears. Set aside 1 pear half and reserve for other use. Cut remaining 5 pear halves into 4 wedges each. Arrange pears in circular pattern around prepared pan with tapered ends pointing inward. Arrange 2 smallest pear wedges in center.

3. FOR THE CAKE: Pulse walnuts, flour, salt, baking powder, and baking soda in food processor until walnuts are finely ground, 8 to 10 pulses. Transfer walnut mixture to bowl.

4. Process eggs and sugar in now-empty processor until very pale yellow, about 2 minutes. With processor running, add melted butter and oil in steady stream until incorporated. Add walnut mixture and pulse to combine, 4 or 5 pulses. Pour batter evenly over pears (some pears may show through; cake will bake up over fruit).

5. Bake until center of cake is set and bounces back when gently pressed and toothpick inserted in center comes out clean, 1 hour 10 minutes to 1¼ hours, rotating pan after 40 minutes. Let cake cool in pan on wire rack for 15 minutes. Run thin knife around edge of pan to loosen cake. Invert cake onto rack set in rimmed baking sheet and remove pan, discarding parchment. Let cake cool for 2 hours. Serve.

RHUBARB UPSIDE-DOWN CAKE

Serves 8 | 8-inch square baking pan

WHY THIS RECIPE WORKS This recipe combines the best attributes of two of our favorite rhubarb cakes: a Scandinavian-style cake and an upside-down cake. An almond streusel reminiscent of the sugary almond topping of the former provided a substantial, crunchy foundation, and lemon and cardamom in the batter delivered warm, floral notes to highlight the tart, vegetal rhubarb. Enriching the cake with butter, eggs, and sour cream yielded a rich, tender texture with enough structure to support the generous rhubarb topping. Making this cake in an upside-down style encouraged the rhubarb to break down and achieve a sweet, compote-like consistency. You can substitute thawed, drained frozen rhubarb for the fresh. Serve the cake with unsweetened whipped cream, if desired. Red currant jelly is worth seeking out; strawberry and raspberry jam won't produce the same effect.

STREUSEL

½ cup (2½ ounces) all-purpose flour
½ cup sliced almonds
¼ cup (1¾ ounces) sugar
4 tablespoons unsalted butter, melted
¼ teaspoon table salt

RHUBARB

¾ cup (5¼ ounces) sugar
1½ teaspoons cornstarch
1 teaspoon grated lemon zest
1 pound rhubarb, trimmed and cut into ½-inch pieces
2 tablespoons unsalted butter, melted

CAKE

1 cup (5 ounces) all-purpose flour
1½ teaspoons ground cardamom
1 teaspoon baking powder
½ teaspoon table salt
1 cup (7 ounces) sugar
2 large eggs
6 tablespoons unsalted butter, melted and cooled
½ cup sour cream
1 teaspoon grated lemon zest plus 1 tablespoon juice
1 teaspoon vanilla extract
2 tablespoons red currant jelly

1. Adjust oven rack to lower-middle position and heat oven to 350 degrees. Grease 8-inch square baking pan, line bottom with parchment paper, and grease parchment.

2. FOR THE STREUSEL: Stir all ingredients in medium bowl until well combined. Set aside.

3. FOR THE RHUBARB: Whisk sugar, cornstarch, and lemon zest together in large bowl. Add rhubarb and stir well to coat. Drizzle with melted butter and stir to incorporate. Transfer rhubarb mixture to prepared pan and press rhubarb pieces into bottom of pan, making sure there are no large gaps (pieces may not fit in single layer).

4. FOR THE CAKE: Whisk flour, cardamom, baking powder, and salt together in medium bowl; set aside. Whisk sugar and eggs in large bowl until thick and homogeneous, about 45 seconds. Whisk in melted butter until combined. Add sour cream, lemon zest and juice, and vanilla; whisk until combined. Add flour mixture and whisk until just combined. Pour batter into pan and spread evenly over rhubarb mixture. Break up streusel with your hands and sprinkle in even layer over batter. Bake until cake is golden brown and toothpick inserted in center comes out clean, 45 to 50 minutes.

5. Transfer pan to wire rack and let cool for 20 minutes. Run knife around edges of pan to loosen cake, then invert onto serving platter. Let cool for about 10 minutes. Microwave jelly in small bowl until fluid, about 20 seconds. Using pastry brush, gently dab jelly over rhubarb topping. Serve warm or at room temperature.

Rhubarb Upside-Down Cake

TORTES AND FLOURLESS CAKES

Often use ground nuts for structure

Get structure and lift from lots of eggs

Springform pan upholds cake

Slice with warm sharp knife

THESE CAKES HAVE A LOW PROFILE WITH TALL FLAVOR. They're rich, lush, and sophisticated and an elegant finale to any dinner. Chocolate is the main ingredient, and it shines through in all these deliciously dense cakes, as most don't include very much flour—some not at all.

Flourless cakes are the only type named for a missing ingredient. Since flour is generally considered the most important component of just about any cake, giving it structure, crumb, and texture, removing all or a portion of it presents some challenges— namely, finding a way to achieve lift and structure without it. Some of these cakes gain structure from ground nuts, but the biggest hero is eggs. With so few ingredients in these decadent desserts, technique matters: The way you incorporate the eggs determines the final texture of the cake. In Flourless Chocolate Cake (page 317) the eggs are simply mixed with the other ingredients for a dense yet velvety texture, while in our showstopping Triple Chocolate Mousse Cake (page 318), the egg whites are whipped and then folded into the other ingredients for a base cake layer that's almost, well, mousse-like.

Some of these cakes and tortes, such as Torta Caprese (page 320), are served as is, with perhaps a dollop of sweet whipped cream or tangy crème fraîche or a dusting of confectioners' sugar. Others, like our Chocolate-Raspberry Torte (page 321), are enrobed in a rich glaze or chocolate ganache that gives the finished cake a glossy sheen and ups the glamour quotient exponentially. These cakes are *fudgy*. To keep slices looking glamorous, cut with care: Dip a sharp knife in hot water and wipe dry before and after each cut, or use a cheese wire.

FLOURLESS CHOCOLATE CAKE

Serves 10 to 12 | 9-inch springform pan

WHY THIS RECIPE WORKS Incredibly rich and impossibly smooth, flourless chocolate cake is elegant, refined, and universally beloved. Our take on this indulgent cake minimizes fuss without sacrificing flavor or texture. We began by gently melting chocolate and butter in the microwave. In the absence of flour, we called on eggs for structure, cornstarch for body, and water for a moist, smooth texture. Ensuring a crack-free surface was as easy as straining and resting the batter before tapping out bubbles that rose to the surface. This cake needs to chill for at least 6 hours. An accurate oven thermometer is essential here. We prefer this cake made with 60 percent bittersweet chocolate; our favorite brands are Ghirardelli and Callebaut. Top servings with Whipped Cream (page 548) and shaved chocolate if desired.

12 ounces bittersweet chocolate, broken into 1-inch pieces
16 tablespoons unsalted butter
6 large eggs
1 cup (7 ounces) sugar
½ cup water
1 tablespoon cornstarch
1 tablespoon vanilla extract
1 teaspoon instant espresso powder
½ teaspoon table salt

1. Adjust oven rack to middle position and heat oven to 275 degrees. Spray 9-inch springform pan with vegetable oil spray. Microwave chocolate and butter in bowl at 50 percent power, stirring occasionally, until melted, about 4 minutes. Let chocolate mixture cool for 5 minutes.

2. Whisk eggs, sugar, water, cornstarch, vanilla, espresso powder, and salt in large bowl until thoroughly combined, about 30 seconds. Whisk in chocolate mixture until smooth and slightly thickened, about 45 seconds. Strain batter through fine-mesh strainer into prepared pan, pressing against strainer with rubber spatula or back of ladle to help batter pass through. Gently tap pan on counter to release air bubbles; let sit on counter for 10 minutes to allow air bubbles to rise to top. Use tines of fork to gently pop any air bubbles that have risen to surface. Bake until edges are set and center jiggles slightly when cake is shaken gently, 45 to 50 minutes.

3. Let cake cool in pan on wire rack for 5 minutes; run thin knife around edge of pan to loosen cake. Let cake cool on rack until barely warm, about 30 minutes. Cover cake tightly with plastic wrap, poke small hole in top, and refrigerate until cold and firmly set, at least 6 hours or up to 2 days. Remove sides of pan and slide thin metal spatula between cake bottom and pan bottom to loosen, then slide cake onto platter. Let cake stand at room temperature for 30 minutes before slicing and serving.

Flourless Chocolate Cake

TRIPLE CHOCOLATE MOUSSE CAKE

Serves 12 to 16 | 9-inch springform pan

WHY THIS RECIPE WORKS This triple-decker stunner becomes incrementally lighter in texture and richness from bottom to top. For the base we opted for flourless chocolate cake, which had enough heft to support the upper two tiers. For the middle layer, we removed the eggs from a traditional chocolate mousse for a lighter, creamier consistency. And for the top tier, we made an easy white chocolate mousse by folding whipped cream into melted white chocolate; a little gelatin helped stabilize this soft mousse. This recipe requires a springform pan that is at least 3 inches high. We recommend using our favorite dark chocolate, Ghirardelli 60% Cacao Bittersweet Chocolate Premium Baking Bar, for the bottom and middle layers; the test kitchen's other highly recommended dark chocolate, Callebaut Intense Dark Chocolate, L-60–40NV, may be used, but it will produce drier, slightly less sweet results. For the best results, chill the mixer bowl before whipping the heavy cream in steps 5 and 8. Top servings with shaved chocolate or chocolate curls, if desired.

BOTTOM LAYER

- 6 tablespoons unsalted butter, cut into 6 pieces
- 7 ounces bittersweet chocolate, chopped fine
- ¾ teaspoon instant espresso powder
- 4 large eggs, separated
- 1½ teaspoons vanilla extract
  Pinch cream of tartar
  Pinch table salt
- ⅓ cup packed (2⅓ ounces) light brown sugar, divided

MIDDLE LAYER

- 5 tablespoons hot water
- 2 tablespoons Dutch-processed cocoa powder
- 7 ounces bittersweet chocolate, chopped fine
- 1½ cups heavy cream, chilled
- 1 tablespoon granulated sugar
- ⅛ teaspoon table salt

TOP LAYER

- ¾ teaspoon unflavored gelatin
- 1 tablespoon water
- 1 cup (6 ounces) white chocolate chips
- 1½ cups heavy cream, chilled, divided
  Shaved semisweet chocolate (optional)

1. FOR THE BOTTOM LAYER: Adjust oven rack to middle position and heat oven to 325 degrees. Grease 9-inch springform pan. Combine butter, chocolate, and espresso powder in large heatproof bowl set over saucepan filled with 1 inch barely simmering water, making sure that water does not touch bottom of bowl and stirring occasionally until butter and chocolate are melted. Remove from heat and let cool slightly, about 5 minutes. Whisk in egg yolks and vanilla; set aside.

2. Using stand mixer fitted with whisk attachment, whip egg whites, cream of tartar, and salt on medium-low speed until foamy, about 1 minute. Add half of sugar and whip until combined, about 15 seconds. Add remaining sugar, increase speed to high, and whip until soft peaks form, about 1 minute longer, scraping down bowl halfway through whipping. Using whisk, fold one-third of whipped whites into chocolate mixture to lighten. Using rubber spatula, fold in remaining whites until no white streaks remain. Carefully pour batter into prepared pan and smooth top with rubber spatula.

3. Bake until cake has risen, is firm around edges, and center springs back when pressed gently with your finger, 13 to 18 minutes, rotating pan halfway through baking. Let cake cool completely in pan on wire rack, about 1 hour, before filling. (Cake will collapse as it cools.) Do not remove cake from pan.

4. FOR THE MIDDLE LAYER: Combine hot water and cocoa in small bowl; set aside. Melt chocolate in large heatproof bowl set over saucepan filled with 1 inch barely simmering water, making sure that water does not touch bottom of bowl and stirring occasionally until smooth. Remove from heat and let cool slightly, 2 to 5 minutes.

5. Using clean, dry mixer bowl and whisk attachment, whip cream, sugar, and salt on medium-low speed until foamy, about 1 minute. Increase speed to high and whip until soft peaks form, 1 to 3 minutes.

6. Whisk cocoa mixture into melted chocolate until smooth. Using whisk, fold one-third of whipped cream into chocolate mixture to lighten. Using rubber spatula, fold in remaining whipped cream until no white streaks remain. Spoon mousse into pan over cooled cake and smooth top with offset spatula. Gently tap pan on counter to release air bubbles. Wipe inside edge of pan with damp cloth to remove any drips. Refrigerate cake for at least 15 minutes.

7. FOR THE TOP LAYER: Sprinkle gelatin over water in small bowl and let sit until gelatin softens, about 5 minutes. Place chocolate chips in medium heatproof bowl. Bring ½ cup cream to simmer in small saucepan over medium-high heat. Remove from heat, add gelatin mixture, and stir until gelatin is fully dissolved. Pour cream mixture over chocolate chips and let sit, covered, for 5 minutes. Whisk mixture gently until smooth. Let cool completely, stirring occasionally (mixture will thicken slightly).

**Triple Chocolate
Mousse Cake**

8. Using clean, dry mixer bowl and whisk attachment, whip remaining 1 cup cream on medium-low speed until foamy, about 1 minute. Increase speed to high and whip until soft peaks form, 1 to 3 minutes. Using hand whisk, fold one-third of whipped cream into white chocolate mixture to lighten. Using rubber spatula, fold in remaining whipped cream until no white streaks remain. Spoon white chocolate mousse into pan over middle layer and smooth top with offset spatula. Refrigerate cake until set, at least 2½ hours. (Cake can be refrigerated for up to 24 hours; let sit at room temperature for up to 45 minutes before releasing from pan and serving.)

9. Garnish top of cake with shaved chocolate, if using. Run thin knife around edge of pan to loosen cake, then remove sides of pan. Run clean knife along outside of cake to smooth. Slice and serve.

TORTA CAPRESE

Serves 12 to 14 | 9-inch springform pan

WHY THIS RECIPE WORKS A simple yet elegant dessert with origins along the Amalfi Coast, torta caprese is a chocolate-almond cake with all the richness and depth of flourless chocolate cake, but it features finely ground almonds that subtly break up the fudgy crumb, making it a lighter final course. Bittersweet chocolate provided a solid chocolate base, and some cocoa powder added complexity. To aerate the heavy batter and provide enough structure and lift, we beat the whites and yolks separately. We also discovered that commercial almond flour worked just as well as nuts we had ground ourselves, which saved us the trouble of using two appliances. This cake tastes great the next day, so it's an excellent make-ahead dessert for entertaining. Either almond flour or almond meal will work in this recipe; we used Bob's Red Mill Almond Flour. We like the cake with Orange Whipped Cream (page 548).

    12 tablespoons unsalted butter, cut into 12 pieces
     6 ounces bittersweet chocolate, chopped
     1 teaspoon vanilla extract
     4 large eggs, separated
     1 cup (7 ounces) granulated sugar, divided
     2 cups (7 ounces) almond flour
     2 tablespoons unsweetened cocoa powder
     ½ teaspoon table salt
        Confectioners' sugar (optional)

1. Adjust oven rack to middle position and heat oven to 325 degrees. Lightly spray 9-inch springform pan with vegetable oil spray.

2. Microwave butter and chocolate in bowl at 50 percent power, stirring occasionally, until melted and smooth, 1½ to 2 minutes. Stir in vanilla and set aside.

3. Using stand mixer fitted with whisk attachment, whip egg whites on medium-low speed until foamy, about 1 minute. Increase speed to medium-high and whip, slowly adding ½ cup granulated sugar, until glossy, stiff peaks form, about 4 minutes. Transfer whites to large bowl.

4. Add egg yolks and remaining ½ cup granulated sugar to now-empty mixer bowl and whip on medium-high speed until thick and pale yellow, about 3 minutes, scraping down bowl as needed. Add chocolate mixture and mix on medium speed until incorporated, about 15 seconds. Add almond flour, cocoa, and salt and mix until incorporated, about 30 seconds.

5. Remove bowl from mixer and stir batter a few times with large rubber spatula, scraping bottom of bowl to ensure almond flour is fully incorporated. Add one-third of whipped whites to bowl, return bowl to mixer, and mix on medium speed until no streaks of white remain, about 30 seconds, scraping down bowl halfway through mixing. Transfer batter to bowl with remaining whites. Using large rubber spatula, gently fold whites into batter until no streaks of white remain. Transfer batter to prepared pan and smooth top with spatula. Place pan on rimmed baking sheet and bake until toothpick inserted in center comes out with few

Torta Caprese

moist crumbs attached, about 50 minutes, rotating sheet halfway through baking. Let cake cool in pan on wire rack for 20 minutes. Remove side of pan and let cake cool completely, about 2 hours. (Cake can be stored at room temperature for up to 3 days.)

6. Dust top of cake with confectioners' sugar, if using. Using offset spatula, transfer cake to serving platter. Cut into wedges and serve.

CHOCOLATE-RASPBERRY TORTE

Serves 12 to 16 | two 9-inch round cake pans

WHY THIS RECIPE WORKS Sacher torte—a Viennese dessert featuring rich chocolate cake layered with apricot jam and enrobed in a refined chocolate glaze—makes a lavish finish to an elegant meal. We give this classic our own unique spin by pairing the chocolate cake with tangy raspberries. We wanted a decadent, fudgy base, and we started with two thin layers of flourless chocolate cake, but the dense cake tore and fell apart. Adding ground almonds (along with a small amount of flour) gave our cake structure. The winning approach for our filling was to combine jam with lightly mashed fresh berries for a sweet-tart mixture that clung to the cake.

CAKE

- 8 ounces bittersweet chocolate, chopped fine
- 12 tablespoons unsalted butter, cut into ½-inch pieces
- 2 teaspoons vanilla extract
- ¼ teaspoon instant espresso powder
- 1¾ cups sliced almonds, toasted, divided
- ¼ cup (1¼ ounces) all-purpose flour
- ½ teaspoon table salt
- 5 large eggs, room temperature
- ¾ cup (5¼ ounces) sugar
- 2 (9-inch) cardboard rounds

FILLING

- 2½ ounces (½ cup) raspberries, plus 16 raspberries for garnishing
- ¼ cup seedless raspberry jam

GLAZE

- 5 ounces bittersweet chocolate, chopped fine
- ½ cup plus 1 tablespoon heavy cream

1. FOR THE CAKE: Adjust oven rack to middle position and heat oven to 325 degrees. Grease two 9-inch round cake pans, line with parchment paper, grease parchment, and flour pans. Melt chocolate and butter in large heatproof bowl set over saucepan filled with 1 inch barely simmering water, making sure that water does not touch bottom of bowl and stirring occasionally until smooth. Let cool completely, about 30 minutes. Stir in vanilla and espresso powder.

2. Pulse ¾ cup almonds in food processor until coarsely chopped, 6 to 8 pulses; transfer to bowl and set aside for garnish. Process remaining 1 cup almonds until very finely ground, about 45 seconds. Add flour and salt and continue to process until combined, about 15 seconds. Transfer almond mixture to second bowl. Process eggs in now-empty processor until lightened in color and almost doubled in volume, about 3 minutes. With processor running, slowly add sugar and process until thoroughly combined, about 15 seconds. Using whisk, gently fold egg mixture into chocolate mixture until some streaks of egg remain. Sprinkle half of ground almond mixture over chocolate mixture and gently whisk until just combined. Sprinkle with remaining ground almond mixture and gently whisk until just combined.

3. Divide batter evenly between prepared pans and smooth tops with rubber spatula. Bake until centers are firm and toothpick inserted in center comes out with few moist crumbs attached, 14 to 16 minutes, rotating pans halfway through baking. Let cakes cool completely in pans on wire rack, about 30 minutes.

4. Run thin knife around edges of pans to loosen cakes, then invert onto cardboard rounds, discarding parchment. Using wire rack, turn 1 cake right side up, then slide from rack back onto cardboard round.

5. FOR THE FILLING: Place ½ cup raspberries in bowl and mash coarse with fork. Stir in jam until just combined.

6. Spread raspberry mixture onto cake layer that is right side up. Top with second cake layer, leaving it upside down. Transfer assembled cake, still on cardboard round, to wire rack set in rimmed baking sheet.

7. FOR THE GLAZE: Melt chocolate and cream in heatproof bowl set over saucepan filled with 1 inch barely simmering water, making sure that water does not touch bottom of bowl and stirring occasionally until smooth. Off heat, gently whisk until very smooth. Pour glaze onto center of assembled cake. Using offset spatula, spread glaze evenly over top of cake, letting it drip down sides. Spread glaze along sides of cake to coat evenly.

8. Using fine-mesh strainer, sift reserved chopped almonds to remove any fine bits. Gently press sifted almonds onto cake sides. Arrange remaining 16 raspberries on top around outer edge. Refrigerate cake on rack until glaze is set, at least 1 hour or up to 24 hours. (If refrigerated for more than 1 hour, let cake sit at room temperature for about 30 minutes before serving.) Transfer cake to platter and serve.

PUDDING CAKES

KEY POINTS

Don't overbake

Serve warm or as soon as
cake is cool

WITH THEIR LAYERS OF CONTRASTING TEXTURES, pudding cakes may seem like a bit of magic—a single batter goes into the oven and emerges as distinct tiers of cake and pudding—but it's really just culinary chemistry at work. Giving the cake batter more structure, with an additional egg or extra flour, is one way to ensure a cake that will separate and rise above a pudding layer. Adding more butter can "waterproof" the batter and encourage it to remain separate from the sauce. Some pudding cakes use a water bath to different effects: Boiling water and a foil cover trap steam, resulting in perfectly spongy, moist cakes soaked with a rich sauce in Sticky Toffee Pudding (page 325), while our Lemon Pudding Cakes (page 323) call for a cold water bath to create a perfectly cooked layer of creamy pudding beneath a light layer of cake. However it's achieved, the melding of rich, creamy pudding or sauce with tender cake makes for one irresistible treat.

HOT FUDGE PUDDING CAKE

Serves 6 to 8 | 10-inch cast-iron skillet

WHY THIS RECIPE WORKS Hot fudge pudding cake begins with a simple yet magical concoction that is transformed upon baking into a decadent two-layer dessert. A chocolate cake batter is sprinkled with a sugar-cocoa layer, followed by liquid poured over the top. As the batter bakes, the cake rises to the top and the bottom turns into a puddinglike chocolate sauce. To make sure ours delivered on flavor as well as looks, we used cocoa powder and bittersweet chocolate for complex chocolate flavor. Replacing some of the water in the pudding layer with coffee deepened the chocolate flavor further. We made this treat in a cast-iron skillet because hot fudge pudding cake is meant to be served hot: Cast iron does a great job of holding on to heat, so there was no worry that the dessert would cool down before it was time to eat. Serve with Whipped Cream (page 548) or ice cream.

Hot Fudge Pudding Cake

6 tablespoons unsalted butter, cut into 6 pieces
2 ounces bittersweet chocolate, chopped
⅔ cup (2 ounces) unsweetened cocoa powder, divided
¾ cup (3¾ ounces) all-purpose flour
2 teaspoons baking powder
¼ teaspoon table salt
⅓ cup packed (2⅓ ounces) light brown sugar
1 cup (7 ounces) granulated sugar, divided
1 cup brewed coffee
½ cup water
⅓ cup whole milk
1 tablespoon vanilla extract
1 large egg yolk

1. Adjust oven rack to middle position and heat oven to 325 degrees. Melt butter, chocolate, and ⅓ cup cocoa together in 10-inch cast-iron skillet over low heat, stirring often, until smooth, 2 to 4 minutes. Set aside to cool slightly.

2. Whisk flour, baking powder, and salt together in bowl. Whisk brown sugar, ⅓ cup granulated sugar, and remaining ⅓ cup cocoa together in second bowl, breaking up any large clumps of brown sugar with fingers. Combine coffee and water in third bowl.

3. Whisk milk, vanilla, egg yolk, and remaining ⅔ cup granulated sugar into cooled chocolate mixture. Whisk in flour mixture until just combined. Sprinkle brown sugar mixture evenly over top, covering entire surface of batter. Pour coffee mixture gently over brown sugar mixture.

4. Transfer skillet to oven and bake until cake is puffed and bubbling and just beginning to pull away from sides of skillet, about 35 minutes, rotating skillet halfway through baking. Using potholders, transfer skillet to wire rack and let cake cool for 15 minutes. Serve.

LEMON PUDDING CAKES

Serves 6 | six 6-ounce ramekins

WHY THIS RECIPE WORKS The appeal of lemon pudding cake lies in the magic of a single batter producing two texturally distinct layers. We wanted tender cake, creamy pudding, and lots of lemon flavor in one individual-size dessert. Whipping egg whites to soft peaks produced a tender cake with some lift. Baking the cakes in a water bath prevented the pudding from curdling and allowed the cakes to cook gently. Lemon zest, steeped in the dairy, and plenty of lemon juice provided balanced flavor. To take the temperature of the pudding, touch the probe tip of a thermometer to the bottom of the ramekin and pull it up ¼ inch. We like this dessert served at room temperature, but it can also be served chilled (the texture will be firmer) with Blueberry Compote (page 550), if desired.

1 cup whole milk
½ cup heavy cream
3 tablespoons grated lemon zest plus ½ cup juice (3 lemons)
1 cup (7 ounces) sugar, divided
¼ cup (1¼ ounces) all-purpose flour
½ teaspoon baking powder
⅛ teaspoon table salt
2 large eggs, separated, plus 2 large whites
½ teaspoon vanilla extract

Lemon Pudding Cakes

POUDING CHÔMEUR

Serves 6 to 8 | 8-inch square baking pan

WHY THIS RECIPE WORKS This Quebecois version of a pudding cake features a coarse-crumbed cake, a luscious sauce of maple syrup and cream, and a caramelized, craggy top. To ensure that the cake remained separate from the maple-cream sauce, we added more flour to provide structure and more butter to "waterproof" the batter from the sauce. We baked the cake in the top half of a 375-degree oven to caramelize the top. The cake is best served hot; for this reason, we prefer using a glass baking dish, which retains heat well, but a metal baking pan will also work. The color of syrup labeled Grade A Dark Amber will contrast best against the yellow cake. Serve with a dollop of crème fraîche or a scoop of vanilla or coffee ice cream.

  1 cup maple syrup, preferably dark amber
  1 cup heavy cream
  1 teaspoon table salt, divided
1¼ cups (6¼ ounces) all-purpose flour
  3 tablespoons sugar
1½ teaspoons baking powder
 ⅔ cup milk
  2 large eggs
 ½ teaspoon vanilla extract
  6 tablespoons unsalted butter, melted

1. Adjust oven rack to middle position and heat oven to 325 degrees. Bring milk and cream to simmer in medium saucepan over medium-high heat. Off heat, whisk in lemon zest, cover saucepan, and let stand for 15 minutes. Meanwhile, fold dish towel in half and place in bottom of large roasting pan. Place six 6-ounce ramekins on top of towel; set aside pan.

2. Strain milk mixture through fine-mesh strainer into bowl, pressing on lemon zest to extract liquid; discard lemon zest. Whisk ¾ cup sugar, flour, baking powder, and salt together in second bowl. Add egg yolks, vanilla, lemon juice, and milk mixture and whisk until combined. (Batter will have consistency of milk.)

3. Using stand mixer fitted with whisk attachment, whip egg whites on medium-low speed until foamy, about 1 minute. Increase speed to medium-high and whip whites to soft, billowy mounds, about 1 minute. Gradually add remaining ¼ cup sugar and whip until glossy, soft peaks form, 1 to 2 minutes.

4. Whisk one-quarter of whites into batter to lighten. Using rubber spatula, gently fold in remaining whites until no clumps or streaks remain. Divide batter evenly among ramekins (ramekins should be nearly full). Pour enough cold water into roasting pan to come one-third of way up sides of ramekins. Bake until cake is set and pale golden brown and pudding layer registers 172 to 175 degrees at center, 50 to 55 minutes. Remove pan from oven and let ramekins stand in water bath for 10 minutes. Transfer ramekins to wire rack and let cool completely. Serve.

1. Adjust oven rack 6 inches from top of oven and heat oven to 375 degrees. Heat maple syrup, cream, and ½ teaspoon salt in medium saucepan over medium heat until simmering, about 5 minutes. Off heat, whisk to combine, then transfer to heatproof 2-cup liquid measuring cup.

2. Whisk flour, sugar, baking powder, and remaining ½ teaspoon salt together in large bowl. Whisk milk, eggs, and vanilla in second bowl until combined. Whisk milk mixture into flour mixture until combined. Add melted butter and whisk until smooth. Transfer batter to 8-inch square baking dish set in rimmed baking sheet and spread into even layer with spatula. Pour syrup mixture slowly down corner of baking dish so it flows gently over top of cake batter.

3. Bake until deep golden brown and toothpick inserted in center of cake layer comes out clean, 30 to 35 minutes. Let cool on wire rack for 10 minutes. Use serving spoon to scoop onto plates, inverting each spoonful so sauce is on top.

STICKY TOFFEE PUDDING

Serves 8 | eight 6-ounce ramekins

WHY THIS RECIPE WORKS Sticky toffee pudding is a British dessert featuring a moist date-studded cake soaked in toffee sauce. These "puddings" are supposed to be sticky, not mushy, so we needed a fairly sturdy cake that would hold up to the sauce. Happily, the easy quick-bread method of combining the ingredients produced the desired dense-yet-springy crumb. Substituting molasses for the traditional sweetener known as treacle overwhelmed the caramel flavor of the dates; brown sugar was a better option, but the dates still needed a flavor boost. Replacing the water that was already in our batter recipe with the date soaking liquid improved the flavor significantly, and pulverizing half the dates in the food processor before mixing them in guaranteed that every bite was laced with date flavor. Baking the cakes in a water bath ensured they remained moist. Be sure to form a tight seal with the foil before baking the cakes.

CAKES
- 8 ounces pitted dates, cut crosswise into ¼-inch-thick slices (1⅓ cups), divided
- ¾ cup warm water (110 degrees)
- ½ teaspoon baking soda
- 1¼ cups (6¼ ounces) all-purpose flour
- ½ teaspoon baking powder
- ½ teaspoon table salt
- ¾ cup packed (5¼ ounces) brown sugar
- 2 large eggs
- 4 tablespoons unsalted butter, melted
- 1½ tablespoons vanilla extract

SAUCE
- 4 tablespoons unsalted butter
- 1 cup packed (7 ounces) brown sugar
- ¼ teaspoon table salt
- 1 cup heavy cream, divided
- 1 tablespoon rum
- ¼ teaspoon lemon juice

1. FOR THE CAKES: Adjust oven rack to middle position and heat oven to 350 degrees. Grease and flour eight 6-ounce ramekins. Fold dish towel in half and place in bottom of large roasting pan. Place prepared ramekins on top of towel; set aside pan. Bring kettle of water to boil.

2. Combine half of dates, warm water, and baking soda in 2-cup liquid measuring cup (dates should be submerged beneath water); soak dates for 5 minutes. Meanwhile, whisk flour, baking powder, and salt together in large bowl.

3. Process sugar and remaining dates in food processor until no large chunks remain and mixture has texture of damp, coarse sand, about 45 seconds, scraping down sides of bowl as needed. Drain soaked dates and add soaking liquid to processor. Add

Sticky Toffee Pudding

eggs, melted butter, and vanilla and process until smooth, about 15 seconds. Transfer sugar mixture to bowl with flour mixture and sprinkle soaked dates on top. Using rubber spatula or wooden spoon, gently fold sugar mixture into flour mixture until just combined and date pieces are evenly dispersed.

4. Divide batter evenly among prepared ramekins (ramekins should be two-thirds full). Quickly pour enough boiling water into roasting pan to come ¼ inch up sides of ramekins. Cover pan tightly with aluminum foil, crimping edges to seal. Bake until cakes are puffed and surfaces are spongy, firm, and moist to touch, about 40 minutes. Immediately transfer ramekins from water bath to wire rack and let cool for 10 minutes.

5. FOR THE SAUCE: While cakes cool, melt butter in medium saucepan over medium-high heat. Whisk in sugar and salt until smooth. Continue to cook, stirring occasionally, until sugar is dissolved and slightly darkened, 3 to 4 minutes. Stir in ⅓ cup cream until smooth, about 30 seconds. Slowly pour in rum and remaining ⅔ cup cream, whisking constantly until smooth. Reduce heat to low; simmer until frothy, about 3 minutes. Remove from heat and stir in lemon juice.

6. Using toothpick, poke 25 holes in top of each cake and spoon 1 tablespoon toffee sauce over each cake. Let cakes sit until sauce is absorbed, about 5 minutes. Invert each ramekin onto plate or shallow bowl; lift off ramekin. Divide remaining toffee sauce evenly among cakes and serve immediately.

CHILLED CAKES

KEY POINTS

Form even crumb crust with bottom of measuring cup

Let cakes set and chill fully before serving

Slice with warm sharp knife

A COOL, CREAMY CAKE IS THE PERFECT FINISH TO A MEAL on a hot summer day. Chilled cakes such as cheesecakes, icebox cakes, and ice cream cakes offer a delicious paradox: They're simultaneously delicate and light yet also rich and creamy. Keeping things breezy, their crusts are generally simple to make, a cookie or cracker crust.

Some of these cakes are baked (cheesecakes), some partially baked, and some merely frozen. But they all have one thing in common: A big chill, of course. Each cake requires time in the refrigerator to set or freeze for creamy sliceability. Depending on how they're made, the cakes can get structure from eggs or gelatin or custard. Chilled cakes are a make-ahead dessert by design, so they're a great choice when entertaining. Like with many tortes and flourless cakes, we like to run a sharp knife under hot water and wipe it clean between each cut of cake for neat, clean slices.

Desserts that are served cold need a flavor boost because cold temperatures can dull taste sensations. And because these cakes are rich and creamy, featuring cheese, custard, or ice cream as their main ingredients, they take well to lively flavors—like the pretzels, lime, and tequila that give Margarita Cake (page 335) its kick. Toppings with different tastes, textures, and temperatures, like the lemon curd on our Lemon Cheesecake (page 330) or the toasted marshmallows on S'Mores Ice Cream Cake (page 336), add further interest.

Cheesecakes

Cheesecakes aren't all about the cheese: A dairy supplement such as heavy cream or sour cream is usually included to help loosen the texture of the filling and give the cake a smoother, more luxurious feel. Eggs help bind the cake and give it structure. Whole eggs are typically called for, although the addition of a couple extra yolks in Foolproof New York Cheesecake (page 329) helps develop its characteristic dense, suede-like texture. A light, crisp crumb crust offers the perfect foil to the plush cake—graham cracker is classic although a cookie crust is the perfect complement to Milk Chocolate Cheesecake (page 331). Paying close attention to both the temperature of the oven and the temperature of the cheesecake is key to cheesecake success, and some, like our Lemon Cheesecake (page 330), make use of a water bath to help regulate these variables.

CREATING THE CRUST

While the cakes in this chapter call for a variety of crumb crusts, the process of forming them is mostly the same: Mix the crumbs with melted butter and press firmly and evenly into the bottom of a springform pan. We like to use the bottom of a dry measuring cup for this step; its flat bottom and generous surface is perfect for packing the crumbs into an even layer, ensuring a crisp, cohesive crust.

PREPARING A WATER BATH

Some cakes and cheesecakes, as well as custards (see pages 184–199), are baked in a water bath (sometimes referred to as a bain-marie). This means that the pan is partially immersed in water to ensure slow, gentle, even baking. A water bath is especially helpful for recipes that use a lot of eggs, which can curdle if they become overheated. The water also increases the humidity inside the oven, preventing the cake or custard from drying out.

To prevent batter from leaking out of the springform pan or water from seeping in, cover the bottom and sides of the pan with two sheets of heavy-duty aluminum foil. Place the pan in the prepared roasting pan.

Lifting a roasting pan filled with boiling water is awkward and dangerous. Instead, place the roasting pan with the springform pan on the oven rack. Next, carefully pour the boiling water into the pan. The water should come halfway up the sides of the cake pan.

KEY CHEESECAKE TIPS

Cheesecake is certainly a project dessert, but the steps to making it are easy if you keep these tips in mind.

USE SOFTENED CREAM CHEESE Cold cream cheese will lead to a dense, lumpy cheesecake. Softening the cream cheese allows it to mix with the other ingredients and aerate properly for a supercreamy cheesecake.

PREBAKE THE CRUST If the crust is not baked until crisp, the cheesecake's base will become soggy under the moist filling while the cake bakes, and it won't hold together.

SCRAPE DOWN THE BOWL If you scrape down the mixer bowl often, you'll prevent clumps of cream cheese from being pulled into the batter and appearing as chalky bits in the final cake.

LOOSEN THE EDGES Running a thin knife around the edge of the springform pan before the cake is cool prevents the cheesecake from sticking to the sides of the pan and the top from cracking as the cheesecake contracts.

DETERMINING DONENESS

Because cheesecakes have a creamy texture and don't brown the way most cakes do, normal cues like checking with a toothpick or lightly touching the top aren't useful. Gently shaking the cheesecake helps—the center should jiggle slightly—but the best method is checking the internal temperature: Usually the cheese-cake should register 150 degrees. The egg proteins begin to coagulate at this point, but the temperature of the dense cake rises and the eggs continue to set once the cake comes out of the oven. (Our ultraset Foolproof New York Cheesecake on page 329 is an exception.)

CHILLING CHEESECAKES

There's a waiting game involved with cheesecakes—and it's essential but worthwhile. After 2 to 3 hours of cooling at room temperature, most cheesecakes require 3 to 5 hours—and even as many as 8 hours—of refrigeration (chilling time depends on the ingredients as well as the thickness and density of the filling). Don't skimp on this time: If cheesecake isn't thoroughly chilled, the filling won't hold its shape. Allowing the cheesecake plenty of time to set up makes for neat, easy slicing and an attractive presentation.

Properly Chilled Cheesecake   **Underchilled Cheesecake**

Icebox Cakes

Originally made from layering cookies with a creamy filling and letting them rest in the refrigerator until the cookies absorbed the moisture from the filling, transforming them into a cake-like layer, icebox cakes started showing up in the 1930s with the advent of the modern-day refrigerator. The most famous recipe involved Nabisco chocolate wafers, and recipes were printed on the back of the wafer boxes. Nowadays, the term "icebox" also covers a broader range of no-bake cakes, which often rely on gelatin for structure. Whipping the softened gelatin into the other ingredients (we add it right to the whipped cream in our Chocolate Éclair Cake on page 334) lightens the cake and gives it a supple, creamy texture.

Ice Cream Cakes

Ice cream cakes are simple to prepare and sure to be a hit at any gathering. They can be dressed up in countless ways—sprinkled with chopped nuts, cookie crumbles, sprinkles, candy, and more— for an over-the-top sundae vibe. However, an easy recipe isn't necessarily a quick recipe. We found that one of the key ingredients for an ice cream cake is patience: The crust should be completely cooled, the ice cream needs time to soften to a spreadable consis-tency, and then each layer must be frozen until firm before the next layer is added.

FOOLPROOF NEW YORK CHEESECAKE

Serves 12 to 16 | 9-inch springform pan

WHY THIS RECIPE WORKS New York cheesecake has a plush, luxurious texture, golden brown surface, and buttery graham cracker crust. This cheesecake is particularly dense, so we created a pastry–graham cracker hybrid crust that wouldn't become soggy beneath the filling. Adding sour cream to our rich filling contributed more tang, and straining and resting the filling eliminated any lumps or air pockets. Traditionally, New York–style cheesecakes start in a hot oven so that a burnished outer skin develops before the temperature is dropped to finish. For more consistent results we flipped the order, baking at a low temperature to set the filling and then removing it before turning up the heat. Once the oven hit 500 degrees, we put the cheesecake on the upper rack to brown the surface. Serve with Fresh Strawberry Topping (page 550), if desired.

CRUST

- 6 whole graham crackers, broken into pieces
- ⅓ cup packed (2⅓ ounces) dark brown sugar
- ½ cup (2½ ounces) all-purpose flour
- ¼ teaspoon table salt
- 7 tablespoons unsalted butter, melted, divided

FILLING

- 2½ pounds cream cheese, cut into chunks and softened
- 1½ cups (10½ ounces) granulated sugar, divided
- ⅛ teaspoon table salt
- ⅓ cup sour cream
- 2 teaspoons lemon juice
- 2 teaspoons vanilla extract
- 6 large eggs plus 2 large yolks

1. FOR THE CRUST: Adjust oven racks to upper-middle and lower-middle positions and heat oven to 325 degrees. Process crackers and sugar in food processor until finely ground, about 30 seconds. Add flour and salt and pulse to combine, about 2 pulses. Add 6 tablespoons melted butter and pulse until crumbs are evenly moistened, about 10 pulses. Brush bottom of 9-inch springform pan with ½ tablespoon melted butter. Using your hands, press crumb mixture evenly into pan bottom. Using bottom of measuring cup, firmly pack crust into pan. Bake on lower rack until fragrant and beginning to brown around edges, about 13 minutes. Transfer to rimmed baking sheet; set aside and let cool completely. Reduce oven temperature to 200 degrees.

2. FOR THE FILLING: Using stand mixer fitted with paddle, beat cream cheese, ¾ cup sugar, and salt on medium-low speed until combined, about 1 minute. Beat in remaining ¾ cup sugar until combined, about 1 minute. Scrape paddle and bowl well; add sour cream, lemon juice, and vanilla and beat at low speed until combined, about 1 minute. Add egg yolks and beat on

Foolproof New York Cheesecake

medium-low speed until thoroughly combined, about 1 minute. Scrape bowl and paddle. Add whole eggs, two at a time, beating until thoroughly combined, about 30 seconds after each addition. Strain filling through fine-mesh strainer set in large bowl, pressing against strainer with rubber spatula or back of ladle to help filling pass through strainer.

3. Brush sides of springform pan with remaining ½ tablespoon melted butter. Pour filling into crust and set aside for 10 minutes to allow air bubbles to rise to top. Gently draw tines of fork across surface of cake to pop air bubbles that have risen to surface.

4. When oven thermometer reads 200 degrees, bake cheesecake on lower rack until center registers 165 degrees, 3 to 3½ hours. Remove cake from oven and increase oven temperature to 500 degrees.

5. When oven is at 500 degrees, bake cheesecake on upper rack until top is evenly browned, 4 to 12 minutes. Let cool for 5 minutes, then run thin knife around edge of pan. Let cheesecake cool in pan on wire rack until barely warm, 2½ to 3 hours. Wrap cheesecake tightly in plastic wrap and refrigerate until cold and firmly set, at least 6 hours or up to 24 hours.

6. To unmold cheesecake, remove sides of pan and slide thin metal spatula between crust and pan bottom to loosen, then slide cheesecake onto platter. Let sit at room temperature for about 30 minutes before slicing and serving. (Leftover cake can be refrigerated for up to 4 days.)

LEMON CHEESECAKE

Serves 12 to 16 | 9-inch springform pan

WHY THIS RECIPE WORKS Lemon provides a bracing tartness that contrasts with the creamy richness of cheesecake. We aimed to develop a lemon cheesecake with maximum lemon flavor. We ground lemon zest with a portion of the sugar, a step that released its flavorful oils. And for an additional hit of bright citrus flavor, we topped our cake with lemon curd. For the crust, we turned to biscuit-type cookies, such as animal crackers, which allowed the lemon flavor to shine. Baking the cake in a water bath gave us an ultracreamy cake that wasn't as dense as New York–style cheesecake (see page 329).

CRUST
5 ounces Nabisco Barnum's Animals Crackers or Social Tea Biscuits
3 tablespoons sugar
5 tablespoons unsalted butter, melted, divided

FILLING
1¼ cups (8¾ ounces) sugar, divided
1 tablespoon grated lemon zest plus ¼ cup juice (2 lemons)
1½ pounds cream cheese, cut into chunks and softened
¼ teaspoon table salt
½ cup heavy cream
2 teaspoons vanilla extract
4 large eggs, room temperature

LEMON CURD
⅓ cup lemon juice (2 lemons)
2 large eggs plus 1 large yolk
½ cup (3½ ounces) sugar
2 tablespoons unsalted butter, cut into ½-inch pieces and chilled
1 tablespoon heavy cream
¼ teaspoon vanilla extract
Pinch table salt

1. FOR THE CRUST: Adjust oven rack to lower-middle position and heat oven to 325 degrees. Process cookies and sugar in food processor until finely ground, about 30 seconds. Add 4 tablespoons melted butter and pulse until crumbs are evenly moistened, about 10 pulses. Using your hands, press crumb mixture evenly into bottom of 9-inch springform pan. Using bottom of measuring cup, firmly pack crust into pan. Bake until fragrant and golden brown, 15 to 18 minutes.

2. Let crust cool completely on wire rack, about 30 minutes, then wrap outside of pan with two 18-inch square pieces heavy-duty aluminum foil. Brush inside of pan with remaining 1 tablespoon melted butter. Set springform pan in roasting pan. Bring kettle of water to boil.

Lemon Cheesecake

3. FOR THE FILLING: Process ¼ cup sugar and lemon zest in food processor until sugar is yellow and zest is broken down, about 15 seconds; transfer to small bowl and stir in remaining 1 cup sugar.

4. Using stand mixer fitted with paddle, beat cream cheese, salt, and half of lemon-sugar mixture on medium-low speed until combined, about 1 minute. Add remaining lemon-sugar mixture and beat until combined, about 1 minute. Scrape bowl and paddle. Add cream, lemon juice, and vanilla and beat on low speed until combined and smooth, 1 to 3 minutes. Add eggs, two at a time, beating until thoroughly combined, about 30 seconds after each addition.

5. Pour filling into crust. Set roasting pan on oven rack and pour enough boiling water into roasting pan to come about halfway up sides of springform pan. Bake until center jiggles slightly, sides just start to puff, surface is no longer shiny, and center of cake registers 150 degrees, 55 minutes to 1 hour.

6. Turn off oven and prop open oven door with potholder or wooden spoon handle; let cake cool in water bath in oven for 1 hour. Transfer springform pan to wire rack, discarding foil. Run thin knife around edge of pan and let cheesecake cool for 2 hours.

7. FOR THE LEMON CURD: While cheesecake bakes, heat lemon juice in small saucepan over medium heat until hot but not boiling. Whisk eggs and yolk together in bowl, then gradually whisk in sugar. Whisking constantly, slowly pour hot lemon juice into eggs, then return mixture to saucepan and cook over medium heat, stirring constantly with wooden spoon, until mixture is thick enough to cling to spoon and registers 170 degrees, about 3 minutes. Immediately remove pan from heat and stir in cold butter until incorporated. Stir in cream, vanilla, and salt, then strain curd through fine-mesh strainer into small bowl. Place plastic wrap directly on surface of curd and refrigerate until needed.

8. When cheesecake is cool, scrape lemon curd onto cheesecake still in springform pan. Using offset spatula, spread curd evenly over top of cheesecake. Wrap cheesecake tightly in plastic and refrigerate for at least 4 hours or up to 24 hours. To unmold cheesecake, wrap hot, damp dish towel around pan and let stand for 1 minute. Remove sides of pan and slide thin metal spatula between crust and pan bottom to loosen, then slide cheesecake onto platter. Slice and serve.

MILK CHOCOLATE CHEESECAKE

Serves 12 to 16 | 9-inch springform pan

WHY THIS RECIPE WORKS While chocolate typically makes everything better, cheesecake is a notable exception. The bitter edge of dark chocolate—our go-to—is a poor match for the tang of cream cheese. After making dozens of versions, we figured out that mild-mannered milk chocolate was the secret to a sweet, creamy cheesecake with just the right balance of chocolate and cheese. A small amount of cocoa powder contributed depth. For an easy, crunchy, chocolaty crust, we used Oreo cookies processed with butter and a bit of sugar. Use the entire Oreo— filling and all—for the crust.

16 Oreo cookies, broken into rough pieces
 1 tablespoon plus ½ cup (3½ ounces) sugar, divided
 2 tablespoons unsalted butter, melted
 8 ounces milk chocolate, chopped, divided
 ⅓ cup heavy cream
 2 tablespoons unsweetened cocoa powder
 ¼ teaspoon table salt
1½ pounds cream cheese, cut into chunks and softened
 4 large eggs, room temperature
 2 teaspoons vanilla extract

1. Adjust oven rack to middle position and heat oven to 350 degrees. Grease bottom and sides of 9-inch springform pan. Process cookies and 1 tablespoon sugar in food processor until finely ground, about 30 seconds. Add melted butter and pulse until crumbs are evenly moistened, about 6 pulses. Using your hands, press crumb mixture evenly into pan bottom. Using bottom of measuring cup, firmly pack crust into pan. Bake until fragrant and set, about 10 minutes. Let crust cool completely on wire rack, about 30 minutes.

2. Reduce oven temperature to 250 degrees. Combine 6 ounces chocolate and cream in bowl and microwave at 50 percent power, stirring occasionally, until melted and smooth, 60 to 90 seconds. Let cool for 10 minutes. Whisk cocoa, salt, and remaining ½ cup sugar in separate bowl until no lumps remain. Using stand mixer fitted with paddle, beat cream cheese and cocoa mixture on medium speed until creamy and smooth, about 3 minutes, scraping down bowl as needed. Reduce speed to medium-low, add chocolate mixture, and beat until combined. Gradually add eggs, one at a time, until incorporated, scraping down bowl as needed. Add vanilla and give batter final stir by hand until no streaks of chocolate remain.

3. Pour filling into crust and smooth top with spatula. Gently tap pan on counter to release air bubbles. Cover pan tightly with aluminum foil (taking care not to touch surface of cheesecake with foil) and place on rimmed baking sheet. Bake for 1 hour, then remove foil. Continue to bake until edges are set and center registers 150 degrees and jiggles slightly when shaken, 30 to 45 minutes. Let cheesecake cool completely in pan on wire rack. Wrap cheesecake tightly in plastic wrap and refrigerate until cold, at least 8 hours or up to 4 days.

4. To unmold cheesecake, remove sides of pan and slide thin metal spatula between crust and pan bottom to loosen, then slide cheesecake onto platter. Microwave remaining 2 ounces chocolate in small bowl at 50 percent power, stirring occasionally, until melted, 60 to 90 seconds. Let cool for 5 minutes. Transfer to small zipper-lock bag, cut small hole in corner, and pipe chocolate in thin zigzag pattern across top of cheesecake. Let cheesecake sit at room temperature for 30 minutes before slicing and serving.

MAPLE CHEESECAKE

Serves 12 to 16 | 9-inch springform pan

WHY THIS RECIPE WORKS We wanted to use maple syrup to sweeten cheesecake for an autumnal twist. Adding pecans to our tried-and-true graham cracker crust provided a nutty accent to a maple-y filling. For maximum maple impact, we needed to use a lot of maple syrup: 1¼ cups for 2 pounds of cream cheese. A 225-degree oven cooked the cheesecake gently, setting the filling to a barely firm, custardy texture completely free of cracks, without the need for a water bath. A border of crunchy granola plus an extra drizzle of maple syrup made this cheesecake look as stunning as it tastes. Do not substitute pancake syrup—which is corn syrup–based and cloying—for the maple syrup. Reduce the oven temperature as soon as the crust is finished baking, and use an oven thermometer to check that it has dropped to 225 degrees before you bake the cheesecake. Thoroughly scrape the processor bowl as you make the filling to eliminate lumps.

CRUST

- 4 whole graham crackers, broken into pieces
- ¼ cup pecans
- ½ cup (2½ ounces) all-purpose flour
- ⅓ cup (2⅓ ounces) sugar
- ¼ teaspoon table salt
- 4 tablespoons unsalted butter, melted

CHEESECAKE

- 2 pounds cream cheese, softened
- 1¼ cups maple syrup
- 4 large eggs

TOPPING

- ⅓ cup granola
- ½ cup maple syrup

1. FOR THE CRUST: Adjust oven rack to middle position and heat oven to 325 degrees. Grease bottom and sides of 9-inch springform pan. Process cracker pieces and pecans in food processor until finely ground, about 30 seconds. Add flour, sugar, and salt and pulse to combine, about 2 pulses. Add melted butter and pulse until crumbs are evenly moistened, about 5 pulses.

Maple Cheesecake

2. Using your hands, press crumbs into even layer on prepared pan bottom. Using bottom of dry measuring cup, firmly pack crumbs into pan. Bake until crust smells toasty and is browned around edges, about 18 minutes. Reduce oven temperature to 225 degrees. Let crust cool completely.

3. FOR THE CHEESECAKE: In clean, dry processor bowl, process cream cheese and maple syrup until smooth, about 2 minutes, scraping down sides of bowl as needed. With processor running, add eggs, one at a time, until just incorporated, about 30 seconds total. Pour batter onto cooled crust.

4. Firmly tap pan on counter and set aside for 10 minutes to allow air bubbles to rise to top. Gently draw tines of fork across surface of batter to pop air bubbles that have risen to surface.

5. Once oven has reached 225 degrees, bake cheesecake on aluminum foil–lined rimmed baking sheet until edges are set and center jiggles slightly when shaken and registers 165 degrees ½ inch below surface, about 3 hours.

6. Transfer pan to wire rack and let cool completely, about 2 hours. Refrigerate cheesecake, uncovered, until cold, about 6 hours. (Once fully chilled, cheesecake can be covered with plastic wrap and refrigerated for up to 4 days.)

7. To unmold cheesecake, run tip of paring knife between cake and side of pan; remove side of pan. Slide thin metal spatula between crust and pan bottom to loosen, then slide cheesecake onto serving platter. Let cheesecake stand at room temperature for 30 minutes.

8. FOR THE TOPPING: Sprinkle granola around top edge of cheesecake. Drizzle maple syrup inside ring of granola. Spread with back of spoon, as needed, to fill area inside granola ring.

9. Cut cheesecake into wedges and serve.

MIGLIACCIO DI SEMOLINO

Serves 8 to 12 | 9-inch springform pan

WHY THIS RECIPE WORKS The category of cakes known as migliaccio ("migliaccio" means "millet") has ancient roots in Italian cuisine. To make it, we started by preparing a sweet porridge flavored with citrus zest and ground cardamom; we then combined it with a mixture of ricotta cheese, eggs, vanilla, and orange liqueur. The result was a highly aromatic, slightly sweet, velvety treat evocative of a traditional yellow cake crossed with a flan. Make the cake a day ahead of serving so that it has ample time to set up in the refrigerator. We developed this recipe using Bob's Red Mill No. 1 Durum Wheat Semolina Flour. If this product is not available, substitute Cream of Wheat cereal, which is similar. Avoid very fine semolina flour that is often sold in small paper bags. We like the richness of whole milk, but feel free to substitute 2 percent or 1 percent if that's what you have; avoid skim milk. Don't use part-skim or skim ricotta. This cake is great served on its own, but you can serve it with fresh berries, if desired.

    4 tablespoons unsalted butter, plus softened butter for pan
   ¾ cup (5¼ ounces) granulated sugar, plus extra for pan
    4 large eggs
  12 ounces (1½ cups) whole-milk ricotta cheese
    2 tablespoons orange liqueur
    2 teaspoons vanilla extract
   ¾ cup (4⅓ ounces) semolina flour
    3 cups whole milk
    2 tablespoons grated lemon zest (2 lemons)
1½ tablespoons grated orange zest
    1 teaspoon ground cardamom
   ½ teaspoon table salt
     Confectioners' sugar

1. Adjust oven rack to middle position and heat oven to 375 degrees. Grease 9-inch springform pan with softened butter; dust with granulated sugar and knock out excess.

2. Using stand mixer fitted with paddle, beat eggs on medium-low speed until combined. Add ricotta, liqueur, and vanilla and mix on medium speed until smooth, 2 to 3 minutes, scraping down bowl as needed.

3. Mix semolina and granulated sugar in small bowl until combined. Heat milk, lemon zest, orange zest, cardamom, salt, and butter in large saucepan over medium-low heat, stirring occasionally, until mixture registers 180 degrees. Off heat, pour semolina mixture into milk mixture in very slow stream, whisking constantly, until smooth. Return saucepan to heat and stir constantly with wooden spoon until mixture pulls away from side of saucepan, 3 to 5 minutes.

4. Add one-third of semolina mixture to ricotta mixture and mix on medium speed until incorporated. Add remaining semolina mixture in 2 additions, mixing after each addition until incorporated. Continue to mix, scraping down bowl as needed, until mostly smooth (it's OK if some small lumps remain), 3 to 5 minutes longer.

5. Set prepared pan in rimmed baking sheet and transfer batter to pan. Bake until top is golden brown, edges are slightly puffed (some slight cracking is OK), and center is slightly jiggly, 50 minutes to 1 hour.

6. Transfer cake, still on sheet, to wire rack and let cool for 10 minutes. Run knife around edge of cake to loosen. Unlock pan ring, but leave ring in place. Let cool completely, 1½ to 2 hours.

Migliaccio di Semolino

Refasten ring. Refrigerate cake until firm and thoroughly chilled, at least 12 hours or up to 24 hours. To unmold cake, remove side of pan. Slide thin metal spatula between cake and pan bottom to loosen, then slide cake onto serving platter. Let cake stand at room temperature for about 30 minutes. Sprinkle top with confectioners' sugar. Cut into wedges and serve.

ICEBOX CHEESECAKE
Serves 10 to 12 | 9-inch springform pan
WHY THIS RECIPE WORKS We love a tall New York–style cheesecake but sometimes we want the essence of a cheesecake with a bit less fuss, and we want the tang of a cream cheese–based cake without the weight—something lighter and creamier to finish a meal. Enter no-bake cheesecake: The filling is lightened with whipped cream and the absence of eggs makes for a less rich cake. We achieved the best flavor and texture when we stuck to the tried-and-true combination of heavy cream and cream cheese thickened with gelatin. Allowing the gelatin to hydrate in a portion of the cream and then bringing it to a boil in the microwave fully activated its thickening power. Lemon juice, lemon zest, and a little vanilla added just enough spark to perk up the tangy cream cheese. Serve with Fresh Strawberry Topping (page 550), if desired.

CRUST

- 8 whole graham crackers, broken into 1-inch pieces
- 1 tablespoon sugar
- 5 tablespoons unsalted butter, melted

FILLING

- 2½ teaspoons unflavored gelatin
- 1½ cups heavy cream, divided
- ⅔ cup (4⅔ ounces) sugar
- 1 pound cream cheese, cut into 1-inch pieces and softened
- 1 teaspoon grated lemon zest plus 2 tablespoons juice
- 1 teaspoon vanilla extract
   Pinch table salt

1. FOR THE CRUST: Adjust oven rack to middle position and heat oven to 325 degrees. Pulse crackers and sugar in food processor until finely ground, about 15 pulses. Transfer crumbs to bowl, drizzle with melted butter, and mix with rubber spatula until mixture resembles wet sand. Using your hands, press crumb mixture evenly into bottom of 9-inch springform pan. Using bottom of measuring cup, firmly pack crust into pan. Bake until fragrant and beginning to brown, about 13 minutes. Let crust cool completely in pan on wire rack, about 30 minutes.

2. FOR THE FILLING: Sprinkle gelatin over ¼ cup cream in 2-cup liquid measuring cup and let sit until gelatin softens, about 5 minutes. Microwave until mixture is bubbling around edges and gelatin dissolves, about 20 seconds; whisk to combine and set aside.

3. Using stand mixer fitted with whisk attachment, whip remaining 1¼ cups cream and sugar on medium-low speed until foamy, about 1 minute. Increase speed to high and whip until soft peaks form, 1 to 3 minutes. Fit stand mixer with paddle, reduce speed to medium-low, add cream cheese, and beat until combined, about 1 minute, scraping down bowl once (mixture may not be completely smooth). Add lemon juice, vanilla, and salt and continue to beat until combined, about 1 minute, scraping down bowl as needed. Increase speed to medium-high and beat until smooth, about 3 minutes. Add dissolved gelatin mixture and lemon zest and continue to beat until smooth and airy, about 2 minutes.

4. Pour filling into crust and spread into even layer with spatula. Wrap cheesecake tightly in plastic wrap and refrigerate until set, at least 6 hours or up to 24 hours.

5. To unmold cheesecake, wrap hot, damp dish towel around pan and let stand for 1 minute. Remove sides of pan and slide thin metal spatula between crust and pan bottom to loosen, then slide cheesecake onto platter. Cut into wedges and serve.

CHOCOLATE ÉCLAIR CAKE

Serves 15 | 13 by 9-inch baking pan

WHY THIS RECIPE WORKS Chocolate éclair cake is an instant dessert classic; this no-bake cake typically features layers of store-bought vanilla pudding and Cool Whip sandwiched between graham crackers and topped off with chocolate frosting. As the graham crackers soften, the whole thing melds into a creamy, sliceable cake. We loved the ease of these convenience items, but our enthusiasm waned when confronted by their flavor. With a couple of easy techniques and very little active time, we produced a from-scratch version that easily trumped its inspiration. Since the cake layers required no more work than lining a pan with graham crackers, we made the effort to prepare a quick stovetop vanilla pudding, folding in whipped cream to lighten it. For the éclair topping, we created a simple microwave-and-stir glaze. Six ounces of finely chopped semisweet chocolate can be used in place of the chips.

- 1¼ cups (8¾ ounces) sugar
- 6 tablespoons cornstarch
- 1 teaspoon table salt
- 5 cups whole milk
- 4 tablespoons unsalted butter, cut into 4 pieces
- 5 teaspoons vanilla extract
- 1¼ teaspoons unflavored gelatin
- 2 tablespoons water
- 2¾ cups heavy cream, chilled, divided
- 14 ounces graham crackers
- 1 cup (6 ounces) semisweet chocolate chips
- 5 tablespoons light corn syrup

1. Combine sugar, cornstarch, and salt in large saucepan. Whisk milk into sugar mixture until smooth and bring to boil over medium-high heat, scraping bottom of pan with heatproof rubber spatula. Immediately reduce heat to medium-low and cook, continuing to scrape bottom, until thickened and large bubbles appear on surface, 4 to 6 minutes. Off heat, whisk in butter and vanilla. Transfer pudding to large bowl and place plastic wrap directly on surface of pudding. Refrigerate until cool, about 2 hours.

2. Sprinkle gelatin over water in bowl and let sit until gelatin softens, about 5 minutes. Microwave until mixture is bubbling around edges and gelatin dissolves, 15 to 30 seconds. Using stand mixer fitted with whisk attachment, whip 2 cups cream on medium-low speed until foamy, about 1 minute. Increase speed to high and whip until soft peaks form, 1 to 3 minutes. Add gelatin mixture and whip until stiff peaks form, about 1 minute.

Chocolate Éclair Cake

3. Whisk one-third of whipped cream into chilled pudding, then gently fold in remaining whipped cream, 1 scoop at a time, until combined. Cover bottom of 13 by 9-inch baking dish with layer of graham crackers, breaking crackers as necessary to line bottom of pan. Top with half of pudding–whipped cream mixture (about 5½ cups) and another layer of graham crackers. Repeat with remaining pudding–whipped cream mixture and remaining graham crackers.

4. Combine chocolate chips, corn syrup, and remaining ¾ cup cream in bowl and microwave on 50 percent power, stirring occasionally, until smooth, 1 to 2 minutes. Let glaze cool completely, about 10 minutes. Spread glaze over top and refrigerate cake for at least 6 hours or up to 2 days before slicing and serving.

MARGARITA CAKE

Serves 10 to 12 | 9-inch springform pan

WHY THIS RECIPE WORKS In this dessert, cool, creamy icebox cheesecake meets the salty, pucker-inspiring flavors of a margarita. We started by dissolving gelatin in a mixture of margarita mix, tequila, and triple sec to create a kind of margarita Jell-O (perhaps the best kind of Jell-O). We mixed some of this into the cheesecake filling for flavor and structure, and we strained the remainder to create a glassy "shot" on top of the cake. For a crust that was more in line with our theme, we

replaced the traditional graham cracker crust with a pretzel one to hint at the salted rim of a margarita glass. To finish, we garnished the sides of the cake with a mixture of coconut and lime zest and topped it off with slices of lime.

1	cup (3 ounces) sweetened shredded coconut
1	teaspoon grated lime zest plus 1 lime, sliced thin
4½	ounces pretzels (3 cups)
6	tablespoons unsalted butter, melted
4	teaspoons unflavored gelatin
¾	cup water, divided
1	(10-ounce) can frozen margarita mix, thawed
¼	cup tequila
¼	cup triple sec
1½	cups heavy cream, chilled
1	(14-ounce) can sweetened condensed milk
4	ounces cream cheese, softened

1. Adjust oven rack to middle position and heat oven to 350 degrees. Grease 9-inch springform pan and line perimeter with 3-inch-wide strip of parchment paper. Process coconut and lime zest in food processor until coarsely ground, 25 to 30 seconds; reserve ½ cup and set aside. Add pretzels to remaining coconut mixture and process until finely ground, about 1 minute. Add melted butter and pulse to combine, about 5 pulses. Using your hands, press crumb mixture evenly into pan bottom. Using bottom of measuring cup, firmly pack crust into pan. Bake until edges are golden, 10 to 12 minutes. Let crust cool completely on wire rack, about 30 minutes.

2. Sprinkle gelatin over ¼ cup water in small saucepan and let sit until gelatin softens, about 5 minutes. Add margarita mix, tequila, and triple sec and cook over low heat, stirring frequently, until gelatin dissolves, about 5 minutes. Let cool for 15 minutes; set aside.

3. Using stand mixer fitted with whisk attachment, whip cream on medium-low speed until foamy, about 1 minute. Increase speed to high and whip until soft peaks form, 1 to 3 minutes. Transfer whipped cream to bowl; set aside. Using clean, dry mixer bowl and whisk attachment, mix condensed milk and cream cheese until combined, about 1½ minutes. Add 1 cup margarita mixture and whip until incorporated, about 25 seconds. Use whisk to gently fold in one-third of whipped cream, then gently fold in remaining whipped cream. Pour filling into crust. Refrigerate until just set, about 1 hour.

4. Stir remaining ½ cup water into remaining margarita mixture. Strain mixture through fine-mesh strainer into 2-cup liquid measuring cup. Pour over filling and refrigerate until set, at least 4 hours or up to 24 hours. Remove sides of pan and parchment. Press reserved coconut mixture onto sides of cake. Top with lime slices. Slide thin metal spatula between crust and pan bottom to loosen, then slide cheesecake onto platter. Cut into wedges and serve.

CLASSIC ICE CREAM CAKE

Serves 8 to 10 | 9-inch springform pan

WHY THIS RECIPE WORKS Ice cream and cake: These two beloved desserts belong together, and we wanted to develop a basic ice cream cake that would be a hit at any party. We started with three crowd-pleasing flavors—chocolate, vanilla, and strawberry—to create a striped Neapolitan cake. Oreo crumbs served as a sturdy bottom crust and also provided chocolaty crunch between each layer of ice cream. For clean lines and to avoid a melty mess, it was essential to freeze each layer before adding the next. We dressed up our cake by pressing party-ready rainbow sprinkles into the sides, but you could also use chopped nuts or crushed candies or cookies. You can also pipe a greeting on top once the cake is fully frozen. Use the entire Oreo—filling and all—for the crust. Before removing the cake from the springform pan, run your paring knife under hot tap water for 10 seconds or so.

- 25 Oreo cookies, broken into rough pieces
- 3 tablespoons unsalted butter, melted
- 1 pint strawberry ice cream
- 1 pint vanilla ice cream
- 1 pint chocolate ice cream
- ½ cup rainbow sprinkles

1. Adjust oven rack to middle position and heat oven to 325 degrees. Process Oreos in food processor until finely ground, about 30 seconds. Add melted butter and process until mixture resembles wet sand, about 10 seconds.

2. Using your hands, press ⅔ cup crumb mixture evenly into bottom of 9-inch springform pan. Using bottom of measuring cup, firmly pack crust into pan. Bake until the crust is fragrant and set, 5 to 10 minutes. Let crust cool completely on wire rack, about 30 minutes.

3. Scoop strawberry ice cream into large bowl and, using large rubber spatula or wooden spoon, break up scoops of ice cream. Stir and fold ice cream to achieve smooth consistency. Spread softened ice cream evenly over crust. Sprinkle ⅔ cup Oreo crumbs over ice cream and pack down lightly. Wrap pan tightly with plastic wrap and freeze until ice cream is just firm, about 30 minutes. Repeat with vanilla ice cream and remaining ⅔ cup Oreo crumbs; wrap tightly and freeze for another 30 minutes. Soften chocolate ice cream, spread evenly in pan, and smooth top. Wrap cake tightly in plastic and freeze until firm, at least 8 hours or up to 1 week.

4. To unmold cake, run hot thin knife around edge of pan. Remove sides of pan and slide thin metal spatula between crust and pan bottom to loosen, then slide cake onto platter. Press sprinkles onto sides of cake. Serve immediately.

S'MORES ICE CREAM CAKE

Serves 8 to 10 | 9-inch springform pan

WHY THIS RECIPE WORKS We wanted to take each element of s'mores and reimagine this beloved campfire snack as a magnificent ice cream cake. The base of our cake was simple: just a graham cracker crust covered with fudge. The fudge layer provided plenty of chocolate flavor, gave the cake a sundae-like quality, and kept the crust from becoming soggy under the remaining layers. Between the fudge-covered crust and a generous filling of chocolate ice cream, we spread a layer of sweet marshmallow crème—but it wouldn't be s'mores without toasted marshmallows, too. We halved large marshmallows so they'd lie flat and covered the top of our cake with them. After we froze the cake until it was very firm, it took just a quick run under a hot broiler to toast the marshmallows without melting the cake. A ring of graham crackers around the outside provided the finishing touch to this playful dessert.

- 4 ounces bittersweet chocolate, chopped fine
- ½ cup heavy cream
- ¼ cup light corn syrup
- 8 whole graham crackers, broken into pieces, plus 8 quartered along dotted seams
- 4 tablespoons unsalted butter, melted
- 1 tablespoon sugar
- 1 cup marshmallow crème
- 3 pints chocolate ice cream
- 26 large marshmallows, halved crosswise

1. Combine chocolate, cream, and corn syrup in bowl and microwave at 50 percent power until melted and smooth, about 1 minute, stirring halfway through microwaving. Let cool completely, about 30 minutes.

2. Adjust oven rack to middle position and heat oven to 325 degrees. Spray 9-inch springform pan with vegetable oil spray and line perimeter with 2½-inch-wide strip of parchment paper. Pulse cracker pieces in food processor until finely ground, about 15 pulses. Combine cracker crumbs, melted butter, and sugar in bowl until mixture resembles wet sand. Using your hands, press crumb mixture evenly into pan bottom. Using bottom of measuring cup, firmly pack crust into pan. Bake until fragrant and beginning to brown, about 12 minutes. Let crust cool completely in pan on wire rack, about 30 minutes.

3. Pour chocolate mixture over crust and smooth into even layer; freeze until firm, about 30 minutes. Spread marshmallow crème over chocolate mixture in even layer; freeze until firm, about 15 minutes. Scoop ice cream into large bowl and, using large rubber spatula or wooden spoon, break up the scoops of ice cream. Stir and fold ice cream to achieve smooth consistency. Spread softened ice cream evenly over marshmallow crème layer. Cover with plastic wrap and freeze until ice cream is very firm, at least 4 hours or up to 24 hours.

S'mores Ice Cream Cake

crunch, we sprinkled the top and sides of the cake with sliced almonds, which we toasted to enhance their nutty flavor. Use the entire Oreo—filling and all—for the crust. Before removing the cake from the springform pan, run your knife under hot tap water for 10 seconds or so.

25	Oreo cookies, broken into rough pieces
3	tablespoons unsalted butter, melted
1	pint chocolate ice cream
1	pint coffee ice cream
1	pint vanilla ice cream
1	teaspoon ground cinnamon
1½	cups sliced almonds, toasted

1. Adjust oven rack to the middle position and heat oven to 325 degrees. Process Oreos in food processor until finely ground, about 30 seconds. Add melted butter and process until mixture resembles wet sand, about 10 seconds.

2. Using your hands, press ⅔ cup crumb mixture evenly into bottom of 9-inch springform pan. Using bottom of measuring cup, firmly pack crust into pan. Bake until crust is fragrant and set, 5 to 10 minutes. Let crust cool completely on wire rack, about 30 minutes.

3. Scoop chocolate ice cream into large bowl and, using large rubber spatula or wooden spoon, break up scoops of ice cream. Stir and fold ice cream to achieve smooth consistency. Spread softened ice cream evenly over crust. Sprinkle ⅔ cup Oreo crumbs over ice cream and pack them down lightly. Wrap pan tightly in plastic wrap and freeze until ice cream is just firm, about 30 minutes. Repeat with coffee ice cream and remaining ⅔ cup Oreo crumbs; wrap tightly and freeze for another 30 minutes. Soften vanilla ice cream, fold in cinnamon, spread evenly in pan, and smooth top. Wrap the cake tightly in plastic and freeze until ice cream is firm, at least 8 hours or up to 1 week.

4. To unmold, run hot thin knife around edge of pan. Remove sides of pan and slide thin metal spatula between crust and pan bottom to loosen, then slide cake onto platter. Press handfuls of almonds gently onto sides of cake, then sprinkle single layer of almonds evenly over top. Serve immediately.

4. Adjust oven rack 6 inches from broiler element and heat broiler. Place cake on rimmed baking sheet, discarding plastic, and arrange marshmallow halves, cut sides down, in snug layer over top. Broil until marshmallows are lightly browned, 30 to 60 seconds, rotating sheet halfway through broiling. (Refreeze cake if necessary.) Working quickly, remove sides of pan, discarding parchment, and slide thin metal spatula between cake bottom and pan bottom to loosen, then slide cake onto platter. Arrange quartered crackers vertically along sides of cake. Serve immediately.

MEXICAN CHOCOLATE ICE CREAM TORTE

Serves 8 to 10 | 9-inch springform pan

WHY THIS RECIPE WORKS Store-bought versions of ice cream cake are typically boring assemblages of bland, icy ingredients and too-sweet frosting. This ice cream cake—an ice cream torte, really—is inspired, truly elegant, and sure to win raves. We love the savory spice that cinnamon adds to earthy disks of Mexican chocolate, so for our torte we paired chocolate ice cream with cinnamon-infused vanilla ice cream and bittersweet coffee ice cream for a grown-up frozen treat. Crushed Oreos ably separated the layers. To up the elegance and add a welcome

PART 05

pies

PIES HAVE BEEN AROUND FOR CENTURIES, but not quite in the form we usually think of them today. In earlier forms, they were predominantly a savory affair, with meat fillings that were heavily spiced. The crust served as baking dish, storage vessel, and means of transport all in one; as its purpose was to protect and preserve the filling, the crust's flavor and texture were not concerns. Sweet pies came along later, and while savory pies are still very much around, it is the dessert pie that dominates recipes—and the crust is just as important as the filling itself. For many of us, pie conjures homespun memories of rolling out dough, piling sweetened slices of fruit—maybe just-picked apples or farmers' market stone fruit—into passed-down pie plates, and baking a rustic pastry that fills the house with aromas of browned butter or spice. Or maybe you remember sitting at the diner counter, longingly staring up at plumes of whipped cream toppings higher than eye level.

At their simplest, dessert pies are baked pastry shells with a sweet filling. They can be tall and deep or thin and wide; richly dense or light and fluffy; as large as a baking sheet or small enough to fit in your hand. That said, you can generally divide the world of pies in two ways: by type of filling or by type of crust. Here we have largely chosen to group pies based on their unique fillings. But it's not simply the ingredients that determine the category; the process for preparing the filled pies is a defining characteristic as well. Fruit pies made with the seasonal bounty of summer and fall feature buttery, flaky top and bottom crusts encasing mounds of perfectly stewed fruit. Apple pie fillings can generally pack the pie after being precooked. More delicate and juicy summer fruits require a top crust with openings such as a lattice to allow moisture to escape and a thickener combined with the unbaked fruit. Cream pies—chocolate and coconut are two classics—feature billowy pastry cream added to a baked pie shell. And custard pies—which include pumpkin, pecan, and old-fashioned buttermilk—feature egg-thickened fillings that are baked with the crust. While many pie fillings rely on the heat of the oven or stovetop to develop just the right texture, others, such as icebox key lime and strawberry chiffon, require a good long chill in the refrigerator to properly set up to a sliceable consistency.

Pie Equipment Corner

There are certain pieces of equipment that make pie baking easier (and more accurate). These are some of the basic pie tools you'll need.

Pie Plate

While Pyrex and good ceramic dishes stand the test of time, the ultimate pie plate is the **Williams-Sonoma Goldtouch Nonstick Pie Dish** ($18.95). This golden-hued metal plate bakes crusts beautifully without overbrowning; even bottom crusts emerge crisp and flaky. Additionally, we liked this plate's nonfluted lip, which allowed for maximum crust-crimping flexibility. One minor drawback: The metal surface is susceptible to cuts and nicks—just be careful when slicing.

Pie Weights

There are innovative substitutes for pie weights on the market, and many home bakers use rice or sugar or coins. We had our best success with the classic: pie weights. We like **Mrs. Anderson's Baking Ceramic Pie Weights** ($5); however, like with most sets, they come with just a cup of weights. We purchase four sets to completely fill an aluminum foil–lined pie shell. With weights piled up and pressing firmly against the dough's walls, the edges of the pie shell remain high and the bottom turns out crisp, flaky, and golden brown.

Rolling Pin

There are many styles of rolling pins, but we like the classic French-style wood pins without handles. They come straight and tapered. We tend to reach for straight pins, which make achieving even dough thickness and rolling out larger rectangles easy. The **J.K. Adams Plain Maple Rolling Dowel** ($16) has a gentle weight and a slightly textured surface for less sticking.

Kitchen Shears

Once pie dough is placed in the pie plate, we trim the edge so it isn't too thick when folded over. Our favorite shears are the **Shun Multi-Purpose Shears** ($50), but if you're using shears just for baking and not for butchering meat, our Best Buy, J.A. Henckels International Take-Apart Kitchen Shears ($15), are very good.

Pastry Brush

We use a pastry brush to paint crusts with egg wash before they enter the oven or to dab jam over fruit tarts. With a thick head of agile bristles, the **Winco Flat Pastry and Basting Brush, 1½ inch** ($6.93) is our winner. That said, it does contain BPA. For those who are concerned about BPA, our runner-up, the Ateco 1.5″ Flat Stainless Steel Ferrule Pastry Brush ($10.99), is a good choice.

Pie Carrier

Traveling with a pie can feel like tempting fate, but a good pie carrier can make the task more secure. The **Prepworks Collapsible Party Carrier** ($28) is a nifty case. This collapsible plastic tote expands to accommodate even our tallest meringue-topped pies. Its large, nonskid base holds 8-, 9-, and 10-inch pies perfectly in place, even on bumpy car rides. Bonus: It comes with two molded inserts for deviled eggs, one of which can be flipped upside down and used as a second tier for transporting two shorter pies at once. Its one slight fault: The latches take a little finessing to secure.

Pie Server

Surprisingly, serving up a slice of pie isn't always the easiest part of pie baking. You can use a knife, but a pie server—essentially a pointed spatula—is specifically designed to cut, remove, and transport pie slices and should produce picturesque, intact pieces. The **OXO Steel Pie Server** ($10) is the best.

PIE THICKENER POWER RANKINGS

A common fear associated with fruit pie baking is that the filling will turn out soupy (and of course the opposite—an overly gelled brick—is a problem, too). That's where thickeners come in; they work with fruit's juices to rein them in. (Additionally, eggs thicken cream and custard fillings.) Here are the thickeners we turn to and why.

1. Tapioca

Easy dissolving and clearly flavorless, tapioca is a near-perfect thickener. It's our preferred choice in most cases. Note that too much can make a filling gluey so be sure to use only the amount called for.

2. Cornstarch

When working with fruits (such as apricots) that don't exude enough moisture for tapioca to dissolve in, we use cornstarch as a thickener. It's a pure starch so it's very effective and it's the perfect choice when a drier consistency is desired.

Honorable Mention: Pectin

Many fruits are naturally high in pectin. Pectin is a complex polysaccharide that acts as a sort of glue, binding mixtures when it comes into contact with liquid. The apple is one such fruit (in fact, we give the tapioca in our Vegan Blueberry Pie on page 371 a helping hand by incorporating shredded apple). But that doesn't mean the natural pectin is released in amounts high enough to thicken fillings. Sometimes we'll bolster natural pectin with commercial pectin, which begins with apple or citrus extract and is chemically processed to produce a dry, powdered substance. Commercial pectin needs to be used in modest doses, however; it's acidic and can result in a mouth-puckering pie, but fruit like sweet peaches, for example, can handle an addition.

Dishonorable Mention: Flour

Flour is only 75 percent starch, so it is less effective than cornstarch. We've also found that it can taste raw in fillings.

COOLING PIES

Pies are not for the impatient. Not only do they take some time to prepare (although, in this book, the methods are made simple), they also need to cool completely. In fact, most pies require around 4 hours of cooling time. Pie is great warm, so why would you wait? The thickeners are activated in the oven, but the pie filling gels further with cooling. If you cut into a pie before it's set, the filling will pour out of the pie rather than slice cleanly. If you want warm pie, simply heat up slices.

Apple pie sliced after 1 hour   **Apple pie sliced after 4 hours**

The first slice of pie always seems to fall apart. To prevent this, make three cuts before slicing. The extra cut allows for movement in the pie, making it easier to tidily wiggle out the first piece.

STORING PIES

Where's the best place to store a pie, whether whole or left over? According to the U.S. Department of Agriculture (USDA), pies containing fillings with perishable ingredients such as eggs or dairy must be refrigerated once cool. As or fruit pies, the USDA says they're food-safe at room temperature for up to two days because they contain plenty of sugar and acid, which retard bacteria growth. The refrigerator is fine for these pies, too, however. While cold typically hastens the staling of baked goods, the low moisture and high fat content of pie crust makes it resistant to staling in a way that leaner, moister items, such as breads, are not. If you don't have a pie carrier, we've had luck overturning a large bowl over a pie plate.

Making Pie Dough

When it comes to pie-making, if you're intimidated by one thing, chances are it's the crust. Maybe you have memories of flaky crusts that were tough, tender crusts that were bland, or of dough shrinking mercilessly as you rolled. These recipes should erase those memories. For pies with traditional, flaky, buttery pastry our go-to is undeniably our Foolproof All-Butter Pie Dough. It's supremely supple and easy to roll out. It bakes up buttery, tender, and flaky. But there is value in other pie dough recipes, like our classic (see page 345) that's a great option for achieving perfect crust if you have experience working with dough, or our vegan and gluten-free doughs, which can turn many naturally plant-based or gluten-free fillings into a friendly-for-all final course.

FOOLPROOF ALL-BUTTER PIE DOUGH

Pie crust and foolproof might not often live in the same sentence but this dough deserves its moniker—and it's exceptionally flaky and flavorful. How did we do it? First we used the food processor to coat two-thirds of the flour with butter, creating a water-resistant paste-like mixture. Next we broke that dough into pieces, coated the pieces with the remaining flour, and tossed in grated butter. By doing this, the water we folded in was absorbed only by the dry flour that coated the butter-flour chunks. Since gluten can develop only when flour is hydrated, this waterproofing method resulted in a crust that was supertender but had enough structure to support flakes. Weigh the flour. If your recipe requires rolling your dough piece(s) to a rectangle, form the dough into a 5-inch square instead of a disk. This dough will be moister than most pie doughs, but it will absorb a lot of excess moisture as it chills. Roll out the dough on a well-floured counter.

FOOLPROOF ALL-BUTTER SINGLE-CRUST PIE DOUGH
Makes one 9-inch single crust

　10　tablespoons unsalted butter, chilled, divided
1¼　cups (6¼ ounces) all-purpose flour, divided
　　1　tablespoon sugar
　½　teaspoon table salt
　¼　cup ice water, divided

1. Grate 2 tablespoons butter on large holes of box grater and place in freezer. Cut remaining 8 tablespoons butter into ½-inch cubes.

2. Pulse ¾ cup flour, sugar, and salt in food processor until combined, 2 pulses. Add cubed butter and process until homogeneous paste forms, about 30 seconds. Using your hands, carefully break paste into 2-inch chunks and redistribute evenly around processor blade. Add remaining ½ cup flour and pulse until mixture is broken into pieces no larger than 1 inch (most pieces will be much smaller), 4 or 5 pulses. Transfer mixture to bowl. Add grated butter and toss until butter pieces are separated and coated with flour.

3. Sprinkle 2 tablespoons ice water over mixture. Toss with rubber spatula until mixture is evenly moistened. Sprinkle remaining 2 tablespoons ice water over mixture and toss to combine. Press dough with spatula until dough sticks together. Transfer dough to sheet of plastic wrap. Draw edges of plastic over dough and press firmly on sides and top to form compact, fissure-free mass. Wrap in plastic and form into 5-inch disk. Refrigerate dough for at least 2 hours or up to 2 days. Let chilled dough sit on counter to soften slightly, about 10 minutes, before rolling. (Wrapped dough can be frozen for up to 1 month. If frozen, let dough thaw completely on counter before rolling.)

Herb Single-Crust Pie Dough
Add 1½ tablespoons minced fresh sage or thyme to flour-sugar mixture.

Lemon Single-Crust Pie Dough
Add 4 teaspoons grated lemon zest to flour-sugar mixture.

Nut Single-Crust Pie Dough
Do not use toasted nuts in this recipe.
　　Reduce cubed butter to 6 tablespoons and reduce first addition of flour to 6 tablespoons. Add ½ cup pecans, walnuts, hazelnuts, almonds, or peanuts, chopped and frozen, to food processor with flour, sugar, and salt and process until finely ground, about 30 seconds.

Whole-Grain Single-Crust Pie Dough
Substitute ¾ cup whole-wheat or rye flour for first addition of all-purpose flour, using ½ cup all-purpose flour for second addition of flour.

Mixing Foolproof All-Butter Single-Crust Pie Dough

1. Pulse ¾ cup flour, sugar, and salt in food processor until combined, 2 pulses. Add cubed butter and process until homogeneous paste forms, about 30 seconds.

2. Carefully break paste into 2-inch chunks and redistribute evenly around processor blade.

3. Add remaining ½ cup flour and pulse until mixture is broken into pieces no larger than 1 inch (most pieces will be much smaller), 4 to 5 pulses. Transfer mixture to bowl.

4. Add grated butter and toss until butter pieces are separated and coated with flour.

5. Sprinkle 2 tablespoons ice water over mixture. Toss with rubber spatula until mixture is evenly moistened. Sprinkle remaining 2 tablespoons ice water over mixture and toss to combine.

6. Transfer dough to sheet of plastic wrap. Draw edges of plastic over dough and press firmly on sides and top to form compact, fissure-free mass. Wrap in plastic and form into 5-inch disk.

Rolling Single-Crust Pie Dough

1. Roll dough into 12-inch circle on floured counter.

2. Loosely roll dough around rolling pin and gently unroll it onto 9-inch pie plate, letting excess dough hang over edge.

3. Ease dough into plate by gently lifting edge of dough with your hand while pressing into plate bottom with your other hand.

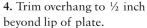

4. Trim overhang to ½ inch beyond lip of plate.

5. Tuck overhang under itself; folded edge should be flush with edge of plate.

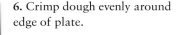

6. Crimp dough evenly around edge of plate.

FOOLPROOF ALL-BUTTER DOUBLE-CRUST PIE DOUGH

Makes one 9-inch double crust

- 20 tablespoons (2½ sticks) unsalted butter, chilled, divided
- 2½ cups (12½ ounces) all-purpose flour, divided
- 2 tablespoons sugar
- 1 teaspoon table salt
- ½ cup (4 ounces) ice water, divided

1. Grate 4 tablespoons butter on large holes of box grater and place in freezer. Cut remaining 16 tablespoons butter into ½-inch cubes.

2. Pulse 1½ cups flour, sugar, and salt in food processor until combined, 2 pulses. Add cubed butter and process until homogeneous paste forms, 40 to 50 seconds. Using your hands, carefully break paste into 2-inch chunks and redistribute evenly around processor blade. Add remaining 1 cup flour and pulse until mixture is broken into pieces no larger than 1 inch (most pieces will be much smaller), 4 or 5 pulses. Transfer mixture to bowl. Add grated butter and toss until butter pieces are separated and coated with flour.

3. Sprinkle ¼ cup ice water over mixture. Toss with rubber spatula until mixture is evenly moistened. Sprinkle remaining ¼ cup ice water over mixture and toss to combine. Press dough with spatula until dough sticks together. Using spatula, divide dough into 2 equal portions. Transfer each portion to sheet of plastic wrap. Working with 1 portion at a time, draw edges of plastic over dough and press firmly on sides and top to form compact, fissure-free mass. Wrap in plastic and form into 5-inch disk. Refrigerate dough for at least 2 hours or up to 2 days. Let chilled dough sit on counter to soften slightly, about 10 minutes, before rolling. (Wrapped dough can be frozen for up to 1 month. If frozen, let dough thaw completely on counter before rolling.)

Herb Double-Crust Pie Dough
Add 3 tablespoons minced fresh sage or thyme to flour-sugar mixture.

Lemon Double-Crust Pie Dough
Add 2½ tablespoons grated lemon zest to flour-sugar mixture.

Rolling Double-Crust Pie Dough

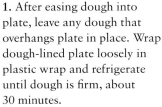

1. After easing dough into plate, leave any dough that overhangs plate in place. Wrap dough-lined plate loosely in plastic wrap and refrigerate until dough is firm, about 30 minutes.

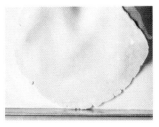

2. Roll other disk of dough into 12-inch circle on well-floured counter, then transfer to parchment paper–lined baking sheet.

3. Fill dough-lined plate; loosely roll remaining dough around rolling pin and gently unroll it onto filling.

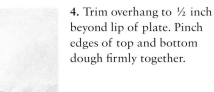

4. Trim overhang to ½ inch beyond lip of plate. Pinch edges of top and bottom dough firmly together.

5. Tuck overhang under itself; folded edge should be flush with edge of plate.

6. Crimp dough evenly around edge of plate.

Nut Double-Crust Pie Dough

Do not use toasted nuts in this recipe.

Reduce cubed butter to 12 tablespoons and reduce first addition of flour in step 2 to ¾ cup. Add 1 cup pecans, walnuts, hazelnuts, almonds, or peanuts, chopped and frozen, to food processor with flour, sugar, and salt and process until finely ground, about 30 seconds.

Whole-Grain Double-Crust Pie Dough

Substitute 1½ cups (8¼ ounces) whole-wheat or rye flour for first addition of all-purpose flour, using 1 cup all-purpose flour (5 ounces) for second addition of flour.

CLASSIC PIE DOUGH

Our Foolproof All-Butter Pie Dough offers reassurance to those who fear pie dough. But maybe you don't need that reassurance. For bakers who want to cut fat into flour and bring it together with water like their grandparents did, we're providing a classic pie dough. It employs a tried-and-true combination of butter (for flavor and flakiness) and shortening (for tenderness and workability). If your recipe requires rolling your dough piece(s) to a rectangle after chilling, form the dough into a 5-inch square instead of a disk.

CLASSIC SINGLE-CRUST PIE DOUGH

Makes one 9-inch single crust

1¼ cups (6¼ ounces) all-purpose flour
1 tablespoon sugar
½ teaspoon table salt
4 tablespoons vegetable shortening, cut into ½-inch pieces and chilled
6 tablespoons unsalted butter, cut into ¼-inch pieces and chilled
3 tablespoons ice water, plus extra as needed

1. Process flour, sugar, and salt in food processor until combined, about 5 seconds. Scatter shortening over top and process until mixture resembles coarse cornmeal, about 10 seconds. Scatter butter over top and pulse until mixture resembles coarse crumbs, about 10 pulses.

2. Transfer mixture to bowl. Sprinkle ice water over mixture. Stir and press dough with spatula until dough sticks together. If dough does not come together, stir in up to 1 tablespoon ice water, 1 teaspoon at a time, until it does.

3. Transfer dough to sheet of plastic wrap and form into 4-inch disk. Wrap tightly in plastic and refrigerate for at least 1 hour or up to 2 days. Let chilled dough sit on counter to soften slightly, about 10 minutes, before rolling. (Wrapped dough can be frozen for up to 1 month. If frozen, let dough thaw completely on counter before rolling.)

Mixing Classic Single-Crust Pie Dough

1. Process flour, sugar, and salt in food processor until combined, about 5 seconds. Scatter shortening over top and process until mixture resembles coarse cornmeal, about 10 seconds.

2. Scatter butter over top and pulse until mixture resembles coarse crumbs, about 10 pulses.

3. Transfer mixture to bowl. Sprinkle ice water over mixture. Stir and press dough with spatula until dough sticks together.

4. Transfer dough to sheet of plastic wrap and form into 4-inch disk.

Beyond Butter

We know butter tastes great and contributes to flakes. So why might you want to use other fats in your crust? Vegetable shortening contains no water, so on its own this fat option creates an almost too-tender short crust with no flakes (not to mention zero flavor). But when you use a combination of shortening and chilled cubes of butter, you can make a very nice crust: The shortening coats the flour to encourage tenderness, while the cubes of butter create flake-forming pockets. To illustrate the difference in how butter and shortening behave, we baked up one all-butter pie crust and one all-shortening pie crust.

Pie dough made with just butter is flaky.

Pie dough made with just shortening is short and dense.

Lard is the fat of pie-baking past—and present if you're a traditionalist. But we don't include recipes that use it because supermarket lard has an unpleasant taste. Higher quality (but harder to find) leaf lard is a different story. It contains very little water so you could use it in place of the shortening in our Classic Pie Dough if you choose.

Coconut oil is the latest fat we've come to associate with pie baking. This is our fat of choice for vegan pie doughs. We incorporate the coconut oil (at room temperature as it's very hard when chilled) much as we do butter in the foolproof all-butter dough. The two additions of flour and fat make two grades of dough: one tender and rich due to its flour being coated in fat and one lean to offer structure that will hold any filling.

CLASSIC DOUBLE-CRUST PIE DOUGH
Makes one 9-inch double crust

2½ cups (12½ ounces) all-purpose flour
2 tablespoons sugar
1 teaspoon table salt
8 tablespoons vegetable shortening, cut into
   ½-inch pieces and chilled
12 tablespoons unsalted butter, cut into
   ¼-inch pieces and chilled
6 tablespoons ice water, plus extra as needed

1. Process flour, sugar, and salt in food processor until combined, about 5 seconds. Scatter shortening over top and process until mixture resembles coarse cornmeal, about 10 seconds. Scatter butter over top and pulse until mixture resembles coarse crumbs, about 10 pulses.

2. Transfer mixture to large bowl. Sprinkle ice water over mixture. Stir and press dough with spatula until dough sticks together. If dough does not come together, stir in up to 2 tablespoons ice water, 1 tablespoon at a time, until it does.

3. Using spatula, divide dough into 2 equal portions. Transfer each portion to sheet of plastic wrap and form each into 4-inch disk. Wrap each piece tightly in plastic and refrigerate for at least 1 hour or up to 2 days. Let chilled dough sit on counter to soften slightly, about 10 minutes, before rolling. (Wrapped dough can be frozen for up to 1 month. If frozen, let dough thaw completely on counter before rolling.)

GLUTEN-FREE PIE DOUGH

Pie dough's structure comes from gluten, so any dough without it is going to be at a disadvantage. Some xanthan gum added to the dry ingredients helped bind the dough and provide structure, giving it the feel of a traditional crust once baked. We used all butter (along with a little sour cream for tenderness) rather than a mix of butter and shortening for rich flavor that stood up to the starchiness of the gluten-free flour. A bit of vinegar provided tenderness. If your recipe requires rolling your dough piece(s) to a rectangle after chilling, form the dough into a 5-inch square instead of a disk. Use the steps that follow to roll out the dough for your recipe. Weigh your ingredients, as the ratios of ingredients are integral to successful gluten-free baking.

GLUTEN-FREE SINGLE-CRUST PIE DOUGH
Makes one 9-inch single crust

 3 tablespoons ice water
1½ tablespoons sour cream
1½ teaspoons rice vinegar
6½ ounces (¾ cup plus ⅔ cup) all-purpose gluten-free flour blend (see page 2)
1½ teaspoons sugar
 ½ teaspoon table salt
 ¼ teaspoon xanthan gum
 8 tablespoons unsalted butter, cut into ¼-inch pieces and frozen for 10 to 15 minutes

1. Combine ice water, sour cream, and vinegar in bowl. Process flour blend, sugar, salt, and xanthan gum in food processor until combined, about 5 seconds. Scatter butter over top and pulse until crumbs look uniform and distinct pieces of butter are no longer visible, 20 to 30 pulses.

2. Pour sour cream mixture over flour mixture and pulse until dough comes together in large pieces around processor blade, about 20 pulses.

3. Transfer dough to sheet of plastic wrap and form into 5-inch disk. Wrap tightly in plastic and refrigerate for at least 1 hour or up to 2 days. Let chilled dough sit on counter to soften slightly, about 30 minutes, before rolling. (Dough cannot be frozen.)

GLUTEN-FREE DOUBLE-CRUST PIE DOUGH
Makes one 9-inch double crust

 6 tablespoons ice water
 3 tablespoons sour cream
 1 tablespoon rice vinegar
13 ounces (2¾ cups plus 2 tablespoons) all-purpose gluten-free flour blend (see page 2)
 1 tablespoon sugar
 1 teaspoon table salt
 ½ teaspoon xanthan gum
16 tablespoons unsalted butter, cut into ¼-inch pieces and frozen for 10 to 15 minutes

1. Combine ice water, sour cream, and vinegar in bowl. Process flour blend, sugar, salt, and xanthan gum in food processor until combined, about 5 seconds. Scatter butter over top and pulse until crumbs look uniform and distinct pieces of butter are no longer visible, 20 to 30 pulses.

2. Pour half of sour cream mixture over flour mixture and pulse to incorporate, about 3 pulses. Add remaining sour cream mixture and pulse until dough comes together in large pieces around processor blade, about 20 pulses.

3. Using spatula, divide dough into 2 equal portions. Transfer each portion to sheet of plastic wrap and form each into 5-inch disk. Wrap each piece tightly in plastic and refrigerate for at least 1 hour or up to 2 days. Let chilled dough sit on counter to soften slightly, about 30 minutes, before rolling. (Dough cannot be frozen.)

Rolling Gluten-Free Pie Dough

1. Roll dough into 12-inch circle between 2 large sheets of plastic wrap.

2. Remove top plastic and gently invert dough over 9-inch pie plate.

3. Working around circumference, ease dough into plate by gently lifting plastic wrap with 1 hand while pressing dough into plate bottom with other hand.

VEGAN PIE DOUGH

Since butter (along with flour, sugar, salt, and maybe shortening) is a key ingredient in traditional pie dough, we thought veganizing this workhorse would be a challenge. Baking with all shortening gave us a tender crust, but it lacked structure and was greasy. Vegetable oil was a failure, delivering a cracker-like crust. We'd hesitated to try coconut oil as it's very hard when chilled—too hard to roll. But when we substituted room-temperature coconut oil for the chilled butter (and passed on chilling the dough itself), we achieved a flaky, nicely browned, rich crust. If you are a strict vegan, use organic sugar. If your recipe requires rolling your dough piece(s) to a rectangle, form the dough into a 4-inch square instead of a disk.

VEGAN SINGLE-CRUST PIE DOUGH
Makes one 9-inch single crust

- 1½ cups (7½ ounces) all-purpose flour, divided
- 1 tablespoon sugar
- ½ teaspoon table salt
- ½ cup plus 1 tablespoon coconut oil
- ¼ cup ice water, plus extra as needed

1. Process ¾ cup flour, sugar, and salt in food processor until combined, about 5 seconds. Pinch off ½-inch pieces of oil into flour mixture and pulse until sticky and dough just begins to clump, 10 to 16 pulses. Redistribute dough evenly around processor blade, add remaining ¾ cup flour, and pulse until just incorporated, 3 to 6 pulses; transfer to large bowl.

2. Sprinkle ice water over mixture. Stir and press dough with spatula until dough sticks together, being careful not to over-mix. If dough does not come together, stir in up to 1 tablespoon ice water, 1 teaspoon at a time, until it does. Transfer dough to sheet of plastic wrap and form into 4-inch disk. (Dough can be wrapped tightly in plastic wrap and refrigerated for up to 2 days or frozen for up to 1 month. Let dough sit at room temperature to soften completely before rolling out, about 2 hours if refrigerated or 4 hours if frozen.)

VEGAN DOUBLE-CRUST PIE DOUGH
Makes one 9-inch double crust

- 3 cups (15 ounces) all-purpose flour, divided
- 2 tablespoons sugar
- 1 teaspoon table salt
- 1 cup plus 2 tablespoons coconut oil
- ½ cup ice water, plus extra as needed

1. Process 1½ cups flour, sugar, and salt in food processor until combined, about 5 seconds. Pinch off ½-inch pieces of oil into flour mixture and pulse until sticky and dough just begins to clump, 12 to 16 pulses. Redistribute dough evenly around processor blade, add remaining 1½ cups flour, and pulse until just incorporated, 3 to 6 pulses; transfer to large bowl.

2. Sprinkle ice water over mixture. Stir and press dough with spatula until dough sticks together, being careful not to overmix. If dough doesn't come together, stir in up to 2 tablespoons ice water, 2 teaspoons at a time, until it does. Using spatula, divide dough into 2 equal portions. Transfer each portion to sheet of plastic wrap and form each into 4-inch disk. (Dough can be wrapped tightly in plastic wrap and refrigerated for up to 2 days or frozen for up to 1 month. Let dough sit at room temperature to soften completely before rolling out, about 2 hours if refrigerated or 4 hours if frozen.)

Blind Baking 101

Blind Baking Tips

Many recipes call for blind-baking a single crust on a baking sheet on the middle rack in a 350-degree oven. This ensures a crisp crust that is golden and flaky in the time the filling bakes.

1. Cover but don't completely enclose the crust edge with foil; it will stick to or steam the dough. Fill the pie with 1 quart of pie weights.

2. To avoid accidents, take the crust out of the oven to remove the pie weights, even if a recipe calls for returning the crust to the oven.

3. Remember to adjust the oven temperature if called for in a recipe after the crust is done parbaking.

Blind-Baking Any Single-Crust Pie Dough

1. Line chilled pie shell with double layer of aluminum foil, covering edges to prevent burning, and fill with pie weights.

2. Bake on rimmed baking sheet until edges are set and just beginning to turn golden, 25 to 30 minutes, rotating sheet halfway through baking.

3. Remove foil and weights, rotate sheet, and continue to bake crust until golden brown and crisp, 10 to 15 minutes longer.

FINISHING YOUR CRUST

Choosing a crust doesn't come down to simply picking a recipe. You also have to decide how to finish your crust's crimped edge (for a single-crust pie) or covered top (for a double-crust pie) before it goes into the oven—and your choice will determine the pie's surface appearance once baked. Below are the methods we use for finishing our crusts; you might find you have a favorite, or you might prefer to change things up every time. Note that a little egg wash goes a long way; you don't want your dough dripping wash and you should have some left once you're done painting.

1. Finish-Free For a rustic appearance with a matte finish and attractive spotting, simply crimp or top your pie and pop it in the oven: That's all this option requires.

2. Egg Wash This is our go-to finishing technique to enhance golden color and give a bit of sophisticated sheen. Our egg wash involves lightly beating an egg with 1 tablespoon of water so it's thinned enough to distribute evenly and not so concentrated that it overbrowns.

3. Water and Sugar For a little sparkle and pleasant exterior crackle, brush the pie with some water before sprinkling on sugar (water helps the sugar adhere).

4. Egg Wash and Sugar This luxe finish gives you the best of all worlds: sparkle and crackle but also golden browning. It's a good choice for quick-baking pies like hand pies because they finish baking before their tops can take on a lot of color.

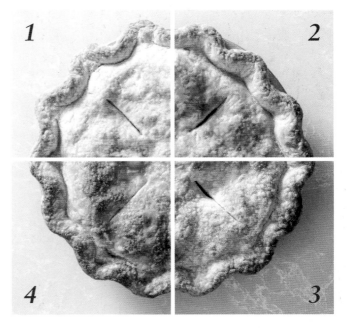

APPLE PIES

KEY POINTS

Choose apple varieties wisely

Parcook apples

Slice apples ¼ inch thick

Pair with aromatic spice

WHEN IT COMES TO PIE, there is perhaps no filling more well-loved than apple. The marriage of sweet-tart, tender apples and crisp, buttery pastry is supremely comforting and satisfying, especially when served alongside a scoop of rich vanilla ice cream. And while a deep-dish double-crust pie may be classic, apple pies come in all shapes and sizes. They can be structured (see page 353), free-form (see page 357), or tall and deep (see page 352). They may have only a bottom crust (see page 354) or feature a streusel-like topping (see page 356). What they all have in common, of course, is the apples. We like tart apples, such as Granny Smith and Empire, because of their bold flavor, but when used alone in a pie their flavor can seem one-dimensional. To achieve a fuller, more balanced flavor, we like to add a sweeter variety, such as Golden Delicious or Braeburn. Another important factor in choosing the right apple is the texture; even with gentle heat, softer varieties such as McIntosh break down readily and turn to mush (for more information on apples, see page 122).

PARCOOKING APPLES

When raw apples are used in a pie, they typically shrink to almost nothing; this is particularly a problem in deep-dish apple pie where the result is a huge gap between the top crust and the filling. Gently precooking the apples eliminates the shrinking problem and actually helps the apples hold their shape once baked in the pie. This seems counterintuitive, but here's what happens: When the apples are gently cooked over moderate heat, their pectin is converted into a heat-stable form that prevents the apples from becoming mushy when cooked further in the oven. The key is to keep the temperature of the apples below 140 degrees during this precooking stage; if you try to speed up the process by using higher heat, the apples will end up mealy. Here's the parcooking procedure we use for many of our apple pies.

1. Cover apples and cook over medium heat, stirring frequently, until apples are tender when poked with a fork but still hold their shape, 15 to 20 minutes.

2. Spread apples and their juices on rimmed baking sheet and let cool completely, about 30 minutes.

3. Drain cooked apples thoroughly in colander.

4. Spread apples into dough-lined pie plate, mounding them slightly in middle.

THE EASIEST WAY TO GRATE APPLES

When a recipe like Marlborough Apple Pie (page 354) or Apple Turnovers (page 510) calls for shredded apples, we occasionally pull out the food processor to do the job, but more often we opt to simply use the large holes of a paddle or box grater. When grating, we find it easiest (and least wasteful) to leave the core intact and use it as a handle.

Grip the apple by the top and the bottom of the core and grate it on the large holes of a paddle or box grater. When you reach the core, turn the apple 90 degrees. Repeat until only the core remains.

DEEP-DISH APPLE PIE

Serves 8 | 9-inch pie plate

WHY THIS RECIPE WORKS If you find yourself with a surplus of fruit after a fall apple-picking extravaganza, we recommend a towering deep-dish pie. But this iconic pie can be tricky to get right, so our goal was to find solutions to the pitfalls: unevenly cooked apples swimming in their own exuded juices atop a pale, soggy bottom crust and a large gap below the top crust. We found that precooking the apples allowed us to cram in lots of them; it also solved the shrinking problem and eliminated excess liquid, thereby protecting the bottom crust. But why didn't the apples then turn to mush during baking? When apples are gently preheated, their pectin is converted to a heat-stable form that keeps them from becoming mushy when cooked further in the oven. Good choices for tart apples are Granny Smiths, Empires, or Cortlands; for sweet, we recommend Golden Delicious, Jonagolds, or Braeburns.

- 1 recipe double-crust pie dough (see pages 342–348)
- 2½ pounds Granny Smith apples, peeled, cored, and sliced ¼ inch thick
- 2½ pounds Golden Delicious apples, peeled, cored, and sliced ¼ inch thick

Apple-Cranberry Pie

- ½ cup (3½ ounces) plus 1 tablespoon granulated sugar, divided
- ¼ cup packed (1¾ ounces) light brown sugar
- ½ teaspoon grated lemon zest plus 1 tablespoon juice
- ¼ teaspoon table salt
- ⅛ teaspoon ground cinnamon
- 1 large egg, lightly beaten with 1 tablespoon water

1. Roll 1 disk of dough into 12-inch circle on floured counter. Loosely roll dough around rolling pin and gently unroll it onto 9-inch pie plate, letting excess dough hang over edge. Ease dough into plate by gently lifting edge of dough with your hand while pressing into plate bottom with your other hand. Leave any dough that overhangs plate in place. Wrap dough-lined plate loosely in plastic wrap and refrigerate until firm, about 30 minutes. Roll other disk of dough into 12-inch circle on floured counter, then transfer to parchment paper–lined baking sheet; cover with plastic and refrigerate for 30 minutes.

2. Toss apples, ½ cup granulated sugar, brown sugar, lemon zest, salt, and cinnamon together in Dutch oven. Cover and cook over medium heat, stirring frequently, until apples are tender when poked with fork but still hold their shape, 15 to 20 minutes.

3. Spread apples and their juices on rimmed baking sheet and let cool completely, about 30 minutes.

4. Adjust oven rack to lowest position and heat oven to 425 degrees. Drain cooled apples thoroughly in colander set over bowl, reserving ¼ cup of juice. Stir lemon juice into reserved juice.

5. Spread apples into dough-lined plate, mounding them slightly in middle, and drizzle with lemon juice mixture. Loosely roll remaining dough round around rolling pin and gently unroll it onto filling.

6. Trim overhang to ½ inch beyond lip of plate. Pinch edges of top and bottom dough firmly together. Tuck overhang under itself; folded edge should be flush with edge of plate.

7. Crimp dough evenly around edge of plate. Cut four 2-inch slits in top of dough. Brush surface with egg wash and sprinkle evenly with remaining 1 tablespoon granulated sugar.

8. Place pie on aluminum foil–lined rimmed baking sheet and bake until crust is light golden brown, about 25 minutes. Reduce oven temperature to 375 degrees, rotate sheet, and continue to bake until juices are bubbling and crust is deep golden brown, 30 to 40 minutes longer. Let pie cool on wire rack until filling has set, about 4 hours. Serve.

APPLE-CRANBERRY PIE

Serves 8 | 9-inch pie plate

WHY THIS RECIPE WORKS Cranberries seem like they would make an ideal addition to classic apple pie, but the tart fruit can disturb the balance of flavors and textures by overwhelming the apples and shedding a lot of liquid. Cooking down the cranberries and using only sweet apples rather than a combination of sweet and tart varieties helped tame the tartness, but the cranberries still overpowered the apples. For the flavor of both elements to come through loud and clear, the solution was to keep the fruits separate by arranging the cooked cranberries and the apples in two layers within the pie. In our Deep-Dish Apple Pie, we learned that precooking the apples made them firmer in the baked pie, but here we wanted to avoid stovetop cooking since we were already cooking the cranberry mixture. Ten minutes in the microwave (and a bit of cornstarch) did the trick.

- 8 ounces (2 cups) fresh or frozen cranberries
- ¼ cup orange juice
- 1 cup (7 ounces) plus 1 tablespoon sugar, divided
- ½ teaspoon ground cinnamon, divided
- ½ teaspoon table salt, divided
- ¼ cup water
- 1 tablespoon cornstarch
- 3½ pounds Golden Delicious apples peeled, cored, and sliced ¼ inch thick
- 1 recipe double-crust pie dough (see pages 342–348)
- 1 large egg, lightly beaten with 1 tablespoon water

1. Bring cranberries, orange juice, ½ cup sugar, ¼ teaspoon cinnamon, and ¼ teaspoon salt to boil in medium saucepan. Cook, stirring occasionally and pressing cranberries against side of pot, until cranberries have completely broken down and juices have thickened to jam-like consistency (wooden spoon scraped across bottom should leave clear trail that doesn't fill in), 10 to 12 minutes. Off heat, stir in water and let cool completely, about 30 minutes.

2. Meanwhile, mix ½ cup sugar, remaining ¼ teaspoon cinnamon, remaining ¼ teaspoon salt, and cornstarch in large bowl. Add apples and toss to combine. Microwave, covered, stirring with rubber spatula every 3 minutes, until apples are just starting to turn translucent around edges and liquid is thick and glossy, 10 to 14 minutes. Let cool completely, about 30 minutes. (Fillings can be refrigerated separately for up to 2 days.)

3. While fillings cool, adjust oven rack to lowest position and heat oven to 425 degrees. Roll 1 disk of dough into 12-inch circle on floured counter. Loosely roll dough around rolling pin and gently unroll it onto 9-inch pie plate, letting excess dough hang over edge. Ease dough into plate by gently lifting edge of dough with your hand while pressing into plate bottom with your other

hand. Leave any dough that overhangs plate in place. Wrap dough-lined plate loosely in plastic wrap and refrigerate until firm, about 30 minutes. Roll other disk of dough into 12-inch circle on floured counter, then transfer to parchment paper–lined rimmed baking sheet; cover with plastic and refrigerate for 30 minutes.

4. Spread cooled cranberry mixture into even layer in dough-lined plate. Spread apple mixture on top, mounding it slightly in center. Loosely roll remaining dough round around rolling pin and gently unroll it onto filling. Trim overhang to ½ inch beyond lip of plate. Pinch edges of top and bottom crusts firmly together. Tuck overhang under itself; folded edge should be flush with edge of plate. Crimp dough evenly around edge of plate. Cut four 2-inch slits in top of dough. Brush surface with egg wash and sprinkle evenly with remaining 1 tablespoon sugar.

5. Place pie on aluminum foil–lined rimmed baking sheet and bake until crust is light golden brown, about 25 minutes. Reduce oven temperature to 375 degrees, rotate sheet, and continue to bake until juices are bubbling and crust is deep golden brown, 30 to 40 minutes longer. Let pie cool on wire rack until filling has set, about 4 hours. Serve.

APPLE PIE WITH CHEDDAR CHEESE CRUST

Serves 8 | 9-inch pie plate

WHY THIS RECIPE WORKS Serving a slice of warm apple pie with a wedge of cheddar on top is commonplace in New England and the Midwest; we thought it would be even better to bake the cheese right into the crust. For ample cheese flavor we found that we had to cut back a bit on butter; otherwise, the cheese-and-butter-filled crust would crumble. Reducing the butter in our double crust to 8 tablespoons allowed us to load half a pound of cheese into the dough. Good choices for tart apples are Granny Smiths, Empires, or Cortlands; for sweet, we recommend Golden Delicious, Jonagolds, or Braeburns. Be sure to use extra-sharp cheddar here. Freezing the butter for 15 minutes promotes flakiness in the crust; do not skip this step.

DOUGH
- 2½ cups (12½ ounces) all-purpose flour
- 1 tablespoon granulated sugar
- 1 teaspoon table salt
- 1 teaspoon dry mustard
- ⅛ teaspoon cayenne pepper
- 8 ounces extra-sharp cheddar cheese, shredded (2 cups)
- 8 tablespoons unsalted butter, cut into ¼-inch pieces and frozen for 15 minutes
- ⅓ cup ice water, plus extra as needed

FILLING

- 2 pounds Granny Smith, Empire, or Cortland apples, peeled, cored, halved, and sliced ¼ inch thick
- 2 pounds Golden Delicious, Jonagold, or Braeburn apples, peeled, cored, halved, and sliced ¼ inch thick
- 6 tablespoons (2⅔ ounces) granulated sugar
- ¼ cup packed (1¾ ounces) light brown sugar
- ½ teaspoon grated lemon zest plus 1 tablespoon juice
- ¼ teaspoon table salt
- ⅛ teaspoon ground cinnamon

1. **FOR THE DOUGH:** Process flour, sugar, salt, mustard, and cayenne in food processor until combined, about 5 seconds. Scatter cheddar and butter over top and pulse until butter is size of large peas, about 10 pulses.

2. Pour half of ice water over flour mixture and pulse until incorporated, about 3 pulses. Repeat with remaining ice water. Pinch dough with your fingers; if dough feels dry and does not hold together, sprinkle 1 to 2 tablespoons extra ice water over mixture and pulse until dough forms large clumps and no dry flour remains, 3 to 5 pulses.

3. Using spatula, divide dough into 2 equal portions. Transfer each portion to sheet of plastic wrap and form each into 4-inch disk. Wrap each piece tightly in plastic and refrigerate for at least 1 hour or up to 2 days. Let chilled dough sit on counter to soften slightly, about 10 minutes, before rolling. (Wrapped dough can be frozen for up to 1 month. If frozen, let dough thaw completely on counter before rolling.)

4. **FOR THE FILLING:** Toss apples, granulated sugar, brown sugar, lemon zest, salt, and cinnamon together in Dutch oven. Cover and cook over medium heat, stirring frequently, until apples are tender when poked with fork but still hold their shape, 10 to 15 minutes. Off heat, stir in lemon juice. Spread apples and their juices on rimmed baking sheet and let cool completely, about 30 minutes. (Filling can be refrigerated for up to 24 hours.)

5. Roll 1 disk of dough into 12-inch circle between 2 sheets of parchment paper. Loosely roll dough around rolling pin and gently unroll it onto 9-inch pie plate, letting excess dough hang over edge. Ease dough into plate by gently lifting edge of dough with your hand while pressing into plate bottom with your other hand. Leave any dough that overhangs plate in place. Wrap dough-lined plate loosely in plastic and refrigerate until firm, about 15 minutes.

6. Adjust oven rack to lowest position and heat oven to 425 degrees. Spread apple mixture into dough-lined plate. Roll other disk of dough into 12-inch circle between 2 sheets of parchment. Loosely roll dough around rolling pin and gently unroll it onto filling.

Marlborough Apple Pie

7. Trim overhang to ½ inch beyond lip of plate. Pinch edges of top and bottom dough firmly together. Tuck overhang under itself; folded edge should be flush with edge of plate. Crimp dough evenly around edge of plate. Cut four 2-inch slits in top of dough.

8. Place pie on aluminum foil–lined rimmed baking sheet and bake for 20 minutes. Reduce oven temperature to 375 degrees, rotate sheet, and continue to bake until juices are bubbling and crust is deep golden brown, 35 to 45 minutes longer. Let pie cool on wire rack until filling has set, about 4 hours. Serve.

MARLBOROUGH APPLE PIE
Serves 8 | 9-inch pie plate

WHY THIS RECIPE WORKS Marlborough pie, an almost-forgotten New England apple pie, combines the comforting apple-and-spice flavors of traditional apple pie with rich, creamy custard. Pre–Civil War bakers turned out these pies as a tasty way to use up the bruised, aging apples from their root cellars. They grated the apples to disguise imperfections and added lemon juice to balance the very sweet nature of old apples before stirring the apples into a custard base. For balanced flavor, we opted for a mix of sweet and tart varieties, along with a bit of complementary lemon zest (rather than juice). We sautéed our grated apples to eliminate moisture that could make the custard wet and weepy and to concentrate the apple flavor. Sherry, cinnamon, and mace rounded out the pie's profile. Shred the apples on the large holes of a box grater.

- 1 recipe single-crust pie dough (see pages 342–348)
- 4 tablespoons unsalted butter
- 2 Granny Smith apples, peeled and shredded (2 cups)
- 2 Fuji, Gala, or Golden Delicious apples, peeled and shredded (2 cups)
- ½ cup (3½ ounces) sugar
- ¼ teaspoon ground cinnamon
- ¼ teaspoon ground mace
- ¼ teaspoon table salt
- 3 large eggs, lightly beaten
- ½ cup heavy cream
- 5 tablespoons dry sherry
- 1 teaspoon grated lemon zest
- 1 teaspoon vanilla extract

1. Roll dough into 12-inch circle on floured counter. Loosely roll dough around rolling pin and gently unroll it onto 9-inch pie plate, letting excess dough hang over edge. Ease dough into plate by gently lifting edge of dough with your hand while pressing into plate bottom with your other hand.

2. Trim overhang to ½ inch beyond lip of plate. Tuck overhang under itself; folded edge should be flush with edge of plate. Crimp dough evenly around edge of plate. Wrap dough-lined plate loosely in plastic wrap and refrigerate until firm, about 30 minutes. Adjust oven rack to middle position and heat oven to 350 degrees.

3. Line chilled pie shell with double layer of aluminum foil, covering edges to prevent burning, and fill with pie weights. Bake on foil-lined rimmed baking sheet until edges are set and just beginning to turn golden, 25 to 30 minutes, rotating sheet halfway through baking. Remove foil and weights, rotate sheet, and continue to bake crust until golden brown and crisp, 10 to 15 minutes longer. Transfer sheet to wire rack. (Crust must still be warm when filling is added.) Adjust oven rack to lower-middle position and reduce oven temperature to 325 degrees.

4. Meanwhile, melt butter in 12-inch skillet over medium heat. Add apples and cook, stirring frequently, until pan is dry and apples have softened, 12 to 14 minutes. Transfer apples to bowl and let cool completely, about 20 minutes.

5. Whisk sugar, cinnamon, mace, and salt together in large bowl. Add eggs, cream, sherry, lemon zest, and vanilla and whisk until smooth. Add cooled apples and stir to combine. With pie still on sheet, pour mixture into warm crust. Bake until center is just set, about 40 minutes. Let pie cool completely on wire rack, about 4hours. Serve. (Pie can be refrigerated for up to 24 hours.)

CRAB APPLE ROSE PIE

Serves 8 | 9-inch pie plate

WHY THIS RECIPE WORKS A crab apple pie is a bit more tart than traditional apple pie, but it's also more complex in flavor and offers a welcome variation on the standard. Crab apples have high levels of pectin, which helps the filling set and makes for an easy-to-slice pie. Since they're so small, we opted to leave the skins on; this made prep easier and contributed a beautiful rosy hue to the filling. A tablespoon of rose water added a floral undertone that brought out the apples' complexity. We don't recommend using an apple corer to core the crab apples; instead, cut around the core using a sharp knife. Crab apples can range from sweet-tart to incredibly sour; use more or less sugar depending on the flavor of your crab apples. Any of the top crusts (see pages 364–367) will allow for enough evaporation to ensure a perfect slice.

- 1 recipe double-crust pie dough (see pages 342–348)
- 3 pounds crab apples, cored and chopped coarse
- 1½–1¾ cups (10½–12¼ ounces) sugar
- ¼ teaspoon table salt
- 1 tablespoon rose water
- 2 tablespoons unsalted butter, cut into ¼-inch pieces
- 1 large egg, lightly beaten with 1 tablespoon water

1. Roll 1 disk of dough into 12-inch circle on floured counter. Loosely roll dough around rolling pin and gently unroll it onto 9-inch pie plate, letting excess dough hang over edge. Ease dough into plate by gently lifting edge of dough with your hand while pressing into plate bottom with your other hand. Leave any dough that overhangs plate in place. Wrap dough-lined plate loosely in plastic wrap and refrigerate until firm, about 30 minutes.

2. Roll other piece of dough into 13 by 10½-inch rectangle on floured counter, then transfer to parchment paper–lined rimmed baking sheet; cover loosely with plastic and refrigerate until firm, about 30 minutes.

3. Using pizza wheel, fluted pastry wheel, or paring knife, trim ¼ inch dough from long sides of rectangle, then cut lengthwise into eight 1¼-inch-wide strips. Cover loosely with plastic and refrigerate until firm, about 30 minutes.

4. Toss apples, sugar, and salt together in Dutch oven. Cover and cook over medium heat, stirring frequently, until apples are tender when poked with fork but still hold their shape, 10 to 15 minutes. Spread apples and their juices on second rimmed baking sheet and let cool completely, about 30 minutes.

5. Drain cooled apples thoroughly in colander, then combine drained apples and rose water in bowl. Spread apples into dough-lined plate and scatter butter over top. Adjust oven rack to middle position and heat oven to 400 degrees.

Crab Apple Rose Pie

PENNSYLVANIA DUTCH APPLE PIE

Serves 8 | 9-inch pie plate

WHY THIS RECIPE WORKS The hallmark of Pennsylvania Dutch apple pie, aside from its crumbly topping, is its creamy apple filling. But rather than rely on the traditional cream to achieve it, we used melted vanilla ice cream (which is essentially custard) for more body and a rich vanilla flavor. We let the sliced apples sit in the melted ice cream along with cinnamon, sugar, and lemon juice until they were soft and pliable; this allowed them to form a cohesive interior that cooked evenly. Melted butter, flour, and brown sugar sprinkled over the top made for a supremely buttery crumble. We prefer sweet Golden Delicious or Gala apples here, but Fuji, Braeburn, or Granny Smith varieties also work well. You may substitute ½ cup of heavy cream for the melted ice cream, if desired. This pie is best when baked a day ahead of time and allowed to rest overnight.

PIE

2½ pounds apples, peeled, cored, halved, and sliced ¼ inch thick
½ cup melted vanilla ice cream
½ cup raisins (optional)
½ cup (3½ ounces) granulated sugar
1 tablespoon lemon juice
1 teaspoon vanilla extract
1 teaspoon ground cinnamon
½ teaspoon table salt
1 recipe single-crust pie dough (see pages 342–348)

TOPPING

1 cup (5 ounces) all-purpose flour
½ cup packed (3½ ounces) light brown sugar
6 tablespoons unsalted butter, melted
½ teaspoon table salt

1. FOR THE PIE: Toss apples; ice cream; raisins, if using; sugar; lemon juice; vanilla; cinnamon; and salt in large bowl until apples are evenly coated. Let sit at room temperature for at least 1 hour or up to 2 hours.

2. Roll dough into 12-inch circle on floured counter. Loosely roll dough around rolling pin and gently unroll it onto 9-inch pie plate, letting excess dough hang over edge. Ease dough into plate by gently lifting edge of dough with your hand while pressing into plate bottom with your other hand.

3. Trim overhang to ½ inch beyond lip of plate. Tuck overhang under itself; folded edge should be flush with edge of plate. Crimp dough evenly around edge of plate. Wrap dough-lined plate loosely in plastic wrap and refrigerate until firm, about 30 minutes. Adjust oven rack to lower-middle position and heat oven to 350 degrees.

6. Remove dough strips from refrigerator; if too stiff to be workable, let sit at room temperature until softened slightly but still very cold. Space 4 strips evenly across top of pie, parallel to counter edge. Fold back first and third strips almost completely. Lay 1 strip across pie, perpendicular to second and fourth strips, keeping it snug to folded edges of dough strips, then unfold first and third strips over top. Fold back second and fourth strips and add second perpendicular strip, keeping it snug to folded edge. Unfold second and fourth strips over top. Repeat weaving remaining strips evenly across pie, alternating between folding back first and third strips and second and fourth strips to create lattice pattern. Shift strips as needed so they are evenly spaced over top of pie. (If dough becomes too soft to work with, refrigerate pie and dough strips until firm.)

7. Trim overhang to ½ inch beyond lip of plate. Pinch edges of bottom crust and lattice strips together firmly to seal. Tuck overhang under itself; folded edge should be flush with edge of plate. Crimp dough evenly around edge of plate. (If dough is very soft, refrigerate for 10 minutes before baking.) Brush surface with egg wash.

8. Place pie on aluminum foil–lined rimmed baking sheet and bake until crust is light golden, 20 to 25 minutes. Reduce oven temperature to 350 degrees, rotate sheet, and continue to bake until juices are bubbling and crust is deep golden brown, 30 to 50 minutes longer. Let pie cool on wire rack until filling has set, about 4 hours. Serve.

4. FOR THE TOPPING: Stir all ingredients in bowl until no dry spots remain and mixture forms clumps. Refrigerate until ready to use.

5. Working with 1 large handful at a time, distribute apple mixture in plate, pressing into even layer and filling in gaps before adding more. Take care not to mound apple mixture in center of plate. Pour any remaining liquid from bowl into pie. Break topping (it will harden in refrigerator) into pea-size crumbs and distribute evenly over apple mixture. Pat topping lightly to adhere.

6. Place pie on aluminum foil–lined rimmed baking sheet. Bake until top is golden brown and paring knife inserted in center meets no resistance, about 1 hour 10 minutes, rotating sheet halfway through baking. Let pie cool on wire rack for at least 4 hours or preferably 8 to 12 hours. Serve.

APPLE PANDOWDY

Serves 6 | 10-inch skillet

WHY THIS RECIPE WORKS One of many old-school New England desserts with funny names, pandowdy is a skillet apple pie with an appealingly caramelized top. We tossed wedges of buttery Golden Delicious apples in cinnamon and brown sugar for sweet-spiced flavor and partially cooked them before simmering in apple cider and lemon juice. Topping the apples with squares of dough allowed steam to escape during baking, preventing the apples from overcooking. "Dowdying," or pressing, the crust partway through baking created the dessert's signature sweet finish by allowing juices from the filling to rise over the crust and caramelize. Do not use store-bought pie crust in this recipe; it yields gummy results.

PIE DOUGH

- 3 tablespoons ice water
- 1 tablespoon sour cream
- ⅔ cup (3⅓ ounces) all-purpose flour
- 1 teaspoon granulated sugar
- ½ teaspoon table salt
- 6 tablespoons unsalted butter, cut into ¼-inch pieces and frozen for 15 minutes

FILLING

- 2½ pounds Golden Delicious apples, peeled, cored, halved, and cut into ½-inch-thick wedges
- ¼ cup packed (1¾ ounces) light brown sugar
- ½ teaspoon ground cinnamon
- ¼ teaspoon table salt
- 3 tablespoons unsalted butter
- ¾ cup apple cider
- 1 tablespoon cornstarch
- 2 teaspoons lemon juice

TOPPING

- 1 tablespoon granulated sugar
- ¼ teaspoon ground cinnamon
- 1 large egg, lightly beaten
  Vanilla ice cream

1. FOR THE PIE DOUGH: Combine ice water and sour cream in bowl. Process flour, sugar, and salt in food processor until combined, about 3 seconds. Add butter and pulse until size of large peas, 6 to 8 pulses. Add sour cream mixture and pulse until dough forms large clumps and no dry flour remains, 3 to 6 pulses, scraping down sides of bowl as needed.

2. Form dough into 4-inch disk, wrap tightly in plastic wrap, and refrigerate for 1 hour. (Wrapped dough can be refrigerated for up to 2 days or frozen for up to 1 month. If frozen, let dough thaw completely on counter before rolling.)

3. Adjust oven rack to middle position and heat oven to 400 degrees. Let chilled dough sit on counter to soften slightly, about 5 minutes, before rolling. Roll dough into 10-inch circle on lightly floured counter. Using pizza cutter, cut dough into four 2½-inch-wide strips, then make four 2½-inch-wide perpendicular cuts to form squares. (Pieces around edges of dough will be smaller.) Transfer dough pieces to parchment paper–lined baking sheet, cover with plastic, and refrigerate until firm, at least 30 minutes.

4. FOR THE FILLING: Toss apples, sugar, cinnamon, and salt together in large bowl. Melt butter in 10-inch skillet over medium heat. Add apple mixture, cover, and cook until apples become slightly pliable and release their juices, about 10 minutes, stirring occasionally.

5. Whisk cider, cornstarch, and lemon juice in bowl until no lumps remain; add to skillet. Bring to simmer and cook, uncovered, stirring occasionally, until sauce is thickened, about 2 minutes. Off heat, press lightly on apples to form even layer.

6. FOR THE TOPPING: Combine sugar and cinnamon in small bowl. Working quickly, shingle dough pieces over filling until mostly covered, overlapping as needed. Brush dough pieces with egg and sprinkle with cinnamon sugar.

7. Bake until crust is slightly puffed and beginning to brown, about 15 minutes. Remove skillet from oven. Using back of large spoon, press down in center of crust until juices come up over top of crust. Repeat 4 more times around skillet. Make sure all apples are submerged and return skillet to oven. Continue to bake until crust is golden brown, about 15 minutes longer.

8. Transfer skillet to wire rack and let cool for at least 20 minutes. Serve with ice cream, drizzling extra sauce over top.

(THE OTHER) FALL FRUIT PIES

KEY POINTS

Parcook fruit

Pair with strong flavors

APPLES MAY CLAIM A PIE CATEGORY ALL THEIR OWN, but there are other fall fruits equally deserving of a starring role in a seasonal pie. One such fruit is sweet, fragrant pears; more commonly associated with tarts and crisps, pears can be an unexpected and welcome addition to your pie repertoire—once you learn how to properly handle this exceptionally juicy fruit. We rein in their juices by precooking them in the microwave. Because pears have a relatively mild flavor, we often like to add a contrasting element such as spicy ginger or another fall favorite: bold, tart cranberries. (During the fall and winter, cranberries are sold fresh, but the frozen ones—available year-round—work equally well for baking.) And if you're looking for something a bit more unique, consider the quince. Once commonplace in American kitchens, this fragrant yellow fruit may be hard, dry, and astringent when eaten raw, but when cooked or baked it is transformed. We poach quinces before adding them to pie, which infuses them with flavor as it softens them. Quinces are a pectin powerhouse, which means they have their own built-in thickener—ideal for a sliceable filling.

GINGER–CRANBERRY PEAR STREUSEL PIE

Serves 8 | 9-inch pie plate

WHY THIS RECIPE WORKS Ripe pears are filled with honey-flavored juices that stream from the fruit when you take a bite. Those same juices also stream out of a pie. We wanted a pear pie, perked up with complementary flavors, that wasn't a watery mess. Microwaving the pears mitigated some moisture, while a streusel topping allowed for evaporation and also provided a nice contrast to the soft fruit. Baking the pie on the bottom rack further encouraged evaporation. By adding a little extra sugar, we were able to distribute 2 cups of cranberries throughout our pie without puckering. And for an alluring final component, we added 1 teaspoon of grated fresh ginger. Some ground ginger and chewy bits of crystallized ginger in the topping tied the components of our seasonal pie together.

- 1 recipe single-crust pie dough (see pages 342–348)
- 3 pounds ripe but firm Bartlett or Bosc pears, peeled, halved, cored, and sliced ¼ inch thick
- ½ cup (3½ ounces) granulated sugar, divided
- ¾ cup (3¾ ounces) all-purpose flour
- ¼ cup packed (1¾ ounces) light brown sugar
- 2 tablespoons crystallized ginger, chopped
- ¾ teaspoon ground ginger
- ⅛ teaspoon table salt
- 5 tablespoons unsalted butter, melted
- 8 ounces (2 cups) fresh or thawed frozen cranberries
- 1 teaspoon grated fresh ginger

1. Roll dough into 12-inch circle on floured counter. Loosely roll dough around rolling pin and gently unroll it onto 9-inch pie plate, letting excess dough hang over edge. Ease dough into plate by gently lifting edge of dough with your hand while pressing into plate bottom with your other hand.

2. Trim overhang to ½ inch beyond lip of plate. Tuck overhang under itself; folded edge should be flush with edge of plate. Crimp dough evenly around edge of plate. Wrap dough-lined plate loosely in plastic wrap and refrigerate until firm, about 30 minutes. Adjust oven rack to lowest position and heat oven to 400 degrees.

3. Toss pears with 2 tablespoons granulated sugar in large bowl. Microwave, covered, until pears turn translucent and release their juices, 4 to 8 minutes, stirring once halfway through microwaving. Uncover and let cool completely, about 30 minutes.

4. Combine flour, brown sugar, crystallized ginger, ground ginger, salt, and 2 tablespoons granulated sugar in bowl. Stir in melted butter until mixture is completely moistened; let sit for 10 minutes.

Ginger–Cranberry Pear Streusel Pie

5. Combine cranberries, fresh ginger, and remaining ¼ cup granulated sugar in food processor and pulse until cranberries are coarsely chopped, about 5 pulses. Drain pears and discard liquid. Return pears to now-empty bowl and add cranberry mixture, stirring to combine. Spread mixture into dough-lined plate. Sprinkle topping over pear mixture, breaking apart any large clumps. Place pie on aluminum foil–lined rimmed baking sheet and bake until juices are bubbling and topping is deep golden brown, 45 to 55 minutes, rotating sheet halfway through baking. Let pie cool on wire rack until filling has set, about 4 hours. Serve.

MULLED WINE QUINCE PIE

Serves 8 | 9-inch pie plate

WHY THIS RECIPE WORKS Quinces have a flavor somewhere between a pear and an apple. Although they're quite tart with hard flesh when raw, quinces soften and sweeten when cooked. We poached them in red wine, along with some spices and citrus zest. We mashed half of the poached quinces and sliced the other half; quinces are loaded with pectin, so this created pie that set up without thickener. It's important to be fastidious when coring quinces, as the core remains tough after cooking. Use a good-quality medium-bodied wine, such as a Côtes du Rhône or Pinot Noir, for this pie. If you don't have cheesecloth, substitute a triple layer of disposable coffee filters. Any of the top crusts (see pages 364–367) will work with this pie.

4 (2-inch) strips orange zest
3 bay leaves
1 cinnamon stick
1 teaspoon allspice berries
¼ teaspoon black peppercorns
1 (750-ml) bottle red wine
2 cups water
1¼ cups (8¾ ounces) sugar, divided
3 pounds quinces, peeled, halved, and cored
1 recipe double-crust pie dough (see pages 342–348)
½ cup dried cherries
¼ teaspoon table salt
1 large egg, lightly beaten with 1 tablespoon water

1. Place orange zest, bay leaves, cinnamon, allspice, and peppercorns in triple layer of cheesecloth and tie closed with kitchen twine. Bring wine, water, ¾ cup sugar, and spice bundle to simmer in Dutch oven over medium-high heat, whisking to dissolve sugar. Add quinces and return to simmer. Reduce heat to medium-low and cook, covered, stirring occasionally, until quince is easily pierced with fork, about 2 hours.

2. While quinces cook, roll 1 disk of dough into 12-inch circle on floured counter. Loosely roll dough around rolling pin and gently unroll it onto 9-inch pie plate, letting excess dough hang over edge. Ease dough into plate by gently lifting edge of dough with your hand while pressing into plate bottom with your other hand. Leave any dough that overhangs plate in place. Wrap dough-lined plate loosely in plastic wrap and refrigerate until firm, about 30 minutes.

3. Roll other piece of dough into 13 by 10½-inch rectangle on floured counter, then transfer to parchment paper–lined rimmed baking sheet; cover loosely with plastic and refrigerate until firm, about 30 minutes.

4. Using pizza wheel, fluted pastry wheel, or paring knife, trim ¼ inch dough from long sides of rectangle, then cut lengthwise into eight 1¼-inch-wide strips. Cover loosely with plastic and refrigerate until firm, about 30 minutes. Adjust oven rack to middle position and heat oven to 400 degrees.

5. Off heat, discard spice bundle from pot. Using slotted spoon, transfer 4 quince halves to large bowl and mash into coarse paste with potato masher. Transfer remaining quince halves to cutting board and let sit until cool enough to handle, about 10 minutes (reserve cooking liquid). Cut quinces in half lengthwise then slice ¼ inch thick crosswise. Add sliced quinces, ½ cup reserved cooking liquid, remaining ½ cup sugar, cherries, and salt to mashed quince mixture in bowl, stirring to combine. Spread quince filling into dough-lined plate.

6. Remove dough strips from refrigerator; if too stiff to be workable, let sit at room temperature until softened slightly but still very cold. Space 4 strips evenly across top of pie, parallel to counter edge. Fold back first and third strips almost completely. Lay 1 strip across pie, perpendicular to second and fourth strips, keeping it snug to folded edges of dough strips, then unfold first and third strips over top. Fold back second and fourth strips and add second perpendicular strip, keeping it snug to folded edge. Unfold second and fourth strips over top. Repeat weaving remaining strips evenly across pie, alternating between folding back first and third strips and second and fourth strips to create lattice pattern. Shift strips as needed so they are evenly spaced over top of pie. (If dough becomes too soft to work with, refrigerate pie and dough strips until firm.)

7. Trim overhang to ½ inch beyond lip of plate. Pinch edges of bottom crust and lattice strips together firmly to seal. Tuck overhang under itself; folded edge should be flush with edge of plate. Crimp dough evenly around edge of plate. (If dough is very soft, refrigerate for 10 minutes before baking.) Brush surface with egg wash.

Mulled Wine Quince Pie

8. Place pie on aluminum foil–lined rimmed baking sheet and bake until crust is light golden, 20 to 25 minutes. Reduce oven temperature to 350 degrees, rotate sheet, and continue to bake until juices are bubbling and crust is deep golden brown, 30 to 50 minutes longer. Let pie cool on wire rack until filling has set, about 4 hours.

9. Once pie is cooled, bring Dutch oven with remaining poaching liquid to boil over medium-high heat. Reduce until sauce has consistency of maple syrup and measures about ¾ cup, 15 to 20 minutes. Let cool slightly, about 20 minutes. Serve pie, passing sauce separately.

PEANUT BUTTER AND CONCORD GRAPE PIE

Serves 8 | 9-inch pie plate

WHY THIS RECIPE WORKS While Concord grapes, which show up in late summer through early fall, are not typically eaten out of hand (they have tough skins and seeds), their bold flavor is ideal in jams, compotes, or fruit fillings. We wanted to incorporate the beloved combination of peanut butter and grape jelly into a pie. We started by cooking down the grapes to create a thick fruit filling. We then spooned a peanut butter mousse into a peanutty pie crust and topped it with our jelly. A peanut butter whipped cream added a pleasantly light layer, and candied peanuts contributed welcome crunch. Look for grapes that are firm, plump, and securely attached to their stems. For fruit pectin we recommend both Sure-Jell for Less or No Sugar Needed Recipes and Ball RealFruit Low or No-Sugar Needed Pectin. We like our nut dough made with peanuts for this pie, but you can use any single-crust pie dough. Use peanuts in the candied nuts.

1 recipe Nut Single-Crust Pie Dough (page 342)

PEANUT BUTTER MOUSSE
½ cup (2 ounces) confectioners' sugar
½ cup creamy peanut butter
4 ounces cream cheese, softened
2 tablespoons plus ½ cup heavy cream, divided

GRAPE FILLING
1 cup (7 ounces) granulated sugar, divided
2 tablespoons low- or no-sugar-needed fruit pectin
1½ pounds Concord grapes, stemmed
1 teaspoon lemon zest plus 1 tablespoon juice
¼ teaspoon table salt
1 recipe Peanut Butter Whipped Cream (page 548)
1 recipe Candied Nuts (page 551)

1. Roll dough into 12-inch circle on floured counter. Loosely roll dough around rolling pin and gently unroll it onto 9-inch pie plate, letting excess dough hang over edge. Ease dough into plate by gently lifting edge of dough with your hand while pressing into plate bottom with your other hand.

2. Trim overhang to ½ inch beyond lip of plate. Tuck overhang under itself; folded edge should be flush with edge of plate. Crimp dough evenly around edge of plate. Wrap dough-lined plate loosely in plastic wrap and refrigerate until firm, about 30 minutes. Adjust oven rack to middle position and heat oven to 350 degrees.

3. Line chilled pie shell with double layer of aluminum foil, covering edges to prevent burning, and fill with pie weights. Bake on foil-lined rimmed baking sheet until edges are set and just beginning to turn golden, 25 to 30 minutes, rotating sheet halfway through baking. Remove foil and weights, rotate sheet, and continue to bake crust until golden brown and crisp, 10 to 15 minutes longer. Transfer sheet to wire rack and let cool completely, about 45 minutes.

4. **FOR THE PEANUT BUTTER MOUSSE:** Using stand mixer fitted with whisk attachment, whip sugar, peanut butter, cream cheese, and 2 tablespoons cream on low speed until combined, about 1 minute. Increase speed to medium-high and whip until fluffy, about 1 minute. Transfer to large bowl; set aside.

5. In now-empty mixer bowl, whip remaining ½ cup cream on medium-low speed until foamy, about 1 minute. Increase speed to high and whip until stiff peaks form, 1 to 3 minutes. Gently fold whipped cream into peanut butter mixture in 2 additions until no white streaks remain. Spoon filling into cooled crust and spread into even layer with spatula. Refrigerate until set, about 1 hour.

6. **FOR THE GRAPE FILLING:** While mousse chills, whisk ¼ cup sugar and pectin together in bowl; set aside. Bring grapes to simmer in large saucepan over high heat. Off heat, coarsely mash grapes with potato masher. Return to simmer over medium-high heat and cook until grapes have softened and pulp has separated from skins, about 5 minutes.

7. Working in batches, strain grapes through fine-mesh strainer into large bowl, pressing firmly on solids to extract as much liquid as possible (you should have about 1¼ cups); discard solids. Return strained grape juice to now-empty saucepan. Bring grape juice, remaining ¾ cup sugar, lemon zest and juice, and salt to boil over medium-high heat. Whisk in pectin mixture, return to boil, and cook for 1 minute, whisking constantly. Let cool off heat until just warm, about 30 minutes. Slowly pour filling over peanut butter mousse, spreading into even layer with rubber spatula. Refrigerate until filling is set, about 2 hours. Spread whipped cream attractively over pie and sprinkle with candied nuts. Serve.

SUMMER FRUIT PIES

Different fruits require different thickeners

Fruit doesn't require parcooking

Top with lattice for evaporation

AT THE HEIGHT OF SUMMER, a berry-picking extravaganza or stop at a roadside farm stand for fresh, ripe stone fruit is bound to inspire a desire for pie. Buttery, flaky top and bottom crusts encase mounds of perfectly stewed fruit in these bright and flavorful summer fruit pies. While the juiciness of summer fruits is part of what makes them so appealing, all that juice can be one of the biggest challenges when trying to incorporate them into a pie. The most traditional crusts feature sliced vents for moisture to escape, although some fruit fillings such as cherry and peach often sport lattice-woven crusts. This allows for maximum evaporation while the pie cooks, which means the juices released by the fruit cook down slowly while baking so that the filling isn't soupy. But because the top crust still shields the filling somewhat, these pies also typically require a thickening agent such as ground tapioca or cornstarch. When sweetening fruit pies, it is important to take into consideration the ripeness of the fruit. Riper fruit will taste sweeter and release more juice than less ripe fruit, so you may want to adjust the amount of sugar in the recipe accordingly. And don't slice them too soon so they have a chance to fully set: If you want a warm slice of pie with ice cream, you can always heat up individual slices

INVOKING APPLES

When making the filling for Blueberry Earl Grey Pie (page 368), we found that if we used more than 2 tablespoons of tapioca, the texture of the filling took on a gummy consistency we didn't like. But less than 2 tablespoons resulted in a filling that was too loose. To solve this problem, we turned to pectin, a gentle thickener that occurs naturally in fruit. Pectin creates structure in a plant by helping bind its cell walls together. This same substance is used to thicken jams and jellies. Apples are a great source of pectin because they contain high levels of high-methoxy pectin, the best natural pectin for making gels. Mashing some of the blueberries and grating a Granny Smith apple released enough pectin from the fruits' cell walls to thicken the pie filling—and as a bonus, the tart flavor of the apple enhanced the fresh fruit flavor of the berries.

THE QUEEN OF FRUITS

Figs are commonly dried: Fig trees thrive in Mediterranean climates, but figs' flavor is desired all year, all around the world. There are more than 700 fresh fig varieties, however. Among the fresh figs you're most likely to find in an American supermarket are jammy, ultrasweet Black Mission figs (a Spanish fig that's one of the most valued); large velvety Brown Turkey figs; and green, globe-like, deliciously sticky-sweet Turkish Calimyrna figs. You can use any variety of figs you can find for our Red Currant and Fig Pie (page 374).

LOVELY LATTICES

Since summer fruit pies often benefit from lattice crusts, you might find yourself slicing strips all season. Each double-crust pie in this chapter is an opportunity to show off a different style of top crust. They're simply beautiful, with the bubbly, deeply hued fruit peeking through buttery, golden strips and shapes of crust. In the following pages, you'll learn the steps to achieving these picture-perfect lattice examples.

Basic Lattice

Cutout Crust

Braided Strips

Free-Form Shapes

Topping Your Pie

We've written every double-crust recipe in this book that requires a lattice crust with the basic lattice crust technique, but we encourage you to use these guides and choose one of your favorite of the following designs. With a photo and description explaining every step, not only will you understand how to weave without fear, but you're guaranteed to get pies that come out of the oven looking as good as they did when they went in.

BASIC LATTICE

This is the classic lattice crust treatment that creates a woven window to the fruit below and allows for moisture evaporation. You can cut your dough strips wider or smaller than indicated here for a tighter (see page 370) or looser (see page 372) look. The wider the dough strips, the less weaving you'll need to do; if you're in a rush or are a beginner, try 2-inch-wide dough strips. For the neatest lattice, take care when cutting the dough rectangle; mark the top and bottom edges of the dough at 1¼-inch intervals (or however wide you'd like your strips) using a bench scraper or a paring knife and then cut along the edge of a ruler, connecting corresponding top and bottom marks.

Making a Basic Lattice

1. Space 4 strips evenly across top of filled pie, parallel to counter edge.

2. Fold back first and third strips almost completely.

3. Lay 1 strip across pie, perpendicular to second and fourth strips, keeping it snug to folded edges of dough strips.

4. Unfold first and third strips over top of perpendicular dough strip.

5. Fold back second and fourth strips and add second perpendicular strip, keeping it snug to folded edge. Unfold second and fourth strips over top.

6. Repeat weaving remaining strips evenly across pie, alternating between folding back first and third strips and second and fourth strips to create lattice pattern. Tuck overhang under itself.

CUTOUT CRUST

For the neatest cutout top crust, we've found it best to roll out your top crust as normal and then use a pie plate as a guide to make an even circle to place on top of the pie. You can use any shape cookie cutter to produce whatever design you can dream up. Be sure to leave at least ¾ inch between each cutout and to leave a 1-inch border around the edge or you may end up with tearing. This design works best with a fruit filling that doesn't need to be mounded. You can save the dough from the cutouts and add them to the top crust for another layer of design; brush the bottom of each cutout with water and press gently but firmly to seal them to the dough before chilling.

Making a Cutout Crust

1. Invert 9-inch pie plate over center of dough round and run paring knife around edge to cut out circle; transfer circle to parchment paper–lined rimmed baking sheet and chill for 30 minutes.

2. Use cookie cutter to cut out shapes from chilled crust in attractive design, leaving 1-inch border around edge and at least ¾ inch between each cutout. Chill dough round for 30 minutes.

3. Fill chilled dough-lined plate. Brush edges of dough with water, then place chilled top crust over top of filling.

4. Using index and middle fingers or palm of your hand, pinch bottom and top crusts firmly together around edge of plate to seal. Tuck overhang under itself; folded edge should be flush with edge of plate.

BRAIDED STRIPS

This showstopping alternative to a top crust shows off your pie dough skills while also showing off plenty of the pie filling. You can vary the width of the dough strips to create fewer thicker braids or more skinnier braids, or alternate braid widths. This technique can take some time, so be sure to keep dough strips you're not working with in the refrigerator. We prefer the look of tightly braided dough strips as they retain their shape better during baking.

Making a Braided Crust

1. Working with 3 strips at a time (and refrigerating remaining dough strips while you work), arrange side by side on counter, perpendicular to counter edge, then firmly pinch tops of strips together to seal.

2. Lift and place right dough strip over center dough strip as close to top as possible. Lift and place left dough strip over center dough strip as close to top as possible. Repeat braiding tightly until you reach bottom of braid.

3. Firmly pinch ends of strips together to secure braid. Return to sheet and chill while braiding remaining strips.

4. Fill chilled dough-lined pie plate. Arrange chilled braids evenly over top of filling, then trim overhang to ½ inch beyond lip of plate.

5. Pinch braids and bottom crust together firmly to seal. Tuck overhang under itself; folded edge should be flush with edge of plate.

FREE-FORM SHAPES

This modern alternative to a woven lattice is deceptively simple. You can cut whatever shapes you like from the dough; we like the dramatic angular look of long triangles. It's important to anchor at least one side of each shape to the dough, and not to overlap more than two shapes, or the crust will bake up doughy. This design doesn't require trimming the dough rectangle before proceeding. These instructions will produce a pie design similar to our Mulled Wine Quince Pie (page 359), but you can use different shapes, or you can use a cookie cutter (see Pear-Butterscotch Slab Pie on page 398).

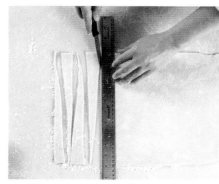

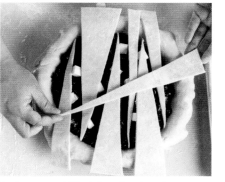

Making Free-Form Shapes
1. Cut 13 by 10½-inch dough rectangle into two 10½-inch-long by ½-inch-wide triangles, two 10½-inch-long by 1-inch-wide triangles, and two 10½-inch-long by 3-inch-wide triangles. Chill for 30 minutes.

2. Arrange chilled dough triangles decoratively over top of filling, with 1 end of each triangle placed at least ½ inch beyond edge of plate and overlapping each triangle no more than once.

3. Trim overhang to ½ inch beyond lip of plate, then pinch edges of bottom crust and triangles together firmly to seal.

Important Tips for Decorating with Dough

The refrigerator is your best friend. You can turn to the fridge whenever you want to. Dough should be firm but malleable during decorating: You don't want butter to melt as your dough will be misshapen, the design won't stay, and overhandled dough won't be flaky once baked. However, you also don't want dough strips to be too cold, as they may crack.

Stay put. The easiest way to track your progress on a design is for you, the pie maker, to stay in one place and to move the pie plate as needed. When crimping an edge (see page 343), rotate the pie plate as you go; if you try to move, the crimps will come out crooked. When weaving a lattice, don't move around the counter; if you stay in the same position, you'll remember which strips one and three are versus two and four.

Flour as needed. If dough sticks to your fingers (or to any implement) while you're working, dip them in a little flour so you can continue working with your hands.

Save your scraps. Any extra dough can be used to make further flourishes. Check out the rosettes on our Crab Apple Rose Pie (page 355). You can also bake your scrap dough (much like individual cookies) and place shapes on the surface of cooled custard pies. While your pie cools, brush dough cutouts with egg wash and bake them on a parchment paper–lined rimmed baking sheet in a 350-degree oven until they're deep golden brown, 8 to 10 minutes. Those scraps also come in handy for patching dough cracks and breaks.

Use an egg wash. We don't always use egg wash, but we like it when applying more intricate designs as it highlights them.

Roll out a larger rectangle. We always roll out our dough to a rectangle size slightly larger than what we need (usually that means a 13 by 10½-inch rectangle) and then trim ¼ inch from the long sides so that our strips are straight and neat.

Strawberry-Rhubarb Pie

STRAWBERRY-RHUBARB PIE

Serves 8 | 9-inch pie plate

WHY THIS RECIPE WORKS Both strawberries and rhubarb are loaded with water. During baking, all this water heats up and causes the rhubarb to blow out, releasing its moisture into the filling and collapsing into mush, while the strawberries become bloated. We microwaved the rhubarb with sugar to draw out some liquid and then stirred a portion of the strawberries into the warm liquid to soften; we then cooked the liquid down with the remaining strawberries to make a jam that we folded into the filling. This allowed us to use less thickener and more fruit for an intense, chunky filling. Brushing the dough with water and sprinkling it with a generous amount of sugar gave it a crackly finish. Measure the tapioca, which may be sold as "minute tapioca," before grinding it. Grind the tapioca to a powder in a spice grinder or a mini food processor.

  1 recipe double-crust pie dough (see pages 342–348)
  2 pounds rhubarb, trimmed and cut into ½-inch pieces (7 cups)
1¼ cups (8¾ ounces) sugar plus 3 tablespoons, divided
  1 pound strawberries, hulled, halved if less than 1 inch, quartered if more than 1 inch (3 to 4 cups), divided
  3 tablespoons instant tapioca, ground

1. Roll 1 disk of dough into 12-inch circle on floured counter. Loosely roll dough around rolling pin and gently unroll it onto 9-inch pie plate, letting excess dough hang over edge. Ease dough into plate by gently lifting edge of dough with your hand while pressing into plate bottom with your other hand. Leave any dough that overhangs plate in place. Wrap dough-lined plate loosely in plastic wrap and refrigerate until firm, about 30 minutes. Roll other disk of dough into 12-inch circle on floured counter, then transfer to parchment paper–lined rimmed baking sheet; cover loosely with plastic and refrigerate until firm, about 30 minutes.

2. While dough chills, combine rhubarb and 1¼ cups sugar in bowl and microwave for 1½ minutes. Stir and continue to microwave until sugar is mostly dissolved, about 1 minute longer. Stir in 1 cup strawberries and set aside for 30 minutes, stirring once halfway through. Drain rhubarb mixture in fine-mesh strainer set over large saucepan. Return drained rhubarb mixture to bowl; set aside. Add remaining strawberries to rhubarb liquid and cook over medium-high heat until strawberries are very soft and mixture is reduced to 1½ cups, 10 to 15 minutes. Mash berries with fork (mixture does not have to be smooth). Add strawberry mixture and tapioca to drained rhubarb mixture and stir to combine; set aside.

3. Adjust oven rack to lowest position and heat oven to 425 degrees. Spread filling into dough-lined plate. Loosely roll remaining dough round around rolling pin and gently unroll it onto filling. Trim overhang to ½ inch beyond lip of plate. Pinch edges of top and bottom crusts firmly together. Tuck overhang under itself; folded edge should be flush with edge of plate. Crimp dough evenly around edge of plate. Cut eight 2-inch slits in top of dough. Brush surface thoroughly with water and sprinkle with remaining 3 tablespoons sugar.

4. Place pie on aluminum foil–lined rimmed baking sheet and bake until crust is set and begins to brown, about 25 minutes. Rotate pie and reduce oven temperature to 375 degrees; continue to bake until crust is deep golden brown and filling is bubbling, 30 to 40 minutes longer. Let pie cool on wire rack until filling has set, about 4 hours. Serve.

BLUEBERRY EARL GREY PIE

Serves 8 | 9-inch pie plate

WHY THIS RECIPE WORKS The sweet, almost earthy flavor of blueberries make them a perfect match for citrusy, slightly musky Earl Grey tea. We ground the tea and added it to the filling with a touch of orange zest to reinforce the tea's citrus notes. We elevated this pie even further with a drizzle of tea-infused glaze. Measure the tapioca, which may be sold as "minute tapioca," before grinding it. Grind both the tapioca and the tea to a powder in a spice grinder or a mini food processor. Use the large holes of a box grater to shred the apple. Any of the top crusts (see pages 364–367) will allow for enough evaporation to ensure a perfect slice.

TUTORIAL
Blueberry Earl Grey Pie

Infusing both the filling and the glaze of this blueberry pie with Earl Grey tea gives the classic an aromatic, floral spin.

1. Place 3 cups blueberries in medium saucepan and set over medium heat. Using potato masher, mash blueberries several times to release juice.

2. Continue to cook, stirring often and mashing occasionally, until about half of blueberries have broken down and mixture is thickened and reduced to 1½ cups, about 8 minutes; let cool slightly.

3. Whisk sugar, tapioca, tea, orange zest, and salt together in large bowl.

4. Place shredded apple in clean dish towel and wring dry.

5. Stir apple, remaining 3 cups blueberries, and cooked blueberries into sugar mixture. Spread mixture into dough-lined pie plate and scatter butter over top.

6. Cover pie with lattice strips (see page 364) and bake. Drizzle glaze attractively over pie.

**Blueberry
Earl Grey Pie**

**Vegan
Blueberry Pie**

1 recipe double-crust pie dough (see pages 342–348)
1 large egg, lightly beaten with 1 tablespoon water

FILLING
30 ounces (6 cups) blueberries, divided
¾ cup (5¼ ounces) granulated sugar
2 tablespoons instant tapioca, ground
2 teaspoons Earl Grey tea leaves, ground
⅛ teaspoon grated orange zest
Pinch table salt
1 Granny Smith apple, peeled and shredded
2 tablespoons unsalted butter, cut into ¼-inch pieces

GLAZE
2 tablespoons milk
1 teaspoon Earl Grey tea leaves, ground
1 cup (4 ounces) confectioners' sugar

1. Roll 1 disk of dough into 12-inch circle on floured counter. Loosely roll dough around rolling pin and gently unroll it into 9-inch pie plate, letting excess dough hang over edge. Ease dough into plate by gently lifting edge of dough with your hand while pressing into plate bottom with your other hand. Leave any dough that overhangs plate in place. Wrap dough-lined plate loosely in plastic wrap and refrigerate until firm, about 30 minutes.

2. Roll other piece of dough into 13 by 10½-inch rectangle on floured counter, then transfer to parchment paper–lined rimmed baking sheet; cover loosely with plastic and refrigerate until firm, about 30 minutes.

3. Using pizza wheel, fluted pastry wheel, or paring knife, trim ¼ inch dough from long sides of rectangle, then cut lengthwise into eight 1¼-inch-wide strips. Cover loosely with plastic and refrigerate until firm, about 30 minutes.

4. FOR THE FILLING: Place 3 cups blueberries in medium saucepan and set over medium heat. Using potato masher, mash blueberries several times to release juice. Continue to cook, stirring often and mashing occasionally, until about half of blueberries have broken down and mixture is thickened and reduced to 1½ cups, about 8 minutes; let cool slightly. Adjust oven rack to middle position and heat oven to 400 degrees.

5. Whisk sugar, tapioca, tea, orange zest, and salt together in large bowl. Place shredded apple in clean dish towel and wring dry. Stir apple, remaining 3 cups blueberries, and cooked blueberries into sugar mixture. Spread mixture into dough-lined pie plate and scatter butter over top.

6. Remove dough strips from refrigerator; if too stiff to be workable, let sit at room temperature until softened slightly but still very cold. Space 4 strips evenly across top of pie, parallel to counter edge. Fold back first and third strips almost completely. Lay 1 strip across pie, perpendicular to second and fourth strips, keeping it snug to folded edges of dough strips, then unfold first and third strips over top. Fold back second and fourth strips and add second perpendicular strip, keeping it snug to folded edge. Unfold second and fourth strips over top. Repeat weaving remaining strips evenly across pie, alternating between folding back first and third strips and second and fourth strips to create lattice pattern. Shift strips as needed so they are evenly spaced over top of pie. (If dough becomes too soft to work with, refrigerate pie and dough strips until firm.)

7. Trim overhang to ½ inch beyond lip of plate. Pinch edges of bottom crust and lattice strips together firmly to seal. Tuck overhang under itself; folded edge should be flush with edge of plate. Crimp dough evenly around edge of plate. (If dough is very soft, refrigerate for 10 minutes before baking.) Brush surface with egg wash.

8. Place pie on aluminum foil–lined rimmed baking sheet and bake until crust is light golden, 20 to 25 minutes. Reduce oven temperature to 350 degrees, rotate sheet, and continue to bake until juices are bubbling and crust is deep golden brown, 30 to 50 minutes longer. Let pie cool on wire rack until filling has set, about 4 hours.

9. **FOR THE GLAZE:** Once pie is cooled, combine milk and tea in bowl. Microwave until steaming, about 30 seconds. Let cool completely, about 10 minutes. Whisk sugar into tea mixture until smooth; let sit until thick but pourable, about 10 minutes. Drizzle glaze over cooled pie; let set for 10 minutes before serving.

VEGAN BLUEBERRY PIE

Serves 8 | 9-inch pie plate

WHY THIS RECIPE WORKS We favor tapioca as a thickener, which allows the blueberry flavor to shine through. Too much of it, though, produces a congealed mess. Cooking and reducing half of the berries helped us cut down on the tapioca, and we added a bit of pectin for gentle thickening. Apples are a great source, so we grated in a Granny Smith. Bonus: The tartness enhanced the berries' fresh fruit flavor. In place of an egg wash, we painted a hot cornstarch slurry over the crust for a golden finish. Use the large holes of a box grater to shred the apple. Measure the tapioca, which may be sold as "minute tapioca," before grinding it. Grind the tapioca to a powder in a spice grinder or a mini food processor. If you are a strict vegan, use organic sugar.

30 ounces (6 cups) blueberries, divided
 1 recipe Vegan Double-Crust Pie Dough (page 348)
 1 Granny Smith apple, peeled and shredded
 ¾ cup (5¼ ounces) plus 1 tablespoon sugar, divided
 2 tablespoons instant tapioca, ground
 2 teaspoons grated lemon zest plus 2 teaspoons juice
   Pinch table salt
 2 tablespoons refined coconut oil or unsalted butter
 ⅔ cup water
 2 teaspoons cornstarch

1. Place 3 cups blueberries in medium saucepan. Cook over medium heat, stirring and mashing occasionally with potato masher, until half of blueberries are broken down and mixture measures 1½ cups, 7 to 10 minutes. Transfer to large bowl and let cool completely, about 20 minutes.

2. Meanwhile, adjust oven rack to lowest position and heat oven to 400 degrees. Line rimmed baking sheet with aluminum foil. Roll 1 disk of dough between 2 large sheets parchment paper into 12-inch circle. Remove parchment on top of dough round and gently flip into 9-inch pie plate; peel off second sheet parchment. Ease dough into plate by gently lifting edge of dough with your hand while pressing into plate bottom with your other hand. Roll other disk of dough between 2 large sheets parchment paper into 12-inch circle.

3. Place shredded apple in center of clean dish towel. Gather ends together and twist tightly to drain as much liquid as possible. Transfer apple to bowl with cooked blueberry mixture and stir in remaining 3 cups uncooked blueberries, ¾ cup sugar, tapioca, lemon zest and juice, and salt until combined. Spread mixture into dough-lined pie plate. Pinch ½-inch pieces of coconut oil and disperse evenly over top of blueberries.

4. Using 1¼-inch round cookie cutter, cut out single round in center of 12-inch dough circle. Cut out 6 more rounds from dough, 1½ inches from edge of center hole and equally spaced around center hole. Loosely roll dough circle around rolling pin and gently unroll it onto filling.

5. Trim overhang to ½ inch beyond lip of plate. Pinch edges of top and bottom crusts firmly together. Tuck overhang under itself; folded edge should be flush with edge of plate. Crimp dough evenly around edge of plate using your fingers. Sprinkle surface evenly with remaining 1 tablespoon sugar.

6. Set pie on prepared baking sheet and bake until crust is light golden brown, about 25 minutes. Reduce oven temperature to 350 degrees, rotate sheet, and continue to bake until juices are bubbling and crust is golden brown, 40 to 50 minutes.

7. Whisk water and cornstarch together in small saucepan. Whisking constantly, bring to boil over high heat; remove pot from heat. Working quickly, brush surface of pie with cornstarch mixture, being careful to avoid pooling. Let pie cool completely on wire rack, about 4 hours, before serving.

SOUR CHERRY–HAZELNUT PIE

Serves 8 | 9-inch pie plate

WHY THIS RECIPE WORKS With their refreshingly tart, complex flavor and vibrant ruby-red color, sour cherries make a brilliant summertime pie filling. We left all of the pitted cherries whole in our pie; they baked down to a tender and juicy filling that really highlighted the fruit. A full cup of sugar balanced the cherries' tartness. To make this pie extra special, we added hazelnut liqueur to our filling; the nuttiness was a round counterpoint to the bracing cherries. Measure the tapioca, which may be sold as "minute tapioca," before grinding it. Grind the tapioca to a powder in a spice grinder or a mini food processor. We like the flavor of our nut dough made with hazelnuts here, but you can use any double-crust pie dough. Any of the top crusts (see pages 364–367) will allow for enough evaporation to ensure a perfect slice.

Sour Cherry–Hazelnut Pie

1 recipe Nut Double-Crust Pie Dough (page 345)
1 cup (7 ounces) sugar
1 teaspoon grated lemon zest plus 2 teaspoons juice
¼ cup instant tapioca, ground
⅛ teaspoon table salt
2 pounds fresh sour cherries, pitted
3 tablespoons hazelnut liqueur (optional)
1 large egg, lightly beaten with 1 tablespoon water

1. Roll 1 disk of dough into 12-inch circle on floured counter. Loosely roll dough around rolling pin and gently unroll it onto 9-inch pie plate, letting excess dough hang over edge. Ease dough into plate by gently lifting edge of dough with your hand while pressing into plate bottom with your other hand. Leave any dough that overhangs plate in place. Wrap dough-lined plate loosely in plastic wrap and refrigerate until firm, about 30 minutes.

2. Roll other piece of dough into 13 by 10½-inch rectangle on floured counter, then transfer to parchment paper–lined rimmed baking sheet; cover loosely with plastic and refrigerate until firm, about 30 minutes.

3. Using pizza wheel, fluted pastry wheel, or paring knife, trim ¼ inch dough from long sides of rectangle, then cut lengthwise into eight 1¼-inch-wide strips. Cover loosely with plastic and refrigerate until firm, about 30 minutes. Adjust oven rack to middle position and heat oven to 400 degrees.

4. Whisk sugar, lemon zest, tapioca, and salt together in large bowl. Stir in cherries; lemon juice; and hazelnut liqueur, if using, and let sit for 15 minutes. Spread cherry mixture into dough-lined plate.

5. Remove dough strips from refrigerator; if too stiff to be workable, let sit at room temperature until softened slightly but still very cold. Space 4 strips evenly across top of pie, parallel to counter edge. Fold back first and third strips almost completely. Lay 1 strip across pie, perpendicular to second and fourth strips, keeping it snug to folded edges of dough strips, then unfold first and third strips over top. Fold back second and fourth strips and add second perpendicular strip, keeping it snug to folded edge. Unfold second and fourth strips over top. Repeat weaving remaining strips evenly across pie, alternating between folding back first and third strips and second and fourth strips to create lattice pattern. Shift strips as needed so they are evenly spaced over top of pie. (If dough becomes too soft to work with, refrigerate pie and dough strips until firm.)

6. Trim overhang to ½ inch beyond lip of plate. Pinch edges of bottom crust and lattice strips together firmly to seal. Tuck overhang under itself; folded edge should be flush with edge of plate. Crimp dough evenly around edge of plate. (If dough is very soft, refrigerate for 10 minutes before baking.) Brush surface with egg wash.

7. Place pie on aluminum foil–lined rimmed baking sheet and bake until crust is light golden, 20 to 25 minutes. Reduce oven temperature to 350 degrees and continue to bake until juices are bubbling and crust is deep golden brown, 30 to 50 minutes longer. Let pie cool on wire rack until filling has set, about 4 hours. Serve.

APRICOT, VANILLA BEAN, AND CARDAMOM PIE

Serves 8 | 9-inch pie plate

WHY THIS RECIPE WORKS The sweet flavor of apricots is balanced with an undertone of musky tartness, which gives apricot pie a distinctive sophistication. Cornstarch tightened our filling but didn't thicken it so much that we lost the meaty texture of the apricots. Vanilla bean heightened the floral notes of the apricots and rounded out their flavor, while a touch of earthy cardamom highlighted the apricots' subtle tang. To make our pie stand out further, we paired it with a rye dough. The nuttiness of our whole-grain pie dough made with rye flour pairs well with the bright filling, but you can use any double-crust pie dough. Any of the top crusts (see pages 364–367) will allow for enough evaporation to ensure a perfect slice.

Apricot, Vanilla Bean, and Cardamom Pie

1 recipe Whole-Grain Double-Crust Pie Dough (page 345)
1 vanilla bean
1 cup (7 ounces) sugar
3 tablespoons cornstarch
1 teaspoon grated lemon zest plus 1 tablespoon juice
¼ teaspoon ground cardamom
¼ teaspoon table salt
2½ pounds apricots, halved, pitted, and cut into
   ½-inch-thick wedges
1 large egg, lightly beaten with 1 tablespoon water

1. Roll 1 disk of dough into 12-inch circle on floured counter. Loosely roll dough around rolling pin and gently unroll it onto 9-inch pie plate, letting excess dough hang over edge. Ease dough into plate by gently lifting edge of dough with your hand while pressing into plate bottom with your other hand. Leave any dough that overhangs plate in place. Wrap dough-lined plate loosely in plastic wrap and refrigerate until firm, about 30 minutes.

2. Roll other piece of dough into 13 by 10½-inch rectangle on floured counter, then transfer to parchment paper–lined rimmed baking sheet; cover loosely with plastic and refrigerate until firm, about 30 minutes.

3. Using pizza wheel, fluted pastry wheel, or paring knife, trim ¼ inch dough from long sides of rectangle, then cut lengthwise into eight 1¼-inch-wide strips. Cover loosely with plastic and refrigerate until firm, about 30 minutes. Adjust oven rack to middle position and heat oven to 400 degrees.

4. Cut vanilla bean in half lengthwise. Using tip of paring knife, scrape out seeds. Whisk vanilla bean seeds, sugar, cornstarch, lemon zest, cardamom, and salt together in large bowl. Stir in apricots and lemon juice and let sit for 15 minutes. Spread apricot mixture into dough-lined plate.

5. Remove dough strips from refrigerator; if too stiff to be workable, let sit at room temperature until softened slightly but still very cold. Space 4 strips evenly across top of pie, parallel to counter edge. Fold back first and third strips almost completely. Lay 1 strip across pie, perpendicular to second and fourth strips, keeping it snug to folded edges of dough strips, then unfold first and third strips over top. Fold back second and fourth strips and add second perpendicular strip, keeping it snug to folded edge. Unfold second and fourth strips over top. Repeat weaving remaining strips evenly across pie, alternating between folding back first and third strips and second and fourth strips to create lattice pattern. Shift strips as needed so they are evenly spaced over top of pie. (If dough becomes too soft to work with, refrigerate pie and dough strips until firm.)

6. Trim overhang to ½ inch beyond lip of plate. Pinch edges of bottom crust and lattice strips together firmly to seal. Tuck overhang under itself; folded edge should be flush with edge of plate. Crimp dough evenly around edge of plate. (If dough is very soft, refrigerate for 10 minutes before baking.) Brush surface with egg wash.

7. Place pie on aluminum foil–lined rimmed baking sheet and bake until crust is light golden, 20 to 25 minutes. Reduce oven temperature to 350 degrees, rotate sheet, and continue to bake until juices are bubbling and crust is deep golden brown, 30 to 50 minutes longer. Let pie cool on wire rack until filling has set, about 4 hours. Serve.

FRESH PEACH PIE

Serves 8 | 9-inch pie plate

WHY THIS RECIPE WORKS Eaten out of hand, a juicy peach is one of summer's greatest pleasures. Incorporate peaches into a pie, however, and you get a soupy mess. We macerated the peaches to draw out their juices. Using both cornstarch and pectin (the latter of which we cooked with some of the peach liquid) as binders gave us a clear, silky filling without the gumminess or gelatinous texture that larger amounts of either one alone produced. If your peaches are too soft to withstand the pressure of a peeler, cut a shallow X in the bottom of the fruit, blanch them in a pot of simmering water for 15 seconds, and then shock them in a bowl of ice water before peeling. For fruit pectin we recommend both Sure-Jell for Less or No Sugar Needed Recipes and Ball RealFruit Low or No-Sugar Needed Pectin. Any of the top crusts (see pages 364–367) will allow for enough evaporation to ensure a perfect slice.

    1   recipe double-crust pie dough (see pages 342–348)
    3   pounds ripe but firm peaches, peeled, halved, pitted,
        and cut into 1-inch pieces
    ½   cup (3½ ounces) plus 2 tablespoons sugar, divided
    1   teaspoon grated lemon zest plus 1 tablespoon juice
    ⅛   teaspoon table salt
    2   tablespoons low- or no-sugar-needed fruit pectin
    ¼   teaspoon ground cinnamon
        Pinch ground nutmeg
    1   tablespoon cornstarch
    1   large egg, lightly beaten with 1 tablespoon water

1. Roll 1 disk of dough into 12-inch circle on floured counter. Loosely roll dough around rolling pin and gently unroll it onto 9-inch pie plate, letting excess dough hang over edge. Ease dough into plate by gently lifting edge of dough with your hand while pressing into plate bottom with your other hand. Leave any dough that overhangs plate in place. Wrap dough-lined plate loosely in plastic wrap and refrigerate until firm, about 30 minutes.

2. Roll other piece of dough into 13 by 10½-inch rectangle on floured counter, then transfer to parchment paper–lined rimmed baking sheet; cover loosely with plastic and refrigerate until firm, about 30 minutes.

3. Using pizza wheel, fluted pastry wheel, or paring knife, trim ¼ inch dough from long sides of rectangle, then cut lengthwise into eight 1¼-inch-wide strips. Cover loosely with plastic and refrigerate until firm, about 30 minutes. Adjust oven rack to middle position and heat oven to 400 degrees.

4. Toss peaches, ½ cup sugar, lemon zest and juice, and salt in bowl and let sit for at least 30 minutes or up to 1 hour. Combine pectin, cinnamon, nutmeg, and remaining 2 tablespoons sugar in small bowl; set aside. Measure out 1 cup peach pieces and mash with fork to coarse paste. Drain remaining peach pieces through colander set in bowl, reserving ½ cup peach juice. Return peach pieces to now-empty bowl and toss with cornstarch.

5. Whisk reserved peach juice and pectin mixture together in 12-inch skillet. Cook over medium heat, stirring occasionally, until thickened slightly and pectin is dissolved (liquid should become less cloudy), 3 to 5 minutes. Transfer peach-pectin mixture and peach paste to bowl with peach pieces and stir to combine. Spread peach mixture into dough-lined plate.

6. Remove dough strips from refrigerator; if too stiff to be workable, let sit at room temperature until softened slightly but still very cold. Space 4 strips evenly across top of pie, parallel to counter edge. Fold back first and third strips almost completely. Lay 1 strip across pie, perpendicular to second and fourth strips, keeping it snug to folded edges of dough strips, then unfold first and third strips over top. Fold back second and fourth strips and add second perpendicular strip, keeping it snug to folded edge. Unfold second and fourth strips over top. Repeat weaving remaining strips evenly across pie, alternating between folding back first and third strips and second and fourth strips to create lattice pattern. Shift strips as needed so they are evenly spaced over top of pie. (If dough becomes too soft to work with, refrigerate pie and dough strips until firm.)

7. Trim overhang to ½ inch beyond lip of plate. Pinch edges of bottom crust and lattice strips together firmly to seal. Tuck overhang under itself; folded edge should be flush with edge of plate. Crimp dough evenly around edge of plate. (If dough is very soft, refrigerate for 10 minutes before baking.) Brush surface with egg wash.

8. Place pie on aluminum foil–lined rimmed baking sheet and bake until crust is light golden, 20 to 25 minutes. Reduce oven temperature to 350 degrees, rotate sheet, and continue to bake until juices are bubbling and crust is deep golden brown, 30 to 50 minutes longer. Let pie cool on wire rack until filling has set, about 4 hours. Serve.

RED CURRANT AND FIG PIE

Serves 8 | 9-inch pie plate

WHY THIS RECIPE WORKS Red currants have a tartness and a flavor more complex than that of other berries. Although their season is short, we wanted to capture their distinctive flavor in a special pie. For a thickened, jammy filling, we cooked down some of the berries and strained them through a fine-mesh strainer (to eliminate any seeds or peels); we stirred the remaining berries in whole. Some orange zest and juice complemented their flavor and ensured it remained bright after

**Red Currant
and Fig Pie**

cooking. But we thought the berries' intense flavor could use some taming and their texture some breaking up with the addition of another fruit. Fresh figs are in season at the same time and added a meatiness and caramel sweetness that made this filling exceptionally unique. Measure the tapioca, which may be sold as "minute tapioca," before grinding it. Grind the tapioca to a powder in a spice grinder or a mini food processor. Any of the top crusts (see pages 364–367) will allow for enough evaporation to ensure a perfect slice.

1   recipe double-crust pie dough (see pages 342–348)
¾   cup (5¼ ounces) sugar
2   tablespoons instant tapioca, ground
1   teaspoon grated orange zest plus 2 tablespoons juice
⅛   teaspoon table salt
1½ pounds fresh red currants, divided
1   pound fresh figs, stemmed and cut into ¼-inch wedges
1   large egg, lightly beaten with 1 tablespoon water

1. Roll 1 disk of dough into 12-inch circle on floured counter. Loosely roll dough around rolling pin and gently unroll it onto 9-inch pie plate, letting excess dough hang over edge. Ease dough into plate by gently lifting edge of dough with your hand while pressing into plate bottom with your other hand. Leave any dough that overhangs plate in place. Wrap dough-lined plate loosely in plastic wrap and refrigerate until firm, about 30 minutes.

2. Roll other piece of dough into 13 by 10½-inch rectangle on floured counter, then transfer to parchment paper–lined rimmed baking sheet; cover loosely with plastic and refrigerate until firm, about 30 minutes.

3. Using pizza wheel, fluted pastry wheel, or paring knife, trim ¼ inch dough from long sides of rectangle, then cut lengthwise into eight 1¼-inch-wide strips. Cover loosely with plastic and refrigerate until firm, about 30 minutes. Adjust oven rack to middle position and heat oven to 400 degrees.

4. Whisk sugar, tapioca, orange zest, and salt together in large bowl; set aside. Bring 1 pound currants to simmer in large saucepan over medium-high heat. Off heat, coarsely mash currants with potato masher. Return to simmer over medium-high heat and cook until currants are softened, about 3 minutes.

5. Strain currants through fine-mesh strainer set over bowl with sugar mixture, pressing firmly on solids to extract as much liquid and pulp as possible; discard solids. Stir in figs, orange juice, and remaining 8 ounces currants and let sit for 15 minutes. Spread currant mixture into dough-lined plate.

6. Remove dough strips from refrigerator; if too stiff to be workable, let sit at room temperature until softened slightly but still very cold. Space 4 strips evenly across top of pie, parallel to counter edge. Fold back first and third strips almost completely. Lay 1 strip across pie, perpendicular to second and fourth strips, keeping it snug to folded edges of dough strips, then unfold first and third strips over top. Fold back second and fourth strips and add second perpendicular strip, keeping it snug to folded edge. Unfold second and fourth strips over top. Repeat weaving remaining strips evenly across pie, alternating between folding back first and third strips and second and fourth strips to create lattice pattern. Shift strips as needed so they are evenly spaced over top of pie. (If dough becomes too soft to work with, refrigerate pie and dough strips until firm.)

7. Trim overhang to ½ inch beyond lip of plate. Pinch edges of bottom crust and lattice strips together firmly to seal. Tuck overhang under itself; folded edge should be flush with edge of plate. Crimp dough evenly around edge of plate. (If dough is very soft, refrigerate for 10 minutes before baking.) Brush surface with egg wash.

8. Place pie on aluminum foil–lined rimmed baking sheet and bake until crust is light golden, 20 to 25 minutes. Reduce oven temperature to 350 degrees, rotate sheet, and continue to bake until juices are bubbling and crust is deep golden brown, 30 to 50 minutes longer. Let pie cool on wire rack until filling has set, about 6 hours. Serve.

CUSTARD PIES

Cook pastry cream to 180 degrees

Bake custard pies to 165 degrees

Use cornstarch to thicken

CUSTARD PIES ARE PURE COMFORT; they should be creamy yet sliceable, with an egg-thickened filling that's a bit firmer than pastry cream (cornstarch is also sometimes added as a thickener) and that contrasts with the crisp crust. Fillings for custard pie vary widely—from chocolate cream to passion fruit curd—but they typically begin with a combination of eggs, dairy, and sugar. For some, the filling is baked in the pie shell until just set; once cooled, the custard is a creamy, lightly eggy filling that coheres with the crust. Other custard fillings don't go into the oven at all; instead, they're cooked on the stovetop and then added to the pie crust and chilled until set. Sometimes—as with our Pecan Pie on page 388—we do both: Gently cooking the custard on the stovetop before adding it to the pie gives it a head start and ensures that it bakes quickly and evenly. Unlike most of our fruit pies, custard pies feature a single crust, the topping instead often clouds of whipped cream. You can have fun with the pie dough for these pies, however, adding a decorative design to the crust's edge or adorning the pie with small cutouts (see page 365). If the filling requires no baking (such as a cream pie), the pie shell is fully baked so the filled pie can be refrigerated (to help set the filling and facilitate neat slicing) and then served. In cases when the filling requires baking (where the heat of the oven causes the eggs to thicken the filling), the pie shell is generally partially baked, filled, and then returned to the oven.

Cream Pies

A crisp crust encasing cool, luscious pastry cream filling and a plume of whipped cream that seemingly lightens the richness of the ingredients below it: All of this makes cream pies a diner special. They're perfect after a greasy-spoon lunch, or as a satisfying after-dinner dessert. For this type of custard pie, the pastry cream is cooked completely on the stove and then spread into a fully baked pie crust before the whole thing goes in the refrigerator to chill until set and perfectly sliceable.

SET IT WITH STARCH

While eggs serve an important function in cream pies—contributing thickening power, rich flavor, and smooth, silky texture—the addition of a starch is key for a sliceable filling. The most common thickeners for cream pie fillings are flour and cornstarch, but we have found that flour makes for a stodgy filling with a heavy, starchy feel. Cornstarch results in a lilting, creamy texture, thickening the filling without announcing its presence. The cornstarch prevents curdling by slowing the coagulation of the egg proteins, so as it cooks, the mixture thickens without overcooking or curdling. When cornstarch is added to a custard, the temperature of the custard needs to come up to around 180 degrees to ensure that the cornstarch-egg mixture is cooked.

WHIPPED TOPPING WHIMSY

With little effort, the addition of whipped cream instantly makes dessert more fun. Some pies, such as cream pies, require it to solidify their identity, while others benefit from a dollop simply as an enhancement or creamy contrast to bolder, heavier ingredients. When you're whipping cream, make sure it's refrigerator-cold; the colder your cream, the more voluptuous it will be once whipped. Sometimes we'll leave the edge of the filling exposed so you know what's inside. But we encourage you to get fancy, too.

Billows

A whipped cream topping is inviting no matter how it's applied, but we most often spread it attractively across the top of the pie—either with a small offset spatula or the back of a spoon for some decorative swoops.

Star-Piped Top

For whipped cream that plays a starring role, fit a pastry bag with a star tip of your desired size and fill the bag with whipped cream. Start around the edge of the pie and pipe in concentric circles until you reach the middle and have covered the whole pie. Hold the bag perpendicular to the surface of the pie, pipe out a small amount of whipped cream, and pull the bag straight away from the pie.

Swirled Top

For rosette-like swirls of whipped cream, fit a pastry bag with a closed star tip of your desired size and fill the bag with whipped cream. Pipe out whipped cream while directing the top in a circular motion, then stop piping and pull the bag straight away from the pie. You can leave as much or as little space as you like.

Baked Custards

Unlike cream pies in which the filling is cooked entirely on the stovetop, the filling for baked custard pies is poured into a warm crust and then baked in the oven. These pies require careful baking—overbaked pies will crack and lose their voluptuous creaminess, while underbaked pies won't set up and will be difficult to slice cleanly. A baked custard pie is done when the center still wobbles gently (165 degrees is typically the sweet spot for doneness)—as it cools it will set to a sliceable consistency.

CHECK TEMPERATURE TWICE

For some custard pies, such as our Lavender Crème Brûlée Pie (page 384) and Salted Caramel Apple Pie (page 385), we check the temperature twice. We check the temperature of the filling on the stovetop to ensure the egg mixture is cooked and again once the pie is in the oven to ensure it's set. Adding the warm custard to the warm, prebaked crust also allows the filling to bake quickly so the edges of the custard don't overcook and curdle before the center sets.

Sugar Pies

Sugar pies are baked egg custard pies with a generous proportion of sugar, which gives them a sweet caramelized flavor and a luxurious soft set with a contrasting crackly sugar top. They frequently make use of a viscous liquid such as corn syrup or maple syrup to both sweeten and help set the filling. To balance the intense sweetness of these pies, a small amount of an acidic ingredient such as lemon or vinegar is sometimes incorporated. Some sugar pies have strong regional ties, such as chess pie (see page 389), which is a Southern classic. Cornmeal is a common ingredient in the former; in addition to thickening, it rises to the top and accentuates the crackly top. Sometimes we gently cook the sugar mixture, as in Pecan Pie (page 388) to increase the caramelization and jump-start cooking.

DEMYSTIFYING CORN SYRUP

Is Karo corn syrup the same thing as the high-fructose corn syrup ubiquitous in soft drinks and other processed foods? In a word, no. Corn syrup (the most popular brand being Karo, introduced in 1902) is made by adding enzymes to a mixture of cornstarch and water to break the long starch strands into glucose molecules. It's valuable in candy making because it discourages crystallization; it also helps baked goods—including some of the pies in this chapter such as Virginia Peanut Pie on page 388—retain moisture. And corn syrup makes an excellent addition to glazes; it's less sweet than granulated sugar, and it contributes body and sticking power. High-fructose corn syrup (HFCS) is a newer product that came on the market in the 1960s. It's made by putting regular corn syrup through an additional enzymatic process that converts a portion of the glucose molecules into fructose, boosting its sweetness to a level even higher than that of cane sugar. Because HFCS is considerably less expensive than cane sugar, it's widely used in processed foods, but it's not sold directly to consumers. Corn syrup comes in light and dark varieties, with dark corn syrup having a deeper flavor. Manufacturers turn light corn syrup into dark by adding caramel color and a molasses-like product.

PLAYING CHESS

Chess pie is really a catchall term for a whole category of one-crust custard pies, from lemon to chocolate. Though it's now best known as a Southern dessert, some culinary historians believe that English settlers brought the pie over to the New World as early as the 17th century. But where did its curious name come from? Theories abound, but the most likely etymology ties chess pie to an archaic English spelling of "cheese," which was often spelled with just one "e" in the middle: chese. According to culinary historian and Southern food expert Damon Lee Fowler, the word "cheese," or "chese," was often used to signify the types of curds and custards commonly used in single-crust pies. Linguistic license, which early Americans were fond of exercising, allowed cheese pie, or chese pie, to become chess pie.

Crumb Crusts

Cream pies are particularly fun because while they can feature a pastry crust, the creamy filling also can come in a crumb crust, a crisp, sweet shell made from graham crackers, Oreos, other cookies, or even saltines.

GRAHAM CRACKER CRUST
Makes one 9-inch crust
We prefer Keebler Grahams Crackers Original in our crust. We don't recommend using store-bought graham cracker crumbs here, as they can often be stale.

- 8 **whole graham crackers, broken into 1-inch pieces**
- 3 **tablespoons sugar**
- 5 **tablespoons unsalted butter, melted and cooled**

1. Adjust oven rack to middle position and heat oven to 325 degrees. Process graham cracker pieces and sugar in food processor to fine, even crumbs, about 30 seconds. Sprinkle melted butter over crumbs and pulse to incorporate, about 5 pulses.

2. Sprinkle mixture into 9-inch pie plate. Using bottom of dry measuring cup, press crumbs into even layer on bottom and sides of pie plate. Bake until crust is fragrant and beginning to brown, 12 to 18 minutes; transfer to wire rack. Following pie recipe, use crust while it is still warm or let it cool completely.

COCONUT COOKIE CRUST
Makes one 9-inch crust
Coconut is a great crust mix-in because, once processed, it doesn't disrupt the texture and it adds a fragrance to the entire crust. Nilla Wafers add complementary vanilla flavor, and a hearty dash of salt enhances all the flavors.

- 2 **cups (4½ ounces) Nilla Wafer cookies (34 cookies)**
- ½ **cup (1½ ounces) sweetened shredded coconut**
- 2 **tablespoons sugar**
- 1 **tablespoon all-purpose flour**
- ¼ **teaspoon table salt**
- 4 **tablespoons unsalted butter, melted**

1. Adjust oven rack to middle position and heat oven to 325 degrees. Process cookies, coconut, sugar, flour, and salt in food processor until finely ground, about 30 seconds. Sprinkle melted butter over crumbs and pulse to incorporate, about 6 pulses.

2. Sprinkle mixture into 9-inch pie plate. Using bottom of dry measuring cup, press crumbs firmly into bottom and up sides of plate. Bake until crust is fragrant and set, 18 to 22 minutes. Following pie recipe, use crust while it is still warm or let it cool completely.

CHOCOLATE COOKIE CRUST
Makes one 9-inch crust
Oreo cookies offer just the right balance of dark, rich chocolate crumbs and a texture that's neither too dry nor too moist once processed. Other brands of chocolate sandwich cookies may be substituted, but avoid "double-filled" cookies.

- 16 **Oreo cookies, broken into rough pieces**
- 4 **tablespoons unsalted butter, melted and cooled**

1. Adjust oven rack to middle position and heat oven to 325 degrees. Pulse cookies in food processor until coarsely ground, about 15 pulses, then process to fine, even crumbs, about 15 seconds. Sprinkle melted butter over crumbs and pulse to incorporate, about 5 pulses.

2. Sprinkle mixture into 9-inch pie plate. Using bottom of dry measuring cup, press crumbs into even layer on bottom and sides of pie plate. Bake until crust is fragrant and appears set, 13 to 18 minutes; transfer to wire rack. Following pie recipe, use crust while it is still warm or let it cool completely.

Nutter Butter Cookie Crust
Substitute 16 Nutter Butter cookies for Oreo cookies.

Chocolate Cream Pie

Butterscotch Cream Pie

CHOCOLATE CREAM PIE

Serves 8 | 9-inch pie plate

WHY THIS RECIPE WORKS A staple of the diner dessert case, chocolate cream pie holds a lot of promise for chocolate fans, but it often fails to deliver. For a pie with well-balanced flavor, we combined two types of chocolate: Bittersweet or semisweet chocolate provided the main chocolate hit, as well as creaminess, and intense unsweetened chocolate lent depth. A set but ultrasilky custard requires a few key steps: tempering the egg mixture with the simmering dairy (to prevent overcooking the eggs), cooking the mixture to 180 degrees (the point at which the custard is properly thickened but before it curdles), and whisking in cold butter so the filling emulsifies. Finally, rather than encasing our custard in a traditional pie dough, we spread it into a chocolate cookie crust to bring home the filling's flavor. Do not combine the egg yolks and sugar in advance of making the filling.

2½ cups half-and-half
⅓ cup (2⅓ ounces) sugar, divided
 Pinch table salt
6 large egg yolks
2 tablespoons cornstarch
6 tablespoons unsalted butter, cut into 6 pieces
6 ounces semisweet or bittersweet chocolate, chopped fine
1 ounce unsweetened chocolate, chopped fine
1 teaspoon vanilla extract
1 recipe Chocolate Cookie Crust (page 379),
 baked and cooled
1 recipe Whipped Cream (page 548)

1. Bring half-and-half, 3 tablespoons sugar, and salt to simmer in medium saucepan over medium heat, stirring occasionally. Whisk egg yolks, cornstarch, and remaining sugar in bowl until smooth.

2. Slowly whisk 1 cup of warm half-and-half mixture into yolk mixture to temper, then slowly whisk tempered yolk mixture into remaining half-and-half mixture in saucepan.

3. Whisking constantly, cook over medium heat until mixture is thickened and registers 180 degrees, 30 to 90 seconds (mixture should have consistency of thick pudding).

4. Off heat, whisk in butter, semisweet chocolate, and unsweetened chocolate until completely smooth and melted. Stir in vanilla.

5. Pour warm filling into cooled crust and spread into even layer. Spray piece of parchment paper with vegetable oil spray and press directly against surface of filling. Refrigerate until chilled and set, at least 4 hours or up to 24 hours. Spread whipped cream attractively over pie. Serve.

COCONUT CREAM PIE

Serves 8 | 9-inch pie plate

WHY THIS RECIPE WORKS With its lofty profile, billowy whipped cream, and golden coconut topping, coconut cream pie is perhaps the queen of rotating glass dessert displays. We wanted to find out how to pack maximum coconut flavor into this retro pie. Coconut milk was too subtle, while coconut extract had an artificial taste. Folding sweetened shredded coconut into a milk custard gave us a clear coconut flavor. A garnish of toasted coconut over the whipped cream topping dressed up our pie and provided welcome texture. Often this pie features a classic flaky crust, but we opted for a coconut cookie crust for snappy, vanilla-scented, salty contrast—and, of course, extra coconut flavor. To toast the small measure of coconut evenly and with ease, we do so in the microwave—no burnt edges. Be sure to let the cookie crust cool completely before you begin making the filling—at least 30 minutes.

    3   cups whole milk, divided
    ½   cup (3½ ounces) sugar
    5   large egg yolks
    5   tablespoons (1¼ ounces) cornstarch
    ¼   teaspoon table salt
    ¾   cup (2¼ ounces) sweetened shredded coconut, divided
    ½   teaspoon vanilla extract
    1   recipe Coconut Cookie Crust (page 379), baked and cooled
    1   recipe Whipped Cream (page 548)

1. Whisk ¼ cup milk, sugar, egg yolks, cornstarch, and salt together in bowl. Bring remaining 2¾ cups milk to simmer in large saucepan over medium heat. Slowly whisk 1 cup of hot milk mixture into yolk mixture to temper, then slowly whisk tempered yolk mixture into remaining milk in saucepan. Cook over medium heat, whisking constantly, until mixture is thickened, bubbling, and registers 180 degrees, 30 to 90 seconds (mixture should have consistency of thick pudding). Strain mixture through fine-mesh strainer into clean bowl, then stir in ½ cup coconut and vanilla.

2. Pour filling into cooled crust, smoothing top with clean spatula into even layer. Spray piece of parchment paper with vegetable oil spray and press directly against surface of filling. Refrigerate until set, at least 4 hours or up to 24 hours.

3. Microwave remaining ¼ cup coconut on large plate until golden, about 2 minutes, stirring every 30 seconds; set aside to cool slightly, about 10 minutes. Once coconut is cooled, spread whipped cream attractively over pie and sprinkle with toasted coconut. Serve.

Golden Milk Coconut Cream Pie

Add 1 teaspoon ground turmeric, ¾ teaspoon ground cinnamon, ½ teaspoon ground cardamom, and ¼ teaspoon ground ginger to milk in saucepan before bringing to simmer in step 1.

BUTTERSCOTCH CREAM PIE

Serves 8 | 9-inch pie plate

WHY THIS RECIPE WORKS Butterscotch cream pie often looks like butterscotch, but it rarely tastes like the buttery brown sugar confection. We made butterscotch sauce by cooking butter, brown and white sugars, corn syrup, lemon juice, and salt together into a deep, dark caramel. We made the process foolproof by first boiling the caramel to jump-start it and then reducing the heat to a low simmer; this approach provided a large window to take the temperature and stop cooking the caramel at the right moment. When taking the temperature of the caramel in step 4, tilt the saucepan and move the thermometer back and forth to equalize hot and cool spots. We like the flavor of whole-wheat pie dough in this recipe, but you can use any single-crust pie dough.

    1   recipe Whole-Grain Single-Crust Pie Dough (page 342)
    6   large egg yolks
    2   tablespoons cornstarch
    8   tablespoons unsalted butter, cut into ½-inch pieces
    ⅓   cup (2⅓ ounces) granulated sugar
    ⅓   cup packed (2⅓ ounces) dark brown sugar
    2   tablespoons water
    2   tablespoons light corn syrup
    1   teaspoon lemon juice
    ¼   teaspoon table salt
    1   cup heavy cream, divided
    1½   cups whole milk
    1   teaspoon vanilla extract
    ½   teaspoon dark rum (optional)
    1   recipe Whipped Cream (page 548)
         Flake sea salt

1. Roll dough into 12-inch circle on floured counter. Loosely roll dough around rolling pin and gently unroll it onto 9-inch pie plate, letting excess dough hang over edge. Ease dough into plate by gently lifting edge of dough with your hand while pressing into plate bottom with your other hand.

2. Trim overhang to ½ inch beyond lip of plate. Tuck overhang under itself; folded edge should be flush with edge of plate. Crimp dough evenly around edge of plate. Wrap dough-lined plate loosely in plastic wrap and refrigerate until firm, about 30 minutes. Adjust oven rack to middle position and heat oven to 350 degrees.

3. Line chilled pie shell with double layer of aluminum foil, covering edges to prevent burning, and fill with pie weights. Bake on foil-lined rimmed baking sheet until edges are set and just beginning to turn golden, 25 to 30 minutes, rotating sheet halfway through baking. Remove foil and weights, rotate sheet, and continue to bake crust until golden brown and crisp, 10 to 15 minutes longer. Transfer sheet to wire rack and let cool completely, about 45 minutes.

4. Whisk egg yolks and cornstarch together in bowl until smooth; set aside. Bring butter, granulated sugar, brown sugar, water, corn syrup, lemon juice, and salt to boil in large saucepan over medium-high heat. Cook, without stirring, until mixture is straw-colored, 4 to 6 minutes. Reduce heat to low and continue to cook, swirling saucepan occasionally, until caramel is color of dark peanut butter and registers 300 degrees, 12 to 16 minutes.

5. Off heat, carefully stir in ¼ cup cream; mixture will bubble and steam. Whisk vigorously, being sure to scrape corners of saucepan, until mixture is completely smooth. Gradually whisk in remaining ¾ cup cream and milk, then bring to simmer over medium heat.

6. Slowly whisk 1 cup hot caramel mixture into yolk mixture to temper, then slowly whisk tempered yolk mixture into remaining caramel mixture in saucepan. Cook, whisking constantly, until mixture is thickened, bubbling, and registers 180 degrees, 4 to 6 minutes (mixture should have consistency of thick pudding). Strain mixture through fine-mesh strainer into clean bowl, then stir in vanilla and rum, if using.

7. Pour custard into cooled crust, smoothing top with clean spatula into even layer. Spray piece of parchment paper with vegetable oil spray and press directly against surface of filling. Refrigerate until set, at least 4 hours or up to 24 hours. Spread whipped cream attractively over pie and sprinkle with sea salt to taste. Serve.

CHOCOLATE–PEANUT BUTTER BANANA CREAM PIE

Serves 8 | 9-inch pie plate

WHY THIS RECIPE WORKS Banana cream pies may be a staple of slapstick comedy, but in our experience they are no laughing matter. The creamiest versions are unsliceable, while those that produce the tidiest slices are starchy and gloppy. We wanted a smooth, creamy, sliceable banana cream pie that actually tasted like banana—and while we were at it, we planned to incorporate chocolate and peanut butter for an over-the-top indulgence. Six egg yolks and just 3 tablespoons of cornstarch gave us a clean slice but limited the banana flavor to the layer of sliced bananas. For banana flavor throughout, we infused the custard by steeping two sliced and sautéed bananas in the half-and-half. Layered with melted chocolate, chopped peanuts, and peanut butter whipped cream, this ultimate banana cream pie is sure to put a smile on your face. Peel and slice the bananas just before using to minimize browning.

1 recipe single-crust pie dough (see pages 342–348)
5 ripe bananas, divided
4 tablespoons unsalted butter, divided
2½ cups plus 1½ tablespoons half-and-half, divided
½ cup (3½ ounces) plus 2 tablespoons sugar
6 large egg yolks
¼ teaspoon table salt
3 tablespoons cornstarch
1 teaspoon vanilla extract
4 ounces milk chocolate, chopped
2 tablespoons orange juice
½ cup salted dry-roasted peanuts, chopped, divided
1 recipe Peanut Butter Whipped Cream (page 548)

1. Roll dough into 12-inch circle on floured counter. Loosely roll dough around rolling pin and gently unroll it onto 9-inch pie plate, letting excess dough hang over edge. Ease dough into plate by gently lifting edge of dough with your hand while pressing into plate bottom with your other hand.

2. Trim overhang to ½ inch beyond lip of plate. Tuck overhang under itself; folded edge should be flush with edge of plate. Crimp dough evenly around edge of plate. Wrap dough-lined plate loosely in plastic wrap and refrigerate until firm, about 30 minutes. Adjust oven rack to middle position and heat oven to 350 degrees.

3. Line chilled pie shell with double layer of aluminum foil, covering edges to prevent burning, and fill with pie weights. Bake on foil-lined rimmed baking sheet until edges are set and just beginning to turn golden, 25 to 30 minutes, rotating sheet halfway through baking. Remove foil and weights, rotate sheet, and continue to bake crust until golden brown and crisp, 10 to 15 minutes longer. Transfer sheet to wire rack and let cool completely, about 45 minutes.

4. Peel and slice 2 bananas ½ inch thick. Melt 1 tablespoon butter in medium saucepan over medium-high heat. Add sliced bananas and cook until they begin to soften, about 2 minutes. Add 2½ cups half-and-half, bring to boil, and cook for 30 seconds. Remove from heat, cover, and let sit for 40 minutes.

5. Whisk sugar, egg yolks, and salt in large bowl until smooth. Whisk in cornstarch. Strain cooled half-and-half mixture through fine-mesh strainer into yolk mixture (do not press on bananas) and whisk until incorporated; discard cooked bananas.

6. Transfer mixture to clean medium saucepan. Cook over medium heat, whisking constantly, until mixture is thickened and registers 180 degrees, 4 to 6 minutes (mixture should have the consistency of thick pudding). Off heat, whisk in vanilla and remaining 3 tablespoons butter. Transfer filling to bowl; spray piece of parchment paper with vegetable oil spray and press directly against surface of filling and let cool for about 1 hour.

7. Meanwhile, combine chocolate and remaining 1 ½ tablespoons half-and-half in bowl and microwave until melted, about 40 seconds, stirring halfway through microwaving. Peel and slice remaining 3 bananas ¼ inch thick and toss with orange juice. Spread melted chocolate mixture evenly in bottom of empty baked pie shell and sprinkle with all but 2 tablespoons peanuts. Whisk filling briefly, then spread half evenly over peanuts. Arrange sliced bananas on filling. Spread remaining filling evenly on top.

8. Refrigerate until set, at least 5 hours or up to 24 hours. Spread whipped cream attractively over pie. Sprinkle with remaining peanuts and serve.

BUTTERMILK PIE

Serves 8 | 9-inch pie plate

WHY THIS RECIPE WORKS A favorite in the South, buttermilk pie has a creamy texture, tangy-sweet flavor, and irresistibly crunchy sugar top. Custards get their richness from egg and heavy cream, so we started by whisking these ingredients together with the standard buttermilk pie components: sugar, vinegar, butter, vanilla, cornstarch, and, of course, plenty of buttermilk. The cornstarch and yolks provided a perfectly wobbly structure, and the vinegar backed up the buttermilk's pleasant tang. Baking the pie at a gentle 300 degrees cooked the filling evenly, but we also wanted a crackly, lightly browned top. A sprinkling of sugar 10 minutes into baking got us on the right track, and increasing the temperature for the last few minutes sealed the deal—the almost-melted sugar caramelized quickly. Use commercial cultured buttermilk (avoid nonfat), as some locally produced, artisanal buttermilks that we tested were prone to curdling during baking.

Buttermilk Pie

1 recipe single-crust pie dough (see pages 342–348)
¾ cup (5 ¼ ounces) plus 2 teaspoons sugar, divided
1 tablespoon cornstarch
¾ teaspoon table salt
2 large eggs plus 5 large yolks
1 ¾ cups buttermilk
¼ cup heavy cream
4 tablespoons unsalted butter, melted
2 teaspoons distilled white vinegar
1 ½ teaspoons vanilla extract

1. Roll dough into 12-inch circle on floured counter. Loosely roll dough around rolling pin and gently unroll it onto 9-inch pie plate, letting excess dough hang over edge. Ease dough into plate by gently lifting edge of dough with your hand while pressing into plate bottom with your other hand.

2. Trim overhang to ½ inch beyond lip of plate. Tuck overhang under itself; folded edge should be flush with edge of plate.

Crimp dough evenly around edge of plate. Wrap dough-lined plate loosely in plastic wrap and refrigerate until firm, about 30 minutes. Adjust oven racks to middle and upper-middle positions and heat oven to 350 degrees.

3. Line chilled pie shell with double layer of aluminum foil, covering edges to prevent burning, and fill with pie weights. Bake on foil-lined rimmed baking sheet on lower rack until edges are set and just beginning to turn golden, 25 to 30 minutes, rotating sheet halfway through baking. Remove foil and weights, rotate sheet, and continue to bake crust until golden brown and crisp, 10 to 15 minutes longer.

4. Meanwhile, whisk ¾ cup sugar, cornstarch, and salt together in large bowl. Whisk eggs and yolks into sugar mixture until well combined. Whisk buttermilk, cream, melted butter, vinegar, and vanilla into sugar-egg mixture until incorporated. Reduce oven temperature to 300 degrees. Whisk buttermilk mixture to recombine and, leaving pie shell in oven, carefully pour buttermilk mixture into hot pie shell. Bake on lower rack for 10 minutes.

5. Sprinkle remaining 2 teaspoons sugar evenly over top of pie. Continue to bake until center jiggles slightly when pie is shaken, 30 to 40 minutes. Remove pie from oven and increase oven temperature to 450 degrees. Once oven comes to temperature, place pie on upper rack and bake until golden brown on top, 5 to 7 minutes. Let pie cool on wire rack for 2 hours. Refrigerate for 3 hours. Serve.

FLORIDA SOUR ORANGE PIE

Serves 8 | 9-inch pie plate

WHY THIS RECIPE WORKS Sour orange pie, with its custard filling featuring the tart, bright juice of wild sour oranges, is northern Florida's answer to Key lime pie. But it's not easy to find these oranges outside of tropical locations, so we made a substitute with lemon juice and orange juice concentrate. We thought a sweet, vanilla-scented crust would provide a pleasant contrast to the creamy, tangy citrus filling, and animal crackers were the perfect cookie to get us there. If sour oranges are available, use ¾ cup of strained sour orange juice in place of the lemon juice and orange juice concentrate. Minute Maid Original Frozen is our favorite orange juice concentrate. Depending on the brand, 5 ounces is between 80 and 90 animal crackers.

CRUST

5 ounces animal crackers
3 tablespoons sugar
  Pinch table salt
4 tablespoons unsalted butter, melted

FILLING

1 (14-ounce) can sweetened condensed milk
6 tablespoons thawed orange juice concentrate
4 large egg yolks
2 teaspoons grated lemon zest plus 6 tablespoons juice (2 lemons)
1 teaspoon grated orange zest
  Pinch table salt
  Orange Whipped Cream (page 548)

1. FOR THE CRUST: Adjust oven rack to middle position and heat oven to 325 degrees. Process crackers, sugar, and salt in food processor to fine, even crumbs, about 30 seconds. Sprinkle melted butter over crumbs and pulse to incorporate, about 8 pulses.

2. Sprinkle mixture into 9-inch pie plate. Using bottom of dry measuring cup, press crumbs into even layer on bottom and sides of pie plate. Bake on aluminum foil–lined rimmed baking sheet until crust is fragrant and beginning to brown, 12 to 14 minutes. Transfer sheet to wire rack and let cool completely, about 30 minutes.

3. FOR THE FILLING: When crust is cool, whisk condensed milk, orange juice concentrate, egg yolks, lemon zest and juice, orange zest, and salt in bowl until fully combined. With pie still on sheet, pour filling into cooled crust.

4. Bake until center of pie jiggles slightly when shaken, 15 to 17 minutes. Let pie cool completely on wire rack, about 2 hours. Refrigerate for at least 3 hours or up to 24 hours. (If refrigerating for more than 3 hours, cover with greased plastic wrap before chilling.) Serve with whipped cream.

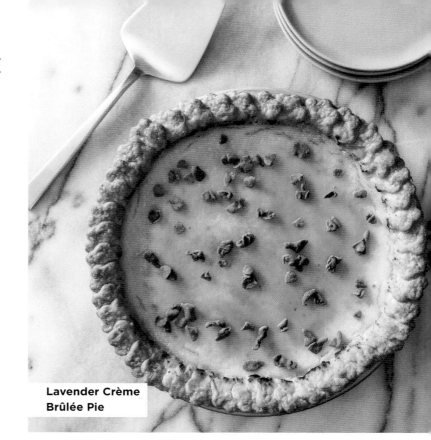

Lavender Crème Brûlée Pie

LAVENDER CRÈME BRÛLÉE PIE

Serves 8 | 9-inch pie plate

WHY THIS RECIPE WORKS Crème brûlée, the light, silky custard with a crackly sugar top, is a mainstay on the dessert menu of fancy restaurants. We thought the textural contrast of the dessert would translate well to pie form, so we set out to develop a recipe for crème brûlée pie that would be practical for the home cook. For a creative twist, we skipped the traditional vanilla bean and instead infused our custard with lavender by steeping (and later straining) dried lavender blossoms in the dairy. For the delicate sugar crust on top, we sprinkled sugar over the chilled custard pie and then torched it. We like the flavor of the lemon pie dough in this recipe, but you can use any single-crust pie dough. Do not use a broiler to caramelize the sugar crust. We love the color candied violets add, but they are optional.

1 recipe Lemon Single-Crust Pie Dough (page 342)
⅔ cup (4⅔ ounces) plus 3 tablespoons sugar, divided
3 large eggs
3 tablespoons cornstarch
¼ teaspoon table salt
2 cups whole milk
1 cup heavy cream
2 teaspoons dried lavender
1 teaspoon vanilla extract
10–12 candied violets (optional)

1. Roll dough into 12-inch circle on floured counter. Loosely roll dough around rolling pin and gently unroll it onto 9-inch pie plate, letting excess dough hang over edge. Ease dough into plate by gently lifting edge of dough with your hand while pressing into plate bottom with your other hand.

2. Trim overhang to ½ inch beyond lip of plate. Tuck overhang under itself; folded edge should be flush with edge of plate. Crimp dough evenly around edge of plate. Wrap dough-lined plate loosely in plastic wrap and refrigerate until firm, about 30 minutes. Adjust oven rack to middle position and heat oven to 350 degrees.

3. Line chilled pie shell with double layer of aluminum foil, covering edges to prevent burning, and fill with pie weights. Bake on foil-lined rimmed baking sheet until edges are set and just beginning to turn golden, 25 to 30 minutes, rotating sheet halfway through baking. Remove foil and weights, rotate sheet, and continue to bake crust until golden brown and crisp, 10 to 15 minutes longer. Transfer sheet to wire rack. (Crust must still be warm when filling is added.)

4. While crust bakes, whisk ⅔ cup sugar, eggs, cornstarch, and salt together in bowl. Bring milk, cream, and lavender to simmer in large saucepan over medium heat. Slowly whisk 1 cup of hot milk mixture into egg mixture to temper, then slowly whisk tempered egg mixture into remaining milk in saucepan. Cook over medium heat, whisking constantly, until custard is thickened, bubbling, and registers 180 degrees, 30 to 90 seconds (custard should have consistency of thick pudding). Strain mixture through fine-mesh strainer into clean bowl, then stir in vanilla.

5. With pie still on sheet, pour custard into warm crust, smoothing top with clean spatula into even layer. Transfer pie to oven and bake until center of pie registers 160 degrees, 14 to 18 minutes. Let pie cool completely on wire rack, about 4 hours. Cover cooled pie loosely with plastic and refrigerate until chilled, at least 4 hours or up to 24 hours. Blot surface of pie dry with paper towels, then sprinkle evenly with remaining 3 tablespoons sugar. Using torch, evenly caramelize sugar until deep golden brown. Sprinkle with candied violets, if using. Serve.

SALTED CARAMEL APPLE PIE

Serves 8 | 9-inch pie plate

WHY THIS RECIPE WORKS We love the chewy caramel-coated apples found at orchards and country fairs; this pie brings these elements together in a grown-up fall dessert. Instead of stewing the fruit in a double crust, we reimagined our apple slices and used them as a fancy garnish to a salted caramel custard pie. We made the filling by whisking basic custard components into

Salted Caramel Apple Pie

homemade caramel. A surprising ingredient—white miso—deepened the flavor of the caramel dramatically, and prevented the custard from being overly sweet. We softened thin apple slices with sugar and a little lemon juice so they could be bent and formed into beautiful roses. Carefully tilt the saucepan to pool the caramel to get a more consistent temperature reading. For best results, use a mandoline to slice the apples paper-thin.

1 recipe single-crust pie dough (see pages 342–348)
1½ cups (10½ ounces) plus 2 tablespoons sugar, divided
3 large eggs
¼ cup (1 ounce) cornstarch
2 tablespoons white miso
½ teaspoon vanilla extract
¼ teaspoon table salt
2 tablespoons water
1 cup heavy cream, divided
1½ cups whole milk
3 Fuji, Gala, or Golden Delicious apples, cored, quartered, and sliced very thin lengthwise
2 tablespoons lemon juice
Flake sea salt

1. Roll dough into 12-inch circle on floured counter. Loosely roll dough around rolling pin and gently unroll it onto 9-inch pie plate, letting excess dough hang over edge. Ease dough into plate by gently lifting edge of dough with your hand while pressing into plate bottom with your other hand.

TUTORIAL
Salted Caramel Apple Pie

This pie displays a silky-smooth baked custard—learning it is a core technique.
The apple rose top gilds the lily—learn how to make that, too.

1. Pour filling into warm crust, smoothing top with spatula into even layer.

2. Bake until center of pie registers 160 degrees, 14 to 18 minutes.

3. Combine apple slices, remaining 2 tablespoons sugar, and lemon juice in bowl. Microwave until apples are pliable, about 2 minutes, stirring halfway through microwaving.

4. Drain apples, then transfer to paper towel–lined sheet and pat dry with paper towels. Shingle 5 apple slices, peel side out, overlapping each slice by about ½ inch on cutting board or counter.

5. Starting at 1 end, roll up slices to form rose shape; place in center of pie.

6. Repeat, arranging apple roses decoratively over top of pie.

2. Trim overhang to ½ inch beyond lip of plate. Tuck overhang under itself; folded edge should be flush with edge of plate. Crimp dough evenly around edge of plate. Wrap dough-lined plate loosely in plastic wrap and refrigerate until firm, about 30 minutes. Adjust oven rack to middle position and heat oven to 350 degrees.

3. Line chilled pie shell with double layer of aluminum foil, covering edges to prevent burning, and fill with pie weights. Bake on foil-lined rimmed baking sheet until edges are set and just beginning to turn golden, 25 to 30 minutes, rotating sheet halfway through baking. Remove foil and weights, rotate sheet, and continue to bake crust until golden brown and crisp, 10 to 15 minutes longer. Transfer sheet to wire rack. (Crust must still be warm when filling is added.)

4. Whisk ¾ cup sugar, eggs, cornstarch, miso, vanilla, and table salt together in bowl; set aside. Bring ¾ cup sugar and water to boil in large saucepan over medium-high heat. Cook, without stirring, until mixture is straw-colored, 4 to 6 minutes. Reduce heat to low and continue to cook, swirling saucepan occasionally, until caramel is amber-colored and registers 360 to 370 degrees, 2 to 5 minutes.

5. Off heat, carefully stir in ¼ cup cream; mixture will bubble and steam. Whisk vigorously, being sure to scrape corners of saucepan, until mixture is completely smooth, at least 30 seconds. Gradually whisk in remaining ¾ cup cream and milk, then bring to simmer over medium heat. Slowly whisk 1 cup hot caramel mixture into egg mixture to temper then slowly whisk tempered egg mixture into remaining caramel mixture in saucepan. Cook, whisking constantly, until mixture is thickened and bubbling and registers 180 degrees, 4 to 6 minutes (mixture should have consistency of thick pudding). Strain mixture through fine-mesh strainer into clean bowl.

6. With pie still on sheet, pour filling into warm crust, smoothing top with clean spatula into even layer. Bake until center of pie registers 160 degrees, 14 to 18 minutes. Let pie cool completely on wire rack, about 4 hours.

7. Before serving, combine apple slices, remaining 2 tablespoons sugar, and lemon juice in bowl. Microwave until apples are pliable, about 2 minutes, stirring halfway through microwaving. Drain apples, then transfer to paper towel–lined sheet and pat dry with paper towels. Shingle 5 apple slices, peel side out, overlapping each slice by about ½ inch on cutting board or counter. Starting at 1 end, roll up slices to form rose shape; place in center of pie. Repeat, arranging apple roses decoratively over top of pie. Sprinkle with sea salt and serve.

PASSION FRUIT CURD PIE
Serves 8 | 9-inch pie plate

WHY THIS RECIPE WORKS Passion fruit packs a tropical punch that, even in the middle of winter, transports us to the beach on a hot, sunny day. We made a smooth passion fruit curd to fill our pie with just the right balance of sweet, tangy, and rich. To complement this special fruit, we had to choose our components carefully—nothing too sour or cloyingly sweet. A coconut cookie crust and toasted coconut sprinkled on top were perfectly sweet and rich. Raspberries made the passion fruit flavor really pop. A schmear of raspberry jam beneath the curd and some puckery fresh raspberries on top were the perfect combination. You can substitute ½ cup frozen passion fruit puree, thawed, for the fresh in this recipe (skip step 1).

1¼ pounds passion fruit, halved
1¼ cups water
¾ cup (5¼ ounces) plus 1½ teaspoons sugar, divided
6 large egg yolks
⅓ cup (1⅓ ounces) cornstarch
⅛ teaspoon table salt
2 tablespoons unsalted butter, cut into 2 pieces
½ cup heavy cream
½ teaspoon vanilla extract
½ cup raspberry jam
1 recipe Coconut Cookie Crust (page 379), baked and cooled
5 ounces (1 cup) raspberries
¼ cup (¾ ounce) sweetened shredded coconut, toasted

1. Scrape pulp (including seeds) from passion fruit into bowl of food processor. Pulse until seeds are separated from pulp, about 4 pulses. Strain puree through fine-mesh strainer into bowl, discarding solids. Measure out ½ cup puree, reserving any remaining for another use.

2. Whisk water, ¾ cup sugar, ½ cup puree, egg yolks, cornstarch, and salt together in large saucepan until combined. Cook over medium-low heat, stirring constantly with rubber spatula, until mixture thickens slightly and registers 170 degrees, 5 to 10 minutes. Off heat, whisk in butter until smooth. Strain curd through clean fine-mesh strainer into large bowl, cover with plastic wrap, and refrigerate until chilled, about 1½ hours.

3. Using stand mixer fitted with whisk attachment, whip cream, vanilla, and remaining 1½ teaspoons sugar on medium-low speed until foamy, about 1 minute. Increase speed to high and whip until soft peaks form, 1 to 3 minutes. Gently whisk one-third whipped cream into chilled puree mixture until lightened. Using rubber spatula, gently fold in remaining whipped cream until homogeneous. Spread raspberry jam evenly over cooled crust, then top with curd mixture, smoothing with clean spatula into even layer. Refrigerate until set, at least 8 hours or up to 24 hours. Arrange raspberries decoratively on top of pie and sprinkle with coconut. Serve.

PECAN PIE

Serves 8 | 9-inch pie plate

WHY THIS RECIPE WORKS Pecan pie can be a beautiful marriage of smooth sweetness and crunchy rich nuttiness, but it is often overwhelmingly sweet, lacking pecan flavor, or weepy and soggy. We used dark brown sugar for deep flavor and reduced the typical amount to tame the saccharine bite and allow the pecan flavor to shine. Some butter added a lush texture to the filling. Adding the hot filling to the partially baked, still-warm pie crust prevented the crust from getting soggy. Cooking the filling over a simulated double-boiler was an easy way to maintain gentle heat and prevent the eggy filling from curdling. Finally, we avoided overbaking the pie—further insurance against curdling—by removing it from the oven when the center was still jiggly. As the pie cooled, the residual heat of the filling cooked the center through. We recommend chopping the toasted pecans by hand.

  1 recipe single-crust pie dough (see pages 342–348)
  6 tablespoons unsalted butter, cut into 1-inch pieces
  1 cup packed (7 ounces) dark brown sugar
  ½ teaspoon table salt
  3 large eggs
  ¾ cup light corn syrup
  1 tablespoon vanilla extract
  2 cups pecans, toasted and chopped fine

1. Roll dough into 12-inch circle on floured counter. Loosely roll dough around rolling pin and gently unroll it onto 9-inch pie plate, letting excess dough hang over edge. Ease dough into plate by gently lifting edge of dough with your hand while pressing into plate bottom with your other hand. Trim overhang to ½ inch beyond lip of plate. Tuck overhang under itself; folded edge should be flush with edge of plate. Crimp dough evenly around edge of plate. Wrap dough-lined plate loosely in plastic wrap and refrigerate until firm, about 30 minutes. Adjust oven rack to lowest position and heat oven to 425 degrees.

2. Line chilled pie shell with double layer of aluminum foil, covering edges to prevent burning, and fill with pie weights. Bake on foil-lined rimmed baking sheet until pie dough looks dry and is pale in color, about 15 minutes. Remove foil and weights, rotate sheet, and continue to bake until crust is light golden brown, 4 to 7 minutes longer. Transfer sheet to wire rack. (Crust must still be warm when filling is added.)

3. While crust is baking, melt butter in heatproof bowl set over saucepan filled with 1 inch of barely simmering water, making sure that water does not touch bottom of bowl. Off heat, stir in sugar and salt until butter is absorbed.

4. Whisk in eggs, then corn syrup and vanilla, until smooth. Return bowl to saucepan and stir until mixture is shiny, hot to touch, and registers 130 degrees. Off heat, stir in pecans.

5. As soon as pie crust comes out of oven, adjust oven rack to lower-middle position and reduce oven temperature to 275 degrees. With pie still on sheet, pour pecan mixture into warm crust.

6. Bake until filling looks set but yields like gelatin when gently pressed with back of spoon, 50 minutes to 1 hour, rotating sheet halfway through baking. Let pie cool completely on wire rack, about 4 hours. Serve.

VIRGINIA PEANUT PIE

Serves 8 | 9-inch pie plate

WHY THIS RECIPE WORKS The contrasting flavors and textures of this pie—a specialty of the bustling Virginia Diner in Wakefield, Virginia—are easy to love. The pie is sweet and salty, with a creamy filling tucked beneath a crunchy top. For our version, we settled on corn syrup and brown sugar as the sweeteners and doubled the amount of nuts called for in most recipes. We also found a way around precooking the filling and prebaking the crust: superchilling the dough and baking the pie on the lowest rack for more than an hour. Salted dry-roasted, cocktail, or honey-roasted peanuts can be used in this recipe. Do not use Spanish red skin peanuts. Crush the peanuts in a zipper-lock bag using a rolling pin or meat pounder for pieces, not dust. Do not use a Pyrex pie plate in this recipe.

  1 recipe single-crust pie dough (see pages 342–348)
  ¾ cup light corn syrup
  ¾ cup packed (5¼ ounces) brown sugar
  3 large eggs
  6 tablespoons unsalted butter, melted
  1 tablespoon vanilla extract
  ½ teaspoon table salt
  2 cups salted dry-roasted peanuts

1. Adjust oven rack to lowest position and heat oven to 350 degrees. Roll dough into 12-inch circle on floured counter. Loosely roll dough around rolling pin and gently unroll it onto 9-inch pie plate, letting excess dough hang over edge. Ease dough into plate by gently lifting edge of dough with your hand while pressing into plate bottom with your other hand.

Virginia Peanut Pie

LEMON CHESS PIE

Serves 8 | 9-inch pie plate

WHY THIS RECIPE WORKS Made from everyday ingredients—namely lots of eggs, lots of sugar, lots of butter, and sometimes milk or cream—chess pie is a rich custard pie that can be incredibly sweet, so a popular variation is lemon chess pie, which offers tartness to balance everything out. To get the filling of this intense pie right, we cut back on the sugar and butter and settled on five eggs for a set pie, while 3 tablespoons of juice and 1 tablespoon of zest contributed a delicately tart flavor. Using cornmeal as our thickener resulted in a particular crackly exterior that we loved. Mixing the custard filling by hand worked best (the food processor aerated the mixture and made the baked filling foamy). Regular yellow cornmeal (not stone ground) works best here. Make the filling before baking the shell so the cornmeal has time to soften.

  1 recipe single-crust pie dough (see pages 342–348)
  5 large eggs
1¾ cups (12¼ ounces) plus 1 teaspoon sugar, divided
  2 tablespoons cornmeal
  1 tablespoon grated lemon zest plus 3 tablespoons juice
 ¼ teaspoon table salt
  8 tablespoons unsalted butter, melted and cooled

2. Trim overhang to ½ inch beyond lip of plate. Tuck overhang under itself; folded edge should be flush with edge of plate. Crimp dough evenly around edge of plate. Wrap dough-lined plate loosely in plastic wrap and freeze until firm, about 15 minutes.

3. Whisk corn syrup, sugar, eggs, melted butter, vanilla, and salt in large bowl until fully combined. Stir in peanuts until incorporated.

4. Place chilled pie shell on aluminum foil–lined rimmed baking sheet. Pour filling into shell. Bake until filling is puffed and set but still jiggles slightly when pie is shaken, 1 hour 5 minutes to 1 hour 10 minutes. Transfer pie to wire rack and let cool completely, at least 4 hours or up to 8 hours. Serve.

1. Roll dough into 12-inch circle on floured counter. Loosely roll dough around rolling pin and gently unroll it onto 9-inch pie plate, letting excess dough hang over edge. Ease dough into plate by gently lifting edge of dough with your hand while pressing into plate bottom with your other hand.

2. Trim overhang to ½ inch beyond lip of plate. Tuck overhang under itself; folded edge should be flush with edge of plate. Crimp dough evenly around edge of plate. Wrap dough-lined plate loosely in plastic wrap and refrigerate until firm, about 30 minutes. Adjust oven rack to middle position and heat oven to 350 degrees.

3. Whisk eggs in large bowl until smooth. Slowly whisk in 1¾ cups sugar, cornmeal, lemon zest and juice, and salt until combined. Whisk in melted butter.

4. Line chilled pie shell with double layer of aluminum foil, covering edges to prevent burning, and fill with pie weights. Bake on foil-lined rimmed baking sheet until edges are set and just beginning to turn golden, 25 to 30 minutes, rotating sheet halfway through baking. Remove foil and weights. (Crust must still be warm when filling is added.) Whisk filling to recombine. With pie still on sheet, transfer filling to hot crust and bake until filling's surface is light brown and center jiggles slightly when shaken, 35 to 40 minutes. Sprinkle with remaining 1 teaspoon sugar. Let pie cool completely on wire rack, about 4 hours. Serve.

SQUASH AND SWEET POTATO PIES

PIES MADE WITH PUMPKIN AND SWEET POTATOES are a type of custard pie (see page 376). Because of their regional ties and associations with the holidays, these pies can carry a certain nostalgia. But sometimes our cravings for them cloud reality: The star ingredient might be buried under an overload of spices and sugar. Using a lighter hand with the spices so they complement rather than overwhelm the filling is easy enough, but the real challenge with these pies is texture. They have a tendency toward graininess rather than the silky-smooth quality we want from them. The type of dairy and quantity of eggs play a role—egg yolks in particular help ensure a rich, sliceable pie—but one of the most important factors is temperature. The temperature of the oven, as well as the temperature of the filling and crust when they are combined, can all affect the final texture of the filling. And although pumpkin and sweet potato pies are classics, you can put a unique spin on these seasonal favorites by using almost any winter squash (see our Butternut Squash Pie with Browned Butter and Sage on page 393).

KEY POINTS

Cook pumpkin fillings to mitigate moisture

Bloom any spices

Bolster pumpkin flavor with sweet potatoes

Add filling to warm parbaked crust

PUMPKIN PROBLEMS

Simmering the filling for pumpkin pie is an unusual step, but it has several benefits.

1. Cooking the pumpkin and sweet potatoes drives off moisture and concentrates their flavor.

2. Cooking the spices along with the pumpkin allows their flavors to bloom.

3. Heating the filling causes it to firm up quickly in the oven rather than soaking into the pastry (which would result in a soggy crust).

POTATO FOR PUMPKIN FLAVOR

The right spices and sweeteners give pumpkin pie good flavor, but when developing our recipe (see page 392) we wanted even more complexity. The addition of a different vegetable, canned sweet potatoes or yams, with their concentrated sweet flavor, actually made our filling taste more like pumpkin than using pumpkin puree alone.

HOT CRUST

Prebaking the pie crust is an essential step with our pumpkin and squash pies. If you skip it, and instead pour the pie filling straight into the raw dough, you'll wind up with a soggy, sad crust when the pie finally exits the oven. This is because the filling is very wet, and the crust needs that extra alone time in the oven to crisp up before encountering all the extra moisture.

PUMPKIN PIE

Serves 8 | 9-inch pie plate

WHY THIS RECIPE WORKS Our pumpkin pie sets the standard: It's velvety smooth, packed with pumpkin flavor, and perfectly spiced. Canned pumpkin puree contains flavor-muting moisture, so to eliminate some of the liquid and concentrate its flavor we cooked the puree before whisking in heavy cream, milk, and eggs to enrich it. Working with this hot filling and a warm prebaked crust helped the custard firm up quickly in the oven and prevented it from soaking into the crust. Nutmeg, cinnamon, and fresh ginger provided just enough spice and warmth, but surprisingly it was another vegetable that really put our pie's flavor over the top. The addition of mashed candied sweet potatoes actually made our filling taste more like pumpkin than when it was made from pumpkin puree alone. If candied sweet potatoes or yams are unavailable, regular canned sweet potatoes or yams can be substituted. When the pie is properly baked, the center 2 inches of the pie should look firm but jiggle slightly.

Pumpkin Pie

1 recipe single-crust pie dough (see pages 342–348)
1 cup heavy cream
1 cup whole milk
3 large eggs plus 2 large yolks
1 teaspoon vanilla extract
1 (15-ounce) can unsweetened pumpkin puree
1 cup drained candied sweet potatoes or yams
¾ cup (5¼ ounces) sugar
¼ cup maple syrup
2 teaspoons grated fresh ginger
1 teaspoon table salt
½ teaspoon ground cinnamon
¼ teaspoon ground nutmeg

1. Roll dough into 12-inch circle on floured counter. Loosely roll dough around rolling pin and gently unroll it onto 9-inch pie plate, letting excess dough hang over edge. Ease dough into plate by gently lifting edge of dough with your hand while pressing into plate bottom with your other hand.

2. Trim overhang to ½ inch beyond lip of plate. Tuck overhang under itself; folded edge should be flush with edge of plate. Crimp dough evenly around edge of plate. Wrap dough-lined plate loosely in plastic wrap and refrigerate until firm, about 30 minutes. Adjust oven rack to middle position and heat oven to 350 degrees.

3. Line chilled pie shell with double layer of aluminum foil, covering edges to prevent burning, and fill with pie weights. Bake on foil-lined rimmed baking sheet until edges are set and just beginning to turn golden, 25 to 30 minutes, rotating sheet halfway through baking.

4. Remove foil and weights, rotate sheet, and continue to bake crust until golden brown and crisp, 10 to 15 minutes longer. Transfer sheet to wire rack. (Crust must still be warm when filling is added.) Increase oven temperature to 400 degrees.

5. While crust is baking, whisk cream, milk, eggs and yolks, and vanilla together in bowl; set aside. Bring pumpkin, sweet potatoes, sugar, maple syrup, ginger, salt, cinnamon, and nutmeg to simmer in large saucepan over medium heat and cook, stirring constantly and mashing sweet potatoes against sides of saucepan, until thick and shiny, 15 to 20 minutes.

6. Remove saucepan from heat and whisk in cream mixture until fully incorporated. Strain mixture through fine-mesh strainer into bowl, using back of ladle or spatula to press solids through strainer.

7. Whisk mixture, then, with pie still on sheet, pour into warm crust. Bake for 10 minutes. Reduce oven temperature to 300 degrees and continue to bake until edges of pie are set and center registers 175 degrees, 20 to 35 minutes longer, rotating sheet halfway through baking. Let pie cool completely on wire rack, about 4 hours. Serve.

PUMPKIN PRALINE PIE

Serves 8 | 9-inch pie plate

WHY THIS RECIPE WORKS Pumpkin praline pie combines the best features of two holiday favorites: It has the spiced custard of a pumpkin pie and the praline-like chew of a pecan pie. We cooked our filling on the stovetop to evaporate excess moisture; this ensured that our pie would have enough structure to support a substantial topping. For the praline, we tossed chopped pecans with sugar and just enough corn syrup to make the topping clump like streusel. We added our praline when the edge of the custard had just begun to crack—a visual cue that meant our filling was set enough to support the topping. After just 10 more minutes of baking, the praline became a crisp contrast to the smooth custardy filling.

- 1 recipe single-crust pie dough (see pages 342–348)

FILLING
- 1 (15-ounce) can unsweetened pumpkin puree
- ¾ cup packed (5¼ ounces) dark brown sugar
- 2 teaspoons ground cinnamon
- 1 teaspoon ground ginger
- ½ teaspoon ground allspice
- ½ teaspoon table salt
   Pinch ground cloves
- 1 cup evaporated milk
- 3 large eggs
- 2 teaspoons vanilla extract

TOPPING
- 1 cup pecans, chopped fine
- ½ cup packed (3½ ounces) dark brown sugar
   Pinch table salt
- 2 teaspoons dark corn syrup
- 1 teaspoon vanilla extract
- 2 teaspoons granulated sugar

1. Roll dough into 12-inch circle on floured counter. Loosely roll dough around rolling pin and gently unroll it onto 9-inch pie plate, letting excess dough hang over edge. Ease dough into plate by gently lifting edge of dough with your hand while pressing into plate bottom with your other hand.

2. Trim overhang to ½ inch beyond lip of plate. Tuck overhang under itself; folded edge should be flush with edge of plate. Crimp dough evenly around edge of plate. Wrap dough-lined plate loosely in plastic wrap and refrigerate until firm, about 30 minutes. Adjust oven rack to middle position and heat oven to 425 degrees.

3. Line chilled pie shell with double layer of aluminum foil, covering edges to prevent burning, and fill with pie weights. Bake on rimmed baking sheet until pie dough looks dry and is pale in color, about 15 minutes. Remove foil and weights and continue

to bake crust until light golden brown, 4 to 7 minutes longer. Transfer to wire rack. (Crust must still be warm when filling is added.) Reduce oven temperature to 350 degrees.

4. FOR THE FILLING: Process pumpkin, sugar, cinnamon, ginger, allspice, salt, and cloves in food processor until smooth, about 1 minute. Transfer mixture to large saucepan and cook over medium-high heat until sputtering and thickened, about 4 minutes. Off heat, whisk evaporated milk into pumpkin mixture, then whisk in eggs and vanilla. With pie still on sheet, pour filling into warm crust. Bake until filling is puffed and cracked around edges and center barely jiggles when pie is shaken, about 35 minutes.

5. FOR THE TOPPING: While pie is baking, toss pecans, brown sugar, and salt together in bowl. Add corn syrup and vanilla, using your fingers to ensure that ingredients are well blended. Scatter topping evenly over puffed filling. Sprinkle with granulated sugar. Bake until pecans are fragrant and topping is bubbling around edges, about 10 minutes. Let pie cool completely on wire rack, about 4 hours. Serve.

BUTTERNUT SQUASH PIE WITH BROWNED BUTTER AND SAGE

Serves 8 | 9-inch pie plate

WHY THIS RECIPE WORKS Pumpkin isn't the only winter squash that works in desserts—slightly earthier butternut is a lovely autumn alternative to the pie norm. To make this pie unique from its cousin, we incorporated browned butter for nutty richness. Mincing some sage and cooking it with the butter before adding it to the filling allowed this classic fall herb to subtly infuse the pie without being too prominent. For even more sage flavor we like to use our herb pie dough, here made with sage, but you can use any single-crust pie dough. If you want to top your pie with cutouts, make a double crust so you have enough dough (see page 367 for more information).

- 1 recipe Herb Single-Crust Pie Dough (page 342)
- 8 tablespoons unsalted butter, cut into 8 pieces
- 1 teaspoon minced fresh sage
- 30 ounces butternut squash, peeled, seeded, and cut into 1-inch pieces (5 cups)
- 1 teaspoon table salt
- 1 teaspoon grated fresh ginger
- ¼ teaspoon ground nutmeg
- ¾ cup packed (5¼ ounces) brown sugar
- ¾ cup heavy cream
- ⅔ cup whole milk
- 2 large eggs plus 2 large yolks
- 1 teaspoon vanilla extract

1. Roll dough into 12-inch circle on floured counter. Loosely roll dough around rolling pin and gently unroll it onto 9-inch pie plate, letting excess dough hang over edge. Ease dough into plate by gently lifting edge of dough with your hand while pressing into plate bottom with your other hand.

2. Trim overhang to ½ inch beyond lip of plate. Tuck overhang under itself; folded edge should be flush with edge of plate. Crimp dough evenly around edge of plate. Wrap dough-lined plate loosely in plastic wrap and refrigerate until firm, about 30 minutes. Adjust oven rack to middle position and heat oven to 350 degrees.

3. Melt butter and sage in 8-inch skillet over medium-high heat. Continue to cook, swirling skillet occasionally, until butter is dark golden brown and has nutty aroma, about 2 minutes; set aside. Microwave squash in covered bowl until very soft and easily pierced with fork, 15 to 18 minutes, stirring halfway through microwaving. Carefully uncover, allowing steam to escape away from you, then drain squash; transfer to food processor. Add browned butter, salt, ginger, and nutmeg and process until smooth, about 1 minute, scraping down sides of bowl as needed. Transfer to large saucepan and set aside.

4. Line chilled pie shell with double layer of aluminum foil, covering edges to prevent burning, and fill with pie weights. Bake on foil-lined rimmed baking sheet until edges are set and just beginning to turn golden, 25 to 30 minutes, rotating sheet halfway through baking. Remove foil and weights, rotate sheet, and continue to bake crust until golden brown and crisp, 10 to 15 minutes longer. Transfer to wire rack. (Crust must still be warm when filling is added.)

5. Meanwhile, cook squash mixture and sugar in saucepan over medium heat until thick, shiny, and reduced to 2½ cups, 10 to 15 minutes, stirring constantly. Return squash mixture to now-empty processor bowl, add cream, milk, eggs and yolks, and vanilla, and process until well combined and smooth, about 15 seconds. Transfer filling to warm crust. Reduce oven temperature to 300 degrees and bake until edges of pie are set but center jiggles slightly and registers 160 degrees, 25 to 35 minutes. Let pie cool completely on wire rack, about 4 hours. Serve.

SWEET POTATO PIE

Serves 8 | 9-inch pie plate

WHY THIS RECIPE WORKS Sweet potatoes commonly star in pie in the American South. It's a delicious tradition, but sweet potato pies sometimes feature heavy, grainy fillings. To fix the heaviness problem, we cooked the sweet potatoes for the puree in the microwave rather than boiling them, which can result in dense, soggy potatoes. For the dairy component, we liked sour cream for its smoothness and subtle tang. In addition to cinnamon and nutmeg we rounded out the pie with vanilla and bourbon. For a layer of caramelly interest, we sprinkled brown sugar over the crust before pouring in the filling.

1 recipe single-crust pie dough (see pages 342–348)
1¼ cups packed (8¾ ounces) light brown sugar, divided
1¾ pounds sweet potatoes, unpeeled
½ teaspoon table salt
4 tablespoons unsalted butter
½ teaspoon ground cinnamon
¼ teaspoon ground nutmeg
1 cup sour cream
3 large eggs plus 2 large yolks
2 tablespoons bourbon (optional)
1 teaspoon vanilla extract

1. Roll dough into 12-inch circle on floured counter. Loosely roll dough around rolling pin and gently unroll it onto 9-inch pie plate, letting excess dough hang over edge. Ease dough into plate by gently lifting edge of dough with your hand while pressing into plate bottom with your other hand.

2. Trim overhang to ½ inch beyond lip of plate. Tuck overhang under itself; folded edge should be flush with edge of plate. Crimp dough evenly around edge of plate. Wrap dough-lined plate loosely in plastic wrap and refrigerate until firm, about 30 minutes. Adjust oven rack to middle position and heat oven to 375 degrees.

3. Line chilled pie shell with double layer of aluminum foil, covering edges to prevent burning, and fill with pie weights. Bake on foil-lined rimmed baking sheet until lightly golden around edges, 18 to 25 minutes, rotating sheet halfway through baking. Remove foil and weights, rotate sheet, and continue to bake until center begins to look opaque and slightly drier, 3 to 6 minutes. Transfer sheet to wire rack and let cool completely, about 45 minutes. Sprinkle ¼ cup sugar over bottom of crust. Reduce oven temperature to 350 degrees.

4. Meanwhile, prick potatoes all over with fork. Microwave on large plate until potatoes are very soft and surface is slightly wet, 15 to 20 minutes, flipping every 5 minutes. Immediately slice potatoes in half. When cool enough to handle, scoop flesh into food processor. Add salt and remaining 1 cup sugar and process until smooth, about 1 minute, scraping down sides of bowl as needed. Microwave butter, cinnamon, and nutmeg in small bowl until melted, 15 to 30 seconds; stir to combine. Add spiced butter; sour cream; eggs and yolks; bourbon, if using; and vanilla to potatoes and process until incorporated, about 10 seconds, scraping down sides of bowl as needed. With pie still on sheet, pour potato mixture into cooled crust. Bake until filling is set around edges but center registers 165 degrees and jiggles slightly when pie is shaken, 35 to 40 minutes. Let pie cool completely on wire rack, about 4 hours. Serve.

Butternut Squash Pie with Browned Butter and Sage

SLAB PIES

KEY POINTS

Carefully seal seams in dough

Create spaces in top crust
for evaporation

Slice into sturdy squares

SLAB PIE IS A FEAT OF BAKING INGENUITY. The impressively large fruit-filled pie is prepared in a baking sheet rather than in a pie plate and can be cut into easy-to-pick-up squares, making pie a big-party possibility. The large surface area of a slab pie gives it a leg up on pies baked in a traditional pie plate because it allows for more moisture evaporation, particularly when topped with a cutout, lattice, or streusel topping. This style of pie is short in stature and the filling is thickened to a consistency that ensures neat slicing, while its flat top is perfect for holding a sweet glaze. But the dough for such a mammoth pie can be a challenge: When rolled into rectangles big enough to fit an 18 by 13-inch rimmed baking sheet, the dough is bound to tear when it's transferred to the pan. Instead of two large pieces of dough, we find it much easier to roll it into four squares, two for the bottom crust and two for the top. By taking two smaller pieces and overlapping them to create one large rectangle, the dough is sturdier and much easier to handle.

Slab Pie Dough

Our slab pie dough is simply a larger yield of our Foolproof All-Butter Pie Dough (page 342). The dough is very workable, which makes it ideal for rolling into large rectangles that fit into a baking sheet to make these large-scale pies.

FOOLPROOF ALL-BUTTER SLAB PIE DOUGH

Makes one 18 by 13-inch single crust

Be sure to weigh the flour for this recipe. In the mixing stage, this dough will be moister than most pie doughs, but as it chills it will absorb much of the excess moisture. Be sure to roll the dough on a well-floured counter.

24 tablespoons (3 sticks) unsalted butter, divided
2¾ cups (13¾ ounces) all-purpose flour, divided
2 tablespoons sugar
1 teaspoon table salt
½ cup ice water, divided

1. Grate 5 tablespoons butter on large holes of box grater and place in freezer. Cut remaining 19 tablespoons butter into ½-inch cubes.

2. Pulse 1¾ cups flour, sugar, and salt in food processor until combined, 2 pulses. Add cubed butter and process until homogeneous paste forms, 40 to 50 seconds. Using your hands, carefully break paste into 2-inch chunks and redistribute evenly around processor blade. Add remaining 1 cup flour and pulse until mixture is broken into pieces no larger than 1 inch (most pieces will be much smaller), 4 to 5 pulses. Transfer mixture to bowl. Add grated butter and toss until butter pieces are separated and coated with flour.

3. Sprinkle ¼ cup ice water over mixture. Toss with rubber spatula until mixture is evenly moistened. Sprinkle remaining ¼ cup ice water over mixture and toss to combine. Press dough with spatula until dough sticks together. Using spatula, divide dough into 2 equal portions. Transfer each portion to sheet of plastic wrap. Working with 1 portion at a time, draw edges of plastic over dough and press firmly on sides and top to form compact, fissure-free mass. Wrap in plastic and form into 5 by 6-inch rectangle. Refrigerate dough for at least 2 hours or up to 2 days. Let chilled dough sit on counter to soften slightly, about 10 minutes, before rolling. (Wrapped dough can be frozen for up to 1 month. If frozen, let dough thaw completely on counter before rolling.)

Fitting Slab Pie Dough

1. Starting at short side of 1 piece of dough, loosely roll around rolling pin, then gently unroll over half of long side of sheet, leaving about 2 inches of dough overhanging 3 edges of sheet.

2. Repeat with second piece of dough, overlapping first piece of dough by ½ inch in center of sheet.

3. Ease dough into sheet by gently lifting edges of dough with your hand while pressing into sheet bottom with your other hand.

4. Brush edge where doughs overlap with water, pressing to seal. Cover loosely with plastic and refrigerate until dough is firm, about 30 minutes.

PEAR-BUTTERSCOTCH SLAB PIE

Serves 18 to 24 | rimmed baking sheet

WHY THIS RECIPE WORKS Pears pair with warm, rich fall flavors in this impressively sized pie. Firm but ripe Bosc pears gave our filling the best texture. We matched their floral sweetness with a trio of warm spices—cinnamon, cloves, and star anise—and then drizzled our fruit filling with butterscotch. This unique slab pie deserved an appealing topper, so we covered it with pie dough cutouts—we particularly loved the autumnal look of fall leaves. Measure the tapioca, which may be sold as "minute tapioca," before grinding it. Grind the tapioca to a powder in a spice grinder or a mini food processor. If you can't find ground star anise, you can grind your own, or substitute five-spice powder. You can toss the pear mixture in step 5 in two bowls if it doesn't fit in one. We use 3-inch cookie cutters for this recipe, but you can use whatever size and shape you prefer. When placing the cutouts on the pie, be sure to leave space for evaporation and don't overlap more than two cutouts.

2 recipes Foolproof All-Butter Slab Pie Dough (page 397)
7 pounds ripe but firm Bosc pears, peeled, halved, cored, and sliced ¼ inch thick
¼ cup (1¾ ounces) sugar
½ teaspoon table salt
¼ cup instant tapioca, ground
1 teaspoon ground cinnamon
¼ teaspoon ground cloves
¼ teaspoon ground star anise
2 recipes Butterscotch Sauce (page 549), divided
1 large egg, lightly beaten with 1 tablespoon water

1. Line rimmed baking sheet with parchment paper. Roll each dough square into 16 by 11-inch rectangle on floured counter; stack on prepared sheet, separated by additional sheets of parchment. Cover loosely with plastic wrap and refrigerate until dough is firm but still pliable, about 10 minutes.

2. Using parchment as sling, transfer 2 chilled dough rectangles to counter; discard parchment. Spray second rimmed baking sheet with vegetable oil spray. Starting at short side of 1 dough rectangle, loosely roll around rolling pin, then gently unroll over half of long side of prepared sheet, leaving about 2 inches of dough overhanging 3 edges. Repeat with second dough rectangle, unrolling it over empty side of sheet and overlapping first dough piece by ½ inch.

3. Ease dough into sheet by gently lifting edges of dough with your hand while pressing into sheet bottom with your other hand. Brush overlapping edge of dough rectangles with water and press to seal. Trim overhang to ½ inch beyond edge of sheet. Tuck overhang under itself; folded edge should rest on edge of sheet. Crimp dough evenly around edge of sheet. Cover loosely with plastic and refrigerate until firm, about 30 minutes.

4. Using parchment as sling, transfer remaining 2 dough rectangles to counter. Using cookie cutters, cut as many shapes from dough rectangles as you can. Reserve dough scraps for another use. Return cutouts to sheet, still on parchment, and cover loosely with plastic. Refrigerate until firm, about 30 minutes.

5. Meanwhile, adjust oven racks to lower-middle and lowest positions and heat oven to 375 degrees. Toss pears, sugar, and salt together in large bowl. Let sit, tossing occasionally, until pears release their juices, about 30 minutes.

Pear-Butterscotch Slab Pie

6. Working in batches, drain pears thoroughly in colander, discarding juices; transfer to large bowl. Whisk tapioca, cinnamon, cloves, and star anise together in small bowl, then add to pears and toss to combine. Spread pear mixture evenly over chilled dough-lined sheet, then drizzle evenly with 1 cup butterscotch sauce. Arrange cutouts evenly over fruit, being careful not to overlap more than 2 cutouts. Brush cutouts with egg wash.

7. Place large sheet of aluminum foil directly on lower rack (to catch any bubbling juices). Place pie on upper rack and bake until crust is deep golden brown and juices are bubbling, 1 hour to 1 hour 10 minutes, rotating sheet halfway through baking. Let pie cool on wire rack until filling has set, about 2 hours. Serve, passing remaining butterscotch sauce separately.

TRIPLE BERRY SLAB PIE WITH GINGER-LEMON STREUSEL

Serves 18 to 24 | rimmed baking sheet

WHY THIS RECIPE WORKS Our berry slab pie is guaranteed to elicit oohs and aahs before the first slice is even cut. And no one will know it's a cinch to prepare. We started by tossing no-prep berries—blueberries, raspberries, and blackberries—with sugar, lemon zest, and tapioca for the filling. Instead of applying a top crust, which would hide the beautiful berry hues and trap moisture, we sprinkled on a streusel that we flavored liberally with more lemon zest as well as some crystallized ginger; the topping added fresh and zingy pops of flavor to the sweet, bright berries peeking through. You can toss the berry mixture in step 5 in two bowls if it doesn't fit in one.

    1 recipe Foolproof All-Butter Slab Pie Dough (page 397)

STREUSEL
1½ cups (7½ ounces) all-purpose flour
 ½ cup packed (3½ ounces) light brown sugar
 ½ cup crystallized ginger, chopped fine
 ¼ cup (1¾ ounces) granulated sugar
  1 tablespoon ground ginger
  1 teaspoon grated lemon zest
 ¼ teaspoon table salt
 10 tablespoons unsalted butter, melted and cooled

FILLING
  1 cup (7 ounces) granulated sugar
  6 tablespoons instant tapioca, ground
  1 teaspoon grated lemon zest
 ¼ teaspoon table salt
1¼ pounds (4 cups) blackberries
1¼ pounds (4 cups) blueberries
1¼ pounds (4 cups) raspberries

1. Line rimmed baking sheet with parchment paper. Roll each dough square into 16 by 11-inch rectangle on floured counter; stack on prepared sheet, separated by second sheet of parchment. Cover loosely with plastic wrap and refrigerate until dough is firm but still pliable, about 10 minutes.

2. Using parchment as sling, transfer chilled dough rectangles to counter; discard parchment. Wipe sheet clean with paper towels and spray with vegetable oil spray. Starting at short side of 1 dough rectangle, loosely roll around rolling pin, then gently unroll over half of long side of prepared sheet, leaving about 2 inches of dough overhanging 3 edges. Repeat with second dough rectangle, unrolling it over empty side of sheet and overlapping first dough piece by ½ inch.

3. Ease dough into sheet by gently lifting edges of dough with your hand while pressing into sheet bottom with your other hand. Brush overlapping edge of dough rectangles with water and press to seal. Trim overhang to ½ inch beyond edge of sheet. Tuck overhang under itself; folded edge should rest on edge of sheet. Crimp dough evenly around edge of sheet. Cover loosely with plastic and refrigerate until firm, about 30 minutes.

4. FOR THE STREUSEL: Meanwhile, adjust oven racks to lower-middle and lowest positions and heat oven to 375 degrees. Combine flour, brown sugar, crystallized ginger, granulated sugar, ground ginger, lemon zest, and salt in bowl. Stir in melted butter until mixture is completely moistened; let sit for 10 minutes.

5. FOR THE FILLING: Whisk sugar, tapioca, lemon zest, and salt together in large bowl. Add blackberries, blueberries, and raspberries and gently toss to combine. Spread berry mixture evenly over chilled dough-lined sheet. Sprinkle streusel evenly over fruit, breaking apart any large chunks. Place large sheet of aluminum foil directly on lower rack (to catch any bubbling juices). Place pie on upper rack and bake until crust and streusel are deep golden brown and juices are bubbling, 45 minutes to 1 hour, rotating sheet halfway through baking. Let pie cool on wire rack until filling has set, about 2 hours. Serve.

INDIVIDUAL PIES

HAND-SIZE, PORTABLE FRUIT PIES have been around in America since colonial times, most likely arriving with British settlers. During that era, the individual pies were generally made from dried fruit—usually peaches or apples—and were typically fried, not baked. Fast-forward to today and individual pies are prepared in a variety of ways and can be found in a multitude of shapes and forms, from hand pies—essentially just a pie in miniature form—to pies baked in muffin tins to pies on a stick. These petite pies are a fun treat for pie lovers of all ages—and anyone who doesn't feel like sharing! They're made to be eaten out of hand and offer a good alternative to traditional pies when ease of serving or transporting is a factor. They're portable, perfect for picnics or on the go, and can easily cross over from dessert to sweet snack.

KEY POINTS

Pretreat fruit to avoid watery fillings

Cooked fillings stay put

Seal dough tight

Steam vents prevent bursting

Hand Pies

Small hand pies are incredibly versatile and a justifiable treat at any time—they can even be breakfast fare if you're feeling indulgent. To make them as easy as they are versatile, we often like to start with store-bought puff pastry and fill it with a simple precooked fruit filling. (An exception is our peach hand pies on page 405, which are fried and require a different treatment.) Freezing the pastries before baking allows the pastry enough time to crisp up without the risk of the filling overcooking or bubbling out in the oven. Even still, cutting sufficient steam vents—three 1-inch-long slits in the tops—is key to preventing the turnovers from bursting open and leaking.

Muffin Tin Pies

These little pies are just what the name suggests: individual pies baked in a muffin tin. The result is a handheld pie with a generous crust-to-filling ratio and a crisp, buttery streusel topping. But while forming these little pies isn't all that different than shaping a larger one, the muffin tin itself presents a challenge: The pies in the middle are insulated by the surrounding ones and can wind up soggy and soft on the bottom. To ensure consistently browned, flaky bottoms on every pie, we leave the two muffin cups in the middle empty.

Pie Pops

Pie pops are the ultimate party starter, party dessert, or party favor—and they're way more kid-friendly than a full-size pie. While they're particularly fun to assemble and eat with children, they're packed with flavor adults will love, too. The process starts with good old pie dough and some rolling; after that, it's a breeze. We skip the fresh fruit and use preserves or fruit butter. Preserves offer concentrated fruit flavor and allow you to skip the hassle of chopping and cooking down fresh fruit. And because preserves are already thickened, they virtually eliminate the risk of leaking. Requiring only pantry ingredients, pie pops are sure to become something you'll love to make and share.

COOL CUTOUTS

When making pie pops, we cut slits in the top crust so moisture can evaporate, but you can go a step further and make a cutout. Using a ½- to ¾-inch cutter, cut a shape out of the center of half the dough rounds before chilling. The cutout will be a window to the filling inside.

MAKING PIE POPS

1. Using 3-inch round cutter, cut 16 rounds from dough circle and transfer to baking sheet. Cover and refrigerate until firm but still pliable, about 10 minutes.

2. Transfer 8 dough rounds to second sheet. Working with 1 round at a time, lay lollipop stick flat on top of dough with one end in center. Press stick firmly into dough.

3. Mound 1 tablespoon filling in center of each dough round on top of stick. Transfer sheet with filled rounds to freezer and chill for 10 minutes.

4. Brush edges of filled dough rounds with egg wash.

5. Top with remaining chilled dough rounds, pressing edges firmly to seal.

6. Crimp edges of each pie with fork. Cut three ½-inch slits in top of each pie and brush with remaining egg wash.

PEAR-ROSEMARY MUFFIN TIN PIES

Serves 10 | muffin tin

WHY THIS RECIPE WORKS These individual pear pies—made in a muffin tin—capture all the scents and flavors of fall in a few bites. We were delighted by the pairing of fragrant, piney rosemary with the sweet, honey-like flavor of Bosc pears in our simple filling. Precooking the pears removed excess moisture; it also reduced the fruit's volume, allowing us to pack the entire dough cup with filling. We topped the pies with a walnut streusel, which added a subtle savory note to the sweet pears. While a muffin tin was perfect for creating mini pies, the middle pies emerged from the oven soggy and soft on the bottom; to resolve this problem, we opted to simply leave the two middle cups empty. Measure the tapioca, which may be sold as "minute tapioca," before grinding it. Grind the tapioca to a powder in a spice grinder or a mini food processor. Be sure to spray both the muffin tin cups and the surface between cups with vegetable oil spray to prevent sticking.

1 recipe double-crust pie dough (see pages 342–348)

FILLING

2½ pounds ripe but firm Bosc pears, peeled, halved, cored, and cut into ½-inch pieces
3 tablespoons packed brown sugar, divided
¼ teaspoon table salt
1 tablespoon instant tapioca, ground
¾ teaspoon minced fresh rosemary

STREUSEL

⅔ cup (3⅓ ounces) all-purpose flour
½ cup walnuts, chopped fine
6 tablespoons packed (2⅔ ounces) brown sugar
½ teaspoon table salt
6 tablespoons unsalted butter

1. Line rimmed baking sheet with parchment paper. Roll each dough piece into 16 by 11-inch rectangle on floured counter; stack on prepared sheet, separated by second sheet of parchment. Cover loosely with plastic wrap and refrigerate until dough is firm but still pliable, about 10 minutes.

2. Spray outer cups of 12-cup muffin tin as well as surface in between cups with vegetable oil spray. Using parchment as sling, transfer chilled dough rectangles to counter. Using 5-inch round biscuit or cookie cutter, cut 5 rounds from each dough rectangle. Reserve dough scraps for another use. Return rounds to sheet, still on parchment, and cover loosely with plastic. Refrigerate until firm but still pliable, about 10 minutes.

3. Center 1 dough round over outer muffin tin cup. Using your fingers, press center of dough into bottom of cup, then press dough into corners and against sides, smoothing out any overlapping creases. (You should have about ½ inch dough overhanging rim of cup.) Fold overhang over itself; fold edge over rim of cup to rest on surface of muffin tin. Repeat with remaining 9 dough rounds and outer muffin tin cups. (If dough rounds become too soft to work with, refrigerate tin and rounds until firm.) Cover and refrigerate muffin tin until dough is firm, about 30 minutes.

4. FOR THE FILLING: Toss pears, 1 tablespoon sugar, and salt together in bowl. Microwave until pears soften slightly and release their juices, 6 to 8 minutes, stirring once halfway through microwaving. Drain pears thoroughly in colander set over bowl; discard juices and return pears to now-empty bowl. Let pears cool completely, about 30 minutes.

5. FOR THE STREUSEL: Meanwhile, adjust oven rack to lower-middle position and heat oven to 375 degrees. Whisk flour, walnuts, sugar, and salt together in medium bowl. Melt butter in 10-inch skillet over medium-high heat and cook, swirling skillet constantly, until butter is browned and has nutty aroma, 3 to 5 minutes. Stir butter into flour mixture until completely moistened.

Pear-Rosemary Muffin Tin Pies

TUTORIAL
Pear-Rosemary Muffin Tin Pies

These petite pies fit plentiful filling within a rimmed pie shell and under a streusel topping. Sound familiar? Learn how to shrink a full-size pie.

1. Center 1 dough round over outer muffin tin cup.

2. Using your fingers, press center of dough into bottom of cup.

3. Press dough into corners and against sides, smoothing out any overlapping creases. (You should have about ½ inch dough overhanging rim of cup.)

4. Fold overhang over itself.

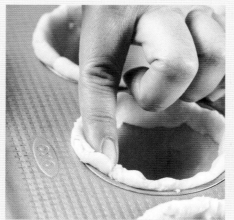

5. Fold edge over rim of cup to rest on surface of muffin tin.

6. Divide pear mixture evenly among dough-lined cups. Sprinkle streusel evenly over fruit, breaking apart any large clumps.

Blueberry Hand Pies

6. Whisk remaining 2 tablespoons sugar, tapioca, and rosemary together in small bowl. Add to pears and toss to combine. Divide pear mixture evenly among dough-lined cups. Sprinkle streusel evenly over fruit, breaking apart any large clumps. Bake until crusts are deep golden brown and juices are bubbling, 35 to 45 minutes, rotating muffin tin halfway through baking. Transfer muffin tin to wire rack and let pies cool for 10 minutes. Run paring knife around edges of pies, transfer to wire rack, and let cool until filling has set, about 2 hours. Serve.

BLUEBERRY HAND PIES

Serves 8 | rimmed baking sheet

WHY THIS RECIPE WORKS For an easy handheld pie bursting with fruit flavor, we started with a precooked filling of blueberries flavored with cinnamon and lemon zest. Frozen blueberries worked as well as fresh, making these petite pies a treat we could enjoy any time of year. Freezing the pastries before baking chilled the filling enough to ensure it wouldn't overcook or leak out before the pies had time to develop a shatteringly crisp exterior. Steam vents provided further insurance against the pies bursting open. Brushed with egg wash and sprinkled with sugar, our hand pies were crispy and flaky on the outside and full of luscious blueberry filling. To thaw frozen puff pastry, let it sit either in the refrigerator for 24 hours or on the counter for 30 minutes to 1 hour.

- 1 pound (3¼ cups) fresh or frozen blueberries
- ½ cup (3½ ounces) plus 1 tablespoon sugar, divided
- 1 teaspoon grated lemon zest
- ¼ teaspoon table salt
- ¼ teaspoon ground cinnamon
- 1 tablespoon cornstarch
- 1 tablespoon water
- 2 (9½ by 9-inch) sheets puff pastry, thawed
- 1 large egg, lightly beaten with 1 tablespoon water

1. Cook blueberries, ½ cup sugar, lemon zest, salt, and cinnamon in medium saucepan over medium heat, stirring occasionally, until blueberries begin to break down and release their juices, about 8 minutes. Reduce heat to medium-low and continue to cook until mixture thickens and spatula starts to leave trail when pulled through, 8 to 10 minutes.

2. Whisk cornstarch and water together in bowl, then stir into blueberry mixture. Cook until mixture has thickened to jam-like consistency, about 1 minute (you should have about 1¼ cups filling). Let cool completely, about 30 minutes.

Fried Peach Hand Pies

3. Adjust oven rack middle position and heat oven to 400 degrees. Line rimmed baking sheet with parchment paper. Working with 1 sheet of pastry at a time, roll into 10-inch square on floured counter. Cut pastry into four 5-inch squares. Place 2 tablespoons blueberry filling in center of each square.

4. Brush edges of squares with egg wash, then fold dough over filling to form rectangle. Using fork, crimp edges of dough to seal. Transfer pies to prepared sheet and cut three 1-inch slits on top (do not cut through filling). Freeze pies until firm, about 15 minutes. (Once frozen, pies can be transferred to airtight container and stored in freezer for up to 1 month.)

5. Brush tops of pies with remaining egg wash and sprinkle with remaining 1 tablespoon sugar. Bake until well browned, about 25 minutes, rotating sheet halfway through baking. Transfer pies to wire rack and let cool slightly, about 15 minutes. Serve warm or at room temperature.

FRIED PEACH HAND PIES

Serves 8 | Dutch oven

WHY THIS RECIPE WORKS There's a lot of peach pie in the South, and it's not unusual to find it in the form of hand pies. But what's even better than a personal peach pie? A fried one, with a crust that's tender and crumbly wrapped around a thick peach filling. We started by cooking sliced peaches with sugar and a pinch of salt on the stovetop before gently mashing the fruit and letting it thicken. We knew we couldn't use traditional pie pastry for frying, so we created a soft dough with melted butter and flour. The addition of baking powder and milk helped us achieve the dainty, almost cake-like crumble we wanted. You can substitute 20 ounces frozen peaches for the fresh peaches; increase the cooking time in step 1 to 15 to 20 minutes. Use a Dutch oven that holds 6 quarts or more for frying.

- 4 ripe peaches, peeled, halved, pitted, and cut into ½-inch wedges
- ½ cup (3½ ounces) sugar
- 1 teaspoon table salt, divided
- 2 teaspoons lemon juice
- 2 cups (10 ounces) all-purpose flour
- 2 teaspoons baking powder
- 6 tablespoons unsalted butter, melted and cooled
- ½ cup whole milk
- 2 quarts peanut or vegetable oil for frying

1. Combine peaches, sugar, and ¼ teaspoon salt in medium saucepan. Cover and cook over medium heat, stirring occasionally and breaking up peaches with spoon, until tender, about 5 minutes.

2. Uncover and continue to cook, stirring and mashing frequently with potato masher to coarse puree, until mixture is thickened and measures about 1⅔ cups, 7 to 13 minutes. Off heat, stir in lemon juice and let cool completely.

3. Line rimmed baking sheet with parchment paper. Pulse flour, baking powder, and remaining ¾ teaspoon salt in food processor until combined, about 3 pulses. Add melted butter and pulse until mixture resembles wet sand, about 8 pulses, scraping down sides of bowl as needed. Add milk and process until no floury bits remain and dough looks pebbly, about 8 seconds.

4. Turn dough onto lightly floured counter, gather into disk, and divide into 8 equal pieces. Roll each piece between your hands into ball, then press to flatten into round. Place rounds on prepared sheet, cover with plastic wrap, and refrigerate for 20 minutes.

5. Working with 1 dough round at a time, roll into 6- to 7-inch circle about ⅛ inch thick on floured counter. Place 3 tablespoons filling in center of circle. Brush edges of dough with water and fold dough over filling to create half-moon shape, lightly pressing out air at seam. Trim any ragged edges and crimp edges with fork to seal. Return pies to prepared sheet, cover with plastic, and refrigerate until ready to fry. (Pies can be covered and refrigerated for up to 24 hours.)

6. Line platter with triple layer of paper towels. Add oil to large Dutch oven until it measures about 1½ inches deep and heat over medium-high heat to 375 degrees. Gently place 4 pies in hot oil and fry until golden brown, about 3 minutes, using slotted spatula or spider skimmer to flip halfway through frying. Adjust burner, if necessary, to maintain oil temperature between 350 and 375 degrees. Transfer pies to prepared platter. Return oil to 375 degrees and repeat with remaining 4 pies. Let cool for 10 minutes before serving.

CHOCOLATE-CHERRY PIE POPS

Serves 8 | 2 rimmed baking sheets

WHY THIS RECIPE WORKS Pie pops—miniature pies on sticks—are festive, handheld desserts perfect for pie lovers, young or old. With their concentrated flavor, fruit preserves made an ideal filling for these two-bite treats. Tasters loved a cherry-chocolate combination, but loosely set cherry preserves leaked out of the pies during baking. Straining the preserves and using only the solids for the filling proved a successful fix. But we didn't let that glossy-pink liquid go to waste; we combined it with confectioners' sugar to create a glaze for drizzling. We found that 3-inch circles of dough gave us the best

Chocolate-Cherry
Pie Pops

filling-to-crust ratio. Quickly chilling the partially assembled pies set the filling enough to prevent it from squeezing out the sides when we pressed on the top crust. You can find lollipop and Popsicle sticks at most craft stores. This recipe can be easily doubled.

1 cup cherry preserves
1 recipe single-crust pie dough (see pages 342–348)
2 tablespoons plus 2 teaspoons chocolate chips
8 (4- to 6-inch) lollipop or Popsicle sticks
1 large egg, lightly beaten with 1 tablespoon water
½ cup (2 ounces) confectioners' sugar

1. Microwave cherry preserves in bowl until fluid, 45 to 60 seconds, stirring halfway through microwaving. Strain preserves through fine-mesh strainer set over bowl, pressing on solids to extract as much liquid as possible; reserve solids (you should have about ⅓ cup) and liquid separately. Set aside to cool.

2. Roll dough into 15-inch circle on floured counter. Using 3-inch round biscuit or cookie cutter, cut 16 rounds from dough circle and transfer to parchment paper–lined rimmed baking sheet. Reserve dough scraps for another use. Cover rounds loosely with plastic wrap and refrigerate until firm but still pliable, about 10 minutes.

3. Line second rimmed baking sheet with parchment. Transfer 8 dough rounds to second prepared sheet, spaced evenly apart. Working with 1 dough round at a time, lay lollipop stick flat on top of dough with 1 end in center of dough round. Press stick firmly into dough. Mound 2 teaspoons cherry solids and 1 teaspoon chocolate chips in center of each dough round on top of stick. Transfer sheet with filled rounds to freezer and chill for 10 minutes.

4. Adjust oven rack to upper-middle position and heat oven to 375 degrees. Brush edges of filled dough rounds with egg wash, then top with remaining chilled dough rounds, pressing edges firmly to seal. Crimp edges of each pie with fork. Cut three ½-inch slits in top of each pie and brush with remaining egg wash. Bake until crusts are golden brown, 22 to 26 minutes, rotating sheet halfway through baking. Transfer sheet to wire rack and let pies cool for 10 minutes. Using spatula, carefully transfer pies to wire rack and let cool completely, about 1 hour.

5. Whisk 2 tablespoons reserved cherry preserve liquid and confectioners' sugar together in small bowl until smooth. Let glaze sit until slightly thickened but still able to be drizzled, about 10 minutes. Adjust thickness with up to 1 teaspoon extra cherry liquid as needed. Drizzle pies with glaze and let sit for 10 minutes. Serve.

APPLE BUTTER PIE POPS

Serves 8 | 2 rimmed baking sheets

WHY THIS RECIPE WORKS Apple pie is a winner no matter what form it takes, from the biggest to the smallest (these pops). But making the best apple pie pops doesn't mean simply putting your favorite apple pie filling on a stick. For starters, peeling, chopping, and precooking were too much hassle for these petite pies. And leaking wasn't OK, whether in the oven or onto our shoes when taking a bite. Using apple butter for the filling addressed these concerns; it stayed thick through baking and offered warm-spiced, deep apple flavor that easily satisfied our apple pie cravings. But we found that apple butter was too sweet on its own; blending in a couple tablespoons of cream cheese added creaminess, richness, and tang. You can find lollipop and Popsicle sticks at most craft stores. To soften cream cheese, microwave it for 10 to 15 seconds. This recipe can be easily doubled.

⅓ cup plus 2 tablespoons apple butter
1 ounce cream cheese, softened
1 recipe single-crust pie dough (see pages 342–348)
8 (4- to 6-inch) lollipop or Popsicle sticks
1 large egg, lightly beaten with 1 tablespoon water

1. Stir apple butter and cream cheese together in small bowl until fully combined. Refrigerate until ready to use.

2. Roll dough into 15-inch circle on floured counter. Using 3-inch round biscuit or cookie cutter, cut 16 rounds from dough circle and transfer to parchment paper–lined rimmed baking sheet. Reserve dough scraps for another use. Cover rounds loosely with plastic wrap and refrigerate until firm but still pliable, about 10 minutes.

3. Line second rimmed baking sheet with parchment. Transfer 8 dough rounds to second prepared sheet, spaced evenly apart. Working with 1 dough round at a time, lay lollipop stick flat on top of dough with 1 end in center of dough round. Press stick firmly into dough. Mound 1 tablespoon apple butter mixture in center of each dough round on top of stick. Transfer sheet with filled rounds to freezer and chill for 10 minutes.

4. Adjust oven rack to upper-middle position and heat oven to 375 degrees. Brush edges of filled dough rounds with egg wash, then top with remaining chilled dough rounds, pressing edges firmly to seal. Crimp edges of each pie with fork. Cut three ½-inch slits in top of each pie and brush with remaining egg wash.

5. Bake until crusts are golden brown, 22 to 26 minutes, rotating sheet halfway through baking. Transfer sheet to wire rack and let pies cool for 10 minutes. Using spatula, carefully transfer pies to wire rack and let cool completely, about 1 hour. Serve.

CHILLED PIES

WHILE CHILLED PIES SUCH AS ICEBOX AND CHIFFON may have an old-fashioned charm, their ease and elegance make them as appealing as ever. For the most part, these pies feature no-bake fillings that set up in the refrigerator with the help of a thickener such as gelatin or cornstarch. Others get most of their structure from whipped egg whites or whipped cream. Finding that sweet spot in terms of texture—neither too soupy nor too dense but rather light yet sliceable—is one of the biggest challenges. Once fully chilled, the result should be a light, creamy, and smooth filling encased in a delicately crisp pastry shell or crunchy cookie crust. Because these pies require ample chilling time, they are make-ahead by nature, which means they are a great addition to a summer gathering or picnic. And for one of the easiest make-ahead desserts out there, it's hard to go wrong with a loaded ice cream pie.

KEY POINTS

Fillings are no-bake

Use combination of thickeners

Lightened with whipped cream
or egg whites

Chill each layer thoroughly

Icebox Pies

Icebox pies date back to the early 1800s in the American South, and they get their name from the iceboxes where they were traditionally kept cool. These recipes were easy and no-bake, which was a relief in the heat of summer. They feature cool, creamy fillings that range from simple (tart, bracing citrus) to decadent (rich peanut butter layered with chocolate, gooey caramel, and crunchy nuts) as well as an easy crumb crust made from cookies or graham crackers. Although they're traditionally made with egg whites, we have gone a couple routes to thickening our icebox fillings to the perfect, sliceable consistency. In each of the desserts, you need to turn on the oven only to bake the crust.

PICKING PECTIN FOR FRUIT

To create a filling for our Fresh Strawberry Pie (page 411) with just enough sticking power to hold the berries together gently, we turned to low-sugar pectin (often used in jam) and used it in combination with cornstarch (see page 341 for more information on types of thickeners). Both products work similarly: When combined with liquid, then heated and cooled, some of their molecules bond together, trapping water and creating a solid, jelly-like structure. But the strength and properties of the two structures differ. Amylose, one of two types of starch molecules in cornstarch, forms a weak structure that easily comes apart under the weight of heavy, juicy-filled strawberries. Low-sugar pectin (which, unlike regular pectin, gels without added sugar and acid) contains bigger molecules that form a firmer structure held together more forcefully by calcium ions. Once created, this matrix resists coming apart. When used independently, neither product resulted in a suitable icebox pie filling, but together they yielded just the right texture.

THROUGH THICK AND THIN

Many fruit icebox pies fail because they're overloaded with thickeners that either gum up the filling or never manage to thicken it at all.

Too Stiff
Thicken the filling with gelatin and the result resembles Jell-O.

Too Runny
Thicken the filling with cornstarch and the result typically turns out gloppy, dull-tasting, and still not firm enough.

Chiffon Pies

When they hit the dessert scene in the early 20th century, chiffon pies were a breakthrough idea. Chiffon pies start with a rich, creamy filling that is typically lightened with whipped egg whites or whipped cream to create its hallmark fluffy, mousse-like consistency. Not only is their filling particularly light and silky, but they come together quickly. Instead of require baking, they're set with gelatin and chilled in the refrigerator. The crust is a snap to make, too: Around the same time that chiffon pies became popular, so did crumb crusts—not only are they easy, but their crisp, delicate texture is the ideal complement to the billowy filling.

THICKENING CHIFFON

While many chiffon pies call for adding only one thickener—usually gelatin or cornstarch—others, such as our Lemon Chiffon Pie (page 413) and Strawberry Chiffon Pie (page 414) use two. Using both gelatin and cornstarch in moderation produces chiffon that sets up reliably but isn't rubbery. The proteins in a small amount of gelatin are enough to form a gel network, while the cornstarch acts as a filler that makes the network more stable without dulling the filling's fruity punch.

Ice Cream Pies

This one is pretty self-explanatory—and pretty delicious. The store-bought ice cream pies you might remember from childhood can't begin to compare with homemade versions, which couldn't be easier to make: Ice cream (or sorbet or gelato) is softened, maybe combined with mix-ins, and spread into a prebaked cookie crust. For pies with more than one layer, like our Coconut-Raspberry Gelato Pie (page 416), we find it's important to freeze the first layer before adding the next to ensure distinct elements. Top these pies with chopped nuts, sprinkles, or maraschino cherries and drizzle them with chocolate sauce for a sundae in sliceable form.

MIX-IN CREAMERY

Mix-ins such as cookie pieces, candy, and nuts are a simple and delicious way to add loads of flavor and texture to ice cream pie. Ice cream needs to be softened to a spreadable consistency before you can add it to the pie crust, but it's also much easier to add any mix-ins when the ice cream isn't straight from the freezer. Leaving the container out to soften results in an unevenly melted mess; instead, we like to transfer the ice cream to a bowl and soften it with a spatula.

SLICING CREAMY PIES

Ice cream pies, plus a number of other pies in this section from custard to icebox, have supercreamy fillings that will stick to the knife, making it difficult to cut neat slices. We like to dip our knife in a container of hot water or run it under a hot tap and quickly dry it before cutting so it glides through the pie. Wipe the knife clean before making another cut. Repeat heating the knife as needed.

ICEBOX KEY LIME PIE

Serves 8 to 10 | 9-inch pie plate

WHY THIS RECIPE WORKS Authentic Key lime pie recipes used to be simple and uncooked, but they contained raw eggs. We wanted to develop an eggless Key lime pie recipe as bright and custardy as the original. In lieu of using egg yolks, we found the right ratio of instant vanilla pudding, gelatin, and cream cheese to thicken our Icebox Key Lime Pie's filling into a perfect, smooth consistency. A full cup of fresh lime juice produced a pie with bracing lime flavor. Lime zest added another layer of flavor, and processing the zest with a little sugar offset its sourness and eliminated the annoying chewy bits. Use instant pudding, which requires no stovetop cooking, for this recipe. Do not be tempted to use bottled lime juice, which lacks depth of flavor.

¼ cup (1¾ ounces) sugar
1 tablespoon grated lime zest plus 1 cup juice (8 limes), divided
8 ounces cream cheese, softened
1 (14-ounce) can sweetened condensed milk
⅓ cup instant vanilla pudding mix
1¼ teaspoons unflavored gelatin
1 teaspoon vanilla extract
1 recipe Graham Cracker Crust (page 379), baked and cooled

1. Process sugar and zest in clean food processor until sugar turns bright green, about 30 seconds. Add cream cheese and process until combined, about 30 seconds. Add condensed milk and pudding mix and process until smooth, about 30 seconds. Scrape down sides of bowl. Sprinkle gelatin over 2 tablespoons lime juice in small bowl and let sit until gelatin softens, about 5 minutes. Heat in microwave for 15 seconds; stir until dissolved. With processor running, pour in gelatin mixture, remaining lime juice, and vanilla and mix until thoroughly combined, about 30 seconds.

2. Pour filling into cooled crust, cover with plastic wrap, and refrigerate for at least 3 hours or up to 2 days. To serve, let pie sit at room temperature for 10 minutes before slicing.

FRESH STRAWBERRY PIE

Serves 8 | 9-inch pie plate

WHY THIS RECIPE WORKS This pie of high-piled gleaming strawberries is an iconic diner dessert. What's the secret to preventing the berry mountain from tumbling? The thickener has to be just right; or rather, thickeners, as we soon discovered. Together, pectin and cornstarch—combined with a puree of some of the strawberries—produced a supple, lightly clingy glaze that held the berries together. To account for imperfect fruit, we call for several more ounces than will be used in the

Fresh Strawberry Pie

pie. If possible, seek out local, in-season berries. For fruit pectin, we recommend both Sure-Jell for Less or No Sugar Needed Recipes and Ball RealFruit Low or No-Sugar Needed Pectin. The pie is at its best after 2 hours of chilling; longer and the glaze becomes softer and wetter, though the pie will taste good.

1 recipe single-crust pie dough (see pages 342–348)
3 pounds strawberries, hulled (9 cups), divided
¾ cup (5¼ ounces) sugar
2 tablespoons cornstarch
1½ teaspoons low- or no-sugar needed fruit pectin
Pinch table salt
1 tablespoon lemon juice

1. Roll dough into 12-inch circle on floured counter. Loosely roll dough around rolling pin and gently unroll it onto 9-inch pie plate, letting excess dough hang over edge. Ease dough into plate by gently lifting edge of dough with your hand while pressing into plate bottom with your other hand.

2. Trim overhang to ½ inch beyond lip of plate. Tuck overhang under itself; folded edge should be flush with edge of plate. Crimp dough evenly around edge of plate. Wrap dough-lined plate loosely in plastic wrap and refrigerate until firm, about 30 minutes. Adjust oven rack to middle position and heat oven to 350 degrees.

3. Line chilled pie shell with double layer of aluminum foil, covering edges to prevent burning, and fill with pie weights. Bake on foil-lined rimmed baking sheet until edges are set and just beginning to turn golden, 25 to 30 minutes, rotating sheet halfway through baking. Remove foil and weights, rotate sheet, and continue to bake crust until golden brown and crisp, 10 to 15 minutes longer. Transfer sheet to wire rack and let cool completely, about 45 minutes.

4. Select 6 ounces misshapen, underripe, or otherwise unattractive berries, halving those that are large; you should have about 1½ cups. Process berries in food processor to smooth puree, 20 to 30 seconds, scraping down bowl as needed (you should have about ¾ cup puree). Whisk sugar, cornstarch, pectin, and salt together in medium saucepan. Stir in berry puree, making sure to scrape corners of pan. Bring to boil over medium-high heat, stirring constantly. Boil, scraping bottom and sides of pan to prevent scorching, for 2 minutes (mixture will appear frothy when it first reaches boil, then will darken and thicken with further cooking). Transfer glaze to large bowl and stir in lemon juice; let cool completely.

5. Meanwhile, pick over remaining berries and measure out 2 pounds of most attractive ones; halve only extra-large berries. Add berries to bowl with glaze and fold gently with rubber spatula until berries are evenly coated. Scoop berries into cooled crust, piling into mound. Turn any cut sides face down. If necessary, rearrange berries so that holes are filled and mound looks attractive. Refrigerate until chilled and set, at least 2 hours or up to 5 hours. Serve.

MISSISSIPPI MUD PIE

Serves 10 to 12 | 9-inch pie plate

WHY THIS RECIPE WORKS This intense chocolate pie is said to be named for the Mississippi River's silty bottom, but there's nothing muddy about its flavor or texture. We started by baking a chewy, gooey brownie layer in a chocolate cookie crust, using melted bittersweet chocolate and moisture-rich dark brown sugar and baking it until it was slightly underdone. Once this layer was chilled, we added our chocolate mousse. For a fluffy-yet-sliceable mixture, we replaced granulated sugar with starchier confectioners' sugar for more stability. We also made sure to let the chocolate cool to between 90 and 100 degrees before incorporating it—any warmer and it deflated the mousse. For a crunchy topping, we toasted chocolate wafer cookie pieces with melted butter, cocoa, and sugar and sprinkled them over the mousse layer to form a cookie streusel. Be sure to use milk chocolate in the mousse, as bittersweet chocolate will make the mousse too firm.

BROWNIE LAYER
- 4 ounces bittersweet chocolate, chopped fine
- 3 tablespoons unsalted butter
- 3 tablespoons vegetable oil
- 1½ tablespoons Dutch-processed cocoa powder
- ⅔ cup packed (4⅔ ounces) dark brown sugar
- 2 large eggs
- 2 teaspoons vanilla extract
- ¼ teaspoon table salt
- 3 tablespoons all-purpose flour
- 1 recipe Chocolate Cookie Crust (page 379), baked and cooled

TOPPING
- 10 chocolate wafer cookies (2 ounces)
- 2 tablespoons confectioners' sugar
- 1 tablespoon Dutch-processed cocoa powder
- ⅛ teaspoon table salt
- 2 tablespoons unsalted butter, melted

MOUSSE
- 6 ounces milk chocolate, chopped fine
- 1 cup heavy cream, chilled, divided
- 2 tablespoons Dutch-processed cocoa powder
- 2 tablespoons confectioners' sugar
- ⅛ teaspoon table salt

1. FOR THE BROWNIE LAYER: Adjust oven rack to middle position and heat oven to 325 degrees. Combine chocolate, butter, oil, and cocoa in bowl and microwave at 50 percent power, stirring often, until melted, about 1½ minutes. Whisk sugar, eggs, vanilla, and salt in second bowl until smooth. Whisk in chocolate mixture until incorporated. Whisk in flour until just combined.

2. Pour brownie batter into crust. Bake pie until edges begin to set and toothpick inserted in center comes out with thin coating of batter attached, about 15 minutes. Do not turn off oven. Transfer pie to wire rack and let cool for 1 hour, then refrigerate until fully chilled, about 1 hour longer.

3. FOR THE TOPPING: While pie cools, line rimmed baking sheet with parchment paper. Place cookies in zipper-lock bag, press out air, and seal bag. Using rolling pin, crush cookies into ½- to ¾-inch pieces. Combine sugar, cocoa, salt, and crushed cookies in bowl. Stir in melted butter until mixture is moistened and clumps begin to form. Spread crumbs in even layer on prepared sheet and bake until fragrant, about 10 minutes, shaking sheet to break up crumbs halfway through baking. Transfer sheet to wire rack and let cool completely.

4. FOR THE MOUSSE: Once brownie layer has fully chilled, microwave chocolate in large bowl at 50 percent power, stirring often, until melted, 1½ to 2 minutes. Let cool until just barely warm and registers between 90 and 100 degrees, about 10 minutes.

Mississippi Mud Pie

chiffon. Our graham cracker crust added just a hint of flavor and made a crisp contrast to the soft and fluffy filling. Before cooking the curd mixture, be sure to whisk thoroughly so that no clumps of cornstarch or streaks of egg white remain. Pasteurized egg whites can be substituted for the three raw egg whites, but you will need to increase the whipping time. Serve with Whipped Cream (page 548).

  1 teaspoon unflavored gelatin, divided
  4 tablespoons water, divided
  5 large eggs (2 whole, 3 separated), divided
1¼ cups (8¾ ounces) sugar, divided
  1 tablespoon cornstarch
 ⅛ teaspoon table salt
  1 tablespoon grated lemon zest plus ¾ cup juice (4 lemons)
 ¼ cup heavy cream
  1 recipe Graham Cracker Crust (page 379), baked and cooled
  4 ounces cream cheese, cut into ½-inch pieces, softened

1. Sprinkle ½ teaspoon gelatin over 2 tablespoons water in small bowl and let sit until gelatin softens, about 5 minutes. Repeat with second small bowl, remaining ½ teaspoon gelatin, and remaining 2 tablespoons water.

2. Whisk 2 eggs and 3 yolks in medium saucepan until thoroughly combined. Whisk in 1 cup sugar, cornstarch, and salt until well combined. Whisk in lemon zest and juice and heavy cream. Cook over medium-low heat, stirring constantly, until thickened and slightly translucent, 4 to 5 minutes (mixture should register 170 degrees). Stir in 1 water-gelatin mixture until dissolved. Remove pan from heat and let stand for 2 minutes.

3. Remove 1¼ cups curd from pan and pour through fine-mesh strainer set in bowl. Transfer strained curd to cooled crust (do not wash out strainer or bowl). Place filled crust in freezer. Add remaining water-gelatin mixture and cream cheese to remaining curd in pan and whisk to combine. (If cream cheese does not melt, briefly return pan to low heat.) Pour through strainer into now-empty bowl.

4. Using stand mixer fitted with whisk attachment, whip 3 egg whites on medium-low speed until foamy, about 2 minutes. Increase speed to medium-high and slowly add remaining ¼ cup sugar. Continue whipping until whites are stiff and glossy, about 4 minutes. Add curd–cream cheese mixture and whip on medium speed until few streaks remain, about 30 seconds. Remove bowl from mixer and, using spatula, scrape sides of bowl and stir mixture until no streaks remain. Remove pie shell from freezer and carefully pour chiffon over curd, allowing chiffon to mound slightly in center. Refrigerate for at least 4 hours or up to 2 days before serving.

5. Microwave 3 tablespoons cream in small bowl until it registers between 105 and 110 degrees, about 15 seconds. Whisk in cocoa until combined. Combine cocoa-cream mixture, sugar, salt, and remaining cream in bowl of stand mixer. Fit mixer with whisk attachment and whip cream mixture on medium speed until beginning to thicken, about 30 seconds, scraping down bowl as needed. Increase speed to high and whip until soft peaks form, 30 seconds to 1 minute.

6. Using whisk, fold one-third of whipped cream mixture into melted chocolate to lighten. Using rubber spatula, fold in remaining whipped cream mixture until no dark streaks remain. Spoon mousse into chilled pie and spread evenly from edge to edge. Sprinkle with cooled topping and refrigerate for at least 3 hours or up to 8 hours. Serve.

LEMON CHIFFON PIE

Serves 8 to 10 | 9-inch pie plate

WHY THIS RECIPE WORKS We love the elegant simplicity of lemon chiffon pie but found the amount of gelatin used in most recipes difficult to work with. We used a combination of cornstarch and gelatin to get a creamy pie and added a burst of lemon flavor by tucking a layer of lemon curd beneath the

Strawberry Chiffon Pie

STRAWBERRY CHIFFON PIE

Serves 8 | 9-inch pie plate

WHY THIS RECIPE WORKS For a light and fluffy chiffon pie with fresh berry flavor, we started with our own strawberry puree, which we strained for a silky-smooth texture. The traditional gelatin supplemented with cornstarch resulted in chiffon that was firmly set and sliceable without being bouncy. Whipped egg whites contributed lift, but for richness we also added whipped cream. After folding the whipped cream into the berry–egg white mixture, we poured the enriched filling into the crust, and chilled it; the result was a fluffy filling with a velvety texture from the added fat. To strengthen the berry flavor while also adding visual appeal, we folded sliced strawberries into the filling right before pouring it into the crust. Finally, a crunchy, buttery crumb crust made from store-bought shortbread cookies was the perfect foil for the cool, creamy filling. You will need about 3 pints of fresh strawberries. Pasteurized egg whites can be substituted for the raw egg whites, but you will need to increase the whipping time.

CRUST

1 (5.3-ounce) box shortbread cookies, broken into 1-inch pieces
2 tablespoons sugar
¼ teaspoon table salt
½ cup slivered almonds, toasted
2 tablespoons unsalted butter, melted

FILLING

2 teaspoons unflavored gelatin
2 tablespoons water
12 ounces strawberries, hulled (2½ cups), plus 8 ounces strawberries, hulled, halved, and sliced thin (1⅓ cups)
¾ cup (5¼ ounces) plus 2 tablespoons sugar, divided
2 tablespoons cornstarch
¼ teaspoon table salt
2 tablespoons lemon juice
2 large egg whites
⅛ teaspoon cream of tartar
½ cup heavy cream, chilled

1. FOR THE CRUST: Adjust oven rack to middle position and heat oven to 325 degrees. Grease 9-inch pie plate. Process cookies, sugar, and salt in food processor until finely ground, about 1 minute. Add almonds and pulse until coarsely chopped, about 8 pulses. Add melted butter and pulse until combined, about 10 pulses. Transfer crumb mixture to pie plate. Using bottom of dry measuring cup, press crumbs evenly into bottom and up sides of plate. Bake until crust is golden brown, 18 to 20 minutes, rotating plate halfway through baking. Let crust cool completely on wire rack, about 30 minutes. (Crust can be wrapped in plastic wrap and stored at room temperature for up to 24 hours.)

2. FOR THE FILLING: Sprinkle gelatin over water in small bowl and let sit until gelatin softens, about 5 minutes. Process whole strawberries in food processor until completely smooth, about 1 minute. Transfer to fine-mesh strainer set over medium bowl and press on solids to extract 1 cup juice; discard solids. Whisk strawberry juice, ¾ cup sugar, cornstarch, and salt together in small saucepan.

3. Bring juice mixture to simmer over medium heat, stirring constantly. Cook until slightly thickened, about 1 minute. Off heat, whisk in gelatin mixture until dissolved. Transfer to large bowl, stir in lemon juice, and let cool completely, about 30 minutes, stirring occasionally.

4. Using stand mixer fitted with whisk attachment, whip egg whites and cream of tartar on medium-low speed until foamy, about 1 minute. Increase speed to medium-high and whip whites to soft, billowy mounds, about 1 minute. Gradually add remaining 2 tablespoons sugar and whip until glossy, stiff peaks form, 2 to 3 minutes. Whisk one-third of meringue into cooled strawberry mixture until smooth. Fold remaining meringue into strawberry mixture until only few white streaks remain.

5. In now-empty mixer bowl, whip cream on medium-low speed until foamy, about 1 minute. Increase speed to high and whip until stiff peaks form, 1 to 3 minutes. Gently fold whipped cream into strawberry mixture until no white streaks remain. Fold in sliced strawberries. Spoon filling into crust and spread into even layer using back of spoon. Refrigerate pie for at least 3 hours or up to 24 hours. Serve.

FRENCH SILK CHOCOLATE PIE

Serves 8 | 9-inch pie plate

WHY THIS RECIPE WORKS French silk pie is a retro no-bake pie that's lighter and less dense than chocolate cream pie, but silky-smooth and packed with richness. Rather than use raw eggs for volume and richness, we cooked the eggs with sugar on the stovetop—whipping them in the process—until the mixture was light and thick. Off the heat, we continued whipping the mixture until it was cooled. However, this filling was much too dense when we beat in the two sticks of softened butter we were using. Cutting the amount of butter in half gave our filling a silkier texture. Bittersweet chocolate, folded into the cooled egg and sugar mixture, boosted the chocolate flavor better than milder varieties. And to lighten the pie, we incorporated whipped cream into the filling before spooning it into the pie shell. We like to serve this pie with Whipped Cream (page 548) and chocolate curls.

    1 recipe single-crust pie dough (see pages 342–348)
    1 cup heavy cream, chilled
    3 large eggs
    ¾ cup (5¼ ounces) sugar
    2 tablespoons water
    8 ounces bittersweet chocolate, melted and cooled
    1 tablespoon vanilla extract
    8 tablespoons unsalted butter, cut into ½-inch pieces
       and softened

1. Roll dough into 12-inch circle on floured counter. Loosely roll dough around rolling pin and gently unroll it onto 9-inch pie plate, letting excess dough hang over edge. Ease dough into plate by gently lifting edge of dough with your hand while pressing into plate bottom with your other hand.

2. Trim overhang to ½ inch beyond lip of plate. Tuck overhang under itself; folded edge should be flush with edge of plate. Crimp dough evenly around edge of plate. Wrap dough-lined plate loosely in plastic wrap and refrigerate until firm, about 30 minutes. Adjust oven rack to middle position and heat oven to 350 degrees.

3. Line chilled pie shell with double layer of aluminum foil, covering edges to prevent burning, and fill with pie weights. Bake on foil-lined rimmed baking sheet until edges are set and just beginning to turn golden, 25 to 30 minutes, rotating sheet halfway through baking. Remove foil and weights, rotate sheet, and continue to bake crust until golden brown and crisp, 10 to 15 minutes longer. Transfer sheet to wire rack and let cool completely, about 30 minutes.

4. Using handheld mixer set at medium-high speed, whip cream to stiff peaks, 2 to 3 minutes. Refrigerate until ready to use.

5. Combine eggs, sugar, and water in large heatproof bowl set over saucepan filled with 1 inch barely simmering water, making sure that water does not touch bottom of bowl. Using handheld mixer on medium speed, beat until egg mixture is thickened and registers 160 degrees, 7 to 10 minutes. Remove bowl from heat and continue to beat until egg mixture is fluffy and cooled completely, about 8 minutes.

6. Add chocolate and vanilla to egg mixture and beat until incorporated. Beat in butter, a few pieces at a time, until incorporated. Using rubber spatula, fold in refrigerated whipped cream until no white streaks remain. Transfer filling to cooled crust, smoothing top with spatula. Refrigerate, uncovered, until set, at least 3 hours. Serve.

PEANUT BUTTER PIE

Serves 8 | 9-inch pie plate

WHY THIS RECIPE WORKS Smooth, creamy peanut butter seems like a natural filling for pie, but keeping its flavor strong and nutty while creating a light, almost airy texture from the dense spread took some finessing. We started by whipping smooth peanut butter with cream cheese (for tang and to aid sliceability), confectioners' sugar, and a touch of cream, which loosened the mixture just enough for a fluffy consistency; folding in some whipped cream lightened the filling even further. Sweet honey roasted peanuts sprinkled directly onto the crust added good flavor and crunch; we then layered in the filling and topped the whole thing with still more whipped cream and a second dose of crunchy nuts. All-natural peanut butters will work in this recipe. You can use our homemade Candied Nuts (page 551) with peanuts in place of the honey roasted peanuts for even deeper flavor and more crunch.

    ½ cup honey roasted peanuts, chopped, divided
    1 recipe Graham Cracker Crust (page 379),
       baked and cooled
    ¾ cup (3 ounces) plus 2 tablespoons confectioners'
       sugar, divided
    ¾ cup creamy peanut butter
    6 ounces cream cheese, softened
    1¾ cups heavy cream, divided
    1 teaspoon vanilla extract

1. Spread ⅓ cup peanuts evenly over bottom of crust.

2. Using stand mixer fitted with whisk attachment, mix ¾ cup sugar, peanut butter, cream cheese, and 3 tablespoons cream on low speed until combined, about 1 minute. Increase speed to medium-high and whip until fluffy, about 1 minute. Transfer to large bowl; set aside.

3. In now-empty mixer bowl, whip ¾ cup cream on medium-low speed until foamy, about 1 minute. Increase speed to high and whip until stiff peaks form, 1 to 3 minutes. Gently fold whipped cream into peanut butter mixture in 2 additions until no white streaks remain. Spoon filling into crust and spread into even layer with spatula.

4. In now-empty mixer bowl, whip vanilla, remaining cream, and remaining 2 tablespoons sugar on medium-low speed until foamy, about 1 minute. Increase speed to high and whip until stiff peaks form, 1 to 3 minutes. Spread whipped cream attractively over pie. Refrigerate until set, about 2 hours. Sprinkle with remaining peanuts. Serve.

COOKIES AND CREAM ICE CREAM PIE

Serves 8 | 9-inch pie plate

WHY THIS RECIPE WORKS This ice cream pie is as tasty as it is whimsical. We used crushed sugar cones to make the crust, turning an ice cream cone into a plated affair. The flavor was a better match for the ice cream than the more conventional graham cracker crust, and it didn't overshadow the texture of the cookies in the pie the way a chocolate cookie crust would. We made our own cookies-and-cream ice cream by adding crushed Oreos to ice cream that we softened in a bowl with a spatula. This allowed us to control the size of the cookie pieces for appealing texture. We like to serve the pie with Classic Hot Fudge Sauce (page 548) for a sundae-like effect.

12 sugar cones
 5 tablespoons unsalted butter, melted
 2 tablespoons sugar
 2 pints vanilla ice cream
 2 cups coarsely chopped Oreo cookies
 2 cups Whipped Cream (page 548)

1. Adjust oven rack to middle position and heat oven to 350 degrees. Process sugar cones in food processor to fine crumbs, about 30 seconds. (You should have 1⅓ cups.) Transfer crumbs to bowl and stir in melted butter and sugar until crumbs are moistened. Press crumb mixture evenly against bottom and sides of 9-inch pie plate, compacting it with your fingertips. Bake crust until crisp, 6 to 8 minutes. Let crust cool completely on wire rack, about 30 minutes. (Crust can be wrapped in plastic wrap and frozen for up to 1 month.)

2. Scoop ice cream into bowl and work with rubber spatula to soften. Add Oreos to bowl and mash mixture with back of spoon until well combined. Spread ice cream mixture into crust in even layer. Place plastic directly on surface of ice cream and freeze until completely frozen, at least 4 hours or up to 1 week.

3. Cut pie into wedges and dollop each piece with whipped cream. Serve.

COCONUT-RASPBERRY GELATO PIE

Serves 8 | 9-inch pie plate

WHY THIS RECIPE WORKS Kids may love ice cream pie, but ice cream pie isn't just for kids; we wanted to make an easy yet sophisticated version using store-bought ingredients, for a layered ice cream pie with complex flavors. Our graham cracker crust was an easy starting point. And for a refreshing twist, we paired a sweet-tart sorbet with coconut gelato for contrasting richness. We spread an even layer of sorbet into the crust followed by the gelato; mashing some fresh raspberries into the gelato allowed the two flavors to meld. Toasted and chopped macadamia nuts sprinkled on top gave a nod to tropical flavors and contributed crunch. We like the rich texture and bold flavor of coconut gelato in this recipe. You can use coconut ice cream in place of gelato in this recipe, but it may be a little icy. Serve the pie with Classic Hot Fudge Sauce (page 548), if desired.

 1 cup raspberry sorbet
 1 recipe Graham Cracker Crust (page 379), baked and cooled
 1 pint coconut gelato
7½ ounces (1½ cups) raspberries, divided
 ½ cup macadamia nuts, toasted and chopped

1. Scoop raspberry sorbet into bowl and work with rubber spatula to soften. Spread raspberry sorbet into crust in even layer. Transfer to freezer while making coconut layer.

2. Scoop coconut gelato into clean bowl and work with rubber spatula to soften. Stir in 1 cup raspberries, mashing mixture with spatula until well combined. Remove pie from freezer and spread gelato mixture over sorbet in even layer. Place plastic wrap directly on surface of gelato and freeze until filling is completely frozen, at least 4 hours or up to 1 week.

3. Let pie sit at room temperature for 30 minutes. Halve remaining ½ cup raspberries, then sprinkle raspberries and macadamia nuts over top of pie. Serve.

Coconut-Raspberry
Gelato Pie

PART 06

tarts

TAKE THE TOP OFF A PIE AND REFINE IT, build it low, make It lush, and you have a tart. Is that all? While pies and tarts share some techniques and some fillings, the elegant tart is a category of dessert in its own right, not just a modified pie partner.

Tarts are centerpiece desserts for special occasions. The idea of tarts as refined likely comes from classic French-style tarts with fluted sides, a short-crust pastry, and a restrained filling—that is, one that doesn't bubble over the sides with fruit juices or sweet caramel but rather is level with the sides and doesn't spill the least bit out of its anchoring crust when the tart is sliced. The filling might be creamy and rich, like a curd or custard, and baked in sync with the tart shell or added after the shell is baked, like a pastry cream. Or the shell can be topped with a modest amount of delicate fruit. With a pie, usually the filling is the story, recipes often decoding how to pile it high without affecting the crust. With a French-style tart, the filling-to-crust ratio is 1 to 1; the buttery, sometimes sweet, crisp crust is an equal player adding character and crunch to the smooth filling.

But tarts aren't always buttoned up. A picture window of flaky dough surrounds oven-baked ruby fruits in galettes for a free-form rustic feel. This still feels like a feature presentation dessert but is easier than a pie to put together. Caramel-painted fruits dribbling perfumed juice sit atop the crust for the French tarte tatin. Puff pastry tarts require less engineering: Some store-bought puff pastry is dessert when it's covered with whipped toppings or roasted fruit. Small-er-size tartlets have a cute playfulness—and take tarts away from the center of the table. These examples show that tarts cover a range of baking abilities, and you'll be the star of the after-dinner show with any one of them.

Many equipment pieces used for tarts are also used for pies (see page 340): rolling pins for shaping dough, a fine-mesh strainer for straining custards and curds, and pie weights for baking. A cake equipment item, a large offset spatula, has a surprising use as an able tool for moving a tart crust from its pan to the platter in one piece. But there's one piece of equipment below that you'll use only for French-style tarts.

Tart Pan

Shallow, fluted tart pans give a home baker's tart a sophisticated look. You should only consider a pan with a removable bottom. It's nearly impossible to chisel a tart out of a solid pan. A nonstick surface helps removal further—its darker interior also holds heat to give your tart a more golden hue. A pan with sharply fluted sides looks best. Our favorite is the **Mafter Steel Non-stick Tart Mold with Removable Bottom** ($27). It is a standard 9 inches, although you may want to invest in 10- and 11-inch pans for specialty recipes like Linzertorte (page 436).

You might also invest in a set of 4-inch tart (tartlet) pans (also go for ones with removable bottoms) if you like the idea of making the individual-size tartlets on pages 460–462. They'll make dessert cute while keeping it elegant with no broken crusts.

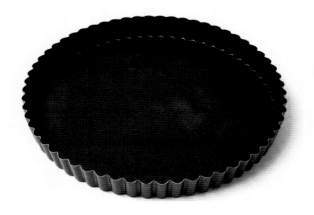

TART PAN SUBSTITUTE

A round tart pan's removable bottom allows you to turn out beautiful crusts without marring the sides. But what if you want to get baking before you own one? We tried various options, including cutting out the bottom of a disposable aluminum pan, but our favorite hack for both press-in and roll-out crusts was a 9-inch springform pan. Its removable collar helped release both crusts without damaging them. And the smooth-sided tarts were just as elegant as those with a flute. Here's how we fit the pans with dough.

FOR A PRESS-IN CRUST Pat dough into pan (with collar fastened), pressing dough 1 inch up sides to approximate height of sides of tart pan, and bake as directed.

FOR A ROLL-OUT CRUST Roll dough into circle approximately 2 inches larger than size of pan and about ¼ inch thick. Gently ease dough into springform pan with collar closed but unfastened. Once dough is fitted into pan, snap collar shut and trim edge to 1-inch height using paring knife.

COOLING AND STORING

Because tarts house much less filling than pies (and the fillings are firm and do all of their thickening and setting through precooking or baking with the tart in oven), tarts generally cool in a shorter time frame, in 1 to 3 hours.

Tarts can be a bit more ephemeral than pies—eat them as soon as you can for them to be at their best, as the crust can soften from contact with the moist filling. A tart that consists of a cooked filling like pastry cream added to a baked tart shell can be more of a make-ahead dessert. You can store the crust, wrapped, at room temperature, and pastry creams do well in the refrigerator for a couple days; fill the tart and top with fresh ingredients just before serving. If you are refrigerating a whole completed tart, you can try placing it on a platter and improvising a cover with an overturned springform pan big enough. A galette, with fruit baked within, stores like a fruit pie—room temperature is OK for a couple of days.

PARSING TARTS

Each category of tart gets its moments of distinction in the pages that follow; however, we recognize that the steps and components of these categories are a bit more varied than those of other categories of desserts. (A pie for example, no matter if a fruit, custard, or sugar pie, will always be round and have a supporting crust baked in a pie pan—how you fill it or top it largely defines it.) Keep the different types of crusts, different fillings, and different vessels straight with this handy at-a-glance tart comparison.

	ALTERNATIVE NAMES	CRUST	FILLING	VESSEL	BAKING TECHNIQUE	POSSIBLE TOPPINGS
Shortcrust Pastry Tart	French tart Tarte	Pâte sucrée (sweetened shortbread-like dough)	Pastry cream Baked custard Frangipane Ganache Curd	Tart pan	Parbake or bake crust, then fill and bake or serve	Thinned jam Confectioners' sugar
Galette	Crostata Free-form tart Open-faced tart	Pie pastry	Fresh fruit	Baking sheet	Wrap fruit with pastry and bake	Whipped cream Ice cream Caramel drizzle
Puff Pastry Tart	Open-faced tart	Puff pastry	Pastry cream or other cool, creamy filling	Baking sheet	Bake pastry shell, then fill	Fresh fruit Roasted fruit Nuts and chocolate
Tarte Tatin	Upside-down tart	Puff pastry Pie pastry	Fruit and caramel	Skillet	Cook fruit, top with dough, bake	Crème fraîche Whipped cream Ice cream
Tartlets	Individual tarts Miniature tarts	Pâte sucrée Pie pastry	Pastry cream Baked custard Frangipane Ganache Curd Fruit	Tartlet pans Baking sheet Muffin tin	Various	Various

SHORTCRUST PASTRY TARTS

Crust is shortbread-like, not flaky
Almost equal ratio of crust to filling
Bake on baking sheet
Remove from pan with care

C'EST FRANÇAIS: The elegant fluted tarts that gleam from behind the glass of Parisian bakeries are defined by the buttery, sandy crust they sport. This is sure to sell their appeal: They're kind of like a big filled cookie, a buttery shortbread that's a hint sweet. That makes shortcrust pastry (or pâte sucrée) a rich contrast to punchy fillings like lemon curd or a match for caramel or custard tarts, drawing out those fillings' buttery flavors. While ultracreamy pastry cream dotted with jam-dribbled fruit (see page 427) is a classic tart shell filling after baking, oftentimes curd (see page 428), custard (see page 434), or nut (see page 428) fillings get baked with the tart. No matter the filling, it has equal presence as the crust, sitting neatly and evenly within its walls, so executing the pastry well matters (see page 424).

Tarts with a shortcrust pastry are often baked in a fluted tart pan (see page 420), and that's what we use in all of our recipes to minimize the specialty equipment you need, although you will find straight-sided tarts in the wild (and you can even use a springform pan; see page 225). Removing a tart from the pan can pose an interesting challenge: You have to slip it out of its pan encasing and slide it onto a platter in one piece. We have tricks that remove the challenge from these steps.

As with most desserts, you should rotate tarts midway through the baking time. Because the crusts are often crumbly and the pans lack edges to grip, you'll want to bake all tarts of this variety on a baking sheet. The tart fillings in our recipes are versatile. Try a chocolate dough where you like. Or choose one of the gluten-free fillings and fill the provided gluten-free tart shell.

PROTECT THE EDGES

Sometimes the edges of a tart shell can burn before the bottom is cooked through and nicely browned. You can cut a circle from a sheet of aluminum foil and place it over the endangered crust with the edges covered. The tart can continue to bake without further coloring of the edges.

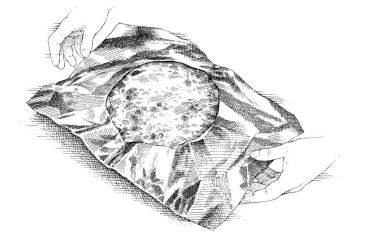

TART UNMOLDING MADE EASY

Lifting up the removable pan bottom with your hand can cause the ring to slide down your arm like a hula hoop. To remove the ring easily, you can try placing a wide can, such as a 28-ounce tomato can, on the counter and setting the cooled tart pan on top of the can. Hold the pan ring and gently pull it downward to safely remove it.

TART TO TABLE

We do not recommend using a pan without a removable bottom. And you should use nonstick if you can (see page 420). But even with these assists, removing a tart without creating a crack is easier if you follow these steps.

1. Let tart cool completely on sheet on wire rack.

2. Remove outer ring of tart pan (see above for a trick).

3. Slide thin metal spatula between tart and tart pan bottom.

4. Carefully slide tart onto serving platter.

Making Shortcrust Dough

Don't let tarts make you tart. We provide instruction on mixing the doughs, rolling them, and fitting pâte sucrée and its variations into or on the pan.

CLASSIC TART DOUGH
Makes one 9-inch tart crust

Classic tart crust is a shortcrust pastry; it should be fine-textured, buttery-rich, crisp, and crumbly. (Unsurprisingly, it's often described as shortbread-like.) And this crust should handle the spotlight. Using a whole stick of butter made tart dough that tasted great and was easy to handle, yet still had a delicate crumb. Instead of using the hard-to-find superfine sugar and pastry flour that many recipes call for, we used confectioners' sugar (the finest of the fine) combined with all-purpose flour to achieve a crisp texture. After rolling, we had ample dough to patch any holes. You need only to lightly flour the counter when rolling out this supple dough.

- 1 large egg yolk
- 1 tablespoon heavy cream
- ½ teaspoon vanilla extract
- 1¼ cups (6¼ ounces) all-purpose flour
- ⅔ cup (2⅔ ounces) confectioners' sugar
- ¼ teaspoon table salt
- 8 tablespoons unsalted butter, cut into ¼-inch pieces and chilled

1. Whisk egg yolk, cream, and vanilla together in bowl. Process flour, sugar, and salt in food processor until combined, about 5 seconds. Scatter butter over top and pulse until mixture resembles coarse cornmeal, about 15 pulses. With processor running, add egg yolk mixture and continue to process until dough just comes together around processor blade, about 12 seconds.

2. Transfer dough to sheet of plastic wrap and form into 6-inch disk. Wrap tightly in plastic and refrigerate for at least 1 hour or up to 2 days. Let chilled dough sit on counter to soften slightly, about 10 minutes, before rolling. (Wrapped dough can be frozen for up to 1 month. If frozen, let dough thaw completely on counter before rolling.)

Chocolate Tart Dough
Substitute ¼ cup Dutch-processed cocoa powder for ¼ cup flour.

Making Classic Tart Dough

1. Process flour, sugar, and salt in food processor until combined, about 5 seconds. Scatter butter over top and pulse until mixture resembles coarse cornmeal, about 15 pulses.

2. Add egg yolk mixture and continue to process until dough just comes together around processor blade, about 12 seconds. Form dough into 6-inch disk and refrigerate.

3. Let dough sit on counter to soften slightly, about 10 minutes. Roll dough into 11-inch circle on floured counter. Refrigerate dough for 30 minutes.

4. Loosely roll dough around rolling pin and gently unroll it onto tart pan, letting excess dough hang over edge.

5. Lift dough and gently press it into corners and fluted sides of pan.

6. Run rolling pin over top of pan to remove any excess dough. Freeze until dough is fully chilled and firm, about 30 minutes.

VEGAN TART DOUGH
Makes one 9-inch tart crust

While tart crusts typically get their shortbread-like texture from butter, we achieved the same effect using melted coconut oil plus a little water. The water replaced the moisture that butter contains and prevented a crumbly crust. The texture of our vegan tart dough requires its own set of steps for fitting it into the pan. If you are a strict vegan, use organic sugar.

1¾ cups (8¾ ounces) all-purpose flour
3 tablespoons sugar
¼ teaspoon table salt
½ cup refined coconut oil, melted and cooled slightly
3 tablespoons water

1. Whisk flour, sugar, and salt together in bowl. Add melted oil and water and stir with rubber spatula until dough forms.

2. Transfer dough to sheet of plastic wrap and form into 6-inch disk. Wrap tightly in plastic and refrigerate for at least 1 hour or up to 2 days. (Wrapped dough can be frozen for up to 2 months. If frozen, let dough thaw completely on counter before rolling.)

Shaping Vegan Tart Dough

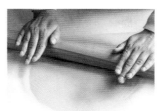

1. Roll dough into 12-inch circle between 2 large sheets of parchment paper.

2. Remove top sheet of parchment and gently invert dough onto tart pan. Center dough over pan letting excess dough hang over edge. Remove parchment.

3. Lift dough and gently press it into corners and fluted sides of pan.

4. Run rolling pin over top of pan to remove any excess dough.

5. Prick dough all over with fork, then wrap pan loosely in plastic wrap and refrigerate for at least 30 minutes or up to 24 hours.

GLUTEN-FREE TART DOUGH
Makes one 9-inch tart crust

Many tart fillings are naturally gluten-free so if you need a gluten-free dessert, you can easily use this dough to hold the filling. Simply substituting a gluten-free flour blend for all-purpose flour made a tart dough that was too sweet (the rice flour found in these blends has a distinct sweetness) and too fragile. Adding xanthan gum helped reinforce the structure, but our tart shell was still too crumbly and too sweet. In the end we found that using a mix of confectioners' sugar and brown sugar did the trick. We strongly recommend that you weigh your ingredients, as the ratios of ingredients are integral to successful gluten-free baking. Our gluten-free tart dough is softer than traditional dough; you will need to roll it out between sheets of plastic wrap. Rolling and shaping is also a bit different than the recipe steps for classic tart dough, so we've included steps you can follow here.

1	large egg yolk
½	teaspoon vanilla extract
7	ounces (1⅓ cups plus ¼ cup) all-purpose gluten-free flour blend (see page 2)
2⅓	ounces (⅓ cup packed) light brown sugar
1	ounce (¼ cup) confectioners' sugar
1	teaspoon xanthan gum (see page 2)
¼	teaspoon table salt
8	tablespoons unsalted butter, cut into ¼-inch pieces and chilled
2	teaspoons ice water

1. Whisk egg yolk and vanilla together in bowl. Process flour blend, brown sugar, confectioners' sugar, xanthan gum, and salt in food processor until combined, about 5 seconds. Scatter butter over top and pulse until mixture resembles coarse cornmeal, about 10 pulses.

2. With processor running, add egg yolk mixture and continue to process until dough just comes together around processor blade, about 15 seconds. Add 1 teaspoon ice water and pulse until dough comes together. If dough does not come together, add remaining 1 teaspoon ice water and pulse until dough comes together.

3. Transfer dough to sheet of plastic wrap and form into 6-inch disk. Wrap tightly in plastic and refrigerate for at least 1 hour or up to 2 days. (Wrapped dough can be frozen for up to 2 months. If frozen, let dough thaw completely on counter before rolling.)

Shaping Gluten-Free Tart Dough

1. Roll dough into 12-inch circle between 2 sheets of plastic wrap. Slide onto baking sheet, then carefully remove top sheet.

2. Place tart pan, bottom side up, in center of dough and press gently so that sharp edge of tart pan cuts dough.

3. Holding tart pan in place, pick up baking sheet and carefully flip it over so that tart pan is right side up on counter. Remove baking sheet and peel off plastic.

4. Run rolling pin over edges of tart pan to cut dough completely. Gently ease and press dough into bottom of pan, reserving scraps.

5. Roll dough scraps into ½-inch-thick rope, line edge of tart pan with rope, and gently press into fluted sides.

6. Line tart pan with plastic and, using measuring cup, gently press and smooth dough to even thickness (sides should be ¼ inch thick). Trim any excess dough with paring knife.

FRESH FRUIT TART

Serves 8 to 10 | 9-inch tart pan

WHY THIS RECIPE WORKS As they sit glistening in the windows and glass cases of patisseries, fresh fruit tarts are things of beauty. For ours, we filled the tart with pastry cream thickened with just enough cornstarch to keep its shape during slicing. The finishing touch: a drizzle with a jelly glaze on perfectly placed fruit. Once filled, the tart should be served within 30 minutes. Don't wash the berries or they will lose their flavor and shape.

PASTRY CREAM

- 2 cups half-and-half
- ½ cup (3½ ounces) granulated sugar
- Pinch salt
- 5 large egg yolks
- 3 tablespoons cornstarch
- 4 tablespoons unsalted butter, cut into 4 pieces
- 1½ teaspoons vanilla extract

- 1 recipe tart dough (see pages 424–426)

FRUIT AND GLAZE

- 2 large kiwis, peeled, halved lengthwise, and cut crosswise into ⅜-inch-thick slices
- 10 ounces (2 cups) raspberries
- 5 ounces (1 cup) blueberries
- ½ cup apple jelly

1. FOR THE PASTRY CREAM: Bring half-and-half, 6 tablespoons sugar, and salt to simmer in medium saucepan over medium heat, stirring occasionally.

2. As half-and-half mixture begins to simmer, whisk egg yolks, cornstarch, and remaining 2 tablespoons sugar in medium bowl until smooth. Whisking constantly, slowly add 1 cup half-and-half mixture to yolk mixture. Then, whisking constantly, slowly return tempered yolk mixture to half-and-half mixture in saucepan. Cook, whisking vigorously, until mixture is thickened and a few bubbles burst on surface, about 30 seconds. Off heat, whisk in butter and vanilla. Transfer mixture to clean bowl, press sheet of plastic wrap directly on surface, and refrigerate pastry cream until chilled and firm, about 3 hours. (Pastry cream can be refrigerated for up to 2 days.)

3. Roll dough into 11-inch circle on floured counter, then transfer to parchment paper–lined rimmed baking sheet; cover loosely with plastic wrap and refrigerate until firm but pliable, about 10 minutes.

4. Loosely roll dough around rolling pin and gently unroll it onto 9-inch tart pan with removable bottom, letting excess dough hang over edge. Ease dough into pan by gently lifting edge of dough with your hand while pressing into corners and fluted sides of pan

Fresh Fruit Tart

with your other hand. Run rolling pin over top of pan to remove any excess dough. Wrap loosely in plastic, place on large plate, and freeze until fully chilled and firm, about 30 minutes. (Dough-lined tart pan can be frozen for up to 1 month.)

5. Adjust oven rack to middle position and heat oven to 375 degrees. Set dough-lined pan on rimmed baking sheet. Spray 1 side of double layer of aluminum foil with vegetable oil spray. Press foil, sprayed side down, into pan, covering edges to prevent burning; fill with pie weights. Bake until tart shell is golden brown and set, about 30 minutes, rotating sheet halfway through baking. Carefully remove foil and weights and continue to bake tart shell until it is fully baked and golden brown, 5 to 10 minutes longer. Transfer baking sheet to wire rack and let tart shell cool completely on sheet, about 1 hour.

6. FOR THE FRUIT AND GLAZE: Spread chilled pastry cream evenly over bottom of cooled tart shell. Shingle kiwi slices around edge of tart, then arrange 3 rows of raspberries inside kiwi ring. Finally, mound blueberries in middle of tart and arrange over raspberries.

7. Melt jelly in small saucepan over medium-high heat, stirring occasionally to smooth out any lumps. Using pastry brush, gently dab melted jelly over fruit. Remove outer metal ring of tart pan, slide thin metal spatula between tart and pan bottom, and carefully slide tart onto serving platter or cutting board. Serve.

LEMON–OLIVE OIL TART

Serves 8 | 9-inch tart pan

WHY THIS RECIPE WORKS Classic lemon tart recipes feature butter in both the crust and the filling, but here we use extra-virgin olive oil instead. It makes the crust a snap: Just mix the flour, sugar, and salt with the oil and a little water until a soft dough forms; crumble it into the tart pan; press it into the sides and bottom; and bake it right away—no rolling or chilling required. Using olive oil in the filling doesn't compromise its firmness or sliceability because the filling gets plenty of structure from eggs. Olive oil does, however, allow lemons' acidity to come to the fore in a way that butter doesn't. That means we can use a bit less juice. Use a fresh, high-quality extra-virgin olive oil here. Make sure that all your metal equipment is nonreactive, or the filling may have a metallic flavor.

CRUST

1½ cups (7½ ounces) all-purpose flour
5 tablespoons (2¼ ounces) sugar
½ teaspoon table salt
½ cup extra-virgin olive oil
2 tablespoons water

FILLING

1 cup (7 ounces) sugar
2 tablespoons all-purpose flour
¼ teaspoon table salt
3 large eggs plus 3 large yolks
1 tablespoon grated lemon zest plus ½ cup juice (3 lemons)
¼ cup extra-virgin olive oil

1. FOR THE CRUST: Adjust oven rack to middle position and heat oven to 350 degrees. Whisk flour, sugar, and salt together in bowl. Add oil and water and stir until uniform dough forms. Using your hands, crumble three-quarters of dough over bottom of 9-inch tart pan with removable bottom. Press dough to even thickness in bottom of pan. Crumble remaining dough and scatter evenly around edge of pan, then press crumbled dough into fluted sides of pan. Press dough to even thickness. Set dough-lined tart pan on rimmed baking sheet and bake until tart shell is deep golden brown and firm to touch, 30 to 35 minutes, rotating sheet halfway through baking.

2. FOR THE FILLING: About 5 minutes before crust is finished baking, whisk sugar, flour, and salt in medium saucepan until combined. Whisk in eggs and yolks until no streaks of egg remain. Whisk in lemon zest and juice. Cook over medium-low heat, whisking constantly and scraping corners of saucepan, until mixture thickens slightly and registers 160 degrees, 5 to 8 minutes.

3. Off heat, whisk in oil until incorporated. Strain curd through fine-mesh strainer set over bowl. Pour curd into warm tart shell.

Lemon–Olive Oil Tart

4. Bake until filling is set and barely jiggles when pan is shaken, 8 to 12 minutes. Transfer baking sheet to wire rack and let tart cool completely, at least 2 hours. Remove outer metal ring of tart pan. Slide thin metal spatula between tart and pan bottom, then carefully slide tart onto serving platter or cutting board. Serve. (Leftovers can be wrapped loosely in plastic wrap and refrigerated for up to 3 days.)

POACHED PEAR AND ALMOND TART

Serves 10 to 12 | 9-inch tart pan

WHY THIS RECIPE WORKS Sliced poached pears, fanned atop light, nutty frangipane (a sweetened, custardy paste of ground almonds) and contained within a sweet crust, make up this stunning classic French tart. The process of poaching doesn't just tenderize the pears; it perfumes them with flavor that complements the almond filling. White wine spiced with a cinnamon stick, black peppercorns, whole cloves, and a vanilla bean created our fragrant poaching liquid. We made sure to dry the pears before setting them on the frangipane (which comes together in the food processor) so they didn't make the dessert sticky and wet. We like the bright, crisp flavor of pears poached in Sauvignon Blanc. Chardonnay-poached pears have a deeper, oakier flavor that we also like.

Poached Pear and
Almond Tart

TUTORIAL
Poached Pear and Almond Tart

This three-component recipe may look intricate, but each is easy to execute. Learn how to fill and top this tart, and give it its trademark pear petal design.

1. Cut 1 dried poached pear half crosswise into ⅜-inch slices (do not separate slices). Pat dry again.

2. Discard first 4 slices from narrow end of sliced pear half.

3. Slide spatula under sliced pear and, steadying it with your hand, slide pear onto center of tart.

4. Cut and dry another pear half. Slide spatula under pear and gently press pear to fan slices toward narrow end.

5. Slide fanned pear half onto filling, narrow end toward center, almost touching center pear.

6. Repeat slicing, fanning, and placing remaining pear halves, spacing them evenly around center pear.

POACHED PEARS

  1 (750-ml) bottle white wine
 ⅔ cup (4⅔ ounces) sugar
  5 (2-inch) strips lemon zest plus 2 tablespoons juice
  1 cinnamon stick
15 black peppercorns
  3 cloves
 ⅛ teaspoon table salt
 ½ vanilla bean (optional)
  4 ripe but firm Bosc or Bartlett pears (8 ounces each),
     peeled, halved, and cored

FILLING

  1 cup slivered almonds
 ½ cup (3½ ounces) sugar
 ⅛ teaspoon table salt
  1 large egg plus 1 large white
 ½ teaspoon almond extract
 ½ teaspoon vanilla extract
  6 tablespoons unsalted butter, cut into 6 pieces and softened

  1 recipe tart dough (see pages 424–426)
 ¼ cup apple jelly

1. FOR THE POACHED PEARS: Combine wine, sugar, lemon zest and juice, cinnamon stick, peppercorns, cloves, and salt in large saucepan. If using, cut vanilla bean in half lengthwise, then, using tip of paring knife, scrape out seeds and add seeds and pod to saucepan. Bring mixture to simmer, stirring occasionally to dissolve sugar. Slide pear halves into simmering wine mixture. Return to simmer, then reduce heat to low, cover, and cook pears, covered, turning them occasionally, until tender and skewer can be inserted into pear with very little resistance, about 10 minutes. Off heat, let pears cool in liquid, partially covered, until pears have turned translucent and are cool enough to handle, about 1 hour. (Cooled pears and liquid can be refrigerated for up to 3 days.)

2. FOR THE FILLING: Pulse almonds, sugar, and salt in food processor until finely ground, about 25 pulses. Continue to process until nut mixture is as finely ground as possible, about 10 seconds. Add egg and white, almond extract, and vanilla and process until combined, about 10 seconds. Add butter and process until no lumps remain, about 20 seconds, scraping down bowl as needed. (Filling can be refrigerated for up to 3 days. Let filling stand at room temperature until softened, about 10 minutes, stirring 3 or 4 times, before using.)

3. Roll dough into 11-inch circle on floured counter, then transfer to parchment paper–lined rimmed baking sheet; cover loosely with plastic wrap and refrigerate until firm but pliable, about 10 minutes.

4. Loosely roll dough around rolling pin and gently unroll it onto 9-inch tart pan with removable bottom, letting excess dough hang over edge. Ease dough into pan by gently lifting edge of dough with your hand while pressing into corners and fluted sides of pan with your other hand. Run rolling pin over top of pan to remove any excess dough. Wrap loosely in plastic, place on large plate, and freeze until fully chilled and firm, about 30 minutes. (Dough-lined tart pan can be frozen for up to 1 month.)

5. Adjust oven rack to middle position and heat oven to 375 degrees. Line chilled tart shell with double layer of aluminum foil and fill with pie weights. Bake on foil-lined rimmed baking sheet until tart shell is golden and set, about 30 minutes, rotating sheet halfway through baking. Remove foil and weights. Transfer sheet to wire rack and let tart shell cool completely, about 1 hour. Reduce oven temperature to 350 degrees.

6. Spread filling evenly over bottom of cooled tart shell. Remove pears from poaching liquid and pat dry with paper towels. Cut 1 poached pear half crosswise into ⅜-inch slices, leaving pear half intact on cutting board (do not separate slices). Pat dry again with paper towels to absorb excess moisture. Discard first 4 slices from narrow end of sliced pear half. Slide spatula under sliced pear and, steadying it with your hand, slide pear off spatula onto center of tart. Cut and dry another pear half. Slide spatula under pear and gently press pear to fan slices toward narrow end. Slide fanned pear half onto filling, narrow end toward center, almost touching center pear. Repeat slicing, fanning, and placing remaining pear halves, spacing them evenly and making flower petal pattern around center pear.

7. Bake tart on sheet until crust is deep golden brown and almond filling is puffed, browned, and firm to the touch, about 45 minutes, rotating sheet halfway through baking. Transfer sheet to wire rack and let tart cool for 10 minutes.

8. Melt jelly in small saucepan over medium-high heat, stirring occasionally to smooth out lumps. Using pastry brush, gently dab jelly over fruit, avoiding crust. Let tart cool completely, about 2 hours. Remove outer ring of tart pan, slide thin metal spatula between tart and tart pan bottom, and carefully slide tart onto serving platter or cutting board. Serve.

FRENCH APPLE TART

Serves 8 | 9-inch tart pan

WHY THIS RECIPE WORKS French apple tart is a visually stunning centerpiece dessert that's all apples—half are cooked down to an applesauce-like mixture—and pastry. We packed our tart with a whopping 5 pounds of Golden Delicious apples; this variety broke down easily to make the puree. To concentrate the apple flavor, we cooked down the puree. For a beautiful presentation, we arranged parcooked apple slices on top of the tart in a flower-like design. A thin coat of preserves and a final run under the broiler provided a caramelized finish. You may have extra apple slices after arranging the apples in step 8. To ensure that the outer ring of the pan releases easily, avoid getting apple puree and apricot glaze on the edge of the crust. The tart is best served the day it is assembled.

1 recipe tart dough (see pages 424–426)
10 large Golden Delicious apples (8 ounces each), peeled and cored
3 tablespoons unsalted butter, divided
1 tablespoon water
½ cup apricot preserves
¼ teaspoon table salt

1. Roll dough into 11-inch circle on floured counter, then transfer to parchment paper–lined rimmed baking sheet; cover loosely with plastic wrap and refrigerate until firm but pliable, about 10 minutes.

2. Loosely roll dough around rolling pin and gently unroll it onto 9-inch tart pan with removable bottom, letting excess dough hang over edge. Ease dough into pan by gently lifting edge of dough with your hand while pressing into corners and fluted sides of pan with your other hand. Run rolling pin over top of pan to remove any excess dough. Wrap loosely in plastic, place on large plate, and freeze until fully chilled and firm, about 30 minutes. (Dough-lined tart pan can be frozen for up to 1 month.) Adjust oven rack to middle position and heat oven to 375 degrees.

3. Line chilled tart shell with double layer of aluminum foil and fill with pie weights. Bake on wire rack set in rimmed baking sheet until tart shell is golden and set, about 30 minutes, rotating sheet halfway through baking. Remove foil and weights; set aside.

4. Cut 5 apples lengthwise into quarters and cut each quarter lengthwise into 4 slices. Melt 1 tablespoon butter in 12-inch skillet over medium heat. Add apple slices and water and toss to combine. Cover and cook, stirring occasionally, until apples begin to turn translucent and are slightly pliable, 3 to 5 minutes. Transfer apples to large plate, spread into single layer, and set aside to cool. Do not clean skillet.

5. Microwave apricot preserves in small bowl until fluid, about 30 seconds. Strain preserves through fine-mesh strainer into bowl, reserving solids. Set aside 3 tablespoons strained preserves for brushing tart.

6. Cut remaining 5 apples into ½-inch-thick wedges. Melt remaining 2 tablespoons butter in now-empty skillet over medium heat. Add remaining apricot preserves, reserved apricot solids, apple wedges, and salt. Cover and cook, stirring occasionally, until apples are very soft, about 10 minutes.

7. Mash apples to puree with potato masher. Continue to cook, stirring occasionally, until puree is reduced to 2 cups, about 5 minutes.

8. Spread filling evenly over bottom of tart shell. Select 5 thinnest slices of sautéed apple and set aside. Starting at outer edge of crust, arrange remaining slices, tightly overlapping, in concentric circles. Bend reserved slices to fit in center. Bake tart, still on wire rack set in sheet, on lower rack for 30 minutes. Remove tart from oven and heat broiler.

French Apple Tart

9. While broiler heats, warm reserved preserves in microwave until fluid, about 20 seconds. Brush evenly over surface of apples, avoiding tart crust. Broil tart, checking every 30 seconds and turning as necessary, until apples are attractively caramelized, 1 to 3 minutes. Let tart cool on wire rack for 1½ hours. Remove outer ring of tart pan, slide thin metal spatula between tart and tart pan bottom, and carefully slide tart onto serving platter or cutting board. Serve.

RICH CHOCOLATE TART

Serves 10 to 12 | 9-inch tart pan

WHY THIS RECIPE WORKS To us, the real draw of a rich chocolate tart is its simple confidence: The best versions boast a flawlessly smooth, truffle-like texture; unadulterated chocolate flavor; and a sophisticated polish. As chocolate is the sole filling, we wanted a custard-style mixture here: one that would be dense and rich, but not as dense as ganache; and plush, so we could eat more than a couple of bites. The ganache we saved for a thin glaze to give the top a pristine sheen. The tart can be garnished with chocolate curls or with a flaky coarse sea salt, such as Maldon. Or, make the chocolate-tahini variation and top with sesame brittle that enforces the sesame flavor and makes a stunning geometric finish.

1 recipe tart dough (see pages 424–426)

FILLING
9 ounces bittersweet chocolate, chopped fine
1¼ cups heavy cream
½ teaspoon instant espresso powder
¼ teaspoon table salt
4 tablespoons unsalted butter, sliced thin and softened
2 large eggs, room temperature

GLAZE
3 tablespoons heavy cream
1 tablespoon light corn syrup
2 ounces bittersweet chocolate, chopped fine
1 tablespoon hot water

1. Roll dough into 11-inch circle on floured counter, then transfer to parchment paper–lined rimmed baking sheet; cover loosely with plastic wrap and refrigerate until firm but pliable, about 10 minutes.

2. Loosely roll dough around rolling pin and gently unroll it onto 9-inch tart pan with removable bottom, letting excess dough hang over edge. Ease dough into pan by gently lifting edge of dough with your hand while pressing into corners and fluted sides of pan with your other hand. Run rolling pin over top of pan to

Chocolate-Tahini Tart

remove any excess dough. Wrap loosely in plastic, place on large plate, and freeze until fully chilled and firm, about 30 minutes. (Dough-lined tart pan can be frozen for up to 1 month.)

3. Adjust oven rack to middle position and heat oven to 375 degrees. Line chilled tart shell with double layer of aluminum foil and fill with pie weights. Bake on foil-lined rimmed baking sheet until tart shell is golden brown and set, about 30 minutes, rotating sheet halfway through baking. Remove foil and weights and continue to bake tart shell until it is fully baked and golden, 5 to 10 minutes longer. Transfer sheet to wire rack and let tart shell cool completely, about 1 hour.

4. **FOR THE FILLING:** Reduce oven temperature to 250 degrees. Place chocolate in large bowl. Bring cream, espresso powder, and salt to simmer in small saucepan over medium heat, whisking to dissolve espresso powder and salt, then pour over chocolate. Cover and let sit until chocolate is softened, about 5 minutes, then whisk to combine. Whisk in butter until smooth, then add eggs and whisk until combined and glossy.

5. Pour filling into cooled tart shell and spread into even layer with rubber spatula, popping any large bubbles with toothpick. Bake until edge of filling is just set but center jiggles slightly and very faint cracks appear on surface, 30 to 35 minutes. Let tart cool completely on sheet on wire rack, about 2 hours. Refrigerate, uncovered, until filling is chilled and set, at least 3 hours. (Tart can be refrigerated for up to 18 hours.)

6. FOR THE GLAZE: Remove tart from refrigerator and let sit at room temperature for 30 minutes. Bring cream and corn syrup to simmer in small saucepan over medium heat, stirring occasionally. Off heat, add chocolate, cover, and let sit until chocolate is softened, about 5 minutes. Whisk to combine, then whisk in hot water (glaze should be homogeneous, shiny, and pourable). Working quickly, pour glaze onto center of tart and tilt tart to allow glaze to run to edge. Pop any large bubbles with toothpick. Let sit at room temperature until glaze is set, at least 1 hour or up to 3 hours. Remove outer ring of tart pan, slide thin metal spatula between tart and tart pan bottom, and carefully slide tart onto serving platter or cutting board. Serve.

Chocolate-Tahini Tart

Be mindful of how you plan to cut the tart when arranging the brittle over the top.

In filling, reduce chocolate to 5 ounces and cream to ¾ cup. Add ¼ cup sugar to saucepan with espresso powder in step 4, whisking until sugar is dissolved. Add ¾ cup tahini to saucepan with butter in step 4, whisking until smooth. Arrange 1 recipe Sesame Brittle (page 551) over finished tart before serving.

BAKED RASPBERRY TART

Serves 8 to 10 | 9-inch tart pan

WHY THIS RECIPE WORKS Rich custard tempers tart raspberries and bakes up golden brown in this balanced, crowd-pleasing tart. We started with a simple butter, egg, sugar, and flour batter for the filling, deepening its flavor by browning the butter for a hint of nuttiness. Lemon zest brightened our custard, and fruity kirsch accented the raspberries. Substituting instant flour (Wondra) for all-purpose produced a smooth and silky (rather than starchy) texture. Wondra is an instant flour sold in canisters in the baking aisle. To minimize waste, reserve the egg white left from making the tart pastry for use in the filling. If your raspberries are very tart or very sweet, adjust the amount of sugar in the filling by about a tablespoon or so. This tart is best eaten the day it is made.

  1 recipe tart dough (see pages 424–426)
  6 tablespoons unsalted butter
  1 large egg plus 1 large white
  ½ cup (3½ ounces) plus 1 tablespoon sugar
  ¼ teaspoon table salt
  1 teaspoon vanilla extract
  1 teaspoon kirsch or framboise (optional)
  ¼ teaspoon grated lemon zest plus 1½ teaspoons juice
  2 tablespoons Wondra flour
  2 tablespoons heavy cream
 10 ounces (2 cups) raspberries

1. Roll dough into 11-inch circle on floured counter, then transfer to parchment paper–lined rimmed baking sheet; cover loosely with plastic wrap and refrigerate until firm but pliable, about 10 minutes.

2. Loosely roll dough around rolling pin and gently unroll it onto 9-inch tart pan with removable bottom, letting excess dough hang over edge. Ease dough into pan by gently lifting edge of dough with your hand while pressing into corners and fluted sides of pan with your other hand. Run rolling pin over top of pan to remove any excess dough. Wrap loosely in plastic, place on large plate, and freeze until fully chilled and firm, about 30 minutes. (Dough-lined tart pan can be frozen for up to 1 month.) Adjust oven rack to middle position and heat oven to 375 degrees.

3. Line chilled tart shell with double layer of aluminum foil and fill with pie weights. Bake on foil-lined rimmed baking sheet until tart shell is golden and set, about 30 minutes, rotating sheet halfway through baking. Remove foil and weights and transfer sheet to wire rack.

4. Melt butter in small saucepan over medium heat, swirling occasionally, until butter is browned and releases nutty aroma, about 7 minutes; transfer to bowl and let cool slightly.

5. Whisk egg and white together in bowl, then vigorously whisk in sugar and salt until light-colored, about 1 minute. Whisk in browned butter until combined. Whisk in vanilla; kirsch, if using; and lemon zest and juice. Whisk in Wondra. Whisk in cream until thoroughly combined.

6. Distribute raspberries in single tightly packed layer in bottom of tart shell. Pour filling mixture evenly over raspberries. Bake tart on sheet until fragrant, filling is set (does not jiggle when shaken) and bubbling lightly around edges, and surface is puffed and deep golden brown, about 30 minutes, rotating sheet halfway through baking.

7. Let tart cool completely on sheet on wire rack, about 2 hours. Remove outer ring of tart pan, slide thin metal spatula between tart and tart pan bottom, and carefully slide tart onto serving platter or cutting board. Serve. (Cooled tart can be wrapped loosely with plastic wrap and kept at room temperature for up to 4 hours before serving.)

VARIATIONS
Baked Blackberry Tart
Substitute 10 ounces blackberries for raspberries.

Baked Blueberry-Raspberry Tart
Replace 5 ounces raspberries with 5 ounces blueberries.

BLOOD ORANGE AND CHOCOLATE TART

Serves 10 to 12 | 9-inch tart pan

WHY THIS RECIPE WORKS Chocolate tart dough and a silky ganache are deeply chocolaty complementary foundations, but the star of this refined tart is a simple jewel-toned layer of jelly that consists of nothing more than fresh blood orange zest and juice, sugar, salt, and gelatin. For the clearest jelly, be sure to strain the orange juice with a fine-mesh strainer and discard any pulp.

1 recipe Chocolate Tart Dough (page 424)

GANACHE
¾ cup heavy cream
1 teaspoon grated blood orange zest
¼ teaspoon table salt
4 ounces bittersweet chocolate, chopped
3 tablespoons unsalted butter, softened
½ teaspoon vanilla extract

JELLY
1 teaspoon unflavored gelatin
1 teaspoon grated blood orange zest plus
   1 cup juice (4 oranges), divided
½ cup (3½ ounces) sugar
¼ teaspoon table salt
1 blood orange

1. Roll dough into 11-inch circle on floured counter, then transfer to parchment paper–lined rimmed baking sheet; cover loosely with plastic wrap and refrigerate until firm but pliable, about 10 minutes.

2. Loosely roll dough around rolling pin and gently unroll it onto 9-inch tart pan with removable bottom, letting excess dough hang over edge. Ease dough into pan by gently lifting edge of dough with your hand while pressing into corners and fluted sides of pan with your other hand. Run rolling pin over top of pan to remove any excess dough. Wrap loosely in plastic, place on large plate, and freeze until fully chilled and firm, about 30 minutes. (Dough-lined tart pan can be frozen for up to 1 month.) Adjust oven rack to middle position and heat oven to 375 degrees.

3. Line chilled tart shell with double layer of aluminum foil and fill with pie weights. Bake on foil-lined rimmed baking sheet until tart is set and fragrant, about 30 minutes, rotating sheet halfway through baking. Remove foil and weights and continue to bake 5 minutes longer. Transfer sheet to wire rack and let tart shell cool completely, about 30 minutes.

4. FOR THE GANACHE: Bring cream, orange zest, and salt to simmer in small saucepan over medium heat. Off heat, add chocolate, cover, and let sit until chocolate is softened,

about 5 minutes, then whisk to combine. Whisk in butter and vanilla until smooth. Pour filling into cooled tart shell, spreading into even layer with rubber spatula. Refrigerate, uncovered, until filling is chilled and set, at least 2 hours or up to 2 days.

5. FOR THE JELLY: Sprinkle gelatin over ¼ cup orange juice in bowl and let sit until gelatin softens, about 5 minutes. Cook orange zest and remaining ¾ cup juice, sugar, and salt in small saucepan over medium-low heat just until sugar dissolves, about 3 minutes, whisking occasionally. Off heat, add softened gelatin and whisk until dissolved. Strain mixture through fine-mesh strainer into bowl and let cool for 15 minutes; discard solids. Slowly pour orange mixture evenly over tart. Refrigerate until jelly is set, about 3 hours. (Tart can be refrigerated for up to 24 hours.)

6. Remove outer ring of tart pan, slide thin metal spatula between tart and tart pan bottom, and carefully slide tart onto serving platter or cutting board. Just before serving, cut away peel and pith from orange. Holding fruit over bowl, use paring knife to slice between membranes to release segments. Arrange orange segments attractively in pinwheel in center of tart. Serve.

Blood Orange and Chocolate Tart

LINZERTORTE

Serves 10 to 12 | 11-inch tart pan

WHY THIS RECIPE WORKS The components of a Linzertorte couldn't be easier to prepare. A buttery nut-enhanced crust comes together easily in the food processor, and the raspberry jam filling is something you buy. Making this holiday tart look special is what takes precision. The hazelnut-and-almond-enriched dough is extra-delicate, so we simply patted it into the tart pan rather than rolling it. As for the lattice, we cut the strips on parchment paper so we could use the parchment to transfer the soft strips to the filled tart. A brush of cream and a sprinkling of turbinado sugar gave the golden-brown tart glitter and glow. Make sure to buy blanched almonds and to use an 11-inch tart pan here (most recipes call for a 9-inch pan). You will have some extra dough when cutting out the lattice strips; we suggest cutting out a few extra lattice strips as backup. If the dough becomes too soft while forming the lattice, refrigerate it for 15 minutes before continuing. The Linzertorte may be served at room temperature the day it is baked, but it's at its best after a night in the refrigerator.

TART DOUGH
- 1 large egg
- 1 teaspoon vanilla extract
- 1 cup hazelnuts, toasted and skinned
- ½ cup plus 2 tablespoons (4⅓ ounces) granulated sugar
- ½ cup whole blanched almonds
- ½ teaspoon table salt
- 1 teaspoon grated lemon zest
- 1½ cups (7½ ounces) all-purpose flour
- ½ teaspoon ground cinnamon
- ⅛ teaspoon ground allspice
- 12 tablespoons unsalted butter, cut into ½-inch pieces and chilled

FILLING
- 1¼ cups raspberry preserves
- 1 tablespoon lemon juice
- 1 tablespoon heavy cream
- 1½ teaspoons turbinado or Demerara sugar (optional)

1. FOR THE TART DOUGH: Whisk egg and vanilla together in bowl. Process hazelnuts, sugar, almonds, and salt in food processor until very finely ground, 45 to 60 seconds. Add lemon zest and pulse to combine, about 5 pulses. Add flour, cinnamon, and allspice and pulse to combine, about 5 pulses. Scatter butter over top and pulse until mixture resembles coarse cornmeal, about 15 pulses. With processor running, add egg mixture and continue to process until dough just comes together, about 12 seconds longer.

2. Transfer dough to counter and form into cohesive mound. Divide dough in half and form each half into 5-inch disk. (If not using immediately, wrap disks tightly in plastic wrap and refrigerate for up to 2 days. Let chilled dough sit on counter until soft and malleable, about 1 hour, before using.)

3. Tear 1 disk into walnut-size pieces, then pat pieces into 11-inch tart pan with removable bottom, pressing dough into corners and ¾ inch up sides of pan. Cover dough with plastic and smooth out any bumps using bottom of measuring cup. Set pan on large plate and freeze until firm, about 30 minutes.

4. Roll second disk into 12-inch square between 2 large sheets of floured parchment paper. (If dough sticks to parchment, gently loosen and lift sticky area with bench scraper and dust parchment with additional flour.) Slide dough, still between parchment, onto rimmed baking sheet and refrigerate until firm, about 15 minutes. Remove top layer of parchment and trim edges of dough to form perfect square, then cut ten ¾-inch-wide strips, cutting through underlying parchment. Cover with parchment and freeze until dough is fully chilled and firm, about 20 minutes.

5. Meanwhile, adjust oven rack to middle position and heat oven to 350 degrees. Set dough-lined tart pan on rimmed baking sheet. Spray 1 side of double layer of aluminum foil with vegetable oil spray. Press foil, greased side down, into frozen tart shell, covering edges to prevent burning, and fill with pie weights. Bake until tart shell is golden brown and set, about 30 minutes, rotating sheet halfway through baking. Remove foil and weights, transfer sheet to wire rack, and let cool completely, about 1 hour.

6. FOR THE FILLING: Stir raspberry preserves and lemon juice together in bowl. Spread filling evenly over bottom of cooled tart shell. Pick up 1 strip of dough by parchment ends, then flip it over onto tart, positioning it near edge of pan. Remove parchment strip and trim ends of dough strip by pressing down on top edge of pan; reserve all dough scraps. Place 2 more strips parallel to first, spacing them evenly so that one is across center and other is near opposite edge of pan. Rotate pan 90 degrees, then place 3 more strips spacing as with first three. Rotate pan 90 degrees again, then place 2 strips across pan, spaced evenly between first three. Rotate pan again and complete lattice by placing last 2 strips between second set of three. Use small scraps of dough to fill in crust around edges between lattice strips. Top of crust should be just below top of pan.

7. Gently brush lattice strips with cream and sprinkle with sugar, if using. Bake on sheet until crust is deep golden brown, about 50 minutes. Let tart cool completely on sheet on wire rack, about 2 hours. Remove outer ring of tart pan, slide thin metal spatula between tart and tart pan bottom, and carefully slide tart onto serving platter or cutting board. Serve or refrigerate overnight.

TUTORIAL

Linzertorte

This holiday stunner has a lattice top but it's not made quite like those for pies. Learn how to place the nut dough on top of the tart.

1. Spread filling evenly over bottom of cooled tart shell.

2. Pick up 1 strip of dough by parchment ends, then flip it over onto tart, positioning it near edge of pan.

3. Remove parchment strip and trim ends of dough strip by pressing down on top edge of pan; reserve all dough scraps.

4. Continue creating lattice design with remaining strips.

5. Use small scraps of dough to fill in crust around edges between lattice strips. Top of crust should be just below top of pan.

6. Gently brush lattice strips with cream and sprinkle with sugar, if using. Bake on sheet until crust is deep golden brown, about 50 minutes.

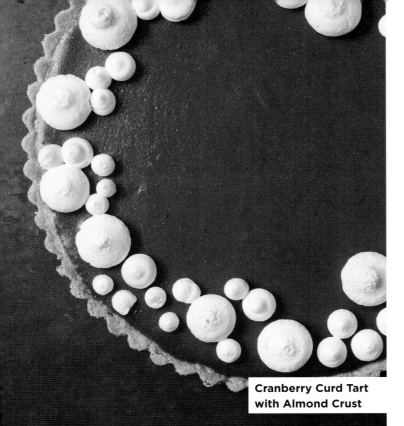

Cranberry Curd Tart with Almond Crust

CRANBERRY CURD TART WITH ALMOND CRUST

Serves 8 | 9-inch tart pan

WHY THIS RECIPE WORKS Our cranberry curd tart showcases cranberries' bold flavor and brilliant color while making use of their ample pectin content to create a nice thick curd. The combination of almond flour and cornstarch kept the crust thin but sturdy (and gluten-free), and the rich nuttiness was a nice contrast to the curd. We pureed butter (to temper the astringency) into the curd, strained it, and poured the mixture over the baked tart crust. This method prevented the filling from developing a thick, rubbery skin. Finally, we whisked up a whipped cream topping stabilized by a small amount of the pectin-rich puree. This topping could be piped onto the tart hours in advance without breaking or weeping. The tart crust will be firm if you serve the tart on the day that it's made; if you prefer a more tender crust, make the tart through step 3 up to two days ahead.

FILLING
- 1 pound (4 cups) fresh or frozen cranberries
- 1¼ cups (8¾ ounces) plus 1 tablespoon sugar, divided
- ½ cup water
  Pinch table salt
- 3 large egg yolks
- 2 teaspoons cornstarch
- 4 tablespoons unsalted butter, cut into 4 pieces and softened

CRUST
- 1 cup (4 ounces) almond flour
- ½ cup (2 ounces) cornstarch
- ⅓ cup (2⅓ ounces) sugar
- ½ teaspoon table salt
- 6 tablespoons unsalted butter, melted and cooled
- ¾ teaspoon almond extract
- 1 cup heavy cream

1. FOR THE FILLING: Bring cranberries, 1¼ cups sugar, water, and salt to boil in medium saucepan over medium-high heat, stirring occasionally. Adjust heat to maintain very gentle simmer. Cover and cook until all cranberries have burst and started to shrivel, about 10 minutes. While cranberries cook, whisk egg yolks and cornstarch in bowl until smooth. Transfer hot cranberry mixture to food processor. Immediately add yolk mixture and process until smooth (small flecks of cranberry skin will be visible), about 1 minute, scraping down sides of bowl as necessary. Let mixture cool in processor bowl until skin forms and mixture registers 120 to 125 degrees, 45 minutes to 1 hour. While mixture cools, make crust.

2. FOR THE CRUST: Adjust oven rack to middle position and heat oven to 350 degrees. Whisk flour, cornstarch, sugar, and salt in bowl until well combined. Add melted butter and almond extract and stir with wooden spoon until uniform dough forms. Crumble two-thirds of mixture over bottom of 9-inch tart pan with removable bottom. Press dough to even thickness in bottom of pan. Crumble remaining dough and scatter evenly around edge of pan. Press crumbled dough into sides of pan. Press edges to even thickness. Set pan on rimmed baking sheet and bake until crust is golden brown, about 20 minutes, rotating sheet halfway through baking.

3. Add softened butter to cranberry puree and process until fully combined, about 30 seconds. Strain mixture through fine-mesh strainer set over bowl, pressing on solids with rubber spatula to extract puree. Transfer 2 tablespoons puree to medium bowl, then stir in cream and remaining 1 tablespoon sugar. Cover and refrigerate. Transfer remaining puree to crust (it's OK if crust is still warm) and smooth into even layer. Let tart sit at room temperature for at least 4 hours. (Cover tart with large bowl and refrigerate after 4 hours if making ahead.)

4. Whisk cream mixture until stiff peaks form, 1 to 3 minutes. Transfer to pastry bag fitted with pastry tip. Pipe decorative border around edge of tart. Transfer any remaining whipped cream to small serving bowl.

5. To serve, remove outer metal ring of tart pan. Slide thin metal spatula between tart and pan bottom to loosen tart. Carefully slide tart onto serving platter or cutting board. Serve, passing extra whipped cream separately. (Leftovers can be covered and refrigerated for up to 3 days.)

VEGAN CHOCOLATE-ESPRESSO TART

Serves 10 to 12 | 9-inch tart pan

WHY THIS RECIPE WORKS This pull-out-all-the-stops chocolate tart with a dreamy espresso "meringue" is magic. We started with our vegan tart dough. Next, we made a superchocolaty ganache with water that set up beautifully glossy at room temperature, and sliced like a dream. The crowning touch was inspired by Dalgona coffee: Instant espresso crystals, when dissolved in water with sugar and then whipped, created a billowy, glossy foam that could be piped or dolloped as an elegant decoration. Not all brands of bittersweet chocolate are vegan, so check ingredient lists carefully. We used bittersweet chocolate with 60 to 70 percent cacao for the filling (higher-percentage cacao will set faster). We had the best results using a stand mixer to whip the topping. If you are a strict vegan, use organic sugar. For an accurate measurement of boiling water, bring a full kettle of water to a boil and then measure out the desired amount.

- 1 recipe Vegan Tart Dough (page 426), fully baked and cooled

FILLING
- 10½ ounces bittersweet chocolate, chopped fine
- ¼ cup (1¾ ounces) sugar
- ¼ teaspoon table salt
- ¾ cup boiling water

TOPPING (OPTIONAL)
- 6 tablespoons (2⅔ ounces) sugar
- ¼ cup ice water
- 4 teaspoons instant espresso powder

  Unsweetened cocoa powder (optional)

1. FOR THE FILLING: Place chocolate, sugar, and salt in bowl. Pour boiling water over chocolate mixture and let sit for 30 seconds, then whisk until mixture is completely smooth. Transfer filling to cooled tart shell, popping any large bubbles that form with a toothpick, and let tart sit at room temperature until chocolate is set, at least 2 hours and up to 24 hours. (Do not refrigerate or crust will become hard.)

2. FOR THE TOPPING: Using stand mixer fitted with whisk attachment, whip sugar, ice water, and espresso powder on high speed until soft peaks form, 2 to 3 minutes. Transfer mixture to pastry bag fitted with star tip and pipe decoratively over filling (or use zipper-lock bag with corner snipped off). Dust with cocoa powder, if using, and serve.

Vegan Chocolate-Espresso Tart

GALETTES

A PICTURE FRAME OF FLAKY, BUTTERY CRUST displays a jewel-hued center of fruit in these open-faced desserts. The French word "galette" refers to essentially any round pastry; when we use the term "galette" in this book, we mean a variety of tart. You may also know it by an Italian name, crostata.

Galettes use pie pastry but they're easier to prepare than pie as they're made free-form (that's why you'll see the names free-form tart and galette used interchangeably) on a baking sheet. They're rustic (rarely if ever a perfect circle, and streaked with fruit juices between the cracks of flaky dough) but they also have a quiet elegance and intense beauty, featuring fabric-like folds of pastry around vibrant fruit. The exposed fruit filling roasts, which gives it beautiful caramelization, an ultraconcentrated flavor, and just the right amount of juiciness— often without the use of a thickener. Galettes are an excellent choice to display bounties of seasonal fruit. And they need little in terms of adornment, although a melting scoop of ice cream or a modest drizzle of caramel or balsamic reduction isn't unwelcome.

KEY POINTS

Crust is flaky but sturdy

Use fraisage to mix dough

Fruit rarely needs thickener

DOUGH DIFFERENCES

Creating tender-flaky crust is a premier pie goal (see pages 342–348). A flaky dough encasing the fruit is important for galettes too, but since they stand free-form, with no supporting pan, there's an extra consideration: sturdiness. Butter is a tenderizer and pieces distributed throughout the dough provide flakes, but too much butter creates a weak, leaky crust. And too little flour makes for a crust that is cracker-like and edging toward tough. In our recipe for free-form tart dough (see page 442), we use a plentiful but appropriate amount of butter. (Shortening, beyond tasting flat, would tenderize too severely.) But just as important is the mixing method. Fraisage is a French method of making pastry and involves smearing the dough with the heel of the hand. This spreads the butter pieces into long streaks between thin layers of flour and water, which results in a stable, yet tender, flaky crust. What happens if you omit this key step? Something like the crust on the bottom, which has short flaky layers that juices can easily leak through. The crust on the top, made with the fraisage method, has long flaky layers and is far less prone to leaking.

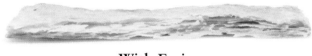

With Fraisage

Without Fraisage

PERFECT PLEATING

Free-form tarts are rustic but the folded pleats around the exposed produce are unquestionably attractive. Here's how to make them perfectly.

1. Fold outermost 2 inches of dough over fruit, pleating every 2 to 3 inches as needed.

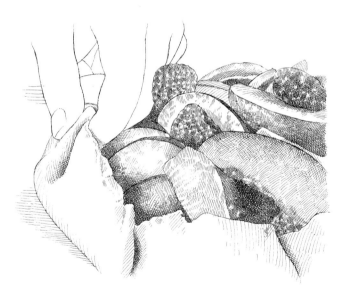

2. Gently pinch pleated dough to secure, but do not press dough into fruit.

Making Galette Dough

Free-form tarts aren't free from sound guidelines. Discover the best crust for these rustic desserts.

FREE-FORM TART DOUGH
Makes enough for one 9-inch tart

Without the support of a pie plate or tart pan, the crust for a free-form tart is prone to leaking juice, resulting in a soggy tart bottom. The answer to satisfying structure is a French pastry method called fraisage; chunks of butter are pressed into the flour in long, thin sheets which creates lots of long, flaky layers when the dough is baked. These long layers are tender for eating yet sturdy and impermeable, making this crust ideal for supporting a generous filling of juicy fruit.

1½ cups (7½ ounces) all-purpose flour
½   teaspoon table salt
10 tablespoons unsalted butter, cut into
     ½-inch cubes and chilled
3–6 tablespoons ice water

1. Process flour and salt in food processor until combined, about 5 seconds. Scatter butter over top and pulse until mixture resembles coarse sand and butter pieces are about size of small peas, about 10 pulses. Continue to pulse, adding ice water 1 tablespoon at a time, until dough begins to form small curds that hold together when pinched with your fingers, about 10 pulses.

2. Transfer mixture to lightly floured counter and gather into rectangular-shaped pile. Starting at farthest end, use heel of your hand to smear small amount of dough against counter. Continue to smear dough until all crumbs have been worked. Gather smeared crumbs together in another rectangular-shaped pile and repeat process.

3. Form dough into 6-inch disk, wrap tightly in plastic wrap, and refrigerate for at least 1 hour or up to 2 days. Let chilled dough sit on counter to soften slightly, about 10 minutes, before rolling. (Wrapped dough can be frozen for up to 1 month. If frozen, let dough thaw completely on counter before rolling.)

Free-Form Tartlet Dough
Using spatula, divide dough into 6 equal portions and form each into 4-inch disk. Wrap tightly in plastic wrap and refrigerate as directed in step 3.

Making Free-Form Tart Dough

1. Process flour and salt in food processor until combined, about 5 seconds. Scatter butter over top and pulse until mixture resembles coarse sand and butter pieces are size of small peas, about 10 pulses.

2. Continue to pulse, adding ice water 1 tablespoon at a time, until dough begins to form small curds that hold together when pinched with your fingers, about 10 pulses.

3. Turn mixture onto lightly floured counter and gather into rectangular-shaped pile.

4. Starting at farthest end, use heel of your hand to smear small amount of dough against counter. Continue to smear dough until all crumbs have been worked.

5. Gather smeared crumbs together in another rectangular-shaped pile and repeat process.

6. Form dough into 6-inch disk, wrap tightly in plastic wrap, and refrigerate for at least 1 hour or up to 2 days.

Free-Form Apple Tart

TUTORIAL

Free-Form Fruit Tart with Plums and Raspberries

These tarts require little more than combining fruit, rolling dough, filling, folding the dough, and baking the beauty—as below

1. Roll dough into 12-inch circle between 2 large sheets of floured parchment paper. Refrigerate until firm.

2. Gently toss plums, raspberries, and sugar together in bowl. Mound fruit in center of dough, leaving 2½-inch border around edge of fruit.

3. Fold outermost 2 inches of dough over fruit, pleating it every 2 to 3 inches as needed; be sure to leave ½-inch border of dough between fruit and edge of tart.

4. Gently pinch pleated dough to secure, but do not press dough into fruit.

5. Brush top and sides of dough lightly with egg wash and sprinkle with sugar. Bake until crust is golden brown and fruit is bubbling, about 1 hour, rotating sheet halfway through baking.

6. Let tart cool on baking sheet for 10 minutes. Using parchment, carefully slide tart onto wire rack and let tart cool until filling thickens, about 25 minutes.

FREE-FORM FRUIT TART WITH PLUMS AND RASPBERRIES

Serves 6 | rimmed baking sheet

WHY THIS RECIPE WORKS Free-form tarts are perfect for making in the summer heat: They're easier than pie, with a short list of ingredients that produce sweet, juicy fruit surrounded by a sturdy crust. Because ripe summer fruit is a treat in itself, a modest ¼ cup of sugar was all our filling needed to enhance the fruit's natural sweetness. Some drips of fruit juice make a free-form tart appealing, but to prevent unsightly leaks or pastry damage we found it crucial to leave a small swath about ½ inch wide between the fruit and the edge of the tart to act as a barrier. We particularly love the pairing of earthy plums and bright raspberries, but we've included two additional combinations of stone fruit and berries. Taste the fruit before adding sugar; use less sugar if the fruit is very sweet, more if it is tart.

  1 recipe Free-Form Tart Dough (page 442)
  1 pound plums, halved, pitted, and cut into ½-inch wedges
  5 ounces (1 cup) raspberries
  ¼ cup (1¾ ounces) plus 1 tablespoon sugar, divided
  1 large egg, lightly beaten with 1 tablespoon water

1. Roll dough into 12-inch circle between 2 large sheets of floured parchment paper. (If dough sticks to parchment, gently loosen dough with bench scraper and dust parchment with additional flour.) Slide dough, still between parchment, onto rimmed baking sheet and refrigerate until firm, 15 to 30 minutes.

2. Adjust oven rack to middle position and heat oven to 375 degrees. Gently toss plums, raspberries, and ¼ cup sugar together in bowl.

3. Remove top sheet of parchment paper from dough. Mound fruit in center of dough, leaving 2½-inch border around edge of fruit.

4. Fold outermost 2 inches of dough over fruit, pleating it every 2 to 3 inches as needed; be sure to leave ½-inch border of dough between fruit and edge of tart. Gently pinch pleated dough to secure, but do not press dough into fruit.

5. Brush top and sides of dough lightly with egg wash and sprinkle with remaining 1 tablespoon sugar. Bake until crust is golden brown and fruit is bubbling, about 1 hour, rotating sheet halfway through baking. Let tart cool on baking sheet for 10 minutes. Using parchment, carefully slide tart onto wire rack and let tart cool until filling thickens, about 25 minutes. Serve slightly warm or at room temperature.

Free-Form Fruit Tart with Plums and Raspberries

VARIATIONS

Free-Form Fruit Tart with Apricots and Blackberries
Substitute 1 pound apricots for plums and 1 cup blackberries for raspberries.

Free-Form Fruit Tart with Peaches and Blueberries
Substitute 1 pound peaches for plums and 1 cup blueberries for raspberries.

FREE-FORM APPLE TART

Serves 6 | rimmed baking sheet

WHY THIS RECIPE WORKS Our French Apple Tart (page 432) has a buttoned-up elegance; it's the black tie attire of the elegant party. A free-form apple tart, with its display of roasted apples framed by a butter dough border, is more laidback but every bit as beautiful. A mix of Granny Smith and McIntosh apples, sliced thin, gave us complex flavor, and just ½ cup of sugar, a bit of lemon juice, and a pinch of cinnamon perfected the filling. We stacked the apples in a ring and then filled the ring with yet more apples to give the finished tart a neater, fuller appearance than if we had just casually piled the apples in the center as we often do with galettes. Finally, we folded and pleated the edge of the dough around the apples before baking the tart until golden brown. We like to serve this tart with Classic Caramel Sauce (page 549).

1 recipe Free-Form Tart Dough (page 442)
1 pound Granny Smith apples, peeled, cored, and sliced ¼ inch thick
1 pound McIntosh apples, peeled, cored, and sliced ¼ inch thick
½ cup (3½ ounces) plus 1 tablespoon sugar, divided
1 tablespoon lemon juice
⅛ teaspoon ground cinnamon

1. Roll dough into 12-inch circle between 2 large sheets of floured parchment paper. (If dough sticks to parchment, gently loosen dough with bench scraper and dust parchment with additional flour.) Slide dough, still between parchment, onto rimmed baking sheet and refrigerate until firm, 15 to 30 minutes.

2. Adjust oven rack to lower-middle position and heat oven to 375 degrees. Toss apples, ½ cup sugar, lemon juice, and cinnamon together in large bowl. Stack some apple slices into circular wall around dough, leaving 2½-inch border around edge. Fill in middle of tart with remaining apples. Fold outermost 2 inches of dough over fruit, pleating it every 2 to 3 inches as needed; be sure to leave ½-inch border of dough between fruit and edge of tart. Gently pinch pleated dough to secure, but do not press dough into fruit.

3. Brush top and sides of dough lightly with water and sprinkle with remaining 1 tablespoon sugar. Bake until crust is golden brown and apples are tender, about 1 hour, rotating sheet halfway through baking.

4. Let tart cool on baking sheet for 10 minutes. Using parchment, carefully slide tart onto wire rack and let tart cool until juices have thickened, about 25 minutes. Serve slightly warm or at room temperature.

Strawberry Galette with Candied Basil and Balsamic

STRAWBERRY GALETTE WITH CANDIED BASIL AND BALSAMIC

Serves 6 to 8 | rimmed baking sheet

WHY THIS RECIPE WORKS Typically free-form tarts need no added thickener. But one with strawberries is an exception: They create a watery mess lacking in strawberry flavor. Tossing cornstarch with the berries did the trick, and incorporating some strawberry jam intensified the berry flavor while adding viscosity. The tart's flavor was further elevated by a drizzle of balsamic glaze. And to gild the lily, we finished with some sugared basil leaves that took less than 2 minutes to candy in the microwave. We love these garnishes, but you could substitute 1 tablespoon chopped fresh basil for all of them if you prefer.

GALETTE
1 recipe Free-Form Tart Dough (page 442)
⅓ cup strawberry jam
¼ cup (1¾ ounces) plus 1 tablespoon sugar, divided
¼ teaspoon table salt
1½ tablespoons cornstarch
1½ pounds strawberries, hulled and halved (5 cups)

GARNISHES
½ cup balsamic vinegar
1½ teaspoons sugar, divided
Vegetable oil spray
¼ cup fresh basil leaves
1 teaspoon coarsely ground pepper

1. **FOR THE GALETTE:** Roll dough into 12-inch circle between 2 large sheets of floured parchment paper. (If dough sticks to parchment, gently loosen dough with bench scraper and dust parchment with additional flour.) Slide dough, still between parchment, onto rimmed baking sheet and refrigerate until firm, 15 to 30 minutes.

2. Adjust oven rack to lower-middle position and heat oven to 375 degrees. Microwave jam, ¼ cup sugar, and salt in large bowl until warm, about 30 seconds. Whisk in cornstarch. Add strawberries and gently toss to coat. Mound fruit in center of chilled dough, leaving 2-inch border around edge. Fold outermost 2 inches of dough over fruit, pleating it every 2 to 3 inches as needed. Gently pinch pleated dough to secure, but do not press dough into fruit.

3. Brush top and sides of dough lightly with water and sprinkle with remaining 1 tablespoon sugar. Bake until crust is deep golden brown and fruit is bubbling, 1 hour to 1 hour 10 minutes. Let tart cool on baking sheet for 10 minutes. Using parchment, carefully slide tart onto wire rack and let cool until just warm, about 30 minutes.

4. FOR THE GARNISHES: While tart cools, bring vinegar and 1 teaspoon sugar to simmer in 8-inch skillet over medium heat. Cook until vinegar is reduced to 2 tablespoons, 5 to 7 minutes; set aside to cool slightly, about 5 minutes. Line large plate with parchment and lightly spray with oil spray. Arrange basil in single layer on plate, then lightly spray with oil spray and sprinkle evenly with remaining ½ teaspoon sugar. Microwave until bright green and crisp, about 90 seconds; transfer to paper towel–lined plate to cool completely, about 5 minutes. Serve tart, topping with basil and pepper and drizzling with balsamic reduction.

NECTARINE AND RASPBERRY SLAB GALETTE

Serves 18 to 24 | rimmed baking sheet

WHY THIS RECIPE WORKS The expansive surface of this extra-large baking-sheet galette highlighted the beauty of the fruit, which was framed like stained glass by just a few inches of crust. Baking the galette on the lower-middle rack helped crisp up the bottom. And the large surface area of the sheet meant the fruit juices evaporated readily and thickened enough on their own after cooking. You can toss the fruit mixture in step 4 in two bowls if it doesn't fit in one.

    1 recipe Foolproof All-Butter Slab Pie Dough (page 397)
  3¼ pounds ripe but firm nectarines, halved, pitted, and sliced ½ inch thick
12½ ounces (2½ cups) raspberries
  ½ cup (3½ ounces) plus 1 tablespoon sugar, divided
  ¼ teaspoon table salt

1. Line rimmed baking sheet with parchment paper. Roll each dough square into 16 by 11-inch rectangle on floured counter; stack on prepared sheet, separated by second sheet of parchment. Cover loosely with plastic wrap and refrigerate until dough is firm but still pliable, about 10 minutes.

2. Using parchment as sling, transfer chilled dough rectangles to counter; discard parchment. Wipe sheet clean with paper towels and spray with vegetable oil spray. Starting at short side of 1 dough rectangle, loosely roll around rolling pin, then gently unroll over half of long side of prepared sheet, leaving about 2 inches of dough overhanging 3 edges. Repeat with second dough rectangle, unrolling it over empty side of sheet and overlapping first dough piece by ½ inch.

Nectarine and Raspberry Slab Galette

3. Ease dough into sheet by gently lifting edges of dough with your hand while pressing into sheet bottom with your other hand. Brush overlapping edge of dough rectangles with water and press to seal. Leave any dough that overhangs sheet in place. Cover loosely with plastic and refrigerate until firm, about 30 minutes.

4. Adjust oven racks to lower-middle and lowest positions and heat oven to 375 degrees. Gently toss nectarines, raspberries, ½ cup sugar, and salt together in bowl. Spread nectarine mixture evenly over chilled dough-lined sheet. Fold overhanging dough over filling, pleating corners, trimming excess dough as needed, and pinching overlapping edges to secure. (If dough is too stiff to fold, let stand at room temperature until pliable.) Brush dough with water and sprinkle evenly with remaining 1 tablespoon sugar.

5. Place large sheet of aluminum foil directly on lower rack (to catch any bubbling juices). Place galette on upper rack and bake until crust is deep golden brown and fruit is bubbling, about 1 hour, rotating sheet halfway through baking. Let galette cool on wire rack until filling has set, about 2 hours. Serve.

PUFF PASTRY TARTS

KEY POINTS

Keep pastry cold

Brush with egg wash

Create platform for filling

Fill with something creamy

PUFF PASTRY TARTS ARE DELICIOUSLY DECEITFUL: Their many flaky layers and elegant golden puffed appearance give the impression that they're difficult to execute. But they're the easiest tarts of them all if you start with store-bought frozen puff pastry as we do.

There's no need to slight store-bought here. While supermarket pie dough may be flat-tasting and short (not flaky), store-bought puff pastry is decidedly buttery and flaky, and it rises more evenly than most can achieve with from-scratch puff pastry dough (we'll show you how to make your own on page 508, however). Using puff pastry made with all butter, such as Dufour brand, makes a difference if you can find it; otherwise, Pepperidge Farm Puff Pastry works fine.

With purchased puff pastry, tart making seems more like assembly than baking. You can create turnovers (see page 510) and other filled pastries and napoleons (see page 511) with this convenient ingredient but it also makes a great base for traditional tarts. Thaw the dough, roll it to the proper dimensions, and then the tart's only as difficult to make as the filling you choose. All of our tarts in this category call for a creamy filling, to which other toppings nicely anchor, although you'll also find puff pastry as a base for Easy Pear Tarte Tatin on page 457 and as an easy dough to fit into muffin tins to re-create Portuguese Egg Tarts on page 462.

PREPARING THE PLATFORM

Puff pastry dough is rolled to a smooth rectangle; what holds the filling is a dropped platform for creating the filling. You create the space after the tart base is baked.

1. Roll dough to desired dimensions. (Sometimes we'll divide dough in half to make 2 units.)

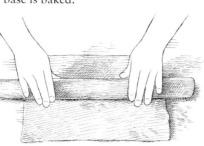

2. Poke dough all over with fork.

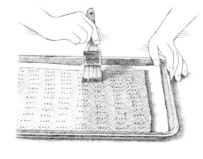

3. Brush with egg wash.

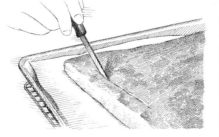

4. Once crust is baked, use tip of paring knife to cut ½-inch-wide border around top edge of pastry (being careful not to cut through bottom).

5. Press center down with your fingertips and then fill.

Roasted Plum and Mascarpone Tart

STRAWBERRY-PINEAPPLE TART

Serves 8 | rimmed baking sheet

WHY THIS RECIPE WORKS We love our Fresh Fruit Tart (page 427), and it's an elegant classic. But making tart dough from scratch and arranging berries with precision aren't always possible when you're preparing other components of a summertime party. Not to worry: A tart featuring gleaming fruit—here a creative combo of pineapple and strawberries—atop a creamy filling and crisp crust can come together easily. Frozen puff pastry proved strong enough to support the filling; we didn't roll it out like our other puff pastry doughs since it had to have the heft to hold a whole lot of fruit here. Folding in the edges of the pastry before baking created a barrier to keep the fruit in place. For the filling, we beat softened cream cheese with a little almond extract. We sprinkled sugar (combined with fragrant cinnamon) over the pastry before baking to form a moisture barrier. To thaw frozen puff pastry, let it sit either in the refrigerator for 24 hours or on the counter for 30 minutes to 1 hour.

- 1 (9½ by 9-inch) sheet puff pastry, thawed
- 2 tablespoons plus 2 teaspoons sugar
- ¼ teaspoon ground cinnamon
- 10 ounces (2 cups) strawberries, hulled and sliced thin
- ¼ teaspoon grated lemon zest
- 4 ounces cream cheese, softened
- ⅛ teaspoon almond extract
- ¾ cup 1-inch pineapple pieces
  Mint leaves (optional)

1. Adjust oven rack to upper-middle position and heat oven to 425 degrees. Line rimmed baking sheet with parchment paper. Unfold thawed pastry onto baking sheet and brush ½-inch border along edges of pastry with water. Fold long edges of pastry over by ½ inch, then fold short edges over by ½ inch. Working lengthwise, lightly score outer edge of all folded edges with paring knife. Poke dough all over with fork.

2. Combine 2 teaspoons sugar and cinnamon and sprinkle mixture over inside of tart shell. Bake until pastry and sugar are deep golden brown, 15 to 22 minutes. Transfer sheet to wire rack and let tart shell cool completely, about 1 hour.

3. While tart shell is baking, stir strawberries, lemon zest, and remaining 2 tablespoons sugar together in bowl. Stir cream cheese and almond extract in second bowl until smooth.

4. Spread cream cheese mixture evenly over bottom of cooled tart shell. Scatter strawberry mixture and pineapple on top. Garnish with mint leaves, if using. Serve immediately.

ROASTED PLUM AND MASCARPONE TART

Serves 6 to 8 | rimmed baking sheet

WHY THIS RECIPE WORKS There's something incredibly appealing about the richly caramelized exterior of roasted fruit adorning pastry. So for this elegant puff pastry tart, we first roasted plums, which gain great complexity from roasting, before adding them to a baked shell for a multilayer tart. We created a lacquering sauce by deglazing the pan of plums with white wine, adding sugar, thyme, and currants. For a rich, plush filling, we incorporated creamy, lightly sweetened mascarpone cheese flavored with a little lemon zest. To thaw frozen puff pastry, let it sit either in the refrigerator for 24 hours or on the counter for 30 minutes to 1 hour. Be gentle when stirring the mascarpone in step 1; stirring aggressively can cause it to become too loose or even break.

- 12 ounces (1½ cups) mascarpone cheese, room temperature
- 2 tablespoons confectioners' sugar
- 1 teaspoon grated lemon zest plus ½ teaspoon juice
- 1 (9½ by 9-inch) sheet puff pastry, thawed
- 1 large egg, lightly beaten with 1 tablespoon water
- 3 tablespoons unsalted butter, divided
- 6 ripe but firm plums, halved and pitted
- ¾ cup dry white wine
- ¼ cup dried currants
- ¼ cup (1¾ ounces) granulated sugar
- 1 teaspoon fresh thyme leaves, divided
- ⅛ teaspoon table salt

1. Adjust oven rack to middle position and heat oven to 425 degrees. Gently stir mascarpone, confectioners' sugar, and lemon zest in bowl until combined, then cover with plastic wrap and refrigerate until ready to serve.

2. Roll pastry into 14 by 10-inch rectangle on floured counter and transfer to parchment paper–lined rimmed baking sheet. Poke dough all over with fork, then brush surface with egg wash. Bake until puffed and golden brown, 12 to 15 minutes, rotating sheet halfway through baking.

3. Using tip of paring knife, cut ½-inch-wide border around top edge of pastry (being careful not to cut through to bottom), then press center down with your fingertips. Transfer tart shell to wire rack and let cool completely, about 30 minutes.

4. Melt 2 tablespoons butter in 12-inch ovensafe skillet over medium-high heat. Place plum halves cut side down in skillet and cook, without moving, until plums are beginning to brown, about 3 minutes. Transfer skillet to oven and roast for 5 minutes. Flip plums cut side up and continue to roast until fork easily pierces fruit, about 5 minutes.

5. Remove skillet from oven and transfer plums to plate. Being careful of hot skillet handle, whisk in wine, currants, granulated sugar, ½ teaspoon thyme, salt, and remaining 1 tablespoon butter. Bring to vigorous simmer over medium-high heat, whisking to scrape up any browned bits, and cook until sauce has consistency of maple syrup and measures about ½ cup, 3 to 5 minutes. Off heat, stir in lemon juice. Let cool slightly, about 10 minutes.

6. Spread mascarpone mixture evenly over cooled tart shell, avoiding raised border, then arrange plums over top. Drizzle with sauce and sprinkle with remaining ½ teaspoon thyme. Serve.

CHOCOLATE-HAZELNUT RASPBERRY MOUSSE TART

Serves 6 to 8 | rimmed baking sheet

WHY THIS RECIPE WORKS This quick tart is filled with pretty pink mousse, packed with berry flavor, and complemented by sophisticated candied hazelnuts. Mousse doesn't have to be an egg white–whipping affair, but simply folding raspberry puree into whipped cream didn't work—it was too loose for a tart. We tried cooking the puree to a thick jam, but the mousse lost its brightness. The solution came with a little cream cheese, which added body and tang. We loved pairing raspberry with hazelnuts, but we wanted even more nut flavor, so we added a slick of Nutella under the mousse. To thaw frozen puff pastry, let it sit either in the refrigerator for 24 hours or on the counter for 30 minutes to 1 hour. Use hazelnuts in the candied nuts.

12½ ounces (2½ cups) raspberries, divided
 ⅓ cup (2⅓ ounces) sugar
1½ ounces cream cheese, cut into ½-inch pieces and softened
 ⅔ cup heavy cream
  1 (9½ by 9-inch) sheet puff pastry, thawed
  1 large egg, lightly beaten with 1 tablespoon water
 ⅓ cup Nutella
  1 recipe Candied Nuts (page 551)
     Shaved chocolate

1. Adjust oven rack to middle position and heat oven to 425 degrees. Using potato masher, mash 1½ cups raspberries and sugar in medium saucepan until raspberries are completely broken down. Cook mixture over medium-low until thickened slightly, about 5 minutes, stirring occasionally.

2. Off heat, whisk in cream cheese until well combined. Strain raspberry mixture through fine-mesh strainer into bowl, pressing on solids with rubber spatula to extract as much puree as possible. Discard solids and refrigerate puree until cooled, about 10 minutes.

Chocolate-Hazelnut Raspberry Mousse Tart

3. Using stand mixer fitted with whisk attachment, whip cream on medium-low speed until foamy, about 1 minute. Increase speed to medium-high and whip until stiff peaks form, 1 to 3 minutes. Gently whisk one-third of whipped cream into chilled raspberry puree until lightened. Using rubber spatula, gently fold in remaining whipped cream until homogeneous. Refrigerate until ready to serve. (Mousse can be refrigerated for up to 24 hours.)

4. Roll pastry into 14 by 10-inch rectangle on floured counter. Cut in half lengthwise and transfer to parchment paper–lined rimmed baking sheet (you should have two 14 by 5-inch rectangles). Poke dough all over with fork and brush surface with egg wash. Bake until puffed and golden brown, 12 to 15 minutes, rotating sheet halfway through baking.

5. Using tip of paring knife, cut ½-inch-wide border around top edge of each tart shell (being careful not to cut through to bottom), then press center down with your fingertips. Transfer tart shells to wire rack and let cool completely, about 30 minutes.

6. Divide Nutella between cooled tart shells and, avoiding raised border, spread into even layer. Repeat with raspberry mixture. Top with remaining 1 cup raspberries, candied hazelnuts, and shaved chocolate. Serve.

TARTE TATINS

KEY POINTS

Make adjustments for different fruits
Let cool before removing
Carefully invert out of pan

A TARTE TATIN IS A BRAVE DESSERT. Caramel-cooked fruits (apples, originally) lay artfully in a hot skillet with a pastry dough on top; then, the maker rolls up their sleeves, accesses their valor, and flips the tart out of the pan so the fruit, glaze and all, falls neatly on top of the pastry on a platter.

While tarte Tatin requires moving with intention, its invention may have been an accident. Other upside-down tarts existed in France previously, but there's a story (two versions, actually) that one of the proprietors of Hotel Tatin in Paris, Stéphanie Tatin, topped her cooking apples with dough by chance when she meant to make a traditional tart. It was a hit.

Sure, hot caramel; moist, sugary fruit; and a hot skillet obviously require attention when cooking and extracting a tart; however, in many ways tarte Tatin can be more simple than a regular apple tart. It's made in one pan, it requires a simple rolled piece of dough, there's no blind-baking, and there's no need to worry about a filling setting up properly.

Impress your guests with the classic, Apple Tarte Tatin (page 454) or a summery peach version (see page 456) with its own set of considerations. Or take an even easier path making a faux Tatin with pears placed over some buttery, flaky store-bought puff pastry (see more puff pastry tarts on pages 450–451).

FLIP OUT

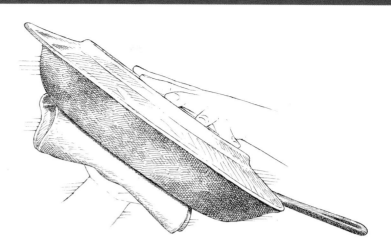

The hardest part about a tarte Tatin is getting it out of the pan. Fear not! While it may seem logical to flip as soon as you can so the tart doesn't stick, letting the tart rest thickens the filling. The key is using a platter that's comfortably larger than the skillet. Even better, one with sloped sides contains excess caramel. After the tart rests, loosen the tart from the skillet and place an inverted large platter on top. Swiftly and carefully flip the tart onto the platter. If the apples shift or stick to the skillet, rearrange with a spoon.

FRUIT JUICE FACTOR

Apple tarte Tatin is the classic. To swap in another fruit—without making a tart awash in juices—you need to follow a slightly different formula. Peaches, for example, are much wetter, sweeter, and more fragile. How to switch from pomme to pêche?

Simmer down on the sweetness: Peaches are sweeter than apples so cooking them with caramel is too cloying. Instead use just a little sugar, sprinkled over a butter paste that coats the skillet.

Reduce the juice: Watery summery peaches leach juices that will sog out the tart and prevent caramelization. Cook the peaches until the juices thicken.

Pour off and repurpose: Before inverting the tart, drain off the juice and then reduce it to create a glaze for the finished tart.

APPLE TARTE TATIN

Serves 6 to 8 | 10-inch ovensafe nonstick skillet

WHY THIS RECIPE WORKS For our version of this classic dessert, we were after big chunks of juicy apples glazed with a sticky, buttery caramel atop a flaky crust. We started with a simplified all-butter pie dough, which we rolled out immediately and then let rest in the fridge, to display the fruit and caramel. Using a separate saucepan to cook the caramel (instead of making the caramel in the skillet with the apples) gave us greater control over the final color of the caramel and the texture of the apples. We poured the amber caramel over the softened apples, topped it with the chilled pastry, and then baked the tart until the caramel was thick and syrupy. Flipping the tart out of the skillet revealed a gorgeous spiral of caramelized apples. We like Gala or Golden Delicious apples here because they retain their shape and provide mild sweetness.

DOUGH
- 1 cup (5 ounces) all-purpose flour
- 2 teaspoons sugar
- ½ teaspoon table salt
- 8 tablespoons unsalted butter, cut into ½-inch pieces and chilled
- ¼ cup ice water

FILLING
- 4 tablespoons unsalted butter, cut into 1-tablespoon pieces, divided
- 5 Gala or Golden Delicious apples (6 to 7 ounces each), peeled, quartered, and cored
- ¼ teaspoon table salt
- ¾ cup (5¼ ounces) sugar
- ¼ cup water
- 2 tablespoons light corn syrup

1. FOR THE DOUGH: Line large, flat plate with parchment paper. Process flour, sugar, and salt in food processor until combined, about 3 seconds. Scatter butter over top and pulse until irregular, large chunks of butter form with some small pieces throughout, about 5 pulses. Add ice water and process until little balls of dough form and almost no dry flour remains, about 10 seconds, scraping down sides of bowl after 5 seconds.

2. Turn out dough onto clean counter and gather into ball. Sprinkle dough and counter generously with flour and shape dough into 5-inch disk, pressing any cracked edges back together. Roll dough into 9-inch circle, reflouring counter and dough as needed. Loosely roll dough around rolling pin and gently unroll it onto prepared plate. Cut three 2-inch slits in center of dough. Cover dough loosely with plastic wrap and refrigerate until dough is very firm, at least 2 hours or up to 2 days.

3. FOR THE FILLING: After dough has chilled for at least 2 hours, adjust oven rack to middle position and heat oven to 350 degrees.

4. Melt 1 tablespoon butter in 10-inch ovensafe nonstick skillet over medium-low heat. Off heat, arrange apple quarters on their sides in melted butter in circular pattern around edge of skillet, nestling fruit snugly. Tuck remaining apples into center (it is not necessary to maintain circular pattern in center). Sprinkle salt over apples.

5. Cover and cook over medium-low heat until apples have released enough juice to cover bottom of skillet and juice just begins to reduce, 10 to 15 minutes. Uncover and continue to cook until liquid has mostly evaporated, 3 to 5 minutes longer (apples may brown on undersides). Remove skillet from heat and set aside.

6. Bring sugar, water, and corn syrup to boil in large heavy-bottomed saucepan over medium-high heat. Cook, without stirring, until mixture begins to turn straw-colored around edge of saucepan, 4 to 8 minutes. Reduce heat to medium-low and continue to cook, swirling saucepan occasionally, until mixture is light amber–colored and registers 355 to 360 degrees, 2 to 5 minutes longer. (To take temperature, remove saucepan from heat and tilt to 1 side; stir with thermometer to equalize hotter and cooler spots, avoiding bottom of saucepan.)

7. Off heat, carefully stir in remaining 3 tablespoons butter (mixture will bubble and steam). Working quickly, pour caramel over apples (caramel will not completely cover apples). Place dough over apples.

8. Bake tart until thick, syrupy bubbles form around edge and crust is golden brown, 50 minutes to 1 hour. Transfer skillet to wire rack and let sit until cool enough to handle, 20 to 30 minutes.

9. Run thin rubber spatula or plastic knife around edge of skillet to loosen tart. Invert large serving platter over skillet (make sure platter is larger than skillet and has sloped sides to catch any excess caramel). Swiftly and carefully invert tart onto platter (if apples shift or stick to skillet, rearrange with spoon). Cut into wedges and serve warm or at room temperature.

TO MAKE AHEAD: Let baked tart cool completely in skillet. Cover and refrigerate for up to 24 hours. To serve, reheat tart in 300-degree oven until hot, about 25 minutes, then cool and invert.

TUTORIAL
Apple Tarte Tatin

Turn tart(e) on its head with this recipe.

1. Arrange apple quarters on their sides in melted butter in circular pattern around edge of skillet, nestling fruit snugly. Tuck remaining apples into center. Sprinkle salt over apples.

2. Cover and cook until apples have released enough juice to cover bottom of skillet and juice just begins to reduce, 10 to 15 minutes. Uncover and cook until liquid has mostly evaporated, 3 to 5 minutes longer.

3. Cook caramel, without stirring, until mixture begins to turn straw-colored around edges, 4 to 8 minutes. Reduce heat and cook, swirling saucepan occasionally, until mixture is light amber and registers 355 to 360 degrees, 2 to 5 minutes longer.

4. Off heat, carefully stir remaining 3 tablespoons butter into caramel. Working quickly, pour caramel over apples.

5. Place dough over apples.

6. Bake tart until thick, syrupy bubbles form around edge and crust is golden brown, 50 minutes to 1 hour. (For information on removing tart from pan, see page 453).

PEACH TARTE TATIN

Serves 8 | 10-inch ovensafe skillet

WHY THIS RECIPE WORKS We wanted to put a summery spin on our Apple Tarte Tatin (page 454), and figured we could substitute peaches for the apples. But peaches produced a cloying tart that was awash in juice; this soft fruit would require a different approach. To make peaches work, we started by cooking them in the skillet for slightly less time. Once our tart was baked, we poured off the excess juice before inverting the tart. Then we reduced the juices with a bit of bourbon and brushed the mixture over the peaches. Firm peaches are important here, as they hold their shape when cooked. Yellow peaches are preferable to white peaches. When pouring off the liquid in step 4, the peaches may shift; shake the skillet to redistribute them.

1 recipe single-crust pie dough (see pages 342–348)
3 tablespoons unsalted butter, softened
½ cup (3½ ounces) plus 2 tablespoons sugar
¼ teaspoon table salt
2 pounds ripe but firm peaches, peeled, quartered, and pitted
1 tablespoon bourbon (optional)

1. Invert rimmed baking sheet and place sheet of parchment paper or waxed paper on top. Roll dough into 10-inch circle on floured counter. Loosely roll dough around rolling pin and gently unroll it onto prepared sheet. Working around circumference, fold ½ inch of dough under itself and pinch to create 9-inch round with raised rim. Cut three 2-inch slits in center of dough and refrigerate until needed.

2. Adjust oven rack to middle position and heat oven to 400 degrees. Smear butter over bottom of 10-inch ovensafe skillet. Sprinkle ½ cup sugar over butter and shake skillet to distribute sugar in even layer. Sprinkle salt over sugar. Arrange peaches in circular pattern around edge of skillet, nestling fruit snugly. Tuck remaining peaches into center, squeezing in as much fruit as possible (it is not necessary to maintain circular pattern in center).

3. Place skillet over high heat and cook, without stirring fruit, until juice is released and turns from pink to deep amber, 8 to 12 minutes. (If necessary, adjust skillet's placement on burner to even out hot spots and encourage even browning.) Off heat, carefully slide prepared dough over fruit, making sure dough is centered and does not touch edge of skillet. Brush dough lightly with water and sprinkle with remaining 2 tablespoons sugar. Transfer skillet to oven and bake until crust is very well browned, 30 to 35 minutes. Transfer skillet to wire rack set in rimmed baking sheet and let cool for 20 minutes.

4. Place inverted plate on top of crust. With your hand firmly securing plate, carefully tip skillet over bowl to drain juice (skillet handle may still be hot). When all juice has been transferred to bowl, return skillet to wire rack, remove plate, and shake skillet firmly to redistribute peaches. Off heat, carefully invert tart onto plate, then slide tart onto wire rack. (If peaches have shifted during unmolding, gently nudge them back into place with spoon.)

5. Pour juice into now-empty skillet (handle may be hot). Stir in bourbon, if using, and cook over high heat, stirring constantly, until mixture is dark and thick and starting to smoke, 2 to 3 minutes. Return mixture to bowl and let cool until mixture is consistency of honey, 2 to 3 minutes. Brush mixture over peaches. Let tart cool for at least 20 minutes. Serve.

Peach Tarte Tatin

EASY PEAR TARTE TATIN

Serves 6 to 8 | rimmed baking sheet

WHY THIS RECIPE WORKS We wanted one more tarte Tatin to satisfy our craving for caramelized fruit in a buttery crust, so we thought we'd create something for a weeknight that didn't require masterfully flipping pastry onto a platter. We first baked a sheet of puff pastry to a beautiful golden brown. While the pastry baked in the oven, we cooked pears in a skillet until they were browned and tender. We then spooned the pears over the pastry, arranging them in three even rows and leaving a ½-inch border around the outside of the pastry. We served the whole thing with whipped sour cream. This easy tarte Tatin was really good, but for a bit more flavor we decided to make a sauce, stirring some of the sour cream topping into the caramelized pear juices left in the pan to make a quick caramel. To thaw frozen puff pastry, let it sit either in the refrigerator for 24 hours or on the counter for 30 minutes to 1 hour. If the pastry rises unevenly during baking, press it flat immediately after removing it from the oven.

1 (9½ by 9-inch) sheet puff pastry, thawed

PEARS
8 tablespoons unsalted butter
¾ cup (5¼ ounces) sugar
2 pounds Anjou or Bartlett pears, peeled, quartered, and cored

TOPPING
1 cup heavy cream
½ cup sour cream
2 tablespoons pear liqueur, such as Poire Williams (optional)

1. Adjust oven rack to middle position and heat oven to 400 degrees. Line rimmed baking sheet with parchment paper. Place puff pastry on parchment, poke dough all over with fork, and bake until golden brown and puffed, 10 to 12 minutes. Transfer crust to serving platter or cutting board.

2. **FOR THE PEARS:** Meanwhile, melt butter in 12-inch skillet over high heat. Off heat, sprinkle sugar evenly over surface, then arrange pears in skillet so they are all resting flat side down. Return skillet to high heat and cook until juices in pan turn rich amber color, about 15 minutes. Using tongs, turn pears over to the other flat side. Cook pears for 8 minutes longer.

Easy Pear Tarte Tatin

3. **FOR THE TOPPING:** Using stand mixer fitted with whisk attachment, whip heavy cream and sour cream on medium-low speed until foamy, about 1 minute. Increase speed to high and whip until soft peaks form, 1 to 3 minutes. Add liqueur, if using, and whip until stiff peaks form.

4. Using tongs, remove pear quarters from pan one at a time and place in 3 overlapping horizontal rows on baked crust. Spoon about three-quarters of pan juices over top of pears. (You can use pastry brush to dab some of liquid onto edges of pastry.) Whisk 2 tablespoons whipped sour cream topping into liquid left in pan.

5. Cut tart in half vertically down center, and then horizontally into 3 or 4 rows (to serve 6 or 8, respectively). Transfer portions to individual plates and top each with a dollop of whipped sour cream and a drizzle of pan sauce. Serve immediately.

TARTLETS

MOST TARTS TRANSLATE TO A SMALL-SCALE FORMAT, even more so than pies because they don't require a top crust. These diminutive desserts are probably among the most elegant you can serve. And the crust-to-filling ratio per dessert increases—ideal for buttery pastry lovers.

Miniaturization isn't tough: The principles you learned for working with other tarts stand. But there are some considerations. First, fillings will cook faster with much less volume contained within the pastry. We'll teach you to create tarts with crusts that are browned in the time it takes to cook the more scant filling. Parbaking helps. Second, there are some equipment needs for miniature tarts. Four-inch tart pans with removable bottoms are an adorable investment. The smaller size of tartlets makes them easier to dislodge from tart pans, but we still highly recommend the removable bottoms as these desserts are prone to sticking. You'll also want a muffin tin, but we suspect you already have one of those.

Rolling dough into small circles for small tarts can be a pain, so we developed a shortbread dough that can be pressed right into the pan (without becoming tough) for fluted tartlets. Other tartlets require only some pleating and folding for galettes (it's easier with the smaller format) or cutting store-bought puff pastry dough to size.

FORMING THE CRUST FOR SHORTCRUST TARTLETS

We take the temperamental out of tiny by creating a dough that can be patted into the pan before baking and filling.

1. Whisk flour, sugar, and salt together in bowl. Add melted butter and stir with wooden spoon until dough forms.

2. Divide dough into 6 equal pieces.

3. Working with 1 piece of dough at a time, press two-thirds of dough into bottom of 1 prepared pan using your fingers.

4. Press remaining dough into fluted sides of pan. Press and smooth dough with your fingers to even thickness.

MAKING MINI GALETTES

Galettes need to be formed right on the baking sheet; you could never transfer these abundantly filled little packages without risk. We give each a parchment square to sit on.

1. Working with 1 disk of dough at a time, roll into 6½-inch circle; stack on baking sheet separated by 7-inch-square sheets of parchment paper.

2. Arrange chilled dough circles with parchment squares on 2 baking sheets.

3. Mound filling in the center of each circle, leaving 1-inch border around edge.

4. Fold dough over filling, pleating every 2 to 3 inches as needed.

NUTELLA TARTLETS

Serves 6 | six 4-inch tart pans

WHY THIS RECIPE WORKS Nutella is an ideal tartlet filling because with just a few more simple ingredients, you can create a decadent—and easy—dessert. In order to transform Nutella into a creamy filling, we amped up its richness and transformed its thick texture by adding heavy cream and butter and a bit of melted bittersweet chocolate for a deeper, more intense flavor. We then microwaved the mixture until it formed a homogeneous filling—essentially a ganache that just needed some time in the fridge to set up. Once chilled, the luscious truffle-like chocolate-hazelnut filling perfectly complemented the crisp, buttery crust. A sprinkling of chopped hazelnuts in the bottom of each tart shell added welcome crunch to the smooth, creamy filling.

CRUST

  2 cups (10 ounces) all-purpose flour
  ½ cup (3½ ounces) sugar
  ¾ teaspoon table salt
 14 tablespoons unsalted butter, melted

FILLING

  1 cup hazelnuts, toasted and skinned
 1½ cups Nutella
  ½ cup plus 1 tablespoon heavy cream
  3 ounces bittersweet chocolate, chopped
  3 tablespoons unsalted butter

1. FOR THE CRUST: Adjust oven rack to lowest position and heat oven to 350 degrees. Spray six 4-inch tart pans with removable bottoms with vegetable oil spray. Whisk flour, sugar, and salt together in bowl. Add melted butter and stir with wooden spoon until dough forms.

2. Divide dough into 6 equal pieces. Working with 1 piece of dough at a time, press two-thirds of dough into bottom of 1 prepared pan using your fingers. Press remaining dough into fluted sides of pan. Press and smooth dough with your fingers to even thickness.

3. Line tart pans with double layer of aluminum foil, covering edges to prevent burning, and fill with pie weights. Place pans on wire rack set in rimmed baking sheet and bake until edges are beginning to turn golden, about 25 minutes. Carefully remove foil and weights, rotate sheet, and continue to bake until crust is golden brown and firm to touch, 10 to 15 minutes; let cool completely, about 1 hour.

4. FOR THE FILLING: Reserve 48 whole hazelnuts for garnish, then chop remaining hazelnuts coarse. Sprinkle chopped hazelnuts evenly among cooled tart shells.

5. Microwave Nutella, cream, chocolate, and butter together in covered bowl at 30 percent power, stirring often, until mixture is smooth and glossy, about 1 minute (do not overheat). Divide warm Nutella filling evenly among cooled tart shells, smoothing tops with clean spatula into even layer.

6. Refrigerate tarts until filling is just set, about 15 minutes. Arrange reserved whole hazelnuts evenly around edge of tarts and continue to refrigerate until filling is firm, about 1½ hours. Remove outer ring of tart pans, slide thin metal spatula between tartlets and pan bottoms, and carefully slide tartlets onto serving platter or individual plates. Serve.

LEMON TARTLETS

Serves 6 | six 4-inch tart pans

WHY THIS RECIPE WORKS Our Lemon–Olive Oil Tart (page 428) is an elegant dessert, but individual tartlets are the darlings of pastry cases and the thought of enjoying a sleek fluted tart all our own was undeniably appealing. We blind-baked our pat-in-the-pan crusts so they wouldn't shrink and would remain crisp under the filling after baking. Once the lemon curd ingredients have been combined, cook the curd immediately; otherwise, its finished texture will be grainy. It is important to add the filling to the tart shells while they are still warm; if the shells have cooled, rewarm them in the oven for 5 minutes before adding the filling.

CRUST

  2 cups (10 ounces) all-purpose flour
  ½ cup (3½ ounces) granulated sugar
  ¾ teaspoon table salt
 14 tablespoons unsalted butter, melted

FILLING

  3 large eggs plus 9 large yolks
  1 cup (7 ounces) granulated sugar
  3 tablespoons grated lemon zest plus ¾ cup juice (4 lemons)
  ¼ teaspoon table salt
  6 tablespoons unsalted butter, cut into 6 pieces
  3 tablespoons heavy cream, chilled
     Confectioners' sugar

1. FOR THE CRUST: Adjust oven racks to middle and lowest positions and heat oven to 350 degrees. Spray six 4-inch tart pans with removable bottoms with vegetable oil spray. Whisk flour, sugar, and salt together in bowl. Add melted butter and stir with wooden spoon until dough forms.

2. Divide dough into 6 equal pieces. Working with 1 piece of dough at a time, press two-thirds of dough into bottom of 1 prepared pan using your fingers. Press remaining dough into fluted sides of pan. Press and smooth dough with your fingers to even thickness. (See page 459.)

3. Line tart pans with double layer of aluminum foil, covering edges to prevent burning, and fill with pie weights. Place pans on wire rack set in rimmed baking sheet and bake on lower rack until edges are beginning to turn golden, about 25 minutes. Carefully remove foil and weights, rotate sheet, and continue to bake until tart shells are golden brown and firm to touch, 10 to 15 minutes; set aside (tart shells must still be warm when filling is added).

4. FOR THE FILLING: Whisk eggs and yolks together in medium saucepan. Whisk in sugar until combined, then whisk in lemon zest and juice and salt. Add butter and cook over medium-low heat, stirring constantly, until mixture thickens slightly and registers 170 degrees, about 5 minutes. Immediately pour mixture through fine-mesh strainer into bowl. Stir in cream.

5. With tarts still on wire rack, divide warm lemon filling evenly among warm tart shells. Bake on upper rack until filling is shiny and opaque and centers jiggle slightly when shaken, about 10 minutes, rotating sheet halfway through baking.

6. Let tartlets cool completely on wire rack in sheet, about 2 hours. Remove outer ring of tart pans, slide thin metal spatula between tartlets and pan bottoms, and carefully slide tartlets onto serving platter or individual plates. Dust with confectioners' sugar. Serve.

INDIVIDUAL FREE-FORM APPLE TARTLETS

Serves 6 | 2 rimmed baking sheets

WHY THIS RECIPE WORKS An individual package of caramel-y apples and buttery pastry is a great gift to receive at the end of the meal, so we made individual free-form tarts. We sliced the apples thin enough to cook through in a short amount of time and tossed them with sugar, a little lemon juice, and a pinch of cinnamon. After we divided our standard free-form tart dough into 6 portions and rolled them into circles, all that was left was to pile in the apple mixture and fold the dough around it before baking these tartlets to crisp, golden-brown perfection. We like to serve these tartlets with Caramel Sauce (page 549).

Nutella Tartlets

Lemon Tartlets

1 recipe Free-Form Tartlet Dough (page 442)
2 McIntosh apples, peeled, cored, halved, and sliced
   ¼ inch thick
1 Granny Smith apple, peeled, cored, halved, and sliced
   ¼ inch thick
½ cup (3½ ounces) sugar, divided
1½ teaspoons lemon juice
   Pinch ground cinnamon

1. Working with 1 disk of dough at a time, roll into 6½-inch circle on floured counter; stack on baking sheet, separated by 7-inch-square sheets of parchment paper. Cover with plastic wrap and refrigerate until firm but pliable, about 10 minutes.

2. Adjust oven racks to upper-middle and lower-middle positions and heat oven to 375 degrees. Toss apples with 7 tablespoons sugar, lemon juice, and cinnamon. Arrange dough circles with parchment squares on 2 baking sheets. Mound apple mixture evenly in center of each circle, leaving 1-inch border around edge. Fold dough over apples, pleating every 2 to 3 inches as needed. Gently pinch pleated dough to secure, but do not press dough into fruit.

3. Brush top and sides of tartlets lightly with water and sprinkle with remaining 1 tablespoon sugar. Bake until crusts are golden brown and apples are tender, about 45 minutes, switching and rotating sheets halfway through baking.

4. Transfer sheets to wire rack and let tartlets cool for 10 minutes. Using metal spatula, loosen tartlets from parchment and carefully slide onto wire rack; let tartlets cool until apple juices have thickened, about 25 minutes. Serve slightly warm or at room temperature.

PORTUGUESE EGG TARTS
Serves 12 | muffin tin
WHY THIS RECIPE WORKS The sweet, creamy vanilla- and lemon-scented custard filling and crisp pastry shell of petite Portuguese egg tarts leave tourists yearning for these iconic pastries. Store-bought puff pastry, parbaked in muffin tin cups, gave us the most shattering crust. To get the classic swirled pastry layers, we rolled the puff pastry dough into logs, sliced it into rounds and pressed it into the muffin cups. While many of our custard recipes use cornstarch as a thickener, we found that flour helped this custard withstand the high oven heat necessary to achieve the traditional spotty brown surface. Serve these tarts warm or at room temperature with a sprinkle of cinnamon and confectioners' sugar as they do in Portugal. To thaw frozen puff pastry, let it sit either in the refrigerator for 24 hours or at room temperature for 30 minutes to 1 hour.

1½ (9½ by 9-inch) sheets puff pastry, thawed
1½ cups whole milk
  1 cup (7 ounces) granulated sugar
  ¾ cup heavy cream
  2 (3-inch) strips lemon zest
  ¼ cup (1¼ ounces) all-purpose flour
  ½ teaspoon table salt
  8 large egg yolks
1½ teaspoons vanilla extract
    Confectioners' sugar
    Ground cinnamon

1. Unfold puff pastry sheets on clean counter. Brush tops lightly with water. Roll full pastry sheet into tight log and pinch seam to seal. Roll short side of half pastry sheet into tight log and pinch seam to seal. Transfer to rimmed baking sheet, cover loosely with plastic wrap, and refrigerate until firm, at least 30 minutes.

2. Spray 12-cup muffin tin with vegetable oil spray. Using serrated knife, trim off uneven ends of each dough log and discard. Cut twelve 1-inch slices from dough logs and place 1 slice in each muffin tin cup, cut side up. Using your moistened fingers, press dough into bottom and up sides of muffin cups so dough reaches top of cups (dough should be very thin). Prick shells all over with fork and refrigerate muffin tin until dough is firm, about 20 minutes.

3. Adjust oven racks to upper-middle and lower-middle positions and heat oven to 350 degrees. Line tart shells with muffin tin liners and fill with pie weights. Place muffin tin on lower rack and bake until pastry is puffed but still pale, about 10 minutes. Cover muffin tin with aluminum foil and continue to bake until pastry is just blond at edges, about 5 minutes. Transfer muffin tin to wire rack, discard foil, and let tart shells cool slightly, 10 to 15 minutes. Remove liners and weights. Increase oven temperature to 500 degrees.

4. Combine milk, granulated sugar, cream, and lemon zest in medium saucepan and cook over medium-low heat, stirring occasionally, until steaming, about 6 minutes. Off heat, let mixture steep for 15 minutes; discard zest. Whisk flour and salt together in bowl, then gradually whisk in milk mixture. Whisk in egg yolks and vanilla until smooth. Return egg mixture to saucepan and cook over medium-low heat, whisking constantly, until mixture begins to thicken, 6 to 8 minutes. Strain mixture through fine-mesh strainer into clean bowl.

5. Divide custard evenly among pastry shells. Bake on upper rack until shells are dark golden brown and crisp and custard is puffed and spotty brown, 8 to 11 minutes. Let tarts cool in muffin tin on wire rack for 10 minutes. Remove tarts from muffin tin and let cool on wire rack for 15 minutes. Dust with confectioners' sugar and cinnamon and serve warm or at room temperature.

TUTORIAL
Portuguese Egg Tarts

A muffin tin and store-bought puff pastry make these custardy tarts with a burnished finish easy to prepare and bake.

1. Roll full pastry sheet into tight log and pinch seam to seal. Roll short side of half pastry sheet into tight log and pinch seam to seal. Refrigerate until firm.

2. Using serrated knife, trim off uneven ends of each dough log and discard. Cut twelve 1-inch slices from dough logs.

3. Place 1 slice in each muffin tin cup, cut side up. Using your moistened fingers, press dough into bottom and up sides of muffin cups so dough reaches top of cups.

4. Prick shells all over with fork. Refrigerate until dough is firm, about 20 minutes. Line tart shells with muffin tin liners and fill with pie weights. Bake until pastry is puffed, but pale, about 10 minutes.

5. Cover with aluminum foil and continue to bake until pastry is just blond at edges, about 5 minutes. Transfer muffin tin to wire rack, discard foil, and let tart shells cool for 10 to 15 minutes. Remove liners.

6. Divide custard evenly among pastry shells. Bake on upper rack until shells are dark golden brown and crisp and custard is puffed and spotty brown, 8 to 11 minutes.

meringue desserts

ONE OF THE GREATEST FEATS OF CULINARY MAGIC is taking a few egg whites, whipping them to billowy clouds, and baking them into a delicate dessert with a texture unlike any other. And so meringue is a little magic. And a lot of science. You'll learn the amazing properties of egg whites and what turns them from an unassuming clear jelly to an impressive foam—and then learn all the things you can do with that foam—in this section.

Many desserts have "meringue" in their title: Whether it's a cookie, a pie, or a cake, the meringue is an indicator that these desserts—no matter how simple, how rich, how dense—will have an extra element of ethereal. Recipes throughout the sections in this book might also have whipped egg whites hidden inside them, like a cake batter that's lightened with or given structure by them, a buttercream that's creamy-fluffy, or a frozen dessert that's lighter than ice cream. But meringue deserves its own category for exploration. For one, making it can be a delicate dance. You need to prep your ingredients right, whip enough but not too much, incorporate heat or a sugar syrup, and work quickly. Take your meringue to higher heights with our instructions that set you up for whipping success.

Unadulterated meringue can be a confectionery treat, as with meringue cookies, or a large and lovely pavlova, or it can be a finishing flourish on a lemon meringue pie or baked Alaska. It tastes like a marshmallow but has a moldable texture that levts it kiss all kinds of desserts.

Meringue has European roots and there are three large categories of it: French meringue (the simplest), Swiss meringue (the most delicate), and Italian meringue (the one that uses a hot sugar syrup). They each serve a purpose and have a place in the recipes in this book. Discover the differences, and then make them all.

Believe it or not, you can even go vegan with meringue. What replaces the whites? Aquafaba, the liquid from a can of chickpeas, can be whipped and baked to a texture that mimics the real thing. Crack some cans and make some marvelous egg meringue replicas.

You won't need additional baking equipment for making meringue. It's all about the whisk—the whisk attachment, that is. With a stand mixer, meringue reaches peaks with ease.

EGG WHITE PLAY-BY-PLAY

The white makes up two-thirds the volume of the entire egg but because of its leanness, it might not garner attention. Egg whites deserve love. When you whip whites, they don't turn from liquid to fluff by mere magic but because of the white's unique properties. Here's how meringue captures air and puts it to use.

1 When egg whites are whipped, the proteins are agitated and start to unfold (denature) and then crosslink to form a mesh-like network (coagulate).

2 The network coats the air bubbles that are also produced by whipping and are suspended in the egg white's liquid.

3 As the whites are beaten further, more air bubbles form and more proteins bond to coat and reinforce them, separating them from the liquid. This increases their stability.

4 Eventually, the whole mix will puff up and take on the firm texture of shaving cream (creating a foam).

5 If you cook the foam, other proteins in the egg whites set and preserve that structure.

THREE TYPES OF MERINGUE

While you may think that meringue is all about the whipping—and much of it is—there are ways of adding sugar and heating techniques that can alter the texture of your meringue and make it more or less stable. Knowing all three types of meringue is handy for understanding when to employ each, for what dessert, and for what outcome.

French Meringue

A French meringue is the classic, the most simple iteration of the confection, and the model often used for teaching egg-white whipping. It's made simply by whipping egg whites, adding granulated sugar (and sometimes a stabilizer; see page 468), and whipping to the desired peaks.

It's folded into batters for cakes like Chiffon Cake (page 284), which relies on those whites for structure; Torta Caprese (page 320) and other flourless cakes made with chocolate and/or nuts, which get some lightness from them; and even our classic yellow cake layers (see page 233), which are fluffier than the rest. It takes soufflés (see pages 210–215) to the sky. Make it and bake it and you have Meringue Cookies (page 472). And a diner pie might feature a mountain of it.

French meringue is a lot but what it isn't is the most refined of the styles. When baked, French meringue can have an openness and a slight coarseness. This is welcome to achieve the light, airy, meltaway nature of a meringue cookie, but you might choose a different style of meringue when creaminess or undetectable smoothness is the goal. It's also the least stable of the meringues: Have you ever seen some moisture beads weeping (pooling of reliquidized egg white that comes from undercooking) from your meringue topping? It's probably a simple French meringue.

While it's just egg whites and sugar (a dry meringue), this mixture can be finicky. The sugar must be added to the whites at precisely the right second: Too soon and the meringue won't inflate properly; too late and it will be gritty.

Swiss Meringue

You can prevent grittiness in meringue altogether if the sugar dissolves right away. A Swiss meringue does this by gently warming sugar and egg whites in a bowl over simmering water until the sugar is dissolved; then the mixture is whipped. You may know this meringue from its eponymous buttercream (see page 242). It's a fairly firm meringue, so it's often used for toppings and frostings that aren't baked. We also use it for pavlova, although the style is not traditional here (for more information, see page 493).

Italian Meringue

Italian meringue gives you the smooth creaminess of Swiss but it's lighter—extra fluffy and billowy. In addition to solving grittiness, the Italian meringue solves weeping even better than Swiss meringue. Boiling-hot sugar syrup is whipped into the egg whites. The hot syrup cooks the whites and helps transform them into a silky-smooth meringue that is stable enough to resist weeping.

How to Whip French Meringue

1. Using stand mixer fitted with whisk attachment, whip egg whites (and cream of tartar, if using) on medium-low until foamy, about 1 minute.

2. Increase speed to medium-high and whip whites to soft, billowy mound, about 1 minute.

3. Gradually add sugar mixture.

4. Whip until glossy, stiff peaks form, 2 to 3 minutes.

How to Whip Swiss Meringue

1. Combine sugar and egg whites in bowl of stand mixer. Place bowl over saucepan filled with 1 inch simmering water.

2. Whisking gently but constantly, heat until sugar is dissolved and mixture registers 160 to 165 degrees (for baked applications; see page 242 for frosting).

3. Fit stand mixer with whisk attachment and whip mixture on high speed until meringue forms stiff peaks, is smooth and creamy, and is bright white with sheen, about 4 minutes.

How to Whip Italian Meringue

1. Bring sugar and water to vigorous rolling boil and cook until mixture is slightly thickened and syrupy. Remove from heat.

2. Using stand mixer fitted with whisk, whip egg whites on medium-low speed until frothy.

3. Add salt and cream of tartar (if using) and whip, gradually increasing speed, until whites hold soft peaks.

4. With mixer running, slowly pour hot syrup into whites.

5. Whip until meringue is cooled, very thick, and shiny.

STABILIZING FOAM FORCES

The proteins in egg whites are impressive molecules that allow a foam to stretch and grow but, as a rule, whipped egg-white foams are temporary things. Whether the foam is raw or cooked, the water surrounding the air bubbles will eventually succumb to the force of gravity and drain away, causing the foam to separate and release liquid. The foam can benefit from other ingredients to help maintain that volume for longer through meringue's various applications.

Sugar

Sugar flavors meringue, but the addition is necessary for other reasons. At the same time that egg whites whip, the sugar dissolves in the water from the whites to form a viscous liquid. In lightly cooked applications like pie toppings, the sugar slows down the drainage of moisture, helping the whites to remain stable as well as achieve maximum volume. In baked applications, the concept goes further. As a meringue bakes, its moisture slowly evaporates, weakening its structure. At the same time, the egg white protein ovalbumin is becoming stronger by bonding with other proteins, providing additional structure for the foam. Because sugar has a tendency to hold on to water molecules, if there is not enough sugar in the meringue, the water evaporates too quickly, causing the cookies to collapse before the ovalbumin has time to strengthen.

Cornstarch

Cornstarch shares the water-clinging property of sugar. Sometimes the amount of sugar needed to adequately stabilize a foam will make the meringue taste too cloying. To cut some of the sugar while keeping the stability, we sneak in cornstarch to play the same role.

Acids

Acids don't make egg foams fluffier or more voluminous, but they do make them stay foams longer. Cream of tartar is the most common; the acid changes the electrical charge on the proteins of egg whites, in turn reducing the interactions between protein molecules. Because this delays the formation of the foam, whipping takes longer but also results in a much more stable foam. You can also add vinegar, as is traditional in a pavlova.

To demonstrate the effects of adding this acid, we whipped cream of tartar into one batch of egg whites and left it out of another. We transferred the fluffy eggs to funnels set over beakers and collected exuded water for 60 minutes, long enough to see significant results. The whites whipped without any stabilizers lost 23mL of liquid on average. The whites stabilized with cream of tartar lost less than half that amount, about 10mL on average.

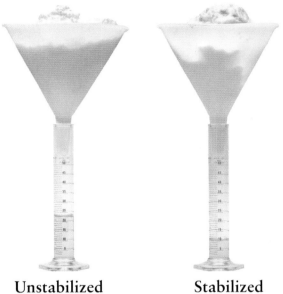

Unstabilized
Whipped with no stabilizer, these egg whites oozed liquid.

Stabilized
Cream of tartar helped these whites to hold on to much more liquid.

DESTABILIZING FORCES

Fats interfere with the creation of the protein network. And, coincidentally, yolk can interfere with whipping more than a pure fat like oil. (Note that fat is a problem while you're whipping an egg white foam but it's OK to add later, whether it's the butter in Swiss meringue buttercream or the chocolate in mousse.)

Fats and oils coat the proteins, preventing them from unfolding and bonding. They also take up valuable space on the surface of the air bubbles created when whipping egg whites, which disrupts and weakens the network of protective proteins, causing the foam to collapse very quickly and resulting in a soggy, deflated mass.

Perfect Peaks

It's important to whip egg whites for meringue exactly to stiff peaks. If whipped just shy of that, their structure will be too weak to provide structure and leaven their applications. But if over-whipped, the same is true. Know when to stop and when to keep going with these visual cues.

SOFT PEAKS

STIFF PEAKS

OVERWHIPPED

SEPARATING AN EGG

Separating each egg over a smaller bowl before adding the yolk or white to another bowl is a safe bet. If there's an issue in separating, you won't have to lose the whole batch because of some intruding egg yolk. Use fresh eggs, cold from the fridge. The yolk membrane of a fresh egg is stronger and a cold yolk is less likely to rupture. If a recipe calls for room-temperature eggs that need to be separated, simply separate them cold and then cover the bowls with plastic wrap (make sure the wrap touches the surface of the eggs to keep them from drying out), and let them sit on the counter until they've lost their chill.

PROCESSED EGG WHITES

Meringue recipes often call for a lot of egg whites and it's tempting to grab a carton sold in the supermarket dairy case or a canister of powdered egg whites in the baking aisle. Do they taste and bake up the same? We've found that fresh eggs produce taller cakes and delicately crisp meringues, whereas egg white substitutes yield shorter cakes and slightly harder, denser meringues.

Given that these products contain nothing but egg whites, what makes the difference? The U.S. Department of Agriculture requires that liquid egg whites be pasteurized, a process that heats the whites enough to kill bacteria without cooking them. Powdered egg whites are made by

evaporating water in a spray dryer. The substitutes can be safely added to uncooked frostings and drinks. But pasteurization changes the nature of the egg proteins enough to compromise their structure, especially in baked goods. The heating process prematurely links the proteins so that they unfold and stretch less readily when whipped. As a result, they cannot hold the same amount of air or achieve the same volume as fresh egg whites. (When we whipped the whites, one product needed 22 minutes to reach soft peaks!)

FREEZING EGG WHITES

Custards or recipes that call for thickening with egg yolks often leave the cook with leftover whites. We've recommended freezing whites for later use in recipes. But do they whip to the same volume and consistency as fresh whites?

We compared frozen egg whites that had been thawed overnight in the refrigerator to fresh whites in Angel Food Cake (page 286) and Mile-High Lemon Meringue Pie (page 488). In both instances, the frozen whites reached the desired consistency (soft peaks for the angel food cake and stiff peaks for the meringue topping) a few seconds faster than the fresh. Research revealed that freezing egg whites begins the process of unwinding their proteins, which the mechanical action of the whip continues. That was the only difference. Otherwise, frozen and fresh whites performed equally well.

MERINGUE COOKIES

YOU WON'T FIND FLOUR OR BUTTER IN THESE COOKIES.
Textures like rich and chewy, thin and crispy, or soft and cakey
describe cookies—but none of these describe meringues.
Meringue cookies are diminutive kisses that are lean and sweet
and delicate and crisp. Usually piped onto the baking sheet,
they look refined with their pointed tips and glossy sheen and
they taste it too, with a fine texture that's dry before it melts
on the tongue.

We use a simple French meringue technique (see page 466).
We've found that using Italian meringue for meringue cookies
results in a dense, candy-like result. The perfect meringue
cookie is perfectly white (browning is a bad sign). Traditionally, meringues are baked at a very low temperature and then
left in the turned-off oven, sometimes for as long as overnight.
The idea is to completely dry out the cookies while allowing
them to remain snow-white.

Fun add-ins take them a bit away from the traditional but are
a way of incorporating other flavors and textures and maybe
some welcome richness in the form of nuts and chocolate.
Restraint is necessary: You don't want to weigh down the foam
and you don't want any pieces too large to interfere with piping.

SWEET TIMING

We've learned that the sugar that's added to whipping egg whites in a French meringue contributes not only sweetness but also stability. And the degree of stability can depend on when you incorporate the sugar.

We made three batches of meringue cookies, adding the sugar to the whites before whipping, after a minute of whipping, or once the foam had reached the soft peak stage. We baked them and compared the results. The timing made a difference. Adding the sugar after a minute of whipping was clearly best. Adding the sugar at the start of mixing produced a cookie that was dull on the exterior, with a too-fine crumb within. The cookies made when the sugar was added near the end had an overly airy texture (tasters compared it to Styrofoam) and a grainy consistency. To top it off, they took on an unappealing brown color.

Too Early
Dull exterior and too-fine crumb.

Too Late
Browned, with grainy, Styrofoam-like texture.

Just Right
Snow-white color and ideal airy texture.

A (LESS) SWEET TRADITION

Traditional meringue cookies can be quite sweet—they're made of just egg whites and sugar, after all. As you learned on page 468, cutting the amount of sugar (which is more important here than, say, in a topping or frosting that's offset by the richness and flavor of other recipe components) without compromising structure can be done by using some cornstarch in place of the reduced sugar.

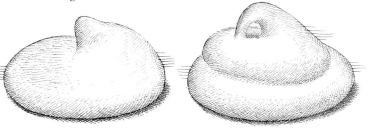

Sugar Withdrawal
Removing too much sugar causes meringues to collapse in the oven.

Fortified Foam
Replacing a little sugar with cornstarch helps meringues keep their shape while baking.

VOLUMINOUS WHITES

When whipping egg whites, the usual approach is to start slow and build up speed for better volume. Does the volume matter?

We found that egg whites whipped slowly at the start produced meringue that was about 10 percent more voluminous than the high-speed-only whites, resulting in meringue cookies and frosting that were lighter and airier (the cookies were also larger). Both batches of mousse and chiffon cake that we made, on the other hand, were indistinguishable.

Beating egg whites slowly to start causes the proteins to loosen up. Like stretching a balloon before inflating it, the improved elasticity allows the proteins to take on air more easily and gain more volume. The extra volume matters when meringue is the main element in a recipe. But when meringue gets folded into a batter or mousse, you won't notice the difference.

Continuous High Speed

Slow Start

MERINGUE COOKIES

Makes about 48 cookies | 2 rimmed baking sheets

WHY THIS RECIPE WORKS Precise timing is required to achieve a classic meringue that emerges from the oven glossy white, with a shattering texture that dissolves instantly once you bite into it. If you're not careful, you'll end up with meringue that's as dense as Styrofoam. Add the sugar too early and it will interfere with the cross-linked egg white proteins that uphold the meringue; add it too late and there isn't enough water in which the sugar can dissolve, resulting in a gritty meringue. The sweet spot is adding the sugar just before the whites reach soft peak stage, when they have gained some volume but still have enough water for the sugar to dissolve. To scale back on the sweetness, we cut the sugar with cornstarch. The meringues may be a little soft immediately after being removed from the oven but will stiffen as they cool. To minimize stickiness on humid or rainy days, let the meringues cool in a turned-off oven for an additional hour (2 hours total) without opening the door, then transfer them immediately to airtight containers and seal.

Meringue Cookies

¾ cup (5¼ ounces) sugar
2 teaspoons cornstarch
4 large egg whites
¾ teaspoon vanilla extract
⅛ teaspoon salt

1. Adjust oven racks to upper-middle and lower-middle positions and heat oven to 225 degrees. Line 2 baking sheets with parchment paper. Whisk sugar and cornstarch together in small bowl.

2. Using stand mixer fitted with whisk attachment, whip egg whites, vanilla, and salt on high speed until very soft peaks start to form (peaks should slowly lose their shape when whisk is removed), 30 to 45 seconds. Reduce speed to medium and slowly add sugar mixture in steady stream down side of mixer bowl (process should take about 30 seconds). Stop mixer and scrape down bowl. Increase speed to high and whip until glossy, stiff peaks form, 30 to 45 seconds.

3. Working quickly, fill pastry bag fitted with ½-inch plain tip or large zipper-lock bag with ½ inch of corner cut off with meringue. Pipe 1¼-inch-wide mounds about 1 inch high on prepared sheets, 4 rows of 6 meringues on each sheet. Bake meringues for 1 hour, switching and rotating sheets halfway through baking. Turn off oven and let meringues cool in oven for at least 1 hour. Transfer sheets to wire rack and let meringues cool completely before serving. (Meringues can be stored at room temperature for up to 2 weeks.)

Chocolate Meringue Cookies
Gently fold 2 ounces finely chopped bittersweet chocolate into meringue mixture at end of step 2.

Espresso Meringue Cookies
Whisk 2 teaspoons instant espresso powder into sugar mixture in step 1.

Orange Meringue Cookies
Whisk 1 teaspoon grated orange zest into sugar mixture in step 1.

Toasted Almond Meringue Cookies
Substitute ½ teaspoon almond extract for vanilla extract. In step 3, sprinkle meringues with ⅓ cup almonds, toasted and coarsely chopped, and 1 teaspoon flake sea salt (optional) before baking.

TUTORIAL
Meringue Cookies

With all of our egg-whipping info (see page 467), making meringue cookies should now be a breeze. Watch when to add the sugar for the last key to success.

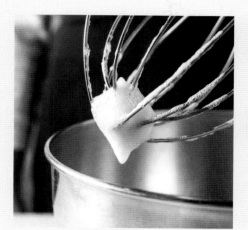

1. Whip egg whites, vanilla, and salt on high speed until very soft peaks start to form (peaks should slowly lose their shape when whisk is removed), 30 to 45 seconds.

2. Reduce speed to medium and slowly add sugar mixture in steady stream down side of mixer bowl (process should take about 30 seconds).

3. Stop mixer and scrape down bowl. Increase speed to high and whip until glossy, stiff peaks form, 30 to 45 seconds.

4. Working quickly, fill pastry bag fitted with ½-inch plain tip or large zipper-lock bag with ½ inch of corner cut off with meringue.

5. Pipe 1¼-inch-wide mounds about 1 inch high on prepared sheets, 4 rows of 6 meringues on each sheet.

6. Bake meringues for 1 hour, switching and rotating sheets halfway through baking. Turn off oven and let meringues cool in oven for at least 1 hour.

CHOCOLATE-PEPPERMINT MERINGUE KISSES

Makes about 72 cookies | 2 rimmed baking sheets

WHY THIS RECIPE WORKS Crisp and light as a feather, sweet peppermint-flavored meringue makes an ideal foil—in both flavor and texture—to a rich, creamy chocolate base in these easy tiny treats. Before piping the meringue onto the baking sheets, we incorporated mini chocolate chips and crushed peppermint candies for festive holiday flair. Once fully cooled, we dipped the bottom of our kisses in melted chocolate chips. Try to work as quickly as possible when shaping the kisses; they'll deflate if they're left to sit for too long before baking. You will need about seven round peppermint candies to make 3 tablespoons crushed candy.

- 2 large egg whites
- ⅛ teaspoon cream of tartar
- ⅛ teaspoon table salt
- ⅔ cup (4⅔ ounces) sugar
- ½ teaspoon vanilla extract
- 2 cups (12 ounces) mini semisweet chocolate chips, divided
- 3 tablespoons crushed peppermint candies
- 2 teaspoons vegetable oil

1. Adjust oven racks to upper-middle and lower-middle positions and heat oven to 275 degrees. Line 2 baking sheets with parchment paper.

2. Using stand mixer fitted with whisk attachment, whip egg whites, cream of tartar, and salt on medium-low speed until foamy, about 1 minute. Increase speed to medium-high and whip whites to soft, billowy mounds, about 1 minute. Gradually add sugar and vanilla and whip until glossy, stiff peaks form, 2 to 3 minutes. Using rubber spatula, gently fold in 1 cup chocolate chips and crushed peppermints.

3. Using spoon or pastry bag fitted with ½-inch tip, dollop or pipe 1-teaspoon mounds of meringue, about 1 inch high, onto prepared sheets, spacing them about 1 inch apart. Bake until exterior begins to crack and turn light golden brown, 25 to 30 minutes, switching and rotating sheets halfway through baking. Transfer sheets to wire rack and let cookies cool completely on sheets.

4. Microwave remaining 1 cup chocolate chips in bowl at 50 percent power, stirring occasionally, until melted, about 1 minute. Stir in oil until incorporated. Dip bottoms of cookies in melted chocolate, scrape off excess, and place cookies on freshly lined baking sheet. Let chocolate set for at least 1 hour before serving.

BUTTERSCOTCH MERINGUE BARS

Makes 24 bars | 13 by 9-inch baking pan

WHY THIS RECIPE WORKS When it comes to meringue, we all know Meringue Cookies (page 472), but here we use meringue as a topping for a rich, chewy, multilayered bar, a cookie with an intriguing contrast of textures. An ultrachewy blondie base was our starting point. To emphasize the blondies' butterscotch flavor, we used brown sugar. We pressed chocolate chips on top before baking so the chocolate got its own fudgy layer. For the final layer, we brought in the meringue, spreading a fluff of the sweet, glossy whites over the chocolate chips. During baking the interior of the meringue stayed soft and airy, while the top developed a crackle that we loved.

- 2 cups (10 ounces) all-purpose flour
- 1 teaspoon baking powder
- ½ teaspoon baking soda
- ½ teaspoon salt
- 16 tablespoons unsalted butter, softened
- 2 cups packed (14 ounces) light brown sugar, divided
- ½ cup (3½ ounces) granulated sugar
- 2 large eggs, separated
- 1 tablespoon water
- 1 teaspoon vanilla extract
- 2 cups (12 ounces) semisweet chocolate chips

1. Adjust oven rack to lower-middle position and heat oven to 350 degrees. Make foil sling for 13 by 9-inch baking pan by folding 2 long sheets of aluminum foil; first sheet should be 13 inches wide and second sheet should be 9 inches wide. Lay sheets of foil in pan perpendicular to each other, with extra foil hanging over edges of pan. Push foil into corners and up sides of pan, smoothing foil flush to pan. Grease foil.

2. Whisk flour, baking powder, baking soda, and salt together in large bowl. Using stand mixer fitted with paddle, beat butter, 1 cup brown sugar, and granulated sugar on medium-high speed until light and fluffy, about 2 minutes. Add egg yolks, water, and vanilla and mix until incorporated. Reduce speed to low and add flour mixture, mixing until combined. Transfer batter to prepared pan and spread into even layer. Press chocolate chips lightly into dough.

3. Using clean, dry mixer bowl and whisk attachment, whip egg whites at medium-high speed until stiff peaks form, about 3 minutes. Reduce speed to medium-low and slowly add remaining 1 cup brown sugar, mixing until smooth and shiny. Gently spread egg white mixture over chocolate chip layer.

4. Bake bars until golden brown, 25 to 30 minutes. Let bars cool completely in pan on wire rack, about 2 hours. Using foil overhang, remove bars from pan. Cut into 24 pieces before serving.

Butterscotch
Meringue Bars

MERINGUE CAKES

Use French or Swiss meringue

Draw outline for
spreading meringue

Bake at low temperature

Decorate quickly

SOME CAKES RELY ON WHIPPED EGG WHITES for structure, from the obvious like light and lovely Angel Food Cake (page 286) to the unassuming like our Fluffy Yellow Layer Cake (page 233), a butter cake that benefits from this technique. In these cases, the end result is still a plush cake with a distinct crumb. Meringue itself, however, can *be* the cake. You can spread and shape it to nearly any layer shape.

A round of meringue in a meringue cake is utterly appealing: It bakes crisp but then fillings of cream or fruit soften it enough so it's sliceable like other layer cakes. It's nice to slather the marshmallowy layers with something rich or tangy to offset their sweetness. Since these cakes are not frosted you can see the beautiful, shiny white layers at every level.

Similarly, a meringue layer can coat or top a traditional cake layer, as with Blitz Torte (page 478) for a remarkable contrast of texture that's built (or baked) right in.

The dacquoise (see page 480) might be the most refined of the meringue cakes. The meringue, sometimes baked in round layers, sometimes baked into slick rectangles, are combined with plenty of nuts for cake layers that are refreshingly rich. Filled with buttercream and ganache and topped with nuts, it's almost like a large candy bar—despite its refinement.

You rarely need to avoid browning in these recipes as you do with meringue cookies, as they're part of a whole composed dessert and a golden hue can be desirable. But we still bake at a low temperature to ensure properly dried interiors.

Another way meringue makes the cake? As a billowy seven-minute frosting that adorns a layer cake (see page 244) or insulates a Baked Alaska (page 483). Swiss meringue is ideal in these applications. It gives the meringue creamy smoothness that's important for any coating, and it boasts stability.

MAKING MERINGUE SHAPES

It's nearly impossible to paint perfect rounds or rectangles of sticky meringue before baking meringue layers. We always bake on a piece of parchment paper. This allows us, when necessary, to use pencil to draw an outline for filling in with whites. You can usually use a cake pan as a guide. If a cake is particularly long or wide, as in the case of our Chocolate-Espresso Dacquoise (page 480), you can do some post-bake construction; we spread the meringue to form the best rectangle we can and then use a serrated knife to trim it and cut out individual rectangle layers. The serrated knife and a sawing motion makes sure the layers don't break haphazardly.

For Circles

1. Using 8-inch cake pan as guide, trace two 8-inch circles on each of 2 sheets of parchment paper; flip sheets over and use to line 2 rimmed baking sheets.

2. Divide meringue evenly among all 4 circles on prepared pans.

3. Gently spread meringue into even layers.

For Rectangles

   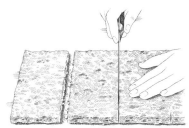

1. Using offset spatula, spread meringue evenly into 13 by 10½-inch rectangle on parchment, using lines on parchment as guide.

2. Once baked and cooled, use serrated knife and gentle, repeated scoring motion to trim edges of meringue to form 12 by 10-inch rectangle.

3. With long side of rectangle parallel to counter, mark both long edges at 3-inch intervals.

4. Repeatedly score surface by gently drawing knife from top mark to bottom mark until cut through. Repeat to make 4 strips.

BLITZ TORTE

Serves 10 to 12 | two 9-inch cake pans

WHY THIS RECIPE WORKS The beauty of blitz torte, a dessert created by German American immigrants, is that you get five impressive layers—cake, meringue, fruit-and-cream filling, more cake, and more meringue—for about the same amount of work as a two-layer cake. Each meringue layer is baked directly atop the yellow cake batter. The recipe is also pleasingly symmetrical; the egg yolks go into the cake, while the whites go into the meringue. In order for the meringue and cake to cook through at the same rate, we baked them for almost an hour in a 325-degree oven—a longer time and lower temperature than we normally would for a yellow cake. For our filling, we folded store-bought lemon curd into whipped cream and stabilized it with gelatin before layering it with raspberries, mimicking the silky richness of a custard without making one. The end result is a masterpiece of flavors and textures: tender cake, soft and crisp meringue, crunchy almonds, and creamy fruit filling.

FILLING

- 1 teaspoon unflavored gelatin
- 2 tablespoons water
- 1 cup heavy cream, chilled
- 1 teaspoon vanilla extract
- ½ cup lemon curd
- 10 ounces (2 cups) raspberries
- 2 tablespoons orange liqueur
- 1 tablespoon sugar

CAKE

- ½ cup whole milk
- 4 large egg yolks
- 1½ teaspoons vanilla extract
- 1¼ cups (5 ounces) cake flour
- 1 cup (7 ounces) sugar
- 1½ teaspoons baking powder
- ½ teaspoon table salt
- 12 tablespoons unsalted butter, cut into 12 pieces and softened

MERINGUE

- 4 large egg whites
- ¼ teaspoon cream of tartar
- ¾ cup (5¼ ounces) sugar
- ½ teaspoon vanilla extract
- ½ cup sliced almonds

1. FOR THE FILLING: Sprinkle gelatin over water in small bowl and let sit until gelatin softens, about 5 minutes. Microwave until mixture is bubbling around edges and gelatin dissolves, 15 to 30 seconds. Using stand mixer fitted with whisk attachment, whip cream and vanilla on medium-low speed until foamy, about 1 minute. Increase speed to medium-high and whip until soft peaks form, about 2 minutes. Add gelatin mixture and whip until stiff peaks form, about 1 minute.

2. Whisk lemon curd in large metal bowl to loosen. Gently fold whipped cream mixture into lemon curd. Refrigerate whipped cream filling for at least 1½ hours or up to 3 hours. (Filling may look slightly curdled before assembling cake.)

3. FOR THE CAKE: Meanwhile, adjust oven rack to middle position and heat oven to 325 degrees. Grease two 9-inch round cake pans, line with parchment paper, grease parchment, and flour pans.

4. Beat milk, egg yolks, and vanilla together in 2-cup liquid measuring cup with fork. Using clean, dry mixer bowl and paddle, mix flour, sugar, baking powder, and salt on low speed until combined, about 5 seconds. Add butter, 1 piece at a time, and mix until only pea-size pieces remain, about 1 minute. Add half of milk mixture, increase speed to medium-high, and beat until light and fluffy, about 1 minute. Reduce speed to medium-low, add remaining milk mixture, and beat until incorporated, about 30 seconds (batter may look slightly curdled). Give batter final stir by hand. Divide batter evenly between prepared pans and spread into even layer using small offset spatula.

5. FOR THE MERINGUE: Using clean, dry mixer bowl and whisk attachment, whip egg whites and cream of tartar on medium-low speed until foamy, about 1 minute. Increase speed to medium-high and whip whites to soft, billowy mounds, 1 to 3 minutes. Gradually add sugar and whip until glossy, stiff peaks form, 3 to 5 minutes. Add vanilla and whip until incorporated.

6. Divide meringue evenly between cake pans and spread evenly over cake batter to edges of pan. Using back of spoon, create peaks in meringue. Sprinkle meringue with almonds. Bake until meringue is golden and has pulled away from sides of pan, 50 to 55 minutes, switching and rotating pans halfway through baking. Let cakes cool completely in pans on wire rack. (Cakes can be stored, uncovered, in pans at room temperature for up to 24 hours.)

7. Ten minutes before assembling cake, gently toss raspberries, liqueur, and sugar together in bowl and let sit, stirring occasionally.

8. Gently remove cakes from pans, discarding parchment. Place 1 cake layer on platter, meringue side up. Spread half of whipped cream filling evenly over top of meringue. Using slotted spoon, spoon raspberries evenly over filling, leaving juice in bowl. Gently spread remaining whipped cream filling over raspberries, covering raspberries completely. Top with second cake layer, meringue side up. Serve cake within 2 hours of assembly.

TUTORIAL
Blitz Torte

This cake is a three-component affair—cake, meringue, and custard. Follow how they come together.

1. Divide meringue evenly between cake pans and spread evenly over cake batter to edges of pan.

2. Using back of spoon, create peaks in meringue. Sprinkle meringue with almonds.

3. Bake until meringue is golden and has pulled away from sides of pan, 50 to 55 minutes.

4. Gently remove cakes from pans, discarding parchment. Place 1 cake layer on platter, meringue side up.

5. Spread half of whipped cream filling evenly over top of meringue. Using slotted spoon, spoon raspberries evenly over filling, leaving juice in bowl.

6. Gently spread remaining whipped cream filling over raspberries, covering raspberries completely. Top with second cake layer, meringue side up.

APRICOT-ALMOND MERINGUE CAKE

Serves 10 to 12 | 2 rimmed baking sheets

WHY THIS RECIPE WORKS Butter cakes aren't the only layers you can stack. Here we fill crisp meringue layers with fruit and cream. We chose apricots, and added almond to our meringue for a complementary pairing. We spread the meringue into disks on parchment–lined baking sheets and then baked in a low oven for nearly 2 hours. Letting our meringues cool in the still-warm oven ensured they were crisp throughout. As the layers absorb the apricots, they softened slightly.

MERINGUE

- 1⅛ cups (7¾ ounces) granulated sugar
- 1 tablespoon cornstarch
- 6 large egg whites
- ¾ teaspoon almond extract
- ¼ teaspoon salt
- 1⅓ cups sliced almonds, lightly toasted

FILLING

- 2 pounds apricots, halved, pitted, and cut into ½-inch wedges
- ½ cup apricot jam
- 2 teaspoons lemon juice

WHIPPED CREAM

- 1½ cups heavy cream, chilled
- 1½ tablespoons confectioners' sugar, plus extra for dusting
- ¾ teaspoon vanilla extract

1. FOR THE MERINGUE: Adjust oven racks to upper-middle and lower-middle positions and heat oven to 225 degrees. Using 8-inch round cake pan as guide, trace two 8-inch circles on each of 2 sheets of parchment paper; flip parchment sheets over and use to line 2 rimmed baking sheets.

2. Combine sugar and cornstarch in bowl. Using stand mixer fitted with whisk attachment, whip egg whites, almond extract, and salt on medium-low speed until foamy, about 1 minute. Increase speed to medium-high and whip whites to soft, billowy mounds, about 1 minute. Gradually add sugar mixture and whip until glossy, stiff peaks form, 2 to 3 minutes.

3. Divide meringue evenly among 4 circles on prepared sheets and gently spread into even layers. Sprinkle each round with ⅓ cup almonds. Bake for 1¾ hours, switching and rotating sheets halfway through baking. Turn off oven and let meringues cool in oven for 1 hour. Remove from oven and let cool completely, about 15 minutes.

4. FOR THE FILLING: Toss apricots, jam, and lemon juice together in bowl.

Apricot-Almond Meringue Cake

5. FOR THE WHIPPED CREAM: Using stand mixer fitted with whisk attachment, whip cream, sugar, and vanilla on medium-low speed until foamy, about 1 minute. Increase speed to high and whip until stiff peaks form, 1 to 3 minutes.

6. Place 1 meringue round on platter. Spread 1 cup whipped cream over top and scatter generous 1 cup apricot filling in even layer over top. Repeat with remaining meringue rounds, whipped cream, and apricot filling, finishing with final meringue layer. Dust with confectioners' sugar. Serve immediately.

CHOCOLATE-ESPRESSO DACQUOISE

Serves 10 to 12 | rimmed baking sheet

WHY THIS RECIPE WORKS It's possible there is no more stunning finale to a meal than a dacquoise, a multilayered showpiece of crisp meringue and rich, silky buttercream coated in a glossy ganache. We swapped the traditional individually piped meringue layers for a single sheet that we trimmed into layers. For the filling, we opted for German buttercream, which requires no thermometer or sugar syrup. Espresso powder and amaretto contributed sophistication. To slice, dip a sharp knife in hot water and wipe it dry before and after each cut.

MERINGUE
- ¾ cup blanched sliced almonds, toasted
- ½ cup hazelnuts, toasted and skinned
- 1 tablespoon cornstarch
- ⅛ teaspoon salt
- 1 cup (7 ounces) sugar, divided
- 4 large egg whites, room temperature
- ¼ teaspoon cream of tartar

BUTTERCREAM
- ¾ cup whole milk
- 4 large egg yolks
- ⅓ cup (2⅓ ounces) sugar
- 1½ teaspoons cornstarch
- ¼ teaspoon salt
- 2 tablespoons amaretto or water
- 1½ tablespoons instant espresso powder
- 16 tablespoons unsalted butter, cut into 16 pieces and softened

GANACHE
- 6 ounces bittersweet chocolate, chopped fine
- ¾ cup heavy cream
- 2 teaspoons corn syrup
- 12 hazelnuts, toasted and skinned
- 1 cup blanched sliced almonds, toasted

1. FOR THE MERINGUE: Adjust oven rack to middle position and heat oven to 250 degrees. Using ruler, draw 13 by 10½-inch rectangle on piece of parchment paper. Grease baking sheet and place parchment on it, marked side down. Process almonds, hazelnuts, cornstarch, and salt in food processor until nuts are finely ground, 15 to 20 seconds. Add ½ cup sugar and pulse to combine, 1 to 2 pulses.

2. Using stand mixer fitted with whisk attachment, whip egg whites and cream of tartar on medium-low speed until foamy, about 1 minute. Increase speed to medium-high and whip whites to soft, billowy mounds, about 1 minute. Gradually add remaining ½ cup sugar and whip until glossy, stiff peaks form, 2 to 3 minutes. Fold nut mixture into egg whites in 2 batches. Using offset spatula, spread meringue evenly into 13 by 10½-inch rectangle on parchment, using lines on parchment as guide. Using spray bottle, evenly mist surface of meringue with water until glistening. Bake for 1½ hours. Turn off oven and let meringue cool in oven for 1½ hours. (Do not open oven during baking or cooling.) Remove from oven and let cool completely, about 10 minutes. (Meringue can be wrapped tightly in plastic wrap and stored at room temperature for up to 2 days.)

3. FOR THE BUTTERCREAM: Bring milk to simmer in small saucepan over medium heat. Meanwhile, whisk egg yolks, sugar, cornstarch, and salt in bowl until smooth. Remove milk from heat and, whisking constantly, add half of milk to yolk mixture to temper. Whisking constantly, return tempered yolk mixture to

remaining milk in saucepan. Return saucepan to medium heat and cook, whisking constantly, until mixture is bubbling and thickens to consistency of warm pudding, 3 to 5 minutes. Transfer pastry cream to bowl and press plastic wrap directly on surface. Refrigerate until cold and set, at least 2 hours or up to 24 hours. Warm to room temperature in microwave at 50 percent power, stirring every 10 seconds, before using.

4. Stir together amaretto and espresso powder; set aside. Using stand mixer fitted with paddle, beat butter at medium speed until smooth and light, 3 to 4 minutes. Add pastry cream in 3 batches, beating for 30 seconds after each addition. Add amaretto mixture and continue to beat until light and fluffy, about 5 minutes longer, scraping down bowl thoroughly halfway through mixing.

5. FOR THE GANACHE: Place chocolate in heatproof bowl. Bring cream and corn syrup to simmer in small saucepan over medium heat. Pour cream mixture over chocolate; let stand for 1 minute, then stir until smooth. Set aside to cool until chocolate mounds slightly when dripped from spoon, about 5 minutes.

6. Carefully invert meringue and peel off parchment. Reinvert meringue and place on cutting board. Using serrated knife and gentle, repeated scoring motion, trim edges of meringue to form 12 by 10-inch rectangle. Discard trimmings. With long side of rectangle parallel to counter, use ruler to mark both long edges of meringue at 3-inch intervals. Using serrated knife, score surface of meringue by drawing knife toward you from mark on top edge to corresponding mark on bottom edge. Repeat scoring until meringue is fully cut through. Repeat until you have four 10 by 3-inch rectangles. (If any meringues break during cutting, use them as middle layers.)

7. Place 3 rectangles on wire rack set in rimmed baking sheet. Spread ¼ cup ganache evenly over each meringue. Refrigerate until ganache is firm, about 15 minutes. Set aside remaining ganache.

8. Using offset spatula, spread top of remaining rectangle with ½ cup buttercream; place rectangle on wire rack with ganache-coated meringues. Invert 1 ganache-coated meringue, place on top of buttercream, and press gently to level. Repeat, spreading meringue with ½ cup buttercream and topping with inverted ganache-coated meringue. Spread top with buttercream. Invert final ganache-coated meringue on top of cake. Use your hand to steady top of cake and spread half of remaining buttercream to lightly coat sides of cake, then use remaining buttercream to coat top of cake. Smooth until cake resembles box. Refrigerate until buttercream is firm, about 2 hours. (Once buttercream is firm, assembled cake may be wrapped tightly in plastic and refrigerated for up to 2 days.)

9. Warm remaining ganache in heatproof bowl set over saucepan filled with 1 inch barely simmering water, making sure that water does not touch bottom of bowl; stir occasionally until mixture is very fluid but not hot. Keeping assembled cake on

TUTORIAL
Chocolate-Espresso Dacquoise

You've learned how to cut the meringue layers. Slather and stack them with the help of this tutorial.

1. Spread ¼ cup ganache evenly over 3 meringues. Refrigerate until ganache is firm. Spread top of remaining rectangle with ½ cup buttercream.

2. Invert 1 ganache-coated meringue, place on top of buttercream, and press gently to level. Repeat, spreading meringue with ½ cup buttercream and topping with inverted ganache-coated meringue.

3. Repeat, then invert final ganache-coated strip on top.

4. Use your hand to steady top of cake and spread half of remaining buttercream to lightly coat sides of cake, then use remaining buttercream to coat top of cake. Smooth until cake resembles box.

5. Pour warmed ganache over top of chilled cake. Spread ganache in thin, even layer over top of cake, letting excess flow down sides. Spread ganache over sides in thin layer.

6. Garnish top of cake with hazelnuts. Holding bottom of cake with your hand, gently press almonds onto cake sides with your other hand.

wire rack, pour ganache over top of cake. Using offset spatula, spread ganache in thin, even layer over top of cake, letting excess flow down sides. Spread ganache over sides in thin layer (top must be completely covered, but some small gaps on sides are OK).

10. Garnish top of cake with hazelnuts. Holding bottom of cake with your hand, gently press almonds onto cake sides with your other hand. Refrigerate on wire rack, uncovered, for at least 3 hours or up to 12 hours. Transfer cake to platter. Serve.

LEMON LAYER CAKE

Serves 10 to 12 | two 9-inch cake pans

WHY THIS RECIPE WORKS Many versions of lemon layer cake are poorly executed concoctions of dense, heavy cake stacked with filling and frosting that taste more like butter than lemon. We wanted a cake with a tangy, creamy lemon filling dividing layers of delicate cake. We found that our Classic White Layer Cake (page 234) was the perfect base: The layers were buttery yet light enough to accommodate the lemon flavor, and their fine crumb and tender texture were ideal. Lemon buttercream fillings have muted flavor; we vastly preferred the brightness of lemon curd, and adding gelatin made for a filling stable enough for this multilayered cake. We also wanted something lighter than buttercream, and eventually landed on seven-minute frosting—a meringue frosting (Swiss-style), essentially. The swirls and swoops brought the lemon-meringue flavor to cake.

FILLING
 1 teaspoon unflavored gelatin
 1 cup lemon juice (6 lemons), divided
 1½ cups (10½ ounces) sugar
 ⅛ teaspoon table salt
 4 large eggs plus 6 large yolks, room temperature
 8 tablespoons unsalted butter, cut into ½-inch pieces and frozen

CAKE
 1 recipe Classic White Layer Cake (page 234), prepared through step 3

FROSTING
 1 cup (7 ounces) sugar
 2 large egg whites
 ¼ cup water
 1 tablespoon lemon juice
 1 tablespoon corn syrup

1. FOR THE FILLING: Sprinkle gelatin over 1 tablespoon lemon juice in small bowl; set aside. Heat sugar, salt, and remaining lemon juice in medium saucepan over medium-high heat, stirring occasionally, until sugar dissolves and mixture is hot but

not boiling. Whisk eggs and yolks together in large bowl. Whisking constantly, slowly pour hot lemon-sugar mixture into eggs, then return mixture to saucepan. Cook over medium-low heat, stirring constantly with heat-resistant spatula, until mixture registers 170 degrees and is thick enough to leave trail when spatula is scraped along saucepan bottom, 4 to 6 minutes. Immediately remove saucepan from heat and stir in gelatin mixture until dissolved. Stir in butter until incorporated. Strain filling through fine-mesh strainer into bowl (you should have 3 cups). Place plastic wrap directly on surface of filling and refrigerate until firm enough to spread, at least 4 hours. (Filling can be refrigerated for up to 24 hours; fold with rubber spatula to loosen before spreading onto cake.)

2. FOR THE CAKE: Using long serrated knife, cut 1 horizontal line around sides of each layer; then, following scored lines, cut each layer into 2 even layers.

3. Line edges of cake platter with 4 strips of parchment paper to keep platter clean. Place 1 cake layer on platter. Spread 1 cup filling evenly over top, leaving ½-inch border around edge of cake. Repeat with 2 more cake layers, pressing lightly to adhere and spreading 1 cup filling evenly over each layer. Top with remaining cake layer, pressing lightly to adhere, and smooth out any filling that has leaked from sides of cake. Cover cake with plastic and refrigerate while preparing frosting.

4. FOR THE FROSTING: Combine all ingredients in bowl of stand mixer and set bowl over medium saucepan filled with 1 inch barely simmering water, making sure that water does not touch bottom of bowl. Cook, whisking constantly, until mixture registers 160 degrees, 5 to 10 minutes. Remove bowl from heat and transfer to stand mixer fitted with whisk attachment. Whip mixture on medium speed until soft peaks form, about 5 minutes. Increase speed to medium-high and continue to whip until mixture has cooled completely and stiff peaks form, 5 to 7 minutes.

5. Immediately spread about 1 cup frosting evenly over top of cake, right to edge of cake. Spread remaining frosting evenly over sides of cake. Carefully remove parchment strips before serving. (Frosted cake can be refrigerated for up to 24 hours; bring to room temperature before serving.)

BAKED ALASKA

Serves 8 to 10 | rimmed baking sheet

WHY THIS RECIPE WORKS Baked Alaska puts on an impressive display: Cake is topped with ice cream and then finished with a burnished plume of meringue—magically, the ice cream doesn't melt through serving. Plenty of insulation was the key. We encased the ice cream entirely in cake; this allowed us to decrease the amount of meringue without sacrificing heat resistance. Using less meringue ensured that our baked Alaska wasn't too sweet. Rather than packing softened ice cream into a mold (refrozen ice cream can be icy, and it can be hard to find a vessel) we simply cut the cardboard off two pints of ice cream and stuck them together to form the core. Coffee ice cream's bitter flavor provided a welcome contrast to the sweetness. To slice, dip a sharp knife in very hot water and wipe dry before and after each cut.

2 (1-pint) containers coffee ice cream

CAKE
1 cup (4 ounces) cake flour
⅔ cup (4⅔ ounces) sugar, divided
⅓ cup (1 ounce) unsweetened cocoa powder
1½ teaspoons baking powder
¼ teaspoon table salt
½ cup vegetable oil
6 tablespoons water
4 large eggs, separated

MERINGUE
¾ cup (5¼ ounces) sugar
⅓ cup light corn syrup
3 large egg whites
2 tablespoons water
Pinch table salt
1 teaspoon vanilla extract

1. Lay 12-inch-square sheet of plastic wrap on counter and remove lids from ice cream. Use scissors to cut cardboard tubs from top to bottom. Peel away cardboard and discard. Place ice cream blocks on their sides in center of plastic with wider ends facing each other. Grasp each side of plastic and firmly press blocks together to form barrel shape. Wrap plastic tightly around ice cream and roll briefly on counter to form uniform cylinder. Place cylinder, standing on end, in freezer until completely solid, at least 1 hour.

2. FOR THE CAKE: Adjust oven rack to middle position and heat oven to 350 degrees. Lightly grease 18 by 13-inch rimmed baking sheet, line with parchment paper, and lightly grease parchment. Whisk flour, ⅓ cup sugar, cocoa, baking powder, and salt together in large bowl. Whisk oil, water, and egg yolks into flour mixture until smooth batter forms.

3. Using stand mixer fitted with whisk attachment, whip egg whites on medium-low speed until foamy, about 1 minute. Increase speed to medium-high and whip whites to soft, billowy mounds, about 1 minute. Gradually add remaining ⅓ cup sugar and whip until glossy, soft peaks form, 1 to 2 minutes. Transfer one-third of whites to batter; whisk gently until mixture is lightened. Using rubber spatula, gently fold remaining egg whites into batter until no white streaks remain.

4. Pour batter into prepared sheet and spread into even layer. Bake until cake springs back when pressed lightly in center, 10 to 13 minutes. Let cake cool in baking sheet on wire rack for 5 minutes. Run knife around edge of sheet, then invert cake onto wire rack. Carefully remove parchment, then reinvert cake onto second wire rack and let cool completely, at least 15 minutes.

5. Transfer cake to cutting board with long side of rectangle parallel to edge of counter. Using serrated knife, trim ¼ inch off left side of cake and discard. Using ruler, measure 4½ inches from cut edge and make mark with knife. Using mark as guide, cut 4½-inch rectangle from cake. Trim piece to create 4½ by 11-inch rectangle and set aside. (Depending on pan size and how much cake has shrunk during baking, it may not be necessary to trim piece to measure 11 inches.) Measure 4 inches from new cut edge and make mark. Using mark as guide, cut 4-inch rectangle from cake. Trim piece to create 4 by 10-inch rectangle, wrap rectangle in plastic, and set aside. Cut 3½-inch round from remaining cake and set aside (biscuit cutter works well); discard scraps.

6. Unwrap ice cream. Trim cylinder to 4½ inches in length; discard scraps. Place ice cream cylinder on 4½ by 11-inch cake rectangle and wrap cake around ice cream. (Cake may crack slightly.) Place cake circle on 1 end of cylinder. Wrap entire cylinder tightly in plastic. Place cylinder, standing on cake-covered end, in freezer until cake is firm, at least 30 minutes. Unwrap cylinder and place on cutting board, standing on cake-covered end, and cut in half lengthwise. Unwrap reserved 4 by 10-inch cake rectangle and place halves on top, ice cream side down, with open ends meeting in middle. Wrap tightly in plastic and press ends gently to close gap between halves. Return to freezer for at least 2 hours or up to 2 weeks.

7. FOR THE MERINGUE: Adjust oven rack to upper-middle position and heat oven to 500 degrees. Spray wire rack set in rimmed baking sheet with vegetable oil spray. Unwrap cake and place on rack. Combine sugar, corn syrup, egg whites, water, and salt in bowl of stand mixer and set bowl over medium saucepan filled with 1 inch barely simmering water, making sure that water does not touch bottom of bowl. Cook, whisking constantly, until mixture registers 160 degrees, 5 to 10 minutes.

8. Remove bowl from heat and transfer to stand mixer fitted with whisk attachment. Whip mixture on medium speed until soft peaks form, about 5 minutes. Increase speed to medium-high and continue to whip until mixture has cooled completely and stiff peaks form, 5 to 7 minutes. Add vanilla and mix until combined. Using offset spatula, spread meringue over top and sides of cake, avoiding getting meringue on rack. Use back of spoon to create peaks all over meringue.

9. Bake until browned and crisp, about 5 minutes. Run offset spatula or thin knife under dessert to loosen from rack, then use two spatulas to transfer to platter. Serve immediately.

TUTORIAL
Baked Alaska

How do you get to the torched meringue finish without the ice cream melting into a puddle on top of mushy cake? Insulate the ice cream with a cake wrapping.

1. Wrap plastic tightly around ice cream halves and roll briefly on counter to form uniform cylinder; freeze.

2. Place ice cream cylinder on 4½ by 11-inch cake rectangle and wrap cake around ice cream.

3. Place cake circle on one end of cylinder. Wrap entire cylinder tightly in plastic. Place cylinder, standing on cake-covered end, in freezer until cake is firm, at least 30 minutes.

4. Unwrap cylinder and place on cutting board, standing on cake-covered end, and cut in half lengthwise.

5. Unwrap reserved 4 by 10-inch cake rectangle and place halves on top, with open ends meeting in middle. Wrap tightly in plastic and press ends gently to close gap between halves. Return to freezer.

6. Using offset spatula, spread meringue over top and sides of cake, avoiding getting meringue on rack. Use back of spoon to create peaks all over meringue.

MERINGUE PIES

Use Italian or Swiss meringue, or
stabilize with cornstatch

Anchor meringue to the crust

Bake or torch for browning

WHEN A PIE IS SKY HIGH it's usually thanks to a generous topping of meringue. Pies are the darlings of the diner case and a slice is often tall enough to obscure a little one's face—maybe that's why they're the ultimate nostalgic enticement. Your fork moves through airy meringue, yielding slightly more into creamy filling, and finally stopping at a crisp crust that offsets it all.

Meringue pies lose their appeal, however, when they're wet and weepy. You know the kind: beading on the surface, a watery layer between meringue and custard, a topping that slides off. We avoid weeping on our meringue pies by employing either Italian or Swiss meringues. And for our Mile-High Lemon Meringue Pie (page 488) we add a heated cornstarch mixture as that recipe requires extra stabilizing to touch the sky.

Baking the meringue briefly on the pie encourages cohesion but it also results in a dessert with unique browning, brush-strokes of brown following the peaks and contours of the malleable meringue. Torching the top also adds this artfulness. Find fascinating ways to decorate with meringue (with more than a spoon sweep) for the most eye-catching pies.

STOP THE SHRINK

Many recipes for meringue pies instruct the baker to spread the meringue to the edges of the crust. Why? We baked two pies: For one we made sure the meringue touched the fluted crust, and for the other we spread the meringue over the filling but stopped short of the crust. When the pies were just out of the oven, we didn't notice much difference, but after they had spent five minutes on the counter, we observed that the meringue topping that had never hugged the crust had shrunk slightly. The difference was even more noticeable after the pies spent a few hours in the refrigerator.

Short Stop
The unbaked meringue didn't touch the crust so the filling peeks through.

Perfect Pie
The unbaked meringue touched the crust.

What's the best way to do this?

1. When the pie is filled and the meringue is ready, immediately dollop meringue evenly around edge of crust, attaching the meringue to the crust.

2. Fill the center of the pie and smooth the top.

WHIPPED WHIMSY

Once briefly baked, the sugars and proteins in meringue caramelize, brown, and highlight any decorative techniques. You can simply smooth meringue over the pie, but we like these flourishes.

Spoon Swoops
This is what you can expect to see in the shiniest dessert cases at diners and bakeries. It creates an appealing contrast between browned ridges and paler valleys. Using a rubber spatula, immediately distribute meringue evenly around the edge and then the center of pie, attaching meringue to the pie crust. Using the back of a spoon, create attractive swirls and peaks in the meringue, lifting the spoon quickly if you'd like taller, sharper peaks. Bake as directed.

The Beehive
This retro look shows off impressively tall meringue and beautifully browned detail. Using a rubber spatula, immediately distribute meringue evenly around the edge, attaching it to the crust and then the center of the pie. Then, working quickly and using your spatula, smooth the meringue around the pie, spreading the meringue inward and upward to create a cone-like mound of meringue. Using the back of a spoon, make an indented swirl starting at the bottom of the pie and working your way up to the top. Bake as directed.

Torched
If you cook a Swiss-style meringue to 160 to 165 degrees, it is very stable, requiring no further baking for structure (see page 466). If topping a pie with an uncooked filling and using Swiss meringue, you can use the broiler or a torch to give it the look of toasted marshmallows with a range of striking browning. We apply this for our Banana Pudding Pie (page 491). Here's how: Ignite torch; continuously sweep flame about 2 inches above meringue until well browned.

MILE-HIGH LEMON MERINGUE PIE

Serves 8 | 9-inch pie plate

WHY THIS RECIPE WORKS Lemon meringue pie is even more fun to eat when the meringue reaches the highest heights. We wanted a pie with a rich, lemony filling that was soft but not runny and firm but not gelatinous—and we wanted it topped with an impressively tall, perfect, airy meringue, one that wouldn't break down and puddle. To stabilize the meringue and keep it from weeping we beat in a small amount of cornstarch. The meringue cooked through and browned in just a short time in the oven. Our lemon curd is bracing enough to balance out all that sweetness and creamy enough to provide a textural contrast between the layers. Use a silicone spatula to spread the meringue and attach it to the edges of the pie crust, which will keep it from shrinking away from the edge as it bakes.

Mile-High Lemon Meringue Pie

1 recipe single-crust pie dough (see pages 342–348)

FILLING

1¼ cups (8¾ ounces) sugar
½ cup water
3 tablespoons cornstarch
¼ teaspoon table salt
8 large egg yolks
2 tablespoons grated lemon zest plus 1 cup juice (5 lemons)
4 tablespoons unsalted butter, cut into 4 pieces and softened

MERINGUE

½ cup water
1 tablespoon cornstarch
4 large egg whites
½ teaspoon cream of tartar
½ teaspoon vanilla extract
1 cup (7 ounces) sugar

1. Roll dough into 12-inch circle on floured counter. Loosely roll dough around rolling pin and gently unroll it onto 9-inch pie plate, letting excess dough hang over edge. Ease dough into plate by gently lifting edge of dough with your hand while pressing into plate bottom with your other hand.

2. Trim overhang to ½ inch beyond lip of plate. Tuck overhang under itself; folded edge should be flush with edge of plate. Crimp dough evenly around edge of plate. Wrap dough-lined plate loosely in plastic wrap and refrigerate until firm, about 30 minutes. Adjust oven rack to middle position and heat oven to 350 degrees.

3. Line chilled pie shell with double layer of aluminum foil, covering edges to prevent burning, and fill with pie weights. Bake on foil-lined rimmed baking sheet until edges are set and just beginning to turn golden, 25 to 30 minutes, rotating sheet halfway through baking. Remove foil and weights, rotate sheet, and continue to bake crust until golden brown and crisp, 10 to 15 minutes longer. Transfer sheet to wire rack and let cool completely, about 45 minutes. Reduce oven temperature to 325 degrees.

4. FOR THE FILLING: Bring sugar, water, cornstarch, and salt to simmer in large saucepan, whisking constantly. When mixture starts to turn translucent, whisk in egg yolks, two at a time. Whisk in lemon zest and juice and butter. Return mixture to brief simmer, then remove from heat. Spray piece of parchment paper with vegetable oil spray and press directly against surface of filling to keep warm and prevent skin from forming.

5. FOR THE MERINGUE: Bring water and cornstarch to simmer in small saucepan and cook, whisking occasionally, until thickened and translucent, 1 to 2 minutes. Remove from heat and let cool slightly.

6. Using stand mixer fitted with whisk attachment, whip egg whites, cream of tartar, and vanilla on medium-low speed until foamy, about 1 minute. Increase speed to medium-high and beat in sugar, 1 tablespoon at a time, until incorporated and mixture forms soft, billowy mounds. Add cornstarch mixture, 1 tablespoon at a time, and continue to beat to glossy, stiff peaks, 2 to 3 minutes.

7. Meanwhile, remove parchment from filling and return to very low heat during last minute or so of beating meringue (to ensure filling is hot).

8. With pie still on sheet, pour warm filling into cooled crust. Using rubber spatula, immediately dollop meringue evenly around edge of crust, spreading meringue so it touches crust (this will prevent the meringue from shrinking), then fill in center with remaining meringue. Using back of spoon, create attractive swirls and peaks in meringue. Bake until meringue is light golden brown, about 20 minutes. Let pie cool on wire rack until filling has set, about 2 hours. Serve.

REALLY GOOD KEY LIME PIE

Serves 8 | 9-inch pie plate

WHY THIS RECIPE WORKS This key lime pie has a soft yet set filling that straddles the fine line between sweet and tart. We started with what many think of as the go-to: the recipe on the back of the bottle of Nellie & Joe's Famous Key West Lime Juice. We increased the ingredient amounts and added heavy cream to make an impressively tall slice of pie that's extra-luscious. For some embellishment, we bolstered a sturdy graham cracker crust with pulverized pretzels. The pretzels added a buttery saltiness that balanced the sweet-tart filling. A pillowy meringue topping added a contrasting texture. Be sure to zest the limes to get the 2 teaspoons of zest needed for the garnish before juicing them. You'll need to buy two 14-ounce cans of sweetened condensed milk to yield the 1½ cups for this recipe. We call for Persian limes in this recipe, but if you'd prefer to use key lime juice you'll need to squeeze about 18 key limes to get ¾ cup of juice.

CRUST
- 6 ounces graham crackers, broken into 1-inch pieces (about 11 crackers)
- 2 ounces mini pretzel twists (about 35 twists)
- ¼ cup packed (1¾ ounces) light brown sugar
- ¼ teaspoon table salt
- 8 tablespoons unsalted butter, melted

FILLING
- 1½ cups sweetened condensed milk
- ¾ cup lime juice (6 limes)
- 6 tablespoons heavy cream
- 4 large egg yolks
- ⅛ teaspoon table salt

MERINGUE
- 2 large egg whites
- ¼ teaspoon table salt
- ¼ teaspoon cream of tartar
- ½ cup (3½ ounces) granulated sugar
- ¼ cup water
- 1 tablespoon vanilla extract
- 2 teaspoons grated lime zest

1. FOR THE CRUST: Adjust oven rack to middle position and heat oven to 350 degrees. Process cracker pieces, pretzels, sugar, and salt in food processor until finely ground, about 30 seconds. Add melted butter and pulse until combined, about 8 pulses.

2. Transfer cracker mixture to 9-inch pie plate. Using bottom of dry measuring cup, press crumbs firmly into bottom and up sides of plate. Place plate on baking sheet and bake until crust is fragrant and set, about 17 minutes. Transfer sheet to wire rack.

3. FOR THE FILLING: Whisk all ingredients in bowl until fully combined. With pie plate still on sheet, carefully pour filling into crust (crust needn't be completely cooled). Transfer sheet to oven and bake pie until edge of filling is set but center still jiggles slightly when shaken, about 30 minutes.

4. Place pie on wire rack and let cool completely, about 1 hour. Refrigerate until fully chilled, at least 4 hours, or cover with greased plastic wrap and refrigerate for up to 24 hours.

5. FOR THE MERINGUE: Using stand mixer fitted with whisk attachment, whip egg whites, salt, and cream of tartar on medium-high speed until soft peaks form, 2 to 4 minutes.

6. Combine sugar and water in small saucepan. Bring to rolling boil over medium-high heat and cook until syrup registers 240 degrees, 1 to 3 minutes.

7. Working quickly, turn mixer to medium speed. With mixer running, slowly and carefully pour hot syrup into egg white mixture (avoid pouring syrup onto whisk, if possible). Add vanilla. Increase speed to medium-high and whip until shiny, stiff peaks form, about 2 minutes.

8. Spread meringue over pie filling, leaving 1-inch border around pie. Working gently, use spatula or spoon to create swirls and cowlicks over surface of meringue. Sprinkle meringue with lime zest. Slice pie into wedges with wet knife, wiping knife clean between slices. Serve.

TUTORIAL
Banana Pudding Pie

Take the banana pudding out of the trifle dish and bake it into a pie. Learn how to perfect layers of cookie crust, creamy pudding, and torched meringue.

1. Bake crust until fragrant and beginning to darken at edges, 18 to 20 minutes. Transfer plate to wire rack.

2. Cook pudding over medium heat, whisking constantly and scraping corners of saucepan, until mixture registers 180 degrees, 5 to 7 minutes. Off heat, whisk in butter, vanilla, and gelatin mixture.

3. Stir bananas into hot filling. Pour filling into crust (crust needn't be completely cooled).

4. Press parchment paper directly onto surface of filling and refrigerate until set, at least 4 hours or up to 24 hours.

5. Gently peel off parchment from filling (if any filling sticks to parchment, scrape off and smooth back over surface of pie). Spread meringue over filling, making sure meringue touches edges of crust.

6. Ignite torch; continuously sweep flame about 2 inches above meringue until well browned.

BANANA PUDDING PIE

Serves 8 | 9-inch pie plate

WHY THIS RECIPE WORKS This pie—our take on the signature dessert at Buxton Hall Barbecue in Asheville, North Carolina—is a reimagining of classic layered banana pudding. For a sturdy crust, we used ground Nilla Wafers (a vanilla-y standard of puddings) plus some additional flour. Some gelatin firmed the pudding layer just enough to get clean slices. A pinch each of ground cinnamon and allspice made the perfect backdrop for sliced fresh bananas. We topped it all off with a cooked meringue, swapping in some brown sugar for added caramel undertones. Browning the meringue topping added a slight toasty bitterness that perfectly offset the sweet pudding underneath. Peel and slice the bananas just before using to help prevent browning. Chilling the topped pie for longer than 4 hours may cause the top to deflate. Don't worry; it will still be delicious.

CRUST

- 4 cups (8⅓ ounces) Nilla Wafer cookies
- 3 tablespoons packed light brown sugar
- 1 tablespoon all-purpose flour
- ¼ teaspoon table salt
- 6 tablespoons unsalted butter, melted

FILLING

- 2 teaspoons unflavored gelatin
- 1¾ cups half-and-half, divided
- ¾ cup (5¼ ounces) granulated sugar
- 5 large egg yolks
- 2 tablespoons all-purpose flour
- ¼ teaspoon table salt
  - Pinch ground cinnamon
  - Pinch ground allspice
- 2 tablespoons unsalted butter, cut into 2 pieces and chilled
- 1 tablespoon vanilla extract
- 2 ripe bananas, peeled and sliced ¼ inch thick (1½ cups)

MERINGUE

- ⅓ cup (2⅓ ounces) granulated sugar
- ⅓ cup packed (2⅓ ounces) light brown sugar
- 4 large egg whites
- ¼ teaspoon cream of tartar
- ⅛ teaspoon table salt

1. FOR THE CRUST: Adjust oven rack 8 inches from broiler element and heat oven to 325 degrees. Pulse cookies, sugar, flour, and salt in food processor until finely ground, about 10 pulses. Add melted butter and pulse until combined, about 8 pulses, scraping down sides of bowl as needed. Transfer mixture to 9-inch pie plate (it will seem like a lot of crumbs).

2. Using your hands, press crumbs firmly up sides of plate, building walls about ¼ inch thick and leveling top edge. Press remaining crumbs into even layer on bottom of plate, firmly pressing crumbs into corners of plate. Bake until fragrant and beginning to darken at edges, 18 to 20 minutes. Transfer plate to wire rack.

3. FOR THE FILLING: Meanwhile, sprinkle gelatin over ½ cup half-and-half in small bowl and let mixture sit until gelatin softens, about 5 minutes. Whisk sugar, egg yolks, flour, salt, cinnamon, allspice, and remaining 1¼ cups half-and-half in large saucepan until fully combined. Cook over medium heat, whisking constantly and scraping corners of saucepan, until mixture thickens, bubbles burst across entire surface, and mixture registers 180 degrees in several places, 5 to 7 minutes. Off heat, whisk in butter, vanilla, and gelatin mixture until combined.

4. Stir bananas into hot filling. Pour filling into crust (crust needn't be completely cooled). Press parchment paper directly onto surface of filling and refrigerate until set, at least 4 hours or up to 24 hours.

5. FOR THE MERINGUE: Whisk all ingredients together in bowl of stand mixer. Place bowl over saucepan filled with 1 inch of barely simmering water, making sure water does not touch bottom of bowl. Whisking gently but constantly, cook until mixture registers 160 to 165 degrees, 5 to 8 minutes. Remove bowl from heat and transfer to stand mixer fitted with whisk attachment. Whip mixture on high speed until meringue forms stiff peaks and is smooth and creamy, 2 to 3 minutes.

6. Gently peel off parchment from filling (if any filling sticks to parchment, scrape off and smooth back over surface of pie). Spread meringue over filling, making sure meringue touches edges of crust. Working gently, use spatula or spoon to create swirls over surface.

7A. FOR A BROILER: Heat broiler. Broil until meringue is well browned, 1 to 2 minutes, rotating plate as needed for even browning.

7B. FOR A TORCH: Ignite torch; continuously sweep flame about 2 inches above meringue until well browned.

8. Slice pie into wedges with wet knife, wiping knife clean between slices. Serve immediately. (Topped pie can be refrigerated for up to 4 hours.)

PAVLOVAS

Employ cornstarch

Finish meringue in turned-off oven

Add creamy fillings

A BASE OF MERINGUE IS A CLOUD-LIKE SHELL for a light and lovely filling in This flourless dessert. It's a multitextured marvel; the drop-dead-gorgeous dessert is named for Anna Pavlova the "incomparable" Russian ballerina who captivated audiences across the world at the turn of the 20th century. Unlike meringue cookies, which are uniformly dry and crunchy throughout, the meringue for pavlova (which can be baked in a single large round or smaller individual disks) offers a range of textures: a crisp outer shell; a tender, marshmallowy interior; and a pleasant chew where the two textures meet. The meringue's sweetness is balanced by whipped cream and tart fresh fruit. This gorgeous jumble is ideal at the end of a rich meal. It usually calls for a French meringue, but we gained great texture benefits from a Swiss meringue that's heated first. Whipped cream ups the ethereal quotient even more.

AN UNCONVENTIONAL PAVLOVA APPROACH

Almost every pavlova recipe starts with a French meringue (see page 466), which is made by whipping raw egg whites and sugar to stiff peaks and then folding in cornstarch and white vinegar, along with a flavoring such as vanilla. The meringue is spread into a disk on a parchment-lined baking sheet and baked in a low oven until the outside is crisp. The oven is then turned off, and the meringue is left to continue drying out until the inside is no longer wet but still soft. A French meringue, with its exacting timing required for adding the sugar, often turned out gritty pavlovas for us. We use Swiss meringue (see page 466).

But there's another departure. Heating the meringue to 140 degrees, as is common for Swiss meringue, resulted in a pavlova that baked up with a pitted, coarse interior. Here's why: Egg white proteins start out as separately wound little molecules, like balls of yarn. They start to knit together at about 140 degrees, but not all the way. As the meringue bakes, the knitted proteins firm and contract, squeezing out water, which then evaporates. The more loosely knit the proteins are, the more they're pushed apart by the escaping steam, which can result in a coarse-textured dessert. Cooking the whites to a higher temperature—160 degrees—before baking causes more coagulation. With the proteins knit into a finer, more cohesive mesh, the structure is not as disrupted by escaping steam during baking and the final product is smooth and fine.

A TRIO OF FUN-TO-EAT TEXTURES

Whereas a meringue cookie is dry and crunchy throughout, pavlova boasts three unique textures that keep things interesting as you eat.

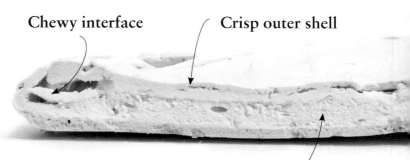

Chewy interface

Crisp outer shell

Tender, marshmallowy center

PAVLOVA WITH FRUIT AND WHIPPED CREAM

Serves 10 | rimmed baking sheet

WHY THIS RECIPE WORKS Pavlova presents a gorgeous jumble of flavors and textures: a large meringue with a crisp outer shell and marshmallowy interior, piled with whipped cream and fresh fruit. A firm Swiss meringue baked up with perfect transitions between textures. Slicing pavlova can be a slightly messy affair, but letting the dessert sit for just 5 minutes will soften the meringue's crust to make cutting easier. Because eggs can vary in size, measuring the egg whites by weight or volume is essential. Open the oven door as infrequently as possible while the meringue is inside. Don't worry when the meringue cracks; this is part of the dessert's charm. The inside of the meringue will remain soft.

MERINGUE
- 1½ cups (10½ ounces) sugar
- ¾ cup (6 ounces) egg whites (5 to 7 large eggs)
- 1½ teaspoons distilled white vinegar
- 1½ teaspoons cornstarch
- 1 teaspoon vanilla extract

WHIPPED CREAM
- 2 cups heavy cream, chilled
- 2 tablespoons sugar
- 1 recipe Orange, Cranberry, and Mint Topping (recipe follows)

1. FOR THE MERINGUE: Adjust oven rack to middle position and heat oven to 250 degrees. Using pencil, draw 10-inch circle in center of 18 by 13-inch piece of parchment paper.

2. Combine sugar and egg whites in bowl of stand mixer and place bowl over saucepan filled with 1 inch simmering water, making sure that water does not touch bottom of bowl. Whisking gently but constantly, heat until sugar is dissolved and mixture registers 160 to 165 degrees, 5 to 8 minutes.

3. Fit stand mixer with whisk attachment and whip mixture on high speed until meringue forms stiff peaks, is smooth and creamy, and is bright white with sheen, about 4 minutes (bowl may still be slightly warm to touch). Stop mixer and scrape down bowl with spatula. Add vinegar, cornstarch, and vanilla and whip on high speed until combined, about 10 seconds.

4. Spoon about ¼ teaspoon meringue onto each corner of rimmed baking sheet. Press parchment, marked side down, onto sheet to secure. Pile meringue in center of circle on parchment. Using circle as guide, spread and smooth meringue with back of spoon or spatula from center outward, building 10-inch disk that is slightly higher around edges. Finished disk should measure about 1 inch high with ¼-inch depression in center.

5. Bake meringue until exterior is dry and crisp and meringue releases cleanly from parchment when gently lifted at edge with thin metal spatula, 1 to 1½ hours. Meringue should be quite pale (a hint of creamy color is OK). Turn off oven, prop door open with wooden spoon, and let meringue cool in oven for 1½ hours. Remove from oven and let cool completely before topping, about 15 minutes. (Cooled meringue can be wrapped tightly in plastic wrap and stored at room temperature for up to 1 week.)

6. FOR THE WHIPPED CREAM: Before serving, whip cream and sugar in chilled bowl of stand mixer fitted with whisk attachment on low speed until small bubbles form, about 30 seconds. Increase speed to medium and whip until whisk leaves trail, about 30 seconds. Increase speed to high and continue to whip until cream is smooth, thick, and nearly doubled in volume, about 20 seconds longer for soft peaks. If necessary, finish whipping by hand to adjust consistency.

7. Carefully peel meringue away from parchment and place on large serving platter. Spoon whipped cream into center of meringue. Top whipped cream with fruit topping. Let stand for at least 5 minutes or up to 1 hour, then slice and serve.

ORANGE, CRANBERRY, AND MINT TOPPING

Makes 4½ cups

You can substitute tangelos or Cara Cara oranges for the navel oranges, if desired. Valencia or blood oranges can also be used, but since they are smaller, increase the number of fruit to six.

- 1½ cups (10½ ounces) sugar, divided
- 6 ounces (1½ cups) frozen cranberries
- 5 navel oranges
- ⅓ cup chopped fresh mint, plus 10 small leaves, divided

1. Bring 1 cup sugar and 1 cup water to boil in medium saucepan over medium heat, stirring to dissolve sugar. Off heat, stir in cranberries. Let cranberries and syrup cool completely, about 30 minutes. (Cranberries in syrup can be refrigerated for up to 24 hours.)

2. Place remaining ½ cup sugar in shallow dish. Drain cranberries, discarding syrup. Working in 2 batches, roll ½ cup cranberries in sugar and transfer to large plate or tray. Let stand at room temperature to dry, about 1 hour.

3. Cut away peel and pith from oranges. Cut each orange into quarters from pole to pole, then cut crosswise into ¼-inch-thick pieces (you should have 3 cups). Just before serving, toss oranges with nonsugared cranberries and chopped mint in bowl until combined. Using slotted spoon, spoon fruit in even layer over pavlova. Garnish with sugared cranberries and mint leaves. Before serving, drizzle pavlova slices with any juice from bowl.

CHOCOLATE PAVLOVA WITH BERRIES AND WHIPPED CREAM

Serves 10 | rimmed baking sheet

WHY THIS RECIPE WORKS Rich bar chocolate balances some of the sweetness of the meringue in this pavlova. Chopped chocolate weighed down the meringue, interrupting the delicate structure and texture. We were able to fold in finely grated bittersweet chocolate to flavor every bite. Because eggs can vary in size, measuring the egg whites by weight or volume is essential. Open the oven door as infrequently as possible. Don't worry when the meringue cracks; this is unavoidable and is part of the dessert's charm. The inside of the meringue will remain soft.

MERINGUE

1½ cups (10½ ounces) sugar
¾ cup (6 ounces) egg whites (5 to 7 large eggs)
1½ teaspoons distilled white vinegar
1½ teaspoons cornstarch
1 teaspoon vanilla extract
2 ounces bittersweet chocolate, grated

TOPPING

2 pounds (5 cups) blackberries, blueberries, and/or raspberries
3 tablespoons sugar, divided
Pinch table salt
2 ounces bittersweet chocolate, chopped fine
2 cups heavy cream, chilled

Chocolate Pavlova with Berries and Whipped Cream

1. FOR THE MERINGUE: Adjust oven rack to middle position and heat oven to 250 degrees. Using pencil, draw 10-inch circle in center of 18 by 13-inch piece of parchment paper. Combine sugar and egg whites in bowl of stand mixer; place bowl over saucepan filled with 1 inch simmering water, making sure that water does not touch bottom of bowl. Whisking gently but constantly, heat until sugar is dissolved and mixture registers 160 to 165 degrees, 5 to 8 minutes.

2. Fit stand mixer with whisk attachment and whip mixture on high speed until meringue forms stiff peaks, is smooth and creamy, and is bright white with sheen, about 4 minutes (bowl may still be slightly warm to touch). Stop mixer and scrape down bowl with spatula. Add vinegar, cornstarch, and vanilla and whip on high speed until combined, about 10 seconds. Remove bowl and, using rubber spatula, fold in grated chocolate.

3. Spoon about ¼ teaspoon meringue onto each corner of rimmed baking sheet. Press parchment, marked side down, onto sheet to secure. Pile meringue in center of circle on parchment. Using circle as guide, spread and smooth meringue with back of spoon or spatula from center outward, building 10-inch disk that is slightly higher around edges. Finished disk should measure about 1 inch high with ¼-inch depression in center.

4. Bake meringue until exterior is dry and crisp and meringue releases cleanly from parchment when gently lifted at edge with thin metal spatula, 1 to 1½ hours. Meringue should be quite pale (a hint of creamy color is OK). Turn off oven, prop door open with wooden spoon, and let meringue cool in oven for 1½ hours. Remove from oven and let cool completely before topping, about 15 minutes. (Cooled meringue can be wrapped tightly in plastic wrap and stored at room temperature for up to 1 week.)

5. FOR THE TOPPING: Toss berries with 1 tablespoon sugar and salt in large bowl. Set aside for 30 minutes. Meanwhile, microwave chocolate in bowl at 50 percent power, stirring occasionally, until melted, about 1 minute. Set aside to cool slightly.

6. Before serving, whip cream and remaining 2 tablespoons sugar in clean, dry bowl of stand mixer fitted with whisk attachment on medium-low speed until foamy, about 1 minute. Increase speed to high and whip until soft peaks form, 1 to 3 minutes.

7. Carefully peel meringue away from parchment and place on large serving platter. Spoon whipped cream into center of meringue. Spoon berries in even layer over whipped cream, then drizzle with melted chocolate. Let sit for at least 5 minutes or up to 1 hour. Slice and serve.

VEGAN MERINGUES

KEY POINTS

Use canned chickpea liquid

Add cream of tartar

Whip longer than egg whites

IF MERINGUE IS EGG WHITES, HOW COULD IT EVER BE VEGAN? We've discussed how the unique structure of egg whites is what's responsible for the magical transformation from water to billowy whip.

Well, the plant-based world has a pretty amazing substitute for egg whites, and it's probably a free ingredient you discard: aquafaba, or the liquid from a can of chickpeas (not other beans, although we've tried that). You've seen starchy aquafaba used as an egg-like binder in our other vegan recipes throughout the book. But what really makes it magic is that it whips and creates a foam, which means it's able to trap air and grow into a meringue nearly identical in appearance to an egg white one that bakes up with a nearly identical texture. It's also a bit easier to work with than conventional meringue: no separating eggs and less guesswork about when it's reached the perfect stiff peaks. Aquafaba does take longer to whip (10 to 15 minutes), but be patient and you'll be rewarded with a glossy, stiff, taffy-like mixture.

We use aquafaba meringue to make cookies with the melt-in-your-mouth texture of our classic meringue cookies (see page 472) and an impressive pavlova with the same contrast of textures of our traditional version (see page 494). Learn all about working with aquafaba and vegan meringue on the following pages.

MEASURING AQUAFABA

To measure out the amount of aquafaba called for in a recipe, start by shaking the unopened can of chickpeas well. Drain the chickpeas through a fine-mesh strainer over a bowl and reserve the beans for another use. Whisk the aquafaba liquid and then measure. While it may not be visible, the starches in the chickpea liquid settle in the can. In order to take advantage of them, you'll want to make sure they're evenly distributed throughout the liquid.

STORING AQUAFABA

For ease, we like to freeze the aquafaba in 1-tablespoon portions in ice cube trays. Once the bean liquid cubes are frozen solid, you can pop them into a freezer bag for future use. Frozen-then-thawed aquafaba whips just as successfully as fresh aquafaba. To speed things along, you can also defrost the aquafaba in the microwave (do not cook). Chickpea liquid stored in the refrigerator will last for 1 week.

WHIPPING AQUAFABA

Just like real eggs, aquafaba needs to reach adequate volume and peaking to be usable in recipes. Underwhipped aquafaba might look glossy white but it'll lack pretty peaks. Properly whipped aquafaba will look like a proper plume.

Underwhipped Aquafaba

Properly Whipped Aquafaba

STABILIZING AQUAFABA

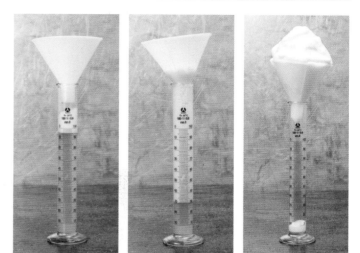

Aquafaba Whipped Alone   **Aquafaba Whipped with Sugar**   **Aquafaba Whipped with Cream of Tartar**

As it does with egg whites, adding a stabilizing ingredient improves the structure of whipped aquafaba. In sweet recipes, that's usually sugar. But there's another ingredient that we often whip with egg whites for stability: cream of tartar (see page 468).

While aquafaba isn't protein-rich like egg whites, we wanted to know if cream of tartar could benefit our vegan baked goods as well. To find out, we conducted an experiment. We whipped 4 ounces of aquafaba to a stiff foam three ways: aquafaba alone, aquafaba with ¼ cup of sugar, and aquafaba with ¼ teaspoon of cream of tartar. We transferred each foam to a funnel set over a graduated cylinder (sound familiar?). We took note of how long it took to whip the aquafaba to a stiff foam on high speed in a stand mixer as well as how much liquid weeped out when the foam was left to sit for 1 hour.

After 1 hour, it was clear that cream of tartar stabilizes aquafaba foams as it does egg foams. The aquafaba whipped alone took 10 minutes to reach stiff foam, and it had completely deflated after just 20 minutes, filling the cylinder almost completely, with about 95 mL of liquid. The aquafaba whipped with sugar fared better; it still took 10 minutes to reach stiff peaks (like egg whites, aquafaba whipped with sugar gets to stiff, sticky peaks rather than just a foam). The mixture filled the cylinder in 1 hour, but it had weeped only about 30 mL of liquid. The aquafaba whipped with cream of tartar was the star, however: It took only 4½ minutes to reach a stiff foam. And after 1 hour, only about 2 mL of liquid collected in the graduated cylinder, and only the slightest amount of foam slid through the funnel.

BEST BEAN

We wanted to see if the liquid in cans of other kinds of beans worked as well as chickpea liquid in baked goods. We made meringues using chickpea liquid, pinto bean liquid, cannellini bean liquid, and inky-dark black bean liquid. Chickpea liquid was by far the winner. We had to whip the other liquids for much longer to see any action, and at that, some didn't reach stiff peaks, resulting in flatter meringues—pancake-flat in the case of black bean liquid. Only chickpea meringues held their peaks and had solid, consistent interiors after baking.

Pinto Bean Liquid Meringues

Cannellini Bean Liquid Meringues

Black Bean Liquid Meringues

Chickpea Liquid Meringues

AQUAFABA MERINGUE COOKIES

Makes 48 cookies | 2 rimmed baking sheets

WHY THIS RECIPE WORKS We hoped whipped aquafaba would bake into ethereal vegan meringues. Unfortunately, our early attempts weren't uplifting. Our meringues deflated and developed a mottled surface and hollow centers. Looking for a solution, we reminded ourselves that while aquafaba might behave like egg whites under some circumstances, it's not the same ingredient. So instead of whipping the aquafaba to soft peaks before adding the sugar, we heated the aquafaba, dissolved the sugar in it, and then whipped the mixture to stiff peaks. This eliminated the mottling. Then, since we also didn't need to worry about overwhipping, we experimented with long mixing times. Taking the mixture beyond just "stiff peaks" and to a denser, taffy-like texture gave us tunnel-free cookies. Do not use Progresso brand chickpeas for the aquafaba; it doesn't whip consistently.

- ¾ cup (5¼ ounces) sugar
- 4 ounces (½ cup) aquafaba
- 2 teaspoons cornstarch
- ¾ teaspoon vanilla extract
- ¼ teaspoon cream of tartar
- ⅛ teaspoon table salt

1. Adjust oven racks to upper-middle and lower-middle positions and heat oven to 225 degrees. Line 2 rimmed baking sheets with parchment paper. Microwave sugar and aquafaba in bowl, whisking occasionally, until sugar is completely dissolved, 30 to 60 seconds (mixture should not begin to bubble). Let mixture cool slightly, about 10 minutes, then whisk in cornstarch.

2. Using stand mixer fitted with whisk, whip aquafaba mixture, vanilla, cream of tartar, and salt on high speed until glossy, stiff peaks form, and mixture is sticky and taffy-like, 9 to 15 minutes. Place meringue in pastry bag fitted with ½-inch plain tip or large zipper-lock bag with ½ inch of corner cut off. Pipe meringues into 1¼-inch-wide mounds about 1 inch high on prepared sheets.

3. Bake for 1 hour, switching and rotating sheets halfway through baking. Turn off oven and let meringues cool in oven for at least 1 hour. Remove from oven and let cool completely before serving, about 10 minutes. (Cooled meringues can be stored in single layer in airtight container at room temperature for up to 2 weeks.)

Aquafaba Meringue Cookies

TUTORIAL
Aquafaba Meringue Cookies

You may have nailed our conventional meringues (see page 472), but these vegan versions without the egg (yes!) require cans of chickpeas and a different—easier—procedure.

1. Microwave sugar and aquafaba in bowl, whisking occasionally, until sugar is completely dissolved, 30 to 60 seconds (mixture should not begin to bubble).

2. Let mixture cool slightly, about 10 minutes, then whisk in cornstarch.

3. Using stand mixer fitted with whisk, whip aquafaba mixture, vanilla, cream of tartar, and salt on high speed until glossy, stiff peaks form, and mixture is sticky and taffy-like, 9 to 15 minutes.

4. Pipe meringues into 1¼-inch-wide mounds about 1 inch high on prepared sheets.

5. Bake for 1 hour, switching and rotating sheets halfway through baking. Turn off oven and let meringues cool in oven for at least 1 hour.

6. Remove from oven and let cool completely before serving, about 10 minutes.

VEGAN TROPICAL FRUIT PAVLOVA

Serves 8 | 2 rimmed baking sheets

WHY THIS RECIPE WORKS Since aquafaba is a magical egg-replacing ingredient, we figured that creating a vegan pavlova by whipping aquafaba and sugar into a stiff, fluffy foam would be a cinch. But were we wrong. The first hurdle was color: The bottoms of our meringues turned spotty brown, which signified sugar crystals sinking to the bottom, so we heated the aquafaba mixture to ensure that the sugar dissolved properly. The second hurdle was appearance: We had mottled meringues from too many air bubbles. Although aquafaba takes longer than egg whites to whip, there was a point when the meringue went from dense and glossy to aerated and cottony—a sign of overwhipping. Chilling the mixture before whipping helped us achieve the proper stage faster, preventing mottling. You will need to refrigerate the unopened cans of coconut milk for the coconut whipped cream for at least 24 hours before use. If you can't find Thai basil, you can use Italian basil.

Vegan Tropical Fruit Pavlova

MERINGUES
- ⅔ cup (4⅔ ounces) sugar
- 4 ounces (½ cup) aquafaba
- ½ teaspoon vanilla extract
- ¼ teaspoon cream of tartar

FRUIT TOPPING
- 1 mango, peeled, pitted, and cut into ¼-inch pieces
- 2 kiwis, peeled, quartered lengthwise, and sliced crosswise ¼ inch thick
- 1½ cups ½-inch pineapple pieces
- 1 tablespoon sugar
- ⅓ cup chopped fresh Thai basil
- 1 recipe Coconut Whipped Cream (page 163)
- ½ cup unsweetened coconut, toasted

1. FOR THE MERINGUES: Adjust oven rack to upper-middle and lower-middle positions and heat oven to 250 degrees. Heat sugar and aquafaba in small saucepan over medium-low heat, whisking until sugar is dissolved, about 5 minutes (mixture should not be bubbling). Transfer to bowl of stand mixer and refrigerate until chilled, about 1 hour.

2. Fit stand mixer with whisk attachment and whip chilled aquafaba mixture, vanilla, and cream of tartar on high speed until stiff peaks form and mixture is dense and bright white, 7 to 9 minutes, scraping down the bowl halfway through. (Do not overwhip.)

3. Spoon about ¼ teaspoon meringue onto each corner of 2 rimmed baking sheets. Line sheets with parchment paper, pressing on corners to secure. Spoon ⅓ cup meringue into 4 evenly spaced piles on each prepared sheet. Evenly distribute any remaining meringue among piles and spread each with back of spoon or spatula from center outward, building 4-inch disks that are slightly higher around edges.

4. Bake meringues for 50 minutes. Without opening oven door, turn off oven and let meringues cool in oven for 1 hour (meringues will still be soft to the touch, but will firm as they continue to cool). Remove meringues from oven and let cool completely before topping, about 15 minutes. (Cooled meringues can be wrapped tightly in plastic wrap and stored at room temperature for up to 2 days.)

5. FOR THE FRUIT TOPPING: Gently toss mango, kiwis, and pineapple with sugar in bowl. Let sit at room temperature until sugar has dissolved and fruit is juicy, about 30 minutes. Just before serving, stir basil into fruit mixture.

6. To assemble, place meringue shells on individual plates and spoon heaping ¼ cup coconut whipped cream into each. Top with about ½ cup fruit (some fruit and juice will fall onto plate) and let sit for about 15 minutes. Sprinkle with toasted coconut and serve.

PART 08

pastries

THE REALM OF PASTRIES IS A WIDE-RANGING ONE: Technically any dessert with some combination of flour, fat, and water could qualify. But when we think of pastry, what typically comes to mind is a tender, crisp, flaky dough layered with or encompassing a filling—anything from luscious pastry cream or ice cream to chopped nuts to tender fruit. Other times, the pastry is truly the star of the show, its buttery, flaky layers adorned with nothing more than a simple glaze or dusting of confectioners' sugar. Many pastries are individual treats with a stunning presentation to match their unique flavors and textures.

Pastries such as this are frequently left in the domain of professional bakers, only to be found at upscale bakeries and fancy patisseries. They are true special-occasion desserts that are packaged with care and presented with fanfare. We hope this section will make them feel more accessible. It's definitely true, however, that pastries can be a labor of love: There's simply no quick way to make a laminated pastry such as Breton Kouign Amann (page 528), in which a block of butter is enclosed in a lean dough and folded and rolled repeatedly into thin sheets to create countless flaky layers. But with the proper instructions and techniques this type of pastry can emerge browned, caramelized, and crisped from your oven if you have a little patience.

Pastries that take a bit of time can often be broken down into more manageable stages or made ahead until they're ready to be filled and assembled. Such is the case for pate a choux, the tender, airy dough used for cream-filled éclairs and for the cream puffs known as profiteroles, which are layered with ice cream and drizzled with chocolate sauce. Other pastries can be assembled and baked without starting from scratch: For many desserts we rely on perfectly good frozen, store-bought pastry dough, which means a warm apple turnover; nutty, honey-sweetened baklava; or crisp strudel can be prepared with minimal fuss.

The art of pastry making may require some time and patience, but for the most part the list of kitchen tools needed is relatively simple: A good rolling pin is key, as is a pastry brush (see page 340) when assembling layer upon layer of phyllo dough, which needs a good coating of butter or oil in between. And for the dough for everything from ice cream–filled Profiteroles (page 514) and elegant Paris-Brest (page 518) to crispy fried Churros (page 521), a piping set (see page 226) is essential.

Serrated knife

There are many uses for a serrated knife in the kitchen when making pastry desserts. The serrations reduce the friction between the knife and the food it's cutting, allowing it to cleanly slice through delicate pastry. It's the perfect tool for slicing puff pastry before stacking and assembling or for cutting cream puffs in half horizontally so they can be filled with pastry cream or ice cream. With the fewest, widest, and deepest serrations as well as a grippy handle, the **Mercer Culinary Millennia 10″ Wide Bread Knife** ($22.10) is a standout.

FREEZER DOUGHS

Two essential doughs of homemade pastry-making—puff pastry and phyllo—can be made from scratch, but the process is typically a time-consuming one. Fortunately, reliable versions of both are readily available in the freezer section at your grocery store. Store-bought frozen puff pastry and phyllo deliver all the advantages of homemade versions without the hours of tricky, temperature-sensitive dough work, so we recommend them for the most consistent results. (While we never make phyllo from scratch, if you are interested in trying your hand at homemade puff pastry, we show you how in our recipe for Napoleons on page 511.)

STORAGE

Some pastry desserts such as turnovers freeze particularly well, while others like Baklava (page 524) require several hours to set before serving. And certain leavened pastries such as Pecan Kringle (page 527) will keep at room temperature for a couple of days once fully baked. That means many of these pastries are great make-ahead options. But others have a short window when they're crisp and fresh once fully assembled, especially if they feature a rich pastry cream or other filling. That said, it's often possible to pause along the way: Once puff pastry is baked, cooled, and cut, it can be stored at room temperature for up to a day. And the dough for pate a choux—the pastry used for cream puffs and éclairs—can be kept in the refrigerator for up to two days, while the baked, cooled pastries can typically be held at room temperature or frozen for a period of time. This allows you to break down the process for these delicate desserts into more manageable steps.

Choux au Craquelin

PUFF PASTRY DESSERTS

Thaw pastry in refrigerator

Chill pastry in between recipe steps for workability

Slice with serrated knife

PUFF PASTRY FEATURES IN A VARIETY OF DESSERTS, from rustic fruit turnovers to elegant Napoleons (page 511). It's extra versatile and can be shaped many ways (you'll even find it in our Tarts section). The multilayered pastry is supremely buttery and tender yet sturdy enough to hold together when eaten out of hand, and its crisp, flaky exterior provides a beautiful contrast to a warm apple filling or layers of cool, silky pastry cream. Puff pastry gets its seemingly endless layers and crispy, flaky texture from a process called lamination. Homemade puff pastry (see page 508) isn't particularly difficult to make, but it is fairly time-intensive (and temperature-sensitive), so we typically reserve it for refined, special-occasion desserts such as Napoleons, although you could use it whenever you want. For most recipes, we turn to store-bought frozen puff pastry, which is convenient, readily available, and provides consistent results. Puff pastry is available in versions made with vegetable shortening as well as all-butter versions, so try both and see which you prefer.

PUFF PASTRY 101

Buttery, flaky puff pastry is fantastic made from scratch, but when we want a more streamlined recipe we use store-bought pastry, which is reliable and produces consistent results. Here are a few tips for working with this dough.

Thaw in Fridge You can thaw puff pastry on the counter for 30 minutes to 1 hour if your kitchen is cool, but the safest bet is to thaw it in the fridge for 24 hours. That way, the pastry defrosts slowly, and there's no risk of it overheating.

Avoid Rolling Over Edges When rolling the puff pastry sheet, try to avoid rolling over the edges of the sheet too much. Flattening the edges could inhibit the "puff" during baking.

Use Sharp Knife A sharp knife edge will make clean, precise cuts that preserve the layers rather than pinch them together.

Rechill Before Baking After you've shaped and cut your puff pastry, it can be a good idea to chill the dough for 15 to 30 minutes before baking to firm it up and help it retain flakiness.

Feel Free to Refreeze If you thaw more puff pastry than you need, simply pop the leftovers back in the freezer. In testing, we've found that there is little difference between dough frozen once and dough frozen twice; all-butter pastry won't rise quite as high after a double freeze as pastry made with shortening will, but the effect is minimal.

AVOIDING TURNOVER EXPLOSIONS

We want the tasty filling inside the turnover, not on the baking sheet. To avoid exploding turnovers, gently cup the filling to center it within the pastry. This technique helps prevent leakage.

EASY FREEZE

Puff pastry desserts freeze beautifully, making turnovers in particular an ideal make-ahead option. After chilling the turnovers, simply transfer them to a zipper-lock bag and freeze for up to one month. When ready to serve, finish according to the recipe and bake the turnovers as indicated (the baking time will not change).

SLICING NAPOLEONS RIGHT

Traditional recipes typically make one large stacked Napoleon and then cut the pastry into individual servings, but this method is fussy and plagued with issues—it not only mars the topping but the filling has a tendency to squirt out the sides during cutting. Instead, once the pastry is cool, we cut it into individual rectangles before filling and stacking. Using a serrated knife ensures clean, neat slices. A serrated knife comes in handy for splitting or portioning a number of other pastries in this section, from Paris-Brest (page 518) to Baklava (page 524).

Puff Pastry School

Making puff pastry from scratch isn't difficult, but it does take a little time. Repeatedly folding and rolling the dough forms multiple sheets of butter and dough that puff into incredibly flaky layers once baked.

PUFF PASTRY DOUGH
Makes 2 pounds

Puff pastry gets its super-flaky, buttery layers from a process called lamination, also known as turning, or folding. Each turn creates paper-thin sheets of butter, and when the dough is baked, the moisture in the butter evaporates into steam, causing the dough to puff and separate into flaky layers. We mix the flour, sugar, salt, lemon juice, and ice water together in a food processor for even, quick distribution and then we chill the dough to allow it to relax for easier rolling. While the dough chills, we make a butter square by gently pounding butter sticks into an even layer. We chill the square so that it does not melt when combined with the dough. If you are making Napoleons (page 511), cut the dough in half (each half will weigh about 1 pound) after it has chilled in step 6; use one piece of dough as directed and refrigerate the rest for up to two days or freeze, wrapped in plastic wrap and then aluminum foil, for up to one month. A half recipe of this homemade Puff Pastry Dough is equal to 2 sheets of frozen puff pastry. If you want to use Premium European butter somewhere, this is the place to do it.

DOUGH
   3   cups (15 ounces) all-purpose flour
1½ tablespoons sugar
1½ teaspoons table salt
   2   teaspoons lemon juice
   1   cup ice water, divided

BUTTER SQUARE
 24 tablespoons (3 sticks) unsalted butter, chilled
  2 tablespoons all-purpose flour

1. FOR THE DOUGH: Process flour, sugar, and salt in food processor until combined, about 5 seconds. With processor running, add lemon juice, followed by ¾ cup water, in slow steady stream. Add remaining ¼ cup water as needed, 1 tablespoon at a time, until dough comes together and no floury bits remain.

2. Turn dough onto sheet of plastic wrap and flatten into 6-inch square. Wrap tightly in plastic and refrigerate for 1 hour.

3. FOR THE BUTTER SQUARE: Lay butter sticks side by side on sheet of parchment paper. Sprinkle flour over butter and cover with second sheet of parchment. Gently pound butter with rolling pin until butter is softened and flour is fully incorporated, then roll it into 8-inch square. Wrap butter square in plastic and refrigerate until chilled, about 1 hour.

4. Roll chilled dough into 13½-inch square on lightly floured counter. Place chilled butter square diagonally in center of dough. Fold corners of dough up over butter square so that corners meet in middle and pinch dough seams to seal.

5. Using rolling pin, gently tap dough, starting from center and working outward, until square becomes larger and butter begins to soften. Gently roll dough into 14-inch square, dusting with extra flour as needed to prevent sticking. Fold dough into thirds like a business letter, then fold rectangle in thirds to form square. Wrap dough in plastic and let rest in refrigerator for 2 hours.

6. Repeat step 5 twice and let folded square of dough rest in refrigerator for 2 hours more before using.

Making Puff Pastry

1. Lay butter sticks side by side on parchment. Sprinkle flour over butter and cover with second sheet of parchment.

2. Using rolling pin, gently pound flour into butter until softened. Roll into 8-inch square. Wrap and refrigerate for 1 hour.

3. Roll chilled dough into 13½-inch square on lightly floured counter. Place chilled butter square diagonally in center of dough.

4. Fold corners of dough square over butter square so that corners meet in middle and pinch dough seams to seal.

5. Using rolling pin, gently tap dough, starting from center and working outward, until square becomes larger and butter begins to soften. Gently roll dough into 14-inch square, dusting with flour as needed.

6. Fold dough into thirds like a business letter, then fold rectangle into thirds to form square. Wrap dough in plastic and refrigerate for 2 hours.

7. Repeat rolling and folding twice and let folded square of dough rest in refrigerator for 2 more hours.

APPLE TURNOVERS

Serves 8 | rimmed baking sheet

WHY THIS RECIPE WORKS These handheld pastries, with puff pastry dough folded over sweet apple filling and baked until golden brown and crisp, have undeniable appeal. Turnovers are quick and easy to make, so we started with good-quality frozen store-bought dough (although you could certainly use homemade). A quick filling made of savory apple butter and freshly grated apples gave our turnovers complex apple flavor. Draining excess moisture from the filling reduced the threat of leakage. Chilling the assembled turnovers in the freezer for about 20 minutes before baking them guaranteed that the pastries rose high. We prefer Granny Smith apples here, but other apple varieties can be used. To thaw frozen puff pastry, let it sit either in the refrigerator for 24 hours or on the counter for 30 minutes to 1 hour.

3–4 Granny Smith apples, peeled
¼ cup (1¾ ounces) plus 2 tablespoons sugar, divided
⅛ teaspoon table salt
½ cup apple butter
2 (9½ by 9-inch) sheets puff pastry, thawed
½ teaspoon ground cinnamon

1. Grate apples on large holes of box grater set inside bowl until you have 3 cups shredded apples. Add ¼ cup sugar and salt to apples and stir to thoroughly combine. Let sit for 5 minutes.

2. Drain apples in fine-mesh strainer set over bowl and press gently with rubber spatula to extract about ⅓ cup juice (do not extract more than ⅓ cup juice or volume of apples will decrease too much). Set aside juice. Transfer apples to now-empty bowl. Add apple butter to apples and stir to combine.

3. Unfold puff pastry sheets onto lightly floured counter and roll each into 10-inch square. Cut each sheet into four 5-inch squares. Mound 3 level tablespoons of apple mixture in center of each square. Brush edges of each dough square with some of reserved juice, then fold 1 corner of each square diagonally over filling. Cup your hands around apple mixture and gently press on dough triangle to seal. Using fork, crimp edges of dough to seal.

4. Transfer pies to 2 large plates and cut two 1-inch slits on top. Freeze pies until firm, about 20 minutes. (Once frozen, pies can be transferred to airtight container and stored in freezer for up to 1 month.)

5. Adjust oven rack to middle position and heat oven to 400 degrees. Line rimmed baking sheet with parchment paper. Combine cinnamon and remaining 2 tablespoons sugar in bowl. Brush tops of turnovers with remaining reserved juice and sprinkle with cinnamon sugar. Transfer turnovers to prepared sheet and bake until well browned, 22 to 24 minutes. Let turnovers cool on wire rack for 10 minutes before serving.

Apple Turnovers

CHERRY TURNOVERS

Serves 8 | rimmed baking sheet

WHY THIS RECIPE WORKS Summer cherry season is fleeting, so we were thrilled to discover that fresh or frozen sweet cherries worked equally well in our cherry turnovers, for a treat we could enjoy year-round. The sweetness and firm texture of sweet cherries was more appealing than softer jarred or canned tart cherries, and chopping the cherries gave the filling more body and ensured every bite of turnover had chunks of fruit. Weigh frozen cherries before thawing and draining. To thaw frozen puff pastry, let it sit either in the refrigerator for 24 hours or on the counter for 30 minutes to 1 hour.

1 pound fresh or frozen sweet cherries, pitted and chopped
¼ cup (1¾ ounces) plus 1 tablespoon sugar, divided
½ teaspoon almond extract
½ teaspoon grated orange zest
⅛ teaspoon table salt
1 tablespoon cornstarch
1 tablespoon water
2 (9½ by 9-inch) sheets puff pastry, thawed
1 large egg, lightly beaten with 1 tablespoon water

1. Cook cherries, ¼ cup sugar, almond extract, orange zest, and salt in medium saucepan over medium heat, stirring occasionally, until cherries release their juices, mixture thickens, and spatula starts to leave trail when pulled through, 6 to 8 minutes.

2. Whisk cornstarch and water together in bowl, then stir into cherry mixture. Cook until mixture has thickened to jam-like consistency, about 1 minute (you should have about 1¼ cups filling). Let cool completely, about 30 minutes.

3. Unfold puff pastry sheets onto lightly floured counter and roll each into 10-inch square. Cut each sheet into four 5-inch squares. Place 2 tablespoons cherry filling in center of each square.

4. Brush edges of squares with egg wash, then fold 1 corner of each square diagonally over filling. Cup your hands around cherry mixture and gently press on dough triangle to seal. Using fork, crimp edges of dough to seal. Transfer pies to prepared sheet and cut three 1-inch slits on top. Freeze pies until firm, about 20 minutes. (Once frozen, pies can be transferred to airtight container and stored in freezer for up to 1 month.)

5. Adjust oven rack to middle position and heat oven to 400 degrees. Line rimmed baking sheet with parchment paper. Brush tops of pies with remaining egg wash and sprinkle with remaining 1 tablespoon sugar. Bake until well browned, about 25 minutes, rotating sheet halfway through baking. Transfer pies to wire rack and let cool slightly, about 15 minutes. Serve warm or at room temperature.

NAPOLEONS

Serves 6 | 2 rimmed baking sheets

WHY THIS RECIPE WORKS Napoleons feature satiny vanilla pastry cream between layers of crisp puff pastry, topped with fanciful icing. It's a multicomponent, special-occasion dessert of fascinating textures, so we chose to go all out with homemade puff pastry (although you could use store-bought). For level pastry layers we rolled the dough, poked holes in it with a fork, slid it onto a baking sheet, and baked it topped with a second, weighted baking sheet. Making one large Napoleon and then cutting it into individual servings was challenging and messy; instead, we cut the cooled pastry into individual rectangles before filling and stacking. If the dough becomes too warm and sticky to work with, cover it with plastic wrap and let it chill in the refrigerator until firm. You can substitute a 1-pound box of store-bought puff pastry dough for homemade puff pastry. The finished dessert can sit for 4 hours before serving.

PASTRY
½ recipe Puff Pastry Dough (page 508)

CHOCOLATE GLAZE
1 ounce bittersweet or semisweet chocolate, chopped fine
2 tablespoons milk
¾ cup (3 ounces) confectioners' sugar

VANILLA GLAZE
¼ cup (1 ounce) confectioners' sugar
1½ teaspoons milk
⅛ teaspoon vanilla extract

1 recipe Pastry Cream (page 186)

1. **FOR THE PASTRY:** Adjust oven rack to middle position and heat oven to 325 degrees. Roll dough into 16 by 12-inch rectangle, about ¼ inch thick, between 2 lightly floured sheets of parchment paper. Remove top sheet of parchment and prick pastry with fork every 2 inches.

2. Replace top sheet of parchment and slide dough onto rimmed baking sheet. Place second rimmed baking sheet on top of dough and weight baking sheet with large ovensafe dish. Bake pastry until cooked through and lightly golden, 50 minutes to 1 hour, rotating baking sheet halfway through baking. Remove weight, top baking sheet, and top sheet of parchment and continue to bake pastry until golden brown, 5 to 10 minutes longer. Let pastry cool completely on baking sheet, about 1 hour.

3. Cut pastry in half lengthwise with serrated knife. Trim edges to make them straight. Cut each pastry half crosswise into 3 rectangles, then cut each rectangle crosswise into 3 small rectangles (you will have 18 rectangles). (Pastry can be wrapped tightly in plastic wrap and stored at room temperature for up to 1 day.)

4. **FOR THE CHOCOLATE GLAZE:** Microwave chocolate at 50 percent power for 15 seconds; stir chocolate, add milk, and continue heating for 10 seconds; stir until smooth. Whisk in confectioners' sugar until smooth.

5. **FOR THE VANILLA GLAZE:** Whisk sugar, milk, and vanilla together in bowl until smooth.

6. Spread chocolate glaze evenly over top of 6 rectangles of pastry and lay them on wire rack set over sheet of parchment (for easy cleanup). Drizzle thin stream of vanilla glaze crosswise over chocolate glaze. Run tip of small knife or toothpick lengthwise through icing to make design. Let icing set, about 20 minutes. Spread about 2½ tablespoons of pastry cream evenly over 6 more rectangles of pastry. Gently top each with one of remaining 6 rectangles and spread remaining pastry cream evenly over tops. Top with glazed rectangles. Serve.

Almond Napoleons
Substitute Almond Pastry Cream (page 186) for Pastry Cream and add 1 drop almond extract to vanilla glaze.

Mocha Napoleons
Substitute Mocha Pastry Cream (page 186) for Pastry Cream and add ¼ teaspoon instant espresso powder or instant coffee powder to chocolate glaze before melting.

PATE A CHOUX DESSERTS

Incorporate eggs with food processor

Leave ample space between pastries on baking sheet

Pastry needs to dry in oven before filling

Serve immediately after filling

ÉCLAIRS AND CREAM PUFFS ARE TWO BELOVED DESSERTS made with the classic French pastry known as pate a choux. Leavened by steam alone, the dough puffs up as it bakes, creating a crisp, hollow shell surrounding a tender, ethereal lining of soft dough—the perfect counterpoint to a silky pastry cream or scoop of ice cream. Creating pate a choux is a particularly rewarding process because it's relatively easy and the results are so dramatic. To make it, milk, water, sugar, and butter are brought to a simmer; flour is stirred in to make a paste; and then the paste is cooked briefly. As it cooks, the paste is stirred constantly, stimulating the development of gluten, the protein that gives dough elasticity and promotes a better, stronger rise in the oven. Once cooked, eggs are whipped into the hot mixture and then the dough is piped out through a pastry bag and baked.

The traditional method of introducing the eggs to the paste is to do so gradually, stirring vigorously after each addition, but we have discovered that this fussy approach is unnecessary; instead, we simply transfer the cooked paste to a food processor and add the eggs in a steady stream. Not only do the eggs incorporate swiftly, but the pastry rises even higher than when mixed by hand. One exception to this is for Churros (page 521); these cinnamon sugar–coated fried fritters have an interior that's less delicate and airy than other pastries, and here we use a stand mixer rather than a food processor to incorporate the eggs. Pate a choux dough can be prepared ahead (as can the baked pastries), so it's an ideal make-ahead option when an occasion call for a showstopping finish to the meal.

Pate a Choux School

PATE A CHOUX
Makes 24 cream puffs or 8 éclairs

Pate a choux, or cream puff pastry, is an elemental type of French pastry, and it forms the basis for éclairs, profiteroles, and more. To make the recipe foolproof, we employed a food processor. In the traditional version, the eggs are added one at a time, and the mixture requires vigorous stirring after each addition. If added all at once, the eggs splash about and require patience and a strong arm to incorporate them into the dough. Instead we transferred the paste to a food processor, let the mixture cool briefly, and then whirred in all the eggs at once. We piped the dough onto the baking sheet in the desired shape. No matter the pastry, we found that crowding during baking pate a choux causes the pastry to collapse. Be sure to leave at least an inch of space between portions of the dough. Be sure to sift the flour after measuring.

- 2 **large eggs plus 1 large white**
- 6 **tablespoons water**
- 5 **tablespoons unsalted butter, cut into ½-inch pieces**
- 2 **tablespoons milk**
- 1½ **teaspoons sugar**
- ¼ **teaspoon table salt**
- ½ **cup (2½ ounces) all-purpose flour, sifted**

1. Beat eggs and white together in 2-cup liquid measuring cup.

2. Bring water, butter, milk, sugar, and salt to boil in small saucepan over medium heat, stirring occasionally. Off heat, stir in flour until incorporated. Return saucepan to low heat and cook, stirring constantly and using smearing motion, until mixture looks like shiny, wet sand, about 3 minutes (mixture should register between 175 and 180 degrees).

3. Immediately transfer hot mixture to food processor and process for 10 seconds to cool slightly. With processor running, gradually add reserved egg mixture in steady stream until incorporated. Scrape down sides of bowl and continue to process until smooth, thick, sticky paste forms, about 30 seconds longer. Proceed with recipe.

Making Pate a Choux

1. Beat eggs and egg white in measuring cup. Bring butter, milk, water, sugar, and salt to boil in small saucepan over medium heat, stirring occasionally.

2. Remove from heat and stir in flour until incorporated and mixture clears sides of saucepan.

3. Return saucepan to low heat and cook, stirring constantly and using smearing motion, until mixture looks like shiny, wet sand, about 3 minutes (mixture should register between 175 and 180 degrees).

4. Immediately transfer hot mixture to food processor and process for 10 seconds to cool slightly.

5. With processor running, gradually add reserved egg mixture in steady stream until incorporated.

6. Scrape down sides of bowl and continue to process until smooth, thick, sticky paste forms, about 30 seconds longer.

DOUBLE CHOCOLATE ÉCLAIRS

Makes 8 éclairs | rimmed baking sheet

WHY THIS RECIPE WORKS We wanted our éclairs—fingerlike French pastries filled with cream and glazed with chocolate— to feature a double dose of chocolate. We incorporated it not only into the glaze but also the pastry cream. Using a pastry bag to pipe our pate a choux onto the baking sheet ensured evenly sized pastries. Once they were baked, we cut a small slit into each pastry and returned them to the turned-off oven until the centers were moist and the surface was crisp. Adding a couple of ounces of bittersweet chocolate to a basic pastry cream ensured chocolaty goodness throughout. A decadent chocolate glaze covered the holes we made to fill our pastries with the chocolate cream. Be sure the pastry cream is thoroughly chilled before filling the pastries. The glaze should still be warm when glazing the éclairs. You will need a large pastry bag with a ½-inch plain tip and a ¼-inch plain tip.

PASTRY CREAM

- 2 cups half-and-half
- ½ cup (3½ ounces) granulated sugar, divided
  Pinch table salt
- 5 large egg yolks
- 3 tablespoons cornstarch
- 4 tablespoons unsalted butter, cut into 4 pieces
- 2 ounces bittersweet chocolate, chopped fine
- ½ teaspoon vanilla extract

PASTRY

- 1 recipe Pate a Choux (page 513), warm

GLAZE

- 2 ounces semisweet or bittersweet chocolate, chopped fine
- 3 tablespoons half-and-half
- 1 cup (4 ounces) confectioners' sugar

1. FOR THE PASTRY CREAM: Bring half-and-half, 6 tablespoons sugar, and salt to simmer in medium saucepan over medium-high heat, stirring occasionally.

2. Meanwhile, whisk egg yolks, cornstarch, and remaining 2 tablespoons sugar together in bowl until smooth. Slowly whisk 1 cup of hot half-and-half mixture into egg mixture to temper, then slowly whisk tempered egg mixture into remaining half-and-half mixture in saucepan. Reduce heat to medium and cook, whisking constantly, until mixture is thickened, smooth, and registers 180 degrees, about 30 seconds. Off heat, whisk in butter, chocolate, and vanilla. Transfer pastry cream to clean bowl and press plastic wrap directly on surface. Refrigerate until cold and set, at least 3 hours or up to 2 days.

3. FOR THE PASTRY: Adjust oven rack to middle position and heat oven to 400 degrees. Line rimmed baking sheet with parchment paper.

4. Fit pastry bag with ½-inch plain tip and fill with warm pate a choux. Pipe pate a choux into eight 5 by 1-inch logs spaced about 1 inch apart on prepared sheet. Use your dampened finger or back of wet teaspoon to even out shape and smooth surface of each log.

5. Bake for 15 minutes (do not open oven door), then reduce oven temperature to 350 degrees and continue to bake until pastries are golden brown and fairly firm (pastries should not be soft and squishy), 8 to 10 minutes longer.

6. Remove sheet from oven. Using paring knife, cut ¾-inch slit into side of each pastry to release steam. Return pastries to oven, turn off oven, and prop door open with handle of wooden spoon. Dry pastries in turned-off oven until centers are just moist (not wet) and surfaces are crisp, about 45 minutes. Transfer pastries to wire rack and let cool completely, about 30 minutes.

7. FOR THE GLAZE: Using tip of paring knife, cut 3 small Xs along top of each pastry. Fit clean pastry bag with ¼-inch plain tip and fill pastry bag with pastry cream. Pipe pastry cream into pastries through each opening until éclairs are completely filled.

8. Microwave chocolate in bowl at 50 percent power until melted, about 30 seconds. Whisk in half-and-half until smooth. Gradually whisk in sugar until smooth.

9. Transfer éclairs to wire rack set in rimmed baking sheet. Spoon warm glaze evenly over tops, making sure to cover holes completely. Let glaze set, about 20 minutes, before serving.

PROFITEROLES

Makes 24 profiteroles | rimmed baking sheet

WHY THIS RECIPE WORKS In profiteroles, delicate pastry encases cold, creamy ice cream to create an elegant, satisfying dessert. To make perfect profiteroles more than a pipe dream, we used both water and milk in the dough for a pastry that crisped up well and colored nicely. For lighter, puffier puffs, we incorporated the eggs all at once using the high speed of a food processor rather than laboriously hand-beating them in one at a time. An initial blast of heat jump-started browning; then lowering the heat let the interior cook through. Prescooping the ice cream makes serving quick and neat. Whisk the chocolate sauce gently so as not to create tiny air bubbles that can mar its appearance. Rewarm the sauce if you make it in advance:

Microwave the sauce at 50 percent power, stirring once or twice, 1 to 3 minutes. Alternatively you can stir it in a heatproof bowl set over a saucepan filled with 1 inch of barely simmering water.)

1 recipe Pate a Choux (page 513), warm
¾ cup heavy cream
3 tablespoons light corn syrup
3 tablespoons unsalted butter, cut into 3 pieces
    Pinch table salt
6 ounces bittersweet chocolate, chopped
1 quart vanilla or coffee ice cream

1. Adjust oven rack to middle position and heat oven to 425 degrees. Spray rimmed baking sheet with vegetable oil spray and line with parchment paper; set aside.

2A. TO PORTION USING PASTRY BAG: Fold down top 3 or 4 inches of 14- or 16-inch pastry bag fitted with ½-inch plain tip to form cuff. Hold bag open with your hand in cuff and fill bag with warm pate a choux. Unfold cuff, lay bag on work surface, and, using your hands or bench scraper, push paste into lower portion of bag. Twist top of bag and pipe paste into 1½-inch mounds on prepared baking sheet, spacing them 1 to 1¼ inches apart (you should be able to fit all 24 mounds on baking sheet).

2B. TO PORTION USING SPOONS: Scoop 1 level tablespoon of dough. Using second small spoon, scrape pate a choux onto prepared sheet into 1½-inch mound. Repeat, spacing mounds 1 to 1¼ inches apart (you should be able to fit all 24 mounds on baking sheet).

3. Using back of teaspoon dipped in bowl of cold water, smooth shape and surface of mounds. Bake for 15 minutes (do not open oven door), then reduce oven temperature to 375 degrees and continue to bake until puffs are golden brown and fairly firm (puffs should not be soft and squishy), 8 to 10 minutes longer. Remove baking sheet from oven. With paring knife, cut ¾-inch slit into side of each puff to release steam; return puffs to oven, turn off oven, and prop oven door open with handle of wooden spoon. Dry puffs in turned-off oven until centers are just moist (not wet) and puffs are crisp, about 45 minutes. Transfer puffs to wire rack and let cool completely. (Cooled puffs can be stored in airtight container at room temperature for up to 24 hours or frozen in zipper-lock bag for up to 1 month. Before serving, crisp room temperature puffs in 300-degree oven for 5 to 8 minutes, or 8 to 10 minutes for frozen puffs.)

4. Line baking sheet with parchment paper; freeze until cold, about 20 minutes. Using 2-inch ice cream scoop (about same diameter as puffs), scoop ice cream onto cold sheet and freeze until firm, then cover with plastic wrap; keep frozen until ready to serve. (Ice cream can be scooped and frozen for up to 1 week.)

5. Bring heavy cream, corn syrup, butter, and salt to boil in small saucepan over medium-high heat. Off heat, add chocolate while gently swirling saucepan. Cover and let stand until chocolate is melted, about 5 minutes. Uncover and whisk gently until combined. (Cooled sauce can be refrigerated for up to 3 weeks.)

6. Use paring knife to split open puffs about ⅜ inch from bottom; set 3 or 4 bottoms on each dessert plate. Place scoop of ice cream on each bottom and gently press tops into ice cream. Pour chocolate sauce over profiteroles and serve immediately.

Profiteroles

CHOUX AU CRAQUELIN

**Makes 24 craquelin | 1 rimless baking sheet,
1 rimmed baking sheet**

WHY THIS RECIPE WORKS For our choux au craquelin—airy, crispy shells, covered with a sweet, crackly coating, encasing smooth, lush pastry cream—we rolled the sugary craquelin dough into a thin sheet from which we cut 24 disks before freezing them. We topped the piped mounds of pate a choux with slim disks of the craquelin dough, which transformed into crackly shells as the puffs baked. We filled the puffs with a pastry cream with extra body (so it wouldn't ooze) lightened with whipped cream. You'll need a 2-inch round cutter, a pastry bag, and two pastry tips—one with a ¼-inch round opening and one with a ½-inch round opening. This recipe can be made over two days: Make the pastry cream and craquelin on day 1 and the puffs on day 2. Use a mixer to whip the cream if you prefer.

PASTRY CREAM
2½ cups whole milk, divided
 ⅔ cup (3⅓ ounces) all-purpose flour
 ½ cup (3½ ounces) granulated sugar
 ¼ teaspoon table salt
 6 large egg yolks
 4 tablespoons unsalted butter, cut into 4 pieces and chilled
 1 tablespoon vanilla extract

CRAQUELIN
 6 tablespoons unsalted butter, softened
 ½ cup packed (3½ ounces) light brown sugar
 ¾ cup (3¾ ounces) all-purpose flour
    Pinch table salt

 1 recipe Pate a Choux (page 513), warm
 1 cup heavy cream

1. FOR THE PASTRY CREAM: Heat 2 cups milk in medium saucepan over medium heat until just simmering. Meanwhile, whisk flour, sugar, and salt in medium bowl until combined. Add egg yolks and remaining ½ cup milk to flour mixture and whisk until smooth. Remove saucepan from heat and, whisking constantly, slowly add ½ cup milk to yolk mixture to temper. Whisking constantly, add tempered yolk mixture to milk in saucepan.

2. Return saucepan to medium heat and cook, whisking constantly, until mixture thickens slightly, about 1 minute. Reduce heat to medium-low and continue to simmer, whisking constantly, for 8 minutes. Increase heat to medium and cook, whisking vigorously, until very thick (mixture dripped from whisk should mound on surface), 1 to 2 minutes. Off heat, whisk in butter and vanilla until butter is melted and incorporated. Transfer to wide bowl. Press lightly greased parchment paper directly on surface and refrigerate until set, at least 2 hours or up to 24 hours.

3. FOR THE CRAQUELIN: Mix butter and sugar in medium bowl until combined. Mix in flour and salt. Transfer mixture to large sheet of parchment and press into 6-inch square. Cover with second piece of parchment and roll dough into 13 by 9-inch rectangle (it's fine to trim and patch dough to achieve correct dimensions). Remove top piece of parchment and use 2-inch round cutter to cut 24 circles. Leaving circles and trim in place, replace top parchment and transfer to rimless baking sheet. Freeze until firm, at least 30 minutes or up to 2 days.

4. Adjust oven rack to middle position and heat oven to 400 degrees. Spray rimmed baking sheet with vegetable oil spray and dust lightly and evenly with flour, discarding any excess. Using 2-inch round cutter, mark 24 circles on sheet. Fit pastry bag with ½-inch round tip.

5. Fill pastry bag with warm pate a choux and pipe into 1½-inch-wide mounds on prepared sheet, using circles as guide. Using small, thin spatula, transfer 1 frozen craquelin disk to top of each mound. Bake for 15 minutes; then, without opening oven door, reduce oven temperature to 350 degrees and continue to bake until golden brown and firm, 7 to 10 minutes longer.

6. Remove sheet from oven and cut ¾-inch slit into side of each pastry with paring knife to release steam. Return pastries to oven, turn off oven, and prop open oven door with handle of wooden spoon. Let pastries dry until center is mostly dry and surface is crisp, about 45 minutes. Transfer pastries to wire rack and let cool completely.

7. Fit pastry bag with ¼-inch round tip. In large bowl, whisk cream to stiff peaks. Gently whisk pastry cream until smooth. Fold pastry cream into whipped cream until combined. Transfer one-third of mixture to pastry bag. To fill choux buns, insert pastry tip ¾ inch into opening and squeeze gently until cream just starts to appear around opening, about 2 tablespoons cream per bun. Refill bag as needed. Serve. (Choux are best eaten up to 2 hours after filling. Leftovers can be refrigerated for up to 3 days but will soften over time.)

Colorful Choux au Craquelin
Substitute granulated sugar for brown sugar in craquelin. Add gel or paste food coloring to craquelin dough until desired color is achieved.

Mocha Choux au Craquelin
Add 5 teaspoons instant espresso powder to hot milk for pastry cream. Decrease flour in craquelin to ⅔ cup and add 1 tablespoon unsweetened cocoa powder.

TUTORIAL
Choux au Craquelin

These might be one of the most precious looking desserts we make, but we've broken down the process for anyone.

1. Using 2-inch round cutter, cut 24 circles from craquelin. Replace top parchment and transfer to rimless baking sheet. Freeze until firm.

2. Fill pastry bag with warm pate a choux and pipe into 1½-inch-wide mounds on prepared sheet, using circles as guide.

3. Using small, thin spatula, transfer 1 frozen craquelin disk to top of each mound.

4. Bake for 15 minutes; reduce oven temperature to 350 degrees and continue to bake until golden brown and firm, 7 to 10 minutes longer.

5. Return pastries to oven, turn off oven, and prop open door with wooden spoon; keep in oven until center is mostly dry and surface is crisp, about 45 minutes.

6. When buns are cool, insert pastry tip ¾ inch into opening and squeeze gently until cream just starts to appear around opening, about 2 tablespoons cream per bun.

PARIS-BREST

Serves 8 to 10 | rimmed baking sheet

WHY THIS RECIPE WORKS Paris-Brest is an elegant French dessert featuring a large ring of pate a choux filled with hazelnut praline pastry cream and sprinkled with chopped nuts and powdered sugar. To fill our pastry ring, we opted for a flour-thickened pastry cream further stabilized with gelatin; we then added pulverized caramel-coated hazelnuts, and folded in whipped cream to lighten it. An equal amount of slivered almonds can be substituted for the hazelnuts. To skin the hazelnuts, simply place them in a clean dish towel after toasting, while they are still warm, and rub gently. Use a serrated knife to cut the dessert.

PRALINE
- ½ cup (3½ ounces) granulated sugar
- ¼ cup water
- 1 teaspoon lemon juice
- 1 cup hazelnuts, toasted and skinned
- 1 tablespoon vegetable oil
- ½ teaspoon table salt

PASTRY
- 3 large eggs
- 6 tablespoons unsalted butter, cut into 12 pieces
- ⅓ cup whole milk
- ⅓ cup water
- 2 teaspoons granulated sugar
- ½ teaspoon table salt
- ¾ cup (3¾ ounces) all-purpose flour
- 2 tablespoons toasted, skinned, and chopped hazelnuts

CREAM FILLING
- 2 teaspoons unflavored gelatin
- ¼ cup water
- 1½ cups half-and-half
- 5 large egg yolks
- ⅓ cup (2⅓ ounces) granulated sugar
- 3 tablespoons all-purpose flour
- 3 tablespoons unsalted butter, cut into 3 pieces and chilled
- 1½ teaspoons vanilla extract
- 1 cup heavy cream, chilled
   Confectioners' sugar

1. **FOR THE PRALINE:** Line rimmed baking sheet with parchment paper; spray parchment with vegetable oil spray and set aside. Bring sugar, water, and lemon juice to boil in medium saucepan over medium heat, stirring once or twice to dissolve sugar. Cook, without stirring, until syrup is golden brown, 10 to 15 minutes. Remove saucepan from heat, stir in hazelnuts, and immediately pour mixture onto prepared sheet. Place sheet on wire rack and allow caramel to harden, about 30 minutes.

2. Break hardened caramel into 1- to 2-inch pieces; process pieces in food processor until finely ground, about 30 seconds. Add oil and salt and process until uniform paste forms, 1 to 2 minutes. Transfer mixture to bowl, cover with plastic wrap, and set aside.

3. **FOR THE PASTRY:** Adjust oven racks to upper-middle and lower-middle positions and heat oven to 400 degrees. Draw or trace 8-inch circle in center of two 12 by 18-inch sheets of parchment paper; flip parchment over. Spray 2 baking sheets with vegetable oil spray and line with parchment (keeping guide rings on underside).

4. Beat eggs in measuring cup or small bowl; you should have ⅔ cup (discard excess). Heat butter, milk, water, sugar, and salt in medium saucepan over medium heat, stirring occasionally. When butter mixture reaches full boil (butter should be fully melted), immediately remove saucepan from heat and stir in flour with heat-resistant spatula or wooden spoon until combined and no mixture remains on sides of pan. Return saucepan to low heat and cook, stirring constantly, using smearing motion, until mixture is slightly shiny and tiny beads of fat appear on bottom of saucepan, about 3 minutes.

Paris-Brest

TUTORIAL
Paris-Brest

This elegant dessert made from pate a choux is baked in rings that resemble cake.
Follow these steps to create a showstopper dessert to end a special meal.

1. Using bag fitted with ⅜-inch round tip, pipe narrow circle of pastry dough directly on top of guide ring traced on parchment.

2. Use ½-inch star tip to pipe circle of dough around inside of remaining guide ring. Then pipe second circle around first so they overlap slightly.

3. Finish outer ring by piping third circle on top of other 2 circles, directly over seam. Sprinkle with nuts and bake.

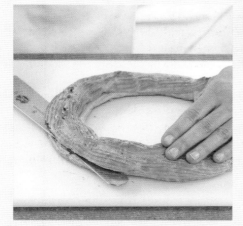

4. After letting outer ring cool, halve horizontally using serrated knife.

5. Using pastry bag fitted with ½-inch star tip, pipe narrow zigzag of praline cream onto bottom half of outer ring.

6. Place inner ring on top of praline cream and press down gently. Pipe remaining praline cream over inner ring in zigzag pattern to cover. Gently place top half of outer ring over filling to cover.

Churros with Mexican Chocolate Sauce

5. Immediately transfer butter mixture to food processor and process with feed tube open for 30 seconds to cool slightly. With processor running, gradually add eggs in steady stream. When all eggs have been added, scrape down sides of bowl, then process for 30 seconds until smooth, thick, sticky paste forms.

6. Transfer ¾ cup dough to pastry bag fitted with ⅜-inch round tip. To make narrow inner ring, pipe single ½-inch-wide circle of dough directly on traced guide ring on 1 baking sheet. For large outer ring, squeeze out any excess dough in pastry bag and change pastry bag tip to ½-inch star tip. Put all remaining dough into pastry bag. Pipe ½-inch-wide circle of dough around inside of traced guide ring on remaining baking sheet. Pipe second ½-inch circle of dough around first so they overlap slightly. Pipe third ½-inch circle on top of other 2 circles directly over seam. Sprinkle hazelnuts evenly over surface of ring.

7. Place sheet with larger outer ring on upper rack and sheet with narrow inner ring on lower rack and bake until narrow ring is golden brown and firm, 22 to 26 minutes. Remove narrow ring and transfer to wire rack. Reduce oven temperature to 350 degrees and continue to bake larger ring 10 minutes longer. Remove sheet from oven and turn off oven. Using paring knife, cut 4 equally spaced ¾-inch-wide slits around edges of larger ring to release steam. Return larger ring to oven and prop oven door open with handle of wooden spoon. Let ring stand in oven until exterior is crisp, about 45 minutes. Transfer ring to wire rack to cool, about 15 minutes.

8. FOR THE CREAM FILLING: Sprinkle gelatin over water in small bowl and let sit until gelatin softens, about 5 minutes. Heat half-and-half in medium saucepan over medium heat until just simmering. Meanwhile, whisk egg yolks and sugar in medium bowl until smooth. Add flour to yolk-sugar mixture and whisk until incorporated. Remove half-and-half from heat and, whisking constantly, slowly add ½ cup to yolk-sugar mixture to temper. Whisking constantly, add tempered yolk-sugar mixture back to half-and-half in saucepan.

9. Return saucepan to medium heat and cook, whisking constantly, until yolk-sugar mixture thickens slightly, 1 to 2 minutes. Reduce heat to medium-low and continue to cook, whisking constantly, 8 minutes longer.

10. Increase heat to medium and cook, whisking vigorously, until bubbles burst on surface, 1 to 2 minutes. Remove saucepan from heat; whisk in butter, vanilla, and softened gelatin until butter is melted and incorporated. Strain pastry cream through fine-mesh strainer set over large bowl. Press lightly greased parchment paper directly on surface and refrigerate until chilled but not set, about 45 minutes.

11. Using stand mixer fitted with whisk attachment, whip cream on medium-low speed until foamy, about 1 minute. Increase speed to high and whip until soft peaks form, 1 to 3 minutes. Whisk praline paste and half of whipped cream into pastry cream until combined. Gently fold in remaining whipped cream until incorporated. Cover and refrigerate until set, at least 3 hours or up to 24 hours.

12. Using serrated knife, slice larger outer ring in half horizontally; place bottom on large serving plate. Fill pastry bag fitted with ½-inch star tip with cream filling. Pipe ½-inch-wide strip of cream filling in narrow zigzag pattern around center of bottom half of ring. Press narrow inner ring gently into cream filling. Pipe cream filling over narrow ring in zigzag pattern to cover. Place top half of larger ring over cream filling, dust with confectioners' sugar, and serve.

CHURROS WITH MEXICAN CHOCOLATE SAUCE

Makes 18 churros | Dutch oven

WHY THIS RECIPE WORKS These fluted pastries are fried until crisp on the outside and soft on the inside, and then rolled in cinnamon sugar and served with a rich, warm chocolate sauce for dipping. Rather than pipe the dough directly into the hot oil—which we found dangerous and hectic—we piped the dough onto a baking sheet and refrigerated the churros for a few minutes to firm them up. This made the process of transferring them to the oil easy. A combination of cocoa powder and unsweetened chocolate kept the sweetness of our sauce in check. We used a closed star #8 pastry tip, ⅝ inch in diameter, to create deeply grooved ridges in the churros. However, you can use any large closed star tip of similar diameter, though your yield may vary slightly. Use a Dutch oven that holds 6 quarts or more.

CHURROS
- 2 cups water
- 2 tablespoons unsalted butter
- 2 tablespoons sugar, plus ½ cup (3½ ounces), divided
- 1 teaspoon vanilla extract
- ½ teaspoon table salt
- 2 cups (10 ounces) all-purpose flour
- 2 large eggs
- 2 quarts vegetable oil
- ¾ teaspoon ground cinnamon

SAUCE
- 1¼ cups (8¾ ounces) sugar
- ⅔ cup whole milk
- ¼ teaspoon table salt
- ¼ teaspoon ground cinnamon
- ¼ teaspoon chipotle chile powder
- ⅓ cup (1 ounce) unsweetened cocoa powder, sifted
- 3 ounces unsweetened chocolate, chopped fine
- 4 tablespoons unsalted butter, cut into 8 pieces and chilled
- 1 teaspoon vanilla extract

1. FOR THE CHURROS: Line rimmed baking sheet with parchment paper and spray with vegetable oil spray. Combine water, butter, 2 tablespoons sugar, vanilla, and salt in large saucepan and bring to boil over medium-high heat. Off heat, add flour all at once and stir with rubber spatula until well combined with no streaks of flour remaining.

2. Transfer dough to bowl of stand mixer. Fit mixer with paddle and mix dough on low speed until cooled slightly, about 1 minute. Add eggs, increase speed to medium, and beat until fully incorporated, about 1 minute.

3. Transfer warm dough to piping bag fitted with ⅝-inch closed star pastry tip. Pipe eighteen 6-inch lengths of dough onto prepared sheet, using scissors to snip dough at tip. Refrigerate uncovered for at least 15 minutes or up to 1 hour.

4. FOR THE SAUCE: Meanwhile, heat sugar, milk, salt, cinnamon, and chile powder in medium saucepan over medium-low heat, whisking gently, until sugar has dissolved and liquid starts to bubble around edges of saucepan, about 6 minutes. Reduce heat to low, add cocoa, and whisk until smooth.

5. Off heat, stir in chocolate and let sit for 3 minutes. Whisk sauce until smooth and chocolate is fully melted. Whisk in butter and vanilla until fully incorporated and sauce thickens slightly. (Sauce can be refrigerated for up to 1 month; gently warm in microwave, stirring every 10 seconds, until pourable, before using.)

6. Adjust oven rack to middle position and heat oven to 200 degrees. Set wire rack in second rimmed baking sheet and place in oven. Line large plate with triple layer of paper towels. Add oil to large Dutch oven until it measures about 1½ inches deep and heat over medium-high heat to 375 degrees.

7. Gently drop 6 churros into hot oil and fry until dark golden brown on all sides, about 6 minutes, turning frequently for even cooking. Adjust burner, if necessary, to maintain oil temperature between 350 and 375 degrees. Transfer churros to prepared plate for 30 seconds to drain off excess oil, then transfer to wire rack in oven. Return oil to 375 degrees and repeat with remaining dough in 2 more batches.

8. Combine cinnamon and remaining ½ cup sugar in shallow dish. Roll churros in cinnamon sugar, tapping gently to remove excess. Transfer churros to platter and serve with sauce.

PHYLLO DOUGH DESSERTS

Keep phyllo from drying out

Brush each layer with butter or oil

THE GREEK PASTRY DOUGH phyllo is famous for its crisp, paper-thin layers, and it's an essential component of both sweet and savory pastries in Greece and beyond—everything from baklava and strudels to bite-size hors d'oeuvres and spanakopita. This delicate, flaky pastry is typically used in one of two ways. Often, phyllo is layered with other ingredients, as it is in baklava: Sheets of the dough are brushed with butter or oil, stacked, and topped with a nut filling; the process is then repeated for alternating layers of flaky pastry and rich, crunchy nuts. Other times the phyllo is wrapped around a filling, as it is for a strudel; here, a lightly sweetened, cohesive fruit filling is placed on the layers of buttered dough and the package is folded and rolled until the filling is completely encased. No matter the approach, the result is an irresistible interplay of flavors and textures.

Unlike puff pastry (see page 506 for more information), which we sometimes make from scratch, phyllo dough requires an exceptionally intricate and time-consuming process; we always opt for store-bought. Fortunately, frozen packaged phyllo dough bakes up into delightful layers of light, flaky pastry. It's available in two sizes: full-size sheets that are 18 by 14 inches (about 20 per box) and half-size sheets that are 14 by 9 inches (about 40 per box). The smaller sheets are more common, so we use those in our recipes. If you buy the large sheets, simply cut them in half. But even with store-bought phyllo, the idea of working with this ultrathin dough can feel intimidating. If that's the case, not to worry: We have plenty of tips for making phyllo much easier to work with.

PHYLLO DOUGH 101

Phyllo dough lends its crisp, flaky, and delicate texture to a variety of sweet and savory pastries. But its tissue-thin structure can make it a bit challenging to handle. Below are some pointers that make working with this delicate dough easier.

Thaw You need to thaw phyllo dough completely before using. This is best achieved by placing the phyllo in the refrigerator overnight for at least 12 hours, but it can also be thawed on the counter for 4 to 5 hours; don't thaw it in the microwave. Allow the phyllo to come to room temperature before using for the easiest handling.

Keep It Covered Phyllo dries out very quickly, so keep it covered. As soon as the phyllo is removed from its plastic sleeve, unfold the dough and carefully flatten it with your hands. Cover with plastic wrap and then a damp dish towel.

Trash Tears Throw out badly torn sheets of dough. Usually each box has one or two badly torn sheets of phyllo that can't be salvaged. But if the sheets have just small cuts or tears, you can still work with them—put them in the middle of the pastry, where imperfections will go unnoticed. If all of the sheets have the exact same tear, alternate the orientation of each sheet when assembling the pastry.

Don't Stick Together When phyllo sheets emerge from the box fused at their edges, don't try to separate the sheets. Instead, trim and discard the fused portion.

Refrigerate Don't refreeze leftover dough. Leftover sheets cannot be refrozen, but they can be rerolled, wrapped in plastic wrap, and stored in the refrigerator for up to five days.

LAYERING PHYLLO DOUGH

Regardless of whether phyllo dough is used in flat sheets or folded and rolled into a tidy package, most phyllo pastries begin with a fairly standard procedure of brushing the sheets of dough with melted butter (or oil) and stacking them.

1. Place sheet of parchment paper on counter with long side facing you. Place 1 phyllo sheet on parchment with long side parallel to edge of counter.

2. Lightly brush phyllo sheet with melted butter.

3. Repeat with phyllo sheets and butter according to recipe, stacking sheets as you go. Fill and fold as directed.

APPLE STRUDEL WITH PINE NUTS

Serves 6 | rimmed baking sheet

WHY THIS RECIPE WORKS Recipes for apple strudel have a reputation for being laborious, calling for kneading an unleavened dough that's rolled, stretched until it's so thin it's transparent, and then wrapped around a lightly sweetened apple filling. Store-bought phyllo dough is a winning replacement for handmade strudel dough and produces equally crispy layers. For the filling, we parcooked the apple pieces in the microwave, which ensured they held their shape while also releasing some of their liquid. Some panko bread crumbs absorbed any extra moisture. Finally, slicing each strudel into thirds after baking allowed excess steam to escape and ensured the phyllo remained flaky. Gala apples can be substituted for the Golden Delicious apples. Phyllo dough is also available in larger 18 by 14-inch sheets; if using, cut them in half to make 14 by 9-inch sheets. Don't thaw phyllo in the microwave; let it sit in the refrigerator overnight or on the counter for 4 to 5 hours.

1¾ pounds Golden Delicious apples, peeled, cored, and cut into ½-inch pieces
 3 tablespoons granulated sugar
 ½ teaspoon grated lemon zest plus 1½ teaspoons juice
 ¼ teaspoon ground cinnamon
 ¼ teaspoon table salt, divided
 ½ cup pine nuts, toasted and chopped
 3 tablespoons golden raisins
1½ tablespoons panko bread crumbs
 7 tablespoons unsalted butter, melted
14 (14 by 9-inch) phyllo sheets, thawed
 1 tablespoon confectioners' sugar, plus extra for serving

1. Toss apples, granulated sugar, lemon zest and juice, cinnamon, and ⅛ teaspoon salt together in large bowl. Cover and microwave until apples are warm to touch, about 2 minutes, stirring once halfway through microwaving. Let apples sit, covered, for 5 minutes. Transfer apples to colander set in second bowl and let drain, reserving liquid. Combine apples, pine nuts, raisins, and panko in now-empty bowl.

2. Adjust oven rack to upper-middle position and heat oven to 375 degrees. Spray rimmed baking sheet with vegetable oil spray. Stir remaining ⅛ teaspoon salt into melted butter.

3. Place 16½ by 12-inch sheet of parchment paper on counter with long side parallel to counter edge. Place 1 phyllo sheet on parchment with long side parallel to counter edge. Place 1½ teaspoons confectioners' sugar in fine-mesh strainer (rest strainer in bowl to prevent making a mess). Lightly brush sheet with melted butter and dust sparingly with confectioners' sugar. Repeat with 6 more phyllo sheets, melted butter, and confectioners' sugar, stacking sheets one on top of the other as you go.

4. Arrange half of apple mixture in 2½ by 10-inch rectangle 2 inches from bottom of phyllo and about 2 inches from each side. Using parchment, fold sides of phyllo over filling, then fold bottom edge of phyllo over filling. Brush folded portions of phyllo with reserved apple liquid. Fold top edge over filling, making sure top and bottom edges overlap by about 1 inch. (If they do not overlap, unfold, rearrange filling into slightly narrower strip, and refold.) Press firmly to seal. Using thin metal spatula, transfer strudel to 1 side of prepared sheet, facing seam toward center of sheet. Lightly brush top and sides of strudel with half of reserved apple liquid. Repeat process with remaining phyllo, melted butter, confectioners' sugar, filling, and apple liquid. Place second strudel on other side of prepared sheet, with seam facing center of sheet.

5. Bake until golden brown, 27 to 35 minutes, rotating sheet halfway through baking. Using thin metal spatula, immediately transfer strudels to cutting board. Let cool for 3 minutes. Slice each strudel into thirds and let cool for at least 20 minutes. Serve warm or at room temperature, dusting with extra confectioners' sugar before serving.

BAKLAVA

Makes 32 to 40 pieces | 13 by 9-inch baking pan

WHY THIS RECIPE WORKS We wanted a classic baklava featuring crisp, flaky pastry, a filling of fragrant nuts and spices, and just enough sweetness. We sprinkled phyllo dough with layers of nuts (we liked a combination of almonds and walnuts) and brushed the phyllo with olive oil to make it crisp and flaky. Cutting the baklava through rather than just scoring it helped it absorb the sugar syrup, and letting it sit overnight dramatically improved its flavor. A straight-sided traditional metal baking pan works best. Phyllo dough is also available in larger 18 by 14-inch sheets; if using, cut them in half to make 14 by 9-inch sheets. Do not thaw the phyllo in the microwave; let it sit in the refrigerator overnight or on the counter for 4 to 5 hours.

SUGAR SYRUP
1¼ cups (8¾ ounces) sugar
 ¾ cup water
 ⅓ cup honey
 3 (2-inch) strips lemon zest plus 1 tablespoon juice
 1 cinnamon stick
 5 whole cloves
 ⅛ teaspoon table salt

NUT FILLING
1¾ cups slivered almonds
 1 cup walnuts
 2 tablespoons sugar

1¼ teaspoons ground cinnamon
¼ teaspoon ground cloves
⅛ teaspoon table salt

PASTRY
1 pound (14 by 9-inch) phyllo, thawed
5 tablespoons extra-virgin olive oil

1. FOR THE SUGAR SYRUP: Bring all ingredients to boil in small saucepan over medium-high heat and cook, stirring occasionally, until sugar has dissolved, about 5 minutes. Transfer syrup to 2-cup liquid measuring cup and let cool completely. Discard spices and zest; set aside.

2. FOR THE NUT FILLING: Pulse almonds in food processor until very finely chopped, about 20 pulses; transfer to bowl. Pulse walnuts in food processor until very finely chopped, about 15 pulses; transfer to bowl with almonds and toss to combine. Measure out 1 tablespoon nuts and set aside for garnish. Add sugar, cinnamon, cloves, and salt to nut mixture and toss well to combine.

3. FOR THE PASTRY: Adjust oven rack to lower-middle position and heat oven to 300 degrees. Lay 1 phyllo sheet in bottom of greased 13 by 9-inch baking pan and brush thoroughly with oil. Repeat with 7 more phyllo sheets, brushing each with oil (you should have total of 8 layers of phyllo).

4. Sprinkle 1 cup nut filling evenly over phyllo. Cover nut filling with 6 more phyllo sheets, brushing each with oil, then sprinkle with 1 cup nut filling. Repeat with 6 phyllo sheets, oil, and remaining 1 cup nut filling.

5. Cover nut filling with 8 more phyllo sheets, brushing each layer, except final layer, with oil. Working from center outward, use palms of your hands to compress layers and press out any air pockets. Spoon remaining oil (about 2 tablespoons) on top layer and brush to cover surface.

6. Using serrated knife with pointed tip, cut baklava into diamonds. Bake until golden and crisp, about 1½ hours, rotating pan halfway through baking. Immediately pour all but 2 tablespoons cooled syrup over cut lines (syrup will sizzle when it hits hot pan). Drizzle remaining 2 tablespoons syrup over surface. Garnish center of each piece with pinch reserved ground nuts. Let baklava cool completely in pan, about 3 hours, then cover with aluminum foil and let sit at room temperature for 8 hours before serving.

Pistachio Baklava with Cardamom and Rose Water
Omit honey, lemon zest, and cinnamon stick in sugar syrup and increase sugar to 1¾ cups. Substitute 10 whole peppercorns for cloves and stir in 1 tablespoon rose water after discarding peppercorns. Substitute 2¾ cups shelled pistachios for almonds and walnuts and 1 teaspoon ground cardamom for cinnamon and cloves in nut filling.

Apple Strudel with Pine Nuts

Baklava

LEAVENED PASTRIES

Employ baking powder and/or yeast

Feature sweet fillings

Chill cubes of butter for lift

Chill dough for workability

SOME PASTRIES LIKE PUFF PASTRY AND PATE A CHOUX
rely on moisture for lift, but this grouping calls on yeast or baking
powder to provide leavening. The result is a dough that's at
once rich, tender, and buttery yet also light and flaky. Leavened
pastries can be old-fashioned and rustic like Blackberry Roly
Poly (page 527), which features swirls of bright blackberry jam
incorporated into the buttery, flaky pastry. Or they can have a
refined elegance like Breton Kouign Amann (page 528): A little
bit croissant and a little bit sticky bun, this pastry uses both yeast
and the process of lamination—enclosing a slab of butter in the
dough and rolling and folding the package to create thin sheets
or layers—to provide lift. While both baking powder and yeast
help dough rise, yeast also contributes subtle yet important
flavor. In the light, airy fritters known as Zeppoles (page 530)
we use both leaveners for maximum flavor and impact. And
while these rich, sweet pastries certainly qualify as dessert, no
one will fault you for enjoying them with a steaming mug of
coffee for breakfast or with afternoon tea.

PECAN KRINGLE

Serves 16 (Makes 2 kringles) | 2 rimmed baking sheets

WHY THIS RECIPE WORKS Traditional recipes for this delightful spiced nut–filled Danish require bakers to fold the dough dozens of times, stopping repeatedly to allow it to chill and relax. Not so delightful. We eliminated this time-consuming step by cutting cubes of cold butter into the dry ingredients before forming the dough. This gave us similar lift. We found that sour cream created a flaky texture by weakening the dough's gluten structure, but, when combined with the butter, it made for a greasy pastry. We solved this by removing some of the butter. To keep the pastry tender, we then replaced a bit of the remaining butter with vegetable shortening. If the capacity of your food processor is less than 11 cups, pulse the butter and shortening into the dry mixture in two batches at the beginning of step 2. You can use whole, 2 percent low-fat, or 1 percent low-fat milk in the glaze, but do not use skim milk.

FILLING
- 1 cup pecans, toasted
- ¾ cup packed (5¼ ounces) light brown sugar
- ¼ teaspoon ground cinnamon
- ⅛ teaspoon table salt
- 4 tablespoons unsalted butter, cut into ½-inch pieces and chilled

DOUGH
- 4 cups (20 ounces) all-purpose flour
- 16 tablespoons unsalted butter, cut into ½-inch pieces and chilled
- 4 tablespoons vegetable shortening, cut into ½-inch pieces and chilled
- 2 tablespoons confectioners' sugar
- 2¼ teaspoons instant or rapid-rise yeast
- ¾ teaspoon table salt
- 2 cups sour cream
- 1–2 tablespoons ice water (optional)
- 1 large egg, lightly beaten

GLAZE
- 1 cup (4 ounces) confectioners' sugar
- 2 tablespoons whole or 2 percent low-fat milk
- ½ teaspoon vanilla extract

1. FOR THE FILLING: Process pecans, sugar, cinnamon, and salt in food processor until pecans are coarsely ground, about 5 seconds. Add butter and pulse until mixture resembles coarse cornmeal, about 9 pulses. Transfer to bowl.

2. FOR THE DOUGH: Add flour, butter, shortening, sugar, yeast, and salt to now-empty food processor and pulse until mixture resembles coarse cornmeal, 15 to 20 pulses. Transfer to bowl and stir in sour cream until smooth dough forms. (If dough appears shaggy and dry, stir in up to 2 tablespoons ice water as needed.) Transfer dough to lightly floured counter and divide in half with bench scraper. Gently press each piece of dough into 7 by 3-inch rectangle and wrap in plastic wrap. Refrigerate dough pieces for 30 minutes, then freeze until firm, about 15 minutes.

3. Line 2 rimmed baking sheets with parchment paper. Transfer 1 piece of dough to lightly floured counter and roll into 28 by 5-inch strip, about ¼ inch thick. With long side facing you, cover bottom half of strip with filling, leaving ½-inch border around bottom and side edges. Brush edge of uncovered dough with water, fold dough over filling, and pinch seams closed. Shape folded dough into oval, tuck 1 end inside other, and pinch to seal. Repeat with remaining dough and filling. Transfer ovals to prepared sheets, cover sheets with plastic, and refrigerate for at least 4 hours or up to 12 hours.

4. Adjust oven racks to upper-middle and lower-middle positions and heat oven to 350 degrees. Remove plastic, brush ovals with egg, and bake until golden brown, 40 to 50 minutes, switching and rotating sheets halfway through baking. Let kringles cool on sheets on wire rack for 10 minutes, then transfer kringles to wire rack and let cool for 30 minutes.

5. FOR THE GLAZE: Whisk sugar, milk, and vanilla in small bowl until smooth. Using soup spoon, drizzle glaze over kringles. Let glaze set for 10 minutes. Serve warm or at room temperature. (Glazed kringles can be stored at room temperature for up to 2 days.)

BLACKBERRY ROLY POLY

Serves 8 | rimmed baking sheet

WHY THIS RECIPE WORKS Buttery, flaky biscuit-like dough gets perked up with a spiral of fruity filling in this centuries-old rolled pastry. In a test of cooking methods, baking the roly poly easily outshined the old-fashioned methods of boiling or steaming. The baked product resembled a jumbo jammy biscuit that tasters loved, while the results of the other two methods were sodden and stodgy. We eliminated shortening from our biscuits and replaced it with butter—and lots of it—for better flavor. A short stay in the freezer firmed the dough (the butter made it too soft to roll out without this step). Both fresh and frozen blackberries will work. Like a biscuit, roly poly tastes best on the day it's baked. Use a serrated knife to slice it.

- 2 cups (10 ounces) blackberries
- ⅔ cup (4⅔ ounces) sugar, divided
- ½ teaspoon grated lemon zest
- 3 cups (15 ounces) all-purpose flour
- 1 tablespoon baking powder
- 1 teaspoon table salt
- 16 tablespoons unsalted butter, cut into ½-inch pieces and chilled, divided
- 1 cup whole or 2 percent low-fat milk

Blackberry Roly Poly

1. Cook blackberries and ¼ cup sugar in saucepan over medium-low heat until berries begin to release juice, about 3 minutes. Increase heat to medium-high and cook, stirring frequently, until blackberries break down and mixture is thick and jam-like, about 10 minutes (mixture should measure ½ cup). Transfer jam to bowl, stir in lemon zest, and let cool completely.

2. Pulse flour, baking powder, salt, ⅓ cup sugar, and 15 tablespoons butter in food processor until mixture resembles coarse meal. Transfer to large bowl and stir in milk until combined.

3. Adjust oven rack to middle position and heat oven to 375 degrees. Line baking sheet with parchment paper. Turn dough out onto lightly floured surface and knead until smooth, 8 to 10 times. Pat dough into 6-inch square, wrap with plastic, and freeze until just firm, about 20 minutes. On lightly floured surface, roll dough into 12 by 10-inch rectangle. Spread jam evenly over dough, leaving ½-inch border around edges. Starting with long edge, roll dough into cylinder. Pinch ends and seam to seal. Arrange dough seam down on prepared sheet.

4. Melt remaining 1 tablespoon butter and brush over dough. Sprinkle with remaining sugar and bake until golden brown, about 45 minutes. Let cool for 10 minutes on sheet, then transfer to wire rack. Serve warm or at room temperature.

BRETON KOUIGN AMANN

Serves 8 to 10 | 9-inch round cake pan

WHY THIS RECIPE WORKS Rustic yet refined and distinctly salty and sweet, Kouign Amann is a croissant-like pastry that celebrates the butter and salt Brittany is famous for. It's a texture marvel: The flaky layers turn more custardy the closer you get to the middle of the cake, and they're contrasted by a crunchy top and a lightly caramelized base. Embedding the sugar into the butter block by paddling the ingredients in a stand mixer prevented the sugar from drawing moisture out of the dough and making it unworkably sticky. We strongly recommend weighing the flour for this recipe. The butter block should be cool but malleable at the beginning of step 4; if your kitchen is cooler than 70 degrees, you may need to leave the butter block on the counter for up to 20 minutes (it's OK to leave the dough in the freezer for the extended time). Once you begin rolling and folding the dough, you'll want to move swiftly and without interruption, so have your ingredients and equipment in place before you start. Keeping plenty of flour under the dough while rolling will help prevent the layers from tearing; brushing away excess flour on top of the dough before folding will help the dough adhere to itself.

2¼ cups (11¼ ounces) all-purpose flour
1¼ teaspoons table salt, divided
½ teaspoon instant or rapid-rise yeast
1 cup water, room temperature
16 tablespoons salted butter, softened
¾ cup (5¼ ounces) plus 1 tablespoon sugar, divided
1 tablespoon milk

1. Using rubber spatula, stir together flour, ¾ teaspoon salt, and yeast in bowl of stand mixer. Add water and mix until most flour is moistened. Attach dough hook and knead on low speed until cohesive dough forms, about 1 minute. Increase speed to medium-low and knead until dough is smooth and elastic, about 5 minutes. Shape dough into ball (scrape out mixer bowl but do not wash). Flatten into rough 5-inch square and transfer to lightly greased plate. Cover dough and refrigerate for at least 1 hour or up to 24 hours. While dough rests, make butter packet.

2. Fold 18-inch length of parchment in half to create rectangle. Fold over 3 open sides of rectangle to form 6 by 9-inch rectangle with enclosed sides. Crease folds firmly. Open parchment packet and set aside. Combine butter, ¾ cup sugar, and remaining ½ teaspoon salt in now-empty mixer bowl. Using paddle, mix on low speed until thoroughly combined, about 1 minute. Transfer butter mixture to prepared parchment rectangle, fold parchment over mixture, and press to ½-inch thickness. Refold parchment at creases to enclose mixture. Turn packet over so flaps are underneath and roll gently until butter mixture fills packet, taking care to achieve even thickness. Refrigerate for at least 45 minutes or up to 24 hours.

TUTORIAL
Breton Kouign Amann

A croissant-like cake layered with rich butter and caramelized sugar could be the ultimate pastry, dessert even, if made according to our easy failproof steps.

1. Fold final 21 by 7-inch rectangle into thirds.

2. Roll dough into 11-inch square. Fold each corner to center, overlapping slightly, and press to adhere.

3. Push right and left corners toward center, and then push top and bottom corners toward center to form rough, crumpled round.

4. Press top to compress. Flip dough so smoother side is up, then tuck edges to form round. Roll into 9½-inch round.

5. Transfer to prepared pan (it's OK if dough is slightly sticky), squishing edges to fit.

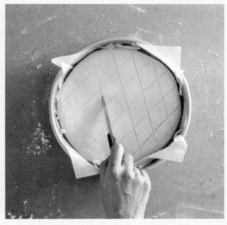

6. Brush top with milk. Using sharp paring knife, score top of pastry in diamond pattern. Sprinkle evenly with remaining 1 tablespoon sugar.

3. Transfer butter block to counter. Transfer dough to freezer and freeze for 10 minutes. Meanwhile, adjust oven rack to middle position and heat oven to 375 degrees. Lightly grease 9-inch round cake pan and line with 12-inch parchment square, pleating parchment so it lines bottom and sides of pan.

4. Transfer dough to well-floured counter and roll into 18 by 6½-inch rectangle with short side parallel to counter edge. Unwrap butter block and place in center of dough. Fold upper and lower sections of dough over butter so they meet in center (it's OK to gently stretch dough). Press center seam and side seams closed. Dust counter with more flour if necessary. Place rolling pin at top edge of dough and press gently to make slight depression across top. Lift pin, move it 1 inch closer to you, and press again. Continue pressing and lifting to bottom edge. Turn rolling pin 90 degrees and make similar depressions across width of dough. Roll dough out lengthwise into 21 by 7-inch rectangle (it's OK if it becomes slightly wider). Pop any bubbles that form. Using dry pastry brush, dust off any flour clinging to surface of dough. Starting at bottom of dough, fold into thirds like a business letter to form 7-inch square. Turn square 90 degrees. Dust counter with more flour if necessary. Roll out lengthwise into 21 by 7-inch rectangle, and pop any bubbles. Using dry pastry brush, dust off any flour clinging to surface of dough, and fold into thirds.

5. Dust counter with more flour if necessary. Roll dough into 11-inch square. Fold each corner to center, overlapping slightly, and press to adhere. Push right and left corners toward center, and then push top and bottom corners toward center to form rough, crumpled round. Press top to compress. Flip dough so smoother side is facing up, then tuck edges under to form round. Flatten gently with your hands, then roll dough into 9½-inch round. Transfer to prepared pan (it's OK if dough is slightly sticky), squishing edges to fit.

6. Brush top with milk. Using sharp paring knife, score top of pastry in diamond pattern. Sprinkle evenly with remaining 1 tablespoon sugar. Using paring knife, pierce dough all the way down to pan surface in 4 places to create air vents. Bake until pastry is deeply browned and crisp, 50 minutes to 1 hour. Let cool in pan on wire rack for 10 minutes. Invert, remove parchment, and reinvert. Let cool for at least 30 minutes before serving. (Kouign amann is best eaten on the day it's made, but leftovers can be wrapped well and stored at room temperature for up to 3 days. Warm leftovers gently in oven before serving.)

ZEPPOLES

Makes 15 to 18 zeppoles | Dutch oven

WHY THIS RECIPE WORKS To make zeppoles, a cross between doughnuts and fried dough, we discovered that two leaveners were better than one. Although typically used independently, in the case of these Italian fritters, a combination of baking powder and yeast created the perfect fluffy confection. The baking powder ensured a light rather than doughy interior, and the yeast provided the requisite flavor and more lift. Frying the wet, sticky dough at 350 degrees yielded a crispy exterior that didn't overcook by the time the interior had finished cooking. These light, tender zeppoles are best served warm with a dusting of powdery confectioners' sugar. The dough is very wet and sticky. If you own a 4-cup liquid measuring cup, you can combine the dough in it to make it easier to tell when it has doubled in volume in step 1.

1⅓ cups (6⅔ ounces) all-purpose flour
1 tablespoon granulated sugar
2 teaspoons instant or rapid-rise yeast
1 teaspoon baking powder
½ teaspoon table salt
1 cup warm water (110 degrees)
½ teaspoon vanilla extract
2 quarts peanut or vegetable oil, for frying
Confectioners' sugar

1. Combine flour, granulated sugar, yeast, baking powder, and salt in large bowl. Whisk water and vanilla into flour mixture until fully combined. Cover tightly with plastic wrap and let rise at room temperature until doubled in size, 15 to 25 minutes.

2. Set wire rack in rimmed baking sheet and line rack with triple layer of paper towels. Adjust oven rack to middle position and heat oven to 200 degrees. Add oil to large Dutch oven until it measures about 1½ inches deep and heat over medium-high heat to 350 degrees.

3. Using greased tablespoon measure, add 6 heaping table-spoonfuls of batter to oil. (Use dinner spoon to help scrape batter from tablespoon if necessary.) Fry until golden brown and toothpick inserted in center of zeppole comes out clean, 2 to 3 minutes, flipping once halfway through frying. Adjust burner, if necessary, to maintain oil temperature between 325 and 350 degrees.

4. Using wire skimmer or slotted spoon, transfer zeppoles to prepared wire rack; roll briefly so paper towels absorb grease. Transfer sheet to oven to keep warm. Return oil to 350 degrees and repeat twice more with remaining batter. Dust zeppoles with confectioners' sugar and serve.

Zeppoles

PART 09

frozen
desserts

FROZEN DESSERTS HAVE BEEN ENJOYED FOR THOUSANDS OF YEARS from Iran to China to the Roman Empire, where snow or ice—frequently harvested from high in the mountains—was flavored with honey or fruit for a cold and refreshing treat. With advances from insulated ice houses to the development of mechanical refrigeration, frozen desserts became much more accessible and plentiful, and today they are beloved all over the world in many forms. Ice cream, gelato, and frozevn custard incorporate milk and/or cream and sometimes eggs for a rich and indulgent treat. Sorbet, ice, and granita are simpler affairs; without the addition of dairy, the fruit flavor takes center stage and really shines. Ice cream sandwiches and ice pops are homey treats that are favorites of kids and adults alike, while decadent semifreddo—a custard-based dessert lightened with whipped cream—makes for an elegant finish to a meal.

Just as the heat of the oven triggers physical changes and chemical reactions to transform ingredients into something with entirely new flavors and textures, the chill of the freezer has a similar effect. The ingredients you use and the way you combine them can alter the structure of the ice crystals that form—which can mean the difference between a hard, icy scoop of ice cream and a luxuriously smooth, creamy one.

There's something for everyone here, from scoops of Rich Vanilla Ice Cream (page 539), Raspberry Sorbet (555), and Ginger-Turmeric Frozen Yogurt (page 545) to a neater, elegant plated affair like Cappuccino Semifreddo with Hazelnuts (page 562).

Frozen Desserts Equipment Corner

There's not a long list of essential equipment specific to frozen desserts, which is all the more reason to ensure that what you do use gets the job done well. In addition to the below tools, a loaf pan is handy for holding ice cream, sorbet, and gelato in the freezer, and an instant-read thermometer is necessary for making bases and determining doneness for frozen desserts.

Ice Cream Maker

All ice cream makers work in a similar fashion. Through a combination of cooling and constant-yet-gentle churning, the machines transform the base mixture into a thick, creamy dessert. There are two types of electric ice cream makers: smaller canister-style machines and larger, more expensive self-refrigerating units. Canister-style makers have smaller footprints but require freezer space for the canister. Canister-style makers also take less time to churn, but making consecutive batches requires prefreezing additional bowls; self-refrigerating models require no prefreezing and can make endless additional batches in succession. Our favorite canister-style maker is the **Cuisinart Frozen Yogurt, Ice Cream & Sorbet Maker** ($53.99): It's relatively inexpensive and easy to use, churns quickly, and produces creamy desserts with minimal ice crystals. For ice cream fanatics who are willing to spend more for the ability to make consecutive batches, we recommend the self-refrigerating Breville Smart Scoop ($399). It has a manual option and a range of automatic settings that create a truly hands-off, walk-away experience.

As for large old-fashioned ice-and-rock-salt-cooling ice cream makers, they can produce a gallon or more in a single batch, handy for large gatherings. But because they have more base to freeze, they take longer, leading to relatively large ice crystals and a grainy texture. These machines require babysitting. What's more, unless you have a large freezer, the tall canisters might not fit. They are also considerably louder than most small ice cream makers, and some models leaked salty water—clearly not meant for indoor use.

Ice Cream Scoop

High-quality dense, hard ice cream requires a sturdy scoop to dig out and release perfectly smooth, round spheres for topping pie and balancing in cones. The gently curved oval bowl of the **Zeroll Original Ice Cream Scoop** ($18.44) forms perfect round orbs that release easily. Even better, its wide, comfortable handle contains heat-conductive fluid that warms up instantly when your hand grips the exterior; when that heat travels to the bowl, the warm metal slightly melts the ice cream or sorbet so that it's particularly easy to scoop.

Refrigerator/Freezer Thermometer

A thermometer helps ensure that you maintain the proper refrigerator and freezer temperature, important for chilling ice creams and bases. Check regularly to ensure that your refrigerator is between 35 and 40 degrees; your freezer should be 0 degrees or below. The **ThermoWorks Fridge/ Freezer Alarm** ($22) not only alerted us when our appliances strayed from the temperatures we designated but also told us when they stayed outside the safe zone for more than 30 minutes.

Ice Pop Molds

There are two basic types of molds. The simpler type is a rectangular frame with the pop molds fixed in place; this type includes a separate lid and usually requires disposable wooden sticks. Another style has individual molds that detach separately from the base or frame; these commonly come with reusable plastic sticks. We prefer the latter, which allows you to remove one or two pops as needed by simply running the desired number under hot water—with the fixed-mold models, you're forced to put the whole frame under the water. They also tend to have clear fill lines and wide openings, making them a breeze to fill and clean. With slender plastic sticks, unobtrusive drip guards, and long, textured handles, **Zoku Classic Pop Molds** ($16.25) were the easiest to use of all those we tested.

FREEZE FAST

For smooth, creamy frozen desserts, fast freezing is key. Smooth ice cream (and sorbet) isn't technically less icy than "icy" ice cream. Instead, its ice crystals are so small that our tongues can't detect them. One way to encourage the creation of small ice crystals is to freeze the base as quickly as possible. Fast freezing, along with agitation, causes the formation of thousands of tiny seed crystals, which in turn promote the formation of more tiny crystals. Commercial producers as well as restaurant kitchens spend tens of thousands of dollars on efficient "continuous batch" churners. They can turn a 40-degree custard base (the coldest temperature it can typically achieve in a refrigerated environment) into soft-serve in 24 seconds, at which point roughly half the base's freezable water has crystallized. To maintain this superfine ice-crystal structure, the churned ice cream is then transferred to a blast freezer in smaller ice cream shops or a hardening room in large commercial operations, where the temperature ranges from 20 to 50 degrees below zero. Under these conditions, the remaining freezable water freezes in a matter of minutes. Here are tricks for faster freezing with resources at home.

Cool the Base

Making sure the temperature of the base you're churning is as cold as it can be—that is, as cold as the refrigerator, about 40 degrees—starts the process with success; a warmer base would take that much longer to freeze.

Superchill

Separating out a small portion of the ice cream or sorbet base and freezing it before adding it back to the rest of the base allows it to freeze quickly. The tiny ice crystals formed in this superchilled portion act as a catalyst, triggering a chain reaction that very rapidly forms equally small crystals in the bigger mixture.

Take the Temperature when Churning

If you know to pull the churning ice cream just when it's ready, you can get it solid in the freezer faster, minimizing the opportunity for large ice crystal formation.

Use a Low Container

Since rate of cooling is a function of both temperature and surface area, transfer the churned ice cream to a wide, shallow container rather than a tall one to expedite freezing.

MANIPULATING ICE CRYSTALS

Many ingredients influence the properties of water and the size—and our perception—of ice crystals. It's worth knowing a few ways to use these ingredients to your advantage for the smoothest, creamiest frozen desserts.

Liquid Ingredients

Milk solids interfere with the formation of ice crystals, so the more milk solids, the better (up to a point—too many create a sandy texture). And since water forms crystals, the less of it, the better (up to a point—too little water leads to gumminess). Cream has more milk solids than milk. And sometimes we employ nonfat dry milk as a trick for upping the milk solids.

Sugar Content and Type

Sugar is used for sweetening, of course, but it also serves another important role: It reduces the tendency of ice crystals to grow large, thus contributing to smoother texture. Replacing some of the granulated sugar with corn syrup results in an even smoother frozen treat. Corn syrup doesn't depress the freezing point of water as much as regular sugar does, which means the ice cream freezes faster and is less affected by the inevitable temperature fluctuations of a home freezer. The result? Minimal large crystal formation.

Alcohol

Because alcohol (tasteless vodka is usually the spirit of choice) has antifreezing properties, it is often added to icy frozen desserts such as Lemon Ice (page 556) to help counter the mixture's solidity and stiffness when frozen. The result is a softer, creamier treat.

Stabilizers

Ingredients such as cornstarch, gelatin, and pectin essentially trap water, which will minimize large water droplets—and thus large ice crystal formation. (Nonfat dry milk serves the same purpose, but it also replaces liquid milk in the mix, effectively decreasing the amount of freezable water.)

CREAMY SCOOPS

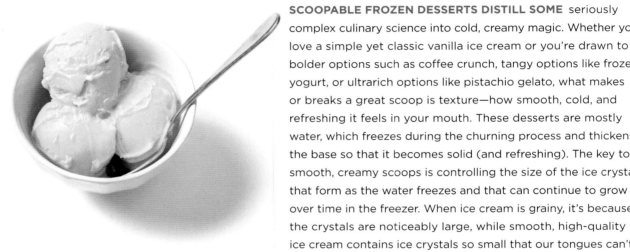

Chill base thoroughly in refrigerator

Use thermometer to determine churning doneness

Freeze in wide, shallow container

SCOOPABLE FROZEN DESSERTS DISTILL SOME seriously complex culinary science into cold, creamy magic. Whether you love a simple yet classic vanilla ice cream or you're drawn to bolder options such as coffee crunch, tangy options like frozen yogurt, or ultrarich options like pistachio gelato, what makes or breaks a great scoop is texture—how smooth, cold, and refreshing it feels in your mouth. These desserts are mostly water, which freezes during the churning process and thickens the base so that it becomes solid (and refreshing). The key to smooth, creamy scoops is controlling the size of the ice crystals that form as the water freezes and that can continue to grow over time in the freezer. When ice cream is grainy, it's because the crystals are noticeably large, while smooth, high-quality ice cream contains ice crystals so small that our tongues can't detect them.

For the smoothest, creamiest desserts, we employ a few tricks, which you previewed in this section's introduction; learn more as you churn through the recipes.

Churning incorporates a small amount of air that is crucial to a smooth, semisoft consistency—without the air, the base would freeze into a hard brick (see how we incorporate air into our no-churn ice creams on page 542). No matter the style of ice cream maker you have (find our favorite on page 534), you'll want to make sure it's good and frozen first: If using a canister-style ice cream maker, freeze the empty canister for at least 24 hours (and preferably 48 hours) before churning. For self-refrigerating ice cream makers, prechill the canister by running the machine for 5 to 10 minutes before pouring in a base.

Have fun putting your own spin on ice creams—the flavor and add-in possibilities are virtually limitless.

Custard-Based Ice Cream

Custard-based ice cream starts with a cooked mixture of milk, cream, and sugar that is thickened with egg yolks. It's a French style of ice cream and is in fact where French vanilla ice cream gets its name—it has nothing to do with the variety of vanilla but rather the technique of using custard as the base. The presence of egg yolks gives the ice cream a denser, richer texture and smooth consistency.

Eggless Ice Cream

This American (also known as Philadelphia) style of ice cream is an uncooked mixture of cream, milk, sugar, and vanilla. Without the egg yolks of a custard-style ice cream, it has a clean-tasting base that really allows the other flavors to shine. To ensure an ultra-creamy, smooth consistency we often incorporate a couple of unusual ingredients: nonfat dry milk powder and cornstarch. These stabilizers increase the viscosity of the base, so there's less chance for ice crystals to cluster into larger, more perceptible crystals.

No-Churn Ice Cream

While it's hard to beat the delightfully rich and luxurious texture of ice cream churned in a machine, sometimes you want to enjoy a cold, creamy treat with less time and fuss. For smooth, scoop-able ice cream without the churning time, whip the cream in a blender. The air trapped within the whipped cream stands in for the air normally incorporated by an ice cream maker. Using a blender to whip the cream is key; a stand mixer will introduce too much air and the resulting texture will be fluffy rather than rich and creamy. Two other secrets to this easy ice cream? Sweetened condensed milk and corn syrup—both of these ingredients help ensure a silky smooth texture.

Dairy-Free Ice Cream

It may seem like a tall order to create a thick, rich, creamy ice cream without milk or cream, but it is in fact possible with the help of one or both of these ingredients: bananas and coconut milk. Overripe bananas make an ideal ice cream base because they remain creamy even when frozen. And because the bananas start frozen, the immediate result is lusciously smooth, like the consistency of soft-serve ice cream, so you can enjoy it right away after blending it in a food processor—no ice cream machine needed. Coconut milk is a great nondairy alternative to heavy cream for ice creams. It's higher in fat than plant-based creamers, and that fat adds richness and helps the ice cream stay supercreamy.

ALL ABOUT COCONUT MILK

Coconut milk products, with their silky texture, richness, and pleasant flavor, have many uses in dairy-free dishes. We turn to canned coconut milk in frozen desserts. Here's how to distinguish liquid coconut items on the market.

Coconut milk sold in a carton near the soy and almond milk that's labeled "coconut milk beverage" is what we're talking about when we call for "coconut milk" in an ingredient list (which is rare). It's made by blending canned coconut milk with water and additives, which make it creamy, despite the water that it contains. Coconut milk has about an eighth of the fat content of canned coconut milk and does not taste strongly of coconut.

What we call canned coconut milk is made by steeping shredded coconut in water and then pressing it to yield a creamy, coconut-flavored liquid. When you open a can of coconut milk, you may find that it's separated—there will be a more solid mass above the watery liquid—but not always. Some recipes require using just the solid part, while others call for the whole thing. If your recipe calls for just the solid part, refrigerate the cans of coconut milk for 24 hours; this will allow you to skim away the thick cream more easily. Do not confuse canned coconut milk with canned coconut cream (the ratio of coconut meat to liquid is higher) or cream of coconut (which is sweetened and contains thickeners and emulsifiers).

Frozen Custard

Frozen custard isn't just a fancy name for ice cream; it's actually a lovely frozen treat in its own right. The popular regional sweet treat (Wisconsin, New York, and Arkansas all claim versions as their own) takes its name from a custard base that includes egg yolks and heavy cream for a luxurious texture. Commercial frozen custard—the thick, soft serve–like treat made famous by the Kohr Brothers in Coney Island and Kopp's in Milwaukee—requires an industrial condenser to produce its supersmooth, almost taffy-like consistency; the machine adds air, and breaks down the ice crystals, by constantly churning the mixture as it freezes. Most machine-free recipes mimic this action by asking the cook to stir or whisk the mixture periodically during freezing, but we use a more hands-off approach and simply whip the custard for a few minutes in a stand mixer.

FROZEN CUSTARD VERSUS ICE CREAM

According to guidelines administered by the U.S. Food and Drug Administration, both ice cream and frozen custard must contain at least 10 percent milk fat (along with milk, cream, sweeteners, flavorings, and so forth). The main difference between them is eggs: While egg yolks are optional in ice cream bases (and occasionally do appear on ingredient lists), they are absolutely required in frozen custard. Frozen custards must contain at least 1.4 percent yolks by weight. The resulting frozen treat is eggier and richer than ice cream.

WHIP IT SMOOTH

Frozen custard is impressively thick and creamy—tip over a cup of it and it's likely to stay in place. To achieve this at home, after cooking the custard we chill it down in the refrigerator to prime it for adding air and then whip the cooled custard to make the final texture especially creamy.

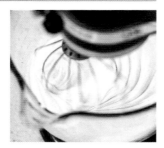

Gelato

Theories as to the origins of gelato abound in Italy, with many believing it evolved from the sorbetto that the Arabs introduced to Southern Italy. The gelato we know today was most certainly birthed in Sicily. And while gelato is a close cousin to ice cream, there are key differences: Gelato typically has less cream and more milk and is served at a warmer temperature than American-style ice cream. The lower fat percentage and higher serving temperature allow its concentrated, pure flavors to taste more intense than those of ice cream; these same factors also keep gelato soft and creamy. For our formula, we have found that using mostly whole milk with just a bit of cream for the custard base results in the ideal dense, rich texture. Cornstarch is a traditional thickener, but we also incorporate egg yolks; while not all recipes include them, we like the rich creaminess they contribute.

Frozen Yogurt

The best frozen yogurt puts the fresh-tasting tartness of yogurt front and center and has a dense, creamy-smooth texture. Most recipes require nothing more than throwing yogurt, sugar, and maybe a few flavorings into an ice cream maker and churning. But frozen yogurt has less fat and more water than ice cream; this means it has a tendency to turn out icy and rock-hard. For a frozen yogurt with a creamy, scoopable texture we take a few simple steps. The first is to strain the yogurt of excess whey to eliminate some water. The type and amount of sweetener is also key. In addition to regular granulated sugar, we include a modest amount of Lyle's Golden Syrup; as a partial invert sugar, Lyle's contains small fructose and glucose molecules that can interfere with ice crystal formation even more readily than the larger sucrose molecules in table sugar can. Finally, we add some gelatin, an ingredient that essentially traps water. All of this translates to fewer ice crystals and a softer, more scoopable product straight from the freezer.

FOR CREAMIER FROYO, FORGO GREEK YOGURT

Making creamy, smooth frozen yogurt is largely about limiting water, since less water translates to fewer large ice crystals. Thus we were surprised when frozen yogurt made with Greek-style yogurt, which has been strained of excess liquid, churned up crumbly and chalky. The reason for these results is twofold: First, Greek-style yogurt has a particularly high protein content (in lab tests, we found that it had almost twice as much protein as regular yogurt we strained ourselves). Second, it's often strained by centrifuge, which can damage these proteins and increase the likelihood of a chalky texture. So while it may seem like a time-saver to reach for Greek when making frozen yogurt, you'll pay for that convenience in texture. That's why we take the time to strain regular yogurt for the creamiest, smoothest results.

RICH VANILLA ICE CREAM

Serves 8 (Makes about 1 quart) | ice cream maker

WHY THIS RECIPE WORKS Thick, rich, and luxuriously creamy, traditional custard-based ice cream is a bit of a project with an elegant payoff. The quicker the ice cream freezes, the smoother and creamier the results, so we took a two-pronged approach. First, we supplemented the sugar with corn syrup, which ensured a faster freezing time, and second, we used a superchilling method, freezing a small amount of the base separately and then adding it back into the rest before churning. The result was an ice cream that remained hard at home-freezer temperatures and was devoid of large ice crystals.

- 1 vanilla bean
- 1¾ cups heavy cream
- 1¼ cups whole milk
- ½ cup plus 2 tablespoons (4⅓ ounces) sugar, divided
- ⅓ cup light corn syrup
- ¼ teaspoon table salt
- 6 large egg yolks

1. Place 8- or 9-inch square baking pan in freezer. Cut vanilla bean in half lengthwise. Using tip of paring knife, scrape out seeds. Combine vanilla bean and seeds, cream, milk, 6 tablespoons sugar, corn syrup, and salt in medium saucepan. Heat over medium-high heat, stirring occasionally, until mixture is steaming steadily and registers 175 degrees, 5 to 10 minutes. Remove saucepan from heat.

2. While cream mixture heats, whisk egg yolks and remaining ¼ cup sugar in bowl until smooth, about 30 seconds. Slowly whisk 1 cup heated cream mixture into egg yolk mixture. Return mixture to saucepan and cook over medium-low heat, stirring constantly, until mixture thickens and registers 180 degrees, 7 to 14 minutes. Immediately pour custard into large bowl and let cool until no longer steaming, 10 to 20 minutes. Transfer 1 cup custard to small bowl. Cover both bowls with plastic wrap. Place large bowl in refrigerator and small bowl in freezer and let cool completely, at least 4 hours or up to 24 hours. (Small bowl of custard will freeze solid.)

3. Remove custards from refrigerator and freezer. Scrape frozen custard from small bowl into large bowl of custard. Stir occasionally until frozen custard has fully dissolved. Strain custard through fine-mesh strainer and transfer to ice cream machine. Churn until mixture resembles thick soft-serve ice cream and registers about 21 degrees, 15 to 25 minutes. Transfer ice cream to frozen baking pan and press plastic on surface. Return to freezer until firm around edges, about 1 hour.

4. Transfer ice cream to airtight container, pressing firmly to remove any air pockets, and freeze until firm, at least 2 hours or up to 5 days. Serve.

Coffee Crunch Ice Cream

Look for chocolate-covered cacao nibs (roasted pieces of the cacao bean) in chocolate shops or well-stocked supermarkets. Freeze the cacao nibs for at least 15 minutes before adding them to the churning ice cream.

Substitute ½ cup coarsely ground coffee for vanilla bean. Add ¾ cup chocolate-covered cacao nibs to ice cream during last minute of churning.

Triple Ginger Ice Cream

Freeze the crystallized ginger for at least 15 minutes before adding it to the churning ice cream.

Substitute one 3-inch piece fresh ginger, peeled and sliced into thin rounds, and 2 teaspoons ground ginger for vanilla bean. Add ½ cup chopped crystallized ginger to ice cream during last minute of churning.

Rich Vanilla Ice Cream

SWEET CREAM ICE CREAM

Serves 8 (Makes about 1 quart) | ice cream maker

WHY THIS RECIPE WORKS Sweet cream ice cream is the most basic of ice cream flavors: It contains no vanilla and no eggs—just milk, heavy cream, and sugar. To ensure a creamy, smooth consistency, we added milk powder, cornstarch, and corn syrup to our sweet cream base. The milk powder replaced a portion of the liquid milk in the mix, decreasing the amount of freezable water, and it also trapped some of the water so that it couldn't freeze (cornstarch performed this function, too). We prefer Carnation Instant Nonfat Dry Milk. Some base may stick to the bottom of the saucepan when pouring it into the strainer in step 2; simply scrape it into the strainer with the rest of the base and press it through with a spatula.

- ½ cup plus ⅓ cup nonfat dry milk powder
- ⅓ cup (2⅓ ounces) sugar
- ¼ teaspoon kosher salt
- 1½ cups whole milk, divided
- 1½ cups heavy cream
- ¼ cup corn syrup
- 5 teaspoons cornstarch

1. Whisk milk powder, sugar, and salt together in small bowl. Whisk 1¼ cups milk, cream, corn syrup, and sugar mixture together in large saucepan. Cook over medium-high heat, whisking frequently to dissolve sugar and break up any clumps, until tiny bubbles form around edge of saucepan and mixture registers 190 degrees, 5 to 7 minutes.

2. Meanwhile, whisk cornstarch and remaining ¼ cup milk together in small bowl. Reduce heat to medium. Whisk cornstarch mixture to recombine, then whisk into milk mixture in saucepan. Cook, constantly scraping bottom of saucepan with rubber spatula, until mixture thickens, about 30 seconds. Immediately pour ice cream base through fine-mesh strainer into large bowl; let cool until no longer steaming, about 20 minutes. Cover bowl, transfer to refrigerator, and chill until base registers 40 degrees, at least 6 hours. (Base can be chilled overnight. Alternatively, base can be chilled to 40 degrees in about 1½ hours by placing bowl in ice bath of 6 cups ice, ½ cup water, and ⅓ cup table salt.)

3. Churn base in ice cream maker until mixture resembles thick soft serve and registers 21 degrees, about 30 minutes. Transfer ice cream to airtight container, pressing firmly to remove air pockets; freeze until firm, at least 2 hours or up to 5 days. Serve.

Strawberry Ripple Ice Cream

Combine 6 ounces fresh strawberries, hulled, ½ cup plus 1 tablespoon sugar, and 1 cup freeze-dried strawberries in blender and blend on high speed until smooth, about 1 minute. Transfer to airtight container and refrigerate until ready to use. After churning base in step 3, spread one-quarter of ice cream in bottom of airtight container and top with ¼ cup ripple. Repeat 3 more times. Press firmly to remove air pockets; freeze until firm, at least 2 hours or up to 5 days. Serve.

PEANUT BUTTER CUP CRUNCH ICE CREAM

Serves 12 (Makes about 1½ quart) | ice cream maker

WHY THIS RECIPE WORKS This ice cream is richer than other eggless recipes because of the addition of crunchy chunky peanut butter. Interestingly, the greater proportion of fat makes this ice cream feel less cold on your tongue than a lower fat ice cream (which contains proportionally more frozen water). Natural peanut butter incorporates easily into our base. We call for freezing the peanut butter cup mix-ins before adding them to the ice cream so they don't melt the nice small ice crystals formed during churning. (That's a good tip for any ice cream add-in.) We prefer Carnation Instant Nonfat Dry Milk. Some ice cream base may stick to the bottom of the saucepan when pouring it into the bowl in step 3; simply scrape it into the bowl with the rest of the base and whisk until smooth.

Sweet Cream Ice Cream

½ cup plus ⅓ cup nonfat dry milk powder
⅓ cup (2⅓ ounces) sugar
¼ teaspoon kosher salt
1½ cups whole milk, divided
1½ cups heavy cream
¼ cup corn syrup
5 teaspoons cornstarch
⅓ cup chunky natural peanut butter
2 cups mini peanut butter cups, halved and frozen

1. Whisk milk powder, sugar, and salt together in small bowl. Whisk 1¼ cups milk, cream, corn syrup, and sugar mixture together in large saucepan. Cook over medium-high heat, whisking frequently to dissolve sugar and break up any clumps, until tiny bubbles form around edge of saucepan and mixture registers 190 degrees, 5 to 7 minutes.

2. Meanwhile, whisk cornstarch and remaining ¼ cup milk together in small bowl. Place peanut butter in large bowl while milk mixture cooks.

3. Reduce heat to medium. Whisk cornstarch mixture to recombine, then whisk into milk mixture in saucepan. Cook, constantly scraping bottom of saucepan with rubber spatula, until mixture thickens, about 30 seconds. Immediately pour ice cream base through fine-mesh strainer into bowl with peanut butter and whisk thoroughly to combine; let cool until no longer steaming, about 20 minutes. Cover bowl, transfer to refrigerator, and chill until base registers 40 degrees, at least 6 hours. (Base can be chilled overnight. Alternatively, base can be chilled to 40 degrees in about 1½ hours by placing bowl in ice bath of 6 cups ice, ½ cup water, and ⅓ cup table salt.)

4. Churn base in ice cream maker until mixture resembles thick soft-serve ice cream and registers 21 degrees, about 30 minutes. Add peanut butter cups and continue to churn until incorporated, 1 to 2 minutes longer. Transfer ice cream to airtight container, pressing firmly to remove air pockets; freeze until firm, at least 2 hours or up to 5 days. Serve.

OLIVE OIL ICE CREAM

Serves 8 to 10 (Makes about 1 quart) | ice cream maker
WHY THIS RECIPE WORKS The grassy, peppery notes of good extra-virgin olive oil pair perfectly with the rich sweetness of ice cream. But olive oil's high fat content led to a pasty, gummy ice cream. We found that we needed to ditch almost all the milk fat in the base (save for the small amount found in the whole milk) by subbing in water for the heavy cream. A little freshly ground pepper reinforced the olive oil's peppery notes. We prefer Carnation Instant Nonfat Dry Milk for this recipe. Go for a premium extra-virgin olive oil with medium pepperiness. Some ice cream base may stick to the bottom of the saucepan when pouring it into the bowl in step 3; simply scrape it into the bowl with the rest of the base and whisk until smooth. We like to drizzle additional extra-virgin olive oil over the top of this ice cream just before serving.

¼ cup plus 2 tablespoons sugar
½ cup plus ⅓ cup nonfat dry milk powder
½ teaspoon pepper
¼ teaspoon kosher salt
1½ cups whole milk, divided
1 cup water
¼ cup corn syrup
2 tablespoons plus 2½ teaspoons cornstarch
¾ cup extra-virgin olive oil

1. In small bowl, whisk sugar, milk powder, pepper, and salt together. Whisk sugar mixture, 1¼ cups milk, water, and corn syrup together in large saucepan. Cook over medium-high heat until tiny bubbles form around edge of saucepan and mixture registers 190 degrees, whisking frequently to dissolve sugar and break up any clumps, 5 to 7 minutes.

2. Meanwhile, whisk remaining ¼ cup milk and cornstarch together in small bowl.

3. Reduce heat to medium. Whisk cornstarch mixture to recombine, then whisk into milk mixture in saucepan. Cook, constantly scraping bottom of saucepan with rubber spatula, until mixture thickens, about 30 seconds. Immediately pour ice cream base through fine-mesh strainer into large bowl; let cool until no longer steaming, about 20 minutes. Whisk in oil in steady stream until smooth. Cover bowl, transfer to refrigerator, and chill to 40 degrees, at least 6 or up to 8 hours. (Base can be refrigerated overnight. Alternatively, base can be chilled in about 1½ hours by placing bowl in ice bath of 6 cups ice, ½ cup water, and ⅓ cup salt.)

4. Churn base in ice cream maker until mixture resembles thick soft-serve ice cream and registers 21 degrees. Transfer to airtight container, cover, transfer to freezer, and freeze until hard, at least 2 hours or up to 8 hours.

No-Churn Ice Cream

KULFI

Serves 8 (Makes about 1 quart) | **eight 6-ounce ramekins**

WHY THIS RECIPE WORKS This frozen milk-based dessert known as kulfi—India's version of ice cream—offers a cooling, sweet finish to heavily spiced meals. It has a distinctive milky flavor and slightly icy texture when compared to ice cream— and it doesn't require an ice cream machine. Many recipes for kulfi require reducing fresh milk on the stovetop, but we shortened the timeline by starting with sweetened condensed milk, which we supplemented with some regular milk for fresh flavor. Do not use low-fat or nonfat milk. Do not omit the vodka; it plays an important role in the frozen texture of the ice milk. When portioning the ice milk into the ramekins, you may have some left over, which can be packed into an airtight container and frozen for up to one week.

    5 cups whole milk
    2 (14-ounce) cans sweetened condensed milk
    ¼ cup vodka
    ½ teaspoon ground cardamom
    ¼ teaspoon table salt
    ½ cup pistachios, 5 tablespoons chopped and 3 tablespoons
       chopped fine, divided

1. Blend milk, condensed milk, vodka, cardamom, and salt in blender until thoroughly combined and emulsified, about 10 seconds. Pour mixture into bowl or container, press plastic wrap flush to surface of mixture, and freeze until mostly frozen but stirrable, 4 to 5 hours.

2. Stir in 5 tablespoons chopped pistachios and ladle mixture evenly into eight 6-ounce ramekins. Cover ramekins tightly with plastic and continue to freeze until solid, at least 5 hours or up to 1 week. Before serving, let kulfi soften slightly at room temperature, about 10 minutes, and sprinkle 3 tablespoons finely chopped pistachios evenly over top.

VANILLA NO-CHURN ICE CREAM

Serves 8 (Makes about 1 quart) | **blender**

WHY THIS RECIPE WORKS With little more than a blender and some basic pantry ingredients, you can have velvety, creamy, scoopable ice cream. Whipping heavy cream in a blender incorporated air in a way that mimicked the effect of churning in an ice cream maker. We added sweetened condensed milk and corn syrup (to keep the ice cream soft) and a hefty 1 tablespoon of vanilla extract and a bit of salt (to enhance the flavor), which produced an intense vanilla ice cream in about a minute of work. Then, we just popped the blended mixture in the freezer and waited.

2 cups heavy cream, chilled
1 cup sweetened condensed milk
¼ cup whole milk
¼ cup light corn syrup
2 tablespoons sugar
1 tablespoon vanilla extract
¼ teaspoon table salt

Process cream in blender until soft peaks form, 20 to 30 seconds. Scrape down sides of blender jar and continue to process until stiff peaks form, about 10 seconds. Using rubber spatula, stir in condensed milk, whole milk, corn syrup, sugar, vanilla, and salt. Process until thoroughly combined, about 20 seconds, scraping down sides of blender jar as needed. Pour cream mixture into 8½ by 4½-inch loaf pan. Press plastic wrap flush against surface of cream mixture. Freeze until firm, at least 6 hours or up to 5 days. Serve.

Dark Chocolate No-Churn Ice Cream

Decrease vanilla to 1 teaspoon. Add 6 ounces melted bittersweet chocolate and ½ teaspoon instant espresso powder with condensed milk.

Malted Milk Chocolate No-Churn Ice Cream

Decrease vanilla to 1 teaspoon. Add 6 ounces melted milk chocolate and 6 tablespoons malted milk powder with condensed milk.

Mint Cookie No-Churn Ice Cream

Substitute ¾ teaspoon peppermint extract for vanilla. Add ⅛ teaspoon green food coloring with condensed milk. After transferring cream mixture to loaf pan, gently stir in ½ cup coarsely crushed Oreo cookies before freezing.

Peach Cobbler No-Churn Ice Cream

Omit sugar. Substitute bourbon for vanilla. Add ½ cup peach preserves and ¼ teaspoon ground cinnamon with condensed milk. After transferring cream mixture to loaf pan, gently stir in ½ cup coarsely chopped shortbread cookies before freezing.

Salted Caramel–Coconut Ice Cream

Reduce vanilla to 1 teaspoon. Increase salt to ½ teaspoon. Substitute caramel sauce for corn syrup. After transferring cream mixture to loaf pan, gently stir in ¼ cup toasted sweetened shredded coconut. Dollop additional ⅓ cup caramel sauce over top and swirl into cream mixture using tines of fork before freezing.

Strawberry Buttermilk No-Churn Ice Cream

Substitute ½ cup buttermilk for whole milk and 1 teaspoon lemon juice for vanilla. After transferring cream mixture to loaf pan, dollop ⅓ cup strawberry jam over top. Swirl jam into cream mixture using tines of fork before freezing.

NO-FUSS BANANA ICE CREAM

Serves 8 (Makes about 1 quart) | food processor

WHY THIS RECIPE WORKS For a lighter alternative to classic ice cream with all the creaminess and flavor of the real thing, we turned to a pair of secret weapons: bananas and our food processor. Bananas are a surprisingly good ice cream base: Their high pectin content allows them to remain creamy when frozen. We started by simply slicing whole, frozen, peeled bananas and then pureeing them in the food processor. The end result had good banana flavor, but it wasn't quite as creamy as tasters wanted. Adding just ½ cup of canned coconut milk produced an unbeatable silky-smooth texture. Ripe, heavily speckled (or even black) bananas contained plenty of sweetness, so we skipped additional sugar. We did, however, add a bit of lemon juice, vanilla, and cinnamon to give our ice cream more dimension. You can skip the freezing in step 2 and serve the ice cream immediately, but the texture will be softer.

6 very ripe bananas
½ cup canned coconut milk
1 tablespoon vanilla extract
1 teaspoon lemon juice
¼ teaspoon table salt
¼ teaspoon ground cinnamon

1. Peel bananas, place in large zipper-lock bag, and press out excess air. Freeze bananas until solid, at least 8 hours.

2. Let bananas sit at room temperature to soften slightly, about 15 minutes. Slice into ½-inch-thick rounds and place in food processor. Add coconut milk, vanilla, lemon juice, salt, and cinnamon and process until smooth, about 5 minutes, scraping down sides of bowl as needed. Transfer to airtight container, press plastic wrap directly on surface of ice cream, and freeze until firm, at least 2 hours or up to 5 days. Serve.

VEGAN COCONUT ICE CREAM

Serves 8 (Makes about 1 quart) | blender

WHY THIS RECIPE WORKS For a thick, creamy plant-based frozen treat with the dense texture of the premium ice creams we love, we started with coconut milk, which has a clean coconut flavor and silky texture. Corn syrup minimized ice crystal formation, as did cornstarch, which also acted as a stabilizer. To fix the grainy, starchy texture from the unemulsified bits of coconut fat, we blended our hot mixture after cooking so that the fat became fully emulsified. We prefer to make this recipe in a canister-style ice cream maker; the ice cream was grainy when made in self-refrigerating models. Be sure to freeze the empty canister for at least 24 hours (or preferably for 48 hours) before churning. Make sure your blender is only two-thirds full or less, open the lid vent, and hold in place with a dish towel in step 2. Do not use light coconut milk in this recipe.

2 (14-ounce) cans coconut milk, divided
2 tablespoons cornstarch
½ cup (3 ½ ounces) sugar
¼ cup light corn syrup
1 teaspoon vanilla extract
¼ teaspoon table salt

1. Shake unopened cans of coconut milk to form homogeneous mixture. Whisk ¼ cup coconut milk and cornstarch together in small bowl and set aside. Combine remaining coconut milk, sugar, corn syrup, vanilla, and salt in large saucepan. Cook over medium-high heat, whisking often to dissolve sugar and break up any clumps, until small bubbles form around edge of saucepan and mixture registers 190 degrees, 5 to 7 minutes. Reduce heat to medium. Whisk cornstarch mixture to recombine, then whisk into coconut milk mixture in pan. Cook, constantly scraping bottom of pan with rubber spatula, until thickened slightly, about 30 seconds.

2. Carefully transfer mixture to blender, let cool slightly, about 1 minute, then process on high speed for 1 minute. Pour ice cream base into large bowl and let cool until no longer steaming, about 20 minutes. Cover with plastic wrap and refrigerate for at least 6 hours or up to 24 hours. (Alternatively, place bowl in ice bath of 6 cups ice, ½ cup water, and ⅓ cup table salt and chill base to 40 degrees, stirring occasionally, about 1 ½ hours.)

3. Whisk chilled ice cream base until recombined and smooth, then transfer to ice cream machine and churn until mixture has consistency of soft-serve ice cream and registers 22 to 23 degrees. Transfer to airtight container, cover, and freeze until firm, at least 6 hours. Serve. (Ice cream is best eaten within 2 weeks.)

Vegan Coconut-Lime Ice Cream
Substitute 1 tablespoon lime juice for vanilla extract. Add 2 teaspoons grated lime zest to coconut milk mixture with lime juice in step 1.

Vegan Horchata Ice Cream
Add ¾ teaspoon ground cinnamon and ⅛ teaspoon ground cloves to coconut milk mixture in saucepan before cooking in step 1. Serve topped with toasted sliced almonds.

Vegan Coconut Ice Cream

VANILLA FROZEN CUSTARD
Serves 8 (Makes about 1 quart) | **stand mixer**
WHY THIS RECIPE WORKS This thick, soft serve–like treat is as refreshing on a hot summer afternoon as it is soothing on a cool autumn evening. While stores use industrial condensers to produce the smoothest custard, we made it supersmooth without a machine. After combining our heated cream and egg yolk mixtures, we strained the custard to remove any pieces of cooked egg. To achieve the smoothest possible custard, we cooled the mixture on ice, let it chill in the refrigerator, and then whipped it in a stand mixer to add air. This prevented ice crystals from building up and made the final texture silky and creamy. We prefer Carnation Instant Nonfat Dry Milk. One teaspoon of vanilla extract can be substituted for the vanilla bean; stir the extract into the strained custard in step 3.

6 large egg yolks
¼ cup (1 ¾ ounces) sugar
2 tablespoons nonfat dry milk powder
1 cup heavy cream
½ cup whole milk
⅓ cup light corn syrup
⅛ teaspoon table salt
1 vanilla bean

1. Whisk egg yolks, sugar, and milk powder in bowl until smooth, about 30 seconds; set aside. Combine cream, milk, corn syrup, and salt in medium saucepan. Cut vanilla bean in half lengthwise. Using tip of paring knife, scrape out vanilla seeds and add to cream mixture, along with vanilla bean. Heat cream mixture over medium-high heat, stirring occasionally, until it steams steadily and registers 175 degrees, about 5 minutes. Remove saucepan from heat.

2. Slowly whisk heated cream mixture into yolk mixture to temper. Return cream-yolk mixture to saucepan and cook over medium-low heat, stirring constantly, until mixture thickens and registers 180 degrees, 4 to 6 minutes.

3. Immediately pour custard through fine-mesh strainer set over large bowl; discard vanilla bean. Fill slightly larger bowl with ice and set custard bowl in bowl of ice. Transfer to refrigerator and let chill until custard registers 40 degrees, 1 to 2 hours, stirring occasionally.

4. Transfer chilled custard to stand mixer fitted with whisk attachment and whip on medium-high speed for 3 minutes, or until mixture increases in volume to about 3¾ cups. Pour custard into airtight 1-quart container. Cover and freeze until firm, at least 6 hours, before serving. (Frozen custard is best eaten within 10 days.)

Chocolate Frozen Custard
Omit vanilla bean. Add ½ ounce finely chopped 60 percent cacao bittersweet chocolate and 1 tablespoon Dutch-processed cocoa powder to cream mixture in step 1 before cooking. Add ½ teaspoon vanilla extract to strained custard in step 3.

FROZEN YOGURT
Serves 8 (Makes about 1 quart) | ice cream maker
WHY THIS RECIPE WORKS Frozen yogurt is a delightful tangy, dense, creamy treat if you can nail that texture. The key is controlling the water in the base to minimize the number of large ice crystals that form during freezing. Since Greek yogurt is strained of excess liquid during processing, it seemed like a logical starting point, but it produced a chalky frozen yogurt. We got much creamier results when we used plain whole-milk yogurt that we strained ourselves. Using Lyle's Golden Syrup and dissolving 1 teaspoon of gelatin in a portion of the strained whey also helped reduce ice crystals, for a frozen yogurt that was scoopable straight from the freezer. This recipe requires draining the yogurt for 8 to 12 hours. We prefer the flavor and texture that Lyle's Golden Syrup lends this frozen yogurt, but if you can't find it, you can substitute light corn syrup. You can substitute low-fat yogurt for whole-milk yogurt, but the results will be less creamy and flavorful.

1 quart plain whole-milk yogurt
1 teaspoon unflavored gelatin
¾ cup (5¼ ounces) sugar
3 tablespoons Lyle's Golden Syrup
⅛ teaspoon table salt

1. Line colander or fine-mesh strainer with triple layer of cheesecloth and place over large bowl or measuring cup. Place yogurt in colander, cover with plastic wrap (plastic should not touch yogurt), and refrigerate until 1¼ cups whey has drained from yogurt, at least 8 hours or up to 12 hours. (If more than 1¼ cups whey drains from yogurt, stir extra back into yogurt.)

2. Discard ¾ cup drained whey. Sprinkle gelatin over remaining ½ cup whey in bowl and let sit until gelatin softens, about 5 minutes. Microwave until mixture is bubbling around edges and gelatin dissolves, about 30 seconds. Let cool for 5 minutes. In large bowl, whisk sugar, syrup, salt, drained yogurt, and cooled whey-gelatin mixture until sugar is completely dissolved. Cover and refrigerate (or place bowl over ice bath) until yogurt mixture registers 40 degrees or less.

3. Churn yogurt mixture in ice cream maker until mixture resembles thick soft-serve frozen yogurt and registers about 21 degrees, 25 to 35 minutes. Transfer frozen yogurt to airtight container and freeze until firm, at least 2 hours or up to 5 days. Serve.

Orange Frozen Yogurt
Substitute ½ cup orange juice for ½ cup whey in step 2. Stir ½ teaspoon grated orange zest into orange juice–gelatin mixture as soon as it is removed from microwave.

Strawberry Frozen Yogurt
Substitute ¾ cup strawberry puree for ½ cup whey in step 2.

GINGER-TURMERIC FROZEN YOGURT
Serves 8 (Makes about 1 quart) | ice cream maker
WHY THIS RECIPE WORKS Frozen yogurt can transcend the single simple flavors you find in a yogurt shop. The tartness takes particularly well to spicing. For a spiced combination inspired by the fragrance of warming golden milk drinks, we incorporated fresh and ground ginger as well as ground turmeric—into a tangy cold treat, of course. The taste was as bright as its sunny yellow color, and it reminded us of a frozen lassi. We prefer richer-tasting Lyle's Golden Syrup, but you can substitute light corn syrup.

1 quart plain whole-milk yogurt
1 teaspoon unflavored gelatin
1½ teaspoons grated fresh ginger
1 teaspoon ground ginger
1 teaspoon ground turmeric
¾ cup (5¼ ounces) sugar
3 tablespoons Lyle's Golden Syrup
⅛ teaspoon table salt

1. Line colander or fine-mesh strainer with triple layer of cheesecloth and place over large bowl or measuring cup. Place yogurt in colander, cover with plastic wrap (plastic should not touch yogurt), and refrigerate until 1¼ cups whey has drained from yogurt, at least 8 hours or up to 12 hours. (If more than 1¼ cups whey drains from yogurt, stir extra back into yogurt.)

2. Discard ¾ cup drained whey. Sprinkle gelatin over remaining ½ cup whey in bowl and let sit until gelatin softens, about 5 minutes. Microwave until mixture is bubbling around edges and gelatin dissolves, about 30 seconds. Stir fresh ginger, ground ginger, and ground turmeric into mixture and let cool for 5 minutes. Strain mixture through fine-mesh strainer set over large bowl, pressing on solids to extract all liquid; discard solids. Whisk drained yogurt, sugar, syrup, and salt into cooled whey-gelatin mixture until sugar is completely dissolved. Cover and refrigerate until yogurt mixture registers 40 degrees or less, about 3 hours.

3. Churn yogurt mixture in ice cream maker until mixture resembles thick soft-serve frozen yogurt and registers about 21 degrees, about 20 minutes. Transfer frozen yogurt to airtight container and freeze until firm, about 2 hours. Serve. (Frozen yogurt can be stored in freezer for up to 5 days.)

PISTACHIO GELATO

Serves 8 (Makes about 1 quart) | ice cream maker
WHY THIS RECIPE WORKS We wanted to make a nutty, elegant gelato that was quintessentially Italian, so we turned to buttery pistachios. Many recipes call for hard-to-find Sicilian pistachio paste, made from sweetened ground pistachios and oil. While pistachio paste is generally delicious and intensely flavored, we found that the percentages of sugar and fat varied from brand to brand, which would affect the texture of the gelato. Instead, we turned to raw pistachios. Grinding the nuts and steeping them in the warmed milk and cream released their volatile oils and deeply flavored the base, and straining the solids through cheesecloth ensured a velvety smooth texture. The gelato stayed within the ideal serving temperature range for up to 6 hours of freezing time, but after that we

needed to temper the frozen gelato in the refrigerator until it warmed to the ideal gelato serving temperature of 10 to 15 degrees for a creamy, intensely pistachio-flavored treat, perfect for bringing sunny Sicilian afternoons home.

2½ cups (11¼ ounces) shelled pistachios
3¾ cups whole milk, divided
¾ cup (5¼ ounces) sugar
⅓ cup heavy cream
⅓ cup light corn syrup
¼ teaspoon table salt
5 teaspoons cornstarch
5 large egg yolks

1. Process pistachios in food processor until finely ground, about 20 seconds. Combine 3½ cups milk, sugar, cream, corn syrup, and salt in large saucepan. Cook, stirring frequently, over medium-high heat until tiny bubbles form around edge of saucepan, 5 to 7 minutes. Off heat, stir in pistachios, cover, and let steep for 1 hour.

2. Line fine-mesh strainer with triple layer of cheesecloth that overhangs edges and set over large bowl. Transfer pistachio mixture to prepared strainer and press to extract as much liquid as possible. Gather sides of cheesecloth around pistachio pulp and gently squeeze remaining liquid into bowl; discard spent pulp.

3. Whisk cornstarch and remaining ¼ cup milk together in small bowl; set aside. Return pistachio-milk mixture to clean saucepan. Whisk in egg yolks until combined. Bring custard to gentle simmer over medium heat and cook, stirring occasionally and scraping bottom of saucepan with rubber spatula, until custard registers 190 degrees, 4 to 6 minutes.

4. Whisk cornstarch mixture to recombine, then whisk into custard. Cook, stirring constantly, until custard thickens, about 30 seconds. Immediately pour custard into bowl and let cool until no longer steaming, about 20 minutes.

5. Cover with plastic wrap and refrigerate for at least 6 hours or up to 24 hours.

6. Whisk custard to recombine, then transfer to ice cream maker and churn until mixture resembles thick soft-serve ice cream and registers 21 degrees, 15 to 30 minutes. Transfer gelato to airtight container, pressing firmly to remove any air pockets, and freeze until firm, at least 6 hours or up to 5 days. Serve. (If frozen for longer than 6 hours, let gelato sit in refrigerator for 1 to 2 hours until it registers 10 to 15 degrees before serving.)

Pistachio Gelato

Toppings and Sauces

You'll learn to make delicious homemade frozen confections in this chapter, but the most fun part about eating ice cream might be topping it off. Making your own homemade sauces and accompaniments elevates your scoops further, tastes richer and less sickly sweet than anything from store, and allows you to personalize dessert. These aren't just for ice cream; we call for adorning all kinds of cakes and spoon desserts with the following recipes.

WHIPPED CREAM
Makes about 2 cups

Whipped cream may be a simple topping, but it's often just the right addition to cut through the richness of a decadent dessert or to lighten its texture. Whipping the ingredients on medium-low speed to start ensures the sugar, vanilla, and salt are evenly dispersed in the cream before we increase the mixer speed to achieve soft peaks (our preference for dolloping).

- 1 cup heavy cream, chilled
- 1 tablespoon sugar
- 1 teaspoon vanilla extract
- Pinch table salt

Using stand mixer fitted with whisk attachment, whip cream, sugar, vanilla, and salt on medium-low speed until foamy, about 1 minute. Increase speed to high and whip until soft peaks form, 1 to 3 minutes. (Whipped cream can be refrigerated in fine-mesh strainer set over small bowl and covered with plastic wrap for up to 8 hours.)

Brown Sugar and Bourbon Whipped Cream
Substitute 3 tablespoons packed brown sugar for granulated. Reduce vanilla to ½ teaspoon. Add 1 tablespoon bourbon to stand mixer with cream. Mix additional 1 tablespoon bourbon into finished whipped cream to taste.

Cocoa Whipped Cream
Increase sugar to 2 tablespoons. Add 2 tablespoons unsweetened cocoa powder, sifted, to stand mixer with cream before whipping.

Orange Whipped Cream
Substitute 2 tablespoons orange juice for vanilla. Add 1 teaspoon grated orange zest to stand mixer with cream before whipping.

Peanut Butter Whipped Cream
Add ¼ cup creamy peanut butter to stand mixer with cream before whipping. Once mixture is foamy, continue to whip on medium-low speed until soft peaks form, 1 to 3 minutes.

Tangy Whipped Cream
Omit sugar, vanilla, and salt. Reduce heavy cream to ¾ cup. Add ½ cup plain Greek yogurt to stand mixer with cream before whipping.

CLASSIC HOT FUDGE SAUCE
Makes about 2 cups

A fudge sauce transforms a simple recipe into an over-the-top dessert. Our classic version relies on cocoa powder and unsweetened chocolate for complexity and richness. Using milk, rather than cream, preserves the intense flavor. Stirring in cold butter creates sheen and a thick consistency. This sauce will make your sundae or ice cream pie ultradecadent.

- 1¼ cups (8¾ ounces) sugar
- ⅔ cup whole milk
- ¼ teaspoon table salt
- ⅓ cup (1 ounce) unsweetened cocoa powder, sifted
- 3 ounces unsweetened chocolate, chopped fine
- 4 tablespoons unsalted butter, cut into 8 pieces and chilled
- 1 teaspoon vanilla extract

1. Heat sugar, milk, and salt in medium saucepan over medium-low heat, whisking gently, until sugar has dissolved and liquid starts to bubble around edges of saucepan, about 6 minutes. Reduce heat to low, add cocoa, and whisk until smooth.

2. Off heat, stir in chocolate and let sit for 3 minutes. Whisk sauce until smooth and chocolate is fully melted. Whisk in butter and vanilla until fully incorporated and sauce thickens slightly. (Sauce can be refrigerated for up to 1 month; gently warm in microwave, stirring every 10 seconds, until pourable before using.)

Orange Hot Fudge Sauce
Bring milk and 8 (3-inch) strips orange zest to simmer in medium saucepan over medium heat. Off heat, cover and let sit for 15 minutes. Strain milk mixture through fine-mesh strainer into bowl, pressing on orange zest to extract as much liquid as possible. Return milk to now-empty saucepan and proceed with recipe as directed.

ALL-PURPOSE CHOCOLATE GLAZE

Makes about 1½ cups

Some of our desserts call for chocolate glaze, but you can also take the lead on glazing other desserts—cakes or even brownies—with this recipe. It's shiny-smooth and the right consistency for pouring and dripping decoratively down the ridges of your dessert.

- ¾ cup heavy cream
- ¼ cup light corn syrup
- 8 ounces bittersweet chocolate, chopped
- ½ teaspoon vanilla extract

Heat cream, corn syrup, and chocolate in small saucepan over medium heat, stirring constantly, until smooth. Stir in vanilla and set aside until slightly thickened, about 30 minutes.

CLASSIC CARAMEL SAUCE

Makes about 2 cups

Nutty, buttery caramel sauce adds a layer of complexity to desserts layered inside or drizzled on top. We made our recipe foolproof by adding water to ensure that the sugar fully dissolved; this helped us avoid the common pitfalls of burning and crystallization (which occur when the sugar cooks unevenly). To ensure an accurate temperature reading, swirl the caramel to even out hot spots and then tilt the pot so that the caramel pools 1 to 2 inches deep. Move the instant-read thermometer back and forth for about 5 seconds before taking a reading.

- 1¾ cups (12¼ ounces) sugar
- ½ cup water
- ¼ cup light corn syrup
- 1 cup heavy cream
- 1 teaspoon vanilla extract
- ¼ teaspoon table salt

1. Bring sugar, water, and corn syrup to boil in large saucepan over medium-high heat. Cook, without stirring, until mixture is straw-colored, 6 to 8 minutes. Reduce heat to low and continue to cook, swirling saucepan occasionally, until caramel is amber-colored, 2 to 5 minutes. (Caramel should register between 360 and 370 degrees.)

2. Off heat, carefully stir in cream, vanilla, and salt; mixture will bubble and steam. Continue to stir until sauce is smooth. Let cool slightly. (Sauce can be refrigerated for up to 2 weeks; gently warm in microwave, stirring every 10 seconds, until pourable, before using.)

Dark Rum Caramel Sauce
Whisk 3 tablespoons dark rum into caramel with cream.

Salted Caramel Sauce
Increase salt to 1 teaspoon.

CHOCOLATE-PORT SAUCE

Makes about ⅔ cup

To create a sophisticated chocolate sauce for ice cream or fruit, we incorporate ruby port. The brilliant red color of this fortified wine adds a subtle but rich hue, and its slightly fruity character balanced the bitter edge of the chocolate.

- ⅔ cup ruby port
- 3 tablespoons heavy cream
- 3 ounces bittersweet chocolate, chopped fine

1. Bring port to simmer in small saucepan over medium heat and cook until reduced to about ⅓ cup, 5 to 7 minutes. Stir in heavy cream and return to simmer.

2. Off heat, add chocolate and let sit for 3 minutes. Whisk sauce until smooth and chocolate is fully melted. (Sauce can be refrigerated for up to 1 month; gently warm in microwave, stirring every 10 seconds, until pourable, before using.)

BUTTERSCOTCH SAUCE

Makes about 1½ cups

Cooking brown sugar and butter gives butterscotch its complexity without the precision required of cooking caramel. In addition to serving butterscotch on ice cream, we fold it into the filling of our Pear-Butterscotch Slab Pie (page 398).

- 1 cup packed (7 ounces) brown sugar
- 2 teaspoons light corn syrup
- 8 tablespoons unsalted butter
- 1 tablespoon water
- ½ cup heavy cream
- 1 teaspoon vanilla extract

Heat sugar, corn syrup, butter, and water in medium saucepan over medium-high heat, stirring often, until sugar is fully dissolved, about 2 minutes. Continue to cook, without stirring, until mixture begins to bubble, 1 to 2 minutes. Off heat, carefully stir in cream and vanilla; mixture will bubble and steam. Continue to stir until sauce is smooth. Let cool slightly. (Sauce can be refrigerated for up to 2 weeks; gently warm in microwave, stirring every 10 seconds, until pourable, before using.)

PEANUT BUTTER SAUCE

Makes 2 cups

We wanted a rich peanut butter sauce that we could spoon over a dish of Chocolate Sorbet (page 555), a lofty Chocolate Soufflé (page 212), or a slice of Chocolate Cream Pie (page 380). Combining ½ cup creamy peanut butter with a stick of butter ensured plenty of peanutty flavor and a silky consistency. We added sugar, evaporated milk, a little vanilla extract, and a dash of salt and cooked our sauce on the stovetop until thickened and smooth. Evaporated milk helps stabilize the sauce, but you should still take care to cook it over low heat; otherwise the peanut butter will cause the sauce to break.

 1 cup (7 ounces) sugar
 ¾ cup evaporated milk
 8 tablespoons unsalted butter
 ½ cup creamy peanut butter
 1 teaspoon vanilla extract
 ⅛ teaspoon table salt

Bring sugar, milk, butter, peanut butter, vanilla, and salt to simmer in medium saucepan over medium heat. Reduce heat to low and cook, stirring often, until sauce is smooth and thick, about 3 minutes. Serve warm. (Sauce can be refrigerated for up to 1 week; gently warm in microwave, stirring every 10 seconds, until pourable, before using.)

MAGIC CHOCOLATE SHELL

Makes about ¾ cup

Magic shell—a chocolate sauce that forms a thin, brittle shell when poured over ice cream—is a childhood soft-serve stand favorite. You can make the magic at home. The secret ingredient? Coconut oil. Coconut oil's high saturated fat content makes it liquid when warm (74 degrees or higher) but solid as soon as it drops to 70 degrees. Because of this quick transition, our satiny sauce solidifies into a shatteringly thin shell when poured over cold ice cream.

 ¼ teaspoon vanilla extract
 ⅛ teaspoon instant espresso powder
    Pinch salt
 4 ounces semisweet chocolate, chopped fine
 ⅓ cup coconut oil
 1 teaspoon unsweetened cocoa powder

Stir vanilla, espresso powder, and salt in small bowl until espresso dissolves. Microwave chocolate and coconut oil in bowl at 50 percent power, stirring occasionally, until melted and smooth, 2 to 4 minutes. Whisk in vanilla mixture and

cocoa until combined. Let cool to room temperature, about 30 minutes, before using. (Sauce can be stored at room temperature in airtight container for up to 2 months; gently warm in microwave, stirring every 10 seconds, until pourable but not hot, before using.)

FRESH STRAWBERRY TOPPING

Makes about 3 cups

Many cheesecakes, buttery cakes, and ice creams pair well with a strawberry topping—but not the shellacked or artificial-tasting toppings seen in bakery cases. We prefer a simple accompaniment, made with fresh berries and jam. This topping is best the day it's made. Do not use frozen strawberries in this recipe.

 1¼ pounds strawberries, hulled and sliced thin (4 cups)
 ¼   cup (1¾ ounces) sugar
     Pinch salt
 ½   cup strawberry jam
 1   tablespoon lemon juice

1. Toss strawberries, sugar, and salt together in bowl and let sit, stirring occasionally, until berries have released their juice and sugar has dissolved, about 30 minutes.

2. Process jam in food processor until smooth, about 8 seconds. Simmer jam in small saucepan over medium heat until no longer foamy, about 3 minutes. Stir warm jam and lemon juice into strawberries. Let cool completely, about 1 hour. Serve at room temperature or chilled.

BLUEBERRY COMPOTE

Makes about 1 cup

This quick-cooking compote adds pleasant color and sweetness. We started with frozen berries, which are consistently sweet and flavorful no matter what time of year it is. We then concentrated the flavor of the berries by cooking them down with a little butter and sugar. To use fresh blueberries, crush one-third of them against the side of the saucepan with a wooden spoon after adding them to the butter and then proceed as directed. You can use regular or wild frozen blueberries in this recipe.

 1   tablespoon unsalted butter
 10 ounces (2 cups) frozen blueberries
 2   tablespoons sugar, plus extra for seasoning
     Pinch salt
 ½   teaspoon lemon juice

Melt butter in small saucepan over medium heat. Add blueberries, 2 tablespoons sugar, and salt; bring to boil. Lower heat and simmer, stirring occasionally, until thickened and about one-quarter of juice remains, 8 to 10 minutes. Remove pan from heat and stir in lemon juice. Season with extra sugar to taste.

CANDIED NUTS
Makes about 1 cup

Many cakes, pies, or cool and creamy desserts could benefit from a little crunch to top things off. A very easy way to achieve this is to sprinkle on some toasted nuts, but to take this topping to the next level we like to candy the nuts for a toasty, sweet, salty treat that's much easier to achieve than you'd think. You can use any nut you'd like in this recipe.

  1 cup nuts, toasted
¼ cup (1¾ ounces) sugar
¼ cup water
½ teaspoon table salt

1. Line rimmed baking sheet with parchment paper. Bring all ingredients to boil in medium saucepan over medium heat. Cook, stirring constantly, until water evaporates and sugar appears dry, opaque, and somewhat crystallized and evenly coats nuts, about 5 minutes.

2. Reduce heat to low and continue to stir nuts until sugar is amber-colored, about 2 minutes. Transfer nuts to prepared sheet and spread in even layer. Let cool completely, about 10 minutes.

CANDIED COFFEE BEANS
Makes about ¼ cup

Nuts aren't the only thing you can candy. Coffee beans make a great alternative accompaniment to a variety of chocolate desserts—not only does their crunch contribute a pleasant texture, but the flavor of the coffee beans highlights and intensifies the flavor of the chocolate. We chop the beans in the food processor first so they're easier to eat. These beans are potent—a small amount goes a long way.

¼ cup coffee beans
  1 tablespoon sugar
1½ teaspoons water
   Pinch table salt

1. Line rimmed baking sheet with parchment paper. Pulse coffee beans in food processor until coarsely chopped, 6 to 8 pulses. Bring all ingredients to boil in medium saucepan over medium heat. Cook, stirring constantly, until water evaporates and sugar appears dry, opaque, and somewhat crystallized and evenly coats coffee beans, about 5 minutes.

2. Reduce heat to low and continue to stir coffee beans until sugar is amber-colored, about 2 minutes. Transfer coffee beans to prepared sheet and spread in even layer. Let cool completely, about 10 minutes.

SESAME BRITTLE
Makes about 2 cups

Sesame brittle gives our Chocolate-Tahini Tart (page 434) a stunning patterned top. But you can break this brittle into shards of any size and top your desired chocolate dessert any way you like. The thin brittle tastes of toasted sesame and caramel. When pouring and rolling out the hot mixture, you will need to work quickly to prevent it from setting before it reaches the right thickness.

2 tablespoons water
2 tablespoons sugar
2 tablespoons light corn syrup
1 tablespoon unsalted butter
⅓ cup sesame seeds, toasted
⅛ teaspoon table salt

1. Place large sheet parchment on cutting board. Heat water, sugar, corn syrup, and butter in small saucepan over medium-high heat, stirring often, until butter is melted and sugar is fully dissolved, about 1 minute. Bring to boil and cook, without stirring, until mixture has faint golden color and registers 300 degrees, 4 to 6 minutes.

2. Reduce heat to medium-low and continue to cook, gently swirling pan, until syrup is amber-colored and registers 350 degrees, 1 to 2 minutes. Off heat, stir in sesame seeds and salt. Working quickly, transfer mixture to prepared parchment, top with second layer of parchment and carefully smooth into ¹⁄₁₆-inch-thick layer using rolling pin.

3. Remove top sheet parchment and let cool completely, about 45 minutes. Break into rough 1-inch pieces before using. (Brittle can be stored in airtight container at room temperature for up to 1 month.)

ICES

Intense, unmasked flavors

Incorporate enough sugar for scoopable product

Use pectin when you want to stabilize

Don't overchurn

A REFRESHING WATER-BASED FROZEN TREAT like sorbet or granita can hold its own against ice cream any day. A well-made batch of sorbet is almost as creamy and smooth as its dairy-based relative, but rather than finishing with mouth-coating richness, it should be delicately icy and dissolve on the tongue, leaving behind an echo of clean, concentrated flavor—whether that's bright summer berries, bracingly tart citrus, or rich bitter-sweet chocolate. A colorful granita intrigues with its bright, palate-cleansing flavors and beautiful pebbly texture. It's shaved ice for adults. A simple ice, like Italian ice, is just flavored water that's frozen—it has a subtle creaminess but also a delightful slushy-like texture. In all cases, as with dairy-based frozen desserts, sugar matters. Sugar depresses the freezing point (see page 535), so using more can result in smoother sorbet, a spoonable ice, or a not-too-solid scrapable granita (of course, as with most things, too much has its problems, too). These recipes are refreshing in more ways than one.

Sorbet

Water and sugar are both crucial in achieving a sorbet with the ideal consistency, one that's delicately icy, velvety smooth, and easily scoopable. The two work in tandem. Some of the water freezes, which creates ice crystals. Sugar reduces the tendency of ice crystals to grow large, thus contributing to a smoother texture. Sugar also depresses the freezing point of water, so some of it remains liquid. This so-called "free" water lubricates the ice crystals, producing a smooth, scoopable texture. To ensure the ice crystals are small and fine, we separate out a small amount of the base and freeze it separately before adding it back into the rest; its tiny crystals act as a catalyst, triggering a chain reaction that very rapidly forms equally small crystals in the bigger mix. Another key ingredient is pectin, which helps stabilize the sorbet—and all that free water—so that it doesn't melt too quickly. Length of churning time is important, too; unlike ice cream, sorbet doesn't contain the fat and protein necessary to stabilize the air that's incorporated during churning. To prevent a loose, crumbly texture, churn your sorbet just until it starts to lighten in color and has the consistency of a thick milkshake.

SOFT ENOUGH TO SCOOP

For sorbet that's soft enough to scoop, some water should freeze but some should remain liquid and "free" to flow between the ice crystals, providing the sensation of creaminess. Added water and sugar are critical. Water ensures that there's enough of it in the mix to remain free. Sugar aids the process by getting in the way of the water freezing.

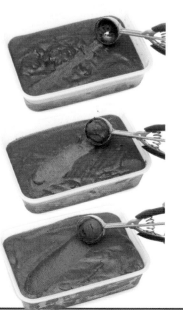

Rock Solid
Straight fruit puree with no added water or sugar freezes into an impenetrable mass.

Getting Softer
A half cup of water plus ¾ cup of sugar creates some free water, and the sorbet starts to soften.

Just Right
One cup of water and nearly 1 cup of sugar and corn syrup produce a creamy, scoopable texture.

CALIBRATING CHURN TIMES

Too much churning has a negative effect on the final texture of sorbet: Because the dessert has no fat or protein to stabilize the air bubbles incorporated during churning, longer churning times produce sorbets that are loose, crumbly, and dull-tasting.

40 Minutes
Overchurned sorbet looks promisingly thick but freezes up crumbly and dull-tasting.

30 Minutes
As the churning time is reduced, less air is incorporated, improving the texture of the final product.

20 Minutes
Churning just long enough for the mixture to reach the consistency of a thick milkshake produces dense, flavorful sorbet.

PERFECT WITH PECTIN

Depressing the freezing point of a frozen dessert, as we do with sorbet, has a downside: Once it sits for even a few minutes at room temperature, it begins to liquefy into a soupy mess. That's because the unfrozen water is literally free to move about and quickly leaks from the mixture, leaving the ice surrounded by syrupy puddles. Professional sorbet manufacturers get around this problem with ingredients like guar gum and locust bean gum. These stabilizers act like sponges, corralling the free water within a loose matrix so that it can remain unfrozen while still not flowing freely. Rather than these additives, we tried two that are readily available: gelatin and pectin. While both curbed melting, the gelatin had a downside: It left the sorbet with an unpalatable plastic-like firmness, even when used sparingly. But a mere teaspoon of pectin (bloomed first in the water) kept the sorbet from immediately puddling without overdoing the firmness.

No Stabilizer
Once out of the freezer, stabilizer-free sorbet quickly melts into a watery mess.

1 Tsp Gelatin
While it greatly improves stability, gelatin creates a sorbet that is strangely rubbery.

1 Tsp Pectin
Pectin, which is also found naturally in berries, slows melting and produces a likable texture.

Granita

Granita is a pleasantly icy dessert typically made by freezing a puree of fruit and sugar, which is then periodically scraped with a fork to produce its characteristic crunchy, granular texture. This frozen treat dates back to ancient times when Arabs occupied Sicily and introduced locals to sharbat, an iced drink made with fruit juice or rose water. Laborers gathered winter snow from the island's mountain peaks and stored it in shallow caves and depressions dotted throughout the landscape. When summer arrived, they divided the ice into large blocks to be grated and drizzled with fruit juices and syrups. Over time, sharbat gave birth to granita ("grana" means "grainy").

Today granita is enjoyed any time of day to beat the heat. While granita is simple to make, the details are important. Using the right amount of sugar is key to a properly crystalline granita—too little and the mixture will freeze solid; too much and it will remain slushy and syrupy. The type of vessel is important as well: It should be wide enough so that the layer of granita is thin and freezes efficiently. We like to use a glass dish because it won't scratch when raked with a fork. Glass also provides insulation from the counter during scraping, which creates a time buffer before the mixture starts to melt.

TOPPING OFF GRANITA

Granita is often enjoyed simply and unadorned, but feel free to add some aromatic intrigue in the form of chopped herbs or citrus zest. For a posh vibe, layer it with unsweetened whipped cream in a martini glass. Or serve a scoop scattered with fresh berries and splashed with prosecco or drizzled with your favorite liqueur.

A CHILLING EVOLUTION

After an hour in the freezer, the edges of the granita will be frozen and the center slushy. Use a fork to scrape the edges, and then stir the icy crystals into the middle of the mixture before returning it to the freezer. Repeat the scraping and stirring process every 30 minutes to 1 hour until the crystals are uniformly light and fluffy, 2 to 3 hours longer.

After 1 Hour

After 2 Hours

After 3+ Hours

Ice Pops

While most frozen desserts are soft enough to be scooped up with a spoon, ice pops and paletas are meant to be frozen solid; not only does this ensure that they remain attached to the stick, but it provides the satisfying experience of sinking your teeth into something cool and bursting with flavor. They require minimal ingredients and no complicated techniques or special equipment (other than an ice pop mold), making them a cinch to prepare. With so few ingredients, quality really matters: If your tap water has an off-flavor, consider filtering it or using bottled. Use fruit of peak ripeness and sweeten accordingly. We like to use honey to sweeten our ice pops; the viscous liquid incorporates seamlessly into the other ingredients and adds a hint of complexity. And if you add a little cream or coconut milk, your ice pops will have a smoother, creamier texture.

RASPBERRY SORBET

Serves 8 (Makes 1 quart) | ice cream maker

WHY THIS RECIPE WORKS To make a light, refreshing raspberry sorbet that was beautifully creamy and smooth, finding the right balance of water and sugar was key; corn syrup helped create a smooth texture without oversweetening. Freezing a small amount of the base and then adding it to the rest helped superchill the mix, making it freeze faster and more smoothly. We added some pectin to bump up the raspberries' natural pectin, which kept the sorbet from turning into a puddle too quickly at room temperature. We recommend both Sure-Jell for Less or No Sugar Needed Recipes and Ball RealFruit Low or No-Sugar Needed Pectin here. You can use a food processor instead of a blender if you prefer.

- 1 cup water
- 1 teaspoon low- or no-sugar-needed fruit pectin
- ⅛ teaspoon table salt
- 1¼ pounds (4 cups) fresh raspberries
- ½ cup plus 2 tablespoons (4⅓ ounces) sugar
- ¼ cup light corn syrup

1. Heat water, pectin, and salt in medium saucepan over medium-high heat, stirring occasionally, until pectin has fully dissolved, about 5 minutes. Remove saucepan from heat and let mixture cool slightly, about 10 minutes.

2. Process raspberries, sugar, corn syrup, and cooled water mixture in blender until smooth, about 30 seconds. Strain mixture through fine-mesh strainer, pressing on solids to extract as much liquid as possible. Transfer 1 cup mixture to small bowl and place remaining mixture in large bowl. Cover both bowls with plastic wrap. Place large bowl in refrigerator and small bowl in freezer and chill for at least 4 hours or up to 24 hours. (Small bowl of base will freeze solid.)

3. Remove mixtures from refrigerator and freezer. Scrape frozen base from small bowl into large bowl of base. Stir occasionally until frozen base has fully dissolved. Transfer mixture to ice cream machine and churn until mixture has consistency of thick milkshake and color lightens, 15 to 25 minutes.

4. Transfer sorbet to airtight container and freeze until firm, at least 2 hours or up to 5 days. Let sorbet sit at room temperature for 5 minutes before serving.

Raspberry Sorbet with Ginger and Mint
Substitute ginger beer for water in step 1. Add 2-inch piece of peeled ginger, thinly sliced, and ¼ cup mint leaves to food processor with raspberries. Decrease amount of sugar to ½ cup.

Chocolate Sorbet

CHOCOLATE SORBET

Serves 8 (Makes 1 quart) | ice cream maker

WHY THIS RECIPE WORKS Without flavor-dulling dairy, chocolate sorbet has the potential to be the most chocolaty, deeply bittersweet of the frozen chocolate desserts. We bloomed a half cup of unsweetened cocoa powder in our base of water, sugar, and corn syrup and then melted in 8 ounces of bittersweet chocolate. Superchilling a cup of the sorbet kept ice crystals to a minimum. Pectin slowed melting and ensured a smooth texture. For fruit pectin be certain you use one engineered for low- or no-sugar recipes. We recommend both Sure-Jell for Less or No Sugar Needed Recipes and Ball RealFruit Low or No-Sugar Needed Pectin here. Allow the sorbet to sit at room temperature for 5 minutes to soften before serving.

- 2¼ cups water
- ½ cup (1½ ounces) unsweetened cocoa powder
- ¾ cup (5¼ ounces) sugar
- ¼ cup corn syrup
- 1 teaspoon low- or no-sugar-needed fruit pectin
- ⅛ teaspoon table salt
- 8 ounces bittersweet chocolate, chopped fine
- ½ teaspoon vanilla extract

1. Combine water, cocoa, sugar, corn syrup, pectin, and salt in medium saucepan. Heat over medium-high heat, stirring occasionally, until simmering and sugar and pectin are fully dissolved, about 5 minutes. Off heat, whisk in chocolate and vanilla until fully combined. Transfer mixture to blender and process until smooth, about 30 seconds.

2. Transfer 1 cup mixture to small bowl and place remaining mixture in large bowl. Cover both bowls with plastic wrap. Place large bowl in refrigerator and small bowl in freezer and let cool completely, at least 4 hours or up to 24 hours. (Small bowl of base will freeze solid.)

3. Remove mixtures from refrigerator and freezer. Scrape frozen base from small bowl into large bowl of base. Stir until frozen base has fully dissolved. Transfer mixture to ice cream machine and churn until mixture has consistency of thick milkshake and color lightens, 15 to 25 minutes.

4. Transfer sorbet to airtight container, pressing firmly to remove any air pockets, and freeze until firm, at least 2 hours or up to 5 days. Serve.

Lemon Ice

LEMON ICE

Serves 8 (Makes 1 quart) | food processor

WHY THIS RECIPE WORKS Lemon ice is sure to quench your thirst on a hot day; it should melt on the tongue with abandon, strike a perfect sweet-tart balance, and hit lots of high notes before quickly disappearing without so much as a trace of bitterness. A cup of sugar gave our lemon ice the ideal amount of sweetness; less sugar left it with a pronounced bitterness, and more sugar made it taste like frozen lemonade. Colorless, odorless, and relatively tasteless vodka was added for its anti-freezing properties—it ensured that the finished ice was soft and creamy, with a slightly slushy texture. Of course, the single most important determinant of the texture of lemon ice is the freezing method. Freezing the mixture in ice cube trays and then processing the cubes in a food processor produced a fluffy, coarse-grained texture. The addition of vodka yields the best texture, but it can be omitted.

2¼ cups water
  1 cup lemon juice (6 lemons)
  1 cup (7 ounces) sugar
  2 tablespoons vodka (optional)
  ⅛ teaspoon table salt

1. Whisk all ingredients together in bowl until sugar has dissolved. Pour mixture into 2 ice cube trays and freeze until solid, at least 3 hours or up to 5 days.

2. Place medium bowl in freezer. Pulse half of ice cubes in food processor until creamy and no large lumps remain, about 18 pulses. Transfer mixture to chilled bowl and return to freezer. Repeat pulsing remaining cubes; transfer to bowl. Serve immediately.

Lemon-Jasmine Ice
Bring 1 cup water, sugar, and salt to simmer in small saucepan over medium-high heat, stirring occasionally. Off heat, add 2 jasmine tea bags; let steep for 5 minutes, then squeeze and discard tea bags and transfer mixture to medium bowl. Stir in remaining 1¼ cups water; lemon juice; and vodka, if using. Let cool to room temperature, about 15 minutes, and freeze as directed.

Lemon-Lavender Ice
Bring 1 cup water, sugar, and salt to simmer in small saucepan over medium-high heat, stirring occasionally. Off heat, stir in 2½ teaspoons dried lavender; let steep for 5 minutes, then strain mixture through fine-mesh strainer into medium bowl. Stir in remaining 1¼ cups water; lemon juice; and vodka, if using. Let cool to room temperature, about 15 minutes, and freeze as directed.

Lemon-Lime Ice
Substitute ½ cup lime juice (4 limes) for ½ cup lemon juice.

BERRY GRANITA

Serves 8 | 13 by 9-inch glass baking dish

WHY THIS RECIPE WORKS For a deeply fruity granita with a light, crystalline texture, we blended berries with enough water to form a silky puree and enough sugar for modest sweetness and to give the puree the proper consistency when frozen. When scraped, this granita yielded light, flaky ice crystals that lingered briefly on the palate for a chilling pause before melting in the mouth in a flood of fruity goodness. If halving this recipe, use an 8-inch glass baking dish. If using fresh strawberries, weigh them after hulling. If using any type of thawed berries, do not drain them before adding them to the blender. If desired, add 2 to 3 tablespoons of chopped fresh mint, 1 to 2 teaspoons of grated fresh ginger, or 1 to 2 teaspoons of grated lemon zest (add only one of these) to the blender in step 1.

> 1 pound fresh or thawed frozen berries
> ¾ cup water
> ½ cup (3½ ounces) sugar
> ¼ cup lemon juice (2 lemons)
>   Pinch table salt

1. Process all ingredients in blender on high speed until very smooth, 1 to 2 minutes. Strain mixture through fine-mesh strainer into 13 by 9-inch glass baking dish. Freeze, uncovered, until edges are frozen and center is slushy, about 1 hour. Using fork, scrape edges to release crystals. Stir crystals into middle of mixture and return dish to freezer. Repeat scraping and stirring, using tines of fork to mash any large chunks, every 30 minutes to 1 hour until granita crystals are uniformly light and fluffy, 2 to 3 hours.

2. Immediately before serving, scrape granita with fork to loosen. Spoon into chilled bowls or glasses and serve. (Any remaining granita can be transferred to airtight container and frozen for up to 1 week. Scrape granita again to loosen before serving.)

BEET GRANITA

Serves 4 | 8-inch square glass baking dish

WHY THIS RECIPE WORKS We wanted to create a truly unique frozen treat by pairing sour beet kvass—a lightly fermented Eastern European beverage traditionally made by fermenting beets in a brine with rye bread—with bitter Campari for a refreshing granita that could serve as a palate cleanser or light dessert at our next dinner party. To balance the sour-salty-bitter-savory combination, we added orange juice, which contributed sweetness and a citrus aroma that helped counter the bitterness. You can temper the intensity of the granita by serving it with lightly whipped cream or a scoop of vanilla ice cream. Use freshly squeezed orange juice here, not

Beet Granita

**Striped Fruit
Ice Pops**

store-bought: It's worth the extra effort. Campari is the Italian liqueur that gives bitterness and depth to the classic Negroni cocktail. You can purchase beet kvass at natural food stores or you can order it online.

    1 cup plus 2 tablespoons beet kvass
    2 tablespoons orange juice
    2 tablespoons sugar
    2 tablespoons Campari

1. Whisk all ingredients in medium bowl until sugar is dissolved. Pour into 8-inch square glass baking dish. Freeze, uncovered, until edges are frozen and center is slushy, about 30 minutes. Using fork, scrape edges to release crystals. Stir crystals into middle of mixture and return dish to freezer. Repeat scraping and stirring, using tines of fork to mash any large chunks, every 30 minutes, until granita crystals are uniformly light and fluffy, 1½ to 2 hours longer.

2. Immediately before serving, scrape granita with fork to loosen. Spoon into chilled bowls or glasses and serve. (Any remaining granita can be transferred to airtight container and frozen for up to 1 week. Scrape granita again to loosen before serving.)

STRIPED FRUIT ICE POPS

Makes 6 ice pops | ice pop mold

WHY THIS RECIPE WORKS Multicolored Popsicles bring to mind carefree summer vacations. But with all that nostalgia comes sugar, corn syrup, and artificial coloring—we wanted an ultraflavorful, naturally colored and sweetened version that we could feel good about. Using honey as our sweetener, we made a vibrant red raspberry puree for one layer and a blueberry puree for a beautifully contrasting purple layer. For a clean-looking white middle layer we tested several bases and settled on using a little bit of cream along with lemon juice for the perfect balance of flavor and texture. A small amount of water in each layer ensured that the ice pops froze solid. For clean, well-defined stripes, be sure to let each layer freeze completely before adding the next layer, and be careful not to spill the mixture onto the sides of the molds when pouring. This recipe was developed using 3-ounce ice pop molds.

RASPBERRY LAYER
    4 ounces (¾ cup) raspberries
    ¼ cup water
    1 tablespoon honey
       Pinch table salt

LEMON LAYER
    ¼ cup water
    3 tablespoons heavy cream
    4 teaspoons honey
    1 tablespoon lemon juice
       Pinch table salt

BLUEBERRY LAYER
    4 ounces (¾ cup) blueberries
    ¼ cup water
    1 tablespoon honey
       Pinch table salt

1. FOR THE RASPBERRY LAYER: Process all ingredients in food processor until smooth, about 1 minute. Using 1-tablespoon measuring spoon, carefully pour 2 tablespoons of raspberry mixture evenly into each of six 3-ounce ice pop molds, being careful to keep walls of molds free from drips. Cover molds and freeze until firm, about 4 hours.

2. FOR THE LEMON LAYER: Whisk all ingredients together in bowl. Using 1-tablespoon measuring spoon, carefully pour 2 tablespoons lemon mixture into each ice pop mold. Cover molds tightly with double layer of aluminum foil. Push craft stick through foil into center of each mold until tip hits frozen raspberry mixture. Freeze until firm, about 4 hours.

3. FOR THE BLUEBERRY LAYER: Process all ingredients in food processor until smooth, about 1 minute. Using 1-tablespoon measuring spoon, carefully pour 2 tablespoons blueberry mixture into each ice pop mold. Cover molds and freeze until solid, at least 6 hours or up to 5 days. To serve, hold mold under warm running water for 30 seconds to thaw.

STRAWBERRY CREAM PALETAS

Makes 6 paletas | ice pop mold

WHY THIS RECIPE WORKS A cousin of Popsicles, paletas are Mexican-style frozen treats that usually rely on fresh fruit juice as their base and often have chunks of fresh fruit stirred in. Inspired by an early summer fruit harvest, we built our recipe using fresh strawberries as the focal point. We used the berries in two ways: First, we pureed half of them to a smooth consistency with a small amount of honey for sweetness. We pulsed the rest of the berries to a coarse chop to ensure bites of fresh fruit throughout our pops. Pops made with milk and half-and-half were too icy, but heavy cream provided just the right velvety texture. We prefer the flavor of fresh strawberries in this recipe; however, you can substitute 1 pound frozen strawberries, thawed and drained on paper towels to dry.

- 1 pound strawberries, hulled (3 cups), divided
- ½ cup heavy cream
- ¼ cup honey
- 1 teaspoon lemon juice
- ⅛ teaspoon table salt

1. Process 1½ cups strawberries, cream, honey, lemon juice, and salt in food processor until smooth, about 30 seconds, scraping down sides of bowl as needed. Add remaining 1½ cups strawberries and pulse until coarsely chopped, about 5 pulses. Transfer mixture to large liquid measuring cup.

2. Divide strawberry mixture evenly among six 3-ounce ice pop molds. Insert craft stick in center of each mold, cover, and freeze until firm, at least 6 hours or up to 5 days. To serve, hold mold under warm running water for 30 seconds to thaw.

COCONUT PALETAS

Makes 6 paletas | ice pop mold

WHY THIS RECIPE WORKS We wanted a pop that was rich, creamy, and decadent. Using richly flavored coconut milk as our base, we added a small amount of honey for sweetness, vanilla extract for deeply nuanced undertones, and salt for balance. For a bolder coconut presence, we also added unsweetened flaked coconut, which not only provided great coconut flavor but also gave our paletas a bit of textural contrast. Our favorite brand of coconut milk is Chaokoh;

Coconut Paletas

other brands may contain different amounts of sugar and fat, which will affect the overall flavor and texture of the paletas. Do not substitute low-fat coconut milk or the paletas will taste watery and have an icy texture.

- 2 cups canned coconut milk
- 3 tablespoons honey
- 1 tablespoon vanilla extract
- ¼ teaspoon table salt
- 3 tablespoons unsweetened flaked coconut

1. Whisk coconut milk, honey, vanilla, and salt together in large liquid measuring cup to dissolve honey and salt. Stir in flaked coconut.

2. Divide coconut mixture evenly among six 3-ounce ice pop molds. Insert craft stick in center of each mold, cover, and freeze until firm, at least 6 hours or up to 5 days. To serve, hold mold under warm running water for 30 seconds to thaw.

Coconut, Lime, and Cardamom Paletas
Add 2 teaspoons grated lime zest, 1 tablespoon lime juice, and ½ teaspoon cardamom to coconut mixture in step 1.

Horchata Paletas
Add ½ teaspoon ground cinnamon and ⅛ teaspoon ground cloves to coconut mixture in step 1. Substitute 3 tablespoons toasted sliced almonds for flaked coconut.

SEMIFREDDO

Lighten with whipped cream

Can sit out without melting rapidly

Offset creaminess with crunchy topping

ITALY'S SEMIFREDDO IS A BROADLY DEFINED CATEGORY of simple chilled desserts prepared from whipped egg whites or yolks, whipped cream, and flavorings—frequently coffee, liqueurs, or chocolate—and studded with cookies, candies, or nuts. Semifreddo is often described as a frozen mousse (though it's fully frozen, its name roughly translates as "half-frozen") and is as elegant and simple as a frozen dessert can be. Most recipes fall loosely into three categories: those that combine uncooked egg yolks and large quantities of whipped cream; custardlike versions that combine cooked egg yolks and a lesser amount of whipped cream; and those that cook the egg whites with a hot sugar syrup. Custard versions have a rich and luxurious texture similar to gelato or ice cream, whereas the cooked meringue style has a more delicate and light consistency. Instead of being churned in an ice cream maker, semifreddo is lightened by the whipped cream and/or beaten egg whites. Then it's typically frozen in a mold (a loaf pan is common) until solid, unmolded, and cut into neat slices (although sometimes it is prepared in individual ramekins). It's soft enough that it easily caves to the pressure of a spoon; better yet, unlike ice cream, it can sit out of the freezer for an extended period of time without melting, which makes it ideal for serving to company.

KEEPING SEMIFREDDO IN SHAPE

Fat and air help semifreddo resist melting and keep its shape once it's out of the freezer. Our semifreddos have an abundance of butterfat, and butterfat melts well above room temperature. Even more important, the air from the whipped cream acts as an insulator, slowing the transfer of ambient heat much like the fluffy feathers in a down jacket. It's this latter factor that allows our semifreddo to retain its shape longer than most ice creams, since whipped cream contains more trapped air than what's introduced into ice cream during churning.

To demonstrate how air acts as an insulator, we compared how quickly 1 cup of frozen unwhipped heavy cream would melt versus 1 cup of heavy cream that we whipped before freezing. The frozen unwhipped heavy cream began to slump and soften after about 15 minutes and was ringed by a puddle of liquid after 45 minutes; meanwhile, the frozen whipped cream remained comparatively firm and exhibited little melting.

No Air = More Melting

Air = Less Melting

SMOOTH IT OUT

Semifreddo made in a loaf pan can emerge with a wrinkled appearance from the plastic wrap lining. To give the log a smooth surface, before slicing, use an offset spatula to smooth any wrinkles on the surface of the semifreddo.

CHOCOLATE SEMIFREDDO

Serves 12 | loaf pan

WHY THIS RECIPE WORKS Semifreddo is a classic Italian dessert that's often described as a frozen mousse. (Though it's fully frozen, its name roughly translates as "half-frozen.") For a chocolate semifreddo that was rich and creamy but not overly complicated, we cooked the custard base directly on the stovetop and then poured it over 8 ounces of finely chopped bittersweet chocolate. Using whole eggs instead of yolks and cutting the cream with a bit of water ensured a cold, refreshing semifreddo that wasn't overly rich. A brilliant cherry sauce provided a bright contrast to the rich chocolate and made this an ultra-elegant dessert. If frozen overnight, the semifreddo should be tempered before serving for the best texture: Place slices on individual plates or a large tray and refrigerate for 30 minutes. For some crunch, sprinkle each serving with Candied Nuts (page 551). If you are freezing the semifreddo for longer than 6 hours before unmolding and serving, wrap the pan in a second layer of plastic wrap.

SEMIFREDDO
- 8 ounces bittersweet chocolate, chopped fine
- 1 tablespoon vanilla extract
- ½ teaspoon instant espresso powder
- 3 large eggs
- 5 tablespoons (2¼ ounces) sugar
- ¼ teaspoon table salt
- 2 cups heavy cream, chilled, divided
- ¼ cup water

CHERRY SAUCE
- 12 ounces frozen sweet cherries
- ¼ cup (1¾ ounces) sugar
- 2 tablespoons kirsch
- 1½ teaspoons cornstarch
- 1 tablespoon lemon juice

1. FOR THE SEMIFREDDO: Lightly spray loaf pan with vegetable oil spray and line with plastic wrap, leaving 3-inch overhang on all sides. Place chocolate in large heatproof bowl; set fine-mesh strainer over bowl and set aside. Stir vanilla and espresso powder in second bowl until espresso powder is dissolved.

2. Whisk eggs, sugar, and salt in third bowl until combined. Heat ½ cup cream (keep remaining 1½ cups chilled) and water in medium saucepan over medium heat until simmering. Slowly whisk hot cream mixture into egg mixture until combined. Return mixture to saucepan and cook over medium-low heat, stirring constantly and scraping bottom of saucepan with rubber spatula, until mixture is very slightly thickened and registers 160 to 165 degrees, about 5 minutes. Do not let mixture simmer.

3. Immediately pour mixture through strainer set over chocolate. Let mixture stand to melt chocolate, about 5 minutes. Whisk until chocolate is melted and smooth, then whisk in vanilla mixture. Let chocolate mixture cool completely, about 15 minutes.

4. Using stand mixer fitted with whisk attachment, whip remaining 1½ cups cream on low speed until bubbles form, about 30 seconds. Increase speed to medium and beat until whisk leaves trail, about 30 seconds. Increase speed to high and continue to beat until nearly doubled in volume and whipped cream forms soft peaks, 30 to 45 seconds.

5. Whisk one-third of whipped cream into chocolate mixture. Using rubber spatula, gently fold remaining whipped cream into chocolate mixture until incorporated and no streaks of whipped cream remain. Transfer mixture to prepared pan and spread evenly with rubber spatula. Fold overhanging plastic over surface. Freeze until firm, at least 6 hours. (Semifreddo can be wrapped tightly in plastic wrap and frozen for up to 2 weeks.)

6. FOR THE CHERRY SAUCE: Combine cherries and sugar in bowl and microwave for 1½ minutes. Stir, then continue to microwave until sugar is mostly dissolved, about 1 minute longer. Combine kirsch and cornstarch in small bowl

7. Drain cherries in fine-mesh strainer set over small saucepan. Return cherries to bowl and set aside.

8. Bring juice in saucepan to simmer over medium-high heat. Stir in kirsch mixture and bring to boil. Boil, stirring occasionally, until mixture has thickened and appears syrupy, 1 to 2 minutes. Remove saucepan from heat and stir in cherries and lemon juice. Let sauce cool completely. (Sauce can be refrigerated for up to 1 week.)

9. When ready to serve, remove plastic from surface and invert pan onto serving platter. Remove plastic from the loaf pan and smooth surface with spatula as necessary. Dip slicing knife in very hot water and wipe dry. Slice semifreddo ¾ inch thick, dipping and wiping knife after each slice. Top individual servings with cherry sauce. Serve immediately.

CAPPUCCINO SEMIFREDDO WITH HAZELNUTS

Serves 8 | eight 4-ounce ramekins

WHY THIS RECIPE WORKS This semifreddo recipe is ultralight, featuring a mousse-like cooked meringue flavored with coffee and speckled with nuts. In this Italian meringue (see page 466), the syrup cooks the whites, making for a stable meringue that can hold up to the additional ingredients. Because it can be made far ahead of time (even up to two weeks) and is frozen in individual ramekins, this semifreddo is both refined and simple to serve. For a milder flavor, instant coffee can be substituted for the instant espresso.

  1 cup heavy cream, chilled
  ½ cup plus 2 tablespoons (4⅓ ounces) sugar, divided
  ¼ cup water
  3 large egg whites, room temperature
     Pinch cream of tartar
  2 tablespoons instant espresso, dissolved in
     1 tablespoon warm water
  1 teaspoon vanilla extract
  ¼ cup hazelnuts, toasted, skinned, and
     chopped coarse, divided
     Chocolate shavings (optional)

1. Using stand mixer fitted with whisk attachment, whip cream on medium-low speed until frothy, about 1 minute. Increase speed to high and whip until soft peaks form, 1 to 3 minutes. Transfer whipped cream to bowl, cover, and refrigerate until needed.

2. Bring ½ cup sugar and water to boil in small saucepan over medium-high heat and cook until mixture is slightly thickened and syrupy and registers 235 degrees, 3 to 4 minutes. Remove syrup from heat and cover to keep warm.

3. Using dry, clean bowl and whisk attachment, whip egg whites and cream of tartar on medium-low speed until foamy, about 1 minute. Increase speed to medium-high and whip whites to soft, billowy mounds, about 1 minute. Gradually add remaining 2 tablespoons sugar and whip until glossy, soft peaks form, 1 to 2 minutes.

4. Reduce speed to medium and slowly add hot syrup, avoiding whisk and sides of bowl. Increase speed to medium-high and continue to whip until meringue has cooled slightly (just warm) and is very thick and shiny, 2 to 5 minutes. Add dissolved espresso and vanilla and continue to whip until incorporated, 30 to 60 seconds.

5. Gently stir one-third of whipped cream into meringue with rubber spatula. Fold in remaining whipped cream and 2 tablespoons hazelnuts until just incorporated.

6. Divide mixture evenly among eight 4-ounce ramekins and gently tap ramekins on counter to settle batter. Cover each ramekin tightly with plastic wrap, pressing it flush to surface of batter, and freeze until firm, at least 8 hours or up to 2 weeks.

7. Before serving, let ramekins sit at room temperature until slightly softened, 5 to 10 minutes. Sprinkle with remaining 2 tablespoons hazelnuts and chocolate shavings, if using.

Cappuccino Semifreddo with Hazelnuts

CONVERSIONS AND EQUIVALENTS

The recipes in this book were developed using standard U.S. measures following U.S. government guidelines. The charts below offer equivalents for U.S. and metric measures. All conversions are approximate and have been rounded up or down to the nearest whole number.

EXAMPLE

1 teaspoon = 4.9292 milliliters, rounded up to 5 milliliters
1 ounce = 28.3495 grams, rounded down to 28 grams

VOLUME CONVERSIONS

U.S.	METRIC
1 teaspoon	5 milliliters
2 teaspoons	10 milliliters
1 tablespoon	15 milliliters
2 tablespoons	30 milliliters
¼ cup	59 milliliters
⅓ cup	79 milliliters
½ cup	118 milliliters
¾ cup	177 milliliters
1 cup	237 milliliters
1¼ cups	296 milliliters
1½ cups	355 milliliters
2 cups (1 pint)	473 milliliters
2½ cups	591 milliliters
3 cups	710 milliliters
4 cups (1 quart)	0.946 liter
1.06 quarts	1 liter
4 quarts (1 gallon)	3.8 liters

WEIGHT CONVERSIONS

OUNCES	GRAMS
½	14
¾	21
1	28
1½	43
2	57
2½	71
3	85
3½	99
4	113
4½	128
5	142
6	170
7	198
8	227
9	255
10	283
12	340
16 (1 pound)	454

CONVERSIONS FOR COMMON BAKING INGREDIENTS

Because measuring by weight is far more accurate than measuring by volume, and thus more likely to produce reliable results, in our recipes we provide ounce measures in addition to cup measures for many ingredients. Refer to the chart below to convert these measures into grams.

INGREDIENT	OUNCES	GRAMS
Flour		
1 cup all-purpose flour*	5	142
1 cup cake flour	4	113
1 cup whole-wheat flour	5½	156
Sugar		
1 cup granulated (white) sugar	7	198
1 cup packed brown sugar (light or dark) sugar	7	198
1 cup confectioners' sugar	4	113
Cocoa Powder		
1 cup cocoa powder	3	85
Butter†		
4 tablespoons (½ stick or ¼ cup)	2	57
8 tablespoons (1 stick or ½ cup)	4	113
16 tablespoons (2 sticks or 1 cup)	8	227

* U.S. all-purpose flour, the most frequently used flour in this book, does not contain leaveners, as some European flours do. These leavened flours are called self-rising or self-raising. If you are using self-rising flour, take this into consideration before adding leaveners to a recipe.
ww
† In the United States, butter is sold both salted and unsalted. We recommend unsalted butter. If you are using salted butter, take this into consideration before adding salt to a recipe.

OVEN TEMPERATURE

FAHRENHEIT	CELSIUS	GAS MARK
225	105	¼
250	120	½
275	135	1
300	150	2
325	165	3
350	180	4
375	190	5
400	200	6
425	220	7
450	230	8
475	245	9

CONVERTING TEMPERATURES FROM AN INSTANT-READ THERMOMETER

We include doneness temperatures in many of the recipes in this book. We recommend an instant-read thermometer for the job. Refer to the table above to convert Fahrenheit degrees to Celsius. Or, for temperatures not represented in the chart, use this simple formula:

Subtract 32 degrees from the Fahrenheit reading, then divide the result by 1.8 to find the Celsius reading.

EXAMPLE
"Cook caramel until it registers 234 degrees."

To convert:
234°F − 32 = 202°
202° ÷ 1.8 = 112.22°C, rounded down to 112°C

INDEX

Note: Page references in *italics* indicate photographs.

P